Getting started with Spring Framework
Fourth Edition

Getting started with Spring Framework is a hands-on guide to begin developing applications using Spring Framework. This book is meant for Java developers with little or no knowledge of Spring Framework. **Getting started with Spring Framework, Fourth Edition** has been updated to reflect changes in **Spring 5** and includes new chapters - **Functional programming with Java** (covers lambda expressions, higher-order functions, `Stream` API and method references), **Reactive programming with RxJava 2** (covers Reactive Streams specification and RxJava 2), and **Developing reactive applications using Spring** (shows a reactive RESTful web service that uses MongoDB's reactive database driver, Spring Data MongoDB's reactive support to build the data access layer, Spring WebFlux module to build the web layer, and Spring Security's reactive support to secure the web service).

The examples that accompany this book are based on **Spring 5.0.1**. You can download the examples (consisting of **85 sample projects**) described in this book from the following GitHub project: `https://github.com/getting-started-with-spring/4thEdition`

Chapter 1 – Introduction to Spring Framework

Chapter 2 – Spring Framework basics

Chapter 3 - Configuring beans

Chapter 4 - Dependency injection

Chapter 5 - Customizing beans and bean definitions

Chapter 6 - Annotation-driven development with Spring

Chapter 7 – Java-based container configuration

Chapter 8 - Database interaction using Spring

Chapter 9 – Spring Data

Chapter 10 - Messaging, emailing, asynchronous method execution, and caching using Spring

Chapter 11 - Aspect-oriented programming

Chapter 12 – Spring Web MVC basics

Chapter 13 – Validation and data binding in Spring Web MVC

Chapter 14 – Developing RESTful web services using Spring Web MVC

Chapter 15 – More Spring Web MVC – internationalization, file upload and asynchronous request processing

Chapter 16 – Securing applications using Spring Security

Chapter 17 – Functional programming with Java **(New)**

Chapter 18 – Reactive programming with RxJava 2 **(New)**

Chapter 19 - Developing reactive RESTful web services using Spring WebFlux, Spring Data and Spring Security **(New)**

Appendix A – Downloading and installing MongoDB database

Appendix B – Importing and deploying sample projects in Eclipse IDE

Ashish Sarin, J Sharma

Table of contents

Preface

How to use this book ?

Download sample projects

This book comes with many sample projects that you can download from the following GitHub project: `https://github.com/getting-started-with-spring/4thEdition`.

You can download the sample projects as a single ZIP file or you can check out the sample projects using Git. For more details, refer to the above URL.

Import sample projects into your Eclipse IDE

If you see **IMPORT** **`chapter<chapter-number>/<project name>`** at any point while reading the book, you should import the specified project into your Eclipse IDE (or any other IDE that you are using). Refer appendix B to see the steps required for importing and running the sample projects.

Refer to code examples

Each example listing specifies the sample project name (using **`Project`** label) and the location of the source file (using **`Source location`** label). If the **`Project`** and **`Source location`** labels are not specified, you can assume that the code shown in the example listing is *not* being used anywhere in the sample projects and it has been shown purely to simplify understanding.

Conventions used in this book

Italics has been used for emphasizing terms

`Consolas` has been used for example listings, Java code, configuration details in XML and properties files, and to show program output

`Consolas` has been used in example listings and program outputs to highlight important parts

> A callout like this highlights an important point or concept

Feedback and questions

You can post your feedback and questions to the authors in the following Google Groups forum: `https://groups.google.com/forum/#!forum/getting-started-with-spring-framework`

About the authors

Ashish Sarin is a Sun Certified Enterprise Architect with more than 18 years of experience in architecting applications. He is the author of *Spring Roo 1.1 Cookbook* (by Packt Publishing) and *Portlets in Action* (by Manning Publications)

J Sharma is a freelance Java developer with extensive experience in developing Spring applications.

Chapter 1 – *Introduction to Spring Framework*

1-1 Introduction

In the traditional Java enterprise application development efforts, it was a developer's responsibility to create well-structured, maintainable and easily testable applications. The developers used myriad design patterns to address these non-business requirements of an application. This not only led to low developer productivity, but also adversely affected the quality of developed applications.

Spring Framework (or 'Spring' in short) is an open source application framework that simplifies developing Java enterprise applications. It provides the infrastructure for developing well-structured, maintainable and easily testable applications. When using Spring Framework, a developer only needs to focus on writing the business logic of the application, resulting in improved developer productivity. You can use Spring Framework to develop standalone Java applications, web applications, applets, or any other type of Java application. You can visit the home page of Spring Framework project (`https://projects.spring.io/spring-framework/`) to view the reference documentation and APIs.

This chapter starts off with an introduction to Spring Framework modules and its benefits. At the heart of Spring Framework is its Inversion of Control (IoC) container, which provides dependency injection (DI) feature. This chapter introduces Spring's DI feature and IoC container, and shows how to develop a standalone Java application using Spring. Towards the end of this chapter, we'll look at the new features and enhancements that form part of Spring Framework 5 release. We'll wrap this chapter up by looking at some of the projects that use Spring Framework as their foundation. This chapter will set the stage for the remaining chapters that delve deeper into the Spring Framework.

> In this book, we'll use an example Internet Banking application, *MyBank*, to introduce Spring Framework features.

1-2 Spring Framework modules

Spring Framework consists of multiple modules that are grouped based on the application development features they address. The following table describes the different module groups in Spring Framework and specifies the purpose served by some of the important modules in these groups:

Module group	Description
`Core container`	Contains modules that form the foundation of Spring Framework. The `spring-core` and `spring-beans` modules in this group provide Spring's DI feature and IoC container implementation. The `spring-expression` module provides support for using *Spring Expression Language* (refer chapter 6) for configuring application objects in Spring applications.
`AOP and instrumentation`	Contains modules that support AOP (Aspect-oriented Programming) and class instrumentation. The `spring-aop` module provides Spring's AOP feature, and the `spring-instrument` module provides class instrumentation support.
`Messaging`	Contains the `spring-messaging` module that simplifies developing messaging-based applications.
`Data Access/Integration`	Contains modules that simplify interaction with databases and messaging providers. The `spring-jdbc` module simplifies database interaction using JDBC, and the `spring-orm` module provides integration with ORM (Object Relational Mapping) frameworks, like JPA and Hibernate. The `spring-jms`

	module simplifies interaction with JMS providers. This module group also contains the `spring-tx` module that provides programmatic and declarative transaction management.
Web	Contains `spring-web`, `spring-webmvc`, `spring-webflux` and `spring-websocket` modules. The `spring-webmvc` module simplifies developing servlet-based (that is, web applications that are *blocking* in nature) web applications and RESTful web services. The `spring-webflux` module supports developing *reactive* (that is, applications that are *non-blocking* in nature) web applications and RESTful web services. The `spring-websocket` module supports developing web applications that use WebSocket protocol. The `spring-web` module defines common classes and interfaces that are used across different web modules.
Test	Contains the `spring-test` module that simplifies creating unit and integration tests.

Spring Framework 5 no longer supports developing portlet applications. If you want to develop portlet applications using Spring, stick to Spring Framework 4.3.x.

The above table shows that Spring covers every aspect of enterprise application development; you can use Spring for developing web applications, accessing databases, managing transactions, creating unit and integration tests, and so on. The Spring Framework modules are designed in such a way that you *only* need to include the modules that your application needs. For instance, to use Spring's DI feature in your application, you only need to include the modules grouped under *Core container*. As you progress through this book, you'll find more details about various Spring modules and examples that show how they are used in developing applications.

The naming convention followed by the JAR files in a Spring Framework distribution is:

`spring-`*<short-module-name>*`-`*<spring-version>*`.jar`.

here, *<short-module-name>* is the short name of the Spring module, like aop, `beans`, `context`, `expressions`, and so on. And, the *<spring-version>* is the Spring Framework version.

Following this naming convention, the names of JAR files in Spring `5.0.1.RELEASE` are: `spring-aop-5.0.1.RELEASE.jar`, `spring-beans-5.0.1.RELEASE.jar`, and so on.

Figure 1-1 shows the inter-dependencies of Spring modules. You can infer from the figure that the modules contained in the *Core container* group are central to the Spring Framework, and other modules depend on it. Equally important are the modules contained in the *AOP and instrumentation* group because they provide AOP features to other modules in the Spring Framework.

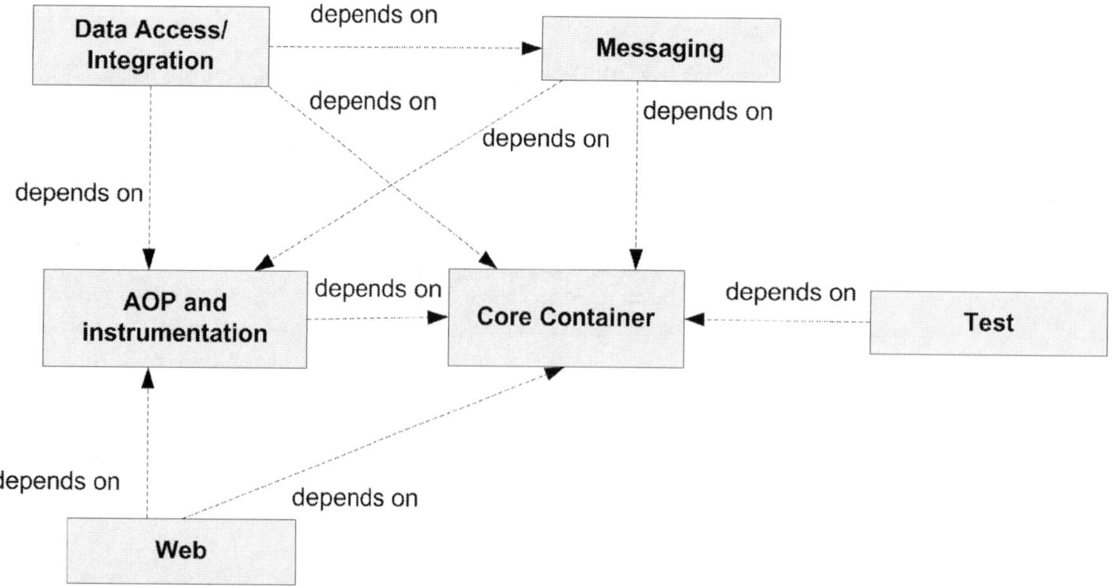

Figure 1-1 Spring modules inter-dependencies

Now that you have some basic idea about the areas of application development covered by Spring, let's look at the Spring IoC container.

1-3 Spring IoC container

A Java application consists of objects that interact with each other to provide application behavior. The objects with which an object interacts are referred to as its *dependencies*. For instance, if an object X interacts with objects Y and Z, then Y and Z are dependencies of object X. DI (short for 'Dependency Injection') is a design pattern in which the dependencies of an object are typically specified as arguments to its constructor and setter methods. And, these dependencies are injected into the object when it's created.

In a Spring application, Spring IoC container (also referred to as 'Spring container') is responsible for creating application objects and injecting their dependencies. The application objects that the Spring container creates and manages are referred as *beans*. As the Spring container is responsible for putting together application objects, you don't need to implement design patterns, like Factory, Service Locator, and so on, to compose your application. DI is also referred to as Inversion of Control (IoC) because the responsibility of creating and injecting dependencies is *not* with the application object, but with the Spring container.

Let's say that the MyBank application (which is the name of our sample application) contains two objects, `FixedDepositController` and `FixedDepositService`. The following example listing shows that the `FixedDepositController` object depends on `FixedDepositService` object:

Example listing 1-1: `FixedDepositController` class

```
public class FixedDepositController {
    private FixedDepositService fixedDepositService;

    public FixedDepositController() {
        fixedDepositService = new FixedDepositService();
    }
    public boolean submit() {
       //-- save the fixed deposit details
        fixedDepositService.save(.....);
    }
```

```
}
```

In the above example listing, FixedDepositController's constructor creates an instance of FixedDepositService which is later used in FixedDepositController's submit method. As FixedDepositController interacts with FixedDepositService, FixedDepositService represents a dependency of FixedDepositController.

To configure FixedDepositController as a Spring bean, you first need to modify the FixedDepositController class of example listing 1-1 such that it accepts FixedDepositService dependency as a constructor argument or as a setter-method argument. The following example listing shows the modified FixedDepositController class:

Example listing 1-2: FixedDepositController class – FixedDepositService is passed as a constructor argument

```
public class FixedDepositController {
    private FixedDepositService fixedDepositService;

    public FixedDepositController(FixedDepositService fixedDepositService) {
        this.fixedDepositService = fixedDepositService;
    }

    public boolean submit() {
       //-- save the fixed deposit details
      fixedDepositService.save(.....);
    }
}
```

The above example listing shows that the FixedDepositService instance is now passed as a constructor argument to the FixedDepositController instance. Now, the FixedDepositController class can be configured as a Spring bean. Notice that the FixedDepositController class doesn't implement or extend from any Spring interface or class.

In Spring-based applications, information about application objects and their dependencies is specified using *configuration metadata*. Spring IoC container reads application's configuration metadata to instantiate application objects and inject their dependencies. The following example listing shows the configuration metadata (in XML format) for MyBank application that consists of FixedDepositController and FixedDepositService classes:

Example listing 1-3: MyBank application's configuration metadata

```
<beans .....>
    <bean id="fdController" class="sample.spring.controller.FixedDepositController">
        <constructor-arg ref="fdService" />
    </bean>

    <bean id="fdService" class="sample.spring.service.FixedDepositService"/>
</beans>
```

In the above example listing, each <bean> element defines an application object that is managed by the Spring container, and the <constructor-arg> element specifies that an instance of FixedDepositService is passed as an argument to FixedDepositController's constructor. The <bean> element is discussed in detail later in this chapter, and the <constructor-arg> element is discussed in chapter 2.

Spring container reads the configuration metadata (like the one shown in example listing 1-3) of an application and creates the application objects defined by <bean> elements and injects their dependencies. Spring container makes use of *Java Reflection API* (http://docs.oracle.com/javase/tutorial/reflect/index.html) to create application objects and inject their dependencies. The following figure summarizes how the Spring container works:

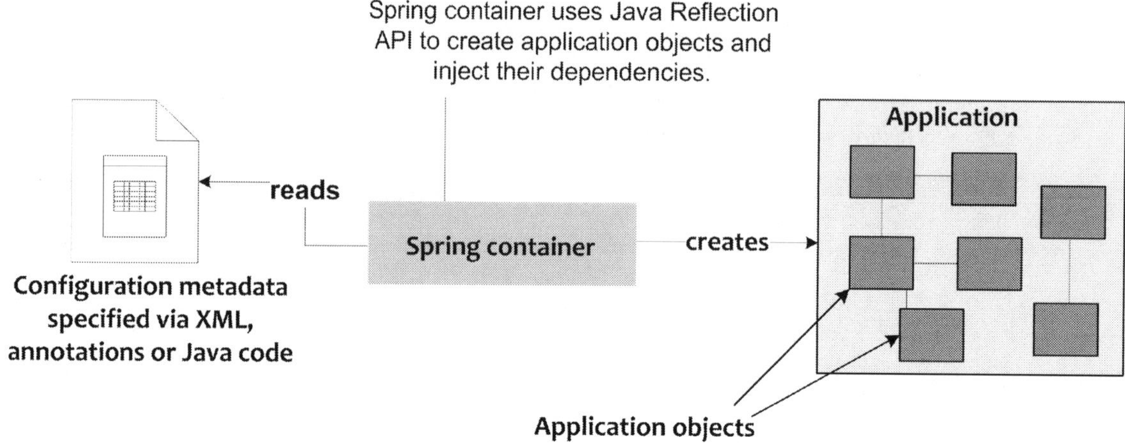

Figure 1-2 Spring container reads application's configuration metadata and creates a fully-configured application

The configuration metadata can be supplied to the Spring container via XML (as shown in example listing 1-3), Java annotations (refer chapter 6) and programmatically through the Java code (refer chapter 7).

As the Spring container is responsible for creating and managing application objects, enterprise services (like transaction management, security, remote access, and so on) can be transparently applied to the objects by the Spring container. The ability of the Spring container to enhance the application objects with additional functionality makes it possible for you to model your application objects as simple Java objects (also referred to as *POJOs* or *Plain Old Java Objects*). Java classes corresponding to POJOs are referred to as *POJO classes*, which are nothing but Java classes that don't implement or extend framework-specific interfaces or classes. The enterprise services, like transaction management, security, remote access, and so on, required by these POJOs are transparently provided by the Spring container.

Now that we know how Spring container works, let's look at some examples that demonstrate benefits of developing applications using Spring.

1-4 Benefits of using Spring Framework

In the previous section, we discussed the following benefits of using Spring:

- Spring simplifies composing Java applications by taking care of creating application objects and injecting their dependencies
- Spring promotes developing applications as POJOs

Spring also simplifies interaction with JMS providers, JNDI, MBean servers, email servers, databases, and so on, by providing a layer of abstraction that takes care of the boilerplate code.

Let's take a quick look at a few examples to better understand the benefits of developing applications using Spring.

Consistent approach to managing local and global transactions

If you are using Spring for developing *transactional* applications, you can use Spring's *declarative transaction management* support to manage transactions.

The following example listing shows the `FixedDepositService` class of MyBank application:

Example listing 1-4 – `FixedDepositService` class

```
public class FixedDepositService {
    public FixedDepositDetails getFixedDepositDetails( ..... ) { ..... }
    public boolean createFixedDeposit(FixedDepositDetails fixedDepositDetails) { ..... }
}
```

`FixedDepositService` class is a POJO class that defines methods to create and retrieve details of fixed deposits. The following figure shows the form for creating a new fixed deposit:

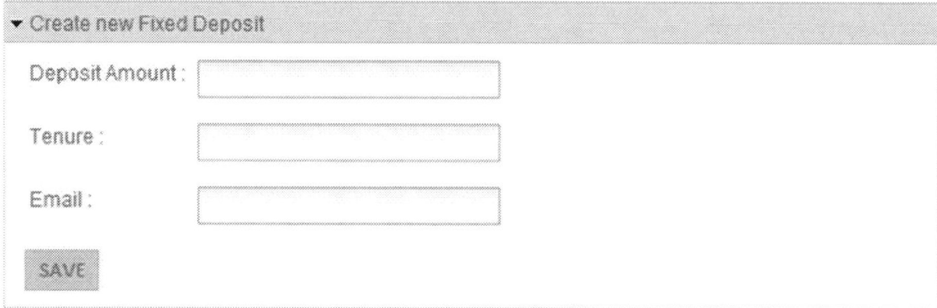

Figure 1-3 HTML form for creating a new fixed deposit

A customer enters the fixed deposit amount, tenure and email id information in the above form and clicks the SAVE button to create a new fixed deposit. The `FixedDepositService`'s `createFixedDeposit` method (refer example listing 1-4) is invoked to create the fixed deposit. The `createFixedDeposit` method debits the amount entered by the customer from his bank account and creates a fixed deposit of the same amount.

Let's say that information about the bank balance of customers is stored in `BANK_ACCOUNT_DETAILS` database table, and the fixed deposit details are stored in `FIXED_DEPOSIT_DETAILS` database table. If a customer creates a fixed deposit of amount x, amount x is subtracted from the `BANK_ACCOUNT_DETAILS` table, and a new record is inserted in `FIXED_DEPOSIT_DETAILS` table to reflect the newly created fixed deposit. If `BANK_ACCOUNT_DETAILS` table is *not* updated or a new record is *not* inserted in `FIXED_DEPOSIT_DETAILS` table, it'll leave the system in an inconsistent state. This means the `createFixedDeposit` method *must* be executed within a transaction.

The database used by the MyBank application represents a *transactional resource*. In the traditional approach to perform a set of database modifications as a single unit of work, you'll first disable auto-commit mode of JDBC connection, then execute SQL statements, and finally commit (or rollback) the transaction. The following example listing shows the `createFixedDeposit` method that uses the traditional approach to managing database transactions:

Example listing 1-5 – Programmatically managing database transactions using JDBC `Connection` object

```
import java.sql.Connection;
import java.sql.SQLException;

public class FixedDepositService {
      public FixedDepositDetails getFixedDepositDetails( ..... ) { ..... }

      public boolean createFixedDeposit(FixedDepositDetails fixedDepositDetails) {
          Connection con = ..... ;
```

```
            try {
                con.setAutoCommit(false);
                //-- execute SQL statements that modify database tables
                con.commit();
            } catch(SQLException sqle) {
                if(con != null) {
                    con.rollback();
                }
            }
            .....
        }
}
```

The above example listing shows that the `createFixedDeposit` method programmatically manages database transactions using JDBC `Connection` object. Transactions that are resource-specific, like the transactions associated with a JDBC `Connection` object, are referred to as *local transactions*.

The approach of using JDBC `Connection` object to manage transactions is suitable for application scenarios in which a single database (that is, a single transactional resource) is involved. When multiple transactional resources are involved, JTA (Java Transaction API) is used for managing transactions. For instance, if you want to send a JMS message to a messaging middleware (a transactional resource) and update a database (another transactional resource) in the same transaction, you must use a JTA transaction manager to manage transactions. JTA transactions are also referred to as *global* (or *distributed*) *transactions*. To use JTA, you fetch `UserTransaction` object (which is part of JTA API) from JNDI and programmatically start and commit (or rollback) transactions.

As you can see, you can either use JDBC `Connection` (for local transactions) or `UserTransaction` (for global transactions) object to programmatically manage transactions. It is important to note that a local transaction *cannot* run within a global transaction. This means that if you want database updates in `createFixedDeposit` method (refer example listing 1-5) to be part of a JTA transaction, you need to modify the `createFixedDeposit` method to use the `UserTransaction` object for transaction management.

Spring simplifies transaction management by providing a layer of abstraction that gives a *consistent* approach to managing both local and global transactions. This means that if you write the `createFixedDeposit` method (refer example listing 1-5) using Spring's transaction abstraction, you don't need to modify the method when you switch from local to global transaction management, or vice versa. Spring's transaction abstraction is explained in chapter 8.

Declarative transaction management

Spring gives you the option to use *declarative transaction management*. You can annotate a method with Spring's `@Transactional` annotation and let Spring handle transactions, as shown here:

Example listing 1-6 – `@Transactional` annotation usage

```
import org.springframework.transaction.annotation.Transactional;

public class FixedDepositService {
    public FixedDepositDetails getFixedDepositDetails( ..... ) { ..... }

    @Transactional
    public boolean createFixedDeposit(FixedDepositDetails fixedDepositDetails) { ..... }
}
```

The above example listing shows that the `FixedDepositService` class doesn't implement or extend from any Spring-specific interface or class to use Spring's transaction management facility. The Spring Framework transparently provides transaction management feature to @Transactional annotated createFixedDeposit method. This shows that Spring is a *non-invasive* framework because it doesn't require your application objects to be dependent upon Spring-specific classes or interfaces. As transaction management is taken care by Spring, you don't need to directly work with transaction management APIs to manage transactions.

Security

Security is an important aspect of any Java application. Spring Security (http://projects.spring.io/spring-security/) is a project that is built on top of Spring Framework. Spring Security provides authentication and authorization features that you can use for securing Java applications.

Let's say that the following 3 user roles have been identified for the MyBank application: LOAN_CUSTOMER, SAVINGS_ACCOUNT_CUSTOMER and APPLICATION_ADMIN. A customer *must* be associated with the SAVINGS_ACCOUNT_CUSTOMER or the APPLICATION_ADMIN role to invoke the createFixedDeposit method of FixedDepositService class (refer example listing 1-6). Using Spring Security you can easily address this requirement by annotating createFixedDeposit method with Spring Security's @Secured annotation, as shown in the following example listing:

Example listing 1-7 – Secured createFixedDeposit method

```
import org.springframework.transaction.annotation.Transactional;
import org.springframework.security.access.annotation.Secured;

public class FixedDepositService {
    public FixedDepositDetails getFixedDepositDetails( ..... ) { ..... }

    @Transactional
    @Secured({ "SAVINGS_ACCOUNT_CUSTOMER", "APPLICATION_ADMIN" })
    public boolean createFixedDeposit(FixedDepositDetails fixedDepositDetails) { ..... }
}
```

If you annotate a method with Spring Security's @Secured annotation, security feature is transparently applied to the method by the Spring Security framework. The above example listing shows that for implementing *method-level* security you don't need to extend or implement any Spring-specific classes or interfaces. Also, you don't need to write security-related code in your business methods.

Spring Security framework is discussed in detail in chapter 16.

JMX (Java Management Extensions)

Spring's JMX support simplifies incorporating JMX technology in your applications.

Let's say that the fixed deposit facility of MyBank application should only be available to customers from 9:00 AM to 6:00 PM every day. To address this requirement, a variable is added to the FixedDepositService class, which acts as a flag indicating whether the fixed deposit service is active or inactive. The following example listing shows the FixedDepositService class that uses such a flag:

Example listing 1-8 – FixedDepositService with active variable

```
public class FixedDepositService {
    private boolean active;

    public FixedDepositDetails getFixedDepositDetails( ..... ) {
        if(active) { ..... }
    }
```

```
    public boolean createFixedDeposit(FixedDepositDetails fixedDepositDetails) {
        if(active) { ..... }
    }
    public void activateService() {
        active = true;
    }
    public void deactivateService() {
        active = false;
    }
}
```

The above example listing shows that a variable named active is added to the FixedDepositService class. If the value of the active variable is true, the getFixedDepositDetails and createFixedDeposit methods work as expected. If the value of the active variable is false, the getFixedDepositDetails and createFixedDeposit methods throw an exception indicating that the fixed deposit service is currently inactive. The activateService and deactivateService methods set the value of active variable to true and false, respectively.

Now, who calls the activateService and deactivateService methods? Let's say a separate scheduler application, *Bank App Scheduler*, runs at 9:00 AM and 6:00 PM to execute activateService and deactivateService methods, respectively. The Bank App Scheduler application uses JMX (Java Management Extensions) API to remotely interact with FixedDepositService instance.

> Refer to the following article to learn more about JMX:
> http://docs.oracle.com/javase/tutorial/jmx/index.html.

As Bank App Scheduler uses JMX to change the value of the active variable of the FixedDepositService instance, you need to register the FixedDepositService instance as a *managed bean* (or *MBean*) with an MBean server, and expose FixedDepositService's activateService and deactivateService methods as JMX operations. In Spring, you register instances of a class with the MBean server by annotating the class with Spring's @ManagedResource annotation, and expose the methods of the class as JMX operations using Spring's @ManagedOperation annotation.

The following example listing shows usage of @ManagedResource and @ManagedOperation annotations to register instances of the FixedDepositService class with the MBean server, and to expose its activateService and deactivateService methods as JMX operations:

Example listing 1-9 – FixedDepositService class that uses Spring's JMX support

```
import org.springframework.jmx.export.annotation.ManagedOperation;
import org.springframework.jmx.export.annotation.ManagedResource;

@ManagedResource(objectName =  "fixed_deposit_service:name=FixedDepositService")
public class FixedDepositService {
    private boolean active;

    public FixedDepositDetails getFixedDepositDetails( ..... ) {
        if(active) { ..... }
    }
    public boolean createFixedDeposit(FixedDepositDetails fixedDepositDetails) {
        if(active) { ..... }
    }

    @ManagedOperation
    public void activateService() {
```

```
        active = true;
    }

    @ManagedOperation
    public void deactivateService() {
        active = false;
    }
}
```

The above example listing shows that the FixedDepositService class doesn't directly use JMX API to register its instances with the MBean server and to expose its methods as JMX operations.

JMS (Java Message Service)

Spring's JMS support simplifies sending and receiving messages from JMS providers.

In MyBank application, when a customer submits a request to receive details of their fixed deposits via email, the FixedDepositService sends the request details to a JMS messaging middleware (like ActiveMQ). The request is later processed by a message listener. Spring simplifies interaction with JMS providers by providing a layer of abstraction. The following example listing shows how FixedDepositService class sends request details to a JMS provider using Spring's JmsTemplate:

Example listing 1-10 – FixedDepositService that sends JMS messages

```
import org.springframework.beans.factory.annotation.Autowired;
import org.springframework.jms.core.JmsTemplate;

public class FixedDepositService {
    @Autowired
    private transient JmsTemplate jmsTemplate;
    .....
    public boolean submitRequest(Request request) {
        jmsTemplate.convertAndSend(request);
    }
}
```

The above example listing shows that the FixedDepositService defines a variable of type JmsTemplate, and is annotated with Spring's @Autowired annotation. For now, you can assume that the @Autowired annotation provides access to a JmsTemplate instance. The JmsTemplate instance knows about the JMS destination to which the JMS message is to be sent. The FixedDepositService's submitRequest method invokes JmsTemplate's convertAndSend method to send request details (represented by Request argument of submitRequest method) as a JMS message to the JMS provider. JmsTemplate is discussed in detail in chapter 10.

Once again, the above example listing shows that if you are using Spring Framework to send messages to JMS providers, then you don't need to directly deal with JMS API.

Caching

Spring's cache abstraction provides a consistent approach to use caching in your application.

It's common to use caching solutions to improve the performance of an application. MyBank application uses a caching product to improve the performance of *read* operations for fixed deposit details. Spring Framework simplifies interacting with different caching solutions by abstracting caching-related logic.

The following example listing shows that the FixedDepositService's getFixedDepositDetails method uses Spring's cache abstraction feature to cache fixed deposit details:

Example listing 1-11 – FixedDepositService that caches fixed deposit details

```
import org.springframework.cache.annotation.Cacheable;

public class FixedDepositService {

    @Cacheable("fixedDeposits")
    public FixedDepositDetails getFixedDepositDetails( ..... ) { ..... }

    public boolean createFixedDeposit(FixedDepositDetails fixedDepositDetails) { ..... }
}
```

In the above example listing, Spring's @Cacheable annotation indicates that the fixed deposit details returned by the getFixedDepositDetails method are *cached*. If the getFixedDepositDetails method is invoked with the same argument value(s), the getFixedDepositDetails method is *not* executed, and the fixed deposit details are returned from the cache. This shows that if you are using Spring Framework, you don't need to write caching-related logic in your classes. Spring's cache abstraction is explained in detail in chapter 10.

In this section, we saw that Spring Framework simplifies developing enterprise applications by transparently providing services to POJOs, thereby shielding developers from lower level API details. Spring also provides easy integration with standard frameworks, like Hibernate, Quartz, JSF, Struts, EJB, and so on, which makes Spring an ideal choice for enterprise application development.

Now that we have looked at some of the benefits of using Spring Framework, let's take a look at how to develop a simple Spring application.

1-5 A simple Spring application

In this section, we'll look at a simple Spring application that uses Spring's DI feature. To use Spring's DI feature in an application, follow these steps:

1. identify application objects and their dependencies
2. create POJO classes corresponding to the application objects identified in step 1
3. create *configuration metadata* that depicts application objects and their dependencies
4. create an instance of Spring IoC container and pass the configuration metadata to it
5. access application objects from the Spring IoC container instance

Let's now look at above mentioned steps in the context of MyBank application.

Identifying application objects and their dependencies

We discussed earlier that the MyBank application shows a form for creating a fixed deposit (refer figure 1-3). The following sequence diagram shows the application objects (and their interaction) that come into picture when a user submits the form:

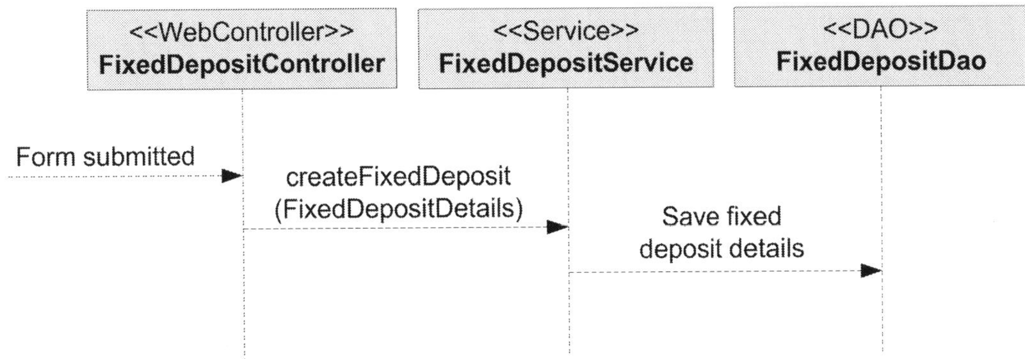

Figure 1-4 MyBank's application objects and their dependencies

In the above sequence diagram, `FixedDepositController` represents a web controller that receives the request when the form is submitted. The fixed deposit details are contained in the `FixedDepositDetails` object. The `FixedDepositController` invokes the `createFixedDeposit` method of `FixedDepositService` (a service layer object). Then, `FixedDepositService` invokes `FixedDepositDao` object (a data access object) to save the fixed deposit details in the application's data store. So, we can interpret from the above diagram that `FixedDepositService` is a *dependency* of `FixedDepositController` object, and `FixedDepositDao` is a *dependency* of `FixedDepositService` object.

IMPORT **chapter 1/ch01-bankapp-xml** (This project shows a simple Spring application that uses Spring's DI feature. To run the application, execute the `main` method of the `BankApp` class of this project)

Creating POJO classes corresponding to identified application objects

Once you have identified application objects, the next step is to create POJO classes corresponding to these application objects. POJO classes corresponding to the `FixedDepositController`, `FixedDepositService` and `FixedDepositDao` application objects are available in `ch01-bankapp-xml` project. The `ch01-bankapp-xml` project represents a simplified version of MyBank application that uses Spring's DI feature. You should import the `ch01-bankapp-xml` project into your IDE as in the remaining steps we'll be looking at the files contained in this project.

In section 1-3, we discussed that a dependency is passed to an application object as a constructor argument or as a setter method argument. The following code listing shows that an instance of `FixedDepositService` (a dependency of `FixedDepositController`) is passed as a setter method argument to the `FixedDepositController` object:

Example listing 1-12 – `FixedDepositController` class
Project – `ch01-bankapp-xml`
Source location - `src/main/java/sample/spring/chapter01/bankapp`

```
package sample.spring.chapter01.bankapp;
.....
public class FixedDepositController {
    .....
    private FixedDepositService fixedDepositService;
    .....
    public void setFixedDepositService(FixedDepositService fixedDepositService) {
        logger.info("Setting fixedDepositService property");
        this.fixedDepositService = fixedDepositService;
    }
    .....
    public void submit() {
        fixedDepositService.createFixedDeposit(new FixedDepositDetails( 1, 10000,
```

```
            365, "someemail@something.com"));
    }
    .....
}
```

In the above example listing, FixedDepositService dependency is passed to FixedDepositController through setFixedDepositService method. We'll soon see that the setFixedDepositService setter method is invoked by Spring.

> If you look at the FixedDepositController, FixedDepositService and FixedDepositDao classes, you'll notice that none of these classes implement any Spring-specific interface or extend from any Spring-specific class.

Let's now look at how application objects and their dependencies are specified in the configuration metadata.

Creating the configuration metadata

We saw in section 1-3 that the configuration metadata specifies application objects and their dependencies, which is read by the Spring container to instantiate application objects and inject their dependencies. In this section, we'll first look at what other information is contained in the configuration metadata, followed by an in-depth look at how configuration metadata is specified in XML format.

The configuration metadata specifies information about the enterprise services (like transaction management, security and remote access) that are required by the application. For instance, if you want Spring to manage transactions, you need to configure an implementation of Spring's PlatformTransactionManager interface in the configuration metadata. PlatformTransactionManager implementation is responsible for managing transactions (refer chapter 8 to know more about Spring's transaction management feature).

If your application interacts with messaging middlewares (like ActiveMQ), databases (like MySQL), e-mail servers, and so on, then Spring-specific objects that simplify interacting with these external systems are also defined in the configuration metadata. For instance, if your application sends or receives JMS messages from ActiveMQ, then you can configure Spring's JmsTemplate class in the configuration metadata to simplify interaction with ActiveMQ. We saw in example listing 1-10 that if you use JmsTemplate for sending messages to a JMS provider, then you don't need to deal with lower-level JMS API (refer chapter 10 to know more about Spring's support for interacting with JMS providers).

You can supply the configuration metadata to the Spring container via an XML file or through annotations in POJO classes. Starting with Spring 3.0, you can also supply the configuration metadata to the Spring container through Java classes annotated with Spring's @Configuration annotation. In this section, we'll see how configuration metadata is specified in XML format. In chapters 6 and 7, we'll see how configuration metadata is supplied via annotations in POJO classes and through @Configuration annotated Java classes, respectively.

You provide the configuration metadata for an application in XML format by creating an *application context XML* file that contains information about the application objects and their dependencies. Example listing 1-3 showed how an application context XML file looks like. The following XML shows the application context XML file of MyBank application that consists of FixedDepositController, FixedDepositService and FixedDepositDao objects (refer figure 1-4 to see how these objects interact with each other):

Example listing 1-13 – applicationContext.xml - MyBank's application context XML file
Project – ch01-bankapp-xml
Source location - src/main/resources/META-INF/spring

```
<?xml version="1.0" encoding="UTF-8" standalone="no"?>
<beans xmlns = "http://www.springframework.org/schema/beans"
    xmlns:xsi = "http://www.w3.org/2001/XMLSchema-instance"
```

```
    xsi:schemaLocation = "http://www.springframework.org/schema/beans
            http://www.springframework.org/schema/beans/spring-beans.xsd">

    <bean id="controller"
            class="sample.spring.chapter01.bankapp.FixedDepositController">
        <property name="fixedDepositService" ref="service" />
    </bean>

    <bean id="service" class="sample.spring.chapter01.bankapp.FixedDepositService">
        <property name="fixedDepositDao" ref="dao" />
    </bean>

    <bean id="dao" class="sample.spring.chapter01.bankapp.FixedDepositDao"/>
</beans>
```

The following are the important points to note about the application context XML file shown above:

- The `<beans>` element is the root element of the application context XML file, and is defined in `spring-beans.xsd` schema (also referred to as Spring's beans schema). The `spring-beans.xsd` schema is contained in `spring-beans-5.0.1.RELEASE.jar` JAR file that comes with the Spring Framework `5.0.1.RELEASE` distribution.

- Each `<bean>` element configures an application object that is managed by the Spring container. In Spring Framework's terminology, a `<bean>` element represents a *bean definition*. The object that the Spring container creates based on the bean definition is referred to as a *bean*. The `id` attribute specifies a unique name for the bean, and the `class` attribute specifies the fully-qualified class name of the bean. You can also use the `name` attribute of `<bean>` element to specify *aliases* for the bean. In MyBank application, the application objects are `FixedDepositController`, `FixedDepositService` and `FixedDepositDao`; therefore, we have 3 `<bean>` elements - one for each application object. As application objects configured by `<bean>` elements are managed by the Spring container, the responsibility for creating them and injecting their dependencies is with the Spring container. Instead of directly creating instances of application objects defined by `<bean>` elements, you should obtain them from the Spring container. Later in this section, we'll look at how to obtain application objects managed by Spring container.

- No `<bean>` element is defined corresponding to the `FixedDepositDetails` domain object of MyBank application. This is because domain objects are *not* typically managed by the Spring container; they are created by the ORM framework (like Hibernate) used by the application, or you create them programmatically using the `new` operator.

- The `<property>` element specifies a dependency (or a configuration property) of the bean configured by the `<bean>` element. The `<property>` element corresponds to a *JavaBean-style setter* method in the bean class which is invoked by the Spring container to set a dependency (or a configuration property) of the bean.

Let's now look at how dependencies are injected via setter methods.

Injecting dependencies via setter methods

To understand how dependencies are injected via setter methods defined in the bean class, let's once again look at the `FixedDepositController` class of MyBank application:

Example listing 1-14 – FixedDepositController class
Project – ch01-bankapp-xml
Source location - src/main/java/sample/spring/chapter01/bankapp

```
package sample.spring.chapter01.bankapp;

import org.apache.logging.log4j.LogManager;
import org.apache.logging.log4j.Logger;

public class FixedDepositController {
    private static Logger logger = LogManager.getLogger(FixedDepositController.class);

    private FixedDepositService fixedDepositService;

    public FixedDepositController() {
       logger.info("initializing");
    }

    public void setFixedDepositService(FixedDepositService fixedDepositService) {
        logger.info("Setting fixedDepositService property");
        this.fixedDepositService = fixedDepositService;
    }
    .....
}
```

The above example listing shows that the FixedDepositController class declares an instance variable named fixedDepositService of type FixedDepositService. The fixedDepositService variable is set by the setFixedDepositService method - a *JavaBean-style setter method* for fixedDepositService variable. This is an example of *setter-based DI*, wherein a setter method satisfies a dependency.

Figure 1-5 describes the bean definition for the FixedDepositController class in the applicationContext.xml file (refer example listing 1-13).

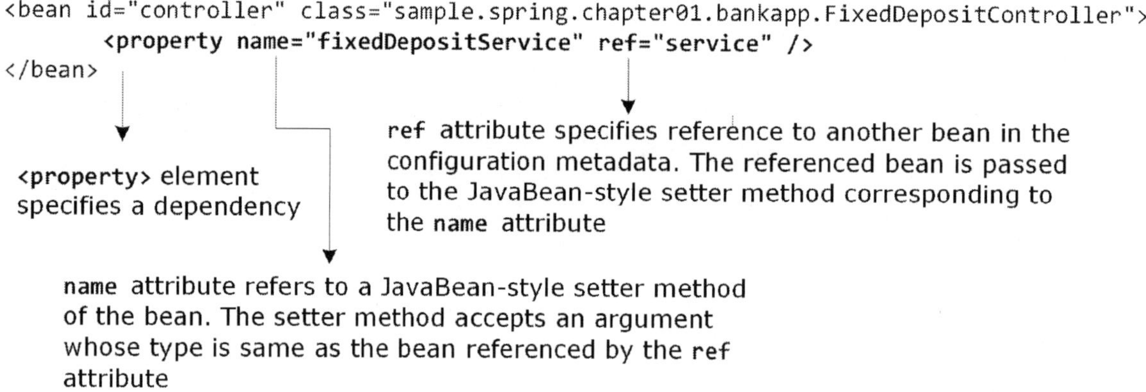

Figure 1-5 Defining dependencies using <property> elements

The above bean definition shows that the FixedDepositController bean defines its dependence on FixedDepositService bean via <property> element. The <property> element's name attribute corresponds to the JavaBean-style setter method in the bean class that is invoked by the Spring container at the time of bean creation. The <property> element's ref attribute identifies the Spring bean whose instance needs to be created and passed to the JavaBean-style setter method. The value of ref attribute must match the id attribute's value (or one of the names specified by the name attribute) of a <bean> element in the configuration metadata.

In figure 1-5, the value of <property> element's name attribute is fixedDepositService, which means that the <property> element corresponds to the setFixedDepositService setter method of FixedDepositController class (refer example listing 1-14). As the value of <property> element's ref attribute is service, the <property> element refers to the <bean> element whose id attribute's value is service. Now, the <bean> element whose id attribute's value is service is the FixedDepositService bean (refer example listing 1-13). Spring container creates an instance of FixedDepositService class (a dependency), and invokes the setFixedDepositService method (a JavaBean-style setter method for fixedDepositService variable) of FixedDepositController (a dependent object), passing the FixedDepositService instance.

In the context of FixedDepositController application object, figure 1-6 summarizes the purpose of name and ref attributes of <property> element.

```
<bean id="controller"
        class="sample.spring.chapter01.bankapp.FixedDepositController">
    <property name="fixedDepositService" ref="service" />
</bean>

        <bean id="service"
                class="sample.spring.chapter01.bankapp.FixedDepositService">
            <property name="fixedDepositDao" ref="dao" />
        </bean>

                public class FixedDepositController {
                        ...
                        private FixedDepositService fixedDepositService;
                        ...
                        public void setFixedDepositService(FixedDepositService
                                        fixedDepositService) {
                                logger.info("Setting fixedDepositService property");
                                this.fixedDepositService = fixedDepositService;
                        }
                        ...
                }
```

Figure 1-6 <property> element's name attribute corresponds to a JavaBean-style setter method that satisfies a bean dependency, and ref attribute refers to another bean.

The above figure shows that fixedDepositService value of name attribute corresponds to the setFixedDepositService method of FixedDepositController class, and service value of ref attribute refers to the bean whose id is service.

Figure 1-7 summarizes how the Spring container creates beans and injects their dependencies based on the configuration metadata supplied by the applicationContext.xml file (refer example listing 1-13) of MyBank application. The figure shows the sequence of steps followed by the Spring IoC container to create FixedDepositController, FixedDepositService and FixedDepositDao beans and inject their dependencies. Before attempting to create beans, the Spring container reads and validates the configuration metadata supplied by the applicationContext.xml file. The order in which the beans are created by the Spring container depends on the order in which they are defined in the applicationContext.xml file. Spring container ensures that the dependencies of a bean are completely configured before the setter method is invoked. For example, the FixedDepositController bean is dependent on FixedDepositService bean; therefore, Spring container configures the FixedDepositService bean before invoking the setFixedDepositService method of FixedDepositController bean.

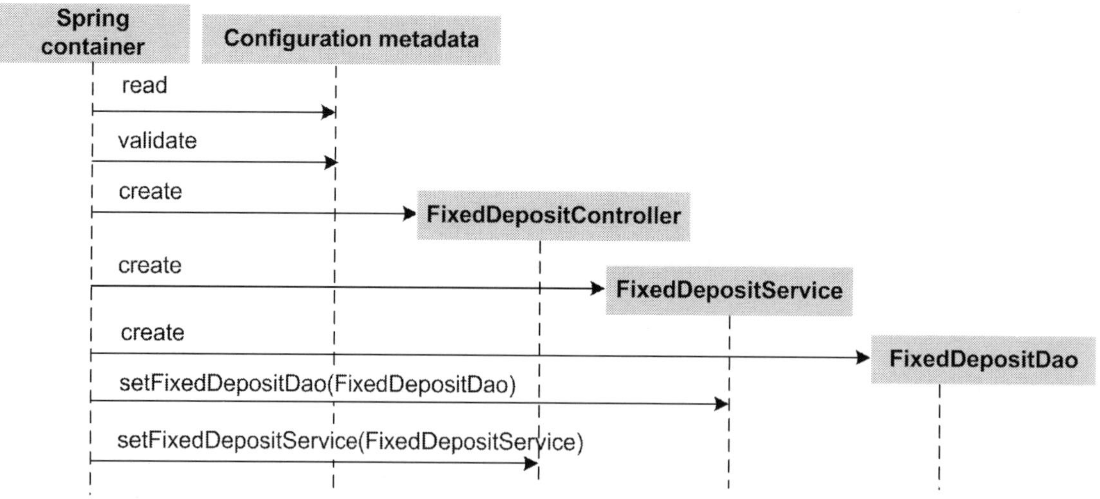

Figure 1-7 - The sequence in which Spring IoC container creates beans and injects their dependencies.

> It is fairly common to refer to a bean definition by its name (which is `id` attribute's value) or type (which is `class` attribute's value) or the interface implemented by the bean class. For instance, you can refer to '`FixedDepositController` bean' as '`controller` bean'. And, if the `FixedDepositController` class implements `FixedDepositControllerIntf` interface, you can refer to '`FixedDepositController` bean' as '`FixedDepositControllerIntf` bean'.

The bean definitions that we have seen so far, instruct Spring container to create bean instances by invoking the *no-argument* constructor of the bean class, and inject dependencies using setter-based DI. In chapter 2, we'll look at bean definitions that instruct Spring container to create a bean instance via a *factory method* defined in a class. Also, we'll look at how to inject dependencies through constructor arguments (referred to as *constructor-based* DI).

Let's now look at how to create an instance of Spring container and pass configuration metadata to it.

Creating an instance of Spring container

Spring's `ApplicationContext` object represents an instance of Spring container. Spring provides a few built-in implementations of `ApplicationContext` interface, like `ClassPathXmlApplicationContext`, `FileSystemXmlApplicationContext`, `XmlWebApplicationContext`, and so on. The choice of the `ApplicationContext` implementation depends on how you have defined the configuration metadata (using XML, annotations or Java code), and the type of your application (standalone or web). For instance, `ClassPathXmlApplicationContext` and `FileSystemXmlApplicationContext` classes are suitable for *standalone* applications in which configuration metadata is supplied in XML format, `XmlWebApplicationContext` is suitable for *web* applications in which the configuration metadata is supplied in XML format, `AnnotationConfigWebApplicationContext` is suitable for *web* applications in which configuration metadata is supplied programmatically through Java code, and so on.

As MyBank application represents a standalone application, we can use either `ClassPathXmlApplicationContext` or `FileSystemXmlApplicationContext` class to create an instance of Spring container. You should note that the `ClassPathXmlApplicationContext` class loads an application context XML file from the specified *classpath* location, and the `FileSystemXmlApplicationContext` class loads an application context XML file from the specified location on the *filesystem*.

The following `BankApp` class of MyBank application shows that an instance of Spring container is created using the `ClassPathXmlApplicationContext` class:

Example listing 1-15 – BankApp class
Project – ch01-bankapp-xml
Source location - src/main/java/sample/spring/chapter01/bankapp

```
package sample.spring.chapter01.bankapp;

import org.springframework.context.ApplicationContext;
import org.springframework.context.support.ClassPathXmlApplicationContext;

public class BankApp {
    .....
    public static void main(String args[]) {
        ApplicationContext context = new ClassPathXmlApplicationContext(
            "classpath:META-INF/spring/applicationContext.xml");
        .....
    }
}
```

The above example listing shows the BankApp's main method, which is responsible for bootstrapping the Spring container. The classpath location of the application context XML file is passed to the constructor of ClassPathXmlApplicationContext class. The creation of ClassPathXmlApplicationContext instance results in creation of those beans in the application context XML file that are *singleton-scoped* and set to be *pre-instantiated*. In chapter 2, we'll discuss *bean scopes*, and what it means to have beans *pre-* or *lazily-instantiated* by Spring container. For now, you can assume that the beans defined in the applicationContext.xml file of MyBank application are singleton-scoped and set to be pre-instantiated. This means that the beans defined in the applicationContext.xml file are created when an instance of ClassPathXmlApplicationContext is created.

Now that we have seen how to create an instance of the Spring container, let's look at how to retrieve bean instances from the Spring container.

Access beans from the Spring container

The application objects defined via <bean> elements are created and managed by the Spring container. You can access instances of these application objects by calling one of the getBean methods of the ApplicationContext interface.

The following example listing shows the main method of BankApp class that retrieves an instance of FixedDepositController bean from the Spring container and invokes its methods:

Example listing 1-16 – BankApp class
Project – ch01-bankapp-xml
Source location - src/main/java/sample/spring/chapter01/bankapp

```
package sample.spring.chapter01.bankapp;

import org.apache.logging.log4j.LogManager;
import org.apache.logging.log4j.Logger;
import org.springframework.context.ApplicationContext;
import org.springframework.context.support.ClassPathXmlApplicationContext;

public class BankApp {
    private static Logger logger = LogManager.getLogger(BankApp.class);

    public static void main(String args[]) {
        ApplicationContext context = new ClassPathXmlApplicationContext(
```

```
            "classpath:META-INF/spring/applicationContext.xml");

        FixedDepositController fixedDepositController =
                (FixedDepositController) context.getBean("controller");
        logger.info("Submission status of fixed deposit : "
                + fixedDepositController.submit());
        logger.info("Returned fixed deposit info : " + fixedDepositController.get());
    }
}
```

At first, the ApplicationContext's getBean method is invoked to retrieve an instance of FixedDepositController bean from the Spring container, followed by invocation of submit and get methods of FixedDepositController bean. The argument passed to the getBean method is the name of the bean whose instance you want to retrieve from the Spring container. The name of the bean passed to the getBean method *must* be the value of the id or name attribute of the bean that you want to retrieve. If no bean with the specified name is registered with the Spring container, an exception is thrown by the getBean method.

In example listing 1-16, to configure the FixedDepositController instance, we didn't programmatically create an instance of FixedDepositService and set it on the FixedDepositController instance. Also, we didn't create an instance of FixedDepositDao and set it on the FixedDepositService instance. This is because the task of creating dependencies, and injecting them into the dependent objects is handled by the Spring container.

If you go to ch01-bankapp-xml project and execute the main method of BankApp class, you'll see the following output on the console:

```
INFO  sample.spring.chapter01.bankapp.FixedDepositController - initializing
INFO  sample.spring.chapter01.bankapp.FixedDepositService - initializing
INFO  sample.spring.chapter01.bankapp.FixedDepositDao - initializing
INFO  sample.spring.chapter01.bankapp.FixedDepositService - Setting fixedDepositDao
property
INFO sample.spring.chapter01.bankapp.FixedDepositController - Setting fixedDepositService
property
INFO  sample.spring.chapter01.bankapp.BankApp - Submission status of fixed deposit : true
INFO  sample.spring.chapter01.bankapp.BankApp - Returned fixed deposit info : id :1,
deposit amount : 10000.0, tenure : 365, email : someemail@something.com
```

The above output shows that the Spring container creates an instance of each of the beans defined in the applicationContext.xml file of MyBank application. Also, Spring container uses setter-based DI to inject an instance of FixedDepositService into FixedDepositController instance, and an instance of FixedDepositDao into the FixedDepositService instance.

Spring Framework 5 introduces many new interesting features and enhancements. Let's look at some of the important changes to Spring Framework 5.

1-6 What's new in Spring Framework 5 ?

The following are some of the notable changes to Spring Framework 5 release:

- compatible with Java 9. This means you can develop applications using Java 9 features and deploy them on Java 9.

- Spring Framework JARs can be added to Java 9's *module path* or classpath. If you add Spring Framework JARs to the module path, they are converted into *automatic modules* that export all their packages.

- embraces *reactive programming* paradigm for developing *asynchronous* and *non-blocking* applications. Spring supports using *reactive types* defined by Reactor 3.1 and RxJava 1.3 and 2.1 libraries. Chapter 18 and 19 discuss developing reactive applications using RxJava 2 and Reactor 3.1.

- source code of the Spring Framework 5 itself is now based on Java 8

- the support for portlets, Velocity templates and JasperReports has been dropped from Spring Framework 5

- `@Nullable`, `@NonNull`, `@NonNullApi` and `@NonNullFields` annotations bring null-safety to Spring applications. `@Nullable` annotation indicates that a field, method argument or a method's return value *can* be `null`. `@NonNull` annotation indicates that a field, method argument or a method's return value *cannot* be `null`. `@NonNullApi` is a package-level annotation that specifies that the methods and their parameters *cannot* be `null`. `@NonNullFields` is a package-level annotation that specifies that the fields *cannot* be `null`. These annotations can be used by static code analysis tools (like FindBugs) to highlight potential issues in the program that can cause `java.lang.NullPointerException` at runtime.

- functional style bean registration and customization using the newly introduced methods in `AnnotationConfigApplicationContext` class (refer chapter 7 for more details)

- generating and reading an index of Spring components from a file (instead of classpath scanning) for faster application startup (refer chapter 7 for more details)

- support for Servlet 4.0's `javax.servlet.http.PushBuilder` as a controller method argument in Spring Web MVC applications. `PushBuilder` allows pushing resources to web clients using HTTP/2 protocol.

- a new web module, `spring-webflux`, for developing *reactive* web applications and RESTful web services using RxJava and Reactor libraries (covered in chapters 18 and 19).

- `AsyncRestTemplate` support is deprecated in favor of the *reactive* `WebClient` (chapter 19 shows how you can use `WebClient` to access a RESTful web service in a *functional* and *reactive* style)

Let's now look at some of the frameworks that are built on top of Spring Framework.

1-7 Frameworks built on top of Spring

Though there are many frameworks that use Spring Framework as the foundation, we'll look at some of the widely popular ones. For a more comprehensive list of frameworks, and for more details about an individual framework, it's recommended that you visit `https://spring.io/projects`.

> As Spring Framework 5 embraces reactive programming paradigm, the framework built on top of Spring have also undergone changes to support developing reactive applications.

The following table provides a high-level overview of the frameworks that are built on top of Spring Framework:

Framework	Description
`Spring Security`	Authentication and authorization framework for enterprise applications. You need to configure a few beans in your application context XML file to incorporate authentication and authorization features into your application.
`Spring Data`	Provides a consistent programming model to interact with different types of databases. For instance, you can use it to interact with non-relational databases, like MongoDB or Neo4j, and you can also use it for accessing relational databases using JPA.
`Spring Batch`	If your application requires bulk processing, this framework is for you.
`Spring Integration`	Provides Enterprise Application Integration (EAI) capabilities to applications.
`Spring Social`	If your application requires interaction with social media websites, like Facebook and Twitter, then you'll find this framework highly useful.

As the frameworks mentioned in the above table are built on top of Spring Framework, before using any of these frameworks make sure that they are compatible with the Spring Framework version that you are using.

1-8 Summary

In this chapter, we looked at the benefits of using Spring Framework. We also looked at a simple Spring application that showed how to specify configuration metadata in XML format, create the Spring container instance and retrieve beans from it. In the next chapter, we'll look at some of the foundation concepts of Spring Framework.

Chapter 2 – *Spring Framework basics*

2-1 Introduction

In the previous chapter, we saw an example in which the Spring container invokes the no-argument constructor of a bean class to create the bean instance, and uses setter-based DI to set bean dependencies. In this chapter, we'll go a step further and look at:

- Spring's support for 'programming to interfaces' design principle
- creating beans using *static* and *instance* factory methods
- constructor-based DI for passing bean dependencies as constructor arguments
- passing simple `String` values as arguments to constructors and setter methods
- bean scopes

Let's begin this chapter by looking at how Spring improves testability of applications by supporting 'programming to interfaces' design principle.

2-2 Programming to interfaces design principle

In section 1-5 of chapter 1, we saw that a dependent POJO class contained reference to the concrete class of the dependency. For example, the `FixedDepositController` class contained reference to the `FixedDepositService` class, and the `FixedDepositService` class contained reference to the `FixedDepositDao` class. If a dependent class has direct reference to the concrete class of the dependency, it results in tight coupling between the classes. This means that if you want to substitute a different implementation of the dependency, it'd require changing the dependent class.

We know that a Java interface defines a contract to which the implementation classes conform. So, if a class depends on the interface implemented by the dependency, no change is required in the class when a different implementation of the dependency is substituted. The application design approach in which a class depends on the interface implemented by the dependency is referred to as 'programming to interfaces'. This design approach results in loose coupling between a dependent class and its dependencies. The interface implemented by the dependency class is referred to as a *dependency interface*.

As it is a good design practice to 'program to interfaces' than to 'program to classes', the following class diagram shows that it is a good design if `ABean` class depends on `BBean` interface and *not* on `BBeanImpl` class (an implementation of `BBean` interface):

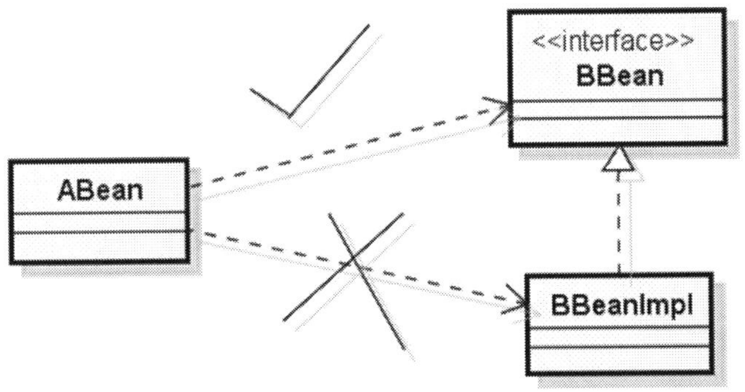

Figure 2-1 – 'Program to interfaces' is a good design practice than to 'program to classes'

The following class diagram shows how the FixedDepositService class makes use of 'programming to interfaces' design approach to easily switch the strategy used for database interaction:

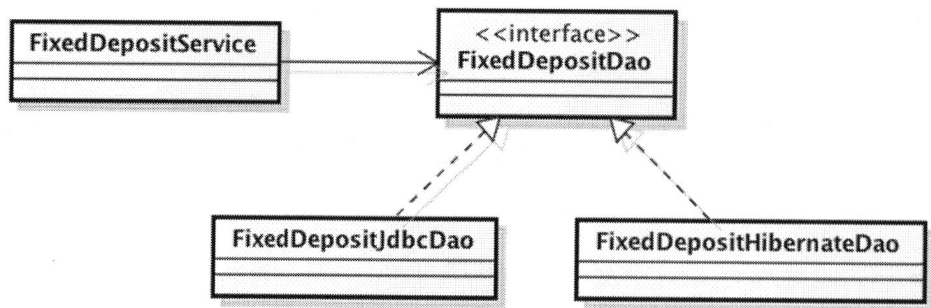

Figure 2-2 – The FixedDepositService depends on FixedDepositDao interface, which is implemented by FixedDepositJdbcDao and FixedDepositHibernateDao classes.

In the above figure, FixedDepositJdbcDao uses plain JDBC and FixedDepositHibernateDao uses Hibernate ORM for database interaction. If FixedDepositService was directly dependent on FixedDepositJdbcDao or FixedDepositHibernateDao, switching the database interaction strategy would have required changes in the FixedDepositService class.

The above figure shows that the FixedDepositService depends on the FixedDepositDao interface (the dependency interface) implemented by FixedDepositJdbcDao and FixedDepositHibernateDao classes. Now, depending on whether you want to use plain JDBC or Hibernate ORM framework, you supply an instance of FixedDepositJdbcDao or FixedDepositHibernateDao to the FixedDepositService instance.

As FixedDepositService depends on FixedDepositDao interface, you can support other database interaction strategies in the future. Let's say that you decide to use iBATIS (now renamed to MyBatis) persistence framework for database interaction. You can use iBATIS without making any changes to FixedDepositService class by simply creating a new FixedDepositIbatisDao class that implements FixedDepositDao interface, and supplying an instance of FixedDepositIbatisDao to the FixedDepositService instance.

Let's now look at how 'program to interfaces' improves testability of dependent classes.

Improved testability of dependent classes

In figure 2-2, we saw that the FixedDepositService class holds reference to the FixedDepositDao interface. FixedDepositJdbcDao and FixedDepositHibernateDao are concrete implementation classes of FixedDepositDao interface. Now, to simplify unit testing of FixedDepositService class, you can substitute a mock implementation of FixedDepositDao interface that doesn't require a database.

If the FixedDepositService class had direct reference to FixedDepositJdbcDao or FixedDepositHibernateDao class, testing FixedDepositService class would have required setting up a database for testing purposes. This shows that by using a mock implementation of dependency interface, you can save the effort to setup the infrastructure for unit testing your dependent classes.

Let's now see how Spring supports 'programming to interfaces' design approach in applications.

Spring's support for 'programming to interfaces' design approach

To use 'programming to interfaces' design approach in your Spring application, you need to do the following things:

- create bean classes that refer to the *dependency interface* and not the concrete implementation class of the dependency
- define <bean> elements that specify the *concrete implementation class* of the dependency that you want to inject into the dependent beans.

Let's now look at the modified MyBank application that follows 'programming to interfaces' design approach.

IMPORT **chapter 2/ch02-bankapp-interfaces** (This project shows how 'programming to interfaces' design approach is used in creating Spring applications. To run the application, execute the `main` method of the `BankApp` class of this project.)

MyBank application that uses 'programming to interfaces' design approach

The following class diagram depicts the modified MyBank application that follows 'programming to interfaces' design approach:

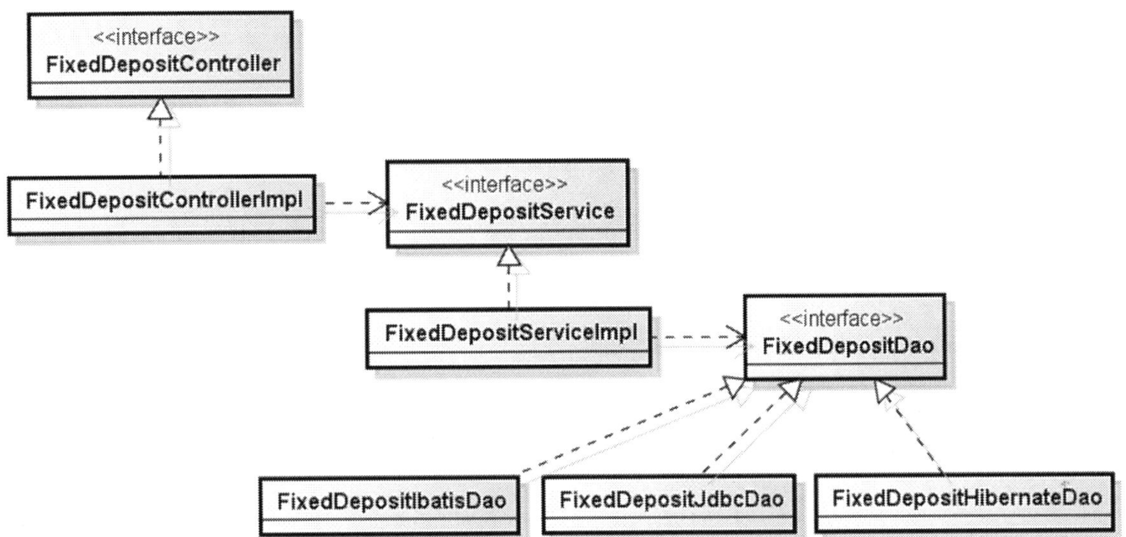

Figure 2-3 - MyBank application that uses 'program to interfaces' design approach

The above figure shows that a class depends on the interface implemented by the dependency, and *not* on the concrete implementation class of the dependency. For instance, the `FixedDepositControllerImpl` class depends on the `FixedDepositService` interface, and the `FixedDepositServiceImpl` class depends on the `FixedDepositDao` interface.

The following example listing shows the `FixedDepositServiceImpl` class based on the design shown in figure 2-3:

Example listing 2-1 – `FixedDepositService` class
Project – `ch02-bankapp-interfaces`
Source location - `src/main/java/sample/spring/chapter02/bankapp`

```
package sample.spring.chapter02.bankapp;

public class FixedDepositServiceImpl implements FixedDepositService {
    private FixedDepositDao fixedDepositDao;
    .....
    public void setFixedDepositDao(FixedDepositDao fixedDepositDao) {
        this.fixedDepositDao = fixedDepositDao;
```

```
    }

    public FixedDepositDetails getFixedDepositDetails(long id) {
        return fixedDepositDao.getFixedDepositDetails(id);
    }

    public boolean createFixedDeposit(FixedDepositDetails fdd) {
        return fixedDepositDao.createFixedDeposit(fdd);
    }
}
```

In the above example listing, the `FixedDepositServiceImpl` class contains reference to the `FixedDepositDao` interface. The `FixedDepositDao` implementation that you want to inject into the `FixedDepositServiceImpl` instance is specified in the application context XML file. As shown in figure 2-3, you can inject any of the following concrete implementations of `FixedDepositDao` interface: `FixedDepositIbatisDao`, `FixedDepositJdbcDao`, `FixedDepositHibernateDao`.

The following example listing shows the `applicationContext.xml` file that injects `FixedDepositHibernateDao` into `FixedDepositServiceImpl`:

Example listing 2-2 – `applicationContext.xml` - MyBank's application context XML file
Project – `ch02-bankapp-interfaces`
Source location - `src/main/resources/META-INF/spring`

```
<?xml version="1.0" encoding="UTF-8" standalone="no"?>
<beans .....>

    <bean id="controller"
            class="sample.spring.chapter02.bankapp.controller.FixedDepositControllerImpl">
        <property name="fixedDepositService" ref="service" />
    </bean>

    <bean id="service"
            class="sample.spring.chapter02.bankapp.service.FixedDepositServiceImpl">
        <property name="fixedDepositDao" ref="dao" />
    </bean>

    <bean id="dao" class="sample.spring.chapter02.bankapp.dao.FixedDepositHibernateDao"/>
</beans>
```

The above `applicationContext.xml` file shows that an instance of `FixedDepositHibernateDao` (an implementation of `FixedDepositDao` interface) is injected into `FixedDepositServiceImpl`. Now, if you decide to use iBATIS instead of Hibernate for persistence, then all you need to do is to change the `class` attribute of the dao bean definition to refer to the fully-qualified name of the `FixedDepositIbatisDao` class.

So far we have seen bean definition examples in which the Spring container creates bean instances by invoking the *no-argument* constructor of the bean class. Let's now look at how static or instance factory methods can be used by the Spring container to create bean instances.

2-3 Creating Spring beans using *static* and *instance* factory methods

Spring container can create and manage instance of any class, irrespective of whether the class provides a no-argument constructor or not. In section 2-4, we'll look at bean definitions in which the constructor of the bean class accepts one or more arguments. If you have an existing Java application that uses factory classes to create object instances, you can still use the Spring container to manage objects created by these factories.

Let's now look at how Spring container invokes a *static* or an *instance* factory method of a class to manage the returned object instance.

Instantiating beans via *static* factory methods

In figure 2-3, we saw that the FixedDepositDao interface is implemented by FixedDepositHibernateDao, FixedDepositIbatisDao and FixedDepositJdbcDao classes. The following example listing shows a FixedDepositDaoFactory class that defines a *static* factory method for creating and returning an instance of FixedDepositDao based on the argument passed to the *static* method:

Example listing 2-3 – FixedDepositDaoFactory class

```
public class FixedDepositDaoFactory {
    private FixedDepositDaoFactory() { }

    public static FixedDepositDao getFixedDepositDao(String daoType, ...) {
        FixedDepositDao fixedDepositDao = null;

        if("jdbc".equalsIgnoreCase(daoType)) {
              fixedDepositDao = new FixedDepositJdbcDao();
        }
        if("hibernate".equalsIgnoreCase(daoType)) {
              fixedDepositDao = new FixedDepositHibernateDao();
        }
        .....
        return fixedDepositDao;
    }
}
```

The above example listing shows that the FixedDepositDaoFactory class defines a getFixedDepositDao *static* method that creates and returns an instance of FixedDepositJdbcDao, FixedDepositHibernateDao or FixedDepositIbatisDao class, depending on the value of the daoType argument.

The following bean definition for the FixedDepositDaoFactory class instructs Spring container to invoke FixedDepositDaoFactory's getFixedDepositDao method to obtain an instance of FixedDepositJdbcDao class:

Example listing 2-4 – Bean definition for the FixedDepositDaoFactory class

```
<bean id="dao" class="sample.spring.FixedDepositDaoFactory"
        factory-method="getFixedDepositDao">
    <constructor-arg index="0" value="jdbc"/>
    ...
</bean>
```

In the above bean definition, the class attribute specifies the fully-qualified name of the class that defines the *static* factory method. The factory-method attribute specifies the name of the *static* factory method that the Spring container invokes to obtain an instance of FixedDepositDao object. The <constructor-arg> element is defined in Spring's beans schema and is used for passing arguments to constructors, and arguments to *static* and *instance* factory methods. The index attribute refers to the location of the argument in the constructor, or in the *static* or *instance* factory method. In the above bean definition, the value 0 of index attribute means that the <constructor-arg> element is supplying value for the first argument (which is daoType) of the getFixedDepositDao factory method. The value attribute specifies the argument value. If a factory method accepts multiple arguments, you need to define a <constructor-arg> element for each of the arguments.

It is important to note that calling ApplicationContext's getBean method to obtain the dao bean (refer example listing 2-4) will result in invocation of the FixedDepositDaoFactory's getFixedDepositDao factory method. This means that calling getBean("dao") returns the FixedDepositDao instance created by the getFixedDepositDao factory method, and *not* an instance of FixedDepositDaoFactory class.

Now that we have seen the configuration of the factory class that creates an instance of FixedDepositDao, the following example listing shows how to inject an instance of FixedDepositDao into FixedDepositServiceImpl class:

Example listing 2-5 – Injecting object created by a *static* factory method

```
<bean id="service" class="sample.spring.chapter02.bankapp.FixedDepositServiceImpl">
    <property name="fixedDepositDao" ref="dao" />
</bean>

<bean id="dao" class="sample.spring.chapter02.basicapp.FixedDepositDaoFactory"
        factory-method="getFixedDepositDao">
    <constructor-arg index="0" value="jdbc"/>
</bean>
```

In the above example listing, <property> element injects the instance of FixedDepositDao returned by FixedDepositDaoFactory's getFixedDepositDao factory method into FixedDepositServiceImpl instance. If you compare the bean definition for the FixedDepositServiceImpl class shown above with the one shown in example listing 2-2, you'll notice that they are exactly the same. This shows that the bean dependencies are specified the same way irrespective of how (using no-argument constructor or *static* factory method) the Spring container creates bean instances.

Let's now look at how Spring container instantiate beans by invoking an *instance* factory method.

Instantiating beans via *instance* factory methods

The following example listing shows the FixedDepositDaoFactory class that defines an *instance* factory method for creating and returning an instance of FixedDepositDao:

Example listing 2-6 – FixedDepositDaoFactory class

```
public class FixedDepositDaoFactory {
    public FixedDepositDaoFactory() {
    }

    public FixedDepositDao getFixedDepositDao(String daoType, ...) {
        FixedDepositDao fixedDepositDao = null;

        if("jdbc".equalsIgnoreCase(daoType)) {
              fixedDepositDao = new FixedDepositJdbcDao();
        }
        if("hibernate".equalsIgnoreCase(daoType)) {
              fixedDepositDao = new FixedDepositHibernateDao();
        }
        .....
        return fixedDepositDao;
    }
}
```

If a class defines an *instance* factory method, the class must define a public constructor so that the Spring container can create an instance of that class. In the above example listing, the FixedDepositDaoFactory class defines a public no-argument constructor. The FixedDepositDaoFactory's getFixedDepositDao method is an *instance* factory method that creates and returns an instance of FixedDepositDao.

The following example listing shows how to instruct Spring container to invoke FixedDepositDaoFactory's getFixedDepositDao method to obtain an instance of FixedDepositDao:

Example listing 2-7 – Configuration to invoke FixedDepositDaoFactory's getFixedDepositDao method

```
<bean id="daoFactory" class="sample.spring.chapter02.basicapp.FixedDepositDaoFactory" />

<bean id="dao" factory-bean="daoFactory" factory-method="getFixedDepositDao">
    <constructor-arg index="0" value="jdbc"/>
</bean>

<bean id="service" class="sample.spring.chapter02.bankapp.FixedDepositServiceImpl">
    <property name="fixedDepositDao" ref="dao" />
</bean>
```

The above example listing shows that the FixedDepositDaoFactory class (a class that contains the *instance* factory method) is configured like a regular Spring bean, and a separate <bean> element is used to configure the *instance* factory method details. To configure details of an *instance* factory method, factory-bean and factory-method attributes of <bean> element are used. The factory-bean attribute refers to the bean that defines the *instance* factory method, and the factory-method attribute specifies the name of the *instance* factory method. In the above example listing, the <property> element injects the instance of FixedDepositDao returned by FixedDepositDaoFactory's getFixedDepositDao factory method into FixedDepositServiceImpl instance.

As with *static* factory methods, you can pass arguments to *instance* factory methods using <constructor-arg> element. It is important to note that invoking ApplicationContext's getBean method to obtain dao bean in the above example listing will result in invocation of the FixedDepositDaoFactory's getFixedDepositDao factory method.

Let's now look at how to set dependencies of beans created by *static* and *instance* factory methods.

Injecting dependencies of beans created by factory methods

You can either pass bean dependencies as arguments to the factory method, or you can use setter-based DI to inject dependencies of the bean instance returned by a *static* or *instance* factory method.

Consider the following FixedDepositJdbcDao class that defines a databaseInfo property:

Example listing 2-8 – FixedDepositJdbcDao class

```
public class FixedDepositJdbcDao {
    private DatabaseInfo databaseInfo;
    .....
    public FixedDepositJdbcDao() { }

    public void setDatabaseInfo(DatabaseInfo databaseInfo) {
        this. databaseInfo = databaseInfo;
    }
    .....
}
```

In the above example listing, the databaseInfo attribute represents a dependency of the FixedDepositJdbcDao class that is fulfilled by the setDatabaseInfo method.

The following FixedDepositDaoFactory class defines a factory method responsible for creating and returning an instance of FixedDepositJdbcDao class:

Example listing 2-9 – FixedDepositDaoFactory class

```
public class FixedDepositDaoFactory {
    public FixedDepositDaoFactory() {
    }

    public FixedDepositDao getFixedDepositDao(String daoType) {
        FixedDepositDao fixedDepositDao = null;

        if("jdbc".equalsIgnoreCase(daoType)) {
            fixedDepositDao = new FixedDepositJdbcDao();
        }
        if("hibernate".equalsIgnoreCase(daoType)) {
            fixedDepositDao = new FixedDepositHibernateDao();
        }
        .....
        return fixedDepositDao;
    }
}
```

In the above example listing, the getFixedDepositDao method is an *instance* factory method for creating FixedDepositDao instances. The getFixedDepositDao method creates an instance of FixedDepositJdbcDao instance if the value of daoType argument is jdbc. It is important to note that the getFixedDepositDao method *doesn't* set the databaseInfo property of the FixedDepositJdbcDao instance.

As we saw in example listing 2-7, the following bean definitions instruct the Spring container to create an instance of FixedDepositJdbcDao by invoking the getFixedDepositDao *instance* factory method of FixedDepositDaoFactory class:

Example listing 2-10 – Configuration to invoke FixedDepositDaoFactory's getFixedDepositDao method

```
<bean id="daoFactory" class="FixedDepositDaoFactory" />

<bean id="dao" factory-bean="daoFactory" factory-method="getFixedDepositDao">
    <constructor-arg index="0" value="jdbc"/>
</bean>
```

The dao bean definition results in invocation of FixedDepositDaoFactory's getFixedDepositDao method, which creates and returns an instance of FixedDepositJdbcDao. But, the FixedDepositJdbcDao's databaseInfo property is *not* set. To set the databaseInfo dependency, you can perform setter-based DI on the FixedDepositJdbcDao instance returned by the getFixedDepositDao method, as shown here:

Example listing 2-11 – Configuration to invoke FixedDepositDaoFactory's getFixedDepositDao method and to set databaseInfo property of returned FixedDepositJdbcDao instance

```
<bean id="daoFactory" class="FixedDepositDaoFactory" />

<bean id="dao" factory-bean="daoFactory" factory-method="getFixedDepositDao">
    <constructor-arg index="0" value="jdbc"/>
    <property name="databaseInfo" ref="databaseInfo"/>
</bean>

<bean id="databaseInfo" class="DatabaseInfo" />
```

In the above bean definition, the `<property>` element is used to set `databaseInfo` property of `FixedDepositJdbcDao` instance returned by the `getFixedDepositDao` *instance* factory method.

> As with the *instance* factory method, you can use the `<property>` element to inject dependencies into the bean instance returned by the *static* factory method.

Let's now look at constructor-based DI.

2-4 Constructor-based DI

In Spring, dependency injection is performed by passing arguments to a bean's constructor and setter methods. We saw earlier that the DI technique in which dependencies are injected via setter methods is referred to as setter-based DI. In this section, we'll look at the DI technique in which dependencies are passed as constructor arguments (referred to as constructor-based DI).

Let's look at an example that compares how bean dependencies are specified in setter- and constructor-based DI techniques.

Revisiting setter-based DI

In setter-based DI, `<property>` elements are used to specify bean dependencies. Let's say that the MyBank application contains a `PersonalBankingService` service that allows customers to retrieve bank account statement, check bank account details, update contact number, change password, and contact customer service. The `PersonalBankingService` class uses `JmsMessageSender` (for sending JMS messages), `EmailMessageSender` (for sending emails) and `WebServiceInvoker` (for invoking external web services) objects to accomplish its intended functionality. The following example listing shows the `PersonalBankingService` class:

Example listing 2-12 – `PersonalBankingService` class

```
public class PersonalBankingService {
    private JmsMessageSender jmsMessageSender;
    private EmailMessageSender emailMessageSender;
    private WebServiceInvoker webServiceInvoker;
    .....
    public void setJmsMessageSender(JmsMessageSender jmsMessageSender) {
        this.jmsMessageSender = jmsMessageSender;
    }

    public void setEmailMessageSender(EmailMessageSender emailMessageSender) {
        this.emailMessageSender = emailMessageSender;
    }

    public void setWebServiceInvoker(WebServiceInvoker webServiceInvoker) {
        this.webServiceInvoker = webServiceInvoker;
    }
    .....
}
```

The above example listing shows that a setter method is defined for each of the dependencies (`JmsMessageSender`, `EmailMessageSender` and `WebServiceInvoker`) of `PersonalBankingService` class.

As the `PersonalBankingService` defines setter-methods for its dependencies, setter-based DI is used, as shown here:

Example listing 2-13 – Bean definitions for PersonalBankingService class and its dependencies

```
<bean id="personalBankingService" class="PersonalBankingService">
    <property name="emailMessageSender" ref="emailMessageSender" />
    <property name="jmsMessageSender" ref="jmsMessageSender" />
    <property name="webServiceInvoker" ref="webServiceInvoker" />
</bean>

<bean id="jmsMessageSender" class="JmsMessageSender">
    .....
</bean>
<bean id="webServiceInvoker" class="WebServiceInvoker" />
    .....
</bean>
<bean id="emailMessageSender" class="EmailMessageSender" />
    .....
</bean>
```

The personalBankingService bean definition shows that a <property> element is specified for each dependency of PersonalBankingService class.

Let's now look at how we can model PersonalBankingService class to use constructor-based DI.

Constructor-based DI

In constructor-based DI, dependencies of a bean are passed as arguments to the bean class's constructor. The following example listing shows a modified version of PersonalBankingService class whose constructor accepts JmsMessageSender, EmailMessageSender and WebServiceInvoker objects:

Example listing 2-14 – PersonalBankingService class

```
public class PersonalBankingService {
    private JmsMessageSender jmsMessageSender;
    private EmailMessageSender emailMessageSender;
    private WebServiceInvoker webServiceInvoker;
    .....
    public PersonalBankingService(JmsMessageSender jmsMessageSender,
        EmailMessageSender emailMessageSender,
        WebServiceInvoker webServiceInvoker) {

        this.jmsMessageSender = jmsMessageSender;
        this.emailMessageSender = emailMessageSender;
        this.webServiceInvoker = webServiceInvoker;
    }
    .....
}
```

The arguments to the PersonalBankingService's constructor represent dependencies of the PersonalBankingService class. The following example listing shows how these dependencies are supplied via <constructor-arg> elements:

Example listing 2-15 – PersonalBankingService bean definition

```
<bean id="personalBankingService" class="PersonalBankingService">
    <constructor-arg index="0" ref="jmsMessageSender" />
    <constructor-arg index="1" ref="emailMessageSender" />
    <constructor-arg index="2" ref="webServiceInvoker" />
```

```
</bean>
<bean id="jmsMessageSender" class="JmsMessageSender">
    .....
</bean>
<bean id="webServiceInvoker" class="WebServiceInvoker" />
    .....
</bean>
<bean id="emailMessageSender" class="EmailMessageSender" />
    .....
</bean>
```

In the above example listing, `<constructor-arg>` elements specify details of the constructor arguments passed to the `PersonalBankingService` instance. The `index` attribute specifies the index of the constructor argument. If the `index` attribute value is `0`, it means that the `<constructor-arg>` element corresponds to the first constructor argument, and if the `index` attribute value is `1`, it means that the `<constructor-arg>` element corresponds to the second constructor argument, and so on. You don't need to specify the `index` attribute if constructor arguments are *not* related by inheritance. For instance, if `JmsMessageSender`, `WebServiceInvoker` and `EmailMessageSender` are distinct objects, you don't need to specify the `index` attribute. As in the case of `<property>` element, the `ref` attribute of `<constructor-arg>` element is used for passing reference to a bean.

Let's now look at how we can use constructor-based DI along with setter-based DI.

Using a mix of constructor- and setter-based DI mechanisms

If a bean class requires both constructor- and setter-based DI mechanisms, you can use a combination of `<constructor-arg>` and `<property>` elements to inject dependencies.

The following example listing shows a version of `PersonalBankingService` class whose dependencies are injected as arguments to constructor and setter methods:

Example listing 2-16 – `PersonalBankingService` class

```
public class PersonalBankingService {
    private JmsMessageSender jmsMessageSender;
    private EmailMessageSender emailMessageSender;
    private WebServiceInvoker webServiceInvoker;
    .....
    public PersonalBankingService(JmsMessageSender jmsMessageSender,
            EmailMessageSender emailMessageSender) {
        this.jmsMessageSender = jmsMessageSender;
        this.emailMessageSender = emailMessageSender;
    }

    public void setWebServiceInvoker(WebServiceInvoker webServiceInvoker) {
        this.webServiceInvoker = webServiceInvoker;
    }
    .....
}
```

In the `PersonalBankingService` class, `jmsMessageSender` and `emailMessageSender` dependencies are injected as constructor arguments, and `webServiceInvoker` dependency is injected via the `setWebServiceInvoker` setter method. The following bean definition shows that both `<constructor-arg>` and `<property>` elements are used to inject dependencies of `PersonalBankingService` class:

Example listing 2-17 – Mixing constructor- and setter-based DI mechanisms

```
<bean id="dataSource" class="PersonalBankingService">
    <constructor-arg index="0" ref="jmsMessageSender" />
    <constructor-arg index="1" ref="emailMessageSender" />
    <property name="webServiceInvoker" ref="webServiceInvoker" />
</bean>
```

We saw that <property> and <constructor-arg> elements are used for passing dependencies (which are references to other beans) to setter methods and constructors. We can also use these elements to pass configuration information (which are simple String values) required by beans.

2-5 Passing configuration details to beans

Consider an EmailMessageSender class that requires email server address, and username and password for authenticating with the email server. The following example listing shows that the <property> element can be used for setting properties of EmailMessageSender bean:

Example listing 2-18 EmailMessageSender class and the corresponding bean definition

```
public class EmailMessageSender {
    private String host;
    private String username;
    private String password;
    .....
    public void setHost(String host) {
        this.host = host;
    }

    public void setUsername(String username) {
        this.username = username;
    }

    public void setPassword(String password) {
        this.password = password;
    }
    .....
}

<bean id="emailMessageSender" class="EmailMessageSender">
    <property name="host" value="smtp.gmail.com"/>
    <property name="username" value="myusername"/>
    <property name="password" value="mypassword"/>
</bean>
```

In the above example listing, <property> elements have been used to set host, username and password properties of EmailMessageSender bean. The value attribute specifies the String value to be set for the bean property identified by the name attribute. The host, username and password properties represent the configuration information required by the EmailMessageSender bean. In chapter 3, we'll see how to set properties of primitive types (like int, long, and so on), collection types (like java.util.List, java.util.Map, and so on) and custom types (like Address).

The following example listing shows the modified version of EmailMessageSender class (and the corresponding bean definition) that accepts configuration information (like, host, username and password) as constructor arguments:

Example listing 2-19 EmailMessageSender class and the corresponding bean definition

```
public class EmailMessageSender {
    private String host;
    private String username;
    private String password;
    .....
    public EmailMessageSender(String host, String username, String password) {
        this.host = host;
        this.username = username;
        this.password = password;
    }
    .....
}

<bean id="emailMessageSender" class="EmailMessageSender">
    <constructor-arg index="0" value="smtp.gmail.com"/>
    <constructor-arg index="1" value="myusername"/>
    <constructor-arg index="2" value="mypassword"/>
</bean>
```

In the above example listing, `<constructor-arg>` elements have been used to pass configuration details required by the `EmailMessageSender` bean. The `value` attribute specifies the `String` value to be set for the constructor argument identified by the `index` attribute.

So far we have seen that `<constructor-arg>` element is used for injecting bean dependencies and passing values for `String` type constructor arguments. In chapter 3, we'll see how to specify values for constructor arguments of primitive type (like `int`, `long`, and so on), collection type (like `java.util.List`, `java.util.Map`, and so on) and custom type (like `Address`).

Now that we have seen how to instruct Spring container to create beans and perform DI, let's look at different scopes that you can specify for beans.

2-6 Bean scopes

You may want to specify the scope of a bean to control whether a shared instance of the bean is created (`singleton` scope), or a new bean instance is created every time the bean is requested (`prototype` scope) from the Spring container. The scope of a bean is defined by the `scope` attribute of the `<bean>` element. If the `scope` attribute is not specified, it means that the bean is a singleton-scoped bean.

In web application scenarios, Spring allows you to specify additional scopes: `request`, `session`, `websocket`, and `application`. These scopes determine the *lifetime* of the bean instance. For instance, a request-scoped bean's lifetime is limited to a single HTTP request. In this chapter, we'll restrict our discussion to `singleton` and `prototype` scopes. The `request`, `session` and `application` scopes are described in chapter 12.

IMPORT **chapter 2/ch02-bankapp-scopes** (This project shows usage of `singleton` and `prototype` bean scopes. To run the application, execute the `main` method of the `BankApp` class of this project. The project also contains 2 JUnit tests, `PrototypeTest` and `SingletonTest` that you can execute)

Singleton

Singleton scope is the *default* scope for all the beans defined in the application context XML file. An instance of a singleton-scoped bean is created when the Spring container is created, and is destroyed when the Spring container is destroyed. Spring container creates a *single* instance of a singleton-scoped bean, which is shared by *all* the beans that depend on it.

The following example listing shows the applicationContext.xml file of ch02-bankapp-scopes project in which all the beans are singleton-scoped:

Example listing 2-20 – applicationContext.xml - Singleton-scoped beans
Project – ch02-bankapp-scopes
Source location - src/main/resources/META-INF/spring

```
<beans ..... >
    <bean id="controller"
           class="sample.spring.chapter02.bankapp.controller.FixedDepositControllerImpl">
        <property name="fixedDepositService" ref="service" />
    </bean>

    <bean id="service"
           class="sample.spring.chapter02.bankapp.service.FixedDepositServiceImpl">
        <property name="fixedDepositDao" ref="dao" />
    </bean>

    <bean id="dao" class="sample.spring.chapter02.bankapp.dao.FixedDepositDaoImpl" />
    .....
</beans>
```

In the above applicationContext.xml file, controller, service and dao beans are singleton-scoped because no scope attribute is specified for the <bean> elements. This means that only a single instance of FixedDepositControllerImpl, FixedDepositServiceImpl and FixedDepositDaoImpl classes is created by the Spring container. As these beans are singleton-scoped, Spring container returns the same instance of the bean every time we retrieve one of these beans using ApplicationContext's getBean method.

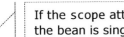

If the scope attribute is not specified or the value of scope attribute is singleton, it means that the bean is singleton-scoped.

The following example listing shows the testInstances method of SingletonTest (a JUnit test class) class of ch02-bankapp-scopes project. The testInstances method tests whether multiple invocations of ApplicationContext's getBean method returns the same instance or different instances of the controller bean:

Example listing 2-21 – SingletonTest JUnit test class
Project – ch02-bankapp-scopes
Source location - src/test/java/sample/spring/chapter02/bankapp

```
package sample.spring.chapter02.bankapp;

import static org.junit.Assert.assertSame;
import org.junit.BeforeClass;
import org.junit.Test;

import sample.spring.chapter02.bankapp.controller.FixedDepositController;

public class SingletonTest {
    private static ApplicationContext context;

    @BeforeClass
    public static void init() {
        context = new ClassPathXmlApplicationContext(
            "classpath:META-INF/spring/applicationContext.xml");
    }
```

```
    @Test
    public void testInstances() {
        FixedDepositController controller1 =
             (FixedDepositController) context.getBean("controller");
        FixedDepositController controller2 =
             (FixedDepositController) context.getBean("controller");
        assertSame("Different FixedDepositController instances", controller1, controller2);
    }
    .....
}
```

In the above example listing, JUnit's `@BeforeClass` annotation specifies that the `init` method is invoked before any of the test methods (that is, methods annotated with JUnit's `@Test` annotation) in the class. This means that the `@BeforeClass` annotated method is invoked only *once*, and the `@Test` annotated methods are executed only *after* the execution of the `@BeforeClass` annotated method. Note that the `init` method is a *static* method. The `init` method creates an instance of `ApplicationContext` object by passing the configuration metadata (shown in example listing 2-20) to the `ClassPathXmlApplicationContext`'s constructor. The `testInstances` method obtains 2 instances of the `controller` bean and checks whether both the instances are the same by using JUnit's `assertSame` assertion. As the `controller` bean is singleton-scoped, `controller1` and `controller2` bean instances are the same. For this reason, `SingletonTest`'s `testInstances` test executes without any assertion errors.

The following figure depicts that the Spring container returns the same instance of `controller` bean when you call the `ApplicationContext`'s `getBean` method multiple times:

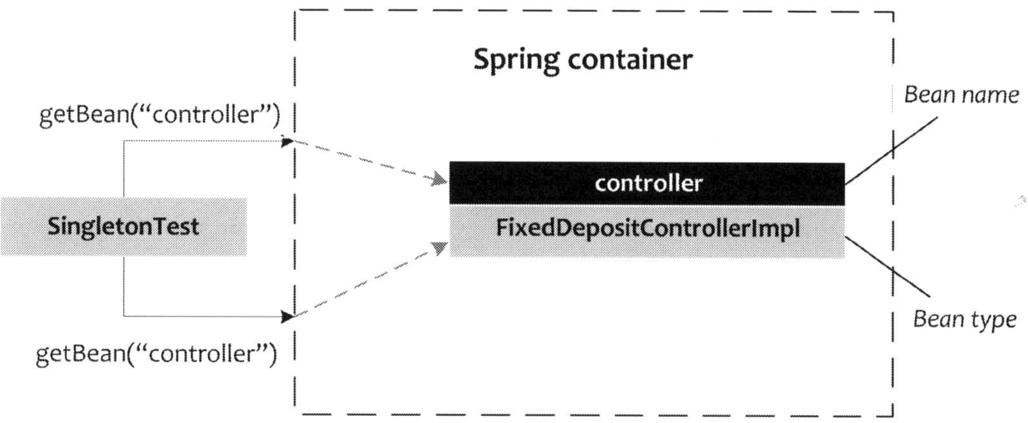

Figure 2-4 Multiple requests for a singleton-scoped bean returns the same bean instance from the Spring container

The above figure shows that multiple calls to obtain `controller` bean returns the *same* instance of the `controller` bean.

> In figure 2-4, the `controller` bean instance is represented by a 2-compartment rectangle. The top compartment shows the *name* of the bean (that is, the value of the `id` attribute of the `<bean>` element) and the bottom compartment shows the *type* of the bean (that is, the value of the `class` attribute of the `<bean>` element). In the rest of this book, we'll use this convention to show bean instances inside a Spring container.

A singleton-scoped bean instance is shared amongst the beans that depend on it. The following example listing shows the `testReference` method of `SingletonTest` (a JUnit test class) that checks if the `FixedDepositDao` instance referenced by the `FixedDepositController` instance is the same as the one obtained by directly calling `ApplicationContext`'s `getBean` method:

Example listing 2-22 – testReference method of SingletonTest JUnit test class
Project – ch02-bankapp-scopes
Source location - src/test/java/sample/spring/chapter02/bankapp

```
package sample.spring.chapter02.bankapp;

import static org.junit.Assert.assertSame;
import org.junit.Test;

public class SingletonTest {
    private static ApplicationContext context;
    .....
    @Test
    public void testReference() {
        FixedDepositController controller =
            (FixedDepositController) context.getBean("controller");

        FixedDepositDao fixedDepositDao1 =
              controller.getFixedDepositService().getFixedDepositDao();
        FixedDepositDao fixedDepositDao2 = (FixedDepositDao) context.getBean("dao");
        assertSame("Different FixedDepositDao instances",
               fixedDepositDao1, fixedDepositDao2);
    }
}
```

In the above example listing, the testReference method first retrieves the FixedDepositDao instance (refer fixedDepositDao1 variable in the above example listing) referenced by the FixedDepositController bean, followed by directly retrieving another instance of FixedDepositDao bean (refer fixedDepositDao2 variable in the above example listing) using ApplicationContext's getBean method. If you execute the testReference test, you'll see that the test completes successfully because the fixedDepositDao1 and fixedDepositDao2 instances are the same.

Figure 2-5 shows that the FixedDepositDao instance referenced by FixedDepositController instance is the same as the one returned by invoking getBean("dao") method on ApplicationContext.

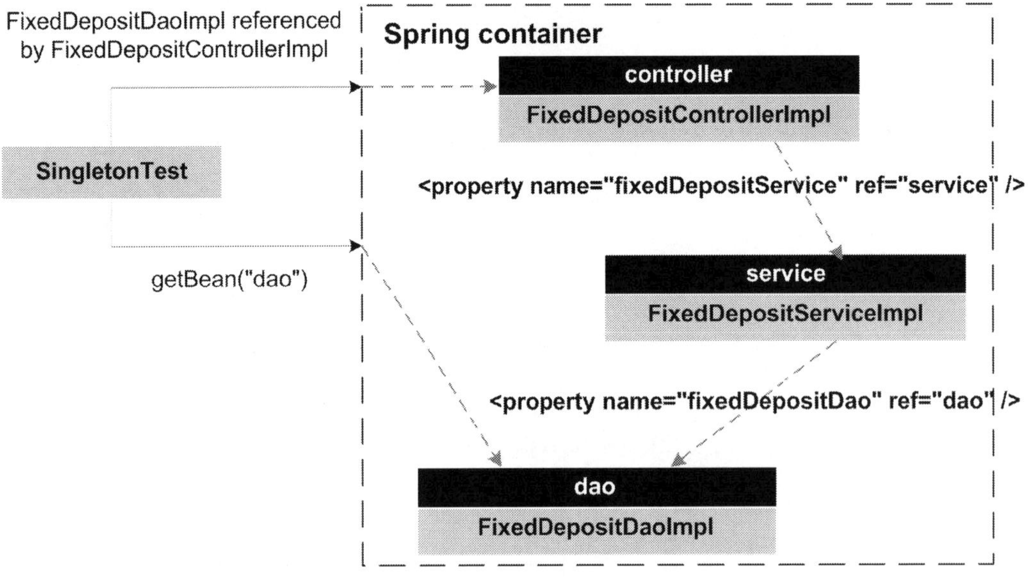

Figure 2-5 Singleton-scoped bean instance is shared between beans that depend on it

The above figure shows that the FixedDepositDao instance referenced by FixedDepositController bean instance and the one retrieved directly by calling ApplicationContext's getBean method are the same. If multiple beans are dependent on a singleton-scoped bean, then all the dependent beans share the same singleton-scoped bean instance.

Let's now look at whether or not the same singleton-scoped bean instance is shared between multiple Spring containers.

Singleton-scoped beans and multiple Spring containers

The scope of a singleton-scoped bean instance is limited to the Spring container instance. This means that if you create 2 instances of the Spring container using the same configuration metadata, each Spring container gets its own set of singleton bean instances.

The following example listing shows the testSingletonScope method of SingletonTest class, which tests whether the FixedDepositController bean instance retrieved from two different Spring container instances are the same or different:

Example listing 2-23 – testSingletonScope method of SingletonTest JUnit test class
Project – ch02-bankapp-scopes
Source location - src/test/java/sample/spring/chapter02/bankapp

```
package sample.spring.chapter02.bankapp;

import static org.junit.Assert.assertNotSame;

public class SingletonTest {
    private static ApplicationContext context;
    .....
    @BeforeClass
    public static void init() {
        context = new ClassPathXmlApplicationContext(
            "classpath:META-INF/spring/applicationContext.xml");
    }

    @Test
    public void testSingletonScope() {
        ApplicationContext anotherContext = new ClassPathXmlApplicationContext(
                "classpath:META-INF/spring/applicationContext.xml");

        FixedDepositController fixedDepositController1 =
                (FixedDepositController) anotherContext.getBean("controller");

        FixedDepositController fixedDepositController2 =
                (FixedDepositController) context.getBean("controller");

        assertNotSame("Same FixedDepositController instances",
                fixedDepositController1, fixedDepositController2);
    }
}
```

The SingletonTest's init method (annotated with JUnit's @BeforeClass annotation) creates an instance of ApplicationContext (identified by context variable) before any @Test annotated method is executed. The testSingletonScope method creates one more instance of Spring container (identified by anotherContext variable) using the same applicationContext.xml file. An instance of FixedDepositController bean is retrieved from both the Spring containers and checked if they are *not* the same. If you execute the testSingletonScope test, you'll find that the test completes successfully because the FixedDepositController bean instance retrieved from the context instance is different from the one retrieved from the anotherContext instance.

The following figure depicts the behavior exhibited by the testSingletonScope method:

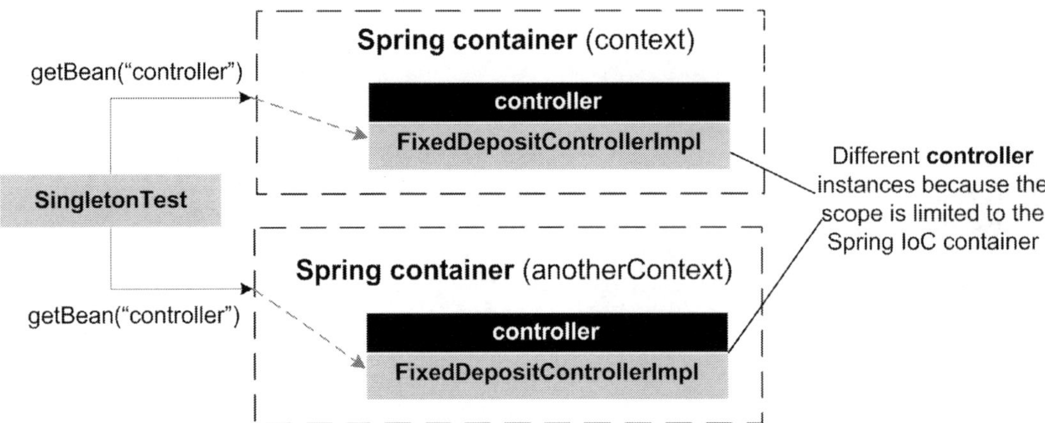

Figure 2-6 Each Spring container creates its own instance of the controller bean

The above figure shows that each Spring container creates its own instance of the controller bean. This is the reason why context and anotherContext return different instances of controller bean when getBean("controller") method is called.

The testSingletonScope method showed that each Spring container created its own instance of the singleton-scoped beans. It is important to note that the Spring container creates an instance of a singleton-scoped bean per bean definition. The following example listing shows multiple bean definitions for the FixedDepositDaoImpl class:

Example listing 2-24 – applicationContext.xml - multiple bean definitions for the same class
Project – ch02-bankapp-scopes
Source location - src/main/resources/META-INF/spring

```
<bean id="dao" class="sample.spring.chapter02.bankapp.dao.FixedDepositDaoImpl" />
<bean id="anotherDao"
      class="sample.spring.chapter02.bankapp.dao.FixedDepositDaoImpl" />
```

The bean definitions shown in the above example listing are for the FixedDepositDaoImpl class. As the scope attribute is *not* specified, bean definitions shown in the above example listing represent singleton-scoped beans. The Spring container treats dao and anotherDao bean definitions as distinct, and creates an instance of FixedDepositDaoImpl corresponding to each bean definition.

The following example listing shows SingletonScope's testSingletonScopePerBeanDef method that tests whether the FixedDepositDaoImpl instances corresponding to dao and anotherDao bean definitions are the same or different:

Example listing 2-25 – testSingletonScopePerBeanDef method of SingletonTest JUnit test class
Project – ch02-bankapp-scopes
Source location - src/test/java/sample/spring/chapter02/bankapp

```
package sample.spring.chapter02.bankapp;

import static org.junit.Assert.assertNotSame;
```

```
public class SingletonTest {
    private static ApplicationContext context;
    .....
    @Test
    public void testSingletonScopePerBeanDef() {
        FixedDepositDao fixedDepositDao1 = (FixedDepositDao) context.getBean("dao");
        FixedDepositDao fixedDepositDao2 = (FixedDepositDao) context.getBean("anotherDao");
        assertNotSame("Same FixedDepositDao instances",
            fixedDepositDao1, fixedDepositDao2);
    }
}
```

In the above example listing, `fixedDepositDao1` and `fixedDepositDao2` variables represent instances of `FixedDepositDaoImpl` class that the Spring container creates corresponding to the dao and anotherDao bean definitions, respectively. If you execute the `testSingletonScopePerBeanDef` test, it'll execute without any assertion errors because the `fixedDepositDao1` instance (corresponding to the dao bean definition) and `fixedDepositDao2` instance (corresponding to the anotherDao bean definition) are distinct.

The following figure summarizes that a singleton-scoped bean is created *per bean definition*:

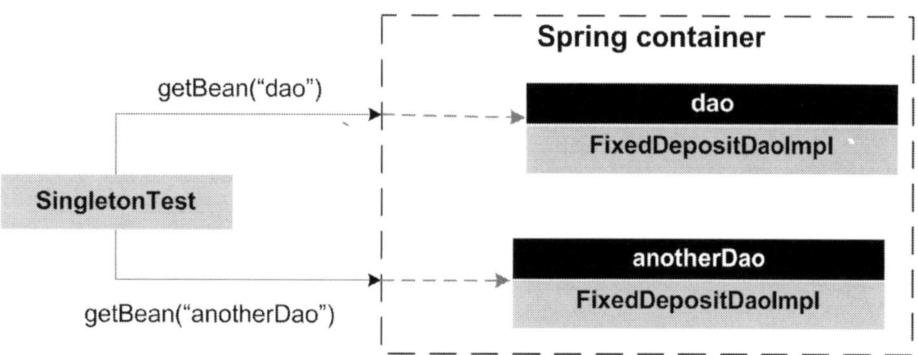

Figure 2-7 There is one singleton-scoped bean instance per bean definition

The above figure shows that there exists one instance of singleton-scoped bean *per bean definition* in the Spring container.

We mentioned earlier that a singleton-scoped bean is *pre-instantiated* by default, which means an instance of a singleton-scoped bean is created when you create an instance of the Spring container. Let's now look at how you can *lazily* initialize a singleton-scoped bean.

Lazily initializing a singleton-scoped bean

You can instruct the Spring container to create an instance of a singleton bean only when it is requested for the *first* time. The following `lazyExample` bean definition shows how to instruct Spring container to lazy initialize `lazyBean` bean:

Example listing 2-26 – Lazily initializing a singleton bean

```
<bean id="lazyBean" class="example.LazyBean" lazy-init="true"/>
```

The `<bean>` element's `lazy-init` attribute specifies whether the bean instance is created lazily or eagerly. If the value is `true` (as in the case of the bean definition shown above), the bean instance is initialized by the Spring container when it receives the request for the bean for the *first* time.

The following sequence diagram shows how `lazy-init` attribute affects the creation of a singleton bean instance:

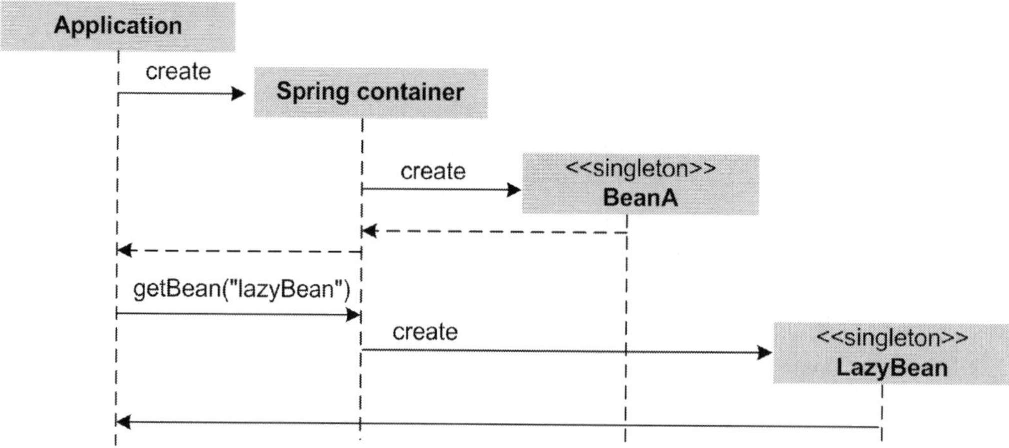

Figure 2-8 A lazily-initialized singleton bean instance is created when it is requested for the first time by the application

In the above diagram, `BeanA` represents a singleton bean that is *not* set to be lazily-initialized, and `LazyBean` represents a singleton bean that is set to be lazily-initialized. When the Spring container is created, `BeanA` is also instantiated because it is *not* set to be lazily-initialized. On the other hand, `LazyBean` is instantiated when `ApplicationContext's getBean` method is invoked for the time first time to retrieve an instance of `LazyBean`.

> You can use `<beans>` element's `default-lazy-init` attribute to specify default initialization strategy for beans defines in the application context XML file. If the `<bean>` element's `lazy-init` attribute specifies a different value than the `<beans>` element's `default-lazy-init`, the value specified by the `lazy-init` attribute applies to the bean.

As a singleton bean can be lazily-initialized or pre-instantiated by the Spring container, you may be thinking at this time whether you should define your singleton beans to be lazily-initialized or pre-instantiated. In most application scenarios, it is beneficial to pre-instantiate singleton beans to discover configuration issues at the time of creation of the Spring container. The following example listing shows an aBean singleton bean that is set to be lazily-initialized, and that depends on bBean bean:

Example listing 2-27 – A lazily-initialized singleton bean

```
public class ABean {
    private BBean bBean;

    public void setBBean(BBean bBean) {
        this.bBean = bBean;
    }
    .....
}
<bean id="aBean" class="ABean" lazy-init="true">
    <property name="bBean" value="bBean" />
</bean>

<bean id="bBean" class="BBean" />
```

In the above example listing, ABean's bBean property refers to the BBean bean. Notice that instead of the ref attribute, the value attribute of <property> element has been used to set ABean's bBean property. If you create an ApplicationContext instance by passing it the XML file containing the above bean definition, no errors will be reported. But, when you try to fetch the aBean bean by invoking ApplicationContext's getBean method, you'll get the following error message:

```
Caused by: java.lang.IllegalStateException: Cannot convert value of type [java.lang.String]
to required type [BBean] for property 'bBean: no matching editors or conversion strategy
found
```

The above error message is shown because the Spring container fails to convert the String value of ABean's bBean property to BBean type. This highlights a simple configuration issue in which instead of specifying <bean> element's ref attribute, value attribute was specified. If aBean was defined as pre-instantiated (instead of lazily-initialized), the above configuration issue could have been caught at the time we created an instance of ApplicationContext, and not when we tried to obtain an instance of aBean bean from the ApplicationContext.

Let's now look at *prototype-scoped* beans in Spring.

Prototype

A prototype-scoped bean is different from a singleton-scoped bean in the sense that the Spring container always returns a *new* instance of a prototype-scoped bean. Another distinctive feature of prototype-scoped beans is that they are *always* lazily-initialized.

The following FixedDepositDetails bean in the applicationContext.xml file of ch02-bankapp-scopes project represents a prototype-scoped bean:

Example listing 2-28 – applicationContext.xml - A prototype-scoped bean example
Project – ch02-bankapp-scopes
Source location - src/main/resources/META-INF/spring

```
<bean id="fixedDepositDetails"
        class="sample.spring.chapter02.bankapp.domain.FixedDepositDetails"
        scope="prototype" />
```

The above example listing shows that the <bean> element's scope attribute value is set to prototype. This means that the fixedDepositDetails bean is a prototype-scoped bean.

The following testInstances method of PrototypeTest JUnit test class shows that the 2 instances of fixedDepositDetails bean retrieved from the Spring container are different:

Example listing 2-29 – testInstances method of PrototypeTest JUnit test class
Project – ch02-bankapp-scopes
Source location - src/test/java/sample/spring/chapter02/bankapp

```
package sample.spring.chapter02.bankapp;

import static org.junit.Assert.assertNotSame;

public class PrototypeTest {
    private static ApplicationContext context;
    .....
    @Test
    public void testInstances() {
        FixedDepositDetails fixedDepositDetails1 =
```

```
                (FixedDepositDetails)context.getBean("fixedDepositDetails");
        FixedDepositDetails fixedDepositDetails2 =
                (FixedDepositDetails) context.getBean("fixedDepositDetails");

        assertNotSame("Same FixedDepositDetails instances",
            fixedDepositDetails1, fixedDepositDetails2);
    }
}
```

If you execute the `testInstances` test, it'll complete without any assertion errors because the 2 `FixedDepositDetails` instances (`fixedDepositDetails1` and `fixedDepositDetails2`) obtained from the `ApplicationContext` are different.

Let's now look at how to choose the right scope (`singleton` or `prototype`) for a bean.

Choosing the right scope for your beans

If a bean doesn't maintain any conversational state (that is, it is stateless in nature), it should be defined as a singleton-scoped bean. If a bean maintains conversational state, it should be defined as a prototype-scoped bean. `FixedDepositServiceImpl`, `FixedDepositDaoImpl` and `FixedDepositControllerImpl` beans of MyBank application are stateless in nature; therefore, they are defined as singleton-scoped beans. `FixedDepositDetails` bean (a *domain object*) of MyBank application maintains conversational state; therefore, it is defined as a prototype-scoped bean.

> If you are using an ORM framework (like Hibenate or iBATIS) in your application, the domain objects are created either by the ORM framework or you create them programmatically in your application code using the `new` operator. It is because of this reason domain objects are not defined in the application context XML file if the application uses an ORM framework for persistence.

2-7 Summary

In this chapter, we discussed some of the basics of Spring Framework. We looked at 'programming to interfaces' design approach, different approaches to create bean instances, constructor-based DI and bean scopes. In the next chapter, we'll look at how to set different types (like `int`, `long`, `Map`, `Set`, and so on) of bean properties and constructor arguments.

Chapter 3 - *Configuring beans*

3-1 Introduction

In previous chapters, we touched upon some of the basic concepts of Spring Framework. We saw how Spring beans and their dependencies are specified in the application context XML file. We also looked at singleton- and prototype-scoped beans, and discussed the implications of assigning these scopes to beans.

In this chapter, we'll look at:

- bean definition inheritance
- how arguments to a bean class's constructor are resolved
- how to configure bean properties and constructor arguments of primitive type (like `int`, `float`, and so on), collection type (like `java.util.List`, `java.util.Map`, and so on), custom type (like `Address`), and so on
- how you can make the application context XML file less verbose by using p-namespace and c-namespace to specify bean properties and constructor arguments, respectively
- Spring's `FactoryBean` interface that allows you to write your own factory class for creating bean instances
- modularizing bean configuration

3-2 Bean definition inheritance

We saw in chapter 1 and 2 that a bean definition in the application context XML file specifies the fully-qualified name of the bean class and its dependencies. In some scenarios, to make a bean definition less verbose, you may want a bean definition to *inherit* configuration information from another bean definition. Let's look at one such scenario in MyBank application.

IMPORT **`chapter 3/ch03-bankapp-inheritance`** (This project shows the MyBank application that uses *bean definition inheritance*. To run the application, execute the `main` method of the `BankApp` class of this project)

MyBank – Bean definition inheritance example

In the previous chapter, we saw that the MyBank application accesses database through DAOs. Let's say that the MyBank application defines a `DatabaseOperations` class that simplifies interacting with the database. So, all the DAOs in the MyBank application depend on `DatabaseOperations` class to perform database operations, as shown in the following figure:

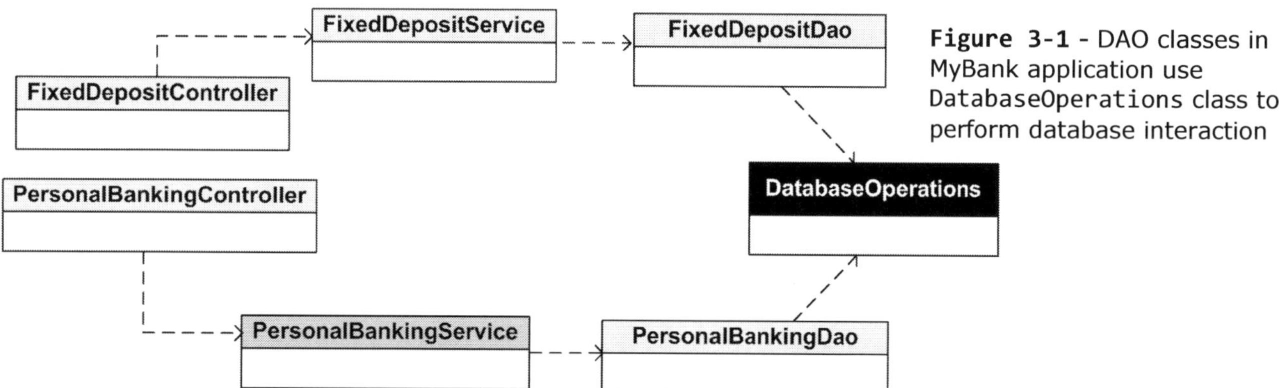

Figure 3-1 - DAO classes in MyBank application use `DatabaseOperations` class to perform database interaction

The above figure shows that the FixedDepositDao and PersonalBankingDao classes are dependent on the DatabaseOperations class. The following application context XML file shows the bean definitions for these classes:

Example listing 3-1 – DAO beans are dependent on DatabaseOperations bean

```
<bean id="databaseOperations"
      class="sample.spring.chapter01.bankapp.utils.DatabaseOperations" />

<bean id="personalBankingDao"
      class="sample.spring.chapter01.bankapp.dao.PersonalBankingDaoImpl">
    <property name="databaseOperations" ref="databaseOperations" />
</bean>

<bean id="fixedDepositDao"
      class="sample.spring.chapter01.bankapp.dao.FixedDepositDaoImpl">
    <property name="databaseOperations" ref="databaseOperations" />
</bean>
```

In the above example listing, both the personalBankingDao and fixedDepositDao bean definitions use the databaseOperations property to refer to the DatabaseOperations instance. This implies that both PersonalBankingDaoImpl and FixedDepositDaoImpl classes define a setDatabaseOperations method to allow Spring container to inject the DatabaseOperations instance.

If multiple beans in your application share a common set of configuration (properties, constructor arguments, and so on), you can create a bean definition that acts as a parent for other bean definitions. In the case of personalBankingDao and fixedDepositDao bean definitions, the common configuration is the databaseOperations property. The following example listing shows how the personalBankingDao and fixedDepositDao bean definitions inherit databaseOperations property from a parent bean definition:

Example listing 3-2 – applicationContext.xml - MyBank's application context XML file
Project – ch03-bankapp-inheritance
Source location - src/main/resources/META-INF/spring

```
<bean id="databaseOperations"
    class="sample.spring.chapter03.bankapp.utils.DatabaseOperations" />

<bean id="daoTemplate" abstract="true">
    <property name="databaseOperations" ref="databaseOperations" />
</bean>

<bean id="fixedDepositDao" parent="daoTemplate"
    class="sample.spring.chapter03.bankapp.dao.FixedDepositDaoImpl" />

<bean id="personalBankingDao" parent="daoTemplate"
    class="sample.spring.chapter03.bankapp.dao.PersonalBankingDaoImpl" />
```

In the above example listing, the daoTemplate bean definition defines the common configuration shared by both the fixedDepositDao and personalBankingDao bean definitions. As both the fixedDepositDao and personalBankingDao bean definitions require the databaseOperations dependency (refer example listing 3-1), the daoTemplate bean definition defines the databaseOperations dependency using the <property> element. The <bean> element's parent attribute specifies the name of the bean definition from which the configuration is inherited. As the parent attribute value is daoTemplate for fixedDepositDao and personalBankingDao bean definitions, they inherit databaseOperations property from the daoTemplate bean definition. The example listings 3-1 and 3-2 are the same, except that the example listing 3-2 makes use of bean definition inheritance.

If the `<bean>` element's `abstract` attribute value is set to `true`, it means that the bean definition is *abstract*. In example listing 3-2, the `daoTemplate` bean definition is *abstract*. It is important to note that the Spring container *doesn't* attempt to create a bean corresponding to an *abstract* bean definition.

> It is important to note that you can't define a bean to be dependent on an *abstract* bean, that is, you can't use `<property>` or `<constructor-arg>` element to refer to an *abstract* bean.

You may have noticed that the `daoTemplate` bean definition doesn't specify the `class` attribute. If a parent bean definition doesn't specify the `class` attribute, child bean definitions (like the `fixedDepositDao` and `personalBankingDao`) specify the `class` attribute. It is important to note that if you don't specify the `class` attribute, you must define the bean definition as *abstract* so that the Spring container doesn't attempt to create a bean instance corresponding to it.

To verify that the `fixedDepositDao` and `personalBankingDao` bean definitions inherit `daoTemplate` bean definition's `databaseOperations` property, execute the `main` method of `BankApp` class of `ch03-bankapp-inheritance` project. `BankApp`'s `main` method invokes methods on the `fixedDepositDao` and `personalBankingDao` beans; those beans in turn invoke methods on the `DatabaseOperations` instance. You'll notice that the `BankApp`'s `main` method runs successfully without any exception. If a `DatabaseOperations` instance was *not* injected into the `fixedDepositDao` and `personalBankingDao` beans, then the code would have thrown `java.lang.NullPointerException`.

The following diagram summarizes how bean definition inheritance works in the case of `fixedDepositDao` and `personalBankingDao` bean definitions:

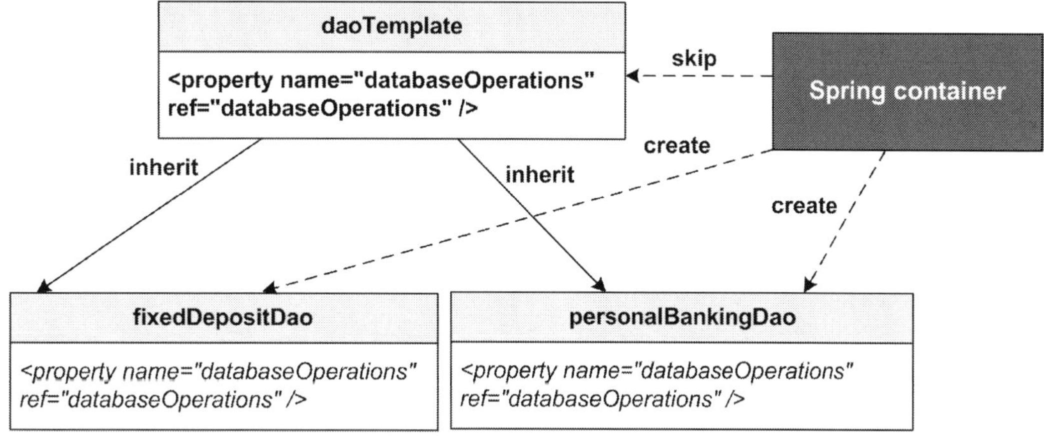

Figure 3-2 – Bean definition inheritance in MyBank application

The above figure shows that the `fixedDepositDao` and `personalBankingDao` bean definitions inherit the `databaseOperations` property (shown in *italics* in the boxes labeled `fixedDepositDao` and `personalBankingDao`) from the `daoTemplate` bean definition. The above figure also depicts that the Spring container doesn't attempt to create a bean instance corresponding to the `daoTemplate` bean definition because it is marked as *abstract*.

Let's now look at what configuration information gets inherited from the parent bean definition.

What gets inherited ?

A child bean definition inherits the following configuration information from the parent bean definition:

- properties – specified via <property> elements
- constructor arguments – specified via <constructor-arg> elements
- method overrides (discussed in section 4-5 of chapter 4)
- initialization and destroy methods (discussed in chapter 5), and
- factory methods – specified via the factory-method attribute of <bean> elements (refer section 2-3 of chapter 2 to know how *static* and *instance* factory methods are used for creating beans)

IMPORT **chapter 3/ch03-bankapp-inheritance-examples** (This project shows the MyBank application that uses bean definition inheritance. In this project, you'll see multiple scenarios in which bean definition inheritance is used. To run the application, execute the main method of the BankApp class of this project)

Let's now look at some of the bean definition inheritance examples.

Bean definition inheritance example – parent bean definition is *not* abstract

The following example listing shows a bean inheritance example in which the parent bean definition is *not* abstract, and the child bean definitions define an additional dependency:

Example listing 3-3 – applicationContext.xml - Bean definition inheritance – parent bean definition is *not* abstract
Project – ch03-bankapp-inheritance-examples
Source location - src/main/resources/META-INF/spring

```
<bean id="serviceTemplate"
        class="sample.spring.chapter03.bankapp.base.ServiceTemplate">
    <property name="jmsMessageSender" ref="jmsMessageSender" />
    <property name="emailMessageSender" ref="emailMessageSender" />
    <property name="webServiceInvoker" ref="webServiceInvoker" />
</bean>

<bean id="fixedDepositService" class=".....FixedDepositServiceImpl"
        parent="serviceTemplate">
    <property name="fixedDepositDao" ref="fixedDepositDao" />
</bean>

<bean id="personalBankingService" class=".....PersonalBankingServiceImpl"
        parent="serviceTemplate">
    <property name="personalBankingDao" ref="personalBankingDao" />
</bean>

<bean id="userRequestController" class=".....UserRequestControllerImpl">
    <property name="serviceTemplate" ref="serviceTemplate" />
</bean>
```

A little background before we delve into the details of the above listed configuration: a service in the MyBank application may send JMS messages to a messaging-middleware or send emails to an email server or it may invoke an external web service. In the above example listing, the jmsMessageSender, emailMessageSender and webServiceInvoker beans simplify these tasks by providing a layer of abstraction. The serviceTemplate bean provides access to jmsMessageSender, emailMessageSender and webServiceInvoker beans. This is the reason why the serviceTemplate bean is dependent on the jmsMessageSender, emailMessageSender and webServiceInvoker beans.

Example listing 3-3 shows that the serviceTemplate bean definition is the parent bean definition of fixedDepositService and personalBankingService bean definitions. Notice that the serviceTemplate bean definition is not *abstract*; the class attribute specifies ServiceTemplate as the class. In our previous bean definition inheritance example (refer example listing 3-2), child bean definitions didn't define any properties. In the above example listing, notice that the fixedDepositService and personalBankingService child bean definitions define fixedDepositDao and personalBankingDao properties, respectively.

As parent bean definition's properties are inherited by the child bean definitions, FixedDepositServiceImpl and PersonalBankingServiceImpl classes *must* define setter methods for jmsMessageSender, emailMessageSender and webServiceInvoker properties. You have the option to either define setter methods in FixedDepositServiceImpl and PersonalBankingServiceImpl classes, or make FixedDepositServiceImpl and PersonalBankingServiceImpl classes as subclasses of ServiceTemplate class. In ch03-bankapp-inheritance-examples, the FixedDepositServiceImpl and PersonalBankingServiceImpl classes are subclasses of ServiceTemplate class.

The following example listing shows the PersonalBankingServiceImpl class:

Example listing 3-4 – PersonalBankingServiceImpl class
Project – ch03-bankapp-inheritance-examples
Source location - src/main/java/sample/spring/chapter03/bankapp/service

```
package sample.spring.chapter03.bankapp.service;

public class PersonalBankingServiceImpl extends ServiceTemplate implements
            PersonalBankingService {

    private PersonalBankingDao personalBankingDao;

   public void setPersonalBankingDao(PersonalBankingDao personalBankingDao) {
      this.personalBankingDao = personalBankingDao;
   }

    @Override
    public BankStatement getMiniStatement() {
        return personalBankingDao.getMiniStatement();
    }
}
```

In example listing 3-3, we saw that the personalBankingService bean definition specifies personalBankingDao as a dependency. In the above example listing, the setPersonalBankingDao setter method corresponds to the personalBankingDao dependency. Also, notice that the PersonalBankingServiceImpl class is a subclass of the ServiceTemplate class.

Figure 3-3 shows that a parent bean definition (like serviceTemplate) need not be *abstract*, child bean definitions (like fixedDepositService and personalBankingService) may define additional properties, and classes represented by parent (like ServiceTemplate class) and child bean definitions (like FixedDepositServiceImpl and PersonalBankingServiceImpl) may themselves be related by inheritance.

Figure 3-3 shows:

- Spring container creates an instance of serviceTemplate bean because it's *not* defined as abstract
- FixedDepositServiceImpl and PersonalBankingServiceImpl classes (corresponding to the child bean definitions) are subclasses of ServiceTemplate class – the class corresponding to the serviceTemplate parent bean definition.

- And, `fixedDepositService` and `personalBankingService` bean definitions define additional properties, `fixedDepositDao` and `personalBankingDao`, respectively. You should note that the child bean definitions can also define additional constructor arguments and *method overrides* (discussed in section 4-5 of chapter 4).

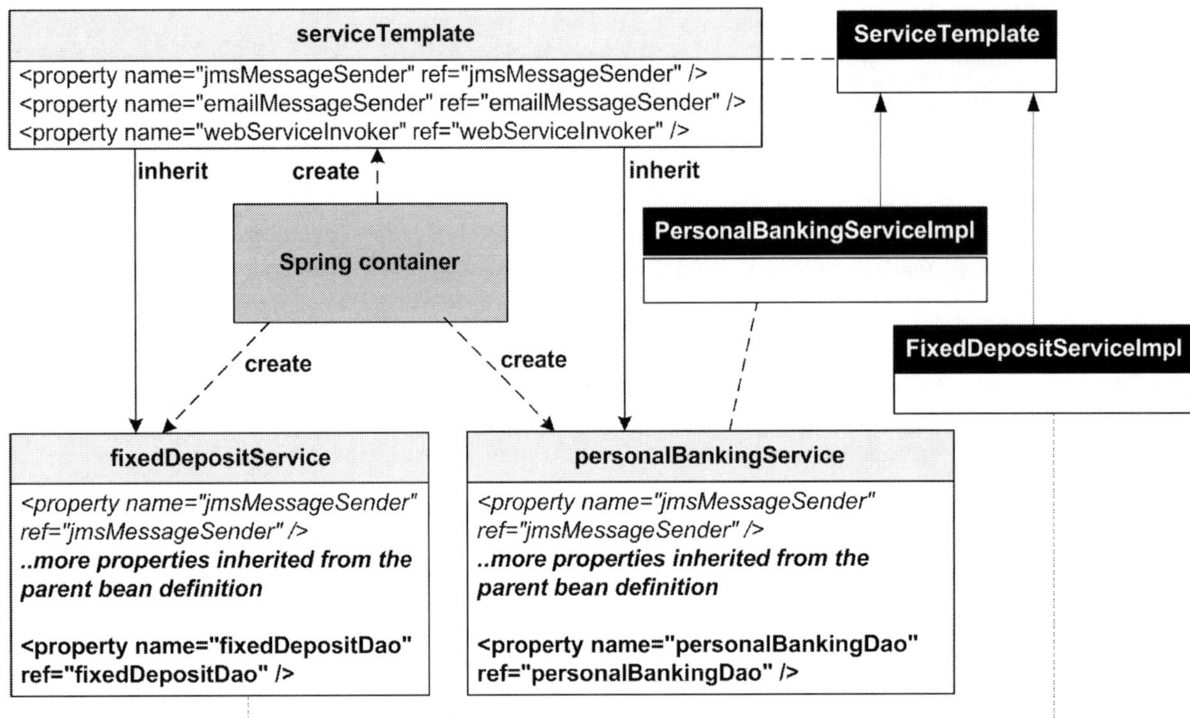

Figure 3-3 – Child bean definitions add additional properties, parent bean definition is *not* abstract, and parent-child relationship exists between the classes represented by the parent and child bean definitions

As `serviceTemplate` bean definition is *not* abstract, other beans can define `serviceTemplate` bean as their dependency. For instance, in example listing 3-3, the `serviceTemplate` bean is a dependency of `userRequestController` bean. You can infer from this discussion that if a parent bean definition is not abstract, the functionality offered by the parent bean can be utilized not only by child beans but also by other beans in the application context.

Bean definition inheritance example – inheriting factory method configuration

Child bean definitions can use bean definition inheritance to inherit factory method configuration from the parent bean definition. Let's look at an example in which the parent's factory method configuration is inherited by child bean definitions.

The following `ControllerFactory` class defines a `getController` *instance* factory method:

Example listing 3-5 – ControllerFactory class
Project – ch03-bankapp-inheritance-examples
Source location - src/main/java/sample/spring/chapter03/bankapp/controller

```
package sample.spring.chapter03.bankapp.controller;

public class ControllerFactory {

    public Object getController(String controllerName) {
        Object controller = null;
```

```
        if ("fixedDepositController".equalsIgnoreCase(controllerName)) {
            controller = new FixedDepositControllerImpl();
        }
        if ("personalBankingController".equalsIgnoreCase(controllerName)) {
            controller = new PersonalBankingControllerImpl();
        }
        return controller;
    }
}
```

The above example listing shows that the getController factory method creates an instance of FixedDepositControllerImpl or PersonalBankingControllerImpl class, depending upon the value of the controllerName argument passed to it. If the value of controllerName argument is fixedDepositController, the getController method creates an instance of FixedDepositControllerImpl class. And, if the value of controllerName argument is personalBankingController, the getController method creates an instance of PersonalBankingControllerImpl class.

The following bean definitions in the applicationContext.xml file of ch03-bankapp-inheritance-example project show that the child bean definitions inherit the getController *instance* factory method configuration from the parent bean definition:

Example listing 3-6 – applicationContext.xml - Bean definition inheritance – inheriting the factory method configuration
Project – ch03-bankapp-inheritance-examples
Source location - src/main/resources/META-INF/spring

```
<bean id="controllerFactory"
      class="sample.spring.chapter03.bankapp.controller.ControllerFactory" />

<bean id="controllerTemplate" factory-bean="controllerFactory"
      factory-method="getController" abstract="true">
</bean>

<bean id="fixedDepositController" parent="controllerTemplate">
    <constructor-arg index="0" value="fixedDepositController" />
    <property name="fixedDepositService" ref="fixedDepositService" />
</bean>

<bean id="personalBankingController" parent="controllerTemplate">
    <constructor-arg index="0" value="personalBankingController" />
    <property name="personalBankingService" ref="personalBankingService" />
</bean>
```

In the above example listing, the ControllerFactory class represents a factory class that defines a getController *instance* factory method. The controllerTemplate bean definition specifies that the ControllerFactory's getController factory method is used for creating bean instances. The getController method (refer example listing 3-5) creates an instance of FixedDepositControllerImpl or PersonalBankingControllerImpl bean, depending on the argument passed to the getController method.

As the controllerTemplate bean definition is *abstract*, it is up to the fixedDepositController and personalBankingController child bean definitions to use the getController factory method configuration. We saw in section 2-3 of chapter 2 that the <constructor-arg> element is used to pass an argument to an *instance* factory method. In example listing 3-6, the <constructor-arg> element has been used by the fixedDepositController and personalBankingController child bean definitions to pass 'fixedDepositController' and 'personalBankingController' values, respectively, to the getController factory method.

So, in the case of fixedDepositController bean definition, the Spring container invokes the getController method with argument 'fixedDepositController', resulting in creation of a FixedDepositControllerImpl instance. And, in the case of personalBankingController bean definition, the Spring container invokes the getController method with argument 'personalBankingController', resulting in creation of a PersonalBankingControllerImpl instance.

It is recommended that you now run the main method of BankApp class of ch03-bankapp-inheritance-examples project to see usage of the bean definition inheritance examples discussed in this section.

Let's now look at how constructor arguments defined in the bean definitions are matched with the arguments defined in the constructor's signature.

3-3 Constructor argument matching

In the previous chapter, we saw that the constructor arguments are specified in the bean definitions using the <constructor-arg> element. In this section, we'll look at how Spring container matches constructor arguments specified by <constructor-arg> elements with the constructor arguments specified in the bean class's constructor.

Before we go into the details of constructor argument matching, let's revisit how we pass arguments to a bean class's constructor.

IMPORT **chapter 3/ch03-bankapp-constructor-args-by-type** (This project shows the MyBank application in which bean class's constructor arguments are matched *by type*. To run the application, execute the main method of the BankApp class of this project)

Passing simple values and bean references using <constructor-arg> element

If a constructor argument is of simple Java type (like int, String, and so on), the <constructor-arg> element's value attribute is used to specify the value of the constructor argument. If a constructor argument is a reference to a bean, you specify the name of the bean using the <constructor-arg> element's ref attribute.

The following example listing shows the UserRequestControllerImpl class of ch03-bankapp-constructor-args-by-type project whose constructor accepts an argument of type ServiceTemplate:

Example listing 3-7 – UserRequestControllerImpl class
Project – ch03-bankapp-constructor-args-by-type
Source location - src/main/java/sample/spring/chapter03/bankapp/controller

```
package sample.spring.chapter03.bankapp.controller;

public class UserRequestControllerImpl implements UserRequestController {
    private ServiceTemplate serviceTemplate;

    public UserRequestControllerImpl(ServiceTemplate serviceTemplate) {
        this.serviceTemplate = serviceTemplate;
    }

    @Override
    public void submitRequest(Request request) {
        //-- do something using ServiceTemplate
```

```
        serviceTemplate.getJmsMessageSender(); //-- For ex., send JMS message
        .....
    }
}
```

The following example listing shows that a reference to ServiceTemplate instance (represented by serviceTemplate bean definition) is passed to UserRequestControllerImpl's constructor using the ref attribute of <constructor-arg> element:

Example listing 3-8 – applicationContext.xml - Passing reference to a Spring bean as constructor argument
Project – ch03-bankapp-constructor-args-by-type
Source location - src/main/resources/META-INF/spring

```
<bean id="serviceTemplate" class="sample.spring.chapter03.bankapp.base.ServiceTemplate">
    .....
</bean>

<bean id="userRequestController"
      class="sample.spring.chapter03.bankapp.controller.UserRequestControllerImpl">
    <constructor-arg index="0" ref="serviceTemplate" />
</bean>
```

With this background information on how to pass simple values and bean references as constructor arguments, let's now look at how Spring container matches constructor argument *types* to locate the bean's constructor to be invoked.

Constructor argument matching based on *type*

If the <constructor-arg> element's index attribute is *not* specified, Spring container locates the constructor to be invoked by matching the types referenced by the <constructor-arg> elements with the argument types specified in the bean class's constructor(s).

Let's first look at how Spring container matches constructor arguments when the constructor arguments are Spring beans that are *not* related by inheritance.

Constructor arguments representing distinct Spring beans

The following example listing shows the ServiceTemplate class that defines a constructor that accepts references to JmsMessageSender, EmailMessageSender and WebServiceInvoker beans:

Example listing 3-9 – ServiceTemplate class
Project – ch03-bankapp-constructor-args-by-type
Source location - src/main/java/sample/spring/chapter03/bankapp/base

```
package sample.spring.chapter03.bankapp.base;

public class ServiceTemplate {
    .....
    public ServiceTemplate(JmsMessageSender jmsMessageSender,
        EmailMessageSender emailMessageSender,
        WebServiceInvoker webServiceInvoker) {
        .....
    }
}
```

The following example listing shows the bean definitions for the ServiceTemplate class and the beans referenced by ServiceTemplate:

Example listing 3-10 – applicationContext.xml - Bean definition for the ServiceTemplate class and its dependencies
Project – ch03-bankapp-constructor-args-by-type
Source location - src/main/resources/META-INF/spring

```
<bean id="serviceTemplate" class="sample.spring.chapter03.bankapp.base.ServiceTemplate">
    <constructor-arg ref="emailMessageSender" />
    <constructor-arg ref="jmsMessageSender" />
    <constructor-arg ref="webServiceInvoker" />
</bean>

<bean id="jmsMessageSender"
        class="sample.spring.chapter03.bankapp.base.JmsMessageSender" />
<bean id="emailMessageSender"
        class="sample.spring.chapter03.bankapp.base.EmailMessageSender" />
<bean id="webServiceInvoker"
        class="sample.spring.chapter03.bankapp.base.WebServiceInvoker" />
```

In the above example listing, the <constructor-arg> elements of serviceTemplate bean *don't* specify the index attribute. The order in which the constructor arguments are specified by the <constructor-arg> elements is: EmailMessageSender, JmsMessageSender, WebServiceInvoker. The order in which constructor arguments are specified in the ServiceTemplate class's constructor is: JmsMessageSender, EmailMessageSender, WebServiceInvoker. As you can see, the order in which constructor arguments are defined by the <constructor-arg> elements is different from the order specified in which they are specified in the ServiceTemplate class's constructor.

If you execute the main method of BankApp class of ch03-bankapp-constructor-args-by-type project, you'll find that the Spring container successfully creates an instance of ServiceTemplate bean. This is because JmsMessageSender, EmailMessageSender and WebServiceInvoker types are distinct in nature (that is, they are *not* related by inheritance), which makes it possible for the Spring container to inject them in the correct order into the ServiceTemplate's constructor.

If the constructor argument types are related by inheritance, the Spring container needs extra instructions to help resolve constructor arguments. Let's look at an example in which beans referenced by the constructor arguments are related by inheritance.

Constructor arguments representing related Spring beans

Consider the following SampleBean bean class whose constructor accepts argument types that are related by inheritance:

Example listing 3-11 – SampleBean class

```
public class SampleBean {
    public SampleBean(ABean aBean, BBean bBean) { ..... }
    .....
}
```

The above example listing shows that the SampleBean class's constructor accepts ABean and BBean types as arguments. ABean and BBean represent Spring beans that are related by inheritance; BBean is a subclass of ABean.

The following application context XML file shows the bean definitions for SampleBean, ABean and BBean classes:

Example listing 3-12 – Bean definitions for SampleBean, ABean and BBean classes

```
<bean id="aBean" class="example.ABean"/>
<bean id="bBean" class="example.BBean"/>

<bean id="sampleBean" class="example.SampleBean">
    <constructor-arg ref="bBean"/>
    <constructor-arg ref="aBean"/>
</bean>
```

As aBean and bBean beans are related by inheritance, the Spring container applies constructor arguments to the SampleBean's constructor in the order in which <constructor-arg> elements appear in the bean definition for the SampleBean class. In the above sampleBean bean definition, the first <constructor-arg> element refers to bBean bean and the second <constructor-arg> element refers to aBean bean. This means that the bBean is passed as the first constructor argument and the aBean is passed as the second constructor argument to the SampleBean constructor. As an instance of ABean (the superclass) can't be passed where BBean (the subclass) instance is expected, the second <constructor-arg> element in the sampleBean bean definition results in exception being thrown by the Spring container. To handle such scenarios, you can use <constructor-arg> element's index or type attribute to identify the constructor argument to which <constructor-arg> element applies. For instance, the following sampleBean bean definition makes use of type attribute to indicate the type of the constructor argument to which the <constructor-arg> element applies:

Example listing 3-13 – <constructor-arg> element's type attribute identifies the type of the constructor argument

```
<bean id="sampleBean" class="example.SampleBean">
    <constructor-arg type="sample.spring.chapter03.bankapp.controller.BBean"
        ref="bBean"/>
    <constructor-arg type="sample.spring.chapter03.bankapp.controller.ABean"
        ref="aBean"/>
</bean>
```

The <constructor-arg> element's type attribute specifies the fully-qualified name of the type to which the <constructor-arg> element applies. In the above example listing, the first <constructor-arg> applies to the constructor argument of type BBean, and the second <constructor-arg> element applies to the constructor argument of type ABean. Specifying the type attribute takes away the ambiguity that arises when constructor arguments are related by inheritance.

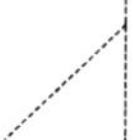

If two or more constructor arguments are of the same type, the only option is to use index attribute to identify the constructor argument to which each <constructor-arg> element applies.

So far we have looked at constructor argument type matching scenarios in which constructor arguments represented distinct or related Spring beans. We'll now look at how constructor argument types are matched for standard Java types (like int, long, boolean, String, Date, and so on) and custom (like Address) types.

Constructor arguments representing standard Java types and custom types

If the type of a constructor argument is a primitive type (like int, long, boolean, and so on) or a String type or a custom type (like Address), the <constructor-arg> element's value attribute is used to specify the value. If there are 2 or more constructor arguments into which the string value specified by the value attribute can be converted, it'll not be possible for the Spring container to derive the type (for example, whether the value represents an int or a long or a String) of the constructor argument. In such scenarios, you need to explicitly specify the type of the constructor argument using the type attribute.

The following example listing shows the TransferFundsServiceImpl class whose constructor accepts arguments of types String, boolean, long and int:

Example listing 3-14 – TransferFundsServiceImpl class
Project – ch03-bankapp-constructor-args-by-type
Source location - src/main/java/sample/spring/chapter03/bankapp/service

```
package sample.spring.chapter03.bankapp.service;

public class TransferFundsServiceImpl implements TransferFundsService {
    public TransferFundsServiceImpl(String webServiceUrl, boolean active, long timeout,
             int numberOfRetrialAttempts) {.....}
     .....
}
```

TransferFundsServiceImpl constructor accepts the following arguments: webServiceUrl, active, timeout and numberOfRetrialAttempts. The following bean definition for the TransferFundsServiceImpl class shows how constructor argument values are passed to the TransferFundsServiceImpl's constructor:

Example listing 3-15 – Bean definition for the TransferFundsServiceImpl class

```
<bean id="transferFundsService"
          class="sample.spring.chapter03.bankapp.service.TransferFundsServiceImpl">
    <constructor-arg value="http://someUrl.com/xyz" />
    <constructor-arg value="true" />
    <constructor-arg value="5" />
    <constructor-arg value="200" />
</bean>
```

Let's assume that the 3rd <constructor-arg> element (value attribute's value is '5') is supposed to supply value for the numberOfRetrialAttempts constructor argument, and the 4th <constructor-arg> element (value attribute's value is '200') is supposed to supply value for the timeout constructor argument. Spring container applies <constructor-arg> elements to the TransferFundsServiceImpl's constructor in the order in which the <constructor-arg> elements appear in the transferFundsService bean definition. This means that the 3rd <constructor-arg> element is applied to the timeout argument, instead of the numberOfRetrialAttempts argument. And, the 4th <constructor-arg> element is applied to the numberOfRetrialAttempts argument, instead of the timeout argument. To handle such scenarios, you can specify the *type* of a constructor argument using <constructor-arg> element's type attribute, as shown in the following example listing:

Example listing 3-16 – applicationContext.xml - <constructor-arg> element's type attribute
Project – ch03-bankapp-constructor-args-by-type
Source location - src/main/resources/META-INF/spring

```
<bean id="transferFundsService"
      class="sample.spring.chapter03.bankapp.service.TransferFundsServiceImpl">
    <constructor-arg type="java.lang.String" value="http://someUrl.com/xyz" />
    <constructor-arg type="boolean" value="true" />
    <constructor-arg type="int" value="5" />
    <constructor-arg type="long" value="200" />
</bean>
```

In the above bean definition for the TransferFundsServiceImpl class, the type attribute is used to specify the constructor argument type. Spring container can now compare constructor argument types to correctly apply them to TransferFundsServiceImpl's constructor.

If two or more constructor arguments are of the same type, the only option is to use index attribute for identifying the constructor argument to which each <constructor-arg> element applies.

In this section, we saw how type matching is performed by Spring to resolve constructor arguments. Let's now look at how you can instruct Spring to perform constructor argument matching based on constructor argument's *name*.

IMPORT **chapter 3/ch03-bankapp-constructor-args-by-name** (This project shows the MyBank application in which bean class's constructor arguments are matched *by name*. To run the application, execute the main method of the BankApp class of this project)

Constructor argument matching based on name

The <constructor-arg> element's name attribute is used for specifying the name of the constructor argument to which the <constructor-arg> element applies. Once again, the following example listing shows the TransferFundsServiceImpl class whose constructor accepts multiple arguments:

Example listing 3-17 – TransferFundsServiceImpl class
Project – ch03-bankapp-constructor-args-by-name
Source location - src/main/java/sample/spring/chapter03/bankapp/service

```
package sample.spring.chapter03.bankapp.service;

public class TransferFundsServiceImpl implements TransferFundsService {
    .....
    public TransferFundsServiceImpl(String webServiceUrl, boolean active, long timeout,
               int numberOfRetrialAttempts) { ..... }
}
```

The above example listing shows that the names of the constructor arguments defined by TransferFundsServiceImpl's constructor are: webServiceUrl, active, timeout and numberOfRetrialAttempts.

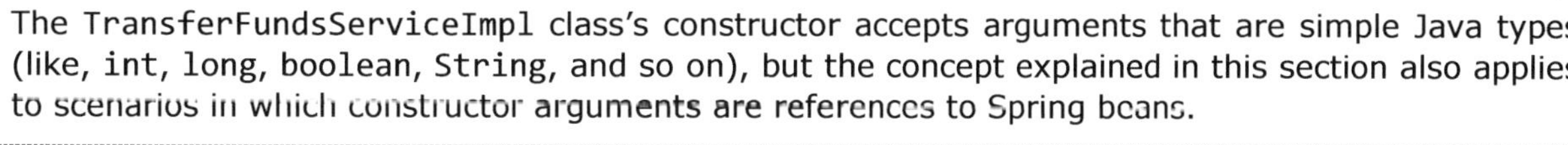

The TransferFundsServiceImpl class's constructor accepts arguments that are simple Java types (like, int, long, boolean, String, and so on), but the concept explained in this section also applies to scenarios in which constructor arguments are references to Spring beans.

The following bean definition for the TransferFundsServiceImpl class uses <constructor-arg> element's name attribute to specify the name of the constructor argument to which the <constructor-arg> element applies:

Example listing 3-18 – applicationContext.xml - <constructor-arg> element's name attribute
Project – ch03-bankapp-constructor-args-by-name
Source location - src/main/resources/META-INF/spring

```
    <bean id="transferFundsService"
            class="sample.spring.chapter03.bankapp.service.TransferFundsServiceImpl">
        <constructor-arg name="webServiceUrl" value="http://someUrl.com/xyz" />
        <constructor-arg name="active" value="true" />
        <constructor-arg name="numberOfRetrialAttempts" value="5" />
        <constructor-arg name="timeout" value="200" />
```

```
    </bean>
```

The above configuration will work only if TransferFundsServiceImpl class is compiled with *debug flag* enabled (refer to -g option of javac) or *'parameter name discovery' flag* enabled (refer to -parameters option of javac in Java 8). When the debug or 'parameter name discovery' flag is enabled, the names of constructor arguments and method parameters are preserved in the generated .class file. If you don't compile your classes with debug or 'parameter name discovery' flag enabled, the constructor argument names are lost during compilation. In the absence of constructor argument names in the generated .class file, Spring has no way to match constructor arguments by name.

If you don't want to compile your classes using debug or 'parameter name discovery' flag enabled, you can use @ConstructorProperties annotation to clearly spell out names of the constructor arguments, as shown here for TransferFundsServiceImpl class:

Example listing 3-19 – @ConstructorProperties annotation
Project – ch03-bankapp-constructor-args-by-name
Source location - src/main/java/sample/spring/chapter03/bankapp/service

```
package sample.spring.chapter03.bankapp.service;

import java.beans.ConstructorProperties;

public class TransferFundsServiceImpl implements TransferFundsService {

    @ConstructorProperties({"webServiceUrl","active","timeout","numberOfRetrialAttempts"})
     public TransferFundsServiceImpl(String webServiceUrl, boolean active, long timeout,
                int numberOfRetrialAttempts) { ..... }
}
```

In the above example listing, @ConstructorProperties annotation specifies the names of constructor arguments in the order in which they appear in the bean class's constructor. You *must* ensure that you use the same constructor argument names in the <constructor-arg> elements.

Let's now look at how the @ConstructorProperties annotation affects bean definition inheritance.

@ConstructorProperties annotation and bean definition inheritance

If the constructor of the class corresponding to the *parent* bean definition is annotated with @ConstructorProperties annotation, the bean class corresponding to the *child* bean definition *must* also be annotated with @ConstructorProperties annotation.

The following example listing shows the serviceTemplate (parent bean definition) and FixedDepositService (child bean definition) bean definitions:

Example listing 3-20 – applicationContext.xml - Parent and child bean definitions
Project – ch03-bankapp-constructor-args-by-name
Source location - src/main/resources/META-INF/spring

```
    <bean id="serviceTemplate"
             class="sample.spring.chapter03.bankapp.base.ServiceTemplate">
        <constructor-arg name="emailMessageSender" ref="emailMessageSender" />
        <constructor-arg name="jmsMessageSender" ref="jmsMessageSender" />
        <constructor-arg name="webServiceInvoker" ref="webServiceInvoker" />
    </bean>

    <bean id="fixedDepositService"
```

```
            class="sample.spring.chapter03.bankapp.service.FixedDepositServiceImpl"
            parent="serviceTemplate">
        <property name="fixedDepositDao" ref="fixedDepositDao" />
    </bean>
```

The above example listing shows that the serviceTemplate bean definition is *not* abstract, which means that the Spring container will create an instance of serviceTemplate bean. The serviceTemplate bean definition specifies 3 <constructor-arg> elements, corresponding to the 3 arguments defined by the ServiceTemplate class (refer example listing 3-21).

As we have specified constructor arguments *by name* in the serviceTemplate bean definition, the ServiceTemplate class's constructor is annotated with the @ConstructorProperties annotation to ensure that constructor argument names are available to Spring at runtime, as shown here:

Example listing 3-21 – ServiceTemplate class
Project – ch03-bankapp-constructor-args-by-name
Source location - src/main/java/sample/spring/chapter03/bankapp/base

```
package sample.spring.chapter03.bankapp.base;

import java.beans.ConstructorProperties;

public class ServiceTemplate {
    .....
    @ConstructorProperties({"jmsMessageSender","emailMessageSender","webServiceInvoker"})
    public ServiceTemplate(JmsMessageSender jmsMessageSender,
             EmailMessageSender emailMessageSender,WebServiceInvoker webServiceInvoker)
                 { ..... }
}
```

As FixedDepositService is a child bean definition of serviceTemplate, the <constructor-arg> configuration in serviceTemplate bean definition is inherited by the FixedDepositService bean definition. This means that the FixedDepositServiceImpl class *must* define a constructor that accepts the same set of arguments as defined by the ServiceTemplate class, and it *must* be annotated with @ConstructorProperties annotation to allow Spring to match constructor arguments by name. If you don't annotate FixedDepositServiceImpl's constructor with @ConstructorProperties annotation, the Spring container will *not* be able to match the inherited <constructor-arg> elements with the constructor arguments specified in the FixedDepositServiceImpl's constructor.

You can't use @ConstructorProperties annotation for passing arguments by name to a *static* or *instance* factory method, as explained next.

@ConstructorProperties annotation and factory methods

We saw in section 2-3 of chapter 2 that the <constructor-arg> elements are also used for passing arguments to *static* and *instance* factory methods. You might think that you can pass arguments by name to *static* and *instance* factory methods by specifying the <constructor-arg> element's name attribute and annotating the factory method with @ConstructorProperties annotation. You should note that the @ConstructorProperties annotation is meant *only* for constructors; you can't annotate methods with @ConstructorProperties annotation. So, if you want to pass arguments by name to a *static* or *instance* factory method, the only option you have is to compile classes with debug or 'parameter name discovery' flag enabled.

> If you compile classes with debug or 'parameter name discovery' flag enabled, it results in `.class` files that are larger in size, but has no impact on the runtime performance of the application. It only results in increased loading time for the classes.

Let's now look at how to enable or disable debug flag in Eclipse IDE.

Enabling (or disabling) the debug or 'parameter name discovery' flag in Eclipse IDE

In Eclipse IDE, follow these steps to enable the debug flag for projects:

1. Go to `Windows` → `Preferences` and select the option `Java` → `Compiler`
2. You'll now see a section titled 'Classfile Generation'.
   a. In this section, if you check the checkbox labeled *'Add variable attributes to generated class files (used by the debugger)'*, the debug flag is *enabled*. Unchecking this checkbox will *disable* the debug flag.
   b. In this section, if you check the checkbox labeled *'Store information about method parameters (usable via reflection)'*, the 'parameter name discovery' flag is enabled. Unchecking this checkbox will *disable* the flag.

So far we have mostly seen bean definition examples in which bean properties and constructor arguments were references to other beans. We'll now look at bean definition examples in which bean properties and constructor arguments are of primitive type, collection type, `java.util.Date`, `java.util.Properties`, and so on.

3-4 Configuring different types of bean properties and constructor arguments

In real world application development scenarios, properties and constructor arguments of a Spring bean could range from a `String` type, to reference to another bean, to any other standard (like `java.util.Date`, `java.util.Map`) or custom (like `Address`) type. So far we have seen examples of how to supply string values for bean properties (using the `value` attribute of `<property>` element) and constructor arguments (using the `value` attribute of `<constructor-arg>` element). We also looked at how to inject dependencies via bean properties (using the `ref` attribute of `<property>` element) and constructor arguments (using the `ref` attribute of `<constructor-arg>` elements).

In this section, we'll look at built-in `PropertyEditor` implementations in Spring that simplify passing bean properties and constructor arguments of types `java.util.Date`, `java.util.Currency`, primitive type, and so on. We'll also look at how to specify values for collection types (like `java.util.List` and `java.util.Map`) in the application context XML file, and how to register a custom `PropertyEditor` implementation with Spring.

Let's now look at bean definition examples that demonstrate use of built-in `PropertyEditor` implementations.

IMPORT **`chapter 3/ch03-simple-types-examples`** (This project shows a Spring application in which bean properties and constructor arguments are of primitive type, `java.util.Date`, `java.util.List`, `java.util.Map`, and so on. This project also shows how to register a custom `PropertyEditor` implementation with the Spring container. To run the application, execute the `main` method of the `SampleApp` class of this project)

Built-in property editors in Spring

JavaBeans PropertyEditors provide the necessary logic for converting a Java type to a string value, and vice versa. Spring provides a couple of built-in PropertyEditors that are used for converting string value of a bean property or a constructor argument (specified via value attribute of <property> and <constructor-arg> elements) to the actual Java type of the property or constructor argument.

Before we look at examples involving built-in PropertyEditors, let's first understand the importance of PropertyEditors in setting values of bean properties and constructor arguments.

Consider the following BankDetails class that we want to configure as a singleton-scoped bean with pre-defined values for its attributes:

Example listing 3-22 – BankDetails class

```
public class BankDetails {
    private String bankName;

    public void setBankName(String bankName) {
        this.bankName = bankName;
    }
}
```

In the above example listing, bankName is an attribute of the BankDetails class, and is of type String. The following bean definition for the BankDetails class shows how to set the value of bankName attribute to 'My Personal Bank':

Example listing 3-23 – Bean definition for the BankDetails class

```
<bean id= "bankDetails" class= "BankDetails">
    <property name= "bankName" value= "My Personal Bank"/>
</bean>
```

In the above bean definition, the <property> element's value attribute specifies a string value for the bankName property. As you can see, if a bean property is of type String, you can simply set that property value using <property> element's value attribute. Similarly, if a constructor argument is of type String, you can set the constructor argument value using <constructor-arg> element's value attribute.

Let's say that the following attributes (along with their setter methods) are added to the BankDetails class: a bankPrimaryBusiness attribute of type byte[], a headOfficeAddress attribute of type char[], a privateBank attribute of type char, a primaryCurrency attribute of type java.util.Currency, a dateOfInception attribute of type java.util.Date, and a branchAddresses attribute of type java.util.Properties. The following example listing shows the modified BankDetails class:

Example listing 3-24 – BankDetails class containing different types of properties
Project – ch03-simple-types-examples
Source location - src/main/java/sample/spring/chapter03/beans

```
package sample.spring.chapter03.beans;
.....
public class BankDetails {
    private String bankName;
    private byte[] bankPrimaryBusiness;
    private char[] headOfficeAddress;
    private char privateBank;
    private Currency primaryCurrency;
```

```
    private Date dateOfInception;
    private Properties branchAddresses;
    .....
    public void setBankName(String bankName) {
        this.bankName = bankName;
    }
    //-- more setter methods
}
```

You can configure the BankDetails class as a Spring bean by specifying string values for the properties, and letting the Spring container convert these string values into the corresponding Java types of the properties by using registered JavaBeans PropertyEditor implementations.

The following bean definition for the BankDetails class shows that simple string values are specified for different property types:

Example listing 3-25 – applicationContext.xml - Bean definition for the BankDetails class
Project – ch03-simple-types-examples
Source location - src/main/resources/META-INF/spring

```
<bean id="bankDetails" class="sample.spring.chapter03.beans.BankDetails">
    <property name="bankName" value="My Personal Bank" />
    <property name="bankPrimaryBusiness" value="Retail banking" />
    <property name="headOfficeAddress" value="Address of head office" />
    <property name="privateBank" value="Y" />
    <property name="primaryCurrency" value="INR" />
    <property name="dateOfInception" value="30-01-2012"></property>
    <property name="branchAddresses">
        <value>
            x = Branch X's address
            y = Branch Y's address
        </value>
    </property>
</bean>
```

In the above example listing, string values are specified for properties of type java.util.Date, java.util.Currency, char[], byte[], char and java.util.Properties. Spring container uses registered PropertyEditors for converting string values of properties and constructor arguments to corresponding Java types. For instance, the Spring container converts the value '30-01-2012' of dateOfInception property to java.util.Date type using CustomDateEditor (a built-in PropertyEditor implementation for java.util.Date type).

If you look at how branchAddresses property (of type java.util.Properties) is configured in example listing 3-25, you'll notice that instead of <property> element's value attribute, <value> sub-element of <property> element has been used to specify the value for the property. In the case of single-valued properties, the use of <property> element's value attribute is preferred over <value> sub-element. But, if you need to specify multiple values for a property or the values need to be specified on separate lines (as in the case of branchAddresses property), the <value> sub-element is preferred over value attribute. In the next section, you'll see that values for properties (or constructor arguments) of type java.util.Properties can also be specified using <props> sub-element of <property> (or <constructor-arg>) element.

Spring comes with couple of built-in PropertyEditor implementations that perform the task of converting values specified in the application context XML file to the Java type of the bean property or constructor argument. The following table describes some of the built-in PropertyEditor implementations in Spring:

Built-in PropertyEditor implementation	Description
CustomBooleanEditor	converts string value to Boolean or boolean type
CustomNumberEditor	converts string value to a number (like int, long, and so on)
CharacterEditor	converts string value to char type
ByteArrayPropertyEditor	converts string value to byte[]
CustomDateEditor	converts string value to java.util.Date type
PropertiesEditor	converts string value to java.util.Properties type

The above table shows only a subset of built-in PropertyEditor implementations in Spring. For a complete list, refer to the org.springframework.beans.propertyeditors package of Spring. It is important to note that not all built-in PropertyEditor implementations in Spring are registered with the Spring container by default. For instance, you need to explicitly register CustomDateEditor to allow Spring container to perform conversion from a string value to a java.util.Date type. Later in this section, we'll look at how you can register property editors with the Spring container.

Let's now look at how to specify values for bean properties (or constructor arguments) of types java.util.List, java.util.Set and java.util.Map.

Specifying values for different collection types

The <list>, <map> and <set> sub-elements (defined in Spring's beans schema) of <property> and <constructor-arg> elements are used to set properties and constructor arguments of types java.util.List, java.util.Map and java.util.Set, respectively.

> Spring's util schema also provides <list>, <set> and <map> elements that simplify setting properties and constructor arguments of different collection types. In section 3-8 of this chapter, we'll look at Spring's util schema elements in detail.

The following DataTypesExample class shows that its constructor accepts arguments of different types:

Example listing 3-26 – DataTypesExample class
Project – ch03-simple-types-examples
Source location - src/main/java/sample/spring/chapter03/beans

```
package sample.spring.chapter03.beans;

import java.beans.ConstructorProperties;
.....
public class DataTypesExample {
    private static Logger logger = LogManager.getLogger(DataTypesExample.class);

    @SuppressWarnings("rawtypes")
    @ConstructorProperties({ "byteArrayType", "charType", "charArray",
            "classType", "currencyType", "booleanType", "dateType", "longType",
            "doubleType", "propertiesType", "listType", "mapType", "setType",
            "anotherPropertiesType" })
    public DataTypesExample(byte[] byteArrayType, char charType,
            char[] charArray, Class classType, Currency currencyType,
            boolean booleanType, Date dateType, long longType,
            double doubleType, Properties propertiesType, List<Integer> listType,
```

```
            Map mapType, Set setType, Properties anotherPropertiesType)  {
        .....
        logger.info("classType " + classType.getName());
        logger.info("listType " + listType);
        logger.info("mapType " + mapType);
        logger.info("setType " + setType);
        logger.info("anotherPropertiesType " + anotherPropertiesType);
    }
}
```

The above example listing shows that the `DataTypesExample` class's constructor accepts arguments of types `java.util.List`, `java.util.Map`, `java.util.Set`, `java.util.Properties`, and so on, and logs the value of each constructor argument.

The following example listing shows the bean definition for the `DataTypesExample` class:

Example listing 3-27 – `applicationContext.xml` - Bean definition for `DataTypesExample` class
Project – `ch03-simple-types-examples`
Source location - `src/main/resources/META-INF/spring`

```
    <bean id="dataTypes" class="sample.spring.chapter03.beans.DataTypesExample">
        .....
        <constructor-arg name="anotherPropertiesType">
          <props>
              <prop key="book">Getting started with the Spring Framework</prop>
          </props>
        </constructor-arg>
        <constructor-arg name="listType">
          <list>
              <value>1</value>
              <value>2</value>
          </list>
        </constructor-arg>
        <constructor-arg name="mapType">
               <map>
                <entry>
                    <key>
                           <value>map key 1</value>
                    </key>
                    <value>map key 1's value</value>
                </entry>
           </map>
        </constructor-arg>
        <constructor-arg name="setType">
            <set>
                 <value>Element 1</value>
                 <value>Element 2</value>
            </set>
        </constructor-arg>
    </bean>
```

The above example listing shows:

- the value of `anotherPropertiesType` (of type `java.util.Properties`) is specified using the `<props>` sub-element of `<constructor-arg>` element. Inside `<props>` element, each `<prop>` sub-element specifies a key-value pair; the `key` attribute specifies the key, and the content of `<prop>` element is the value for the key. Instead of using <props> element, you can use the <value> sub-element of <constructor-arg> element to specify the value for anotherPropertiesType argument (refer example listing 3-25).

- the value of listType constructor argument (of type java.util.List<Integer>) is specified using the <list> sub-element of <constructor-arg>. The <value> sub-elements of <list> element specify items contained in the list. As the listType constructor argument is of type List<Integer>, the Spring container uses CustomNumberEditor (a PropertyEditor that is registered by default with the Spring container) to convert the string values specified by <value> elements to java.lang.Integer type.

- the value of mapType constructor argument (of type java.util.Map) is specified using the <map> sub-element of <constructor-arg>. The <entry> sub-element of <map> specifies a key-value pair contained in the Map; the <key> element specifies the key and the <value> element specifies the value for the key. If the constructor argument was defined as a parameterized Map (like, Map<Integer, Integer>), the Spring container had used the registered property editors to perform conversion of keys and values to the types accepted by the parameterized Map.

- the value of the setType constructor argument (of type java.util.Set) is specified using the <set> sub-element of <constructor-arg>. Each <value> sub-element of <set> specifies an element contained in the Set. If the constructor argument was defined as a parameterized Set (like, Set<Integer>), the Spring container had used registered property editors to perform conversion of values to the type accepted by the parameterized Set.

In DataTypesExample class (refer example listing 3-26 and 3-27), constructor arguments of types List, Map and Set contained elements of type String or Integer. In an application, a collection may contain elements of type Map, Set, Class, Properties, or any other Java type. The elements contained in the collection can also be bean references. To address such scenarios, Spring allows you to use elements like <map>, <set>, <list>, <props>, <ref>, and so on, as sub-elements of <list>, <map> and <set> elements.

Let's now look at examples that demonstrate how to add different types of elements to Map, List and Set type constructor arguments and bean properties.

Adding elements of type List, Map, Set and Properties to collection types

If a bean property or constructor argument is of type List<List>, simply use a nested <list> element, as shown here:

Example listing 3-28 – Configuration example: List inside a List

```
<constructor-arg name="nestedList">
    <list>
        <list>
            <value>A simple String value in the nested list</value>
            <value>Another simple String value in nested list</value>
        </list>
    </list>
</constructor-arg>
```

In the above example listing, the <constructor-arg> element supplies value for a constructor argument named nestedList and is of type List<List>. The nested <list> element represents an element of type List. Similarly, you can use <map>, <set> and <props> elements inside a <list> element to set value of properties or constructor arguments of types List<Map>, List<Set> and List<Properties>, respectively. Like the <list> element, a <set> element can contain <set>, <list>, <map> or <props> element. In the case of a <map> element, you can use <map>, <set>, <list> or <props> element to specify key and value of an entry.

The following example listing shows how you can specify values for a Map<List, Set> type constructor argument:

Example listing 3-29 – Configuration example: Map containing List type as key and Set type as value

```
    <constructor-arg name="nestedListAndSetMap">
        <map>
            <entry>
                <key>
                    <list>
                        <value>a List element</value>
                    </list>
                </key>
                <set>
                    <value>a Set element</value>
                </set>
            </entry>
        </map>
    </constructor-arg>
```

The above example listing shows that the nestedListAndSetMap constructor argument is of Map type whose key is of type List and value is of type Set. The <key> element can contain any of the following elements as its sub-element: <map>, <set>, <list> and <props>. The key value can be defined using <map>, <set>, <list> or <props> element.

Adding bean references to collection types

You can add references to Spring beans into properties and constructor arguments of types List and Set by using <ref> elements inside <list> and <set> elements.

The following example listing shows how references to beans are added to a List type constructor argument:

Example listing 3-30 – Configuration example: List containing reference to beans

```
<bean .....>
    <constructor-arg name="myList">
        <list>
            <ref bean="aBean" />
            <ref bean="bBean" />
        </list>
    </constructor-arg>
</bean>

<bean id="aBean" class="somepackage.ABean" />
<bean id="bBean" class="somepackage.BBean" />
```

The above example listing shows that the myList constructor argument is of type List and it contains 2 elements - a reference to aBean bean and a reference to bBean bean. The <ref> element's bean attribute specifies the name of the bean referenced by the <ref> element.

As in the case of <list> elements, you can use <ref> elements inside <set> elements to add bean references to Set type constructor arguments or bean properties. In the case of <map> element, you can use <ref> element inside a <key> element to specify a bean reference as a key, and use the <ref> element to specify a bean reference as the key value. The following example listing shows a Map type constructor argument that contains a single key-value pair in which both key and value are references to beans:

Example listing 3-31 – Configuration example: Map containing bean references as keys and values

```
<bean .....>
    <constructor-arg name="myMapWithBeanRef">
         <map>
              <entry>
                  <key>
                      <ref bean="aBean" />
                  </key>
                  <ref bean="bBean" />
              </entry>
         </map>
    </constructor-arg>
</bean>

<bean id="aBean" class="somepackage.ABean" />
<bean id="bBean" class="somepackage.BBean" />
```

In the above example listing, the <constructor-arg> supplies value for a Map type constructor argument. A single key-value pair is supplied, in which the key is a reference to aBean bean and the value is a reference to bBean bean.

Adding bean names to collection types

If you want to add a bean name (as specified by the id attribute of <bean> element) to a List, Map or Set type constructor argument or bean property, you can use the <idref> element inside <map>, <set> and <list> elements. In the following example listing, <constructor-arg> element supplies a single key-value pair to a Map type constructor argument, where bean name is the key and bean reference is the value:

Example listing 3-32 – Configuration example: Map containing bean name as key and bean reference as value

```
    <constructor-arg name="myExample">
        <map>
            <entry>
                <key>
                    <idref bean="sampleBean" />
                </key>
                <ref bean="sampleBean" />
            </entry>
        </map>
    </constructor-arg>

    <bean id="sampleBean" class="somepackage.SampleBean" />
```

In the above example listing, <constructor-arg> supplies a single key-value pair to the Map type constructor argument, where key is the string value 'sampleBean' and value is the sampleBean bean. We could have used <value> element to set 'sampleBean' string value as the key, but <idref> element is used because the Spring container verifies existence of the sampleBean bean when the application is deployed.

You can use the <idref> element inside a <property> or <constructor-arg> element to set a bean name as the value of a bean property or constructor argument.

Adding `null` values to collection types

You can add a `null` value to collections of type `Set` and `List` using the `<null>` element. The following example listing shows how to add a `null` value to a `Set` type constructor argument using the `<null>` element:

Example listing 3-33 – Configuration example: `Set` containing a `null` element

```
<constructor-arg name="setWithNullElement">
    <set>
        <value>Element 1</value>
        <value>Element 2</value>
        <null />
    </set>
</constructor-arg>
```

In the above example listing, `setWithNullElement` constructor argument contains 3 elements: `Element 1`, `Element 2` and `null`.

To add a `null` key to a `Map` type constructor argument or property, you can use the `<null>` element inside the `<key>` element. And, to add a `null` value, you can add the `<null>` element inside the `<entry>` element. The following example listing shows a `Map` type constructor argument that contains a `null` key and a `null` value:

Example listing 3-34 – Configuration example: `Map` containing a `null` key and a `null` value

```
<constructor-arg name="mapType">
    <map>
        <entry>
            <key>
                <null />
            </key>
            <null />
        </entry>
    </map>
</constructor-arg>
```

The above example listing shows that an element with `null` key and `null` value is added to the `mapType` constructor argument using `<null>` element.

You can also use `<null>` element inside `<property>` and `<constructor-arg>` elements to set `null` values for properties and constructor arguments, respectively.

Let's now look at how to specify values for array type properties and constructor arguments.

Specifying values for arrays

You can set value for an array type property (or constructor argument) by using the `<array>` sub-element of `<property>` (or `<constructor-arg>`) element.

The following example listing shows how you can set a bean property of type `int[]`:

Example listing 3-35 – Configuration example: Setting value of a bean property of type `int[]`

```
<property name="numbersProperty">
    <array>
```

```
        <value>1</value>
        <value>2</value>
    </array>
</property>
```

In the above example listing, each <value> sub-element of the <array> element represents an element in the numbersProperty array. The CustomNumberEditor property editor is used by the Spring container to convert the string value specified by each of the <value> element to int type. You can use the <array> element inside <list>, <set> and <map> elements. You can also use <list>, <set>, <map>, <props> and <ref> elements inside an <array> element to create arrays of List, Set, Map, Properties and bean references, respectively. If you want to create an array of arrays, you can use <array> elements inside an <array> element.

We discussed that <list>, <map> and <set> elements are used to set properties or constructor arguments of types List, Map and Set, respectively. Let's now look at the default collection implementation that is created by Spring corresponding to each of these elements.

Default implementations corresponding to <list>,<set> and <map> elements

The following table shows the default collection implementations created by Spring for <list>, <set> and <map> elements:

Collection element	Default collection implementation
<list>	java.util.ArrayList
<set>	java.util.LinkedHashSet
<map>	java.util.LinkedHashMap

The above table suggests:

- if a property's (or a constructor argument's) value is specified using <list> element, Spring creates an instance of ArrayList and assigns it to the property (or the constructor argument).

- if a property's (or a constructor argument's) value is specified using <set> element, Spring creates an instance of LinkedHashSet and assigns it to the property (or the constructor argument).

- if a property's (or a constructor argument's) value is specified using <map> element, Spring creates an instance of LinkedHashMap and assigns it to the property (or the constructor argument).

It is likely that you may want to substitute a different implementation of List, Set or Map to a bean property or a constructor argument. For instance, instead of java.util.ArrayList, you may want to assign an instance of java.util.LinkedList to a bean property of type List. In such scenarios, it is recommended to use <list>, <map> and <set> elements of Spring's util schema (explained in section 3-8). The <list>, <set> and <map> elements of Spring's util schema provide the option to specify the fully-qualified name of the concrete collection class that you want to assign to the property or constructor argument of the bean.

Let's now look at some of the built-in property editors provided by Spring.

3-5 Built-in property editors

Spring provides a couple of built-in property editors that are useful when setting bean properties and constructor arguments. In this section, we'll look at CustomCollectionEditor, CustomMapEditor and CustomDateEditor built-in property editors.

In ch03-simple-types-examples project, some of the other built-in property editors that are utilized by beans include:

- ByteArrayPropertyEditor - for converting a string value to byte[] (refer bankPrimaryBusiness attribute of BankDetails class in example listing 3-24),
- CurrencyEditor – for converting a currency code to a java.util.Currency object (refer primaryCurrency attribute of BankDetails class in example listing 3-24),
- CharacterEditor – for converting a string value to a char[] (refer headOfficeAddress attribute of BankDetails class in example listing 3-24), and so on.

To view the complete list of built-in property editors, refer to org.springframework.beans.propertyeditors package.

CustomCollectionEditor

CustomCollectionEditor property editor is responsible for converting a source Collection (like, java.util.LinkedList) type to the target Collection (like, java.util.ArrayList) type. By default, CustomCollectionEditor is registered for Set, SortedSet and List types.

Consider the following CollectionTypesExample class that defines attributes (and corresponding setter methods) of type Set and List:

Example listing 3-36 – CollectionTypesExample class
Project – ch03-simple-types-examples
Source location - src/main/java/sample/spring/chapter03/beans

```
package sample.spring.chapter03.beans;

import java.util.List;
import java.util.Set;

public class CollectionTypesExample {
    private Set setType;
    private List listType;
    .....
    //-- setter methods for attributes
    public void setSetType(Set setType) {
        this.setType = setType;
    }
    .....
}
```

CollectionTypesExample class defines setType and listType attributes of type Set and List, respectively. The following example listing shows the bean definition for CollectionTypesExample class:

Example listing 3-37 – applicationContext.xml - Bean definition for CollectionTypesExample class
Project – ch03-simple-types-examples
Source location - src/main/resources/META-INF/spring

```
    <bean class="sample.spring.chapter03.beans.CollectionTypesExample">
        <property name="listType">
            <set>
                <value>set element 1</value>
                <value>set element 2</value>
            </set>
```

```
        </property>
        <property name="setType">
            <list>
                <value>list element 1</value>
                <value>list element 2</value>
            </list>
        </property>
        .....
    </bean>
```

You might think that the above configuration is incorrect because `<set>` element has been used to set the value of `listType` property (of type `List`), and `<list>` element has been used to set the value of `setType` property (of type `Set`).

The above configuration is completely legal, and the Spring container does *not* complain. This is because `CustomCollectionEditor` converts the `ArrayList` instance (created corresponding to the `<list>` type element) to `LinkedHashSet` type (an implementation of `Set` type) *before* setting the `setType` property. Also, `CustomCollectionEditor` converts the `LinkedHashSet` instance (created corresponding to the `<set>` type element) to `ArrayList` type (an implementation of `List` type) *before* setting the `listType` property.

Figure 3-4 shows that the `CustomCollectionEditor` converts the `LinkedHashSet` type to `ArrayList` to set the value of `CollectionTypesExample`'s `listType` property. The figure shows the sequence of steps that are performed by Spring to set the value of `listType` property. First, Spring creates an instance of `LinkedHashSet` corresponding to the `<set>` element. As the `listType` property is of type `List` (refer example listing 3-36), the `CustomCollectionEditor` comes into picture for setting the `listType` property's value. `CustomCollectionEditor` creates an instance of `ArrayList` and populates it with the elements from the `LinkedHashSet`. In the end, the value of the `listType` variable is set to the `ArrayList` implementation created by `CustomCollectionEditor`.

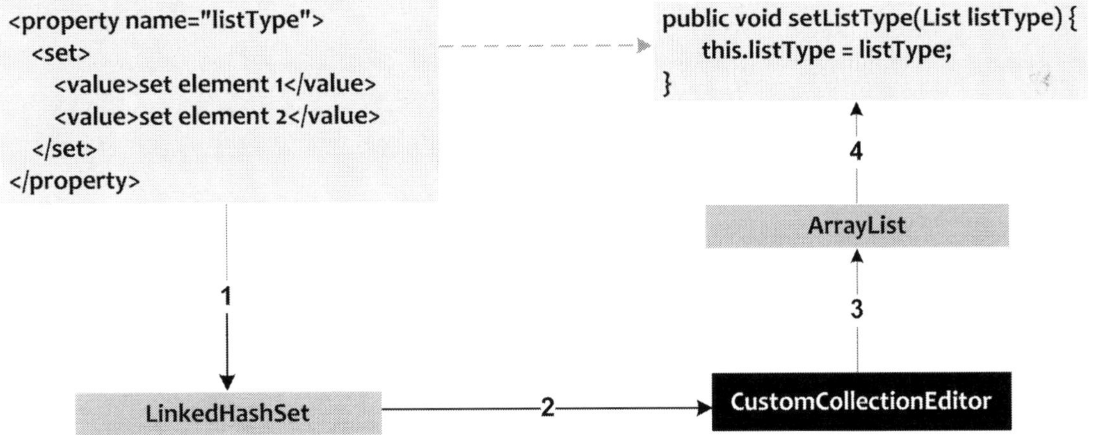

Figure 3-4 – `CustomCollectionEditor` converts the `LinkedHashSet` to `ArrayList` type

It is important to note that if a property or constructor argument type is a concrete collection class (like `LinkedList`), the `CustomCollectionEditor` property editor simply creates an instance of the concrete collection class and adds elements to it from the source collection. The following figure shows a scenario in which the bean property is of type `java.util.Vector` (a concrete collection class):

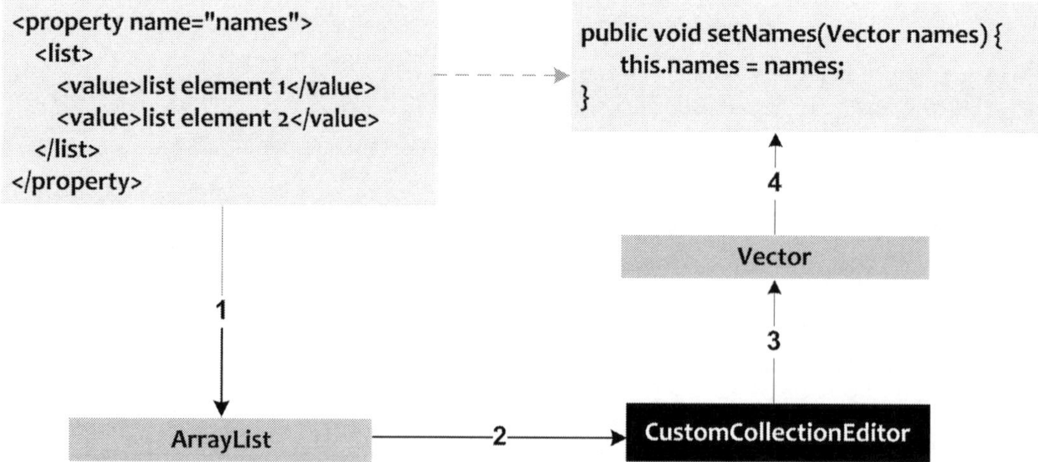

Figure 3-5 `CustomCollectionEditor` converts the `ArrayList` to `Vector` type

The above figure shows that the `CustomCollectionEditor` creates an instance of `Vector` (a concrete collection class) and adds elements to it from the source collection, `ArrayList`.

Let's now look at `CustomMapEditor` property editor.

CustomMapEditor

`CustomMapEditor` property editor deals with converting a source `Map` type (like `HashMap`) to a target `Map` type (like `TreeMap`). By default, `CustomMapEditor` is registered only for `SortedMap` type.

Figure 3-6 shows a scenario in which `CustomMapEditor` converts `LinkedHashMap` (the source `Map` type) to `TreeMap` (an implementation of `SortedMap` type). The figure shows the sequence of steps performed by Spring to set the value of `mapType` property. At first, Spring creates an instance of `LinkedHashMap` corresponding to the `<map>` element. As the `mapType` property is of type `SortedMap`, the `CustomMapEditor` comes into the picture while setting the value of `mapType` property. `CustomMapEditor` creates an instance of `TreeMap` (a concrete implementation of `SortedSet` interface), adds key-value pairs from the `LinkedHashMap` to the newly created `TreeMap` instance and assigns the `TreeMap` instance to the `mapType` property.

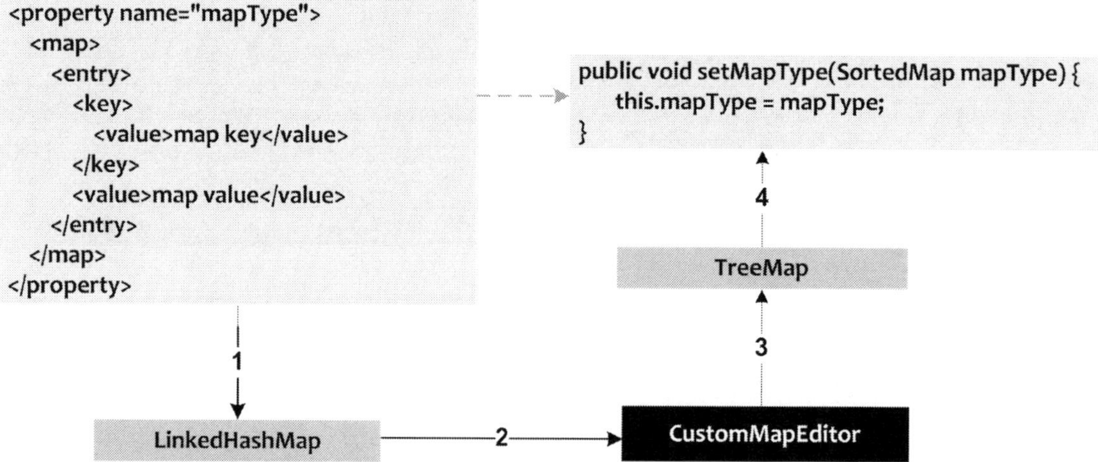

Figure 3-6 `CustomMapEditor` converts the `LinkedHashMap` (the source `Map` type) to `TreeMap` (the target `Map` type) type

CustomDateEditor

CustomDateEditor is a property editor for java.util.Date type bean properties and constructor arguments. CustomDateEditor supports a custom java.text.DateFormat that is used for formatting a date/time string to a java.util.Date type object, and parsing a java.util.Date type object to a date/time string.

In the next section, we'll see how CustomDateEditor is used for setting bean properties and constructor arguments of type java.util.Date. In ch03-simple-types-examples project, CustomDateEditor converts the string value of the BankDetails' dateOfInception property (refer example listings 3-24 and 3-25) and DataTypesExample's dateType constructor argument (refer example listing 3-26) to java.util.Date type.

Let's now look at how to register property editors with the Spring container.

3-6 Registering property editors with the Spring container

Spring's BeanWrapperImpl class registers a couple of built-in property editors with the Spring container. For instance, CustomCollectionEditor, CustomMapEditor, CurrencyEditor, ByteArrayPropertyEditor and CharacterEditor property editors are registered by default with the Spring container. But, the CustomDateEditor property editor is *not* registered by default with the Spring container.

To register property editors with the Spring container, you can use Spring's CustomEditorConfigurer *special* bean. CustomEditorConfigurer class implements Spring's BeanFactoryPostProcessor interface (explained in detail in section 5-4 of chapter 5), and it is automatically detected and executed by the Spring container.

In ch03-simple-types-examples project, BankDetails class (refer example listing 3-24) defines a dateOfInception property of type java.util.Date. The value specified for the dateOfInception property is '30-01-2012' (refer example listing 3-25). To convert the string value '30-01-2012' to java.util.Date type, you *must* register a property editor for java.util.Date type. As Spring provides the CustomDateEditor property editor for java.util.Date type, you can register it with the Spring container.

To register property editors with the Spring container, you need to do the following:

1. Create a class that implements Spring's PropertyEditorRegistrar interface. This class is responsible for registering property editors with the Spring container.

2. Configure the PropertyEditorRegistrar implementation as a Spring bean in the application context XML file.

3. Configure Spring's CustomEditorConfigurer *special* bean in the application context XML file, and provide it with reference to the PropertyEditorRegistrar implementation that you created in step 1 and configured in step 2.

Let's now see how CustomDateEditor is registered with the Spring container in ch03-simple-types-examples project.

Creating a PropertyEditorRegistrar implementation

The following example listing shows the MyPropertyEditorRegistrar class that implements the PropertyEditorRegistrar interface:

Example listing 3-38 – MyPropertyEditorRegistrar class
Project – ch03-simple-types-examples
Source location - src/main/java/sample/spring/chapter03/beans

```
package sample.spring.chapter03.beans;
```

```
import java.text.SimpleDateFormat;
import java.util.Date;

import org.springframework.beans.PropertyEditorRegistrar;
import org.springframework.beans.PropertyEditorRegistry;
import org.springframework.beans.propertyeditors.CustomDateEditor;

public class MyPropertyEditorRegistrar implements PropertyEditorRegistrar {

    @Override
    public void registerCustomEditors(PropertyEditorRegistry registry) {
        registry.registerCustomEditor(Date.class,
                new CustomDateEditor(new SimpleDateFormat("dd-MM-yyyy"), false));
    }
}
```

In the above example listing, MyPropertyEditorRegistrar class implements Spring's PropertyEditorRegistrar interface, and provides implementation for the PropertyEditorRegistrar's registerCustomEditors method. PropertyEditorRegistrar's registerCustomEditors method accepts a PropertyEditorRegistry instance whose registerCustomEditor method is used for registering property editors with the Spring container. In the above example listing, PropertyEditorRegistry's registerCustomEditor registers the CustomDateEditor property editor with the Spring container.

Configuring the CustomEditorConfigurer class

The following example listing shows how the CustomEditorConfigurer class is configured in the application context XML file:

Example listing 3-39 – applicationContext.xml - CustomEditorConfigurer configuration
Project – ch03-simple-types-examples
Source location - src/main/resources/META-INF/spring

```
    <bean id="myPropertyEditorRegistrar"
            class="sample.spring.chapter03.beans.MyPropertyEditorRegistrar" />

    <bean id="editorConfigurer"
          class="org.springframework.beans.factory.config.CustomEditorConfigurer">
        <property name="propertyEditorRegistrars">
            <list>
                <ref bean="myPropertyEditorRegistrar"/>
            </list>
        </property>
    </bean>
```

In the above example listing, myPropertyEditorRegistrar bean definition configures the MyPropertyEditorRegistrar class (shown in example listing 3-38) as a Spring bean. MyPropertyEditorRegistrar class implements Spring's PropertyEditorRegistrar interface, and is responsible for registering the CustomDateEditor property editor with the Spring container. CustomEditorConfigurer's propertyEditorRegistrars property specifies a list of PropertyEditorRegistrar implementations. In the above example listing, myPropertyEditorRegistrar is specified as one of the values of propertyEditorRegistrars property. The CustomEditorConfigurer bean is automatically detected and executed by the Spring container, resulting in the registration of property editors by the MyPropertyEditorRegistrar instance.

Let's now look at how to use p-namespace (for bean properties) and c-namespace (for constructor arguments) to write concise bean definitions in application context XML files.

3-7 Concise bean definitions with p and c namespaces

To make bean definitions less verbose in application context XML files, Spring provides p and c namespaces to specify values for bean properties and constructor arguments, respectively. The p and c namespaces are alternatives to using `<property>` and `<constructor-arg>` elements, respectively.

Let's first look at p-namespace.

IMPORT **chapter 3/ch03-namespaces-example** (This project shows a Spring application in which bean properties and constructor arguments are set using p- and c-namespaces, respectively. To run the application, execute the `main` method of the `SampleApp` class of this project)

p-namespace

To set bean properties using p-namespace, specify bean properties as attributes of the `<bean>` element, and specify each bean property to be in the p-namespace.

The following bean definition shows how to use p-namespace to set bean properties:

Example listing 3-40 – `applicationContext.xml` - p-namespace example
Project – `ch03-namespaces-example`
Source location - `src/main/resources/META-INF/spring`

```
<beans xmlns="http://www.springframework.org/schema/beans"
    xmlns:p="http://www.springframework.org/schema/p" xsi:schemaLocation=".....">

    <bean id="bankDetails" class="sample.spring.chapter03.beans.BankDetails"
        p:bankName="My Personal Bank" p:bankPrimaryBusiness="Retail banking"
        p:headOfficeAddress="Address of head office" p:privateBank="Y"
        p:primaryCurrency="INR" p:dateOfInception="30-01-2012"
        p:branchAddresses-ref="branchAddresses"/>
    .....
</beans>
```

In the application context XML file shown above, p-namespace is specified via `xmlns` attribute. The `bankDetails` bean definition uses the p prefix (for the p-namespace) to specify bean properties.

If you compare the above example listing with the example listing 3-25, you'll notice that the above example listing is *less* verbose. Even though it is possible to use a mix of `<property>` elements and p-namespace to specify bean properties, it's recommended that you choose one style for specifying bean properties and use it consistently.

> As p-namespace is implemented as part of Spring, there is *no* schema corresponding to p-namespace. For this reason, you don't see any schema reference corresponding to p-namespace in example listing 3-40. If you want your IDE to auto-complete bean property names when using p-namespace, consider using IntelliJ IDEA or Spring Tool Suite (STS).

If a bean property is *not* a reference to another bean, it is specified using the following syntax:

```
p:<property-name>="<property-value>"
```

here, *<property-name>* is the name of the bean property, and *<property-value>* is the value of the bean property.

If a bean property is a reference to another bean, it is specified using the following syntax:

```
p:<property-name>-ref="<bean-reference>"
```

here, *<property-name>* is the name of the bean property, and *<bean-reference>* is the id (or name) of the referenced bean. It is important to note that the name of the bean property is followed by -ref. As the branchAddresses property of BankDetails bean represents a reference to the branchAddresses bean, the branchAddresses property is specified as p:branchAddresses-ref in example listing 3-40.

Let's now look at how c-namespace is used for setting values of constructor arguments.

c-namespace

To set constructor arguments using c-namespace, specify constructor arguments as attributes of the <bean> element, and specify each constructor argument to be in the c-namespace.

The following example listing shows the BankStatement class that we'll configure as a Spring bean using c-namespace.

Example listing 3-41 – BankStatement class
Project – ch03-namespaces-example
Source location - src/main/java/sample/spring/chapter03/beans

```
package sample.spring.chapter03.beans;

import java.beans.ConstructorProperties;

public class BankStatement {
    .....
    @ConstructorProperties({ "transactionDate", "amount", "transactionType",
            "referenceNumber" })
    public BankStatement(Date transactionDate, double amount, String transactionType,
            String referenceNumber) {
        this.transactionDate = transactionDate;
        this.amount = amount;
        .....
    }
    .....
}
```

The following bean definition for the BankStatement class shows usage of c-namespace for setting values of constructor arguments:

Example listing 3-42 – applicationContext.xml - c-namespace example
Project – ch03-namespaces-example
Source location - src/main/resources/META-INF/spring

```
<beans xmlns="http://www.springframework.org/schema/beans"
   xmlns:c="http://www.springframework.org/schema/c"
    xsi:schemaLocation=".....">
    .....
    <bean id="bankStatement" class="sample.spring.chapter03.beans.BankStatement"
        c:transactionDate = "30-01-2012"
        c:amount = "1000"
        c:transactionType = "Credit"
        c:referenceNumber = "1110202" />
    .....
</beans>
```

In the above example listing, c-namespace is specified via xmlns attribute. The bankStatement bean definition makes use of the c prefix (for the c-namespace) to specify constructor arguments. The syntax followed for specifying constructor arguments using c-namespace is similar to what we saw in the case of p-namespace.

> As c-namespace is implemented as part of Spring, there is *no* schema corresponding to c-namespace. For this reason, you don't see any schema reference corresponding to c-namespace in example listing 3-42. If you want your IDE to autocomplete constructor argument names when using c-namespace, consider using IntelliJ IDEA or Spring Tool Suite (STS).

If a constructor argument is *not* a reference to another bean, it is specified using the following syntax:

```
c:<constructor-argument-name>="<constructor-argument-value>"
```

here, *<constructor-argument-name>* is the name of the constructor argument, and *<constructor-argument-value>* is the value of the constructor argument.

If a constructor argument is a reference to another bean, it is specified using the following syntax:

```
c:<constructor-argument-name>-ref="<bean-reference>"
```

here, *<constructor-argument-name>* is the name of the constructor argument, and *<bean-reference>* is the id (or name) of the referenced bean. It is important to note that the name of the constructor argument is followed by -ref. For instance, if a constructor argument named myargument represents a reference to a bean with id 'x', you specify myargument constructor argument as:

```
c:myargument-ref = "x"
```

As mentioned earlier, if a class is compiled with debug or 'parameter name discovery' flag enabled, constructor argument names are preserved in the generated .class file. If the BankStatement class is *not* compiled with the debug or 'parameter name discovery' flag enabled, the configuration shown in example listing 3-42 will not work. In such cases, you supply values for constructor arguments using their index, as shown here:

Example listing 3-43 – Supplying values for constructor arguments using their index

```
<beans xmlns="http://www.springframework.org/schema/beans"
   xmlns:c="http://www.springframework.org/schema/c"
    xsi:schemaLocation=".....">
    .....
    <bean id="bankStatement" class="sample.spring.chapter03.beans.BankStatement"
        c:_0 = "30-01-2012"
        c:_1 = "1000"
        c:_2 = "Credit"
        c:_3 = "1110202" />
      .....
</beans>
```

The above bean definition for the BankStatement class uses the index (instead of name) of constructor arguments to supply values. It is important to note that the index of the constructor argument is prefixed with an *underscore* because attribute names in XML *cannot* begin with a numeric value. If a constructor argument is a reference to another bean, -ref *must* be added to the index of the constructor argument. For instance, if the constructor argument at index 0 represents reference to another bean, it is specified as c:_0-ref. Even though it's possible to use both <constructor-arg> elements and c-namespace to specify constructor arguments, it's recommended that you choose one style of specifying constructor arguments and use it consistently.

We saw earlier how <list>, <map> and <set> elements are used to set properties or constructor arguments of types List, Map and Set, respectively. Let's now look at Spring's util schema that simplifies creating collection types, Properties type, constants, and so on, and exposing them as a Spring beans.

3-8 Spring's util schema

Spring's util schema simplifies configuring beans by providing a concise way to perform common configuration tasks. The following table describes the various elements of util schema:

Element	Description
<list>	creates a java.util.List type and exposes it as a bean
<map>	creates a java.util.Map type and exposes it as a bean
<set>	creates a java.util.Set type and exposes it as a bean
<constant>	exposes a public static field on a Java type as a bean
<property-path>	exposes a bean property as a bean
<properties>	creates a java.util.Properties object from a properties file and exposes it as a bean

All the elements of Spring's util schema accept a scope attribute that specifies the scope of the exposed bean. By default, the exposed bean is singleton-scoped.

Spring provides a FactoryBean interface that can be implemented to create a factory for creating bean instances. Spring offers many built-in FactoryBean implementations that you can use instead of util schema elements to perform the same functionality. As using util schema elements is much simpler that using the built-in FactoryBeans, we'll limit our discussion to util schema elements.

IMPORT **chapter 3/ch03-util-schema-examples** (This project shows a Spring application that makes use of Spring's util schema elements to create shared instances of List, Set, Map, and so on. To run the application, execute the main method of the SampleApp class of this project)

Let's first look at the <list> element.

<list>

The <list> element of Spring's util schema is used for creating objects of type java.util.List, as shown here:

Example listing 3-44 – applicationContext.xml - util schema's <list> element
Project – ch03-util-schema-examples
Source location - src/main/resources/META-INF/spring

```
<beans xmlns="http://www.springframework.org/schema/beans"
       xmlns:util="http://www.springframework.org/schema/util"
       xsi:schemaLocation="..... http://www.springframework.org/schema/util
       http://www.springframework.org/schema/util/spring-util.xsd">

    <bean id="dataTypes" class="sample.spring.chapter03.beans.DataTypesExample">
```

```
        .....
        <constructor-arg name="listType" ref="listType" />
        .....
    </bean>

    <util:list id="listType" list-class="java.util.ArrayList">
        <value>A simple String value in list</value>
        <value>Another simple String value in list</value>
    </util:list>
</beans>
```

At first, you need to include Spring's util schema to access its elements. In the above example listing, the <list> element of util schema creates an instance of java.util.ArrayList (specified by the list-class attribute) and exposes it as a bean named listType (specified by the id attribute) The list-class attribute specifies the concrete implementation of java.util.List interface that is created by the <list> element. If you don't specify the list-class attribute, an instance of java.util.ArrayList is created by default. Notice that the <value> element of Spring's beans schema has been used to add items to the list created by the <list> element.

As util schema's <list> element exposes a List instance as a bean, you can inject the exposed List instance as a dependency into any other bean. For instance, in the above example listing, the <constructor-arg> element passes the ArrayList instance created by the <list> element to DataTypesExample's listType (of type java.util.List) constructor argument.

For instance, in the above example listing, the listType constructor argument (which is of type java.util.List) of DataTypesExample bean refers to the List instance created by the util schema's <list> element.

An alternative to using util schema's <list> element is Spring's ListFactoryBean – a factory that is used for creating instances of java.util.List and making them available as Spring beans. The util schema's <list> element offers a more concise configuration for creating List instances than the ListFactoryBean.

<map>

The <map> element of Spring's util schema is used for creating an object of type java.util.Map and exposing it as a bean, as shown here:

Example listing 3-45 – applicationContext.xml - util schema's <map> element
Project – ch03-util-schema-examples
Source location - src/main/resources/META-INF/spring

```
<beans .....
      xmlns:util="http://www.springframework.org/schema/util"
    xsi:schemaLocation="..... http://www.springframework.org/schema/util
    http://www.springframework.org/schema/util/spring-util.xsd">

    <bean id="dataTypes" class="sample.spring.chapter03.beans.DataTypesExample">
        .....
        <constructor-arg name="mapType" ref="mapType" />
        .....
    </bean>

    <util:map id="mapType" map-class="java.util.TreeMap">
        <entry key="map key 1" value="map key 1's value"/>
    </util:map>
     .....
```

```
</beans>
```

In the above example listing, util schema's <map> element creates an instance of java.util.TreeMap (specified by the map-class attribute) and exposes it as a bean named mapType (specified by the id attribute). The map-class attribute specifies the fully-qualified name of the concrete implementation of java.util.Map interface that is created by the <map> element. If you don't specify the map-class attribute, the Spring container creates an instance of java.util.LinkedHashMap by default. Notice that the <entry> element of Spring's beans schema has been used to add a key-value pair to the Map instance created by the <map> element.

As the <map> element exposes a Map instance as a bean, the exposed Map instance can be injected like a dependency into any other bean. For instance, in the above example listing, the <constructor-arg> element passes the TreeMap instance created by the <map> element to DataTypesExample's mapType (which is of type java.util.Map) constructor argument.

Instead of using util schema's <map> element, you can use Spring's MapFactoryBean – a factory for creating instances of java.util.Map and making them available as Spring beans. The util schema's <map> element offers a more concise configuration for creating Map instances than the MapFactoryBean.

<set>

The <set> element of Spring's util schema is used for creating an object of type java.util.Set and exposing it as a bean, as shown here:

Example listing 3-46 – applicationContext.xml - util schema's <set> element
Project – ch03-util-schema-examples
Source location - src/main/resources/META-INF/spring

```
<beans .....
     xmlns:util="http://www.springframework.org/schema/util"
     xsi:schemaLocation="..... http://www.springframework.org/schema/util
     http://www.springframework.org/schema/util/spring-util.xsd">

     <bean id="dataTypes" class="sample.spring.chapter03.beans.DataTypesExample">
          .....
          <constructor-arg name="setType" ref="setType" />
     </bean>
     <util:set id="setType" set-class="java.util.HashSet">
          <value>Element 1</value>
          <value>Element 2</value>
     </util:set>
     .....
</beans>
```

In the above example listing, util schema's <set> element creates an instance of HashSet (specified by the set-class attribute) and exposes it as a bean named setType (specified by the id attribute). The set-class attribute specifies the concrete implementation class of java.util.Set interface that is created by the <set> element. The <value> element of Spring's beans schema adds an element into the Set instance.

The Set instance created by the <set> element can be injected like a dependency into any other bean. For instance, in the above example listing, the <constructor-arg> element passes the HashSet instance created by the <set> element to DataTypesExample's setType (which is of type java.util.Set) constructor argument.

Instead of using util schema's <set> element, you can use Spring's SetFactoryBean to create a Set instance and expose it as a Spring bean. The <set> element is preferred over the SetFactoryBean because it offers a more concise configuration for creating Set instances.

<properties>

The util schema's <properties> element is useful if you want to create an instance of java.util.Properties object from a properties file and expose it as a bean.

The following example listing shows how the <properties> element is used:

Example listing 3-47 – applicationContext.xml - util schema's <properties> element
Project – ch03-util-schema-examples
Source location - src/main/resources/META-INF/spring

```
<beans .....
    xmlns:util="http://www.springframework.org/schema/util"
    xsi:schemaLocation=".....http://www.springframework.org/schema/util
    http://www.springframework.org/schema/util/spring-util.xsd">

    <bean id="bankDetails" class="sample.spring.chapter03.beans.BankDetails">
        .....
        <property name="branchAddresses" ref="branchAddresses" />
    </bean>
    .....
    <util:properties id="branchAddresses"
            location="classpath:META-INF/addresses.properties" />
</beans>
```

In the above example listing, util schema's <properties> element creates an instance of java.util.Properties using the properties defined in the addresses.properties file (specified by the location attribute) and exposes the java.util.Properties instance as a bean named branchAddresses (specified by the id attribute). The Properties instance created by the <properties> element can be injected like a dependency into any other bean. In the above example listing, the <property> element sets BankDetails' branchAddresses property (which is of type java.util.Properties) to the Properties instance created by the util schema's <properties> element.

An alternative to using the <properties> element is Spring's PropertiesFactoryBean but for brevity it's preferred to use the <properties> element.

<constant>

The util schema's <constant> element is used for exposing an object's public static field as a Spring bean.

The following example listing shows an example usage of <constant> element:

Example listing 3-48 – applicationContext.xml - util schema's <constant> element
Project – ch03-util-schema-examples
Source location - src/main/resources/META-INF/spring

```
<beans ..... xmlns:util="http://www.springframework.org/schema/util"
      xsi:schemaLocation="..... http://www.springframework.org/schema/util
      http://www.springframework.org/schema/util/spring-util.xsd">

    <bean id="dataTypes" class="sample.spring.chapter03.beans.DataTypesExample">
        .....
```

```
        <constructor-arg name="booleanType" ref="booleanTrue" />
        .....
    </bean>

    <util:constant id="booleanTrue" static-field="java.lang.Boolean.TRUE" />
    .....
</beans>
```

The util schema's <constant> element exposes the value specified by its static-field attribute as a Spring bean. In the above example listing, <constant> element exposes a bean whose value is java.lang.Boolean.TRUE and id is booleanTrue. You can specify any public static field as the value of the static-field attribute and refer to it from other beans in the Spring container. For instance, in the above example listing, booleanType bean is referenced by DataTypesExample's booleanType constructor argument of type boolean.

A rather less concise way to expose public static fields as Spring beans is to use Spring's FieldRetrievingFactoryBean.

<property-path>

The util schema's <property-path> element is used to expose a bean property value as a bean.

The following example listing shows an example usage of <property-path> element:

Example listing 3-49 – applicationContext.xml - util schema's <property-path> element
Project – ch03-util-schema-examples
Source location - src/main/resources/META-INF/spring

```
<beans .....
    xmlns:util="http://www.springframework.org/schema/util"
    xsi:schemaLocation="..... http://www.springframework.org/schema/util
    http://www.springframework.org/schema/util/spring-util.xsd">

    <bean id="bankDetails" class="sample.spring.chapter03.beans.BankDetails">
        .....
        <property name="dateOfInception" ref="dateType" />
        .....
    </bean>

    <util:property-path id="dateType" path="dataTypes.dateType" />

    <bean id="dataTypes" class="sample.spring.chapter03.beans.DataTypesExample">
        .....
        <property name="dateType" value="30-01-2012" />
        .....
    </bean>
</beans>
```

In the above example listing, DataTypesExample's dateType property (of type java.util.Date) value is specified as '30-01-2012'. The <property-path> element retrieves the DataTypesExample's dateType property (specified by the path attribute) and exposes it as a bean named dateType (specified by the name attribute). The path attribute of <property-path> element has the following syntax:

```
<bean-name>.<bean-property>
```

Here, *<bean-name>* is the id or name of the bean, and *<bean-property>* is the name of the property to be exposed.

As the <property-path> element exposes a bean, the exposed bean can be injected into any other bean in the Spring container. For instance, in the above example listing, the dateType bean is referenced by the dateOfInception property of BankDetails bean.

A rather less concise way to expose bean properties as Spring beans is to use Spring's PropertyPathFactoryBean.

Now that we have taken an in-depth look at util schema elements, let's look at Spring's FactoryBean interface.

3-9 FactoryBean interface

Spring's FactoryBean interface is implemented by classes that act as a factory for creating bean instances. The classes that implement the FactoryBean interface are configured in the application context XML file like any other bean. FactoryBean is particularly useful if you want to perform complicated conditional checks to decide on which bean type to create, and to execute complex bean initialization logic.

Let's now look at an application scenario in which a FactoryBean is used for selecting a bean type and then creating it.

MyBank application – Storing events in the database

In MyBank application, important events (like credit and debit transactions, open and liquidate fixed deposits, and so on) are saved in the database. MyBank may save these events directly into the database or indirectly by first sending the events to a messaging middleware or a web service. The following table describes the classes that are defined by the MyBank application for directly or indirectly saving events:

Class	Description
DatabaseEventSender	saves events in the database
MessagingEventSender	sends events to a messaging middleware
WebServiceEventSender	sends events to a remote web service

The decision to directly save the events in the database or to send them to a messaging middleware or to a web service is based on configuration. For instance, if MyBank finds that there exists a database.properties file, MyBank reads the configuration information (like database url, username and password) from the database.properties file and creates the DatabaseEventSender instance. Similarly, if a messaging.properties file exists, MyBank creates an instance of MessagingEventSender instance, and if a webservice.properties file exists, an instance of WebServiceEventSender is created.

Initializing DatabaseEventSender, MessagingEventSender and WebServiceEventSender instances may require executing complex initialization logic. For instance, you need to create (or obtain from JNDI) javax.jms.ConnectionFactory and javax.jms.Destination instances and set them on the MessagingEventSender instance so that the MessagingEventSender can send JMS messages to the messaging middleware.

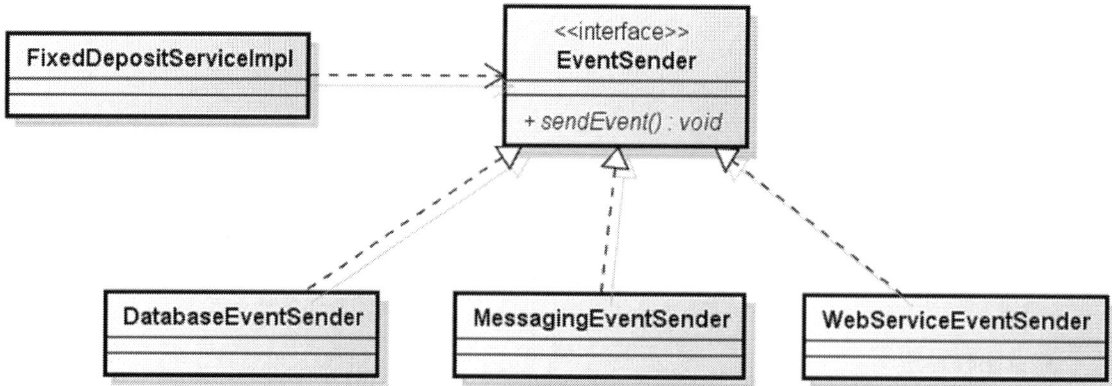

Figure 3-7 FixedDepositServiceImpl class uses one of the implementations of EventSender interface.

Figure 3-7 shows that the FixedDepositServiceImpl class of MyBank uses DatabaseEventSender or MessagingEventSender or WebServiceEventSender instance to directly or indirectly save events related to fixed deposits in the database. In the class diagram, the sendEvent method of EventSender interface defines the contract for directly or indirectly saving events in the database. DatabaseEventSender, MessagingEventSender and WebServiceEventSender classes implement the EventSender interface and provide implementation for the sendEvent method.

Let's now look at how FactoryBean simplifies choosing the right implementation of EventSender interface and initializing it.

IMPORT **chapter 3/ch03-bankapp-factorybean** (This project shows the MyBank application that uses a FactoryBean implementation to create objects of type EventSender. To run the application, execute the main method of the BankApp class of this project)

MyBank – FactoryBean example

In MyBank, selecting the correct EventSender implementation and initializing it is an involved task; therefore, it represents an ideal scenario for using a FactoryBean implementation. FactoryBean interface defines the following methods that you need to implement:

- getObjectType: returns the *type* of the object managed by the FactoryBean implementation. In MyBank application, the FactoryBean implementation creates and returns objects of type EventSender.

- getObject: returns the object managed by the FactoryBean implementation. In MyBank application, the getObject method returns an instance of DatabaseEventSender or MessagingEventSender or WebServiceEventSender.

- isSingleton: returns true if the FactoryBean implementation is a factory for singleton-scoped objects. If the isSingleton method returns true, the object returned by the getObject method is cached by the Spring container and the same instance is returned on subsequent requests. If the FactoryBean implementation is a factory for prototype-scoped objects, return false from the isSingleton method. If the isSingleton method returns false, a fresh instance is created by the getObject method on every request. In MyBank application, the FactoryBean implementation returns an instance of DatabaseEventSender or MessagingEventSender or WebServiceEventSender class. Once created, the same instance is used throughout the lifetime of the MyBank application; therefore, the isSingleton method must be defined to return true.

The following example listing shows the EventSenderFactoryBean – the FactoryBean implementation that creates and returns objects of type EventSender:

Example listing 3-50 – EventSenderFactoryBean class
Project – ch03-bankapp-factorybean
Source location - src/main/java/sample/spring/chapter03/bankapp/event

```
package sample.spring.chapter03.bankapp.event;

import org.springframework.beans.factory.FactoryBean;
import org.springframework.beans.factory.FactoryBeanNotInitializedException;
import org.springframework.core.io.ClassPathResource;
.....
public class EventSenderFactoryBean implements FactoryBean<EventSender> {
    private String databasePropertiesFile;
    private String webServicePropertiesFile;
    private String messagingPropertiesFile;
     .....
    public EventSender getObject() throws Exception {
        EventSender eventSender = null;
        Properties properties = new Properties();
        ClassPathResource databaseProperties = null;

        if(databasePropertiesFile != null) {
            databaseProperties = new ClassPathResource(databasePropertiesFile);
        }
        .....
        if (databaseProperties != null && databaseProperties.exists()) {
            InputStream inStream = databaseProperties.getInputStream();
            properties.load(inStream);
            eventSender = new DatabaseEventSender(properties);
        }
        else if (webServiceProperties != null  && webServiceProperties.exists()) {.....}
        else if (messagingProperties != null  && messagingProperties.exists()) {.....}

        return eventSender;
    }

    public Class<?> getObjectType() {
        return EventSender.class;
    }

    public boolean isSingleton() {
        return true;
    }
}
```

The above example listing shows that the EventSenderFactoryBean implements the FactoryBean interface. The EventSender parameter in the FactoryBean<EventSender> declaration indicates that the FactoryBean's getObject method returns objects of type EventSender. The databasePropertiesFile, webServicePropertiesFile and messagingPropertiesFile are properties of the EventSenderFactoryBean class, and they represent the location of database.properties, webservice.properties and messaging.properties files in the classpath.

The getObject method uses Spring's ClassPathResource class to verify whether the specified properties file exists in the classpath or not. If the properties file exists, properties from that file are loaded and passed to the EventSender implementation class's constructor. For instance, in the above example listing, if the database.properties file (represented by the databasePropertiesFile property) exists, properties are loaded from the database.properties file and passed as an argument to the DatabaseEventSender's constructor. The getObjectType method returns EventSender type because the EventSenderFactoryBean's getObject method returns objects of type EventSender. The isSingleton method returns true, which means that the object returned by the getObject method is cached by Spring and the same instance is returned every time EventSenderFactoryBean's getObject method is invoked.

Now that you have seen how EventSenderFactoryBean class is implemented in MyBank application, you can guess how Spring's built-in FactoryBean implementations, like ListFactoryBean (for creating instances of List type), MapFactoryBean (for creating instances of Map type), SetFactoryBean (for creating instances of Set type), and so on, are implemented.

The following example listing shows how the EventSenderFactoryBean class is configured in the application context XML file:

Example listing 3-51 – applicationContext.xml - EventSenderFactoryBean configuration
Project – ch03-bankapp-factorybean
Source location - src/main/resources/META-INF/spring

```
<beans .....>

    <bean id="service"
        class="sample.spring.chapter03.bankapp.service.FixedDepositServiceImpl">
        .....
        <property name="eventSender" ref="eventSenderFactory" />
    </bean>
    .....
    <bean id="eventSenderFactory"
           class="sample.spring.chapter03.bankapp.event.EventSenderFactoryBean">
        <property name="databasePropertiesFile"
                        value="META-INF/config/database.properties"/>
   </bean>
</beans>
```

The above example listing shows that the EventSenderFactoryBean class is configured like any other Spring bean. Even though a FactoryBean implementation is configured like any other Spring bean, it is treated *differently* by the Spring container. One of the most important differences is - if a bean is dependent on a FactoryBean implementation, the Spring container invokes the getObject method of the FactoryBean implementation and injects the returned object into the dependent bean.

> You should note that FactoryBean's getObject method is invoked only once by the Spring container if the isSingleton method returns true.

In the above example listing, bean definition for the FixedDepositServiceImpl class shows that it is dependent on the EventSenderFactoryBean – a FactoryBean implementation. So, the Spring container invokes the EventSenderFactoryBean's getObject method and injects the returned EventSender object into the FixedDepositServiceImpl instance.

The following example listing shows the FixedDepositServiceImpl class that requires EventSender instance created by the EventSenderFactoryBean bean:

Example listing 3-52 – FixedDepositServiceImpl class
Project – ch03-bankapp-factorybean
Source location - src/main/java/sample/spring/chapter03/bankapp/service

```
package sample.spring.chapter03.bankapp.service;

import sample.spring.chapter03.bankapp.event.EventSender;

public class FixedDepositServiceImpl implements FixedDepositService {
    .....
    private EventSender eventSender;

    public void setEventSender(EventSender eventSender) {
        this.eventSender = eventSender;
    }
    .....
    public void createFixedDeposit(FixedDepositDetails fixedDepositDetails) {
        .....
        eventSender.sendEvent(event);
    }
}
```

The above example listing shows that the FixedDepositServiceImpl class depends on an EventSender instance and *not* on the EventSenderFactoryBean instance. The Spring container obtains the EventSender instance by invoking the EventSenderFactoryBean's getObject method, and injects the obtained EventSender instance into the FixedDepositServiceImpl instance.

Let's now look at how to access the FactoryBean itself and *not* the bean it creates and returns via the getObject method.

Accessing the FactoryBean instance

If you want to obtain the FactoryBean itself from the Spring container, prefix the name (or id) of the factory bean with ampersand '&'.

Let's say that the FixedDepositServiceImpl class requires access to the EventSenderFactoryBean itself, as shown here:

Example listing 3-53 – FixedDepositServiceImpl class that depends on the EventSenderFactoryBean itself

```
package sample.spring.chapter03.bankapp.service;

import sample.spring.chapter03.bankapp.event.EventSenderFactoryBean;
import sample.spring.chapter03.bankapp.event.EventSender;

public class FixedDepositServiceImpl implements FixedDepositService {
    .....
    private EventSenderFactoryBean eventSenderFactoryBean;

    public void setEventSenderFactoryBean (EventSenderFactoryBean eventSenderFactoryBean) {
        this. eventSenderFactoryBean = eventSenderFactoryBean;
    }
    .....
    public void createFixedDeposit(FixedDepositDetails fixedDepositDetails) {
        .....
        EventSender eventSender = eventSenderFactoryBean.getObject();
```

```
        evenSender.sendEvent(event);
    }
}
```

In the above example listing, the FixedDepositServiceImpl class depends on the EventSenderFactoryBean itself. FixedDepositServiceImpl explicitly calls the EventSenderFactoryBean's getObject method to obtain an EventSender object.

We saw in example listing 3-51 that when you define the EventSenderFactoryBean bean as a dependency of FixedDepositServiceImpl bean, the Spring container invokes EventSenderFactoryBean's getObject method and injects the returned EventSender object into the FixedDepositServiceImpl bean. To instruct the Spring container to inject the EventSenderFactoryBean itself, add ampersand '&' prefix to the id (or name) of the bean specified by the ref attribute, as shown in the following example listing:

Example listing 3-54 – Injecting the EventSenderFactoryBean instance into the FixedDepositServiceImpl bean

```
<beans .....>

    <bean id="service"
            class="sample.spring.chapter03.bankapp.service.FixedDepositServiceImpl">
        .....
        <property name="eventSenderFactoryBean" ref="&amp;eventSenderFactory" />
    </bean>
    .....
    <bean id="eventSenderFactory"
          class="sample.spring.chapter03.bankapp.event.EventSenderFactoryBean">
        <property name="databasePropertiesFile"
                value="META-INF/config/database.properties"/>
    </bean>
</beans>
```

In the above example listing, the following <property> element specifies that the FixedDepositServiceImpl bean is dependent on EventSenderFactoryBean:

```
<property name="eventSenderFactoryBean" ref="&amp;eventSenderFactory" />
```

Notice that the ref attribute's value is "&eventSenderFactory". The & prefix instructs the Spring container to inject the EventSenderFactoryBean instance itself into the FixedDepositServiceImpl bean.

The use of ampersand '&' is also required when you want to retrieve the FactoryBean instance itself using ApplicationContext's getBean method. The following example listing shows the BankApp class of MyBank application that retrieves the EventSender object (created by the EventSenderFactoryBean) and the EventSenderFactoryBean instance itself:

Example listing 3-55 – BankApp class
Project – ch03-bankapp-factorybean
Source location - src/main/java/sample/spring/chapter03/bankapp

```
package sample.spring.chapter03.bankapp;
.....
public class BankApp {
    private static Logger logger = LogManager.getLogger(BankApp.class);

    public static void main(String args[]) {
        ApplicationContext context = new ClassPathXmlApplicationContext(
```

```
        .....
        logger.info("Invoking getBean(\"eventFactory\") returns : " +
            context.getBean("eventSenderFactory"));
        logger.info("Invoking getBean(\"&eventFactory\") returns : " +
            context.getBean("&eventSenderFactory"));
    }
}
```

If you execute the main method of the BankApp class shown above, you'll find that calling the getBean("eventSenderFactory") returns an instance of DatabaseEventSender class, and the getBean("&eventSenderFactory") returns the EventSenderFactoryBean instance.

3-10 Modularizing bean configuration

You may define beans across multiple application context XML files to bring modularity or structure to your application configuration. For instance, you may define a myapp-dao.xml file that defines data access objects (DAOs) of your application, a myapp-service.xml that defines services, and a myapp-controller.xml that defines application controllers. In such scenarios, you can either pass all configuration XML files to the ClassPathXmlApplicationContext's constructor, or you can import all the XML files into one XML file and pass that file to ClassPathXmlApplicationContext's constructor.

IMPORT **chapter 3/ch03-bankapp-modular** (This project shows the MyBank application in which beans are configured in multiple application context XML files: bankapp-controller.xml (defines controllers), bankapp-dao.xml (defines DAOs), and bankapp-service.xml (defines services). To run the application, execute the main method of the BankApp class of this project)

The following example listing shows the bankapp-controller.xml file that uses beans schema's <import> element to import bankapp-dao.xml and bankapp-service.xml files:

Example listing 3-56 – bankapp-controller.xml
Project – ch03-bankapp-modular
Source location - src/main/resources/META-INF/spring

```
<beans .....">
    <import resource="bankapp-dao.xml" />
    <import resource="bankapp-service.xml" />

    <bean id="controller"
          class="sample.spring.chapter03.bankapp.controller.FixedDepositControllerImpl">
        <property name="fixedDepositService" ref="service" />
    </bean>
</beans>
```

The <import> element imports the application context XML file specified by the resource attribute. The location of XML files (as specified by the resource attribute) is relative to the file containing the <import> element. The inter-dependencies that exist between beans defined in different XML files are resolved at application startup-time by the Spring container. For instance, the controller bean defined above is dependent on the service bean defined in bankapp-service.xml file. Spring container resolves these dependencies while creating beans defined in application context XML files.

As we've imported bankapp-dao.xml and bankapp-service.xml files into bankapp-controller.xml, we only need to pass the bankapp-controller.xml to the ClassPathXmlApplicationContext's constructor. If you don't want to use the importing feature, you can pass all the XML files to the ClassPathXmlApplicationContext's constructor.

3-11 Summary

In this chapter, we saw how you can use bean definition inheritance to create less verbose and easily manageable bean definitions. We looked at how to set different types of bean properties and constructor arguments, use Spring's `util` schema, create bean factories using the `FactoryBean` interface, and write concise bean definitions using `p`- and `c`-namespaces. We also looked at some of the built-in `PropertyEditor` implementations in Spring and how to register additional property editors with the Spring container. In the next chapter, we'll take an in-depth look at dependency injection feature of Spring.

Chapter 4 - *Dependency injection*

4-1 Introduction

In the previous chapter, we looked at Spring's `util` schema, p- and c-namespaces, `FactoryBean` interface, and so on. In this chapter, we'll focus on challenges that are typically encountered in real world application development efforts, and how Spring addresses them.

We'll begin this chapter with a look at *inner beans* - an alternative to using the `ref` attribute of `<property>` and `<constructor-arg>` elements. We'll then look at `depends-on` attribute of the `<bean>` element. In the second half of this chapter, we'll look at issues that may arise when singleton- and prototype-scoped beans collaborate to provide application functionality. We'll wrap this chapter up with an in-depth look at Spring's *autowiring* feature.

IMPORT **chapter 4/ch04-bankapp-dependencies** (This project shows usage of inner beans and the `<bean>` element's `depends-on` attribute. This project also shows implications of defining dependence of singleton-scoped beans on prototype-scoped beans, and vice versa. To run the application, execute the `main` method of the `BankApp` class of this project)

4-2 Inner beans

If a bean dependency is *not* shared by multiple beans, you can consider defining that dependency as an *inner bean*. An inner bean is defined inside a `<property>` or `<constructor-arg>` element by using the `<bean>` element of Spring's `beans` schema. You should note that an inner bean is accessible only to the bean definition enclosing it, and *not* to the other beans registered with the Spring container.

The following example listing shows how we commonly represent bean dependencies:

Example listing 4-1 – Dependency specified using `<property>` element's `ref` attribute

```
<bean id="service"
      class="sample.spring.chapter04.bankapp.service.FixedDepositServiceImpl">
    <property name="fixedDepositDao" ref="dao" />
</bean>

<bean id="dao" class="sample.spring.chapter04.bankapp.dao.FixedDepositDaoImpl" />
```

In the above example listing, the `service` bean is dependent on the dao bean. If the `service` bean is the only bean that is dependent on the dao bean, then you can define the dao bean as an *inner bean* of the `service` bean.

Example listing 4-2 – `applicationContext.xml` - Inner bean example
Project – `ch04-bankapp-dependencies`
Source location - `src/main/resources/META-INF/spring`

```
<bean id="service"
      class="sample.spring.chapter04.bankapp.service.FixedDepositServiceImpl">
    <property name="fixedDepositDao">
        <bean class="sample.spring.chapter04.bankapp.dao.FixedDepositDaoImpl" />
    </property>
</bean>
```

In the above example listing, the bean definition for the `FixedDepositDaoImpl` class is inside the `<property>` element of the `service` bean. If you compare the above example listing with 4-1, you'll notice that the

<property> element no longer specifies the ref attribute, and the <bean> element corresponding to the FixedDepositDaoImpl class doesn't have the id attribute anymore.

The <bean> element corresponding to an inner bean definition doesn't specify an id attribute because an inner bean is *not* registered with the Spring container. If you specify an id attribute for an inner bean definition, it is ignored by the Spring container. An inner bean is *always* prototype-scoped; therefore, if the <bean> element corresponding to an inner bean definition specifies the scope attribute, then it is ignored by the Spring container. It is important to note that an inner bean is *anonymous* in nature, and it's not accessible to other beans (except the bean that contains the inner bean definition) in the Spring container.

As in the case of normal bean definition, you can use <property>, <constructor-arg>, and so on, elements inside the <bean> element of the inner bean definition.

In the previous chapter, we saw that Spring's util schema elements are used to create beans that represent a List, Set, Map, and so on. We saw that the beans created by Spring's util schema elements are defined as dependencies of other beans. The concept of inner beans makes it possible to use Spring's util schema elements inside <property> and <constructor-arg> elements also, as shown in the following example listing:

Example listing 4-3 – util schema's <list> element defines an inner bean

```
<beans xmlns="http://www.springframework.org/schema/beans"
              xmlns:util="http://www.springframework.org/schema/util"
              xsi:schemaLocation="..... http://www.springframework.org/schema/util
                     http://www.springframework.org/schema/util/spring-util.xsd">

    <bean id="someBean" class="com.sample.SomeBean">
        .....
        <constructor-arg name="listType">
            <util:list list-class="java.util.ArrayList">
                <value>A simple String value in list</value>
                <value>Another simple String value in list</value>
            </util:list>
        </constructor-arg>
        .....
    </bean>
</beans>
```

In the above example listing, the listType constructor argument is of type java.util.List. The value passed to the listType constructor argument is specified by the util schema's <list> element. Note that we didn't specify the id attribute of the <list> element because Spring container ignores ids of inner beans.

Let's now look at the depends-on attribute of <bean> element.

4-3 Controlling the bean initialization order with depends-on attribute

In section 1-5 of chapter 1, we discussed that beans are created in the order in which they are defined in the application context XML file. The order in which beans are created is also decided based on the inter-dependencies of beans. For instance, if bean A accepts an instance of bean B as a constructor argument, the Spring container will create bean B *before* bean A irrespective of the order in which they are defined in the application context XML file. This behavior of the Spring container ensures that the dependencies of a bean are completely configured before they are injected into the dependent bean.

In the examples that we've seen so far, bean dependencies were explicitly specified using <property> and <constructor-arg> elements. If bean dependencies are *implicit*, you can use <bean> element's depends-on attribute to control the order in which beans are created by the Spring container. The Spring container ensures that the dependencies specified by the depends-on attribute are initialized *before* the bean that specifies the depends-on attribute.

Let's now look at an example scenario in which the depends-on attribute is used to control the initialization order of beans.

MyBank – implied dependencies between beans

In the MyBank application of the previous chapter, a FactoryBean implementation created an EventSender object that was used by the FixedDepositServiceImpl instance to directly or indirectly store events in the database (refer section 3-9 of chapter 3 for details). Let's say that instead of using a FactoryBean implementation for creating an EventSender implementation, the approach shown in the following diagram is adopted:

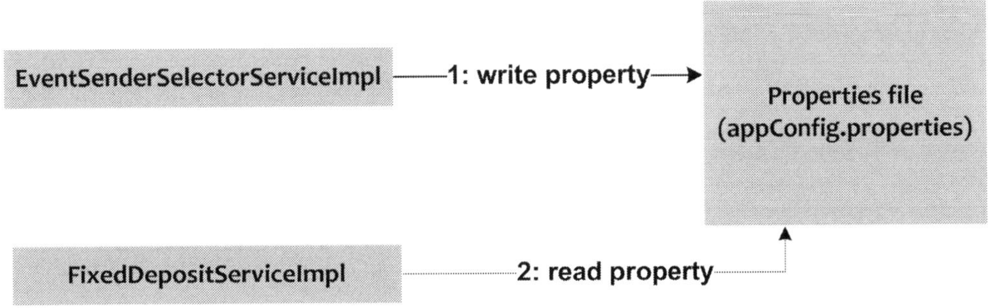

Figure 4-1 – EventSenderSelectorServiceImpl class writes the name of the EventSender implementation in the appConfig.properties file, which is later read by the FixedDepositServiceImpl instance

In the above diagram:

- EventSenderSelectorServiceImpl's constructor decides the EventSender implementation (DatabaseEventSender or WebServiceEventSender or MessagingEventSender) to be used by the FixedDepositServiceImpl class.
- EventSenderSelectorServiceImpl's constructor stores the fully-qualified name of the EventSender implementation in the appConfig.properties file
- FixedDepositServiceImpl's constructor reads the fully-qualified name of the EventSender implementation from the appConfig.properties file, creates the EventSender object and uses it for storing fixed deposit events in the database

If FixedDepositServiceImpl attempts to read from the appConfig.properties file *before* EventSenderSelectorServiceImpl has written the name of the EventSender implementation, then the above approach will fail. As reading from and writing to appConfig.properties file happens in the constructors of EventSenderSelectorServiceImpl and FixedDepositServiceImpl classes, the FixedDepositServiceImpl instance must be created *after* the EventSenderSelectorServiceImpl instance. This means that FixedDepositServiceImpl is *implicitly* dependent on EventSenderSelectorServiceImpl.

Let's now look at the effect of implicit dependence of FixedDepositServiceImpl on EventSenderSelectorServiceImpl.

Implicit dependency problem

Consider the following application context XML file that contains bean definitions for `FixedDepositServiceImpl` and `EventSenderSelectorServiceImpl` classes:

Example listing 4-4 – applicationContext.xml - Implicit dependency example
Project – ch04-bankapp-dependencies
Source location - src/main/resources/META-INF/spring

```
<beans .....>
    <bean id="service"
          class="sample.spring.chapter04.bankapp.service.FixedDepositServiceImpl">
       .....
       <constructor-arg index="0" value="META-INF/config/appConfig.properties" />
    </bean>

    <bean id="eventSenderSelectorService"
          class="sample.spring.chapter04.bankapp.service.EventSenderSelectorServiceImpl">
       <constructor-arg index="0" value="META-INF/config/appConfig.properties" />
    </bean>
</beans>
```

The above application context XML file shows that both `FixedDepositServiceImpl` and `EventSenderSelectorServiceImpl` class's constructor accept location of the `appConfig.properties` file. The `EventSenderSelectorServiceImpl` instance uses the `appConfig.properties` file for communicating the fully-qualified name of the `EventSender` implementation class to the `FixedDepositServiceImpl` instance.

As an explicit dependence *doesn't* exist between `service` and `eventSenderSelectorService` beans, the Spring container creates their instances in the order in which they are defined in the application context XML file. As the `service` bean is defined *before* the `eventSenderSelectorService` bean, the `FixedDepositServiceImpl` instance is created *before* the `EventSenderSelectorServiceImpl` instance. If the `FixedDepositServiceImpl` instance is created *before* the `EventSenderSelectorServiceImpl` instance, the `FixedDepositServiceImpl` instance will *not* be able to read the name of the fully-qualified `EventSender` implementation class from the `appConfig.properties` file.

Let's look at `EventSenderSelectorServiceImpl` and `FixedDepositServiceImpl` classes, and the `appConfig.properties` file.

EventSenderSelectorServiceImpl – the writer

The following example listing shows the `EventSenderSelectorServiceImpl` class:

Example listing 4-5 – EventSenderSelectorServiceImpl class
Project – ch04-bankapp-dependencies
Source location - src/main/java/sample/spring/chapter04/bankapp/service

```
package sample.spring.chapter04.bankapp.service;

import org.springframework.core.io.ClassPathResource;
import sample.spring.chapter04.bankapp.Constants;

public class EventSenderSelectorServiceImpl {

    public EventSenderSelectorServiceImpl(String configFile) throws Exception {
        ClassPathResource resource = new ClassPathResource(configFile);
        OutputStream os = new FileOutputStream(resource.getFile());
```

```
        Properties properties = new Properties();
        properties.setProperty(Constants.EVENT_SENDER_CLASS_PROPERTY,
            "sample.spring.chapter04.bankapp.event.DatabaseEventSender");
        properties.store(os, null);
        .....
    }
}
```

The above example listing shows that the location of appConfig.properties file is passed as an argument to the EventSenderSelectorServiceImpl class's constructor. The EventSenderSelectorServiceImpl class's constructor writes a property named eventSenderClass (which is the value of EVENT_SENDER_CLASS_PROPERTY constant defined in the Constants class) to the appConfig.properties file. The eventSenderClass property specifies the fully-qualified name of the EventSender implementation to be used by the FixedDepositServiceImpl instance for saving events in the database. For the sake of simplicity, the EventSenderSelectorServiceImpl class's constructor sets the fully-qualified name of the DatabaseEventSender class as the value of eventSenderClass property.

appConfig.properties

The following entry gets added to the appConfig.properties file by the EventSenderSelectorServiceImpl class:

```
eventSenderClass=sample.spring.chapter04.bankapp.event.DatabaseEventSender
```

FixedDepositServiceImpl – the reader

The eventSenderClass property, written by the EventSenderSelectorServiceImpl instance, is read by the FixedDepositServiceImpl instance, as shown in the following example listing:

Example listing 4-6 – FixedDepositServiceImpl class
Project – ch04-bankapp-dependencies
Source location - src/main/java/sample/spring/chapter04/bankapp/service

```
package sample.spring.chapter04.bankapp.service;

import org.springframework.core.io.ClassPathResource;
import sample.spring.chapter04.bankapp.Constants;

public class FixedDepositServiceImpl implements FixedDepositService {
    private FixedDepositDao fixedDepositDao;
    private EventSender eventSender;

    public FixedDepositServiceImpl(String configFile) throws Exception {
        ClassPathResource configProperties = new ClassPathResource(configFile);

        if (configProperties.exists()) {
            InputStream inStream = configProperties.getInputStream();
            Properties properties = new Properties();
            properties.load(inStream);

            String eventSenderClassString =
                properties.getProperty(Constants.EVENT_SENDER_CLASS_PROPERTY);

            if (eventSenderClassString != null) {
                Class<?> eventSenderClass = Class.forName(eventSenderClassString);
```

```
                eventSender = (EventSender) eventSenderClass.
                                  getDeclaredConstructor().newInstance();
                logger.info("Created EventSender class");
            } else {
                logger.info("appConfig.properties file doesn't contain the information "
                        + "about EventSender class");
            }
        }
    }

    public void createFixedDeposit(FixedDepositDetails fixedDepositDetails)
            throws Exception {
        .....
        eventSender.sendEvent(event);
    }
}
```

The above example listing shows that the following actions are performed by the FixedDepositServiceImpl class's constructor:

- loads properties from the appConfig.properties file, and obtains the eventSenderClass property (represented by the EVENT_SENDER_CLASS_PROPERTY constant) from it. The configFile constructor argument represents the location of the appConfig.properties file. The value of eventSenderClass property is the fully-qualified name of the EventSender implementation class that FixedDepositServiceImpl needs to use. The value of eventSenderClass property is stored in the eventSenderClassString local variable.

- creates an instance of the EventSender implementation class using the value of eventSenderClassString variable, and stores the instance into the variable named eventSender. The eventSender variable is later used by the FixedDepositServiceImpl's createFixedDeposit method (refer to the createFixedDeposit method in the above example listing) to store events in the database.

If a property named eventSenderClass is *not* found in the appConfig.properties file, the eventSenderClassString variable is *not* set. In this case, the FixedDepositServiceImpl's constructor prints the following message on the console: 'appConfig.properties file doesn't contain the information about EventSender class'. As the Spring container creates the FixedDepositServiceImpl instance *before* the EventSenderSelectorServiceImpl instance (refer example listing 4-4), the FixedDepositServiceImpl instance will *not* find any eventSenderClass property in the appConfig.properties file (refer example listing 4-5 and 4-6). This means that the FixedDepositServiceImpl bean is *implicitly* dependent on the EventSenderSelectorServiceImpl bean.

How to address the implicit dependency problem?

We can solve the implicit dependency problem in two ways:

- change the order in which bean definitions for EventSenderSelectorServiceImpl and FixedDepositServiceImpl classes are defined in the application context XML file. If the bean definition for the EventSenderSelectorServiceImpl class appears *before* the bean definition for the FixedDepositServiceImpl class, the EventSenderSelectorServiceImpl instance will be created *before* the FixedDepositServiceImpl instance.

- use the <bean> element's depends-on attribute to *explicitly* specify that the service bean (corresponding to the FixedDepositServiceImpl class) is dependent on the eventSenderSelectorService bean (corresponding to the EventSenderSelectorServiceImpl class).

The following example listing shows the usage of <bean> element's depends-on attribute:

Example listing 4-7 – <bean> element's depends-on attribute

```
<beans .....>
    <bean id="service"
           class="sample.spring.chapter04.bankapp.service.FixedDepositServiceImpl"
        depends-on="eventSenderSelectorService">
        .....
    </bean>

    <bean id="eventSenderSelectorService"
           class="sample.spring.chapter04.bankapp.service.EventSenderSelectorServiceImpl">
        .....
    </bean>
</beans>
```

In the above example listing, the service bean uses the depends-on attribute to explicitly specify that it is dependent on the eventSenderSelectorService bean. The depends-on attribute specifies the ids or names of the beans on which the bean is dependent. As the service bean specifies that it is dependent on the eventSenderSelectorService bean, the Spring container creates the eventSenderSelectorService bean (corresponding to the EventSenderSelectorServiceImpl class) instance *before* the service bean (corresponding to the FixedDepositServiceImpl class) instance.

> If you execute the main method of the BankApp class of ch04-bankapp-dependencies project, you'll find that the FixedDepositServiceImpl instance is created *before* the EventSenderSelectServiceImpl instance. For this reason, the following message is printed on the console: 'appConfig.properties file doesn't contain the information about EventSender class'.

Multiple implicit dependencies

If a bean has multiple implicit dependencies, you can specify ids or names of all those dependencies as the value of depends-on attribute, as shown here:

Example listing 4-8 – depends-on attribute example - multiple implicit dependencies

```
<beans .....>
    <bean id="abean" ..... depends-on="bBean, cBean">
        .....
    </bean>
    .....
</beans>
```

depends-on attribute and bean definition inheritance

It is important to note that the depends-on attribute is *not* inherited by child bean definitions. The following example listing shows an *abstract* serviceTemplate parent bean definition that uses the depends-on attribute to specify dependency on baseService bean:

Example listing 4-9 – depends-on attribute – bean definition inheritance

```
<bean id="serviceTemplate" class=".....ServiceTemplate" depends-on="baseService"
        abstract="true"/>

<bean id="someService" class=".....SomeServiceImpl" parent="serviceTemplate"/>

<bean id="someOtherService" class=".....SomeOtherServiceImpl"
        parent="serviceTemplate"/>

<bean id="baseService" class=".....BaseServiceImpl" />
```

In the above example listing, someService and someOtherService child bean definitions of serviceTemplate don't inherit the depends-on attribute from the serviceTemplate bean definition. As the Spring container creates beans in the order in which they are defined in the application context XML file, the baseService bean is created *after* the creation of someService and someOtherService beans.

Let's now look at how the Spring container manages dependencies of singleton- and prototype-scoped beans.

4-4 Singleton- and prototype-scoped bean's dependencies

A singleton bean (and its singleton dependencies) is created when the ApplicationContext instance is created. And, a prototype bean (and its prototype dependencies) is created each time ApplicationContext's getBean method is invoked to obtain the prototype bean.

In an application, if a singleton bean is dependent on a prototype bean, or vice versa, things get a bit complicated. To understand such application scenarios, let's look at how dependencies of singleton and prototype beans are managed by the Spring container.

Singleton bean's dependencies

The following example listing shows the singleton-scoped customerRequestService bean and its dependencies:

Example listing 4-10 – applicationContext.xml - Dependencies of customerRequestService bean
Project – ch04-bankapp-dependencies
Source location - src/main/resources/META-INF/spring

```
<bean id="customerRequestService"
      class="sample.spring.chapter04.bankapp.service.CustomerRequestServiceImpl">
    <constructor-arg name="customerRequestDetails" ref="customerRequestDetails" />
    <constructor-arg name="customerRequestDao" ref="customerRequestDao" />
</bean>

<bean id="customerRequestDetails"
      class="sample.spring.chapter04.bankapp.domain.CustomerRequestDetails"
    scope="prototype" />

<bean id="customerRequestDao"
    class="sample.spring.chapter04.bankapp.dao.CustomerRequestDaoImpl" />
```

The above example listing shows that the singleton-scoped customerRequestService bean depends on prototype-scoped customerRequestDetails and singleton-scoped customerRequestDao beans.

CustomerRequestService object (represented by the customerRequestService bean) is a service that is invoked when a bank customer creates a new request, like a check book request. CustomerRequestService puts the details of the customer request into a CustomerRequestDetails object (represented by the customerRequestDetails bean) and saves it in the data store using CustomerRequestDao object (represented by the customerRequestDao bean).

The following example listing shows the main method of BankApp class that loads the bean definitions shown in example listing 4-10:

Example listing 4-11 – BankApp class
Project – ch04-bankapp-dependencies
Source location - src/main/java/sample/spring/chapter04/bankapp

```
package sample.spring.chapter04.bankapp;

import org.springframework.context.ApplicationContext;
import org.springframework.context.support.ClassPathXmlApplicationContext;

public class BankApp {
    private static Logger logger = LogManager.getLogger(BankApp.class);

    public static void main(String args[]) throws Exception {
        ApplicationContext context = new ClassPathXmlApplicationContext(
             "classpath:META-INF/spring/applicationContext.xml");
        .....
        logger.info("Beginning with accessing CustomerRequestService");
        CustomerRequestService customerRequestService_1 =
              context.getBean(CustomerRequestService.class);
        .....
        CustomerRequestService customerRequestService_2 =
              context.getBean(CustomerRequestService.class);
        .....
        logger.info("Done with accessing CustomerRequestService");
    }
}
```

The above example listing shows that after the ApplicationContext instance is created, ApplicationContext's getBean method is invoked twice to obtain reference to the customerRequestService bean.

If you execute the main method of the BankApp class, you'll see the following output:

```
Created CustomerRequestDetails instance
Created CustomerRequestDaoImpl instance
Created CustomerRequestServiceImpl instance
.....
Beginning with accessing CustomerRequestService
Done with accessing CustomerRequestService
```

The 'Created.....' messages are printed by the constructors of the respective bean classes. The output shows that the prototype-scoped customerRequestDetails and singleton-scoped customerRequestDao dependencies of the singleton-scoped customerRequestService bean are created and injected into the customerRequestService instance when the Spring container is created.

As no 'Created .....' message was printed on the console between 'Beginning .....' and 'Done .....' messages, no bean instances were created by the Spring container when ApplicationContext's getBean method was invoked to retrieve the customerRequestService bean.

Figure 4-2 shows the sequence diagram that depicts the following sequence of events occur when BankApp's main method is executed:

- when the Spring container is created, the prototype-scoped customerRequestDetails and singleton-scoped customerRequestDao beans are first created, followed by the creation of singleton-scoped customerRequestService
- customerRequestDetails and customerRequestDao beans are passed as constructor argument to the customerRequestService bean.

As a singleton bean is created *only once* by the Spring container, the Spring container has *only one* opportunity to inject customerRequestService bean's dependencies. For this reason, the Spring container injects prototype-scoped customerRequestDetails bean instance into the customerRequestService bean *only once*. The effect of this behavior is that the customerRequestService bean ends up holding reference to the *same* customerRequestDetails bean instance throughout its lifetime.

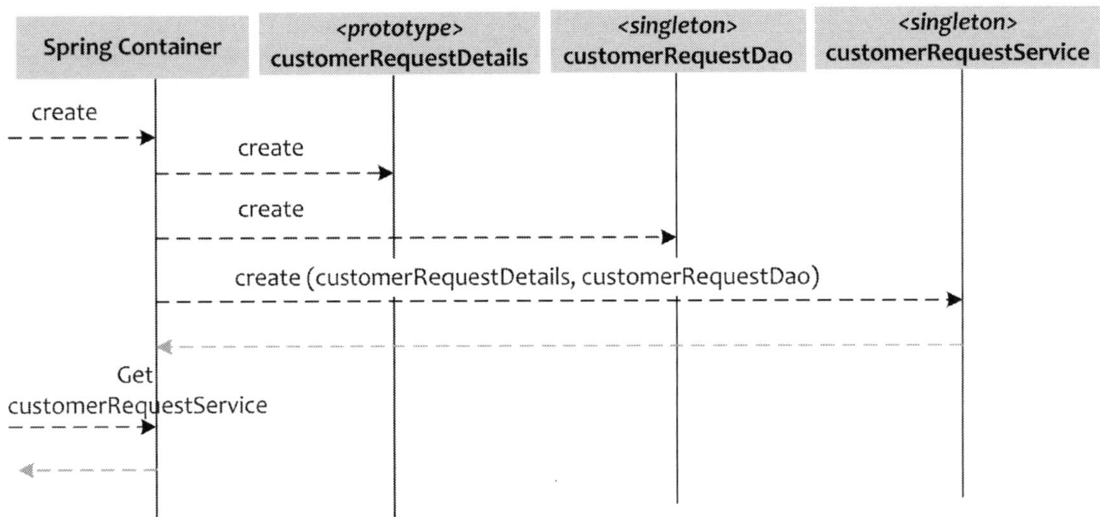

Figure 4-2 - The sequence of events that occur when the Spring container is created and the customerRequestService bean is retrieved from the Spring container

It is important to note that even if setter-based DI was used to inject the prototype-scoped customerRequestDetails dependency of the customerRequestService bean, the Spring container would have called the setter method *only once* during the lifetime of the customerRequestService bean. This means that irrespective of whether setter- or constructor-based DI is used, a singleton bean holds reference to the same prototype bean instance throughout its lifetime.

Now, once the Spring container is created, any request for the singleton-scoped customerRequestService bean returns the same cached instance of the customerRequestService bean. For this reason, no 'Created .....' message was written out to the console between 'Beginning .....' and 'Done .....' messages when we executed BankApp's main method (refer example listing 4-11).

As the customerRequestService bean always holds reference to the *same* prototype-scoped customerRequestDetails bean, it may adversely affect the behavior of MyBank application. For instance, if multiple customers simultaneously submit request to the CustomerRequestServiceImpl instance, all the requests will result in modifying the same instance of the CustomerRequestDetails object held by the CustomerRequestService.

Ideally, CustomerRequestServiceImpl should create a new instance of CustomerRequestDetails object on every request. In section 4-5, we'll see what modifications we need to make to the bean class of a singleton bean so that it can retrieve a new instance of a prototype bean on every method call.

Let's now look at how the Spring container manages prototype and singleton dependencies of a prototype bean.

Prototype bean's dependencies

In MyBank, a customer registers with the MyBank application by following a sequence of steps. For instance, a customer first enters personal information and his account details, and if the MyBank application finds a matching record, the customer is asked for his debit card details. The CustomerRegistrationServiceImpl class of MyBank application contains the necessary business logic to register customers. As a sequence of steps is followed to register with the MyBank application, the CustomerRegistrationServiceImpl object maintains conversational state between method calls.

The following example listing shows the prototype-scoped customerRegistrationService bean (representing the CustomerRegistrationServiceImpl class) of MyBank application, and its dependencies:

Example listing 4-12 – applicationContext.xml - customerRegistrationService bean and its dependencies
Project – ch04-bankapp-dependencies
Source location - src/main/resources/META-INF/spring

```
<bean id="customerRegistrationService"
    class="sample.spring.chapter04.bankapp.service.CustomerRegistrationServiceImpl"
    scope="prototype">
   <constructor-arg
          name="customerRegistrationDetails" ref="customerRegistrationDetails" />
   <constructor-arg name="customerRegistrationDao" ref="customerRegistrationDao" />
</bean>
<bean id="customerRegistrationDetails"
    class="sample.spring.chapter04.bankapp.domain.CustomerRegistrationDetails"
    scope="prototype" />

<bean id="customerRegistrationDao"
    class="sample.spring.chapter04.bankapp.dao.CustomerRegistrationDaoImpl" />
```

The above example listing shows that the prototype-scoped customerRegistrationService bean depends on prototype-scoped customerRegistrationDetails and singleton-scoped customerRegistrationDao beans.

CustomerRegistrationServiceImpl instance maintains progress of the registration process, and stores information provided by the customer during the registration process in a CustomerRegistrationDetails object (represented by the customerRegistrationDetails bean). As both CustomerRegistrationServiceImpl and CustomerRegistrationDetails objects are stateful in nature, both customerRegistrationService and customerRegistrationDetails beans are defined as prototype-scoped beans.

The following example listing shows the main method of BankApp class that loads customer registration related beans (refer example listing 4-12) and performs registrations for 2 customers:

Example listing 4-13 – BankApp class
Project – ch04-bankapp-dependencies
Source location - src/main/java/sample/spring/chapter04/bankapp

```
package sample.spring.chapter04.bankapp;

import org.springframework.context.ApplicationContext;
import org.springframework.context.support.ClassPathXmlApplicationContext;

public class BankApp {
    private static Logger logger = LogManager.getLogger(BankApp.class);

    public static void main(String args[]) throws Exception {
        ApplicationContext context = new ClassPathXmlApplicationContext(
                "classpath:META-INF/spring/applicationContext.xml");
        .....
        logger.info("Beginning with accessing CustomerRegistrationService");

        CustomerRegistrationService customerRegistrationService_1 = context
                 .getBean(CustomerRegistrationService.class);
        customerRegistrationService_1.setAccountNumber("account_1");
        customerRegistrationService_1.setAddress("address_1");
        customerRegistrationService_1.setDebitCardNumber("debitCardNumber_1");
        customerRegistrationService_1.register();
        logger.info("registered customer with id account_1");

        CustomerRegistrationService customerRegistrationService_2 = context
                 .getBean(CustomerRegistrationService.class);

        .....
        logger.info("registered customer with id account_2");
        logger.info("Done with accessing CustomerRegistrationService");
    }
}
```

The above example listing shows that the BankApp's main method calls ApplicationContext's getBean method twice to obtain reference to customerRegistrationService bean. Once the customerRegistrationService bean instance is retrieved, the setAccountNumber, setAddress, setDebitCardNumber and register methods are invoked on it. If you execute BankApp's main method, you'll see the following output on the console:

```
Created CustomerRegistrationDaoImpl instance
.....
Beginning with accessing CustomerRegistrationService
Created CustomerRegistrationDetails instance
Created CustomerRegistrationServiceImpl instance
registered customer with id account_1
Created CustomerRegistrationDetails instance
Created CustomerRegistrationServiceImpl instance
registered customer with id account_2
Done with accessing CustomerRegistrationService
```

The 'Created.....' messages shown in the above output are printed by the constructors of the respective bean classes. The above output shows that the singleton-scoped customerRegistrationDao bean (representing the CustomerRegistrationDaoImpl class) is created *only once* when the ApplicationContext instance is created.

The 'Created.....' messages between 'Beginning.....' and 'Done.....' messages indicate that each time ApplicationContext's getBean method is invoked to obtain the prototype-scoped customerRegistrationService bean, a new instance of the customerRegistrationService bean and its prototype-scoped dependency, customerRegistrationDetails, is created by the Spring container.

Figure 4-3 shows the sequence diagram that depicts the sequence of events that occur when BankApp's main method (refer example listing 4-13) is executed. The figure shows:

- the singleton-scoped customerRegistrationDao bean is created *only once* when ApplicationContext instance is created.
- when the prototype-scoped customerRegistrationService bean is requested from the Spring container, the Spring container first creates an instance of customerRegistrationDetails bean (which is the prototype-scoped dependency of the customerRegistrationService bean), followed by the creation of the customerRegistrationService bean.

This shows that if a prototype bean X is dependent on another prototype bean Y, the Spring container will create a new instance of X and Y each time you request bean X from the Spring container.

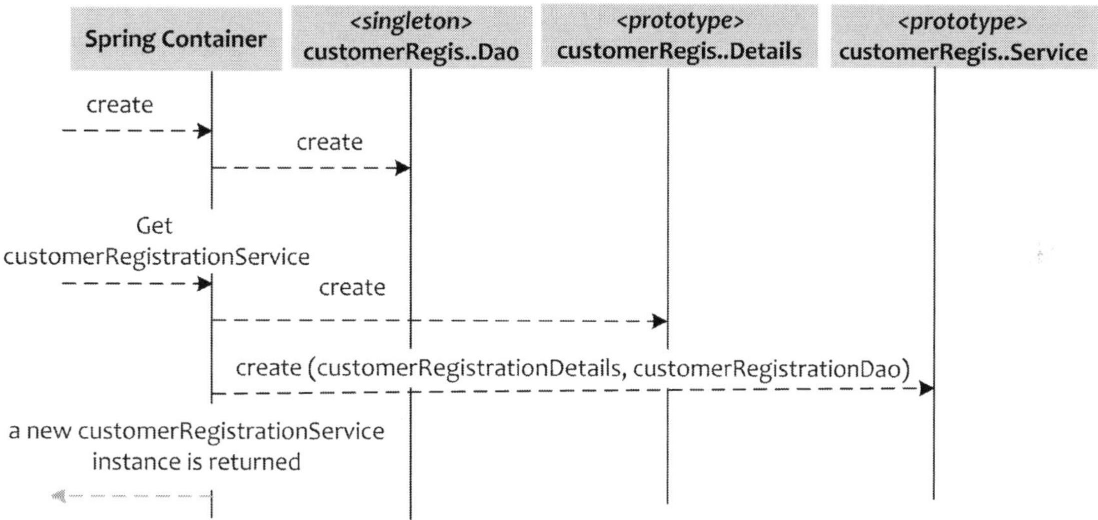

Figure 4-3 – The sequence of events that occur when the Spring container is created and the customerRegistrationService bean is retrieved from the Spring container

Earlier in this section, we saw that if a singleton bean is dependent on a prototype bean, then throughout its lifetime the singleton bean is associated with the *same* instance of the prototype bean. Let's now look at different ways in which a singleton bean can retrieve a new instance of a prototype bean from the Spring container.

4-5 Obtaining new instances of prototype beans inside singleton beans

In the previous section, we saw that the prototype-scoped dependency of a singleton bean is injected at the time of creation of the singleton bean (refer figure 4-2). As the Spring container creates instance of a singleton bean *only once*, the singleton bean holds reference to the *same* prototype bean instance throughout its lifetime. A singleton bean's methods can retrieve a new instance of their prototype-scoped dependency from the Spring container using any one of the following approaches:

- make the singleton bean's class implement Spring's `ApplicationContextAware` interface
- use the `<lookup-method>` element of Spring's `beans` schema
- use the `<replaced-method>` element of Spring's `beans` schema

> If you follow annotation-driven development approach (explained in chapter 6) to create your Spring application, you can use `@Lazy` annotation (refer section 6-7 of chapter 6) to obtain a fresh instance of a prototype bean inside a singleton bean.

IMPORT **`chapter 4/ch04-bankapp-context-aware`** (This project shows a scenario in which a singleton bean's class implements Spring's `ApplicationContextAware` interface to obtain instances of a prototype bean from the Spring container. To run the application, execute the `main` method of the `BankApp` class of this project)

Let's first begin by looking at the `ApplicationContextAware` interface.

ApplicationContextAware interface

Spring's `ApplicationContextAware` interface is implemented by beans that require access to the `ApplicationContext` instance in which they are running. The `ApplicationContextAware` interface defines a single method, `setApplicationContext`, which provides the implementing beans with an instance of the `ApplicationContext` object. The `setApplicationContext` method is called by the Spring container at the time of bean creation.

`ApplicationContextAware` interface is a *lifecycle interface*. A lifecycle interface defines one or more callback methods that are invoked by the Spring container at appropriate times during the bean's lifetime. For instance, `ApplicationContextAware`'s `setApplicationContext` method is called by the Spring container *after* the bean instance is created but *before* the bean instance is completely initialized. In chapter 5, we'll look at some more lifecycle interfaces in Spring.

> A bean instance is considered completely initialized only after its *initialization method* (refer section 5-2 of chapter 5) is called by the Spring container. It's only after a bean instance is completely initialized that it is injected into the dependent bean instances by the Spring container.

A bean that implements the `ApplicationContextAware` interface can access other beans registered with the `ApplicationContext` instance by calling `ApplicationContext`'s `getBean` method. This means that if a singleton bean implements the `ApplicationContextAware` interface, it can explicitly obtain its prototype-scoped dependency by calling `ApplicationContext`'s `getBean` method.

The following example listing shows the `CustomerRequestServiceImpl` class (a singleton bean) that needs a new instance of `CustomerRequestDetails` object (a prototype bean) each time `CustomerRequestImpl`'s `submitRequest` method is called:

Example listing 4-14 – `CustomerRequestServiceImpl` class that implements Spring's `ApplicationContextAware` interface
Project – `ch04-bankapp-context-aware`
Source location - `src/main/java/sample/spring/chapter04/bankapp/service`

```
package sample.spring.chapter04.bankapp.service;
```

```
import org.springframework.context.ApplicationContext;
import org.springframework.context.ApplicationContextAware;

public class CustomerRequestServiceImpl implements
        CustomerRequestService, ApplicationContextAware {

    private CustomerRequestDao customerRequestDao;
    private ApplicationContext applicationContext;

    @ConstructorProperties({ "customerRequestDao" })
    public CustomerRequestServiceImpl(CustomerRequestDao customerRequestDao) {
        this.customerRequestDao = customerRequestDao;
    }

    public void setApplicationContext(ApplicationContext applicationContext)
            throws BeansException {
        this.applicationContext = applicationContext;
    }

    public void submitRequest(String requestType, String requestDescription) {
        CustomerRequestDetails customerRequestDetails = applicationContext
                .getBean(CustomerRequestDetails.class);
        customerRequestDetails.setType(requestType);
        customerRequestDetails.setDescription(requestDescription);
        customerRequestDao.submitRequest(customerRequestDetails);
    }
}
```

In the above example listing, the `setApplicationContext` method provides `CustomerRequestServiceImpl` with an instance of `ApplicationContext` object. The `ApplicationContext` instance is later used by the `submitRequest` method to obtain an instance of `CustomerRequestDetails` object from the Spring container.

If you go to `ch04-bankapp-context-aware` project and execute `BankApp`'s `main` method, you'll find that on each invocation of `submitRequest` method a new instance of `CustomerRequestDetails` object is fetched from the Spring container.

In the context of MyBank application, we saw that the `ApplicationContextAware` interface is useful if a bean requires access to other beans. The downside of implementing the `ApplicationContextAware` interface is that it couples your bean class to Spring Framework. You can avoid coupling your bean classes with Spring Framework and still access other beans from the Spring container by using *method injection* techniques offered by `<lookup-method>` and `<replaced-method>` elements of Spring's beans schema.

Let's first look at the `<lookup-method>` element.

IMPORT **chapter 4/ch04-bankapp-lookup-method** (This project shows the MyBank application that uses the `<lookup-method>` element of Spring's beans schema. To run the application, execute the `main` method of the `BankApp` class of this project)

<lookup-method> element

If a bean class defines a *bean lookup method* whose return type represents a bean, the `<lookup-method>` element instructs Spring to provide implementation for this method. The method implementation provided by Spring is responsible for retrieving the bean instance from the Spring container and returning it.

The <lookup-method> element's bean attribute specifies the name of the bean to be looked-up, and the name attribute specifies the name of the method whose implementation is to be provided by Spring. It is important to note that the bean lookup method defined by the bean class can be an abstract or a concrete method.

> The use of <lookup-method> element to lookup beans is referred to as a *'Method Injection'* technique because the <lookup-method> element injects a bean lookup method implementation into the bean class.

In example listing 4-14, we saw that the CustomerRequestServiceImpl needs a new instance of CustomerRequestDetails object each time CustomerRequestServiceImpl's submitRequest method is invoked. The following example listing shows a variant of CustomerRequestServiceImpl class that defines an *abstract* bean lookup method, getCustomerRequestDetails, whose return type is CustomerRequestDetails. The submitRequest method calls the getCustomerRequestDetails method to obtain a new instance of CustomerRequestDetails instance.

Example listing 4-15 – CustomerRequestServiceImpl class – defining a bean lookup method
Project – ch04-bankapp-lookup-method
Source location - src/main/java/sample/spring/chapter04/bankapp/service

```
package sample.spring.chapter04.bankapp.service;

public abstract class CustomerRequestServiceImpl implements CustomerRequestService {
    private CustomerRequestDao customerRequestDao;

    @ConstructorProperties({ "customerRequestDao" })
    public CustomerRequestServiceImpl(CustomerRequestDao customerRequestDao) {
        this.customerRequestDao = customerRequestDao;
    }

    public abstract CustomerRequestDetails getCustomerRequestDetails();

    @Override
    public void submitRequest(String requestType, String requestDescription) {
        // -- populate CustomerRequestDetails object and save it
        CustomerRequestDetails customerRequestDetails = getCustomerRequestDetails();
        .....
    }
}
```

You should note that we could have defined the getCustomerRequestDetails method as a concrete method. As the getCustomerRequestDetails method is overridden by Spring, it doesn't matter if you perform any action inside the method or keep it empty.

The following example listing shows bean definitions for CustomerRequestServiceImpl and CustomerRequestDetails classes:

Example listing 4-16 – applicationContext.xml - <lookup-method> element usage
Project – ch04-bankapp-lookup-method
Source location - src/main/resources/META-INF/spring

```
    <bean id="customerRequestService"
          class="sample.spring.chapter04.bankapp.service.CustomerRequestServiceImpl">
        <constructor-arg name="customerRequestDao" ref="customerRequestDao" />
        <lookup-method bean="customerRequestDetails" name="getCustomerRequestDetails"/>
    </bean>
```

```
    <bean id="customerRequestDetails"
          class="sample.spring.chapter04.bankapp.domain.CustomerRequestDetails"
      scope="prototype" />
```

In the above example listing, the bean definition for the CustomerRequestServiceImpl class contains a <lookup-method> element. The value of <lookup-method> element's name attribute is getCustomerRequestDetails, which instructs Spring to provide implementation for the getCustomerRequestDetails lookup method. The value of <lookup-method> element's bean attribute is customerRequestDetails, which means that the implementation of getCustomerRequestDetails method retrieves a bean with id (or name) as customerRequestDetails from the Spring container and returns it. As the customerRequestDetails bean represents a CustomerRequestDetails object, the implementation of getCustomerRequestDetails method returns a CustomerRequestDetails object.

In example listing 4-15, the CustomerRequestServiceImpl's submitRequest method calls the getCustomerRequestDetails bean lookup method to obtain a CustomerRequestDetails instance. As the CustomerRequestDetails is defined as a prototype bean in the application context XML file (refer example listing 4-16), each invocation of the submitRequest method results in retrieval of a new instance of CustomerRequestDetails object from the Spring container.

To check that the <lookup-method> element provides correct implementation for the CustomerRequestServiceImpl's getCustomerRequestDetails bean lookup method, the main method of BankApp class obtains an instance of CustomerRequestServiceImpl from the Spring container and invokes its submitRequest method multiple times. If each invocation of the submitRequest method results in retrieval of a fresh instance of CustomerRequestDetails object from the Spring container, then it means that the <lookup-method> element provides the correct implementation for the getCustomerRequestDetails method.

The following example listing shows the BankApp's main method that invokes CustomerRequestServiceImpl's submitRequest method multiple times:

Example listing 4-17 – BankApp class
Project – ch04-bankapp-lookup-method
Source location - src/main/java/sample/spring/chapter04/bankapp

```
package sample.spring.chapter04.bankapp;
.....
public class BankApp {
    private static Logger logger = LogManager.getLogger(BankApp.class);

    public static void main(String args[]) throws Exception {
        ApplicationContext context = new ClassPathXmlApplicationContext(
                "classpath:META-INF/spring/applicationContext.xml");
        .....
        logger.info("Beginning with accessing CustomerRequestService");
        CustomerRequestService customerRequestService_1 = context
                .getBean(CustomerRequestService.class);
        customerRequestService_1.submitRequest("checkBookRequest",
                "Request to send a 50-leaf check book");
        customerRequestService_1.submitRequest("checkBookRequest",
                "Request to send a 100-leaf check book");
        .....
        logger.info("Done with accessing CustomerRequestService");
    }
}
```

If you execute the BankApp's main method, you'll see the following output on the console:

```
Beginning with accessing CustomerRequestService
Created CustomerRequestDetails instance
Created CustomerRequestDetails instance
.....
Done with accessing CustomerRequestService
```

The 'Created.....' messages are printed by the constructors of the respective bean classes. The above output shows that each invocation of CustomerRequestServiceImpl's submitRequest method results in creation of a new CustomerRequestDetails instance by the Spring container.

As the implementation of the bean lookup method is provided by the Spring container, some restrictions apply to the signature of the bean lookup methods. For instance, the bean lookup method *must* be defined as public or protected, and it *must not* accept any arguments. As the bean class containing the bean lookup method is subclassed at runtime by Spring to provide the implementation for the bean lookup method, the bean class and the bean lookup method *must not* be defined as final.

> As the bean class containing the bean lookup method needs to be subclassed at runtime by Spring to provide implementation for the bean lookup method, Spring uses CGLIB (http://cglib.sourceforge.net/) library to perform subclassing of the bean class. Starting with Spring 3.2, the CGLIB classes are packaged within the spring-core JAR file itself; therefore, you don't need to explicitly specify that your project is dependent on CGLIB JAR file.

Instead of using the <lookup-method> element, you can use the <replaced-method> element of Spring's beans schema to obtain beans from the Spring container.

IMPORT **chapter 4/ch04-bankapp-replaced-method** (This project shows the MyBank application that uses the <replaced-method> element of Spring's beans schema. To run the application, execute the main method of the BankApp class of this project)

<replaced-method> element

The <replaced-method> element allows you to replace any arbitrary method in a bean class with a different implementation. The following example listing shows a variant of CustomerRequestServiceImpl class that we'll be using as an example to demonstrate the use of <replaced-method> element:

Example listing 4-18 – CustomerRequestServiceImpl class
Project – ch04-bankapp-replaced-method
Source location - src/main/java/sample/spring/chapter04/bankapp/service

```
package sample.spring.chapter04.bankapp.service;
.....
public class CustomerRequestServiceImpl implements CustomerRequestService {
    private CustomerRequestDao customerRequestDao;
    .....
    public Object getMyBean(String beanName) {
        return null;
    }

    @Override
    public void submitRequest(String requestType, String requestDescription) {
        // -- populate CustomerRequestDetails object and save it
```

```
        CustomerRequestDetails customerRequestDetails =
                (CustomerRequestDetails) getMyBean("customerRequestDetails");
        customerRequestDetails.setType(requestType);
        customerRequestDetails.setDescription(requestDescription);
        customerRequestDao.submitRequest(customerRequestDetails);
    }
}
```

The above example listing shows that the `CustomerRequestServiceImpl` class defines a `getMyBean` method. The `getMyBean` method accepts name of a bean as an argument, and instead of returning the corresponding bean instance, the `getMyBean` method returns `null`. The `submitRequest` method passes 'customerRequestDetails' bean name as argument to the `getMyBean` method, and assumes that the `getMyBean` method returns an instance of `customerRequestDetails` bean. By using the `<replaced-method>` element, we can override the `getMyBean` method to return the bean instance corresponding to the bean name argument.

The `<replaced-method>` element needs information about the *overridden* method (which is `CustomerRequestServiceImpl`'s `getMyBean` method) and the *overriding* method. The overriding method is provided by the class that implements Spring's `MethodReplacer` interface. The following example listing shows `MyMethodReplacer` class that implements the `MethodReplacer` interface:

Example listing 4-19 – MyMethodReplacer class
Project – ch04-bankapp-replaced-method
Source location - src/main/java/sample/spring/chapter04/bankapp/service

```
package sample.spring.chapter04.bankapp.service;

import org.springframework.beans.factory.support.MethodReplacer;
import org.springframework.context.ApplicationContextAware;

public class MyMethodReplacer implements MethodReplacer, ApplicationContextAware {
    private ApplicationContext applicationContext;

    @Override
    public Object reimplement(Object obj, Method method, Object[] args) throws Throwable {
        return applicationContext.getBean((String) args[0]);
    }


    @Override
    public void setApplicationContext(ApplicationContext applicationContext)
            throws BeansException {
        this.applicationContext = applicationContext;
    }
}
```

Spring's `MethodReplacer` interface defines a `reimplement` method whose implementation is provided by the `MyMethodReplacer` class. The `reimplement` method represents the *overriding* method. `MyMethodReplacer` class also implements Spring's `ApplicationContextAware` interface so that the `reimplement` method can use the `ApplicationContext` instance to obtain bean instances from the Spring container.

The `reimplement` method accepts the following arguments:

- `Object obj` – the object whose method we are overriding. In our case, the `obj` object is the `CustomerRequestServiceImpl` object.

- Method method – the bean method that is overridden by the reimplement method. In our case, this is CustomerRequestServiceImpl's getMyBean method.

- Object[] args – arguments passed to the bean method being overridden. In our case, args represents the arguments passed to the CustomerRequestServiceImpl's getMyBean method. In example listing 4-19, args[0] in the reimplement method refers the bean name argument passed to the CustomerRequestServiceImpl's getMyBean method.

If you now look at MyMethodReplacer's reimplement method in example listing 4-19, you can infer that it uses the args argument to obtain the bean name passed to the CustomerRequestServiceImpl's getMyBean method, and then calls ApplicationContext's getBean method to obtain the corresponding bean instance. As MyMethodReplacer's reimplement method overrides CustomerRequestServiceImpl's getMyBean method, call to getMyBean method at runtime returns the bean instance whose name was passed to the getMyBean method.

As shown in the following example listing, the <replaced-method> element informs Spring that MyMethodReplacer's reimplement method overrides CustomerRequestServiceImpl's getMyBean method:

Example listing 4-20 – applicationContext.xml - <replaced-method> element usage
Project – ch04-bankapp-replaced-method
Source location - src/main/resources/META-INF/spring

```
<bean id="customerRequestService"
      class="sample.spring.chapter04.bankapp.service.CustomerRequestServiceImpl">
    <constructor-arg name="customerRequestDao" ref="customerRequestDao" />
    <replaced-method name="getMyBean" replacer="methodReplacer" />
</bean>

<bean id="methodReplacer"
    class="sample.spring.chapter04.bankapp.service.MyMethodReplacer" />
```

The above example listing shows bean definitions for MyMethodReplacer and CustomerRequestServiceImpl classes. The <replace-method> element's name attribute specifies name of the method that you want to override, and the replacer attribute specifies reference to the bean that implements the MethodReplacer interface. The method specified by the name attribute is overridden by the reimplement method of the bean referenced by the replacer attribute.

BankApp class of ch04-bankapp-replaced-method project is same as the one we saw in example listing 4-17 for ch04-bankapp-lookup-method project. If you execute the main method of the BankApp class, you'll find that the <replaced-method> element overrides CustomerRequestServiceImpl's getMyBean method with MyMethodReplacer's reimplement method; therefore, a fresh instance of CustomerRequestDetails instance is retrieved from the Spring container each time CustomerRequestServiceImpl's submitRequest method (refer example listing 4-18) is invoked.

It is important to note that you can use the <replaced-method> element to replace any abstract or concrete method of a bean class with a different method implementation. For instance, we could have defined getMyBean method as an abstract method and used the <replaced-method> element in the same way as described in this section.

Let's now look at how the <replaced-method> element uniquely identifies the bean method to be overridden.

Uniquely identifying the bean method

You may come across scenarios in which the bean method that you want to replace using the <replaced-method> element can't be uniquely identified by name. For instance, the following example listing shows a bean class that contains overloaded perform methods:

Example listing 4-21 – Overloaded methods in a bean class

```
public class MyBean {
    public void perform(String task1, String task2) { ..... }
    public void perform(String task) { ..... }
    public void perform(MyTask task) { ..... }
}
```

In the above example listing, the MyBean class contains multiple methods named perform. To uniquely identify the bean method to be overridden, the <replaced-method> element uses <arg-type> sub-elements to specify method argument types. For instance, the following example listing shows how the <replaced-method> element specifies that the perform(String, String) method of MyBean class should be overridden:

Example listing 4-22 – <replaced-method> element with <arg-type> sub-elements

```
<bean id="mybean" class="MyBean">
    <replaced-method name="perform" replacer=".....">
        <arg-type>java.lang.String</arg-type>
        <arg-type>java.lang.String</arg-type>
    </replaced-method>
</bean>
```

Instead of specifying the fully-qualified name of the argument type as the value of <arg-type> element, you can specify a substring of the fully-qualified name as the value. For instance, instead of java.lang.String, you can specify Str or String as the value of <arg-type> element in the above example listing.

Let's now look at Spring's autowiring feature that saves the effort of specifying bean dependencies in the application context XML file.

4-6 Autowiring dependencies

In Spring, you have the option to either explicitly specify bean dependencies using <property> and <constructor-arg> elements or let Spring automatically resolve bean dependencies. The process in which dependencies are automatically resolved by Spring is referred to as 'autowiring'.

IMPORT **chapter 4/ch04-bankapp-autowiring** (This project shows the MyBank application that uses Spring's *autowiring* feature for dependency injection. To run the application, execute the main method of the BankApp class of this project)

The <bean> element's autowire attribute specifies how a bean's dependencies are automatically resolved by Spring. The autowire attribute can take any one of the following values: default, byName, byType, constructor and no. Let's now look at each of these attribute values in detail.

> You should note that the <bean> element's autowire attribute is not inherited by child bean definitions.

byType

If you specify autowire attribute's value as byType, Spring autowires bean properties based on their type. For instance, if a bean A defines a property of type X, Spring finds a bean of type X in the ApplicationContext and injects it into bean A. Let's look at an example usage of byType autowiring in the MyBank application.

The following example listing shows the MyBank application's CustomerRegistrationServiceImpl class:

Example listing 4-23 – CustomerRegistrationServiceImpl class
Project – ch04-bankapp-autowiring
Source location - src/main/java/sample/spring/chapter04/bankapp/service

```
package sample.spring.chapter04.bankapp.service;

public class CustomerRegistrationServiceImpl implements CustomerRegistrationService {

    private CustomerRegistrationDetails customerRegistrationDetails;
    private CustomerRegistrationDao customerRegistrationDao;
    ....
    public void setCustomerRegistrationDetails(
            CustomerRegistrationDetails customerRegistrationDetails) {
        this.customerRegistrationDetails = customerRegistrationDetails;
    }
    public void setCustomerRegistrationDao(
            CustomerRegistrationDao customerRegistrationDao) {
        this.customerRegistrationDao = customerRegistrationDao;
    }
    .....
}
```

The above example listing shows that the CustomerRegistrationServiceImpl class defines CustomerRegistrationDetails and CustomerRegistrationDao objects as its dependencies.

The following example listing shows bean definitions for CustomerRegistrationServiceImpl, CustomerRegistrationDetails and CustomerRegistrationDaoImpl (an implementation of CustomerRegistrationDao interface) classes:

Example listing 4-24 – applicationContext.xml - autowiring byType configuration
Project – ch04-bankapp-autowiring
Source location - src/main/resources/META-INF/spring

```
<bean id="customerRegistrationService"
        class="sample.spring.chapter04.bankapp.service.CustomerRegistrationServiceImpl"
      scope="prototype" autowire="byType" />

<bean id="customerRegistrationDetails"
        class="sample.spring.chapter04.bankapp.domain.CustomerRegistrationDetails"
      scope="prototype" />

<bean id="customerRegistrationDao"
      class="sample.spring.chapter04.bankapp.dao.CustomerRegistrationDaoImpl" />
```

In the above example listing, the customerRegistrationService bean definition doesn't contain <property> elements for setting customerRegistrationDetails and customerRegistrationDao properties (refer example listing 4-23). Instead, the <bean> element specifies autowire attribute's value as byType to instruct Spring to automatically resolve dependencies of the customerRegistrationService bean based on their *type*. Spring looks for beans of types CustomerRegistrationDetails and CustomerRegistrationDao in the ApplicationContext, and injects them into the customerRegistrationService bean.

It may happen that Spring doesn't find any bean registered with the ApplicationContext whose type matches the property type. In such cases, no exception is thrown and the bean property is *not* set. For instance, if a bean defines a property x of type Y and there is no bean of type Y registered with the ApplicationContext instance, the property x is not set.

If Spring finds multiple beans in the ApplicationContext that match the property type, an exception is thrown. In such cases, instead of using autowiring feature, use <property> elements to explicitly identify bean dependencies or set a bean as the *primary candidate* for autowiring by setting its <bean> element's primary attribute value to true.

constructor

If you specify autowire attribute's value as constructor, Spring autowires bean class's constructor arguments based on their type. For instance, if bean A's constructor accepts arguments of types X and Y, Spring finds beans of types X and Y in the ApplicationContext and injects them as arguments to bean A's constructor. Let's look at an example usage of constructor autowiring.

The following example listing shows the MyBank application's CustomerRequestServiceImpl class:

Example listing 4-25 – CustomerRequestServiceImpl class
Project – ch04-bankapp-autowiring
Source location - src/main/java/sample/spring/chapter04/bankapp/service

```
package sample.spring.chapter04.bankapp.service;

public class CustomerRequestServiceImpl implements CustomerRequestService {
    private CustomerRequestDetails customerRequestDetails;
    private CustomerRequestDao customerRequestDao;

    @ConstructorProperties({ "customerRequestDetails", "customerRequestDao" })
    public CustomerRequestServiceImpl(CustomerRequestDetails customerRequestDetails,
            CustomerRequestDao customerRequestDao) {
        this.customerRequestDetails = customerRequestDetails;
        this.customerRequestDao = customerRequestDao;
    }
    .....
}
```

The CustomerRequestServiceImpl class defines a constructor that accepts arguments of types CustomerRequestDetails and CustomerRequestDao.

The following example listing shows bean definitions for CustomerRequestServiceImpl, CustomerRequestDetails and CustomerRequestDaoImpl (an implementation of CustomerRequestDao interface) classes:

Example listing 4-26 – applicationContext.xml - constructor autowiring
Project – ch04-bankapp-autowiring
Source location - src/main/resources/META-INF/spring

```
<bean id="customerRequestService"
    class="sample.spring.chapter04.bankapp.service.CustomerRequestServiceImpl"
    autowire="constructor">
</bean>
```

```
    <bean id="customerRequestDetails"
          class="sample.spring.chapter04.bankapp.domain.CustomerRequestDetails"
        scope="prototype" />

    <bean id="customerRequestDao"
        class="sample.spring.chapter04.bankapp.dao.CustomerRequestDaoImpl" />
```

In the above example listing, the customerRequestService bean definition specifies autowire attribute's value as constructor, which means that Spring locates beans of types CustomerRequestDetails and CustomerRequestDao in the ApplicationContext, and passes them as arguments to CustomerRequestServiceImpl class's constructor. As customerRequestDetails and customerRequestDao beans are of type CustomerRequestDetails and CustomerRequestDao, Spring automatically injects instances of these beans into CustomerRequestServiceImpl class's constructor.

If Spring doesn't find any bean in the ApplicationContext whose type matches the constructor argument type, the constructor argument is not set. If Spring finds multiple beans in the ApplicationContext that match the constructor argument type, an exception is thrown. In such scenarios, use <constructor-arg> elements to explicitly specify bean dependencies or set a bean as the *primary candidate* for autowiring by setting its <bean> element's primary attribute value to true.

byName

If you specify the autowire attribute's value as byName, Spring autowires bean properties based on their names. For instance, if a bean A defines a property named x, Spring finds a bean named x in the ApplicationContext and injects it into bean A. Let's look at an example usage of byName autowiring.

The following example listing shows the MyBank application's FixedDepositServiceImpl class:

Example listing 4-27 – FixedDepositServiceImpl class
Project – ch04-bankapp-autowiring
Source location - src/main/java/sample/spring/chapter04/bankapp/service

```
package sample.spring.chapter04.bankapp.service;

import sample.spring.chapter04.bankapp.dao.FixedDepositDao;
import sample.spring.chapter04.bankapp.domain.FixedDepositDetails;

public class FixedDepositServiceImpl implements FixedDepositService {
    private FixedDepositDao myFixedDepositDao;

    public void setMyFixedDepositDao(FixedDepositDao myFixedDepositDao) {
        this.myFixedDepositDao = myFixedDepositDao;
    }
    .....
}
```

The above example listing shows that the FixedDepositServiceImpl class defines a property named myFixedDepositDao of type FixedDepositDao.

The following example listing shows bean definitions for FixedDepositServiceImpl and FixedDepositDaoImpl (an implementation of FixedDepositDao interface) classes:

Example listing 4-28 – applicationContext.xml - byName autowiring
Project – ch04-bankapp-autowiring
Source location - src/main/resources/META-INF/spring

```
<bean id="fixedDepositService"
      class="sample.spring.chapter04.bankapp.service.FixedDepositServiceImpl"
      autowire="byName" />

<bean id="myFixedDepositDao"
    class="sample.spring.chapter04.bankapp.dao.FixedDepositDaoImpl" />
```

In the above example listing, the fixedDepositService bean definition specifies the autowire attribute's value as byName, which means the properties of fixedDepositService bean are automatically resolved by Spring based on their names. In listing 4-27, we saw that the FixedDepositServiceImpl class defines a property named myFixedDepositDao; therefore, Spring injects an instance of myFixedDepositDao bean into the fixedDepositService bean.

default / no

If you specify the autowire attribute's value as default or no, autowiring feature is *disabled* for the bean. As Spring's default behavior is to use *no* autowiring for beans, specifying autowire attribute's value as default or no means no autowiring will be performed for the bean.

You can change the default autowiring behavior of all the beans by setting the default-autowire attribute of <beans> element. For instance, if you set default-autowire attribute's value to byType, it effectively means setting the value of autowire attribute of all the <bean> elements in the application context XML file to byType. A bean can override the default-autowire attribute's value by specifying a different value for the autowire attribute. For instance, if the default-autowire attribute's value is byType, a bean can specify that no autowiring should be performed for its properties by setting its autowire attribute's value to default/no.

So far in this section we have seen different ways in which bean dependencies can be autowired by Spring. Let's now look at how we can make a bean *unavailable* for autowiring purposes using <bean> element's autowire-candidate attribute.

Making beans unavailable for autowiring

The default behavior of the Spring container is to make beans available for autowiring. You can make a bean unavailable to other beans for autowiring purposes by setting the <bean> element's autowire-candidate attribute's value to false.

In MyBank application, the AccountStatementServiceImpl class defines a property of type AccountStatementDao. The following example listing shows the AccountStatementServiceImpl class:

Example listing 4-29 – AccountStatementServiceImpl class
Project – ch04-bankapp-autowiring
Source location - src/main/java/sample/spring/chapter04/bankapp/service

```
package sample.spring.chapter04.bankapp.service;

import sample.spring.chapter04.bankapp.dao.AccountStatementDao;
import sample.spring.chapter04.bankapp.domain.AccountStatement;

public class AccountStatementServiceImpl implements AccountStatementService {
    private AccountStatementDao accountStatementDao;

    public void setAccountStatementDao(AccountStatementDao accountStatementDao) {
```

```
        this.accountStatementDao = accountStatementDao;
    }
    .....
}
```

The following example listing shows bean definitions for AccountStatementServiceImpl and AccountStatementDaoImpl (an implementation of AccountStatementDao interface) classes:

Example listing 4-30 – applicationContext.xml - autowire-candidate attribute
Project – ch04-bankapp-autowiring
Source location - src/main/resources/META-INF/spring

```
<bean id="accountStatementService"
        class="sample.spring.chapter04.bankapp.service.AccountStatementServiceImpl"
        autowire="byType" />

<bean id="accountStatementDao"
        class="sample.spring.chapter04.bankapp.dao.AccountStatementDaoImpl"
        autowire-candidate="false" />
```

In the above example listing, the accountStatementService bean definition specifies autowire attribute's value as byType, which means the AccountStatementDao property of accountStatementService bean is autowired by Spring. As the accountStatementDao bean is of type AccountStatementDao, you might expect that Spring will inject an instance of accountStatementDao bean into accountStatementService bean. But, Spring won't consider accountStatementDao bean for autowiring purposes because the accountStatementDao bean definition specifies autowire-candidate attribute's value as false.

> You should note that a bean that is unavailable to other beans for autowiring purposes can itself make use of Spring's autowiring feature to automatically resolve its dependencies.

As mentioned earlier, the default behavior of Spring is to make beans available for autowiring purposes. To make only a select group of beans available for autowiring purposes, set <beans> element's default-autowire-candidates attribute. The default-autowire-candidates attribute specifies a bean name *pattern*, and only beans whose names match the specified pattern are made available for autowiring. The following example listing shows an example usage of default-autowire-candidates attribute:

Example listing 4-31 – default-autowire-candidates attribute example

```
<beans default-autowire-candidates="*Dao" >
    .....
    <bean id="customerRequestDetails"
        class="sample.spring.chapter04.bankapp.domain.CustomerRequestDetails"
        scope="prototype" autowire-candidate="true"/>

    <bean id="customerRequestDao"
        class="sample.spring.chapter04.bankapp.dao.CustomerRequestDaoImpl" />

    <bean id="customerRegistrationDao"
        class="sample.spring.chapter04.bankapp.dao.CustomerRegistrationDaoImpl" />
    .....
</beans>
```

In the above example listing, default-autowire-candidates value is set to *Dao, which means that beans whose names end with Dao (like customerRequestDao and customerRegistrationDao beans) will be available for autowiring purposes. If a bean name doesn't match the pattern specified by the default-autowire-candidates attribute (like customerRequestDetails bean), you can still make it available for autowiring purposes by setting its <bean> element's autowire-candidate attribute to true.

Let's now look at limitations of using autowiring in applications.

Autowiring limitations

We saw that autowiring feature saves the effort to explicitly specify bean dependencies using <property> and <constructor-arg> elements. The downsides of using autowiring feature are:

- You can't use autowiring to set properties or constructor arguments that are of simple Java types (like int, long, boolean, String, Date, and so on). You can autowire arrays, typed collections and maps if the autowire attribute's value is set to byType or constructor.
- As bean dependencies are automatically resolved by Spring, it results in hiding the overall structure of the application. If you use <property> and <constructor-arg> elements to specify bean dependencies, it results in explicitly documenting the overall structure of the application. You can easily understand and maintain an application in which bean dependencies are explicitly documented. For this reason, it is not recommended to use autowiring in large applications.

4-7 Summary

In this chapter, we looked at how Spring caters to different dependency injection scenarios. We looked at how you can use ApplicationContextAware interface, <replaced-method> and <lookup-method> sub-elements of <bean> element to programmatically retrieve a bean instance from the ApplicationContext. We also looked at how Spring's autowiring feature can save the effort for explicitly specifying bean dependencies in the application context XML file. In the next chapter, we'll look at how to customize beans and bean definitions.

Chapter 5 - *Customizing beans and bean definitions*

5-1 Introduction

So far in this book we have seen examples in which the Spring container created a bean instance based on the bean definition specified in the application context XML file. In this chapter, we'll go a step further and look at:

- how to incorporate custom initialization and destruction logic into a bean
- how to interact with a newly created bean instance by implementing Spring's BeanPostProcessor interface
- how to modify bean definitions by implementing Spring's BeanFactoryPostProcessor interface

5-2 Customizing bean's initialization and destruction logic

We saw in the earlier chapters that the Spring container is responsible for creating a bean instance and injecting its dependencies. After creating a bean instance by invoking the constructor of the bean class, the Spring container sets bean properties by invoking bean's setter methods. If you want to execute custom initialization logic (like opening a file, creating a database connection, and so on) *after* the bean properties are set but *before* the bean is completely initialized by the Spring container, specify the name of the initialization method as the value of init-method attribute of the <bean> element. Similarly, if you want to execute custom cleanup logic *before* the Spring container containing the bean instance is destroyed, you can specify the name of the cleanup method as the value of destroy-method attribute of <bean> element.

IMPORT **chapter 5/ch05-bankapp-customization** (This project shows the MyBank application that uses <bean> element's init-method and destroy-method attributes to specify custom initialization and destruction methods. To test whether the initialization method is executed, execute the main method of the BankApp class of this project. To test whether the destruction method is executed, execute the main method of the BankAppWithHook class of this project.)

The following example listing shows the MyBank's FixedDepositDaoImpl class that defines an initialization method named initializeDbConnection for obtaining a connection to MyBank's database, and a destruction method named releaseDbConnection for releasing the connection:

Example listing 5-1 – FixedDepositDaoImpl class - Custom initialization and destruction logic
Project – ch05-bankapp-customization
Source location - src/main/java/sample/spring/chapter05/bankapp/dao

```
package sample.spring.chapter05.bankapp.dao;

public class FixedDepositDaoImpl implements FixedDepositDao {
    private static Logger logger = LogManager.getLogger(FixedDepositDaoImpl.class);
    private DatabaseConnection connection;

    public FixedDepositDaoImpl() {
        logger.info("FixedDepositDaoImpl's constructor invoked");
    }

    public void initializeDbConnection() {
        logger.info("FixedDepositDaoImpl's initializeDbConnection method invoked");
        connection = DatabaseConnection.getInstance();
    }
```

```
    public boolean createFixedDeposit(FixedDepositDetails fixedDepositDetails) {
        logger.info("FixedDepositDaoImpl's createFixedDeposit method invoked");
        // -- save the fixed deposits and then return true
        return true;
    }

    public void releaseDbConnection() {
        logger.info("FixedDepositDaoImpl's releaseDbConnection method invoked");
        connection.releaseConnection();
    }
}
```

In the above example listing, the DatabaseConnection object is used for interacting with the MyBank's database. FixedDepositDaoImpl class defines an initializeDbConnection method that initializes the DatabaseConnection object, which is later used by the createFixedDeposit method for saving fixed deposit details in the MyBank's database.

The following example listing shows the MyBank's FixedDepositServiceImpl class that uses FixedDepositDaoImpl instance to create new fixed deposits:

Example listing 5-2 – FixedDepositServiceImpl class
Project – ch05-bankapp-customization
Source location - src/main/java/sample/spring/chapter05/bankapp/service

```
package sample.spring.chapter05.bankapp.service;

public class FixedDepositServiceImpl implements FixedDepositService {
    private static Logger logger = LogManager.getLogger(FixedDepositServiceImpl.class);
    private FixedDepositDao myFixedDepositDao;

    public void setMyFixedDepositDao(FixedDepositDao myFixedDepositDao) {
        logger.info("FixedDepositServiceImpl's setMyFixedDepositDao method invoked");
        this.myFixedDepositDao = myFixedDepositDao;
    }

    @Override
    public void createFixedDeposit(FixedDepositDetails fixedDepositDetails)
          throws Exception {
        // -- create fixed deposit
        myFixedDepositDao.createFixedDeposit(fixedDepositDetails);
    }
}
```

The above example listing shows that the FixedDepositDaoImpl instance is a dependency of FixedDepositServiceImpl, and is passed as an argument to the setMyFixedDepositDao setter-method. And, if FixedDepositServiceImpl's createFixedDeposit method is invoked, it results in invocation of FixedDepositDaoImpl's createFixedDeposit method.

The following example listing shows bean definitions for FixedDepositDaoImpl and FixedDepositServiceImpl classes:

Example listing 5-3 – applicationContext.xml – usage of init-method and destroy-method attributes
Project – ch05-bankapp-customization
Source location - src/main/resources/META-INF/spring

```
<beans .....>
    <bean id="fixedDepositService"
```

```
        class="sample.spring.chapter05.bankapp.service.FixedDepositServiceImpl">
      <property name="myFixedDepositDao" ref="myFixedDepositDao" />
  </bean>

  <bean id="myFixedDepositDao"
      class="sample.spring.chapter05.bankapp.dao.FixedDepositDaoImpl"
      init-method="initializeDbConnection" destroy-method="releaseDbConnection" />
</beans>
```

The above example listing shows that the <bean> element corresponding to the FixedDepositDaoImpl class specifies initializeDbConnection and releaseDbConnection as the values of init-method and destroy-method attributes, respectively.

> It is important to note that the initialization and destruction methods specified by init-method and destroy-method attributes of <bean> element *must not* accept any arguments, but can be defined to throw exceptions.

The following example listing shows BankApp class whose main method retrieves FixedDepositServiceImpl instance from the ApplicationContext and invokes FixedDepositServiceImpl's createFixedDeposit method:

Example listing 5-4 – BankApp class
Project – ch05-bankapp-customization
Source location - src/main/java/sample/spring/chapter05/bankapp

```
package sample.spring.chapter05.bankapp;

public class BankApp {
    public static void main(String args[]) throws Exception {
        ApplicationContext context = new ClassPathXmlApplicationContext(
                "classpath:META-INF/spring/applicationContext.xml");

        FixedDepositService fixedDepositService =
            context.getBean(FixedDepositService.class);
        fixedDepositService.createFixedDeposit(new FixedDepositDetails(1, 1000, 12,
            "someemail@somedomain.com"));
    }
}
```

If you now execute the BankApp's main method, you'll see the following output on the console:

```
FixedDepositDaoImpl's constructor invoked
FixedDepositDaoImpl's initializeDbConnection method invoked
FixedDepositServiceImpl's setMyFixedDepositDao method invoked
FixedDepositDaoImpl's createFixedDeposit method invoked
```

The above output shows that the Spring container creates an instance of FixedDepositDaoImpl and invokes its initializeDbConnection method. After the invocation of initializeDbConnection method, the FixedDepositDaoImpl instance is injected into the FixedDepositServiceImpl instance. This shows that the Spring container injects a dependency (the FixedDepositDaoImpl instance) into the dependent bean (the FixedDepositServiceImpl instance) *after* the initialization method of the dependency is invoked by the Spring container.

You may have noticed that the output from executing BankApp's main method didn't contain the following message: FixedDepositDaoImpl's releaseDbConnection method invoked (refer FixedDepositDaoImpl's releaseDbConnection method in example listing 5-1). This means that the FixedDepositDaoImpl's releaseDbConnection method was *not* called by the Spring container when BankApp's main method exited. In a real world application development scenario, this means that the database connection held by the FixedDepositDaoImpl instance is never released.

Let's now see how you can make Spring gracefully destroy singleton bean instances by calling the cleanup method specified by the <bean> element's destroy-method attribute.

Making Spring invoke cleanup method specified by the destroy-method attribute

The web version of ApplicationContext implementation is represented by Spring's WebApplicationContext object. WebApplicationContext implementation has the necessary logic to invoke the cleanup method (specified by the destroy-method attribute) of singleton bean instances *before* the web application is shutdown.

> The approach described in this section on making Spring gracefully destroy singleton bean instances by calling the cleanup method is specific to standalone applications.

The following example listing shows the BankAppWithHook class (a modified version of BankApp class shown in example listing 5-4) whose main method ensures that cleanup methods (specified by <bean> element's destroy-method attribute) of all singleton beans registered with the Spring container are invoked when the main method exits:

Example listing 5-5 – BankAppWithHook class – registering a shutdown hook with JVM
Project – ch05-bankapp-customization
Source location - src/main/java/sample/spring/chapter05/bankapp

```
package sample.spring.chapter05.bankapp;

public class BankAppWithHook {
    public static void main(String args[]) throws Exception {
        ConfigurableApplicationContext context = new ClassPathXmlApplicationContext(
                "classpath:META-INF/spring/applicationContext.xml");
        context.registerShutdownHook();

        FixedDepositService fixedDepositService =
            context.getBean(FixedDepositService.class);
        fixedDepositService.createFixedDeposit(new FixedDepositDetails(1, 1000, 12,
            "someemail@somedomain.com"));
    }
}
```

Spring's ConfigurableApplicationContext (a sub-interface of ApplicationContext) defines a registerShutdownHook method that registers a shutdown hook with the JVM. The shutdown hook is responsible for closing the ApplicationContext when the JVM is shutdown. In the above example listing, you'll notice that the ClassPathXmlApplicationContext instance is assigned to ConfigurableApplicationContext type, and the ConfigurableApplicationContext's registerShutdownHook is called to register a shutdown hook with the JVM. When the BankAppWithHook's main method exists, the shutdown hook destroys all cached singleton bean instances and closes the ApplicationContext instance.

If you execute BankAppWithHook's main method of ch05-bankapp-customization project, you'll see the following output on the console:

```
FixedDepositDaoImpl's constructor invoked
```

```
FixedDepositDaoImpl's initializeDbConnection method invoked
FixedDepositServiceImpl's setMyFixedDepositDao method invoked
FixedDepositDaoImpl's createFixedDeposit method invoked
FixedDepositDaoImpl's releaseDbConnection method invoked
```

The message 'FixedDepositDaoImpl's releaseDbConnection method invoked' on the console confirms that the FixedDepositDaoImpl's releaseDbConnection method (refer example listing 5-1) was invoked. As you can see, registering a shutdown hook with the JVM resulted in invocation of the cleanup method of the singleton-scoped myFixedDepositDao bean (corresponding to the FixedDepositDaoImpl class).

> An alternative to using the registerShutdownHook method is to use ConfigurableApplicationContext's close method, which you can call to explicitly close the ApplicationContext.

Let's now look at what happens to prototype beans when the ApplicationContext is closed.

Cleanup methods and prototype beans

In the case of prototype-scoped beans, destroy-method attribute is ignored by the Spring container. The destroy-method attribute is ignored because the Spring container expects that the object that fetches the prototype bean instance from the ApplicationContext is responsible for explicitly calling the cleanup method on the prototype bean instance.

> Lifecycles of prototype- and singleton-scoped beans are same, except that the Spring container will *not* call the cleanup method (specified by the destroy-method attribute) of the prototype-scoped bean instance.

Let's now look at how you can specify default initialization and destruction methods for all the beans contained in the application context XML file.

Specifying default bean initialization and destruction methods for all beans

You can use the default-init-method and default-destroy-method attributes of <beans> element to specify default initialization and destruction methods for beans, as shown in the following example listing:

Example listing 5-6 – default-init-method and default-destroy-method attributes

```
<beans  ..... default-init-method="initialize" default-destroy-method="release">
    <bean id="A" class="....." init-method="initializeService" />
    <bean id="B" class="....." />
</beans>
```

If multiple beans define initialization or cleanup methods with the same name, it makes sense to use default-init-method and default-destroy-method attributes. By specifying init-method and destroy-method attributes, a <bean> element can override the values specified by <beans> element's default-init-method and default-destroy-method attributes. For instance, in the above example listing, bean A specifies the init-method attribute's value as initializeService, which means the initializeService method (and *not* the initialize method specified by the default-init-method attribute of <beans> element) is the initialization method of bean A.

Instead of using init-method and destroy-method attributes of <bean> element to specify custom initialization and destruction methods, you can use Spring's InitializingBean and DisposableBean lifecycle interfaces.

InitializingBean and DisposableBean lifecycle interfaces

A bean that implements lifecycle interfaces, like ApplicationContextAware (refer section 4-5 of chapter 4), InitializingBean and DisposableBean, receives callbacks from the Spring container. These callbacks give an opportunity to the bean instance to perform some action, or they provide information required by the bean instance. For instance, if a bean implements ApplicationContextAware interface, container invokes setApplicationContext method of the bean instance to provide the bean with a reference to the ApplicationContext in which the bean is deployed.

InitializingBean interface defines an afterPropertiesSet method that is invoked by the Spring container after the bean properties are set. Beans perform initialization work in the afterPropertiesSet method, like obtaining connection to a database, opening a flat file for reading, and so on. DisposableBean interface defines a destroy method that is invoked by the Spring container when the bean instance is destroyed.

As with the ApplicationContextAware lifecycle interface, beans should avoid implementing InitializingBean and DisposableBean interfaces because it couples application code with Spring.

Let's now look at JSR 250's @PostConstruct and @PreDestroy annotations for specifying bean initialization and destruction methods.

JSR 250's @PostConstruct and @PreDestroy annotations

JSR 250 (Common Annotations for the Java Platform) defines standard annotations that are used across different Java technologies. JSR 250's @PostConstruct and @PreDestroy annotations identify initialization and destruction methods of an object. A bean class in Spring can set a method as an initialization method by annotating it with @PostConstruct, and set a method as a destruction method by annotating it with @PreDestroy annotation.

Refer JSR 250 home page (http://jcp.org/en/jsr/detail?id=250) for more details.

IMPORT chapter 5/ch05-bankapp-jsr250 (This project shows the MyBank application that uses JSR 250's @PostConstruct and @PreDestroy annotations to identify custom initialization and destruction methods, respectively. To test whether the initialization method is executed, execute the main method of the BankApp class of this project. To test whether the destruction method is executed, execute the main method of the BankAppWithHook class of this project.)

The following example listing shows the FixedDepositDaoImpl class of ch05-bankapp-jsr250 project that uses @PostConstruct and @PreDestroy annotations:

Example listing 5-7 – FixedDepositDaoImpl class - @PostConstruct and @PreDestroy annotations
Project – ch05-bankapp-jsr250
Source location - src/main/java/sample/spring/chapter05/bankapp/dao

```
package sample.spring.chapter05.bankapp.dao;

import javax.annotation.PostConstruct;
import javax.annotation.PreDestroy;

public class FixedDepositDaoImpl implements FixedDepositDao {
    private DatabaseConnection connection;
    .....
    @PostConstruct
    public void initializeDbConnection() {
        logger.info("FixedDepositDaoImpl's initializeDbConnection method invoked");
        connection = DatabaseConnection.getInstance();
```

```
    }
    .....
    @PreDestroy
    public void releaseDbConnection() {
        logger.info("FixedDepositDaoImpl's releaseDbConnection method invoked");
        connection.releaseConnection();
    }
}
```

In the above example listing, the FixedDepositDaoImpl class uses @PostConstruct and @PreDestroy annotations to identify initialization and destruction methods. As of Java 9, @PostConstruct and @PreDestroy annotations are no longer part of Java SE. For this reason, ch05-bankapp-jsr250 project defines dependency on jsr250-api JAR file.

To use @PostConstruct and @PreDestroy annotations in your Spring application, you need to configure Spring's CommonAnnotationBeanPostProcessor class in the application context XML file, as shown here:

Example listing 5-8 – applicationContext.xml – CommonAnnotationBeanPostProcessor configuration
Project – ch05-bankapp-jsr250
Source location - src/main/resources/META-INF/spring

```
<beans .....>
   <bean id="fixedDepositService"
         class="sample.spring.chapter05.bankapp.service.FixedDepositServiceImpl">
       <property name="myFixedDepositDao" ref="myFixedDepositDao" />
   </bean>

   <bean id="myFixedDepositDao"
       class="sample.spring.chapter05.bankapp.dao.FixedDepositDaoImpl" />

   <bean class="org.springframework.context.annotation.CommonAnnotationBeanPostProcessor"/>
</beans>
```

CommonAnnotationBeanPostProcessor implements Spring's BeanPostProcessor interface (explained in the next section), and is responsible for processing JSR 250 annotations.

If you execute the main method of BankApp and BankAppWithHook classes, you'll notice that the @PostConstruct and @PreDestroy annotated methods of FixedDepositDaoImpl class are executed at creation and destruction of FixedDepositDaoImpl instance, respectively.

We'll now look at Spring's BeanPostProcessor interface that allows you to interact with newly created bean instances *before* and/or *after* they are initialized by the Spring container.

5-3 Interacting with newly created bean instances using a BeanPostProcessor

A BeanPostProcessor is used to interact with newly created bean instances *before* and/or *after* their initialization method is invoked by the Spring container. You can also use a BeanPostProcessor to execute custom logic *before* and/or *after* a bean's initialization method is invoked by the Spring container.

> A bean that implements Spring's BeanPostProcessor interface is a special bean type; the Spring container automatically detects and executes a BeanPostProcessor bean.

BeanPostProcessor interface defines the following methods:

- `Object postProcessBeforeInitialization(Object bean, String beanName)` – this method is invoked *before* the initialization method of a bean instance is invoked
- `Object postProcessAfterInitialization(Object bean, String beanName)` – this method is invoked *after* the initialization method of a bean instance is invoked

`BeanPostProcessor`'s methods accept the newly created bean instance and its name as arguments, and they may return the same or modified bean instance. For instance, if you have configured a `FixedDepositDaoImpl` class as a bean with `id` value as `myFixedDepositDao` (refer example listing 5-8), the `BeanPostProcessor`'s methods receive an instance of `FixedDepositDaoImpl` class and 'myFixedDepositDao' string value as arguments. The `BeanPostProcessor`'s methods may return the original bean instance as-is or a modified bean instance or an object that wraps the original bean instance.

You configure a `BeanPostProcessor` implementation in the application context XML file like any other Spring bean. Spring container automatically detects beans that implement the `BeanPostProcessor` interface, and creates their instance *before* creating instance of any other bean defined in the application context XML file. Once the `BeanPostProcessor` beans are created, the Spring container invokes `BeanPostProcessor`'s `postProcessBeforeInitialization` and `postProcessAfterInitialization` methods for each bean instance created by the Spring container.

Let's say that you have defined a singleton bean `ABean` and a `BeanPostProcessor` bean, `MyBeanPostProcessor`, in the application context XML file. Figure 5-1 shows a sequence diagram that depicts the sequence in which `MyBeanPostProcessor`'s methods are invoked by the Spring container.

The `init` method call in the sequence diagram represents a call to the initialization method of a bean. The sequence diagram shows that the `MyBeanPostProcessor` instance is created before the `ABean` bean instance. As a `BeanPostProcessor` implementation is configured like any other bean, if `MyBeanPostProcessor` defines an initialization method, container invokes the initialization method of the `MyBeanPostProcessor` instance. After `ABean`'s instance is created, setter methods of the `ABean` instance are invoked by the Spring container to satisfy its dependencies and to provide the bean instance with the required configuration information. After properties are set, but *before* `ABean`'s initialization method is invoked, the Spring container invokes `MyBeanPostProcessor`'s `postProcessBeforeInitialization` method. After `ABean`'s initialization method is invoked, `MyBeanPostProcessor`'s `postProcessAfterInitialization` method is called by the Spring container.

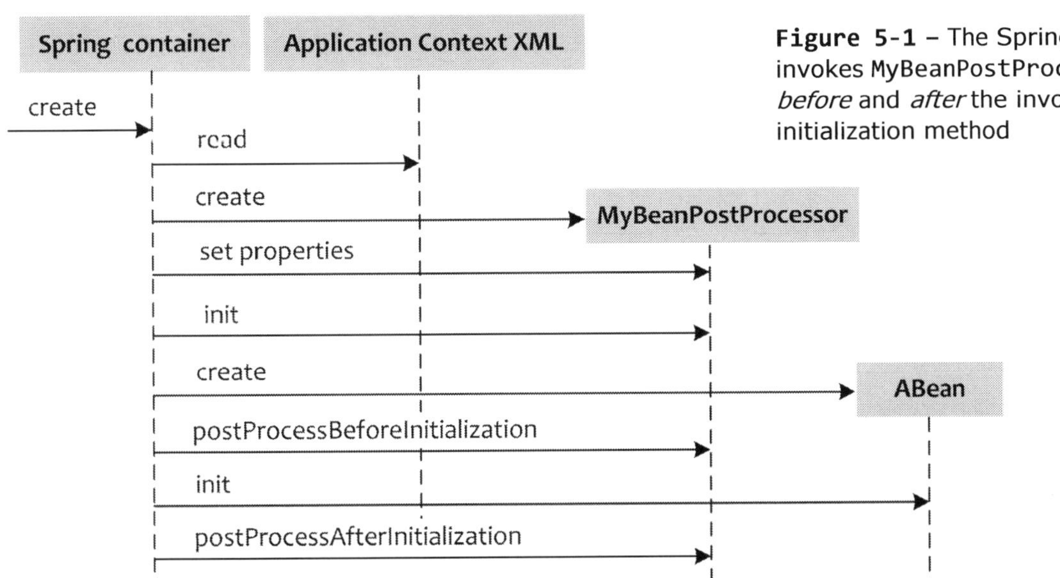

Figure 5-1 – The Spring container invokes `MyBeanPostProcessor`'s methods *before* and *after* the invocation of `ABean`'s initialization method

It's only after the invocation of postProcessAfterInitialization method that a bean instance is considered completely initialized by the Spring container. For this reason, if a ABean bean is dependent on BBean, container will inject BBean instance into ABean only after MyBeanPostProcessor's postProcessAfterInitialization method has been invoked for BBean instance.

You should note that if the bean definition for a BeanPostProcessor bean specifies that it should be lazily created (refer <bean> element's lazy-init attribute or <beans> element's default-lazy-init attribute in section 2-6 of chapter 2), the Spring container ignores lazy initialization configuration and creates the BeanPostProcessor bean instance *before* creating instances of singleton-scoped beans defined in the application context XML file. You should note that the beans that implement the BeanFactoryPostProcessor interface (explained in section 5-4 of chapter 5) are created *before* the beans that implement the BeanPostProcessor interface.

Let's now look at some example scenarios in which you can use Spring's BeanPostProcessor.

IMPORT **chapter 5/ch05-bankapp-beanpostprocessor** (This project shows the MyBank application that uses BeanPostProcessor implementations to validate bean instances and to resolve bean dependencies. To verify that the BeanPostProcessor implementations function correctly, execute the main method of the BankApp class of this project.)

BeanPostProcessor example – Validating bean instances

In a Spring application, you may want to verify that a bean instance is configured correctly *before* it is injected into dependent beans or accessed by other objects in the application. Let's see how we can use a BeanPostProcessor implementation to give an opportunity to each bean instance to validate its configuration before the bean instance is made available to dependent beans or other application objects.

The following example listing shows the MyBank's InstanceValidator interface that *must* be implemented by beans whose configurations we want to validate using a BeanPostProcessor implementation:

Example listing 5-9 – InstanceValidator interface
Project – ch05-bankapp-beanpostprocessor
Source location - src/main/java/sample/spring/chapter05/bankapp/common

```
package sample.spring.chapter05.bankapp.common;

public interface InstanceValidator {
    void validateInstance();
}
```

InstanceValidator interface defines a validateInstance method that verifies whether the bean instance was correctly initialized or not. We'll soon see that the validateInstance method is invoked by a BeanPostProcessor implementation.

The following example listing shows the FixedDepositDaoImpl class that implements the InstanceValidator interface:

Example listing 5-10 – FixedDepositDaoImpl class
Project – ch05-bankapp-beanpostprocessor
Source location - src/main/java/sample/spring/chapter05/bankapp/dao

```
package sample.spring.chapter05.bankapp.dao;

import sample.spring.chapter05.bankapp.common.InstanceValidator;

public class FixedDepositDaoImpl implements FixedDepositDao, InstanceValidator {
```

```
    private static Logger logger = LogManager.getLogger(FixedDepositDaoImpl.class);
    private DatabaseConnection connection;

    public FixedDepositDaoImpl() {
        logger.info("FixedDepositDaoImpl's constructor invoked");
    }

    public void initializeDbConnection() {
        logger.info("FixedDepositDaoImpl's initializeDbConnection method invoked");
        connection = DatabaseConnection.getInstance();
    }

    @Override
    public void validateInstance() {
        logger.info("Validating FixedDepositDaoImpl instance");
        if(connection == null) {
            logger.error("Failed to obtain DatabaseConnection instance");
        }
    }
}
```

In the above example listing, the initializeDbConnection method is the initialization method that retrieves an instance of DatabaseConnection by calling getInstance *static* method of DatabaseConnection class. The connection attribute is null if FixedDepositDaoImpl instance fails to retrieve an instance of DatabaseConnection. If connection attribute is null, the validateInstance method logs an error message indicating that the FixedDepositDaoImpl instance is not correctly initialized. As the initializeDbConnection initialization method sets the value of connection attribute, the validateInstance method *must* be invoked *after* the initializeDbConnection method. In a real world application development scenario, if a bean instance is not configured correctly, the validateInstance method may take some corrective action or throw a runtime exception to stop the application from starting up. For simplicity's sake, the validateInstance method logs an error message if a bean instance is not configured correctly.

The following example listing shows the InstanceValidationBeanPostProcessor class that implements Spring's BeanPostProcessor interface, and is responsible for invoking validateInstance method of newly created beans:

Example listing 5-11 – InstanceValidationBeanPostProcessor class
Project – ch05-bankapp-beanpostprocessor
Source location - src/main/java/sample/spring/chapter05/bankapp/postprocessor

```
package sample.spring.chapter05.bankapp.postprocessor;

import org.springframework.beans.BeansException;
import org.springframework.beans.factory.config.BeanPostProcessor;
import org.springframework.core.Ordered;

public class InstanceValidationBeanPostProcessor implements BeanPostProcessor, Ordered {
    private static Logger logger =
         LogManager.getLogger(InstanceValidationBeanPostProcessor.class);
    private int order;

    public InstanceValidationBeanPostProcessor() {
        logger.info("Created InstanceValidationBeanPostProcessor instance");
    }
```

```
    @Override
    public Object postProcessBeforeInitialization(Object bean, String beanName)
            throws BeansException {
        logger.info("postProcessBeforeInitialization method invoked");
        return bean;
    }

    @Override
    public Object postProcessAfterInitialization(Object bean, String beanName)
            throws BeansException {
        logger.info("postProcessAfterInitialization method invoked");
        if (bean instanceof InstanceValidator) {
            ((InstanceValidator) bean).validateInstance();
        }
        return bean;
    }

    public void setOrder(int order) {
        this.order = order;
    }

    @Override
    public int getOrder() {
        return order;
    }
}
```

The above example listing shows that the `InstanceValidationBeanPostProcessor` class implements Spring's `BeanPostProcessor` and `Ordered` interfaces. The `postProcessBeforeInitialization` method simply returns the bean instance passed to the method. In the `postProcessAfterInitialization` method, if the bean instance is found to be of type `InstanceValidator`, the bean instance's `validateInstance` method is invoked. This means that if a bean implements `InstanceValidator` interface, `InstanceValidationBeanPostProcessor` calls the `validateInstance` method of the bean instance *after* the initialization method of the bean instance is invoked by the Spring container.

The `Ordered` interface defines a `getOrder` method which returns an integer value. The integer value returned by the `getOrder` method determines the priority of a `BeanPostProcessor` implementation with respect to other `BeanPostProcessor` implementations configured in the application context XML file. A `BeanPostProcessor` with *higher* order value is considered at a *lower* priority, and is executed *after* the `BeanPostProcessor` implementations with *lower* order values are executed. As we want the integer value returned by the `getOrder` method to be configured as a bean property, a `setOrder` method and an `order` instance variable are defined in the `InstanceValidationBeanPostProcessor` class.

The following example listing shows bean definition for `InstanceValidationBeanPostProcessor` class:

Example listing 5-12 – `InstanceValidationBeanPostProcessor` bean definition
Project – `ch05-bankapp-beanpostprocessor`
Source location - `src/main/resources/META-INF/spring`

```
<bean class="...bankapp.postprocessor.InstanceValidationBeanPostProcessor">
    <property name="order" value="1" />
</bean>
```

In the above bean definition, `<bean>` element's `id` attribute is *not* specified because we typically don't want a `BeanPostProcessor` to be a dependency of any other bean. The `<property>` element sets the value of `order` property to `1`.

Let's now look at a BeanPostProcessor implementation that is used for resolving bean dependencies.

BeanPostProcessor example – Resolving bean dependencies

In chapter 4, we saw that if a bean implements Spring's ApplicationContextAware interface, it can programmatically obtain bean instances using ApplicationContext's getBean method. Implementing the ApplicationContextAware interface couples the application code with Spring; therefore, it is not recommended to implement ApplicationContextAware interface. In this section, we'll look at a BeanPostProcessor implementation that provides beans with an object that wraps an ApplicationContext instance, resulting in application code that is *not* directly dependent on ApplicationContextAware and ApplicationContext interfaces of Spring.

The following example listing shows the MyBank's DependencyResolver interface that is implemented by beans who want to programmatically retrieve their dependencies from the ApplicationContext:

Example listing 5-13 – DependencyResolver interface
Project – ch05-bankapp-beanpostprocessor
Source location - src/main/java/sample/spring/chapter05/bankapp/common

```
package sample.spring.chapter05.bankapp.common;

public interface DependencyResolver {
    void resolveDependency(MyApplicationContext myApplicationContext);
}
```

DependencyResolver defines a resolveDependency method that accepts a MyApplicationContext object – a wrapper around ApplicationContext object. We'll soon see that the resolveDependency method is invoked by a BeanPostProcessor implementation.

The following example listing shows the FixedDepositServiceImpl class that implements the DependencyResolver interface:

Example listing 5-14 – FixedDepositServiceImpl class
Project – ch05-bankapp-beanpostprocessor
Source location - src/main/java/sample/spring/chapter05/bankapp/service

```
package sample.spring.chapter05.bankapp.service;

import sample.spring.chapter05.bankapp.common.DependencyResolver;
import sample.spring.chapter05.bankapp.common.MyApplicationContext;

public class FixedDepositServiceImpl implements FixedDepositService, DependencyResolver {
    private FixedDepositDao fixedDepositDao;
    .....
    @Override
    public void resolveDependency(MyApplicationContext myApplicationContext) {
        fixedDepositDao = myApplicationContext.getBean(FixedDepositDao.class);
    }
}
```

FixedDepositServiceImpl defines a fixedDepositDao attribute of type FixedDepositDao. The resolveDependency method obtains an instance of FixedDepositDao object from MyApplicationContext (a wrapper around Spring's ApplicationContext object) and assigns it to the fixedDepositDao attribute.

The following example listing shows the DependencyResolutionBeanPostProcessor class that invokes resolveDependency method of beans that implement the DependencyResolver interface:

Example listing 5-15 – DependencyResolutionBeanPostProcessor class
Project – ch05-bankapp-beanpostprocessor
Source location - src/main/java/sample/spring/chapter05/bankapp/postprocessor

```
package sample.spring.chapter05.bankapp.postprocessor;

import org.springframework.beans.factory.config.BeanPostProcessor;
import org.springframework.core.Ordered;
import sample.spring.chapter05.bankapp.common.MyApplicationContext;

public class DependencyResolutionBeanPostProcessor implements BeanPostProcessor, Ordered {
    private MyApplicationContext myApplicationContext;
    private int order;

    public void setMyApplicationContext(MyApplicationContext myApplicationContext) {
        this.myApplicationContext = myApplicationContext;
    }

    public void setOrder(int order) {
        this.order = order;
    }


    @Override
    public int getOrder() {
        return order;
    }

    @Override
    public Object postProcessBeforeInitialization(Object bean, String beanName)
            throws BeansException {
        if (bean instanceof DependencyResolver) {
            ((DependencyResolver) bean).resolveDependency(myApplicationContext);
        }
        return bean;
    }

    @Override
    public Object postProcessAfterInitialization(Object bean, String beanName)
            throws BeansException {
        return bean;
    }
}
```

DependencyResolutionBeanPostProcessor implements Spring's BeanPostProcessor and Ordered interfaces. The myApplicationContext attribute (of type MyApplicationContext) represents a dependency of DependencyResolutionBeanPostProcessor. The postProcessBeforeInitialization method invokes resolveDependency method of beans that implement the DependencyResolver interface, passing the MyApplicationContext object as an argument. The postProcessAfterInitialization method simply returns the bean instance passed to the method.

The following example listing shows the MyApplicationContext class that acts as a wrapper around Spring's ApplicationContext object:

Example listing 5-16 – MyApplicationContext class
Project – ch05-bankapp-beanpostprocessor
Location - src/main/java/sample/spring/chapter05/bankapp/common

```
package sample.spring.chapter05.bankapp.common;

import org.springframework.context.ApplicationContext;
import org.springframework.context.ApplicationContextAware;

public class MyApplicationContext implements ApplicationContextAware {
    private ApplicationContext applicationContext;

    @Override
    public void setApplicationContext(ApplicationContext applicationContext)
            throws BeansException {
        this.applicationContext = applicationContext;
    }

    public <T> T getBean(Class<T> klass) {
        return applicationContext.getBean(klass);
    }
}
```

The MyApplicationContext class implements Spring's ApplicationContextAware interface to obtain reference to the ApplicationContext object in which the bean is deployed. The MyApplicationContext class defines a getBean method that returns a bean instance with the given name from the ApplicationContext instance.

The following example listing shows the bean definitions for DependencyResolutionBeanPostProcessor and MyApplicationContext classes:

Example listing 5-17 – applicationContext.xml
Project – ch05-bankapp-beanpostprocessor
Source location - src/main/resources/META-INF/spring

```
    <bean class=".....postprocessor.DependencyResolutionBeanPostProcessor">
        <property name="myApplicationContext" ref="myApplicationContext" />
        <property name="order" value="0" />
    </bean>

    <bean id="myApplicationContext" class=".....bankapp.common.MyApplicationContext" />
```

The bean definition for DependencyResolutionBeanPostProcessor class shows that its order property value is set to 0. Example listing 5-12 showed that the InstanceValidationBeanPostProcessor's order property value was set to 1. As *lower* order property value means *higher* priority, the Spring container applies DependencyResolutionBeanPostProcessor to a bean instance *before* the InstanceValidationBeanPostProcessor.

The following example listing shows the main method of BankApp class that checks the functionality of DependencyResolutionBeanPostProcessor and InstanceValidationBeanPostProcessor:

Example listing 5-18 – BankApp class
Project – bankapp-beanpostprocessor
Location - src/main/java/sample/spring/chapter05/bankapp

```
package sample.spring.chapter05.bankapp;
```

```
public class BankApp {
    public static void main(String args[]) throws Exception {
        ConfigurableApplicationContext context = new ClassPathXmlApplicationContext(
                "classpath:META-INF/spring/applicationContext.xml");

        FixedDepositService fixedDepositService =
            context.getBean(FixedDepositService.class);
        fixedDepositService.createFixedDeposit(new FixedDepositDetails(1, 1000, 12,
             "someemail@somedomain.com"));
        .....
    }
}
```

BankApp's main method retrieves an instance of fixedDepositService from the ApplicationContext and executes FixedDepositService's createFixedDeposit method. When you execute BankApp's main method, you'll notice that the Spring container creates instances of DependencyResolutionBeanPostProcessor and InstanceValidationBeanPostProcessor beans *before* creating an instance of any other bean defined in the application context XML file. And, the DependencyResolutionBeanPostProcessor (order value 0) is applied to a newly created bean instance *before* the InstanceValidationBeanPostProcessor (order value 1) is applied.

You should note that the Spring container doesn't apply a BeanPostProcessor implementation to other BeanPostProcessor implementations. For instance, in the MyBank application, DependencyResolutionBeanPostProcessor's postProcessBeforeInitialization and postProcessAfterInitialization methods are *not* invoked by the Spring container when an instance of InstanceValidationBeanPostProcessor is created.

Let's now look at the behavior of a BeanPostProcessor implementation for a bean that implements the FactoryBean interface.

BeanPostProcessor behavior for FactoryBeans

In section 3-9 of chapter 3, we discussed that a bean that implements Spring's FactoryBean interface represents a factory for creating bean instances. In this section, we'll see that a BeanPostProcessor's postProcessBeforeInitialization and postProcessAfterInitialization methods are invoked when a FactoryBean instance is created by the Spring container. And, *only* postProcessAfterInitialization method is invoked for bean instances created by a FactoryBean.

The following example listing shows the EventSenderFactoryBean (a FactoryBean implementation) class of MyBank application that creates instances of EventSender bean:

Example listing 5-19 – EventSenderFactoryBean class
Project – ch05-bankapp-beanpostprocessor
Location - src/main/java/sample/spring/chapter05/bankapp/factory

```
package sample.spring.chapter05.bankapp.factory;

import org.springframework.beans.factory.FactoryBean;
import org.springframework.beans.factory.InitializingBean;

public class EventSenderFactoryBean implements FactoryBean<EventSender>, InitializingBean {
    .....
    @Override
    public EventSender getObject() throws Exception {
        logger.info("getObject method of EventSenderFactoryBean invoked");
```

```
        return new EventSender();
    }

    @Override
    public Class<?> getObjectType() {
        return EventSender.class;
    }

    @Override
    public boolean isSingleton() {
        return false;
    }

    @Override
    public void afterPropertiesSet() throws Exception {
        logger.info("afterPropertiesSet method of EventSenderFactoryBean invoked");
    }
}
```

EventSenderFactoryBean class implements Spring's InitializingBean and FactoryBean interfaces. The getObject method returns an instance of EventSender object. As the isSingleton method returns false, EventSenderFactoryBean's getObject method is invoked each time EventSenderFactoryBean receives request for an EventSender object.

The following example listing shows the main method of BankApp class of ch05-bankapp-beanpostprocessor project that retrieves EventSender instances from the EventSenderFactoryBean:

Example listing 5-20 – BankApp class
Project – ch05-bankapp-beanpostprocessor
Location - src/main/java/sample/spring/chapter05/bankapp

```
package sample.spring.chapter05.bankapp;

public class BankApp {
    public static void main(String args[]) throws Exception {
        ConfigurableApplicationContext context = new ClassPathXmlApplicationContext(
                "classpath:META-INF/spring/applicationContext.xml");
        .....
        context.getBean("eventSenderFactory");
        context.getBean("eventSenderFactory");
        context.close();
    }
}
```

In the above example listing, the ApplicationContext's getBean method is called twice to retrieve two distinct EventSender instances from the EventSenderFactoryBean. If you execute BankApp's main method, you'll see the following messages on the console:

```
Created EventSenderFactoryBean
DependencyResolutionBeanPostProcessor's postProcessBeforeInitialization method invoked
for.....EventSenderFactoryBean
InstanceValidationBeanPostProcessor's postProcessBeforeInitialization method invoked for
.....EventSenderFactoryBean
afterPropertiesSet method of EventSenderFactoryBean invoked
```

```
DependencyResolutionBeanPostProcessor's postProcessAfterInitialization method invoked for.....EventSenderFactoryBean
InstanceValidationBeanPostProcessor's postProcessAfterInitialization method invoked for bean .....EventSenderFactoryBean
```

The above output shows that a BeanPostProcessor's postProcessBeforeInitialization and postProcessAfterInitialization methods are invoked for the EventSenderFactoryBean instance created by the Spring container.

Execution of BankApp's main method also shows the following output on the console:

```
getObject method of EventSenderFactoryBean invoked
DependencyResolutionBeanPostProcessor's postProcessAfterInitialization method invoked for.....EventSender
getObject method of EventSenderFactoryBean invoked
DependencyResolutionBeanPostProcessor's postProcessAfterInitialization method invoked for.....EventSender
```

The above output shows that *only* the postProcessAfterInitialization method of a BeanPostProcessor is invoked for the EventSender instance created by the EventSenderFactoryBean. If you want, you can make modifications to an EventSender instance in the postProcessAfterInitialization method.

Let's now look at Spring's built-in RequiredAnnotationBeanPostProcessor that you can use to ensure that *required* (or mandatory) bean properties are configured in the application context XML file.

RequiredAnnotationBeanPostProcessor

If the setter-method for a bean property is annotated with Spring's @Required annotation, Spring's RequiredAnnotationBeanPostProcessor (a BeanPostProcessor implementation) checks if the bean property is configured in the application context XML file.

> You should note that the RequiredAnnotationBeanPostProcessor is not automatically registered with the Spring container, you need to register it explicitly by defining it in the application context XML file.

The following example listing shows an example usage of @Required annotation:

Example listing 5-21 – @Required annotation usage

```
import org.springframework.beans.factory.annotation.Required;

public class FixedDepositServiceImpl implements FixedDepositService {
    private FixedDepositDao fixedDepositDao;

    @Required
    public void setFixedDepositDao(FixedDepositDao fixedDepositDao) {
        this.fixedDepositDao = fixedDepositDao;
    }
    .....
}
```

In the above example listing, the setFixedDepositDao setter-method for fixedDepositDao property is annotated with @Required annotation. If you have defined RequiredAnnotationBeanPostProcessor in the application context XML file, the RequiredAnnotationBeanPostProcessor will check if you have specified a <property> element (or used p-namespace) to set the value of fixedDepositDao property. If you haven't configured the fixedDepositDao property in the application context XML file, it'll result in an exception. This shows that you can use RequiredAnnotationBeanPostProcessor to ensure that all the beans in your application are configured properly in the application context XML file.

RequiredAnnotationBeanPostProcessor only ensures that a bean property is configured in the bean definition. It *doesn't* ensure that the configured property value is correct. For instance, you can configure a property's value as null, instead of a valid value. For this reason, beans may still need to implement initialization methods to check if the properties are correctly set.

Let's now look at Spring's DestructionAwareBeanPostProcessor interface that is a sub-interface of Spring's BeanPostProcessor interface.

DestructionAwareBeanPostProcessor

So far we have seen that a BeanPostProcessor implementation is used for interacting with newly created bean instances. In some scenarios you may also want to interact with a bean instance before it is destroyed. To interact with a bean instance before it is destroyed, configure a bean that implements Spring's DestructionAwareBeanPostProcessor interface in the application context XML file. DestructionAwareBeanPostProcessor is a sub-interface of BeanPostProcessor interface and defines the following method:

```
void postProcessBeforeDestruction(Object bean, String beanName)
```

The postProcessBeforeDestruction method accepts the bean instance, which is about to be destroyed by the Spring container, and its name as arguments. Spring container invokes the postProcessBeforeDestruction method for each singleton bean instance *before* the bean instance is destroyed by the Spring container. Usually, the postProcessBeforeDestruction method is used to invoke custom destruction methods of bean instances. It is important to note that the postProcessBeforeDestruction method is *not* called for prototype beans.

We'll now look at Spring's BeanFactoryPostProcessor interface, which allows you to make modifications to bean definitions.

5-4 Modifying bean definitions using BeanFactoryPostProcessor

Spring's BeanFactoryPostProcessor interface is implemented by classes that want to make modifications to bean definitions. A BeanFactoryPostProcessor is executed *after* bean definitions are loaded by the Spring container, but before any bean instance is created. A BeanFactoryPostProcessor is created *before* any other bean defined in the application context XML file, giving the BeanFactoryPostProcessor an opportunity to make modifications to bean definitions of other beans. You configure a BeanFactoryPostProcessor implementation in the application context XML file like any other Spring bean.

> Instead of bean definitions, if you want to modify or interact with bean instances, use a BeanPostProcessor (refer to section 5-3) and *not* a BeanFactoryPostProcessor.

BeanFactoryPostProcessor interface defines a single method - postProcessBeanFactory. This method accepts an argument of type ConfigurableListableBeanFactory that can be used to obtain and modify bean definitions loaded by the Spring container. It is possible to create a bean instance inside postProcessBeanFactory method itself by calling ConfigurableListableBeanFactory's getBean method, but bean creation inside postProcessBeanFactory method is *not* recommended. It is important to note that BeanPostProcessors (refer section 5-3) are *not* executed for bean instances created inside postProcessBeanFactory method.

It is important to note that a ConfigurableListableBeanFactory provides access to the Spring container just like the ApplicationContext object. ConfigurableListableBeanFactory additionally allows you to configure the Spring container, iterate over beans, and modify bean definitions. For instance, using ConfigurableListableBeanFactory object you can register PropertyEditorRegistrars (refer section 3-6 of chapter 3), register BeanPostProcessors, and so on. Later in this section, we'll see how ConfigurableListableBeanFactory object is used to modify bean definitions.

Let's now look at how we can use a BeanFactoryPostProcessor to modify bean definitions.

IMPORT **chapter 5/ch05-bankapp-beanfactorypostprocessor** (This project shows the MyBank application that uses a BeanFactoryPostProcessor implementation to disable autowiring across the application, and log an error message if a singleton bean is found to be dependent on a prototype bean. To verify that the BeanFactoryPostProcessor implementation functions correctly, execute the main method of the BankApp class of this project.)

BeanFactoryPostProcessor example

In the previous chapter, we saw that autowiring hides the overall structure of the application (refer section 4-6 of chapter 4). We also discussed that instead of using <property> element to specify that a singleton bean is dependent on a prototype bean, you should use <lookup-method> or <replaced-method> element (refer section 4-4 and 4-5 of chapter 4 for more details) to programmatically obtain a prototype-scoped dependency of a singleton bean. We'll now look at a BeanFactoryPostProcessor implementation that makes beans *unavailable* for autowiring (refer <bean> element's autowire-candidate attribute described in section 4-6 of chapter 4) and logs an error message if it finds that a singleton bean is dependent on a prototype bean. For simplicity's sake, we assume that a singleton bean uses the <property> element to specify that it is dependent on a prototype bean.

> A bean that implements Spring's BeanFactoryPostProcessor interface is a *special* bean type; the Spring container automatically detects and executes a BeanFactoryPostProcessor bean.

The following example listing shows the MyBank's ApplicationConfigurer class that implements BeanFactoryPostProcessor interface:

Example listing 5-22 – ApplicationConfigurer class – a BeanFactoryPostProcessor implementation
Project – ch05-bankapp-beanfactorypostprocessor
Source location - src/main/java/sample/spring/chapter05/bankapp/postprocessor

```
package sample.spring.chapter05.bankapp.postprocessor;

import org.springframework.beans.factory.config.BeanDefinition;
import org.springframework.beans.factory.config.BeanFactoryPostProcessor;
import org.springframework.beans.factory.config.ConfigurableListableBeanFactory;

public class ApplicationConfigurer implements BeanFactoryPostProcessor {

    public ApplicationConfigurer() {
        logger.info("Created ApplicationConfigurer instance");
    }

    @Override
    public void postProcessBeanFactory(ConfigurableListableBeanFactory beanFactory)
           throws BeansException {
        String[] beanDefinitionNames = beanFactory.getBeanDefinitionNames();

        // -- get all the bean definitions
```

```
        for (int i = 0; i < beanDefinitionNames.length; i++) {
            String beanName = beanDefinitionNames[i];
            BeanDefinition beanDefinition = beanFactory.getBeanDefinition(beanName);
            beanDefinition.setAutowireCandidate(false);

            // -- obtain dependencies of a bean
            if (beanDefinition.isSingleton()) {
                if (hasPrototypeDependency(beanFactory, beanDefinition)) {
                    logger.error("Singleton-scoped " + beanName
                            + " bean is dependent on a prototype-scoped bean.");
                }
            }
        }
    }
    .....
}
```

The following sequence of actions is performed by the postProcessBeanFactory method:

1. First, the postProcessBeanFactory method calls ConfigurableListableBeanFactory's getBeanDefinitionNames method to obtain names of all the bean definitions loaded by the Spring container. You should note that the name of a bean definition is the value of <bean> element's id attribute.

2. Once the names of all the bean definitions are obtained, the postProcessBeanFactory method invokes ConfigurableListableBeanFactory's getBeanDefinition method to obtain the BeanDefinition object corresponding to each bean definition. The getBeanDefinition method accepts a bean definition name (obtained in step 1) as argument.

3. A BeanDefinition object represents a bean definition, and can be used to modify bean configuration. For each bean definition loaded by the Spring container, the postProcessBeanFactory method invokes BeanDefinition's setAutowireCandidate method to make *all* the beans unavailable for autowiring.

4. BeanDefinition's isSingleton method returns true if a bean definition is for a singleton bean. If a bean definition is for a singleton bean, the postProcessBeanFactory method invokes hasPrototypeDependency method to check if the singleton bean is dependent on any prototype bean. And, if the singleton bean is dependent on a prototype bean, the postProcessBeanFactory method logs an error message.

The following example listing shows the implementation of ApplicationConfigurer's hasPrototypeDependency method that returns true if a bean is dependent on a prototype bean:

Example listing 5-23 – ApplicationConfigurer's hasPrototypeDependency method
Project – ch05-bankapp-beanfactorypostprocessor
Source location - src/main/java/sample/spring/chapter05/bankapp/postprocessor

```
import org.springframework.beans.MutablePropertyValues;
import org.springframework.beans.PropertyValue;
import org.springframework.beans.factory.config.RuntimeBeanReference;

public class ApplicationConfigurer implements BeanFactoryPostProcessor {
    .....
    private boolean hasPrototypeDependency(ConfigurableListableBeanFactory beanFactory,
            BeanDefinition beanDefinition) {
        boolean isPrototype = false;
        MutablePropertyValues mutablePropertyValues = beanDefinition.getPropertyValues();
```

```
        PropertyValue[] propertyValues = mutablePropertyValues.getPropertyValues();

        for (int j = 0; j < propertyValues.length; j++) {
            if (propertyValues[j].getValue()   instanceof    RuntimeBeanReference) {
                String dependencyBeanName = ((RuntimeBeanReference) propertyValues[j]
                        .getValue()).getBeanName();
                BeanDefinition dependencyBeanDef =
                        beanFactory.getBeanDefinition(dependencyBeanName);
                if (dependencyBeanDef.isPrototype()) {
                    isPrototype = true;
                    break;
                }
            }
        }
        return isPrototype;
    }
}
```

The hasPrototypeDependency method checks if the bean represented by BeanDefinition argument is dependent on a prototype bean. The ConfigurableListableBeanFactory argument provides access to bean definitions loaded by the Spring container. The following sequence of actions is performed by hasPrototypeDependency method to find if the bean represented by the BeanDefinition argument has a prototype-scoped dependency:

1. First, hasPrototypeDependency method calls BeanDefinition's getPropertyValues method to obtain bean properties defined by <property> elements. BeanDefinition's getPropertyValues returns an object of type MutablePropertyValues which you can use to modify bean properties. For instance, you can add additional properties to the bean definition by using addPropertyValue and addPropertyValues methods of MutablePropertyValues.

2. As we want to iterate over all the bean properties and check if any bean property refers to a prototype bean, the getPropertyValues method of MutablePropertyValues is invoked to retrieve an array of PropertyValue objects. A PropertyValue object holds information about a bean property.

3. If a bean property refers to a Spring bean, calling PropertyValue's getValue method returns an instance of RuntimeBeanReference object that holds name of the referenced bean. As we are interested in bean properties that reference Spring beans, the return value of PropertyValue's getValue method is checked if it represents an instance of RuntimeBeanReference type. If it does, the object returned by PropertyValue's getValue method is cast to RuntimeBeanReference type, and the name of the referenced bean is obtained by calling the RuntimeBeanReference's getBeanName method.

4. Now that we have the name of the bean referenced by the bean property, the BeanDefinition object for the referenced bean is obtained by calling ConfigurableListableBeanFactory's getBeanDefinition method. You can check if the referenced bean is a prototype bean by calling BeanDefinition's isPrototype method.

The following sequence diagram summarizes how `hasPrototypeDependency` method works:

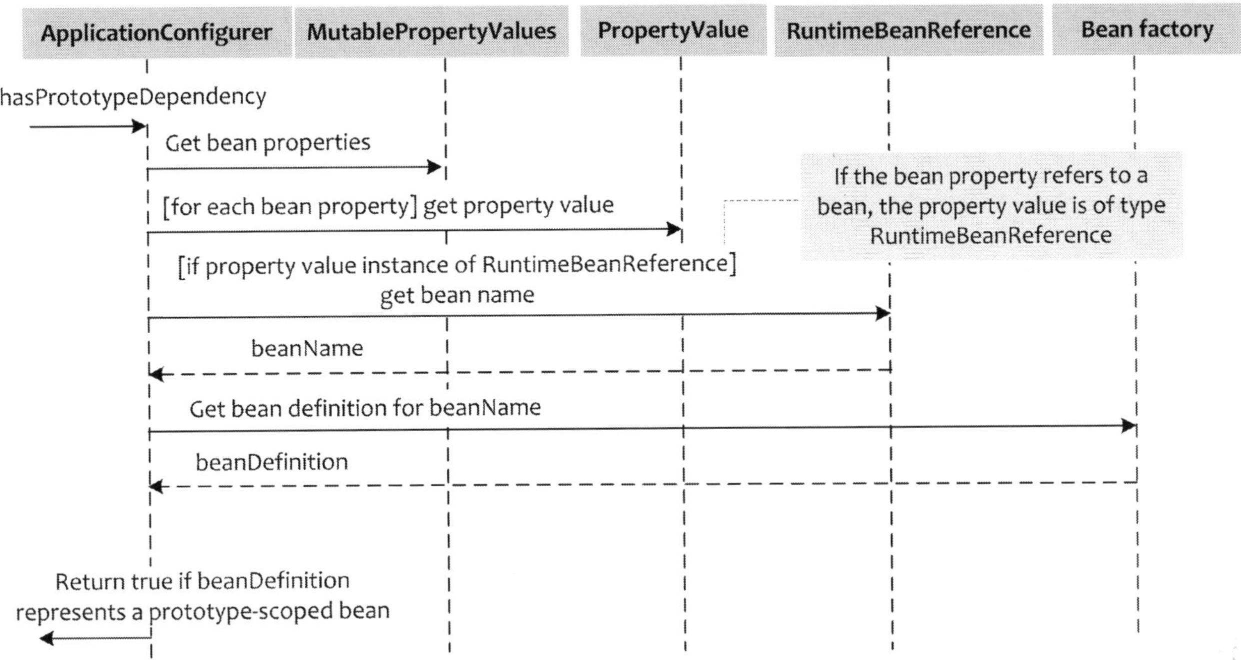

Figure 5-2 – `hasPrototypeDependency` method iterates over bean definitions of dependencies, and returns `true` if a prototype-scoped dependency is found

In the above sequence diagram `ConfigurableListableBeanFactory` object has been depicted as 'Bean factory' object.

The following example listing shows the application context XML file of `ch05-bankapp-beanfactorypostprocessor` project that contains bean definitions for `ApplicationConfigurer` class (a `BeanFactoryPostProcessor` implementation), `InstanceValidationBeanPostProcessor` class (a `BeanPostProcessor` implementation), along with bean definitions for application-specific objects:

Example listing 5-24 – `applicationContext.xml` - `BeanFactoryPostProcessor` bean definition
Project – `ch05-bankapp-beanfactorypostprocessor`
Source location - `src/main/resources/META-INF/spring`

```
<beans .....>
    .....
    <bean id="fixedDepositDao"
        class="sample.spring.chapter05.bankapp.dao.FixedDepositDaoImpl"..... >
        <property name="fixedDepositDetails" ref="fixedDepositDetails" />
    </bean>

    <bean id="fixedDepositDetails"
        class="sample.spring.chapter05.bankapp.domain.FixedDepositDetails"
        scope="prototype" />

    <bean class=".....postprocessor.InstanceValidationBeanPostProcessor">
        <property name="order" value="1" />
    </bean>

    <bean class="sample.spring.chapter05.bankapp.postprocessor.ApplicationConfigurer" />
</beans>
```

In the bean definitions shown above, the singleton fixedDepositDao bean is dependent on the prototype fixedDepositDetails bean.

If you execute the main method of BankApp class of ch05-bankapp-beanfactorypostprocessor project, you'll see the following output on the console:

```
Created ApplicationConfigurer instance
Singleton-scoped fixedDepositDao bean is dependent on a prototype-scoped bean.
Created InstanceValidationBeanPostProcessor instance
```

The above output shows that the Spring container creates ApplicationConfigurer (a BeanFactoryPostProcessor) and executes ApplicationConfigurer's postProcessBeanFactory method *before* creating InstanceValidationBeanPostProcessor (a BeanPostProcessor) instance. It is important to note that the beans that implement the BeanFactoryPostProcessor interface are processed *before* beans that implement the BeanPostProcessor interface. For this reason, you *can't* use a BeanPostProcessor to make modifications to a BeanFactoryPostProcessor instance. The BeanFactoryPostProcessor gives you the opportunity to modify bean definitions loaded by the Spring container, and the BeanPostProcessor gives you the opportunity to make modifications to newly created bean instances.

Let's now look at some of the similarities between BeanPostProcessors and BeanFactoryPostProcessors:

- you can configure multiple BeanFactoryPostProcessors in the application context XML file. To control the order in which BeanFactoryPostProcessors are executed by the Spring container, implement Spring's Ordered interface (refer section 5-3 to know more about the Ordered interface).
- even if you specify that a BeanFactoryPostProcessor implementation is lazily initialized by the Spring container, BeanFactoryPostProcessors are created when the Spring container instance is created.

In chapter 3, we looked at CustomEditorConfigurer - a BeanFactoryPostProcessor implementation that Spring provides out-of-the-box for registering custom property editors. Let's now look at some more BeanFactoryPostProcessor implementations that Spring provides out-of-the-box.

PropertySourcesPlaceholderConfigurer

So far we have seen bean definition examples in which <property> or <constructor-arg> element's value attribute is used to specify the actual string value of a bean property or a constructor argument. PropertySourcesPlaceholderConfigurer (a BeanFactoryPostProcessor) lets you specify the actual string value of bean properties and constructor arguments in a properties file. In the bean definition, you only specify *property placeholders* (of the form ${*<property_name_in_properties_file>*}) as the value of <property> or <constructor-arg> element's value attribute. When bean definitions are loaded by the Spring container, the PropertySourcesPlaceholderConfigurer pulls the actual values from the properties file and replaces the property placeholders in the bean definitions with actual values.

IMPORT **chapter 5/ch05-propertySourcesPlaceholderConfigurer-example** (This project shows a Spring application that uses Spring's PropertySourcesPlaceholderConfigurer to set bean properties from the properties specified in external properties files. To verify that the PropertySourcesPlaceholderConfigurer functions correctly, execute the main method of the SampleApp class of this project.)

The following example listing shows bean definitions for DataSource and WebServiceConfiguration classes that use property placeholders:

Example listing 5-25 – applicationContext.xml - Bean definitions that use property placeholders
Project – ch05-propertySourcesPlaceholderConfigurer-example
Source location - src/main/resources/META-INF/spring

```
<bean id="datasource" class="sample.spring.chapter05.domain.DataSource">
    <property name="url" value="${database.url}" />
    <property name="username" value="${database.username}" />
    <property name="password" value="${database.password}" />
    <property name="driverClass" value="${database.driverClass}" />
</bean>

<bean id="webServiceConfiguration"
        class="sample.spring.chapter05.domain.WebServiceConfiguration">
    <property name="webServiceUrl" value="${webservice.url}" />
</bean>
```

The above example listing shows that each <property> element's value attribute specifies a property placeholder. When bean definitions are loaded by the Spring container, PropertySourcesPlaceholderConfigurer replaces property placeholders with values from a properties file. For instance, if a database.username property is defined in a properties file, the value of database.username property replaces the ${database.username} property placeholder of dataSource bean.

The bean definition for the PropertySourcesPlaceholderConfigurer specifies properties files to be searched for finding replacement for a property placeholder, as shown in the following example listing:

Example listing 5-26 – applicationContext.xml - PropertySourcesPlaceholderConfigurer bean definition
Project – ch05-propertySourcesPlaceholderConfigurer-example
Source location - src/main/resources/META-INF/spring

```
<bean class="org.springframework.context.support.PropertySourcesPlaceholderConfigurer">
    <property name="locations">
        <list>
            <value>classpath:database.properties</value>
            <value>classpath:webservice.properties</value>
        </list>
    </property>
    <property name="ignoreUnresolvablePlaceholders" value="false" />
</bean>
```

PropertySourcesPlaceholderConfigurer's locations property specifies properties files to be searched for finding the value for a property placeholder. In the above example listing, PropertySourcesPlaceholderConfigurer looks for the value of a property placeholder in database.properties and webservice.properties files. The ignoreUnresolvablePlaceholders property specifies whether PropertySourcesPlaceholderConfigurer silently ignores or throws an exception in case a property placeholder value is not found in any of the properties files specified by the locations property. The value false indicates that the PropertySourcesPlaceholderConfigurer will throw an exception if value for a property placeholder is not found in database.properties or webservice.properties files.

The following example listing shows the properties defined in database.properties and webservice.properties files:

Example listing 5-27 – Properties defined in database.properties and webservice.properties files
Project – ch05-propertySourcesPlaceholderConfigurer-example
Source location - src/main/resources/META-INF

```
---------------- database.properties file ------------------
database.url=some_url
database.username=some_username
database.password=some_password
database.driverClass=some_driverClass

---------------- webservice.properties file ------------------
webservice.url=some_url
```

If you compare the properties defined in database.properties and webservice.properties files with the property placeholders specified in datasource and webServiceConfiguration bean definitions (refer example listing 5-25), you'll notice that for each property placeholder a property is defined in one of the properties files.

The main method of SampleApp class of ch05-propertySourcesPlaceholderConfigurer-example project retrieves WebServiceConfiguration and DataSource beans from the ApplicationContext and prints their properties on the console. If you execute SampleApp's main method, you'll see the following output on the console:

```
DataSource [url=some_url, username=some_username, password=some_password,
driverClass=some_driverClass]
WebServiceConfiguration [webServiceUrl=some_url]
```

The above output shows:

- DataSource's url property is set to some_url, username to some_username, password to some_password and driverClass to some_driverClass.
- WebServiceConfiguration's webServiceUrl property is set to some_url.

If you remove a property from either database.properties or webservice.properties file, executing SampleApp's main method will result in an exception.

Let's now look at localOverride property of PropertySourcesPlaceholderConfigurer.

localOverride property

If you want local properties (set via <props> element) to override properties read from properties file, you can set PropertySourcesPlaceholderConfigurer's localOverride property to true.

IMPORT **chapter 5/ch05-localoverride-example** (This project shows a Spring application that uses PropertySourcesPlaceholderConfigurer's localOverride property. To run the application, execute the main method of the SampleApp class of this project.)

The following example listing shows bean definitions for DataSource and WebServiceConfiguration classes:

Example listing 5-28 – applicationContext.xml - Bean definitions that use property placeholders
Project – ch05-localOverride-example
Source location - src/main/resources/META-INF/spring

```
<bean id="datasource" class="sample.spring.chapter05.domain.DataSource">
    <property name="url" value="${database.url}" />
```

```
        <property name="username" value="${database.username}" />
        <property name="password" value="${database.password}" />
        <property name="driverClass" value="${database.driverClass}" />
    </bean>

    <bean id="webServiceConfiguration"
            class="sample.spring.chapter05.domain.WebServiceConfiguration">
        <property name="webServiceUrl" value="${webservice.url}" />
    </bean>
```

The bean definitions for DataSource and WebServiceConfiguration classes are the same as we saw in example listing 5-25.

The following example listing shows the properties defined in database.properties and webservice.properties files:

Example listing 5-29 – Properties defined in database.properties and webservice.properties files
Project – ch05-localOverride-example
Source location - src/main/resources/META-INF

```
---------------- database.properties file ------------------
database.url=some_url
database.username=some_username

---------------- webservice.properties file ------------------
webservice.url=some_url
```

If you compare the properties defined in database.properties and webservice.properties files with the property placeholders specified in datasource and webServiceConfiguration bean definitions (refer example listing 5-28), you'll notice that properties are not defined for ${database.password} and ${database.driverClass} placeholders in the database.properties file.

The following example listing shows the bean definition for PropertySourcesPlaceholderConfigurer class:

Example listing 5-30 - applicationContext.xml - PropertySourcesPlaceholderConfigurer bean definition
Project – ch05-localOverride-example
Source location - src/main/resources/META-INF/spring

```
    <bean
        class="org.springframework.context.support.PropertySourcesPlaceholderConfigurer">
        <property name="locations">
            <list>
                <value>classpath:database.properties</value>
                <value>classpath:webservice.properties</value>
            </list>
        </property>
        <property name="properties">
            <props>
                <prop key="database.password">locally-set-password</prop>
                <prop key="database.driverClass">locally-set-driverClass</prop>
                <prop key="webservice.url">locally-set-webServiceUrl</prop>
            </props>
        </property>
        <property name="ignoreUnresolvablePlaceholders" value="false" />
        <property name="localOverride" value="true" />
    </bean>
```

The properties property of PropertySourcesPlaceholderConfigurer defines *local* properties. The database.password, database.driverClass and webservice.url properties are local properties. The localOverride property specifies whether local properties take precedence over properties read from external properties files. As the value of localOverride property is true, local properties take precedence.

> Instead of using PropertySourcesPlaceholderConfigurer's properties property, you can use <properties> element of Spring's util schema (refer section 3-8 of chapter 3) to define local properties.

The main method of SampleApp class in ch05-localOverride-example project retrieves WebServiceConfiguration and DataSource beans from the ApplicationContext and prints their properties on the console. If you execute SampleApp's main method, you'll see the following output on the console:

```
DataSource [url=some_url, username=some_username, password=locally-set-password,
driverClass=locally-set-driverClass]
WebServiceConfiguration [webServiceUrl=locally-set-webServiceUrl]
```

The output shows that the value of DataSource's password and driverClass properties are locally-set-password and locally-set-driverClass, respectively. This means that the values for DataSource's password and driverClass properties come from the local properties defined by the PropertySourcesPlaceholderConfigurer bean (refer example listing 5-30). This shows that if the PropertySourcesPlaceholderConfigurer can't find a property for a placeholder in the external properties files, it searches for the property in the local properties defined by PropertySourcesPlaceholderConfigurer bean. The output also shows that the WebServiceConfiguration's webServiceUrl property value comes from the local properties defined by the PropertySourcesPlaceholderConfigurer bean (refer example listing 5-30). The value of PropertySourcesPlaceholderConfigurer's localOverride property is set to true; therefore, the locally defined webservice.url property takes *precedence* over the webservice.url property read from the webservice.properties file.

Instead of directly configuring the PropertySourcesPlaceholderConfigurer bean in your application context XML file, you can use the <property-placeholder> element of Spring's context schema. The <property-placeholder> element configures a PropertySourcesPlaceholderConfigurer instance. Let's now look at the <property-placeholder> element in detail.

IMPORT **chapter 5/ch05-property-placeholder-element-example** (This project shows a Spring application that uses the <property-placeholder> element. To run the application, execute the main method of the SampleApp class of this project.)

<property-placeholder> element

The following example listing shows how the <property-placeholder> element is used to configure a PropertySourcesPlaceholderConfigurer instance with the same configuration as the one we configured in example listing 5-30:

Example listing 5-31 – applicationContext.xml - <property-placeholder> element
Project – ch05-property-placeholder-element-example
Source location - src/main/resources/META-INF/spring

```
<beans xmlns="http://www.springframework.org/schema/beans"
    xmlns:context="http://www.springframework.org/schema/context"
    xmlns:util="http://www.springframework.org/schema/util" .....>
    .....
    <context:property-placeholder ignore-unresolvable="false"
        location="classpath:database.properties, classpath:webservice.properties"
        local-override="true" order="1" properties-ref="localProps" />
```

```
    <util:properties id="localProps">
        <prop key="database.password">locally-set-password</prop>
        <prop key="database.driverClass">locally-set-driverClass</prop>
        <prop key="webservice.url">locally-set-webServiceUrl</prop>
    </util:properties>
</beans>
```

In the above example listing, reference to Spring's `context` schema is included so that its elements are accessible. The above example listing shows that the use of `<property-placeholder>` element results in a less verbose configuration of `PropertySourcesPlaceholderConfigurer`. The `ignore-unresolvable`, `location` and `local-override` attributes correspond to `ignoreUnresolvablePlaceholders`, `locations` and `localOverride` properties of `PropertySourcesPlaceholderConfigurer`. As the `PropertySourcesPlaceholderConfigurer` class implements Spring's `Ordered` interface, the `order` attribute's value is used to set the `order` property of `PropertySourcesPlaceholderConfigurer` instance. The `properties-ref` attribute refers to a `java.util.Properties` object that represents the *local properties*. In the above example listing, the `<properties>` element of Spring's `util` schema (refer section 3-8 of chapter 3) creates an instance of `java.util.Properties` object, which is referenced by the `properties-ref` attribute of `<property-placeholder>` element.

Let's now look at Spring's `PropertyOverrideConfigurer` (a `BeanFactoryPostProcessor`) which allows you to specify values for bean properties in external properties files.

PropertyOverrideConfigurer

`PropertyOverrideConfigurer` is similar to `PropertySourcesPlaceholderConfigurer` in the sense that it allows you to specify a bean property value in external properties file. When using `PropertyOverrideConfigurer`, bean property value is specified in the following format in external properties files:

<bean-name>.<bean-property-name>=<value>

here, *<bean-name>* is the name of the bean, *<bean-property-name>* is the name of the bean property, and *<value>* is the value that you want to assign to the bean property.

The notable differences between `PropertyOverrideConfigurer` and `PropertySourcesPlaceholderConfigurer` classes are:

- You can use `PropertyOverrideConfigurer` only for externalizing values of bean properties, that is, you can't use `PropertyOverrideConfigurer` to externalize values of constructor arguments.

- `PropertySourcesPlaceholderConfigurer` *doesn't* provide you with an option to specify default values for properties. But, `PropertyOverrideConfigurer` allows you to specify default values for bean properties.

Let's now look at an example usage of `PropertyOverrideConfigurer`.

IMPORT **chapter 5/ch05-propertyOverrideConfigurer-example** (This project shows a Spring application that uses Spring's `PropertyOverrideConfigurer`. To run the application, execute the `main` method of the `SampleApp` class of this project.)

PropertyOverrideConfigurer example

The following example listing shows bean definitions for `DataSource` and `WebServiceConfiguration` classes whose properties we'll set using `PropertyOverrideConfigurer`:

Example listing 5-32 - applicationContext.xml - Bean definitions for DataSource and WebServiceConfiguration
Project – ch05-propertyOverrideConfigurer-example
Source location - src/main/resources/META-INF/spring

```
<bean id="datasource" class="sample.spring.chapter05.domain.DataSource">
    <property name="url" value="test url value" />
    <property name="username" value="test username value" />
    <property name="password" value="test password value" />
    <property name="driverClass" value="test driverClass value" />
</bean>

<bean id="webServiceConfiguration"
        class="sample.spring.chapter05.domain.WebServiceConfiguration">
    <property name="webServiceUrl" value="this webservice url needs to be replaced" />
</bean>
```

In the above example listing, the <property> element's value attribute specifies default value of a bean property.

The following example listing shows the bean definition for the PropertyOverrideConfigurer class that replaces the default values of bean properties (as shown in example listing 5-32) with values read from database.properties and webservice.properties files:

Example listing 5-33 – applicationContext.xml - PropertyOverrideConfigurer configuration
Project – ch05-propertyOverrideConfigurer-example
Source location - src/main/resources/META-INF/spring

```
<bean class="org.springframework.beans.factory.config.PropertyOverrideConfigurer">
    <property name="locations">
        <list>
            <value>classpath:database.properties</value>
            <value>classpath:webservice.properties</value>
        </list>
    </property>
</bean>
```

In the above example listing, PropertyOverrideConfigurer's locations property specifies the properties files that contain values for bean properties.

> Instead of directly configuring PropertyOverrideConfigurer, you can use <property-override> element of Spring's context schema to configure a PropertyOverrideConfigurer instance.

The following example listing shows database.properties and webservice.properties files that contain values of bean properties:

Example listing 5-34 – Properties defined in database.properties and webservice.properties
Project – ch05-propertyOverrideConfigurer-example
Source location - src/main/resources/META-INF

```
---------------- database.properties file ------------------
datasource.url=some_url
datasource.username=some_username
datasource.password=some_password
```

```
---------------- webservice.properties file -----------------
webServiceConfiguration.webServiceUrl=some_url
```

The entries in the database.properties and webservice.properties files show that the property name follows the pattern: *<bean-name>.<property-name>*. When bean definitions are loaded by the Spring container, PropertyOverrideConfigurer replaces the default value of a bean property with the value read for that bean property from the database.properties and webservice.properties files. For instance, the url property of datasource bean is set to the value of datasource.url property defined in the database.properties file. Similarly, webServiceUrl property of webServiceConfiguration bean is set to the value of webServiceConfiguration.webServiceUrl property defined in the webservice.properties file.

If no value is found for a bean property in the external properties files, the bean property retains its default value. Example listing 5-32 shows that the driverClass property of datasource bean has the default value 'test driverClass value'. Example listing 5-34 shows that there is no property named datasource.driverClass defined in the database.properties or webservice.properties file; therefore, the driverClass bean property retains its default value.

The main method of SampleApp class of ch05-propertyOverrideConfigurer-example project retrieves WebServiceConfiguration and DataSource beans from the ApplicationContext and prints their properties on the console. If you execute SampleApp's main method, you'll see the following output on the console:

```
DataSource [url=some_url, username=some_username, password=some_password, driverClass=test driverClass value]
WebServiceConfiguration [webServiceUrl=some_url]
```

The above output shows that the default values of all bean properties, except that of driverClass, are replaced by the property values specified in the external properties files.

As PropertyOverrideConfigurer and PropertySourcesPlaceholderConfigurer inherit from Spring's PropertyResourceConfigurer class, you'll notice that both of these classes share many common configuration options. For instance, you can set PropertyOverrideConfigurer's localOverride property to control whether the local properties get precedence over properties read from external properties files, you can set PropertyOverrideConfigurer's properties property to define local properties, and so on.

5-5 Summary

In this chapter, we saw how to add custom initialization and destruction logic to a bean instance. We also looked at how you can modify newly created bean instances using BeanPostProcessor implementations, and modify bean definitions using BeanFactoryPostProcessor implementations. Spring internally makes use of BeanPostProcessors and BeanFactoryPostProcessors to provide many framework features. In the next chapter, we'll look at Spring's support for annotation-driven development.

Chapter 6 – *Annotation-driven development with Spring*

6-1 Introduction

In previous chapters, we saw that the bean definitions contained in the application context XML file are used as a blueprint by the Spring container to create bean instances. A bean definition specifies information about bean dependencies, initialization and destruction methods of a bean, lazy or eager initialization strategy for the bean instance, bean scope, and so on. In this chapter, we'll look at annotations that you can use to specify the same information in the bean class itself, thereby saving the effort to explicitly configure a bean in the application context XML file. We'll also touch upon *Spring Expression Language* (SpEL), how to validate objects and methods using Spring's `Validator` interface and through JSR 380 annotations, and bean definition profiles.

Let's first begin with looking at Spring's `@Component` annotation that indicates that a particular class represents a Spring bean.

6-2 Identifying Spring beans with @Component

Spring's `@Component` annotation is a type-level annotation, which indicates that a class represents a Spring bean (also referred to as a Spring *component*). It is recommended that you use the specialized forms of `@Component` annotation to annotate controllers, services and data access objects (DAOs) of your application. For instance, annotate controllers with `@Controller`, services with `@Service`, and DAOs with `@Repository` annotation.

You should note that `@Service`, `@Controller` and `@Repository` annotations are *meta-annotated* with `@Component` annotation, that is, they are themselves annotated with `@Component` annotation. For example, the following definition of `@Service` annotation shows that it is meta-annotated with `@Component` annotation:

```
@Target({ElementType.TYPE})
@Retention(RetentionPolicy.RUNTIME)
@Documented
@Component
public @interface Service {
    String value() default "";
}
```

IMPORT **chapter 6/ch06-bankapp-annotations** (This project shows the MyBank application that uses annotations for registering beans with the Spring container and for autowiring dependencies. To run the application, execute the `main` method of the `BankApp` class of this project.)

The following example listing shows the MyBank's `FixedDepositServiceImpl` class that makes use of `@Service` annotation:

Example listing 6-1 – `FixedDepositServiceImpl` class - `@Service` annotation usage
Project – ch06-bankapp-annotations
Source location - src/main/java/sample/spring/chapter06/bankapp/service

```
package sample.spring.chapter06.bankapp.service;

import org.springframework.stereotype.Service;

@Service(value="fixedDepositService")
public class FixedDepositServiceImpl implements FixedDepositService { ..... }
```

As the FixedDepositServiceImpl class is annotated with @Service annotation, FixedDepositServiceImpl class represents a Spring bean. @Service annotation accepts a value attribute that specifies the name with which the bean is registered with the Spring container. The value attribute serves the same purpose as the <bean> element's id attribute. In the above example listing, the FixedDepositServiceImpl class is registered with the Spring container as a bean named fixedDepositService.

Like @Service annotation, @Component, @Repository and @Controller annotations specify the bean name via value attribute. You can specify the bean name without explicitly specifying the value attribute; @Service(value="fixedDepositService") is same as @Service("fixedDepositService"). If you don't specify the bean name, Spring assumes that the bean name is same as the name of the class beginning with the *lowercase* letter. You should specify a custom bean name because it's particularly helpful when autowiring dependencies 'by name'.

If you enable *classpath scanning* feature of Spring, bean classes annotated with @Component, @Controller, @Service or @Repository annotations are automatically registered with the Spring container. You enable classpath scanning feature of Spring by using the <component-scan> element of Spring's context schema. The following example listing shows usage of <component-scan> element:

Example listing 6-2 – applicationContext.xml
Project – ch06-bankapp-annotations
Source location - src/main/resources/META-INF/spring

```
<beans xmlns="http://www.springframework.org/schema/beans"
    xmlns:context="http://www.springframework.org/schema/context"
    xsi:schemaLocation=".....http://www.springframework.org/schema/context
        http://www.springframework.org/schema/context/spring-context.xsd">

    <context:component-scan base-package="sample.spring"/>
</beans>
```

In the above example listing, reference to Spring's context schema is included so that its elements are accessible. The <component-scan> element's base-package attribute specifies comma-separated list of packages that should be searched for Spring beans. As the base-package attribute's value is sample.spring, Spring beans are searched inside sample.spring package and its sub-packages. As the FixedDepositServiceImpl class shown in example listing 6-1 is annotated with @Service annotation and is located in package sample.spring.chapter06.bankapp.service, the <component-scan> element in the above example listing automatically registers FixedDepositServiceImpl class as a bean with the Spring container. This is equivalent to the following bean definition for the FixedDepositServiceImpl class in the application context XML file:

Example listing 6-3 – Bean definition for the FixedDepositServiceImpl class

```
<bean id="fixedDepositService"
          class="sample.spring.chapter06.bankapp.service.FixedDepositServiceImpl" />
```

If you want to filter the bean classes that should be considered for automatic registration with the Spring container, use the resource-pattern attribute of <component-scan> element. The default value of resource-pattern attribute is **/*.class, which means all the bean classes under the package(s) specified by the base-package attribute will be considered for automatic registration. The <include-filter> and <exclude-filter> sub-elements of <component-scan> element provide a more concise way to specify component classes that should be considered for automatic registration, and the classes that should be ignored. For instance, the following example listing shows an example usage of <include-filter> and <exclude-filter> elements:

Example listing 6-4 – <include-filter> and <exclude-filter> elements

```
<beans .....>
    <context:component-scan base-package="sample.example">
         <context:include-filter type="annotation"
               expression="example.annotation.MyAnnotation"/>
         <context:exclude-filter type="regex" expression=".*Details"/>
    </context:component-scan>
</beans>
```

The <exclude-filter> and <include-filter> elements define a type attribute that specifies the strategy used for filtering bean classes, and the expression attribute specifies the corresponding filter expression. In the above example listing, the <include-filter> element specifies that the bean classes that are annotated with MyAnnotation type-level annotation are automatically registered with the Spring container, and the <exclude-filter> element specifies that the bean classes whose names end with Details are ignored by the <component-scan> element.

The following table describes the possible values that the type attributes of <include-filter> and <exclude-filter> elements can accept:

Value of type attribute	Description
annotation	If the type attribute's value is annotation, the expression attribute specifies the fully-qualified class name of the annotation that a bean class *must* be annotated with. For instance, if the expression attribute's value is example.annotation.MyAnnotation, bean classes that are annotated with MyAnnotation annotation are considered for inclusion (in the case of <include-filter> element) or exclusion (in the case of <exclude-filter> element).
assignable	If the type attribute's value is assignable, the expression attribute specifies the fully-qualified name of a class or interface to which a bean class must be assignable.
aspectj	If the type attribute's value is aspectj, the expression attribute specifies an AspectJ expression that is used for filtering the bean classes.
regex	If the type attribute's value is regex, the expression attribute specifies a regular expression that is used for filtering bean classes by their names.
custom	If the type attribute's value is custom, an implementation of org.springframework.core.type.TypeFilter interface is specified by the expression attribute for filtering the bean classes.

In this section, we looked at an example usage of @Service annotation. @Component, @Controller and @Repository annotations are specified the same way as @Service annotation. Refer CustomerRegistrationDetails and CustomerRequestDetails classes of ch06-bankapp-annotations project to see usage of @Component annotation. Refer DAO classes contained in ch06-bankapp-annotations project to see usage of @Repository annotation.

As we don't define annotated bean classes in the application context XML file, we don't have the option to use <property> or <constructor-arg> element to specify their dependencies. For this reason, annotated bean classes make use of annotations like @Autowired, @Inject, and so on, to specify their dependencies.

Let's now look at Spring's @Autowired annotation.

6-3 @Autowired - autowiring dependencies *by type*

@Autowired annotation is used to autowire dependencies 'by type'. Spring's @Autowired annotation provides the same functionality as the Spring's autowiring feature that we discussed in chapter 4, but @Autowired annotation offers a cleaner and flexible approach to autowiring bean dependencies. @Autowired annotation can be used at *constructor-level*, *method-level* and *field-level*.

The following example listing shows the AccountStatementServiceImpl class that uses the @Autowired annotation at the field-level:

Example listing 6-5 – AccountStatementServiceImpl class - @Autowired annotation usage at the field-level
Project – ch06-bankapp-annotations
Source location - src/main/java/sample/spring/chapter06/bankapp/service

```
package sample.spring.chapter06.bankapp.service;

import org.springframework.beans.factory.annotation.Autowired;
import org.springframework.stereotype.Service;

@Service(value="accountStatementService")
public class AccountStatementServiceImpl implements AccountStatementService {

    @Autowired
    private AccountStatementDao accountStatementDao;

    @Override
    public AccountStatement getAccountStatement(Date from, Date to) {
        return accountStatementDao.getAccountStatement(from, to);
    }
}
```

In the above example listing, the accountStatementDao field (of type AccountStatementDao) is annotated with @Autowired annotation. When an instance of AccountStatementServiceImpl is created, Spring's AutowiredAnnotationBeanPostProcessor (a BeanPostProcessor implementation) is responsible for autowiring accountStatementDao field. The AutowiredAnnotationBeanPostProcessor retrieves reference to an AccountStatementDao type bean from the Spring container and assigns it to the accountStatementDao field. It is important to note that the field annotated with @Autowired annotation need *not* be public or have a corresponding public setter method.

> Spring's AutowiredAnnotationBeanPostProcessor performs autowiring of fields, methods and constructors that are annotated with Spring's @Autowired or JSR 330's @Inject (explained in section 6-5) annotation.

The following example listing shows the CustomerRegistrationServiceImpl class that uses the @Autowired annotation at the method-level:

Example listing 6-6 – CustomerRegistrationServiceImpl class - @Autowired annotation usage at the method-level
Project – ch06-bankapp-annotations
Source location - src/main/java/sample/spring/chapter06/bankapp/service

```
package sample.spring.chapter06.bankapp.service;

@Service("customerRegistrationService")
@Scope(value = ConfigurableBeanFactory.SCOPE_PROTOTYPE)
```

```
public class CustomerRegistrationServiceImpl implements CustomerRegistrationService {

    private CustomerRegistrationDetails customerRegistrationDetails;
    .....
    @Autowired
    public void obtainCustomerRegistrationDetails(
            CustomerRegistrationDetails customerRegistrationDetails) {
        this.customerRegistrationDetails = customerRegistrationDetails;
    }
    .....
    @Override
    public void setAccountNumber(String accountNumber) {
        customerRegistrationDetails.setAccountNumber(accountNumber);
    }
    .....
}
```

In the above example listing, `obtainCustomerRegistrationDetails` method is annotated with `@Autowired` annotation. If a method is annotated with `@Autowired` annotation, the arguments of the method are autowired. As `obtainCustomerRegistrationDetails` method is annotated with `@Autowired` annotation, its `CustomerRegistrationDetails` argument is autowired *by type*. It is important to note that an `@Autowired` annotated method need *not* be `public`.

> A method annotated with `@Autowired` annotation is *automatically* invoked *after* the bean instance is created and the fields annotated with `@Autowired` annotation are injected with matching bean instances.

The following example listing shows the `CustomerRequestServiceImpl` class that defines a constructor annotated with `@Autowired` annotation:

Example listing 6-7 – `CustomerRequestServiceImpl` class - `@Autowired` annotation usage at constructor-level
Project – `ch06-bankapp-annotations`
Source location - `src/main/java/sample/spring/chapter06/bankapp/service`

```
package sample.spring.chapter06.bankapp.service;

@Service(value="customerRequestService")
public class CustomerRequestServiceImpl implements CustomerRequestService {
    private CustomerRequestDetails customerRequestDetails;
    private CustomerRequestDao customerRequestDao;

    @Autowired
    public CustomerRequestServiceImpl(CustomerRequestDetails customerRequestDetails,
            CustomerRequestDao customerRequestDao) {
        this.customerRequestDetails = customerRequestDetails;
        this.customerRequestDao = customerRequestDao;
    }
    .....
}
```

In the above example listing, the `CustomerRequestServiceImpl`'s constructor is annotated with `@Autowired` annotation. If a constructor is annotated with `@Autowired` annotation, the arguments of the constructor are autowired. As `CustomerRequestServiceImpl`'s constructor is annotated with `@Autowired` annotation, its `CustomerRequestDetails` and `CustomerRequestDao` arguments are autowired *by type*. It is important to note that an `@Autowired` annotated constructor need *not* be `public`.

> Since Spring 4.3, if the bean class defines only one constructor, you *don't* need to annotate the constructor with @Autowired annotation; the Spring container performs autowiring of the constructor arguments by default.

When using the @Autowired annotation, exception is thrown if a bean matching the required type is *not* found. For instance, in example listing 6-7, if a bean of type CustomerRequestDetails or CustomerRequestDao is not found to be registered with the Spring container, an exception is thrown while creating the CustomerRequestServiceImpl instance.

@Autowired's required attribute specifies whether the dependency is mandatory or optional. If you set @Autowired's required attribute value to false, dependency is considered *optional*. This means that if the required attribute's value is set to false, exception is not thrown if no bean matching the required type is found in the Spring container. By default, value of required attribute is true; dependencies *must* be satisfied by the Spring container.

If a bean class defines an @Autowired annotated constructor with required attribute's value set to true, it *can't* have another @Autowired annotated constructor. For instance, consider the following example listing that defines two constructors annotated with the @Autowired annotation:

Example listing 6-8 – A bean class that defines two @Autowired annotated constructors

```
@Service(value="customerRequestService")
public class CustomerRequestServiceImpl implements CustomerRequestService {
    .....
    @Autowired(required=false)
    public CustomerRequestServiceImpl(CustomerRequestDetails customerRequestDetails) {
       .....
    }

    @Autowired
    public CustomerRequestServiceImpl(CustomerRequestDetails customerRequestDetails,
            CustomerRequestDao customerRequestDao) { ..... }
}
```

As autowiring of dependencies is required (@Autowired's required attribute is set to true) for one of the constructors and optional (@Autowired's required attribute is set to false) for the other in the above example listing, it results in an exception thrown by Spring.

A bean class can define multiple @Autowired annotated constructors with required attribute's value set to false. In such a case, one of the constructors will be invoked by Spring to create an instance of the bean class. The following example listing shows a bean class that defines two constructors annotated with @Autowired (required = false), and a default constructor:

Example listing 6-9 – A bean class that defines multiple @Autowired annotated constructors with required attribute value set to false

```
@Service(value="customerRequestService")
public class CustomerRequestServiceImpl implements CustomerRequestService {
    public CustomerRequestServiceImpl() { ..... }

    @Autowired(required=false)
    public CustomerRequestServiceImpl(CustomerRequestDetails customerRequestDetails) {
        .....
    }
```

```
    @Autowired(required=false)
    public CustomerRequestServiceImpl(CustomerRequestDetails customerRequestDetails,
            CustomerRequestDao customerRequestDao) {
        .....
    }
}
```

In the above example listing, both the @Autowired annotated constructors are candidates for autowiring by Spring to create an instance of the CustomerRequestServiceImpl class. The constructor with the largest number of satisfied dependencies is chosen. In the case of CustomerRequestServiceImpl class, if beans of types CustomerRequestDetails and CustomerRequestDao are registered with the Spring container, Spring invokes CustomerRequestServiceImpl(CustomerRequestDetails, CustomerRequestDao) constructor. If a bean of type CustomerRequestDetails is registered with container but no bean of type CustomerRequestDao is registered, CustomerRequestServiceImpl(CustomerRequestDetails) constructor is invoked. In case none of the dependencies are found, the default constructor of CustomerRequestServiceImpl class is invoked.

Let's now look at how you can use Spring's @Qualifier annotation along with @Autowired annotation to autowire dependencies *by name*.

6-4 @Qualifier – autowiring dependencies *by name*

You can use Spring's @Qualifier annotation along with @Autowired annotation to autowire dependencies *by name*. The @Qualifier annotation can be used at field-level, method-parameter-level and constructor-argument-level for autowiring dependencies *by name*.

The following example listing shows the FixedDepositServiceImpl class that uses @Qualifier annotation:

Example listing 6-10 – FixedDepositServiceImpl class - @Qualifier annotation usage
Project – ch06-bankapp-annotations
Source location - src/main/java/sample/spring/chapter06/bankapp/service

```
package sample.spring.chapter06.bankapp.service;

import org.springframework.beans.factory.annotation.Autowired;
import org.springframework.beans.factory.annotation.Qualifier;

@Service(value="fixedDepositService")
.....
public class FixedDepositServiceImpl implements FixedDepositService {

    @Autowired
    @Qualifier(value="myFixedDepositDao")
    private FixedDepositDao myFixedDepositDao;
    .....
}
```

In the above example listing, myFixedDepositDao field is annotated with @Autowired and @Qualifier annotations. @Qualifier annotation's value attribute specifies the name of the bean whose instance is assigned to the myFixedDepositDao field.

Spring first finds autowiring candidates 'by type' for the fields, constructor arguments and method arguments that are annotated with @Autowired annotation. Then, Spring uses the bean name specified by @Qualifier annotation to locate a *unique* bean from the list of autowiring candidates. For example, in example listing 6-

10, Spring first finds beans of type FixedDepositDao for myFixedDepositDao field, and then locates the bean named myFixedDepositDao from the list of autowiring candidates. If a bean named myFixedDepositDao is found, Spring assigns it to the myFixedDepositDao field.

@Qualifier(value="myFixedDepositDao") is same as @Qualifier("myFixedDepositDao"); you don't need to use the value attribute to specify the name of the bean to be autowired.

The following example listing shows usage of @Qualifier annotation at method-parameter-level and constructor-argument-level:

Example listing 6-11 – @Qualifier usage at method-parameter-level and constructor-argument-level

```
public class Sample {

    @Autowired
    public Sample(@Qualifier("aBean") ABean bean) { .... }

    @Autowired
    public void doSomething(@Qualifier("bBean") BBean bean, CBean cBean) { ..... }
}
```

In the above example listing, @Qualifier annotation is specified for a constructor argument and a method argument. When creating an instance of Sample class, Spring finds a bean of type ABean with name aBean and passes it as an argument to the Sample class's constructor. When Sample's doSomething method is called, Spring finds a bean of type BBean (whose name is bBean) and another bean of type CBean, and passes both these beans as arguments to the doSomething method. It is important to note that the BBean dependency is autowired *by name*, and CBean dependency is autowired *by type*.

Instead of using bean names, you can use *qualifiers* for autowiring bean dependencies. Let's now look at how qualifiers are used for finding autowiring candidates.

Autowiring beans using qualifiers

A qualifier is a string value that you associate with a bean using @Qualifier annotation, and it need *not* be unique across beans registered with the Spring container. The following example listing shows usage of @Qualifier annotation to associate a qualifier with the bean:

Example listing 6-12 –TxDaoImpl class – associating qualifiers with beans
Project – ch06-bankapp-annotations
Source location - src/main/java/sample/spring/chapter06/bankapp/dao

```
package sample.spring.chapter06.bankapp.dao;
.....
@Repository(value = "txDao")
@Qualifier("myTx")
public class TxDaoImpl implements TxDao {
    .....
}
```

In the above example listing, myTx (specified by @Qualifier) is the qualifier and txDao (specified by @Repository) is the bean name. The following example listing shows how the txDao bean is autowired using the qualifier value:

Example listing 6-13 –TxServiceImpl class – autowiring using qualifiers
Project – ch06-bankapp-annotations
Source location - src/main/java/sample/spring/chapter06/bankapp/service

```
package sample.spring.chapter06.bankapp.service;
.....
@Service("txService")
public class TxServiceImpl implements TxService {
    @Autowired
    @Qualifier("myTx")
    private TxDao txDao;
    .....
}
```

In the above example listing, @Qualifier specifies the qualifier value myTx instead of the bean name txDao to autowire the txDao bean.

You can autowire all beans associated with a qualifier by defining a *typed collection*, as shown here:

Example listing 6-14 – Services class – obtaining all beans associated with service qualifier
Project – ch06-bankapp-annotations
Source location - src/main/java/sample/spring/chapter06/bankapp/service

```
package sample.spring.chapter06.bankapp.service;
.....
@Component
public class Services {
    @Autowired
    @Qualifier("service")
    private Set<MyService> services;
    .....
}
```

In the above example listing, Set<MyService> collection represents services that implement the MyService interface. @Qualifier autowires all beans associated with qualifier value service into Set<MyService> collection. In ch06-bankapp-annotations project, all services implement the MyService marker interface and are annotated with @Qualifier("service") annotation; therefore, all the services defined in ch06-bankapp-annotations project are autowired into the Set<MyService> collection.

Instead of using simple qualifier values and bean names, you can create custom qualifier annotations that define attributes based on which you can filter autowiring candidates. Let's look at how to create and use such annotations.

IMPORT **chapter 6/ch06-custom-qualifier** (This project shows the MyBank application that uses a custom qualifier annotation. To run the application, execute the main method of the BankApp class of this project.)

Creating custom qualifier annotations

MyBank allows its customers to transfer funds from one account to another. The following class diagram shows the MyBank application's classes that come into picture when transferring funds:

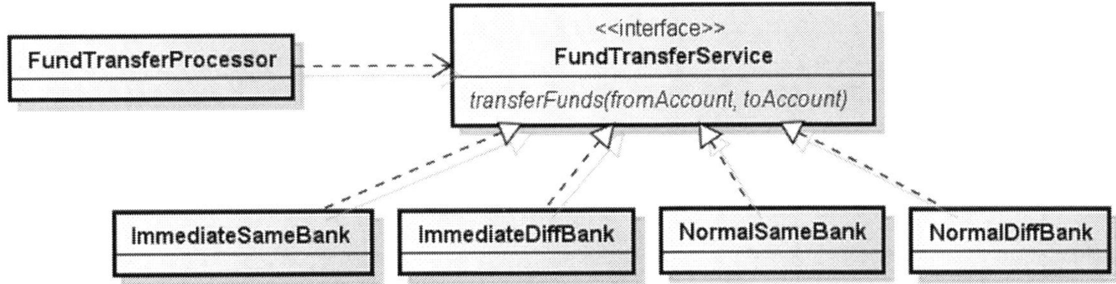

Figure 6-1 – FundTransferProcessor uses the FundTransferService to process fund transfers

In the above class diagram, the FundTransferProcessor is responsible for processing fund transfer requests. An appropriate implementation of FundTransferService is used depending upon whether the recipient's bank account is in the same or different bank, and whether the fund transfer needs to be done immediately or not. For instance, if the recipient's account is in the same bank (that is, MyBank) and the customer selects immediate fund transfer option, the ImmediateSameBank implementation is used for transferring funds.

The following example listing shows @FundTransfer custom qualifier annotation that defines transferSpeed and bankType attributes. We'll use this custom qualifier annotation later to autowire an appropriate implementation of FundTransferService into FundTransferProcessor instance.

Example listing 6-15 – @FundTransfer – a custom qualifier annotation
Project – ch06-bankapp-annotations
Source location - src/main/java/sample/spring/chapter06/bankapp/service

```
package sample.spring.chapter06.bankapp.annotation;
.....
import org.springframework.beans.factory.annotation.Qualifier;

@Target({ElementType.FIELD,ElementType.PARAMETER,ElementType.TYPE,
ElementType.ANNOTATION_TYPE })
@Retention(RetentionPolicy.RUNTIME)
@Qualifier
public @interface FundTransfer {
    TransferMode transferSpeed();
    BankType bankType();
}
```

@FundTransfer annotation is meta-annotated with Spring's @Qualifier annotation, which means that the @FundTransfer annotation is a custom qualifier annotation. If you don't meta-annotate @FundTransfer annotation with @Qualifier, then you need to explicitly register @FundTransfer annotation with the Spring container using Spring's CustomAutowireConfigurer (a BeanFactoryPostProcessor) bean. @FundTransfer serves the same purpose as Spring's @Qualifier annotation; it allows autowiring of beans based on transferSpeed and bankType attributes.

The following example listing shows the ImmediateSameBank bean class that implements the FundTransferService interface:

Example listing 6-16 –ImmediateSameBank – @FundTransfer annotation
Project – ch06-bankapp-annotations
Source location - src/main/java/sample/spring/chapter06/bankapp/service

```
package sample.spring.chapter06.bankapp.service;

import sample.spring.chapter06.bankapp.annotation.BankType;
```

```
import sample.spring.chapter06.bankapp.annotation.FundTransfer;
import sample.spring.chapter06.bankapp.annotation.TransferSpeed;
.....
@Service
@FundTransfer(transferSpeed = TransferSpeed.IMMEDIATE, bankType=BankType.SAME)
public class ImmediateSameBank implements FundTransferService {
    .....
}
```

ImmediateSameBank is annotated with @FundTransfer annotation which specifies values for transferSpeed and bankType attributes as TransferSpeed.IMMEDIATE and BankType.SAME, respectively. Similarly, ImmediateDiffBank, NormalSameBank and NormalDiffBank bean classes are implemented.

As shown in the following example listing, FundTransferProcessor uses the @FundTransfer annotation to autowire different implementations of FundTransferService into its fields:

Example listing 6-17 – FundTransferProcessor
Project – ch06-bankapp-annotations
Source location - src/main/java/sample/spring/chapter06/bankapp/service

```
package sample.spring.chapter06.bankapp.service;

import sample.spring.chapter06.bankapp.annotation.BankType;
import sample.spring.chapter06.bankapp.annotation.FundTransfer;
import sample.spring.chapter06.bankapp.annotation.TransferSpeed;
.....
@Component
public class FundTransferProcessor {
    @Autowired
    @FundTransfer(transferSpeed=TransferSpeed.IMMEDIATE, bankType=BankType.SAME)
    private FundTransferService sameBankImmediateFundTransferService;

    @Autowired
    @FundTransfer(transferSpeed=TransferSpeed.IMMEDIATE, bankType=BankType.DIFFERENT)
    private FundTransferService diffBankImmediateFundTransferService;
    .....
}
```

In the above example listing, @FundTransfer annotation autowires an instance of ImmediateSameBank into sameBankImmediateFundTransferService field, and an instance of ImmediateDiffBank into diffBankImmediateFundTransferService field.

If a custom qualifier annotation is *not* meta-annotated with @Qualifier, then you need to explicitly register it with the Spring container using Spring's CustomAutowireConfigurer (a BeanFactoryPostProcessor), as shown here:

Example listing 6-18 – registering custom qualifier annotations with CustomAutowireConfigurer

```
<bean class="org.springframework.beans.factory.annotation.CustomAutowireConfigurer">
    <property name="customQualifierTypes">
        <set>
            <value>sample.MyCustomQualifier</value>
        </set>
    </property>
</bean>
```

CustomAutowireConfigurer's customQualifierTypes property accepts custom qualifier annotations that you want to register with the Spring container. In the above example listing, CustomAutowireConfigurer registers MyCustomQualifier annotation with the Spring container.

Let's now look at JSR 330's @Inject and @Named annotations that you can use instead of Spring's @Autowired and @Qualifier annotations.

6-5 JSR 330's @Inject and @Named annotations

JSR 330 (Dependency Injection for Java) standardizes dependency injection annotations for the Java platform. JSR 330 defines @Inject and @Named annotations that are similar to Spring's @Autowired and @Qualifier annotations, respectively. Spring provides support for @Inject and @Named annotations.

IMPORT **chapter 6/ch06-bankapp-jsr330** (This project shows the MyBank application that uses JSR 330's @Inject and @Named annotations for autowiring dependencies. To run the application, execute the main method of the BankApp class of this project.)

The following example listing shows the FixedDepositServiceImpl class that makes use of JSR 330's @Inject and @Named annotations:

Example listing 6-19 – FixedDepositServiceImpl class
Project – ch06-bankapp-jsr330
Source location - src/main/java/sample/spring/chapter06/bankapp/service

```
package sample.spring.chapter06.bankapp.service;

import javax.inject.Inject;
import javax.inject.Named;

@Named(value="fixedDepositService")
public class FixedDepositServiceImpl implements FixedDepositService {

    @Inject
    @Named(value="myFixedDepositDao")
    private FixedDepositDao myFixedDepositDao;
    .....
}
```

If you compare the FixedDepositServiceImpl class shown in the above example listing with the FixedDepositServiceImpl class in example listing 6-10, you'll notice that JSR 330's @Named annotation has been used in place of @Service and @Qualifier annotations, and JSR 330's @Inject annotation has been used in place of @Autowired annotation.

@Autowired and @Inject annotations have the same semantics; they are used for autowiring dependencies *by type*. Like @Autowired annotation, @Inject can be used at method-level, constructor-level and field-level. Dependency injection of constructors is performed first, followed by fields, and then methods.

If @Named annotation is used at the type-level, it acts like Spring's @Component annotation. And, if @Named annotation is used at the method-parameter-level or constructor-argument-level, it acts like Spring's @Qualifier annotation. If a class is annotated with @Named annotation, <component-scan> element of Spring's context schema treats it like a bean class annotated with @Component annotation.

To use @Named and @Inject annotations, you need to include JSR 330 JAR file in your project. The ch06-bankapp-jsr330 project includes JSR 330 JAR file through the following <dependency> element in the pom.xml file:

```
<dependency>
    <groupId>javax.inject</groupId>
    <artifactId>javax.inject</artifactId>
    <version>1</version>
</dependency>
```

We discussed earlier that if you set @Autowired annotation's required attribute value to false, the dependency becomes *optional*; the Spring container doesn't throw an exception if the dependency is not found. @Inject doesn't have an equivalent of @Autowired annotation's required attribute, but you can use Java 8's Optional type to achieve the same behavior.

Java 8's Optional type

Spring supports autowiring of Optional type fields, constructor arguments and method parameters. The following example listing shows usage of Optional type for a dependency that is autowired using @Inject annotation:

Example listing 6-20 – Using Java 8's Optional type

```
import java.util.Optional;
.....
@Named(value="myService")
public class MyService {

    @Inject
    private Optional<ExternalService> externalServiceHolder;

    public void doSomething(Data data) {
        if(externalServiceHolder.isPresent()) {
            //-- save data using the external service
            externalServiceHolder.get().save(data);
        }
        else {
            //--save the data locally
            saveLocally(data);
        }
    }

    private void saveLocally(Data data) { ..... }
}
```

In the above example listing, MyService represents a bean that uses ExternalService bean for storing data remotely. If the ExternalService bean is not found, the data is stored locally. As ExternalService is an optional dependency (that is, it may not be available in some setups), MyService defines its dependency on the ExternalService bean using the externalServiceHolder field of type Optional<ExternalService>. An Optional type holds a non-null value, which is reference to an instance of ExternalService bean in the above example.

If the Spring container finds an ExternalService bean, it is stored in the externalServiceHolder field. Optional's isPresent method returns true if it contains a value, and false if it doesn't. In the above example listing, if the isPresent method returns true, the contained ExternalService instance is obtained by calling Optional's get method. The ExternalService's save method is then called to save the data remotely. If isPresent method returns false, the data is saved locally by calling the saveLocally method.

In chapter 5, we looked at JSR 250's @PostConstruct and @PreDestroy annotations that are used to identify initialization and destruction methods of a bean. Let's now look at JSR 250's @Resource annotation that you can use for autowiring dependencies *by name*.

6-6 JSR 250's @Resource annotation

Spring supports autowiring 'by name' of fields and setter methods via JSR 250's @Resource annotation. @Resource annotation is processed by CommonAnnotationBeanPostProcessor (a BeanPostProcessor implementation). @Resource annotation's name attribute specifies the name of the bean to be autowired. It is important to note that you can't use @Resource annotation for autowiring constructor arguments and methods that accept multiple arguments.

The following example listing shows how FixedDepositServiceImpl class from example listing 6-19 can be rewritten using @Resource annotation:

Example listing 6-20 – @Resource annotation usage at field-level

```
import javax.annotation.Resource;

@Named(value="fixedDepositService")
public class FixedDepositServiceImpl implements FixedDepositService {

    @Resource(name="myFixedDepositDao")
    private FixedDepositDao myFixedDepositDao;
    .....
}
```

In the above example listing, @Resource annotation has been used for autowiring myFixedDepositDao field. As the value of name attribute is myFixedDepositDao, Spring locates a bean named myFixedDepositDao in the Spring container and assigns it to myFixedDepositDao field.

Instead of using @Autowired and @Qualifier annotations, you should use @Resource annotation for autowiring dependencies 'by name'. As mentioned earlier, if you are using @Autowired-@Qualifier combination to perform autowiring 'by name', Spring first finds beans based on the type of the field (or the type of the method argument or constructor argument) to be autowired, followed by narrowing down to a unique bean based on the bean name specified by @Qualifier annotation. But, if you are using @Resource annotation, Spring uses bean name specified by @Resource annotation to locate a unique bean. This means that when you use @Resource annotation, type of the field (or setter method argument) to be autowired is *not* taken into consideration by Spring.

@Autowired annotation doesn't work for beans that are themselves of collection or Map type. For instance, if you define a bean using util schema's map element, you can't autowire it using @Autowired annotation. In such scenarios, you should use @Resource annotation for autowiring beans.

> As @Autowired, @Inject and @Resource annotations are processed by BeanPostProcessors, you should not use these annotations in component classes that implement BeanFactoryPostProcessor or BeanPostProcessor interface.

If @Resource's name attribute is not specified, the field name or the property name is used as the default value of the name attribute. The following example listing shows a bean class that doesn't use @Resource annotation with name attribute:

Example listing 6-21 – @Resource usage without name attribute value

```
@Named(value="mybean")
```

```
public class MyService {

    @Resource
    private MyDao myDao;
    private SomeService service;

    @Resource
    public void setOtherService(SomeService service) {
        this.service = service;
    }
}
```

In the above example listing, the default value of the first `@Resource` element's `name` attribute is `myDao` (the field name), and the default value of the second `@Resource` element's `name` attribute is `otherService` (the property name derived from the `setOtherService` setter-method name). If a bean named `myDao` is not found, `@Resource` annotation behaves the same way as the `@Autowired` annotation; the Spring container looks for a bean whose type is `MyDao` (which is the field type). Similarly, if a bean named `otherService` is not found, the Spring container looks for a bean whose type is `SomeService` (the setter-method argument type).

Let's now look at `@Scope`, `@Lazy`, `@DependsOn` and `@Primary` annotations.

6-7 @Scope, @Lazy, @DependsOn and @Primary annotations

The following table describes the purpose served by `@Scope`, `@Lazy`, `@DependsOn` and `@Primary` annotations:

Annotation	Description
@Scope	specifies the bean scope (same as `<bean>` element's `scope` attribute)
@Lazy	specifies that the bean is lazily created by the Spring container (same as `<bean>` element's `lazy-init` attribute)
@DependsOn	specifies implicit dependencies of the bean (same as `<bean>` element's `depends-on` attribute)
@Primary	specifies the bean as the primary candidate for autowiring (same as `<bean>` element's `primary` attribute)

Let's now look at each of the above mentioned annotations in detail.

@Scope

You specify the scope of a bean using Spring's `@Scope` annotation. By default, Spring beans are singleton-scoped. If you want to specify a different scope for a bean, you have to specify it via `@Scope` annotation. `@Scope` annotation plays the same role as the `<bean>` element's `scope` attribute (refer section 2-6 of chapter 2 to know more about the `scope` attribute).

The following example listing shows the `CustomerRequestDetails` class that uses `@Scope` annotation:

Example listing 6-22 – `@Scope` annotation usage
Project – `ch06-bankapp-jsr330`
Source location - `src/main/java/sample/spring/chapter06/bankapp/domain`

```
package sample.spring.chapter06.bankapp.domain;

import javax.inject.Named;
import org.springframework.beans.factory.config.ConfigurableBeanFactory;
```

```
import org.springframework.context.annotation.Scope;

@Named(value="customerRequestDetails")
@Scope(value=ConfigurableBeanFactory.SCOPE_PROTOTYPE)
public class CustomerRequestDetails { ..... }
```

@Scope annotation accepts a value attribute that specifies the scope of the bean. For instance, you can set value attribute's value to prototype to indicate that the bean is prototype-scoped. You can also specify value attribute's value using SCOPE_* constants defined in ConfigurableBeanFactory (defines constants for singleton and prototype scopes) and WebApplicationContext (defines constants for application, session and request scopes) interfaces.

If you are using Spring 4.2 or later, then instead of using the value attribute, you can use the scopeName attribute of @Scope annotation to specify the bean scope. Spring 4.2 added *attribute alias* to most of its annotations (like @RequestMapping, @RequestParam, and so on) to allow referring to the value attribute with a more meaningful name. For instance, in the case of @Scope annotation, scopeName is an attribute alias for the value attribute.

@Lazy

By default, singleton-scoped Spring beans are *eagerly* initialized, that is, they are instantiated when the Spring container is created. If you want a singleton bean to be lazily created, annotate the bean class of a singleton bean with @Lazy annotation.

> @Lazy annotation on the bean class serves the same purpose as the <bean> element's lazy-init attribute. Refer section 2-6 of chapter 2 to know more about lazy-init attribute.

The following example listing shows usage of @Lazy annotation:

Example listing 6-23 – @Lazy annotation usage

```
@Lazy(value=true)
@Component
public class Sample { ..... }
```

@Lazy annotation's value attribute specifies whether the bean is lazily or eagerly initialized. If the value attribute's value is true, it means that the bean is lazily initialized. If you don't specify the value attribute, the bean is considered to be lazily initialized.

@Lazy annotation can also be used to *lazily autowire* dependencies.

IMPORT **chapter 6/ch06-lazy-dependencies** (This project shows an application that uses @Lazy annotation along with @Autowired annotation for lazily autowiring dependencies. To run the application, execute the main method of the SampleApp class of this project.)

Lazily autowiring dependencies

You can use @Lazy annotation along with autowiring annotations (like @Autowired, @Inject and @Resource) to lazily autowire dependencies (that is, dependencies are autowired when they are accessed by the dependent bean). Let's look at an example that shows how to lazily autowire dependencies.

The following figure shows the beans contained in the ch06-lazy-dependencies project:

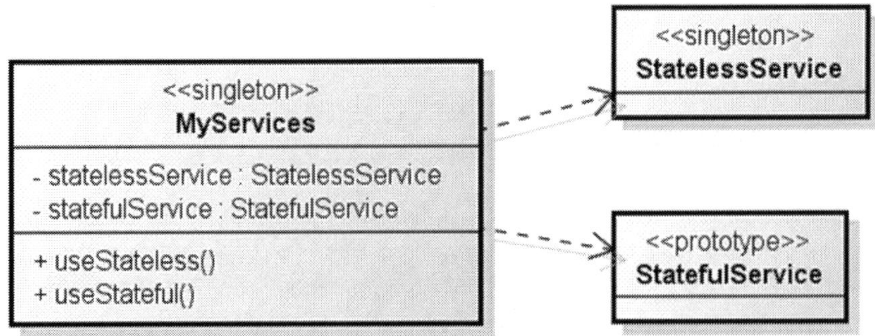

Figure 6-2 – MyServices depends on StatelessService (a singleton bean) and StatefulService (a prototype bean) beans

MyServices is a singleton bean that depends on singleton-scoped StatelessService and prototype-scoped StatefulService beans. MyServices class defines statelessService (of type StatelessService) and statefulService (of type StatefulService) fields that are autowired. The useStateless and useStateful methods access StatelessService and StatefulService beans, respectively. It is expected that the StatelessService and StatefulService beans are autowired into MyServices only when they are accessed by useStateless and useStateful methods.

The following example listing shows the MyServices class:

Example listing 6-24 – MyServices class – lazily autowiring dependencies
Project – ch06-lazy-dependencies
Source location - src/main/java/sample/spring

```
package sample.spring;
.....
@Service
public class MyServices {
    private static Logger logger = LogManager.getLogger(MyServices.class);

    @Autowired
    @Lazy
    private StatelessService statelessService;

    @Autowired
    @Lazy
    private StatefulService statefulService;

    public void useStateless() {
        logger.info(" --> " + statelessService);
    }

    public void useStateful() {
        logger.info(" --> " + statefulService);
    }
}
```

As we want StatelessService and StatefulService dependencies to be lazily autowired into the MyServices bean, statelessService and statefulService fields are annotated with both @Autowired and @Lazy annotations. The useStateless and useStateful methods don't do anything interesting; they simply write the StatelessService and StatefulService bean instances to the console.

StatefulService bean (refer StatefulService class in ch06-lazy-dependencies project) is prototype-scoped; therefore, it is lazily created by the Spring container. StatelessService bean (refer StatelessService class in ch06-lazy-dependencies project) is singleton-scoped but it is annotated with @Lazy, which instructs the Spring container to lazily create it.

As both StatelessService and StatefulService beans are defined to be *lazily created*, only MyServices singleton bean is created when the Spring container is created. As both StatelessService and StatefulService are specified to be *lazily autowired* into the MyServices bean, the Spring container doesn't attempt to autowire them when MyServices bean is created. When useStateless and useStateful methods of MyServices are invoked, only then the autowiring of StatelessService and StatefulService beans is performed by the Spring container, resulting in creation of StatefulService and StatelessService beans.

The following example listing shows the SampleApp class whose main method calls useStateless and useStateful methods of MyServices bean:

Example listing 6-25 – SampleApp class
Project – ch06-lazy-dependencies
Source location - src/main/java/sample/spring

```
package sample.spring;
.....
public class SampleApp {
    private static Logger logger = LogManager.getLogger(SampleApp.class);

    public static void main(String args[]) throws Exception {
        ConfigurableApplicationContext context = new ClassPathXmlApplicationContext(
                "classpath:META-INF/spring/applicationContext.xml");
        MyServices services = context.getBean(MyServices.class);

        logger.info("Calling --> useStateless");
        services.useStateless();

        logger.info("Calling again --> useStateless");
        services.useStateless();

        logger.info("Calling --> useStateful");
        services.useStateful();

        logger.info("Calling again --> useStateful");
        services.useStateful();

        context.close();
    }
}
```

SampleApp's main method calls both the useStateless and useStateful methods twice to demonstrate how lazy autowiring of MyServices dependencies are performed by the Spring container. If you run the main method, you'll see the following output on the console:

```
INFO  sample.spring.SampleApp - Calling --> useStateless
INFO  sample.spring.StatelessService - Created StatelessService
INFO  sample.spring.MyServices -  --> sample.spring.StatelessService@4445629
INFO  sample.spring.SampleApp - Calling again --> useStateless
INFO  sample.spring.MyServices -  --> sample.spring.StatelessService@4445629
```

```
INFO  sample.spring.SampleApp - Calling --> useStateful
INFO  sample.spring.StatefulService - Created StatefulService
INFO  sample.spring.MyServices -  --> sample.spring.StatefulService@4df50bcc
INFO  sample.spring.SampleApp - Calling again --> useStateful
INFO  sample.spring.StatefulService - Created StatefulService
INFO  sample.spring.MyServices -  --> sample.spring.StatefulService@63a65a25
```

The output shows that the first call to useStateless method results in creation of StatelessService bean (indicated by the 'Created StatelessService' message written by StatelessService's constructor). The second call to useStateless method doesn't result in creation of StatelessService bean because it's a singleton bean. On the other hand, both calls to useStateful results in creation of StatefulService bean (indicated by the 'Created StatefulService' message written by StatefulService's constructor) because it's a prototype bean. This shows that StatelessService and StatefulService beans are autowired by the Spring container only when they are accessed by the methods defined in MyServices bean. This also shows that if you have a singleton bean (which is MyService in our example) that depends on a prototype bean (which is StatefulService in our example), then you can use the lazy autowiring approach to access a new instance of prototype bean each time it is accessed by the methods defined in the singleton bean.

@DependsOn

You specify implicit bean dependencies using @DependsOn annotation. The following example listing shows usage of @DependsOn annotation:

Example listing 6-26 – @DependsOn annotation usage

```
@DependsOn(value = {"beanA", "beanB"})
@Component
public class Sample { ..... }
```

In the above example listing, @DependsOn annotation on the Sample class instructs the Spring container to create beanA and beanB beans before creating an instance of Sample class.

> @DependsOn annotation serves the same purpose as the <bean> element's depends-on attribute. Refer section 4-3 of chapter 4 to know more about depends-on attribute.

@Primary

If multiple autowiring candidates are available for a dependency, @Primary annotation designates a bean as a primary candidate for autowiring. The following example listing shows usage of @Primary annotation:

Example listing 6-27 – @Primary annotation usage

```
@Primary
@Component
public class Sample { ..... }
```

> @Primary annotation serves the same purpose as the <bean> element's primary attribute. Refer section 4-6 of chapter 4 to know more about primary attribute.

Let's now look at Spring's @Value annotation that simplifies configuring annotated bean classes.

6-8 Simplifying configuration of annotated bean classes using @Value annotation

In previous chapters, we saw examples in which configuration information required by beans was specified via value attribute of <property> and <constructor-arg> elements. As annotated Spring beans are not defined in the application context XML file, Spring's @Value annotation is used to serve the same purpose as the value attribute of <property> and <constructor-arg> elements. You should note that the @Value annotation can be used at field-level, method-level, method-parameter-level and constructor-argument-level. Spring's AutowiredAnnotationBeanPostProcessor, which handles @Autowired and @Inject annotations, is responsible for handling the @Value annotation.

IMPORT **chapter 6/ch06-value-annotation** (This project shows an application that uses Spring's @Value annotation to configure Spring components. To run the application, execute the main method of the SampleApp class of this project.)

The following example listing shows an example usage of @Value annotation at field-level:

Example listing 6-28 – Sample class - @Value annotation usage
Project – ch06-value-annotation
Source location - src/main/java/sample/spring/chapter06/beans

```
package sample.spring.chapter06.beans;

import org.springframework.beans.factory.annotation.Value;

@Component(value="sample")
public class Sample {
    @Value("Some currency")
    private String currency;
    .....
}
```

In the above example listing, currency field is annotated with @Value annotation. The @Value annotation's value attribute specifies the default value for the field. It is optional to specify the value attribute; therefore, @Value(value="Some currency") is same as @Value("Some currency").

> @Value annotation is processed by a BeanPostProcessor; therefore, you should not use @Value annotation in bean classes that implement BeanFactoryPostProcessor or BeanPostProcessor interface.

Instead of specifying a string value, you can specify a Spring Expression Language (SpEL) expression as the value of @Value annotation's value attribute.

Using Spring Expression Language (SpEL) with @Value annotation

SpEL is an *expression language* that you can use to query and manipulate objects at runtime. The following example listing shows the Sample bean class that specifies @Value annotations that make use of SpEL expressions:

Example listing 6-29 – Sample class - using SpEL expressions with @Value annotations
Project – ch06-value-annotation
Source location - src/main/java/sample/spring/chapter06/beans

```
package sample.spring.chapter06.beans;
```

```
import org.springframework.beans.factory.annotation.Value;

@Component(value="sample")
public class Sample {
    @Value("#{configuration.environment}")
    private String environment;
    .....
    @Value("#{configuration.getCountry()}")
    private String country;

    @Value("#{configuration.state}")
    private String state;
    .....
}
```

The above example listing shows that the @Value annotation specifies a value that has the syntax #{<spel-expression>}. The SpEL expression specified by @Value annotation is processed by AutowiredAnnotationBeanPostProcessor (a BeanPostProcessor). The SpEL expressions can make use of <beanName>.<field or property or method> format to obtain its value. For instance, #{configuration.environment} means obtain value of environment property of bean named configuration, and #{configuration.getCountry()} means invoke getCountry method of bean named configuration.

The following example listing shows the configuration bean's class that was referenced by SpEL expressions shown in example listing 6-29:

Example listing 6-30 – Configuration bean class
Project – ch06-value-annotation
Source location - src/main/java/sample/spring/chapter06/beans

```
package sample.spring.chapter06.beans;

import org.springframework.stereotype.Component;

@Component("configuration")
public class Configuration {
    public static String environment = "DEV";

    public String getCountry() {
        return "Some country";
    }

    public String getState() {
        return "Some state";
    }

    public String[] splitName(String name) {
        return name.split(" ");
    }

    public String getCity() {
        return "Some city";
    }
}
```

Configuration bean class defines fields and methods. If you compare example listing 6-29 with 6-30, you'll notice that #{configuration.environment} expression refers to the static environment variable defined in the Configuration class, #{configuration.getCountry()} expression refers to Configuration's getCountry method, and #{configuration.state} expression refers to Configuration's getState method.

The main method of SampleApp class in ch06-value-annotation project retrieves an instance of Sample bean from the ApplicationContext and prints the value of various attributes of Sample bean instance. If you execute SampleApp's main method, you'll see the following output:

```
environment --> DEV

country --> Some country

state --> Some state
```

The above output shows:

- #{configuration.environment} expression sets Sample's environment field value to 'DEV', which is the value of public static field environment of Configuration class.

- #{configuration.getCountry()} expression sets Sample's country field value to 'Some country', which is the value returned by invoking Configuration's getCountry method.

- #{configuration.state} expression sets Sample's state field value to 'Some state', which is the value returned by invoking Configuration's getState method.

The above example shows that you can use SpEL to retrieve configuration information from other beans.

Using @Value annotation at method-level and method-parameter-level

The following example listing shows usage of @Value annotation at method-level and method-parameter-level:

Example listing 6-31 – Sample class - @Value annotation usage at method-level and method-parameter-level
Project – ch06-value-annotation
Source location - src/main/java/sample/spring/chapter06/beans

```
package sample.spring.chapter06.beans;

import org.springframework.beans.factory.annotation.Autowired;
import org.springframework.beans.factory.annotation.Value;

@Component(value="sample")
public class Sample {
    .....
    private String[] splitName;
    private String city;

    @Autowired
    public void splitName(@Value("#{configuration.splitName('FirstName LastName')}")
                                                String[] splitName) {
        this.splitName = splitName;
    }

    @Autowired
    @Value("#{configuration.getCity()}")
    public void city(String city) {
```

```
        this.city = city;
    }
    .....
}
```

The above example listing shows that the methods that are annotated with @Autowired annotation make use of @Value annotation at method-level and method-parameter-level. You should note that the @Value annotation can be used at method-level and method-parameter-level *only if* the method is annotated with @Autowired or @Resource or @Inject annotation. SpEL expression #{configuration.splitName('FirstName LastName')} results in invocation of Configuration's splitName method with 'FirstName LastName' as argument. This shows that SpEL expressions can be used to invoke methods that accept arguments.

The output from executing SampleApp's main method shows the following values of splitName and city attributes:

```
city --> Some city
splitName --> FirstName LastName
```

Using mathematical, relational and logical operators in SpEL

You can use mathematical, relational and logical operators in SpEL expressions, as shown in the following example listing:

Example listing 6-32 – Sample class – using different operators
Project – ch06-value-annotation
Source location - src/main/java/sample/spring/chapter06/beans

```
package sample.spring.chapter06.beans;
.....
@Component(value = "sample")
public class Sample {
    .....
    @Value("#{101 > 100}")
    private boolean isGreaterThan;

    @Value("#{3 > 2 && 4 > 3}")
    private boolean isConditionTrue;

    @Value("#{100 + 200 - 300*1 + 4/2}")
    private int totalAmount;
    .....
}
```

The output from executing SampleApp's main method shows the following values of isGreaterThan, isConditionTrue and totalAmount attributes:

```
isGreaterThan --> true
isConditionTrue --> true
totalAmount --> 2
```

Obtaining bean reference using SpEL

You can obtain reference to a bean by simply specifying the bean name in the `@Value` annotation, as shown here:

Example listing 6-33 – Sample class – obtaining bean reference
Project – ch06-value-annotation
Source location - src/main/java/sample/spring/chapter06/beans

```
package sample.spring.chapter06.beans;
.....
@Component(value = "sample")
public class Sample {
    .....
    @Value("#{configuration}")
    private Configuration myConfiguration;
    .....
}
```

In the above example listing, the reference to bean named `configuration` is assigned to `myConfiguration` attribute.

Using regular expressions in SpEL

Regular expressions are also supported by SpEL via `matches` operator, as shown in the following example listing:

Example listing 6-34 – Sample class – using regular expressions
Project – ch06-value-annotation
Source location - src/main/java/sample/spring/chapter06/beans

```
package sample.spring.chapter06.beans;
.....
@Component(value = "sample")
public class Sample {
    .....
    @Value("#{('abcd@xyz.com' matches '^[A-Za-z0-9+_.-]+@(.+)$') == true ? true : false}")
    private boolean isEmailId;
    .....
}
```

In the above example listing, `abcd@xyz.com` email id is matched to the regular expression `^[A-Za-z0-9+_.-]+@(.+)$` using the `matches` operator. The above example also shows that you can also use the ternary operator (`condition : trueExpression : falseExpression`) with SpEL.

Working with maps and lists in SpEL

You can also work with maps and lists using SpEL. The following example listing shows configuration of `mapType` (of type `Map`) and `listType` (of type `List`) beans in the application context XML file using Spring's `util` schema:

Example listing 6-35 – applicationContext.xml
Project – ch06-value-annotation
Source location - src/main/resources/META-INF/spring

```
    <util:list id="listType" list-class="java.util.ArrayList">
        <value>A simple String value in list</value>
        <value>Another simple String value in list</value>
```

```
    </util:list>
    <util:map id="mapType" map-class="java.util.TreeMap">
        <entry key="map key 1" value="map key 1's value" />
    </util:map>
```

You can access items contained in `listType` and `mapType` beans using SpEL, as shown in the following example listing:

Example listing 6-36 – Sample class – working with lists and maps
Project – ch06-value-annotation
Source location - src/main/java/sample/spring/chapter06/beans

```
package sample.spring.chapter06.beans;
.....
@Component(value = "sample")
public class Sample {
    .....
    @Value("#{listType[0]}")
    private String listItem;

    @Value("#{mapType['map key 1']}")
    private String mapItem;
    .....
}
```

In the above example listing, `#{listType[0]}` expression retrieves the first element from the `listType`, and `#{mapType['map key 1']}` expression retrieves the value corresponding to 'map key 1' key.

The output from executing `SampleApp`'s `main` method shows the following values of `listItem`, and `mapItem` attributes:

```
listItem --> A simple String value in list
mapItem --> map key 1's value
```

Specifying SpEL expressions in XML-based bean definitions

Usage of SpEL is *not* limited to `@Value` annotations, you can use SpEL in bean definitions contained in application context XML files.

IMPORT **chapter 6/ch06-spel-example** (This project shows an application that uses SpEL expressions in bean definitions contained in an application context XML file. To run the application, execute the `main` method of the `SampleApp` class of this project.)

The following example listing shows how SpEL is used in XML-based bean definitions:

Example listing 6-37 – applicationContext.xml – SpEL expressions in bean definitions
Project – ch06-spel-example
Source location - src/main/resources/META-INF/spring

```
<beans ..... >
    <bean id="sample" class="sample.spring.chapter06.beans.Sample">
        <property name="environment" value="#{configuration.environment}" />
        <property name="currency" value="Some currency" />
        <property name="country" value="#{configuration.getCountry()}" />
        <property name="state" value="#{configuration.state}" />
    </bean>
```

```
    <bean id="configuration" class="sample.spring.chapter06.beans.Configuration" />
</beans>
```

The above example listing shows that the bean definition for the `Sample` class makes use of SpEL expressions (that refer to `Configuration` bean) to set default values for `environment`, `currency`, `country` and `state` properties.

> SpEL is a very powerful expression language, and it offers many more capabilities than described in this book. It is recommended that you refer to Spring reference documentation to know more about SpEL.

Let's now look at how you can perform validation of objects in Spring applications using Spring's `Validator` interface.

6-9 Validating objects using Spring's `Validator` interface

Spring's `Validator` interface is part of Spring Validation API that allows you to perform validation of objects. You can use the `Validator` interface for performing validation of objects in any of the application layers. For instance, you can use the `Validator` interface to validate objects in the web layer as well as in the persistence layer.

> An alternative to using the `Validator` interface is to use JSR 380 annotations to specify constraints that apply on an object. JSR 380 annotations are explained in the next section.

IMPORT **`chapter 6/ch06-validator-interface`** (This project shows the MyBank application that uses Spring's `Validator` interface to validate `FixedDepositDetails` object. To run the application, execute the `main` method of the `BankApp` class of this project.)

The `FixedDepositDetails` object of MyBank application represents details of a fixed deposit. The following example listing shows the `FixedDepositDetails` class:

Example listing 6-38 – `FixedDepositDetails` class
Project – `ch06-validator-interface`
Source location - `src/main/java/sample/spring/chapter06/bankapp/domain`

```
package sample.spring.chapter06.bankapp.domain;

public class FixedDepositDetails {
    private long id;
    private float depositAmount;
    private int tenure;
    private String email;

    public FixedDepositDetails(long id, float depositAmount, int tenure,
            String email) {
        this.id = id;
        this.depositAmount = depositAmount;
        this.tenure = tenure;
        this.email = email;
    }
    .....
    //-- getters and setters for instance variables
    public float getDepositAmount() {
        return depositAmount;
    }
```

```
    .....
}
```

The above example listing shows that the `FixedDepositDetails` class defines `id`, `depositAmount`, `tenure` and `email` instance variables. Let's say that before the fixed deposit details are saved in the system, we need to make sure that the fixed deposit amount (represented by the `depositAmount` instance variable) is not `0`.

To validate the `FixedDepositDetails` object's `depositAmount` property, we need to create an implementation of Spring's `Validator` interface. The following example listing shows a validator for objects of type `FixedDepositDetails`:

Example listing 6-39 – `FixedDepositValidator` class – Spring's `Validator` interface implementation
Project – `ch06-validator-interface`
Source location - `src/main/java/sample/spring/chapter06/bankapp/validator`

```
package sample.spring.chapter06.bankapp.validator;

import org.springframework.validation.Errors;
import org.springframework.validation.Validator;

public class FixedDepositValidator implements Validator {

    @Override
    public boolean supports(Class<?> clazz) {
        return FixedDepositDetails.class.isAssignableFrom(clazz);
    }

    @Override
    public void validate(Object target, Errors errors) {
        FixedDepositDetails fixedDepositDetails = (FixedDepositDetails) target;
        if (fixedDepositDetails.getDepositAmount() == 0) {
            errors.reject("zeroDepositAmount");
        }
    }
}
```

The `Validator` interface defines `supports` and `validate` methods. The `supports` method checks if the supplied object instance (represented by the `clazz` attribute) can be validated. If the `supports` method returns `true`, the `validate` method is used to validate the object. In the above example listing, the `FixedDepositValidator`'s `supports` method checks if the supplied object instance is of type `FixedDepositDetails`. If the `supports` method returns `true`, the `FixedDepositValidator`'s `validate` method validates the object. The `validate` method accepts the object instance to be validated, and an `Errors` instance. The `Errors` instance's `reject` method is used to store errors that occur during validation. You can later inspect the `Errors` instance to know more about the validation errors.

The following example listing shows that the `FixedDepositServiceImpl`'s `createFixedDeposit` method uses the `FixedDepositValidator` (refer example listing 6-39) to validate `FixedDepositDetails` objects:

Example listing 6-40 – `FixedDepositServiceImpl` class – Validating `FixedDepositDetails` object
Project – `ch06-validator-interface`
Source location - `src/main/java/sample/spring/chapter06/bankapp/service`

```
package sample.spring.chapter06.bankapp.service;

import org.springframework.validation.BeanPropertyBindingResult;
import sample.spring.chapter06.bankapp.validator.FixedDepositValidator;
```

```
@Service(value="fixedDepositService")
public class FixedDepositServiceImpl implements FixedDepositService {

    @Autowired
    @Qualifier(value="myFixedDepositDao")
    private FixedDepositDao myFixedDepositDao;

    @Override
    public void createFixedDeposit(FixedDepositDetails fixedDepositDetails)
          throws Exception {
        BeanPropertyBindingResult bindingResult =
                new BeanPropertyBindingResult(fixedDepositDetails, "Errors");
        FixedDepositValidator validator = new FixedDepositValidator();
        validator.validate(fixedDepositDetails, bindingResult);

        if(bindingResult.getErrorCount() > 0) {
            logger.error("Errors were found while
                   validating FixedDepositDetails instance");
        } else {
            myFixedDepositDao.createFixedDeposit(fixedDepositDetails);
            logger.info("Created fixed deposit");
        }
    }
}
```

FixedDepositServiceImpl's createFixedDeposit method validates the FixedDepositDetails object (represented by fixedDepositDetails argument) before it is saved into the data store by FixedDepositDao. The createFixedDeposit method shown in the above example listing performs the following tasks:

- creates an instance of FixedDepositValidator and Spring's BeanPropertyBindingResult - a default implementation of Errors interface provided out-of-the-box by Spring
- invokes FixedDepositValidator's validate method, passing FixedDepositDetails object and the BeanPropertyBindingResult instance
- invokes BeanPropertyBindingResult's getErrorCount method to check if any validation errors were reported. If no validation errors are reported, FixedDepositDao's createFixedDeposit method is called to save fixed deposit details in the data store.

The following example listing shows BankApp's main method that invokes FixedDepositServiceImpl's createFixedDeposit method (refer example listing 6-40) to check if the validation is performed correctly by FixedDepositValidator's validate method:

Example listing 6-41 – BankApp class
Project – ch06-validator-interface
Source location - src/main/java/sample/spring/chapter06/bankapp

```
package sample.spring.chapter06.bankapp;

public class BankApp {
    public static void main(String args[]) throws Exception {
        ApplicationContext context = new ClassPathXmlApplicationContext(
                "classpath:META-INF/spring/applicationContext.xml");

        FixedDepositService fixedDepositService =
```

```
            context.getBean(FixedDepositService.class);

        fixedDepositService.createFixedDeposit(new FixedDepositDetails(1, 0,
                12, "someemail@somedomain.com"));
        fixedDepositService.createFixedDeposit(new FixedDepositDetails(1, 1000,
                12, "someemail@somedomain.com"));
    }
}
```

First, FixedDepositService's createFixedDeposit method is passed a FixedDepositDetails object with depositAmount value as 0, followed by a FixedDepositDetails object with depositAmount value as 1000.

If you execute BankApp's main method, you'll see the following output on the console:

```
Errors were found while validating FixedDepositDetails instance
Created fixed deposit
```

The output 'Errors were found while validating FixedDepositDetails instance' shows that FixedDepositValidator reported errors when the FixedDepositDetails instance with 0 as the depositAmount value was validated. The output 'Created fixed deposit' shows that no errors were reported when the FixedDepositDetails instance with 1000 as the depositAmount value was validated.

> Spring's Validator interface is typically used in Spring MVC based web applications while binding information entered by a user in the HTML form to the corresponding form-backing object.

Let's now look at how you can specify constraints on beans using JSR 380 annotations, and let Spring perform the validation.

6-10 Specifying constraints using JSR 380 (Bean Validation 2.0) annotations

JSR 380 (Bean Validation 2.0) allows you to use annotations to specify constraints on JavaBeans components. When using JSR 380 with Spring, you annotate bean properties, methods and container (like, collections and maps) elements with JSR 380 annotations, and Spring takes care of validating the bean and providing the validation result.

> Spring 5 supports JSR 349 (Bean Validation 1.1) and JSR 380 (Bean Validation 2.0). Spring 4.x supports JSR 303 (Bean Validation 1.0) and JSR 349 (Bean Validation 1.1).

IMPORT **chapter 6/ch06-jsr380-validation** (This project shows the MyBank application that uses JSR 380 annotations. To run the application, execute the main method of the BankApp class of this project.)

The following example listing shows the FixedDepositDetails class that makes use of JSR 380 annotations:

Example listing 6-42 – FixedDepositDetails class – JSR 380 annotations
Project – ch06-jsr380-validation
Source location - src/main/java/sample/spring/chapter06/bankapp/domain

```
package sample.spring.chapter06.bankapp.domain;

import javax.validation.constraints.*;
import javax.validation.constraints.NotBlank;

public class FixedDepositDetails {
    @NotNull
```

```
    private long id;

    @Min(1000)
    @Max(500000)
    private float depositAmount;

    @Min(6)
    private int tenure;

    @NotBlank
    @Size(min=5, max=100)
    private String email;

    public FixedDepositDetails(long id, float depositAmount, int tenure, String email) {
        this.id = id;
        this.depositAmount = depositAmount;
        this.tenure = tenure;
        this.email = email;
    }
    .....
}
```

`@NotNull`, `@Min`, `@Max`, `@NotBlank` and `@Size` are some of the annotations defined by JSR 380 Bean Validation API. The above example listing shows that by using JSR 380 annotations `FixedDepositDetails` class clearly specifies the constraints that apply on its fields. On the other hand, if you are using Spring Validation API to validate an object, constraint information is contained in the `Validator` implementation (refer example listing 6-39).

The following table describes the constraints enforced by JSR 380 annotations on the `FixedDepositDetails` object shown in example listing 6-42:

JSR 380 annotation	Constraint description
@NotNull	The annotated field must not be null. For instance, `FixedDepositDetails'` id field must not be null.
@Min	The annotated field's value must be greater than or equal to the specified minimum value. For instance, `@Min(1000)` annotation on `depositAmount` field of `FixedDepositDetails` object means that `depositAmount`'s value must be greater than or equal to `1000`.
@Max	The annotated field's value must be less than or equal to the specified value. For instance, `@Max(500000)` annotation on `depositAmount` field of `FixedDepositDetails` object means that the `depositAmount`'s value must be less than or equal to `500000`.
@NotBlank	The annotated field's value must not be null or empty. For instance, `FixedDepositDetails'` `email` field must not be empty or null.
@Size	The annotated field's size must be between the specified `min` and `max` attributes. For instance, `@Size(min=5, max=100)` annotation on `email` field of `FixedDepositDetails` object means that the size of the `email` field must be greater than or equal to 5 and less than or equal to `100`.

> To use JSR 380 annotations, `ch06-jsr380-validation` project specifies dependency on JSR 380 API JAR file (`validation-api-2.0.0.FINAL`) and Hibernate Validator framework (`hibernate-validation-6.0.4.Final`). Hibernate Validator framework provides the reference implementation for JSR 380. As Hibernate Validator requires an implementation of the Unified Expression language (JSR 341), `ch06-jsr380-validation` project specifies dependency on `javax.el-api` (the API) and `javax.el` (the reference implementation).

The annotations shown in the above table are defined by JSR 380. Hibernate Validator framework provides additional constraint annotations (like `@Currency`, `@CreditCardNumber`, and so on) that you can use along with JSR 380 annotations.

Now that we have specified JSR 380 constraints on `FixedDepositDetails` class, let's look at how to validate `FixedDepositDetails` object using Spring.

JSR 380 support in Spring

Spring supports validating objects that make use of JSR 380 constraints. Spring's `LocalValidatorFactoryBean` class is responsible for detecting the presence of a JSR 380 provider (like Hibernate Validator) in the application's classpath and initializing it. It is important to note that the `LocalValidatorFactoryBean` implements JSR 380's `Validator` and `ValidatorFactory` interfaces, and also Spring's `Validator` interface.

The following example listing shows the configuration of `LocalValidatorFactoryBean` class in the application context XML file:

Example listing 6-43 – `applicationContext.xml` – Spring's `LocalValidatorFactoryBean` configuration
Project – `ch06-jsr380-validation`
Source location - `src/main/resources/META-INF/spring`

```
<bean id="validator"
        class="org.springframework.validation.beanvalidation.LocalValidatorFactoryBean" />
```

As you can see, `LocalValidatorFactoryBean` is configured like any other Spring bean. Now that we have configured `LocalValidatorFactoryBean`, let's see how it is used to perform validation.

The following example listing shows `FixedDepositServiceImpl`'s `createFixedDeposit` method that validates the `FixedDepositDetails` object before saving fixed deposit details in the data store:

Example listing 6-44 – `FixedDepositServiceImpl` class – validating `FixedDepositDetails` object
Project – `ch06-jsr380-validation`
Source location - `src/main/java/sample/spring/chapter06/bankapp/service`

```
package sample.spring.chapter06.bankapp.service;

import org.springframework.validation.BeanPropertyBindingResult;
import org.springframework.validation.Validator;
.....
@Service(value="fixedDepositService")
public class FixedDepositServiceImpl implements FixedDepositService {

    @Autowired
    private Validator validator;

    @Autowired
    @Qualifier(value="myFixedDepositDao")
    private FixedDepositDao myFixedDepositDao;
```

```
    @Override
    public void createFixedDeposit(FixedDepositDetails fixedDepositDetails)
          throws Exception {
        BeanPropertyBindingResult bindingResult =
              new BeanPropertyBindingResult(fixedDepositDetails, "Errors");
        validator.validate(fixedDepositDetails, bindingResult);

        if(bindingResult.getErrorCount() > 0) {
            logger.error("Errors were found while validating
                  FixedDepositDetails instance");
        } else {
            myFixedDepositDao.createFixedDeposit(fixedDepositDetails);
            logger.info("Created fixed deposit");
        }
    }
}
```

The above example listing shows that Spring's `Validator` implementation is referenced by the `validator` field. As `LocalValidatorFactoryBean` implements Spring's `Validator` interface, `LocalValidatorFactoryBean` instance is assigned to the `validator` field. `FixedDepositServiceImpl`'s `createFixedDeposit` method invokes `Validator`'s `validate` method to perform validation of `FixedDepositDetails` object.

One of the interesting things to notice in example listing 6-44 is that we are *not* dealing with JSR 380 API to perform validation of `FixedDepositDetails` object. Instead, we have used Spring Validation API to perform validation. This is possible because `LocalValidatorFactoryBean` implements `validate` method of Spring's `Validator` interface to use JSR 380 API to perform validation of objects, shielding developers from JSR 380-specific API details.

The following example listing shows `BankApp`'s `main` method that invokes `FixedDepositServiceImpl`'s `createFixedDeposit` method (refer example listing 6-44) to check if the validation is performed correctly:

Example listing 6-45 – `BankApp` class
Project – `ch06-jsr380-validation`
Source location - `src/main/java/sample/spring/chapter06/bankapp`

```
package sample.spring.chapter06.bankapp;
.....
public class BankApp {
    private static Logger logger = LogManager.getLogger(BankApp.class);

    public static void main(String args[]) throws Exception {
        ConfigurableApplicationContext context = new ClassPathXmlApplicationContext(
                "classpath:META-INF/spring/applicationContext.xml");
        logger.info("Validating FixedDepositDetails object using Spring Validation API");

        FixedDepositService fixedDepositService =
              (FixedDepositService)context.getBean("fixedDepositService");
        fixedDepositService.createFixedDeposit(new FixedDepositDetails(1, 0, 12,
              "someemail@somedomain.com"));
        fixedDepositService.createFixedDeposit(new FixedDepositDetails(1, 1000, 12,
              "someemail@somedomain.com"));
        .....
    }
}
```

First, FixedDepositService's createFixedDeposit method is passed a FixedDepositDetails object with depositAmount value as 0, followed by a FixedDepositDetails object with depositAmount value as 1000.

If you execute BankApp's main method, you'll see the following output on the console:

```
Validating FixedDepositDetails object using Spring Validation API
Errors were found while validating FixedDepositDetails instance
Created fixed deposit
```

The output 'Errors were found while validating FixedDepositDetails instance' shows that FixedDepositValidator reported errors when the FixedDepositDetails instance with 0 as the depositAmount value was validated. The output 'Created fixed deposit' shows that no errors were reported when the FixedDepositDetails instance with 1000 as the depositAmount value was validated.

As LocalValidatorFactoryBean also implements JSR 380's Validator and ValidatorFactory interfaces, you have the option to use JSR 380 API to perform validation of FixedDepositDetails object. The following example listing shows an alternative implementation of FixedDepositServiceImpl class that makes use of JSR 380's Validator to perform validation:

Example listing 6-46 – FixedDepositServiceJsr380Impl class - validating FixedDepositDetails object
Project – ch06-jsr380-validation
Source location - src/main/java/sample/spring/chapter06/bankapp/service

```
package sample.spring.chapter06.bankapp.service;

import javax.validation.ConstraintViolation;
import javax.validation.Validator;

@Service(value = "fixedDepositServiceJsr380")
public class FixedDepositServiceJsr380Impl implements FixedDepositService {
    .....
    @Autowired
    private Validator validator;

    @Autowired
    @Qualifier(value = "myFixedDepositDao")
    private FixedDepositDao myFixedDepositDao;

    @Override
    public void createFixedDeposit(FixedDepositDetails fixedDepositDetails)
          throws Exception {
        Set<ConstraintViolation<FixedDepositDetails>> violations =
             validator.validate(fixedDepositDetails);

        Iterator<ConstraintViolation<FixedDepositDetails>> itr = violations.iterator();

        if (itr.hasNext()) {
            logger.error("Errors were found while
                       validating FixedDepositDetails instance");
        } else {
            myFixedDepositDao.createFixedDeposit(fixedDepositDetails);
            logger.info("Created fixed deposit");
        }
    }
}
```

The above example listing shows that JSR 380's Validator implementation is referenced by the validator field. As LocalValidatorFactoryBean implements JSR 380's Validator interface, LocalValidatorFactoryBean instance is assigned to the validator field. The createFixedDeposit method validates FixedDepositDetails object by calling Validator's validate method. The validate method returns a java.util.Set object that contains the constraint violations reported by JSR 380 provider. You can check the java.util.Set<ConstraintViolation> object returned by the validate method to know if any constraint violations were reported. Each constraint violation is represented by the ConstraintViolation object contained in the returned java.util.Set. For instance, in the above example listing, the createFixedDeposit method calls FixedDepositDao's createFixedDeposit method only if java.util.Set doesn't contain any constraint violations.

Let's now look at how to validate methods using JSR 380.

Validating methods

JSR 380 supports validation of methods – their arguments and return values. To enable method validation, you need to configure Spring's MethodValidationPostProcessor – a BeanPostProcessor that delegates method validation to the available JSR 380 provider. The following example listing shows configuration of MethodValidationPostProcessor in applicationContext.xml file:

Example listing 6-47 – applicationContext.xml – MethodValidationPostProcessor configuration
Project – ch06-jsr380-validation
Source location - src/main/resources/META-INF/spring

```
<bean
    class="org.springframework.validation.beanvalidation.MethodValidationPostProcessor" />
```

By default, MethodValidationPostProcessor looks for bean classes annotated with Spring's @Validated annotation and adds validation support for methods that use JSR 380 constraint annotations.

The following example listing shows the CustomerRequestService interface that defines a submitRequest method:

Example listing 6-48 – CustomerRequestService interface – validating method arguments and return values
Project – ch06-jsr380-validation
Source location - src/main/java/sample/spring/chapter06/bankapp/service

```
package sample.spring.chapter06.bankapp.service;

import javax.validation.constraints.*;
import org.springframework.validation.annotation.Validated;

@Validated
public interface CustomerRequestService {
    @Future
    Calendar submitRequest(@NotBlank String type, @Size(min=20, max=100)
        String description, @Past Calendar accountOpeningDate);
}
```

In the above example listing, JSR 380 constraints are specified on submitRequest method's arguments and its return value. @Past annotation specifies that the date passed as the value of accountOpeningDate argument must be in the past. @Future annotation on the submitRequest method specifies that the date returned by the submitRequest method must be in the future. @Validated annotation on the CustomerRequestService interface indicates that it contains methods with JSR 380 constraints.

CustomerRequestServiceImpl implements the CustomerRequestService interface and provides implementation for the submitRequest method. As JSR 380 constraints are inherited, the overridden submitRequest method in CustomerRequestServiceImpl class must meet the constraints specified on CustomerRequestService's submitRequest method. The following example listing shows implementation of CustomerRequestServiceImpl's submitRequest method:

Example listing 6-49 – CustomerRequestServiceImpl
Project – ch06-jsr380-validation
Source location - src/main/java/sample/spring/chapter06/bankapp/service

```
package sample.spring.chapter06.bankapp.service;
.....
@Service("customerRequestService")
public class CustomerRequestServiceImpl implements CustomerRequestService {
    @Override
    public Calendar submitRequest(String type, String description,
            Calendar accountSinceDate) {
        .....
        customerRequestDao.submitRequest(details);
        Calendar cal = Calendar.getInstance();
        cal.add(Calendar.MONTH, -1);
        return cal;
    }
}
```

In the above example listing, the submitRequest method saves the request and returns a date which is one month behind the current date.

The following example listing shows BankApp's main method that invokes CustomerRequestServiceImpl's submitRequest method multiple times with different set of arguments:

Example listing 6-50 – BankApp class
Project – ch06-jsr380-validation
Source location - src/main/java/sample/spring/chapter06/bankapp

```
package sample.spring.chapter06.bankapp;

import javax.validation.ConstraintViolation;
import javax.validation.ConstraintViolationException;
.....
public class BankApp {
    private static Logger logger = LogManager.getLogger(BankApp.class);

    public static void main(String args[]) throws Exception {
        .....
        logger.info("Validating CustomerRequestDetails object using JSR 380 Validator");
        CustomerRequestService customerRequestService =
                context.getBean(CustomerRequestService.class);
        try {
            customerRequestService.submitRequest("request type", "description < 20",
                Calendar.getInstance());
        } catch (ConstraintViolationException ex) {
            printValidationErrors(ex);
        }
        .....
        Calendar futureDate = Calendar.getInstance();
        futureDate.add(Calendar.MONTH, 1);
```

```
        customerRequestService.submitRequest("request type", "description size > 20",
             futureDate);
        .....
        Calendar pastDate = Calendar.getInstance();
        pastDate.add(Calendar.MONTH, -1);
        customerRequestService.submitRequest("request type", "description size > 20",
            pastDate);
        .....
    }
    .....
}
```

In the above example listing, CustomerRequestServiceImpl's submitRequest method is called three times. In the first call, the description argument's length is less than 20, which means that the @Size(min=20, max=100) constraint on the argument will fail. In the second call, the date passed as argument to the accountOpeningDate argument is in the future, which means that the @Past constraint on the argument will fail. In the third call, all arguments satisfy the constraints, but the date returned by the submitRequest method is in the past (refer example listing 6-49); therefore, the @Future constraint on the submitRequest method's return value will fail. When a JSR 380 constraint fails, ConstraintViolationException is thrown. In the above example listing, the ConstraintViolationException is caught and its details are written to the console using printValidationErrors method.

If you run the BankApp's main method, you'll see the following output on the console:

```
Validating CustomerRequestDetails object using JSR 380 Validator
ConstraintViolationImpl{interpolatedMessage='size must be between 20 and 100', .....}
ConstraintViolationImpl{interpolatedMessage='must be a past date' .....}
ConstraintViolationImpl{interpolatedMessage='must be a future date'.....}
```

The output shows the error messages that are reported corresponding to each call to CustomerRequestServiceImpl's submitRequest method.

What's new in JSR 380 ?

Even though Spring 5 supports both JSR 349 and JSR 380, you should consider using JSR 380 for developing applications. JSR 380 offers the following new features that were not available in JSR 349:

- you can specify validation constraints for elements contained in container elements (like, collections and maps)
- you can specify constraints on java.util.Optional type variables
- new validation constraints: @NotBlank, @Email, @Positive, @PositiveOrZero, and so on

> For a complete list of changes in JSR 380, refer to the JSR 380 specification document (https://jcp.org/en/jsr/detail?id=380)

IMPORT **chapter 6/ch06-jsr380-newfeatures** (This project shows a sample application that uses some of the new features of JSR 380. To run the application, execute the main method of the SampleApp class of this project.)

The following example listing shows the Profile class that uses some of the new features offered by JSR 380:

Example listing 6-51 – Profile class – JSR 380 new features
Project – ch06-jsr380-newfeatures
Source location - src/main/java/sample/spring/chapter06/newfeatures/domain

```
package sample.spring.chapter06.newfeatures.domain;

import java.util.List;
import java.util.Optional;
import javax.validation.constraints.*;
import org.hibernate.validator.constraints.Length;
.....
public class Profile {
    private List<@Size(min = 5) String> friendNames;

    private Optional<@Length(min = 10, max = 10) String> phoneNumber;

    @PositiveOrZero
    private Integer income;

    @Positive
    private Integer age;

    .....getters/setters and constructor.....
}
```

In the above example listing:

- List<@Size(min = 5) String> friendNames – the @Size annotation specifies that *each* String value contained in the friendNames list must have minimum length of 5.
- Optional<@Length(min = 10, max = 10) String> phoneNumber – the Hibernate Validator's @Length annotation (serves the same purpose as JSR 380's @Size annotation) specifies that length of phoneNumber field must be 10.
- @PositiveOrZero annotation specifies that the value of income field must be greater than or equal to 0
- @Positive annotation specifies that the value of age field must be greater than 0

The following listing shows the SampleApp's main method that creates an instance of Profile object, validates it by calling Validator's validate method, and prints the validation error messages:

Example listing 6-52 – SampleApp class – validating a Profile object
Project – ch06-jsr380-newfeatures
Source location - src/main/java/sample/spring/chapter06/newfeatures

```
package sample.spring.chapter06.newfeatures;

import javax.validation.*;
import sample.spring.chapter06.newfeatures.domain.Profile;
.....
public class SampleApp {
    .....
    public static void main(String args[]) throws Exception {
        .....
        List<String> friends = new ArrayList<String>();
        friends.add("Johnson");
```

```
        friends.add("John");
        Profile profile = new Profile(friends, Optional.of("123456789"), -1, 0);

        Validator validator = context.getBean(Validator.class);
        Set<ConstraintViolation<Profile>> violations = validator.validate(profile);
        .....
    }
}
```

If you run SampleApp's main method, you'll see the following output:

```
ConstraintViolationImpl{interpolatedMessage='must be greater than 0', propertyPath=age,
.....}
ConstraintViolationImpl{interpolatedMessage='length must be between 10 and 10',
propertyPath=phoneNumber.....}
ConstraintViolationImpl{interpolatedMessage='size must be between 5 and 2147483647',
propertyPath=friendNames[1].<list element>.....}
ConstraintViolationImpl{interpolatedMessage='must be greater than or equal to 0',
propertyPath=income.....}
```

ConstraintViolationImpl's (an implementation of ConstraintViolation interface) propertyPath attribute identifies the field that failed validation. The output shows that the friendNames[1] (that is, the 2nd element of friendNames list) failed validation. This is because the 2nd element in friendNames list is "John" and its length doesn't meet the @Size(min = 5) constraint (refer listing 6-51).

In this section, we saw how to use Spring's support for JSR 380 to perform validation of objects and methods. It is important to note that JSR 380 allows you to create custom constraints and use them in your application. For instance, you can create a @MyConstraint custom constraint and a corresponding validator to enforce that constraint on objects.

Let's now look at the concept of bean definition profiles.

6-11 Bean definition profiles

The bean definition profiles feature of Spring allows you to associate a set of beans with a *profile*. A profile is nothing but a logical name given to a set of beans. If a profile is active, the Spring container creates beans associated with that profile. To set a profile as active, you specify its name as the value of spring.profiles.active property. The spring.profiles.active property can be defined as a system property, an environment variable, a JVM system property, a servlet context parameter (in case of web applications), or as a JNDI entry.

You typically associate beans with profiles when you want different set of beans to be used in different environments. For instance, you may want to use an embedded database in the development environment, and a standalone database in the production environment.

IMPORT **chapter 6/ch06-bean-profiles** (This project shows the MyBank application that uses bean definition profiles. To run the application, execute BankAppWithProfile's main method or BankAppWithoutProfile's main method of this project.)

Let's look at an example scenario in which we'll use bean definition profiles.

Bean definition profiles example

The MyBank application of ch06-bean-profiles project uses bean definition profiles to address the following application requirements:

- the application should use an embedded database in development, and a standalone database in production environment
- the application should support both Hibernate and MyBatis ORM frameworks for database interaction. At the time of deployment, you specify whether the application uses Hibernate or MyBatis for database interaction. If nothing is specified, Hibernate is used by default.

Let's now look at how each of these requirements are met by using bean definition profiles.

Different databases in development and production environments

The DataSource class of ch06-bean-profiles project holds the database configuration (like, driver class, username, and so on) and is used by DAOs for connecting with the database and executing SQLs. The following example listing shows the DataSource class:

Example listing 6-53 – DataSource class
Project – ch06-bean-profiles
Source location - src/main/java/sample/spring/chapter06/bankapp/domain

```
package sample.spring.chapter06.bankapp.domain;
.....
@Component
public class DataSource {
    @Value("#{dbProps.driverClassName}")
    private String driverClass;

    @Value("#{dbProps.url}")
    private String url;
    .....
}
```

The above example listing shows that the DataSource bean obtains database configuration from dbProps bean. The dbProps bean is configured in the application context XML file, as shown here:

Example listing 6-54 – applicationContext.xml
Project – ch06-bean-profiles
Source location - src/main/resources/META-INF/spring

```
<beans .....
    xmlns:util="http://www.springframework.org/schema/util".....>
    .....
    <beans profile="dev, default">
        <util:properties id="dbProps" location="classpath:META-INF/devDB.properties" />
    </beans>

    <beans profile="production">
        <util:properties id="dbProps"
               location="classpath:META-INF/productiondDB.properties" />
    </beans>
</beans>
```

In the above example listing, nested <beans> tags define beans that are associated with one or more profiles. The profile attribute specifies the profile(s) to which the beans belong. For instance, the dbProps bean created by the first <properties> element of util schema is associated with dev and default profiles, and the dbProps bean created by the second <properties> element is associated with production profile. The devDB.properties file contains database configuration for the development environment; therefore, the dbProps bean created by the first <properties> element contains database configuration applicable to the development environment. Similarly, the dbProps bean created by the second <properties> element contains database configuration (contained in productionDB.properties file) applicable to the production environment.

> You should note that nested <beans> tags must appear at the end of the application context XML file.

This means that if dev or default profile is active, the DataSource bean is supplied with database configuration defined in devDB.properties, and if production profile is active, the DataSource bean is supplied with database configuration defined in productionDB.properties.

Supporting both Hibernate and MyBatis

To support both Hibernate and MyBatis for database interaction, separate DAOs (FixedDepositHibernateDao and FixedDepositMyBatisDao) have been created for Hibernate and MyBatis.

The following example listing shows FixedDepositHibernateDao class (an implementation of FixedDepositDao) that uses Hibernate for database interaction:

Example listing 6-55 – FixedDepositHibernateDao – Hibernate-specific DAO implementation
Project – ch06-bean-profiles
Source location - src/main/java/sample/spring/chapter06/bankapp/dao

```
package sample.spring.chapter06.bankapp.dao;

@Profile({ "hibernate", "default" })
@Repository
public class FixedDepositHibernateDao implements FixedDepositDao {
    private DataSource dataSource;
    .....
    @Autowired
    public FixedDepositHibernateDao(DataSource dataSource) {
        this.dataSource = dataSource;
    }
    .....
}
```

In the above example listing, the @Profile annotation specifies that FixedDepositHibernateDao bean is registered with the Spring container only if the active profile is hibernate or default. This means, if the active profile is not hibernate or default, the Spring container will not create an instance of FixedDepositHibernateDao bean. Notice that the FixedDepositHibernateDao's constructor accepts DataSource as argument that is used by Hibernate for connecting with the database and executing SQLs.

The following example listing shows the FixedDepositMyBatisDao class (another implementation of FixedDepositDao) that uses MyBatis for database interaction:

Example listing 6-56 – FixedDepositMyBatisDao – MyBatis-specific DAO implementation
Project – ch06-bean-profiles
Source location - src/main/java/sample/spring/chapter06/bankapp/dao

```
package sample.spring.chapter06.bankapp.dao;

import org.springframework.context.annotation.Profile;
```

```
.....
@Profile("mybatis")
@Repository
public class FixedDepositMyBatisDao implements FixedDepositDao {
    private DataSource dataSource;
    .....
    @Autowired
    public FixedDepositMyBatisDao(DataSource dataSource) {
        this.dataSource = dataSource;
    }
    .....
}
```

In the above example listing, the @Profile annotation specifies that the FixedDepositMyBatisDao is registered with the Spring container only if the active profile is mybatis. FixedDepositMyBatisDao's constructor accepts DataSource as argument which is used by MyBatis for connecting with the database and executing SQLs.

Setting the active profile

The following example listing shows BankAppWithProfile's main method that sets mybatis and production as active profiles:

Example listing 6-57 – BankAppWithProfile – setting mybatis and production as active profiles
Project – ch06-bean-profiles
Source location - src/main/java/sample/spring/chapter06/bankapp

```
package sample.spring.chapter06.bankapp;

public class BankAppWithProfile {
    public static void main(String args[]) {
        System.setProperty("spring.profiles.active", "mybatis, production");
        ConfigurableApplicationContext context = new ClassPathXmlApplicationContext(
                "classpath:META-INF/spring/applicationContext.xml");
        .....
    }
}
```

In the above example listing, System's setProperty method sets spring.profiles.active system property to 'mybatis, production'. This effectively sets mybatis and production profiles as active. As FixedDepositMyBatisDao bean (refer example listing 6-56) and the dbProps bean that holds database configuration read from productionDB.properties file (refer example listing 6-54) are associated with mybatis and production profiles, respectively, they are created by the Spring container.

If you run BankAppWithProfile's main method, you'll see the following messages in the output:

```
INFO  .....FixedDepositMyBatisDao - initializing
INFO  ..... dbProps bean -> {password=root, driverClassName=com.mysql.jdbc.Driver,
url=jdbc:mysql://production:3306/spring_bank_app_db, username=root}
```

The above output shows that FixedDepositMyBatisDao bean is created by the Spring container. Also, the dbProps bean that holds database configuration contained in productionDB.properties file is created by the Spring container.

If no profiles are active, the Spring container considers default profile as the active profile. The BankAppWithoutProfile's main method doesn't set any active profile. If you run BankAppWithoutProfile's main method, you'll see the following output on the console:

```
INFO .....FixedDepositHibernateDao - initializing
INFO ..... dbProps bean -> {password=devDBPassword, driverClassName=devDBDriver, url=devDBURL, username=devDBUsername}
```

We saw earlier that the dbProps bean that holds database configuration contained in devDB.properties file (refer example listing 6-54) and FixedDepositHibernateDao bean (refer example listing 6-55) are associated with default profile. For this reason, the Spring container creates FixedDepositHibernateDao bean and dbProps bean that holds configuration from devDB.properties file.

> You can change the default active profile's name from default to something else by setting the spring.profiles.default property.

We saw earlier that nested <beans> tag's profile attribute specifies the profile to which the enclosing beans belong. If all the beans in your application context XML file belong to the same profile(s), then you can use the profile attribute of the top-level <beans> element to specify the profile(s) to which all the beans belong. The following example listing shows a scenario in which all the beans defined in the application context XML file belong to dev profile:

Example listing 6-58 – Setting the same profile for all the beans

```
<beans profile="dev" .....>
    <bean id="aBean" class="A"/>
    <bean id="bBean" class="B" />
</beans>
```

In the above example listing, aBean and bBean are associated with dev profile.

If you don't associate any profile with a bean, then the bean is registered irrespective of the active profile. Consider the following example listing in which aBean is not associated with any profile:

Example listing 6-59 – Bean with no profile is available in all profiles

```
<beans .....>
    .....
    <bean id="aBean" class="A"/>

    <beans profile="dev">
        <bean id="bBean" class="B"/>
    </beans>

    <beans profile="prod">
        <bean id="cBean" class="C"/>
    </beans>
</beans>
```

In the above example listing, aBean is available (that is, registered with the Spring container) irrespective of whether dev or prod profile is active.

You can prefix a profile name with ! operator to indicate that the bean should be registered with the Spring container if the profile is *not* active. In the following example listing, aBean is registered only if profile dev is *not* active:

Example listing 6-60 – Using ! operator with profile names

```
<beans .....>
    .....
```

```
    <beans profile="!dev">
        <bean id="aBean" class="A"/>
    </beans>

    <beans profile="prod, default">
        <bean id="bBean" class="B"/>
    </beans>
</beans>
```

If prod profile (or any other profile except dev) is active or no profile is active, only then aBean is considered for registration by the Spring container.

> You can use the ! operator with `@Profile` annotation also to make the bean available only if a profile is *not* active. For instance, `@Profile("!dev")` annotation on a bean makes the bean available only if dev profile is *not* active.

6-12 Summary

In this chapter, we saw how to use annotations (like `@Component`, `@Inject`, `@Lazy`, `@Autowired`, and so on) to configure Spring beans. We also looked at SpEL expressions that simplify bean configuration, bean definition profiles, and Spring's Validation API and JSR 380. In the next chapter, we'll look at how to programmatically configure the Spring container and register beans with it.

Chapter 7 – *Java-based container configuration*

7-1 Introduction

In the examples that we've seen so far, the Spring container was configured using either the application context XML file or by using Java annotations. In this chapter, we'll see how to programmatically configure the Spring container. The programmatic approach to configuring beans and the Spring container is also referred to as 'Java-based container configuration'. Depending on your preference, you can choose XML or Java annotations or Java-based configuration approach for developing your applications. Spring allows you to use a combination of these approaches for developing an application, but it's recommended to stick to a single approach.

Let's begin this chapter by looking at `@Configuration` and `@Bean` annotations that are central to Java-based configuration.

7-2 Configuring beans using `@Configuration` and `@Bean` annotations

`@Configuration` and `@Bean` annotations are used to programmatically configure Spring beans. If you annotate a class with `@Configuration` annotation, it indicates that the class contains one or more `@Bean` annotated methods that create and return bean instances. The bean instances returned by `@Bean` annotated methods are managed by the Spring container.

IMPORT **`chapter 7/ch07-bankapp-configuration`** (This project shows the MyBank application that uses `@Configuration` and `@Bean` annotations to programmatically configure beans. To run the application, execute the `main` method of the `BankApp` class of this project.)

The following example listing shows the `BankAppConfiguration` class that is annotated with `@Configuration` annotation:

Example listing 7-1 – BankAppConfiguration class - `@Configuration` and `@Bean` annotations
Project – ch07-bankapp-configuration
Source location - src/main/java/sample/spring/chapter07/bankapp

```
package sample.spring.chapter07.bankapp;

import org.springframework.context.annotation.Bean;
import org.springframework.context.annotation.Configuration;
.....
@Configuration
public class BankAppConfiguration {
    .....
    @Bean(name = "fixedDepositService")
    public FixedDepositService fixedDepositService() {
        return new FixedDepositServiceImpl();
    }
    .....
}
```

`BankAppConfiguration` class defines `@Bean` annotated methods that create and return bean instances. `@Bean`'s `name` attribute specifies the name with which the returned bean instance is registered with the Spring container. In the above example listing, the `fixedDepositService` method creates and returns an instance of `FixedDepositServiceImpl` bean that is registered with the Spring container as a bean named `fixedDepositService`. The `fixedDepositService` method has the same effect as the following bean definition in the application context XML file:

```
<bean id="fixedDepositService"
      class="sample.spring.chapter07.bankapp.service.FixedDepositServiceImpl" />
```

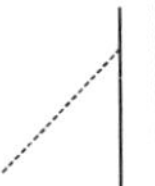

@Bean's name attribute can accept an array of names representing *aliases* for the bean. The aliases are used when you want to refer to the same bean with different names.

To use @Configuration annotated classes for defining beans, CGLIB library is required. CGLIB library extends @Configuration annotated classes to add behavior to the @Bean annotated methods. Starting with Spring 3.2, the CGLIB classes are packaged within the spring-core JAR file itself; therefore, you don't need to explicitly specify that your project is dependent on the CGLIB JAR file. As @Configuration annotated classes are subclassed by CGLIB, you must *not* define them as final, and they must provide a no-argument constructor.

Apart from the name attribute, @Bean annotation defines the following attributes that you can use to configure the returned bean instance:

Attribute	Description
autowire	serves the same purpose as the <bean> element's autowire attribute (refer section 4-6 of chapter 4 to know more about the autowire attribute). If the bean returned by the @Bean annotated method is dependent on other beans, you can use the autowire attribute to instruct Spring to perform autowiring of dependencies by name or type. By default, autowiring is disabled for the returned bean.
initMethod	serves the same purpose as the <bean> element's init-method attribute (refer section 5-2 of chapter 5 to know more about init-method attribute)
destroyMethod	serves the same purpose as the <bean> element's destroy-method attribute (refer section 5-2 of chapter 5 to know more about destroy-method attribute)

If you don't specify the @Bean's name attribute, the name of the method is considered as the bean name. In the following example listing, the FixedDepositDao instance is registered as a bean named fixedDepositDao:

Example listing 7-2 – BankAppConfiguration class - @Bean without name attribute
Project – ch07-bankapp-configuration
Source location - src/main/java/sample/spring/chapter07/bankapp

```
    @Bean
    public FixedDepositDao fixedDepositDao() {
        return new FixedDepositDaoImpl();
    }
```

It is important to note that @Bean annotated methods may also be annotated with @Lazy, @DependsOn, @Primary and @Scope annotations. When specified on an @Bean annotated method, these annotations apply to the bean instance returned by the @Bean annotated method. For instance, @DependsOn annotation specifies the implicit dependencies of the bean instance returned by the @Bean annotated method. The following example listing shows usage of @DependsOn annotation:

Example listing 7-3 – SomeConfig class - @DependsOn annotation

```
import org.springframework.context.annotation.DependsOn;
.....
@Configuration
public class SomeConfig {
    .....
```

```
    @Bean(name = "someBean")
    @DependsOn({"aBean", "bBean"})
    public SomeBean someBean() {
        return new SomeBean();
    }
    .....
}
```

In the above example listing, @DependsOn annotation specifies that aBean and bBean beans are implicit dependencies of someBean; therefore, they must be created before someBean instance is created.

By default, beans returned by @Bean annotated methods are singleton-scoped. You can set a different scope for the returned bean using @Scope annotation, as shown in the following example listing:

Example listing 7-4 – BankAppConfiguration class - @Scope annotation
Project – ch07-bankapp-configuration
Source location - src/main/java/sample/spring/chapter07/bankapp

```
package sample.spring.chapter07.bankapp;

import org.springframework.context.annotation.Scope;
.....
@Configuration
public class BankAppConfiguration {
    .....
    @Bean(name = "customerRegistrationService")
    @Scope(scopeName = ConfigurableBeanFactory.SCOPE_PROTOTYPE)
    public CustomerRegistrationService customerRegistrationService() {
        return new CustomerRegistrationServiceImpl();
    }
    .....
}
```

In the above example listing, @Scope annotation specifies that the customerRegistrationService bean is a prototype-scoped bean.

Defining @Bean methods in @Component and JSR 330's @Named classes

You can also define @Bean methods in bean classes annotated with @Component or JSR 330's @Named annotation. The following example listing shows an @Service annotated bean class that defines an @Bean method:

Example listing 7-5 – TransactionServiceImpl – defining @Bean methods in @Component classes
Project – ch07-bankapp-configuration
Source location - src/main/java/sample/spring/chapter07/bankapp/service

```
package sample.spring.chapter07.bankapp.service;
.....
@Service
public class TransactionServiceImpl implements TransactionService {
    @Autowired
    private TransactionDao transactionDao;

    @Override
    public void getTransactions(String customerId) {
        transactionDao.getTransactions(customerId);
    }
```

```
    @Bean
    public TransactionDao transactionDao() {
        return new TransactionDaoImpl();
    }
}
```

In the above example listing, TransactionServiceImpl bean class defines an @Bean annotated transactionDao method that returns an instance of TransactionDaoImpl (an implementation of TransactionDao interface). TransactionServiceImpl uses the @Autowired annotation to autowire the TransactionDaoImpl instance. This might look a little confusing as too many things are going on inside the bean class. The other issue with defining @Bean annotated methods in bean classes is that you might inadvertently call the @Bean annotated method thinking of it as just another method of the bean class. For this reason, it is recommended to use @Configuration classes to define @Bean annotated methods.

> @Configuration annotation is meta-annotated with @Component. This is the reason why @Configuration and @Component classes have so much in common. For instance, you can define @Bean annotated methods in them, both can use autowiring, Spring container creates and registers instances of both @Configuration and @Component classes as beans, and so on.

Searching and registering beans using @ComponentScan

@ComponentScan annotation serves the same purpose as the <component-scan> element that we discussed in chapter 6. An @Configuration annotated class can use @ComponentScan annotation to search and register @Component classes.

The following code shows an @Configuration annotated class that uses @ComponentScan annotation:

```
@Configuration
@ComponentScan(basePackages = "com.sample")
public class ABean {
    .....
}
```

The basePackages attribute specifies the package(s) that should be searched for @Component annotated classes. If @Component annotated classes are found, they are registered with the Spring container.

Like <component-scan> element, @ComponentScan defines excludeFilters and includeFilters attributes that serve the same purpose as the <exclude-filter> and <include-filter> sub-elements of <component-scan> element.

IMPORT **chapter 7/ch07-indexed-annotation** (This project shows an application that generates an index of Spring components at the time of compilation. To generate the index, execute mvn clean compile from the project directory. And, to run the application, execute the main method of the SampleApp class of this project.)

Using component index instead of classpath scanning

Spring 5 has a new spring-context-indexer module that you can add to your project to generate an *index* of Spring components at *compile* time. At application startup, the index is used (instead of classpath scanning) to load Spring components.

To enable component index generation, you need to add your project's dependency on spring-context-indexer module and configure CandidateComponentsIndexer annotation processor (defined in spring-context-indexer module) with Maven compiler plugin (https://maven.apache.org/plugins/maven-compiler-plugin/). The following code shows how CandidateComponentsIndexer is configured with Maven compiler plugin:

Example listing 7-6 – pom.xml – configuring CandidateComponentsIndexer annotation processor
Project – ch07-indexed-annotation

```
<plugin>
  <groupId>org.apache.maven.plugins</groupId>
  <artifactId>maven-compiler-plugin</artifactId>
  <version>3.7.0</version>
  <configuration>
    .....
    <annotationProcessors>
      <annotationProcessor>
        org.springframework.context.index.CandidateComponentsIndexer
      </annotationProcessor>
    </annotationProcessors>
  </configuration>
</plugin>
```

The <annotationProcessors> element uses <annotationProcessor> sub-elements to specify the annotation processors to run during compilation. In the above listing, CandidateComponentsIndexer is specified as the annotation processor to run during compilation.

If you go to the command line and execute mvn clean compile command (or select pom.xml file in Eclipse IDE, right-click and select Run As → Maven build) from ch07-indexed-annotation folder, compilation process generates a spring.components file in ch07-indexed-annotation/target/classes/META-INF folder. The spring.components file contains an index of Spring components, as shown here:

```
com.sample.functionalstyle.domain.MyConfiguration=org.springframework.stereotype.Component
com.sample.functionalstyle.domain.BeanB=org.springframework.stereotype.Component
com.sample.functionalstyle.domain.BeanA=org.springframework.stereotype.Component
```

Any class that is annotated with Spring's @Indexed annotation, is indexed by the CandidateComponentsIndexer. In Spring 5, @Configuration and @Component annotations are meta-annotated with @Indexed annotation; therefore, MyConfiguration class (annotated with @Configuration and @ComponentScan) and BeanA and BeanB classes (both annotated with @Component annotation) are indexed when we compile the ch07-indexed-annotation project.

When you run SampleApp's main method, MyConfiguration class's @ComponentScan (which has runtime semantics) annotation is ignored. Instead, components contained in spring.components file are loaded by the Spring Framework. As Spring components are loaded from the spring.components file and no classpath scanning is performed, you'll notice significant improvement in application startup time for large applications.

7-3 Injecting bean dependencies

When using Java-based configuration approach, @Bean methods are used to create beans. To satisfy dependencies of a bean created by an @Bean method, you have the following options:

- obtain the dependencies by explicitly calling the @Bean methods that create and return the dependencies.
- specify bean dependencies as arguments to the @Bean method. The Spring container takes care of calling the @Bean methods corresponding to the dependencies and supplying the dependencies as method arguments.

- autowire dependencies by using `@Autowired`, `@Inject` and `@Resource` annotations in the bean class.

The following example listing shows a scenario in which bean dependencies are obtained by calling the corresponding @Bean methods:

Example listing 7-7 – BankAppConfiguration class – obtaining dependencies by calling @Bean methods
Project – ch07-bankapp-configuration
Source location - src/main/java/sample/spring/chapter07/bankapp

```
package sample.spring.chapter07.bankapp;
.....
@Configuration
public class BankAppConfiguration {
    @Bean(name = "accountStatementService")
    public AccountStatementService accountStatementService() {
        AccountStatementServiceImpl accountStatementServiceImpl =
              new AccountStatementServiceImpl();
        accountStatementServiceImpl.setAccountStatementDao(accountStatementDao());
        return accountStatementServiceImpl;
    }

    @Bean(name = "accountStatementDao")
    public AccountStatementDao accountStatementDao() {
        return new AccountStatementDaoImpl();
    }
    .....
}
```

In the above example listing, the accountStatementService method creates AccountStatementServiceImpl bean, and the accountStatementDao method creates AccountStatementDaoImpl bean. As AccountStatementServiceImpl depends on AccountStatementDaoImpl, we explicitly call the accountStatementDao method to obtain an instance of AccountStatementDaoImpl bean and set it on the AccountStatementServiceImpl instance.

You should note that the behavior of an @Bean method conforms to the specified bean configuration. For instance, if you call accountStatementService method multiple times, it'll *not* result in creation of multiple instances of AccountStatementServiceImpl bean. The accountStatementService method will return the same AccountStatementServiceImpl bean instance because it is singleton-scoped. This behavior is possible because @Configuration classes are subclassed and their @Bean methods are overridden. For example, BankAppConfiguration class is subclassed by CGLIB and the accountStatementService method is overriden to first check the Spring container for AccountStatementServiceImpl bean before calling the parent accountStatementService method to create a new instance of AccountStatementServiceImpl bean.

Instead of obtaining dependencies by explicitly calling @Bean methods, you can specify dependencies as arguments to @Bean methods. The following example listing shows a variant of accountStatementService method that specifies dependencies of AccountStatementServiceImpl bean as method arguments:

Example listing 7-8 – Dependencies as arguments to @Bean methods

```
@Configuration
public class BankAppConfiguration {
    @Bean(name = "accountStatementService")
    public AccountStatementService accountStatementService(
                        AccountStatementDao accountStatementDao) {
        AccountStatementServiceImpl accountStatementServiceImpl =
                new AccountStatementServiceImpl();
```

```
        accountStatementServiceImpl.setAccountStatementDao(accountStatementDao);
        return accountStatementServiceImpl;
    }

    @Bean(name = "accountStatementDao")
    public AccountStatementDao accountStatementDao() {
        return new AccountStatementDaoImpl();
    }
    .....
}
```

In the above example listing, AccountStatementDao bean (a dependency of AccountStatementServiceImpl bean) is defined as an argument of accountStatementService method. Behind the scenes, the Spring container calls the accountStatementDao method and provides the accountStatementService method with an instance of AccountStatementDao bean.

Instead of explicitly setting bean dependencies, you can autowire dependencies by using @Autowired, @Inject and @Resource annotations. The following example listing shows the @Bean methods that create FixedDepositService and FixedDepositDao beans:

Example listing 7-9 – BankAppConfiguration class
Project – ch07-bankapp-configuration
Source location - src/main/java/sample/spring/chapter07/bankapp

```
package sample.spring.chapter07.bankapp;
.....
@Configuration
public class BankAppConfiguration {
    .....
    @Bean(name = "fixedDepositService")
    public FixedDepositService fixedDepositService(FixedDepositDao fixedDepositDao) {
        return new FixedDepositServiceImpl();
    }
    @Bean
    public FixedDepositDao fixedDepositDao() {
        return new FixedDepositDaoImpl();
    }
    .....
}
```

In the above example listing, fixedDepositService method creates an instance of FixedDepositServiceImpl and fixedDepositDao method creates an instance of FixedDepositDaoImpl. Even though FixedDepositServiceImpl depends on FixedDepositDaoImpl, we don't set the FixedDepositDaoImpl instance on FixedDepositServiceImpl. Instead, FixedDepositServiceImpl's dependency on FixedDepositDaoImpl is specified using @Autowired annotation, as shown in the following example listing:

Example listing 7-10 – FixedDepositServiceImpl class
Project – ch07-bankapp-configuration
Source location - src/main/java/sample/spring/chapter07/bankapp/service

```
package sample.spring.chapter07.bankapp.service;
.....
public class FixedDepositServiceImpl implements FixedDepositService {
    @Autowired
    private FixedDepositDao fixedDepositDao;
```

```
    @Override
    public void createFixedDeposit(FixedDepositDetails fdd) throws Exception {
        fixedDepositDao.createFixedDeposit(fdd);
    }
}
```

In the above example listing, @Autowired annotation autowires the FixedDepositDao bean created by fixedDepositDao method of BankAppConfiguration class (refer example listing 7-8).

Now that we've seen how dependency injection of beans created by @Bean methods is performed, let's look at how to configure the Spring container when using Java-based configuration.

7-4 Configuring the Spring container

In the examples that we have seen so far, we created an instance of ClassPathXmlApplicationContext class (an implementation of ApplicationContext interface) to represent the Spring container. If you are using an @Configuration annotated class as the source of beans, you need to create an instance of AnnotationConfigApplicationContext class (another implementation of ApplicationContext interface) to represent the Spring container.

The following example listing shows the BankApp class that creates an instance of AnnotationConfigApplicationContext class and retrieves beans from it:

Example listing 7-11 – BankApp class - AnnotationConfigApplicationContext usage
Project – ch07-bankapp-configuration
Source location - src/main/java/sample/spring/chapter07/bankapp

```
package sample.spring.chapter07.bankapp;

import org.springframework.context.annotation.AnnotationConfigApplicationContext;

public class BankApp {

    public static void main(String args[]) throws Exception {
        AnnotationConfigApplicationContext context =
              new AnnotationConfigApplicationContext(BankAppConfiguration.class);
        .....
        FixedDepositService fixedDepositService =
                context.getBean(FixedDepositService.class);
        fixedDepositService.createFixedDeposit(new FixedDepositDetails(1, 1000,
                12, "someemail@somedomain.com"));
        .....
    }
}
```

In the above example listing, the BankAppConfiguration class is passed as an argument to the AnnotationConfigApplicationContext's constructor. As AnnotationConfigApplicationContext class implements ApplicationContext interface, you can access registered beans in the same way as in the case of ClassPathXmlApplicationContext. If you have defined @Bean methods across multiple @Configuration classes, then pass all the @Configuration classes to AnnotationConfigApplicationContext's constructor.

> @Configuration classes are also registered as Spring beans; therefore, you can obtain an instance of BankAppConfiguration class by calling getBean(BankAppConfiguration.class) on AnnotationConfigApplicationContext instance.

If you have also defined @Bean methods in @Component and JSR 330's @Named annotated classes, you can pass these classes to AnnotationConfigApplicationContext's constructor, as shown in the following example listing:

Example listing 7-12 – BankAppMixed class
Project – ch07-bankapp-configuration
Source location - src/main/java/sample/spring/chapter07/bankapp

```
package sample.spring.chapter07.bankapp;

import org.springframework.context.annotation.AnnotationConfigApplicationContext;
.....
public class BankAppMixed {
    public static void main(String args[]) throws Exception {
        AnnotationConfigApplicationContext context =
        new AnnotationConfigApplicationContext(BankAppConfiguration.class,
                TransactionServiceImpl.class);
        .....
    }
}
```

In the above example listing, BankAppConfiguration (an @Configuration annotated class) and TransactionServiceImpl (an @Service annotated class) classes are passed to AnnotationConfigApplicationContext's constructor.

If you want to programmatically configure the AnnotationConfigApplicationContext instance, call the no-args constructor of AnnotationConfigApplicationContext and then add @Configuration (or @Component or @Named) classes using the AnnotationConfigApplicationContext's register method. The following example listing shows a scenario in which the value of configClass JVM property is used to decide which @Configuration classes are added to the AnnotationConfigApplicationContext instance:

Example listing 7-13 – Programmatically configuring AnnotationConfigApplicationContext

```
public class MyApp {
    public static void main(String args[]) throws Exception {
        AnnotationConfigApplicationContext context =
                new AnnotationConfigApplicationContext();
        if(context.getEnvironment().getProperty("configClass")
             .equalsIgnoreCase("myConfig")) {
            context.register(MyConfig.class);
            context.register(MyOtherConfig.class);
        } else {
            context.register(YourConfig.class);
        }
        context.refresh();
        .....
    }
}
```

AnnotationConfigApplicationContext's getEnvironment method returns an Environment instance that contains JVM properties. In the above example listing, if the value of configClass JVM property is myConfig, then MyConfig and MyOtherConfig classes are added to AnnotationConfigApplicationContext, else YourConfig class is added. You should note that after adding @Configuration classes you must call the refresh method so that the classes are processed by AnnotationConfigApplicationContext instance.

Instead of explicitly adding @Configuration classes to AnnotationConfigApplicationContext, you can use the AnnotationConfigApplicationContext's scan method to specify the packages to be scanned. The scan method serves the same purpose as the Spring's context schema's <component-scan> element; it looks for @Component (or @Named) annotated classes and registers them with the Spring container. As @Configuration is meta-annotated with @Component annotation, scan method also adds any @Configuration classes found to AnnotationConfigApplicationContext.

The following example listing shows usage of scan method:

Example listing 7-14 – AnnotationConfigApplicationContext's scan method

```
public class MyApp {
    public static void main(String args[]) throws Exception {
        AnnotationConfigApplicationContext context =
              new AnnotationConfigApplicationContext();
        context.scan("sample.spring", "com.sample");
        context.refresh();
        .....
    }
}
```

AnnotationConfigApplicationContext's scan method specifies the list of packages that should be searched for @Component classes. In the above example listing, @Component classes are searched inside sample.spring and com.sample packages and their sub-packages. If @Component classes are found, they are added to the AnnotationConfigApplicationContext instance.

Let's now look at how beans created by @Bean methods receive lifecycle callbacks from the Spring container.

7-5 Lifecycle callbacks

We saw earlier that JSR 250's @PostConstruct and @PreDestroy annotations identify initialization and destruction methods of a bean. If a bean created by an @Bean method defines @PostConstruct and @PreDestroy methods, then they are called by the Spring container.

Also, if a bean created by an @Bean annotated method implements lifecycle interfaces (like InitializingBean and DisposableBean), and Spring's *Aware interfaces (like ApplicationContextAware, BeanNameAware, and so on), it'll receive callbacks from the Spring container.

As mentioned earlier, @Bean defines initMethod and destroyMethod attributes that you can use to specify custom initialization and destruction methods. The following example listing shows use of initMethod and destroyMethod attributes:

Example listing 7-15 – SomeConfig class – @Bean's initMethod and destroyMethod attributes

```
@Configuration
public class SomeConfig {
    .....
    @Bean(initMethod = "initialize", destroyMethod  = "close")
    public SomeBean someBean() {
        return new SomeBean();
    }
    .....
```

```
}
```

In the above example listing, SomeBean's initialize and close methods are called on initialization and destruction, respectively.

Instead of asking the Spring container to call SomeBean's initialize method, you can call it explicitly during construction, as shown here:

Example listing 7-16 – SomeConfig class – explicitly calling the initialize method

```
@Configuration
public class SomeConfig {
    .....
    @Bean(initMethod = "initialize", destroyMethod  = "close")
    public SomeBean someBean() {
        SomeBean bean =  new SomeBean();
        bean.initialize();
        return bean;
    }
    .....
}
```

In the above example listing, SomeBean's initialize method is called explicitly to initialize the bean instance.

If the destroyMethod attribute is not specified and the bean returned by an @Bean method defines a public close or shutdown method, then the Spring container considers the close or shutdown method as the default destruction method of the bean. You can override this default behavior by setting the destroyMethod attribute's value to an empty string, as shown here:

```
    @Bean(destroyMethod  = "")
    public SomeBean someBean() {
        return new SomeBean();
    }
```

In the above @Bean method, destroyMethod attribute's value is set to ""; therefore, even if SomeBean defines a public close or shutdown method, it is *not* called when the Spring container is shutdown. This feature is particularly useful if your application obtains resources (like javax.sql.DataSource) from JNDI whose lifecycles are *not* managed by the Spring container.

7-6 Importing Java-based configurations

To modularize your application, you may define beans across multiple @Configuration files. To combine one or more @Configuration files, you can use @Import annotation. The @Import annotation serves the same purpose as the <import> element (refer section 3-10 of chapter 3) of beans schema.

IMPORT **chapter 7/ch07-bankapp-import-configs** (This project shows the MyBank application that uses multiple @Configuration files to defines beans. To run the application, execute the main method of the BankApp class of this project.)

In ch07-bankapp-import-configs project, beans are defined across three different @Configuration files – BankServicesConfig (defines services), BankDaosConfig (defines DAOs) and BankOtherObjects (defines domain objects). The BankServicesConfig imports BankDaosConfig and BankOtherObjects files, as shown in the following example listing:

Example listing 7-17 – BankServicesConfig class – @Import annotation usage
Project – ch07-bankapp-import-configs
Source location - src/main/java/sample/spring/chapter07/bankapp

```
package sample.spring.chapter07.bankapp;

import org.springframework.context.annotation.Import;
.....
@Configuration
@Import({BankDaosConfig.class, BankOtherObjects.class})
public class BankServicesConfig {
    .....
}
```

If your application contains @Component classes, you can import them as well into @Configuration classes using @Import annotation, as shown here:

Example listing 7-18 – BankOtherObjects class – importing @Component classes using @Import
Project – ch07-bankapp-import-configs
Source location - src/main/java/sample/spring/chapter07/bankapp

```
package sample.spring.chapter07.bankapp;
.....
@Import({ TransactionServiceImpl.class, TransactionDaoImpl.class })
public class BankOtherObjects {
    .....
}
```

In the above example listing, TransactionServiceImpl and TransactionDaoImpl are @Component annotated classes.

Resolving dependencies

You can handle inter-dependencies between beans defined in different @Configuration files using any of the following approaches:

- specify bean dependencies as arguments to @Bean methods
- autowire the imported @Configuration class as a bean and call its @Bean methods to fetch dependencies

The following example listing shows both the approaches being used in BankServicesConfig class:

Example listing 7-19 – BankServicesConfig class – injecting dependencies
Project – ch07-bankapp-import-configs
Source location - src/main/java/sample/spring/chapter07/bankapp

```
package sample.spring.chapter07.bankapp;
.....
@Configuration
@Import({BankDaosConfig.class, BankOtherObjects.class})
public class BankServicesConfig {
    @Autowired
    private BankDaosConfig bankAppDao;

    @Bean(name = "accountStatementService")
    public AccountStatementService accountStatementService(
            AccountStatementDao accountStatementDao) {
```

```
        AccountStatementServiceImpl accountStatementServiceImpl =
              new AccountStatementServiceImpl();
        accountStatementServiceImpl.setAccountStatementDao(accountStatementDao);
        return accountStatementServiceImpl;
    }
    .....
    @Bean(name = "fixedDepositService")
    public FixedDepositService fixedDepositService() {
        return new FixedDepositServiceImpl(bankAppDao.fixedDepositDao());
    }
}
```

In the above example listing, the accountStatementService method creates an instance of AccountStatementServiceImpl bean that depends on AccountStatementDao bean created by BankDaosConfig's accountStatementDao method. As the AccountStatementServiceImpl depends on AccountStatementDao, the accountStatementDao method is defined to accept an argument of type AccountStatementDao. The Spring container takes care of supplying the accountStatementService method with an instance of AccountStatementDao bean. The downside of using this approach is that you can't easily identify the @Configuration class that creates the AccountStatementDao bean.

The fixedDepositService method creates an instance of FixedDepositServiceImpl that depends on FixedDepositDao bean created by BankDaosConfig's fixedDepositDao method. As @Configuration classes are treated like any other bean class, we've autowired the BankDaosConfig bean. The BankDaosConfig's fixedDepositDao method is explicitly called to obtain an instance of FixedDepositDao bean. The benefit with explicitly calling @Bean methods on @Configuration classes to obtain bean dependencies is that it clearly identifies which @Configuration class owns creation of a dependency.

Let's now look at how to address some of the application requirements when using Java-based configuration.

7-7 Additional topics

In this section, we'll look at:

- how to override @Bean methods
- how to configure BeanPostProcessors and BeanFactoryPostProcessors
- import application context XML files into @Configuration classes
- conditionally import @Bean methods and @Configuration classes
- functional-style bean registration

Let's look at how each of these requirements are addressed.

Overriding @Bean methods

You can override an @Bean method by re-defining it in a new @Configuration class and passing that class to AnnotationConfigApplicationContext's constructor. You need to make sure that in the constructor argument list your new @Configuration class comes *after* the @Configuration class containing the @Bean method that you want to override. If you are using AnnotationConfigApplicationContext's register method to add @Configuration classes, then add the new @Configuration class *after* adding the @Configuration class containing the @Bean method that you want to override.

IMPORT **chapter 7/ch07-bankapp-more** (This project shows the MyBank application that shows how @Bean methods can be overriden. @Bean methods defined in *HibernateDaoImpl classes are overriden by

*MyBatisDaoImpl classes. To run the application, execute the main method of the BankApp class of this project.)

In ch07-bankapp-more project, beans are defined across these @Configuration classes:

- BankServicesConfig – contains @Bean methods that create services
- BankHibernateDaosConfig – contains @Bean methods that create DAOs that use Hibernate ORM for data access
- BankMyBatisDaosConfig – contains the same @Bean methods that are defined in BankHibernateDaosConfig class. But, the methods in this class create DAOs that use MyBatis ORM for data access
- BankOtherObjects – contains @Bean methods that create domain objects, BeanPostProcessors and BeanFactoryPostProcessors

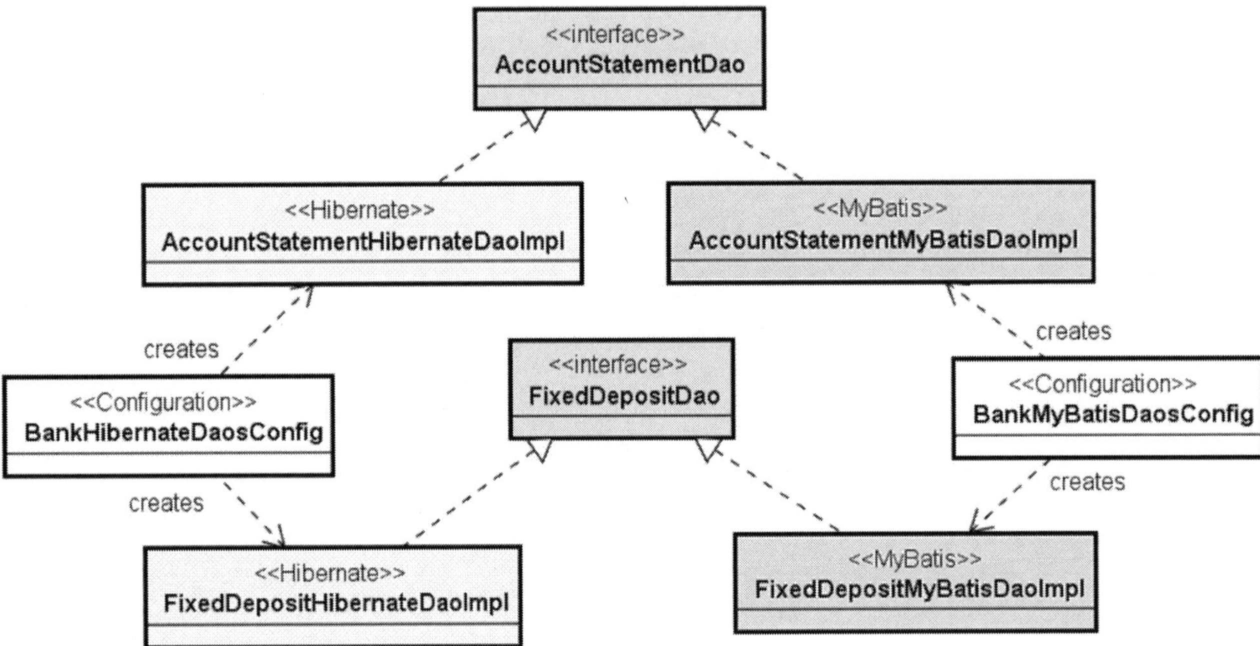

Figure 7-1 : BankHibernateDaosConfig creates Hibernate-specific DAOs, and BankMyBatisDaosConfig creates MyBatis-specific DAOs

Figure 7-1 shows the beans created by @Configuration annotated BankHibernateDaosConfig and BankMyBatisDaosConfig classes.

The following example listing shows some of the @Bean methods defined in BankHibernateDaosConfig class:

Example listing 7-20 – BankHibernateDaosConfig class
Project – ch07-bankapp-more
Source location - src/main/java/sample/spring/chapter07/bankapp

```
package sample.spring.chapter07.bankapp;
.....
@Configuration
public class BankHibernateDaosConfig {

    @Bean
```

```
    public AccountStatementDao accountStatementDao() {
        return new AccountStatementHibernateDaoImpl(.....);
    }
    .....
    @Bean
    public FixedDepositDao fixedDepositDao() {
        return new FixedDepositHibernateDaoImpl(.....);
    }
}
```

In the above example listing, accountStatementDao and fixedDepositDao methods create and return instances of AccountStatementHibernateDaoImpl and FixedDepositHibernateDaoImpl beans, respectively. AccountStatementHibernateDaoImpl and FixedDepositHibernateDaoImpl are DAO implementations that use Hibernate ORM for data access.

BankMyBatisDaosConfig class contains the same accountStatementDao and fixedDepositDao methods, but these methods create and return DAO implementations that use MyBatis ORM for data access. The following example listing shows accountStatementDao and fixedDepositDao methods of BankMyBatisDaosConfig class:

Example listing 7-21 – BankMyBatisDaosConfig class
Project – ch07-bankapp-more
Source location - src/main/java/sample/spring/chapter07/bankapp

```
package sample.spring.chapter07.bankapp;
.....
@Configuration
public class BankMyBatisDaosConfig {

    @Bean
    public AccountStatementDao accountStatementDao() {
        return new AccountStatementMyBatisDaoImpl(.....);
    }
    .....
    @Bean
    public FixedDepositDao fixedDepositDao() {
        return new FixedDepositMyBatisDaoImpl(.....);
    }
}
```

The accountStatementDao and fixedDepositDao methods of BankMyBatisDaosConfig class create and return instances of AccountStatementMyBatisDaoImpl and FixedDepositMyBatisDaoImpl beans, respectively.

If we pass BankHibernateDaosConfig and BankMyBatisDaosConfig classes to AnnotationConfigApplicationContext's constructor, then the class that comes *later* in the constructor argument list will override the @Bean methods of the earlier class. If we use AnnotationConfigApplicationContext's register method to add @Configuration classes, then the class that is added *later* overrides the @Bean methods of the class that was added earlier.

The following example listing shows the BankApp class of ch07-bankapp-more project whose main method creates an instance of AnnotationConfigApplicationContext and adds @Configuration classes to it:

Example listing 7-22 – BankApp class
Project – ch07-bankapp-more
Source location - src/main/java/sample/spring/chapter07/bankapp

```
package sample.spring.chapter07.bankapp;
```

```
.....
public class BankApp {
    public static void main(String args[]) throws Exception {
        AnnotationConfigApplicationContext context =
             new AnnotationConfigApplicationContext();
        context.register(BankServicesConfig.class);
        context.register(BankHibernateDaosConfig.class);
        context.register(BankOtherObjects.class);
        context.register(BankMyBatisDaosConfig.class);
        context.refresh();
        .....
        FixedDepositService fixedDepositService =
            context.getBean(FixedDepositService.class);
        fixedDepositService.createFixedDeposit(new FixedDepositDetails(1, 1000, 12,
            "someemail@somedomain.com"));
        .....
        context.close();
    }
}
```

In the above example listing, BankMyBatisDaosConfig is added *after* BankHibernateDaosConfig class; therefore, @Bean methods defined in BankMyBatisDaosConfig override @Bean methods defined in BankHibernateDaosConfig. If you run the BankApp's main method, you'll see the following output on the console:

```
INFO  .....CustomerRegistrationMyBatisDaoImpl - Registering customer
INFO  .....FixedDepositMyBatisDaoImpl - Saving fixed deposit details
INFO  .....AccountStatementMyBatisDaoImpl - Getting account statement
```

The output shows that DAOs specific to MyBatis are used by the application for data access.

If you modify BankApp's main method such that BankMyBatisDaosConfig is added *before* BankHibernateDaosConfig to AnnotationConfigApplicationContext, then running BankApp's main method will result in the following output:

```
INFO  .....CustomerRegistrationHibernateDaoImpl - Registering customer
INFO  .....FixedDepositHibernateDaoImpl - Saving fixed deposit details
INFO  .....AccountStatementHibernateDaoImpl - Getting account statement
```

The output shows that DAOs specific to Hibernate are now used by the application for data access.

Configuring BeanPostProcessors and BeanFactoryPostProcessors

You can use @Bean methods to configure BeanPostProcessors and BeanFactoryPostProcessors. The @Bean methods that configure BeanPostProcessors and BeanFactoryPostProcessors *must* be defined static, as shown in the following example listing:

Example listing 7-23 – BankOtherObjects class
Project – ch07-bankapp-more
Source location - src/main/java/sample/spring/chapter07/bankapp

```
package sample.spring.chapter07.bankapp;
.....
public class BankOtherObjects {
    .....
    @Bean
```

```
    public static BeanNamePrinter beanNamePrinter() {
        return new BeanNamePrinter();
    }

    @Bean
    public static MyBeanPostProcessor myBeanPostProcessor() {
        return new MyBeanPostProcessor();
    }
}
```

In the above example listing, beanNamePrinter method creates an instance of BeanNamePrinter (a BeanFactoryPostProcessor) and myBeanPostProcessor method creates an instance of MyBeanPostProcessor (a BeanPostProcessor). The BeanNamePrinter's postProcessBeanFactory method writes bean names on the console, and MyBeanPostProcessor's postProcessBeforeInitialization and postProcessAfterInitialization methods simply write the name and class of the bean instance being processed. Also, notice that both beanNamePrinter and myBeanPostProcessor methods are defined as static.

If you don't define beanNamePrinter and myBeanPostProcessor methods as static, the Spring container will create an instance of BankOtherObjects before creating instances of BeanNamePrinter and MyBeanPostProcessor beans. This means that the BankOtherObjects bean will not be processed by BeanNamePrinter and MyBeanPostProcessor beans.

If you run the main method of BankApp class of ch07-bankapp-more project, you'll see the following output on the console:

```
INFO  .....BeanNamePrinter - Created BeanNamePrinter instance
INFO  .....BeanNamePrinter - Found bean named: bankServicesConfig
INFO  .....BeanNamePrinter - Found bean named: bankHibernateDaosConfig
INFO  .....BeanNamePrinter - Found bean named: customerRegistrationService
INFO  .....BeanNamePrinter - Found bean named: myBeanPostProcessor
.....
INFO  .....MyBeanPostProcessor - Created MyBeanPostProcessor
INFO  .....MyBeanPostProcessor - postProcessBeforeInitialization method invoked for bean
bankOtherObjects of type class sample.spring.chapter07.bankapp.BankOtherObjects
INFO  .....MyBeanPostProcessor - postProcessBeforeInitialization method invoked for bean
fixedDepositDao of type class
sample.spring.chapter07.bankapp.mybatis.dao.FixedDepositMyBatisDaoImpl
```

The above output shows that BeanNamePrinter processes bean definitions corresponding to @Configuration and @Bean annotated methods. And, MyBeanPostProcessor interacts with bean instances created by @Bean methods and the bean instances created by the Spring container corresponding to @Configuration classes.

Importing application context XML files

Even if you are using Java-based configuration approach, you may have situations in which some configuration information is also contained in application context XML files. In such situations, you can use @ImportResource annotation to import application context XML files into @Configuration classes. The beans defined in the imported application context XML file are registered with the Spring container.

The DAOs in ch07-bankapp-more project need access to database properties (like driver class, username, and so on) to connect to the database. As these database properties are defined in an external db.properties file, they can be easily loaded using Spring's util schema. The following example listing shows the application context XML file that uses Spring's util schema to load db.properties file:

Example listing 7-24 – applicationContext.xml – loading database properties from db.properties
Project – ch07-bankapp-more
Source location - src/main/resources/META-INF/spring

```
<beans ..... xmlns:util="http://www.springframework.org/schema/util"....>
    <util:properties id="dbProps" location="classpath:META-INF/db.properties" />
</beans>
```

The <properties> element loads properties from db.properties file and exposes them as a bean named dbProps. The contents of db.properties file are:

```
driverClassName=com.mysql.jdbc.Driver
url=jdbc\:mysql\://localhost\:3306/spring_bank_app_db
username=root
password=root
```

As DAOs are created by BankHibernateDaosConfig and BankMyBatisDaosConfig classes, both the classes need access to the dbProps bean. For this reason, both the classes use @ImportResource annotation to import the applicationContext.xml file. The following example listing shows that BankHibernateDaosConfig class uses dbProps bean to obtain database properties for creating DAOs:

Example listing 7-25 – BankHibernateDaosConfig class - @ImportResource usage
Project – ch07-bankapp-more
Source location - src/main/java/sample/spring/chapter07/bankapp

```
package sample.spring.chapter07.bankapp;

import org.springframework.context.annotation.ImportResource;
import sample.spring.chapter07.bankapp.domain.DataSource;
.....
@Configuration
@ImportResource(locations = "classpath:META-INF/spring/applicationContext.xml")
public class BankHibernateDaosConfig {
    @Value("#{dbProps.driverClassName}")
    private String driverClass;

    @Value("#{dbProps.url}")
    private String url;
    .....
    @Bean
    public AccountStatementDao accountStatementDao() {
        return new AccountStatementHibernateDaoImpl(
            new DataSource(driverClass, url,username, password)
        );
    }
    .....
}
```

In the above example listing, @ImportResource imports the applicationContext.xml file that defines the dbProps bean (refer example listing 7-24). The locations attribute specifies the location of application context XML file that needs to be imported. You can import multiple application context XML files by specifying their locations as the value of locations attribute. The database properties are retrieved from the dbProps bean using @Value annotation. These database properties are later used to create the DataSource object and pass it to AccountStatementHibernateDaoImpl's constructor.

Conditionally including @Bean and @Configuration classes

You can use @Profile annotation to conditionally include @Bean methods and @Configuration classes for processing by the Spring container.

IMPORT chapter 7/ch07-bankapp-profiles (This project is a modified version of ch06-bean-profiles project that uses Java-based configuration for developing the MyBank application. To run the application, execute BankAppWithProfile's main method or BankAppWithoutProfile's main method of this project.)

Let's look at MyBank application of ch07-bankapp-profiles project that uses @Profile annotation to conditionally include @Bean methods and @Configuration classes for registration with the Spring container.

The requirements addressed by MyBank application of ch07-bean-profiles project are:

- the application should use an embedded database in development, and a standalone database in production environment
- the application should support both Hibernate and MyBatis ORM frameworks for database interaction. At the time of deployment, you specify whether the application uses Hibernate or MyBatis for database interaction. If nothing is specified, Hibernate is used by default.

Let's now look at how each of these requirements are met by MyBank application.

Different databases in development and production environments

The DataSource class of ch07-bankapp-profiles project holds the database configuration (like, driver class, username, and so on) and is used by DAOs for connecting to the database and executing SQLs. The following example listing shows the DataSource class:

Example listing 7-26 – DataSource class
Project – ch07-bankapp-profiles
Source location - src/main/java/sample/spring/chapter07/bankapp/domain

```
package sample.spring.chapter07.bankapp.domain;

public class DataSource {
    private String driverClass;
    private String url;
    .....
    public DataSource(String driverClass, String url, .....) {
        this.driverClass = driverClass;
        this.url = url;
        .....
    }
    .....
}
```

DataSource's constructor accepts database configuration (like driver class, URL, and so on). The database configuration is stored in devDB.properties file for the development environment and in productionDB.properties file for the production environment. As database configuration needs to be loaded from different properties files depending on which environment the MyBank application is deployed, we've defined two different @Configuration classes, DevDBConfiguration and ProdDBConfiguration, for creating DataSource beans.

The following example listing shows DevDBConfiguration class that creates DataSource bean with properties defined in devDB.properties file:

Example listing 7-27 – DevDBConfiguration class
Project – ch07-bankapp-profiles
Source location - src/main/java/sample/spring/chapter07/bankapp

```
package sample.spring.chapter07.bankapp;
.....
import org.springframework.context.annotation.PropertySource;
import org.springframework.context.support.PropertySourcesPlaceholderConfigurer;

@Configuration
@Profile({ "dev", "default" })
@PropertySource("classpath:/META-INF/devDB.properties")
public class DevDBConfiguration {
    private static Logger logger = LogManager.getLogger(DevDBConfiguration.class);

    @Value("${driverClassName}")
    private String driverClass;

    @Value("${url}")
    private String url;
    .....
    @Bean
    public DataSource dataSource() {
        return new DataSource(driverClass, url, username, password);
    }

    @Bean
    public static PropertySourcesPlaceholderConfigurer
            propertySourcesPlaceholderConfigurer() {
        return new PropertySourcesPlaceholderConfigurer();
    }
}
```

In the above example listing, @Profile annotation specifies that the DevDBConfiguration class is processed by Spring only if dev or default profile is active. @PropertySource annotation reads database configuration from the devDB.properties file and adds them to Spring's Environment object. For instance, the driverClassName, url, username and password properties defined in devDB.properties file are added to Environment object. The propertySourcesPlaceholderConfigurer method configures PropertySourcesPlaceholderConfigurer (a BeanFactoryPostProcessor) that resolves ${.....} placeholders specified by @Value annotations against the Environment object. For instance, @Value("${driverClassName}") annotation on driverClass field sets the value of driverClass field to the value of driverClassName property in the Environment object. The dataSource method creates an instance of DataSource that contains configuration read from devDB.properties file.

The following example listing shows ProdDBConfiguration class that creates DataSource bean with properties defined in productionDB.properties file:

Example listing 7-28 – ProdDBConfiguration class
Project – ch07-bankapp-profiles
Source location - src/main/java/sample/spring/chapter07/bankapp

```
package sample.spring.chapter07.bankapp;
.....
@Configuration
@Profile("production")
@PropertySource("classpath:/META-INF/productionDB.properties")
public class ProdDBConfiguration {
```

```
    @Autowired
    private Environment env;
    .....
    @Bean
    public DataSource dataSource() {
        return new DataSource(env.getProperty("driverClass"),
            env.getProperty("url"), env.getProperty("username"),
            env.getProperty("password"));
    }
}
```

In the above example listing, @Profile annotation specifies that the ProdDBConfiguration class is processed by Spring only if production profile is active. @PropertySource adds database configuration read from productionDB.properties file to Spring's Environment object. Instead of @Value annotation, Environment's getProperty method has been used to retrieve database configuration from the Environment object. As we are not using @Value annotation to obtain properties from the Environment object, the ProdDBConfiguration doesn't configure a PropertySourcesPlaceholderConfigurer. The dataSource method creates an instance of DataSource that contains database configuration read from productionDB.properties file by @PropertySource.

Supporting both Hibernate and MyBatis

To support both Hibernate and MyBatis for database interaction, separate DAOs (FixedDepositHibernateDao and FixedDepositMyBatisDao) have been created for Hibernate and MyBatis.

The following example listing shows FixedDepositHibernateDao class (an implementation of FixedDepositDao) that uses Hibernate for database interaction:

Example listing 7-29 – FixedDepositHibernateDao class
Project – ch07-bankapp-profiles
Source location - src/main/java/sample/spring/chapter07/bankapp/dao

```
package sample.spring.chapter07.bankapp.dao;
.....
public class FixedDepositHibernateDao implements FixedDepositDao {
    private DataSource dataSource;
    .....
    public FixedDepositHibernateDao(DataSource dataSource) {
        this.dataSource = dataSource;
    }
    .....
}
```

FixedDepositHibernateDao's constructor accepts DataSource as argument that is used by Hibernate for connecting with the database and executing SQLs. FixedDepositMyBatisDao (another implementation of FixedDepositDao) is similar to FixedDepositHibernateDao except that it uses MyBatis for database interaction.

The following example listing shows the BankAppConfiguration class that puts together the MyBank application objects:

Example listing 7-30 – BankAppConfiguration class
Project – ch07-bankapp-profiles
Source location - src/main/java/sample/spring/chapter07/bankapp

```
package sample.spring.chapter07.bankapp;
.....
```

```
@Configuration
public class BankAppConfiguration {
    private static Logger logger = LogManager.getLogger(BankAppConfiguration.class);

    @Bean
    public FixedDepositController fixedDepositController(
          FixedDepositService fixedDepositService) {
        .....
    }

    @Bean
    @Profile({ "hibernate", "default" })
    public FixedDepositDao fixedDepositHibernateDao(DataSource dataSource) {
        logger.info("creating FixedDepositHibernateDao. Database URL is - "
            + dataSource.getUrl());
        return new FixedDepositHibernateDao(dataSource);
    }

    @Bean
    @Profile({ "mybatis" })
    public FixedDepositDao fixedDepositMyBatisDao(DataSource dataSource) {
        logger.info("creating FixedDepositMyBatisDao. Database URL is - "
            + dataSource.getUrl());
        return new FixedDepositMyBatisDao(dataSource);
    }

    @Bean
    public FixedDepositService fixedDepositService(FixedDepositDao fixedDepositDao) {
        .....
    }
}
```

In the above example listing, `@Profile` annotation on `fixedDepositHibernateDao` method specifies that the method is considered for invocation by Spring only if `hibernate` or `default` profile is active. Similarly, `@Profile` annotation on `fixedDepositMyBatisDao` method specifies that the method is considered for invocation by Spring only if `mybatis` profile is active. Notice that the `fixedDepositService` method accepts an argument of type `FixedDepositDao` (the interface implemented by both `FixedDepositHibernateDao` and `FixedDepositMyBatisDao`). If both `fixedDepositHibernateDao` and `fixedDepositMyBatisDao` methods are called by the Spring container, it'll result in creation of two objects of `FixedDepositDao` type; therefore, you must ensure that only one profile out of `mybatis`, `hibernate` and `default` is active.

The following example listing shows `BankAppWithProfile`'s `main` method that sets `mybatis` and `production` profiles as active:

Example listing 7-31 – `BankAppWithProfile` – setting `mybatis` and `production` as active profiles
Project – `ch07-bankapp-profiles`
Source location - `src/main/java/sample/spring/chapter07/bankapp`

```
package sample.spring.chapter07.bankapp;
.....
public class BankAppWithProfile {
    public static void main(String args[]) {
        AnnotationConfigApplicationContext context =
            new AnnotationConfigApplicationContext();
        context.getEnvironment().setActiveProfiles("mybatis", "production");
        context.register(BankAppConfiguration.class, DevDBConfiguration.class,
              ProdDBConfiguration.class);
```

```
        context.refresh();
        .....
    }
}
```

In the above example listing, AnnotationConfigApplicationContext's getEnvironment method returns Spring's Environment object whose setActiveProfiles method is used to set active profiles. If you run BankAppWithProfile's main method, you'll see the following output on the console:

```
INFO  .....ProdDBConfiguration - initializing
INFO  .....BankAppConfiguration - creating FixedDepositMyBatisDao. Database URL is - jdbc:mysql://production:3306/spring_bank_app_db
INFO  .....FixedDepositMyBatisDao - initializing
INFO  .....FixedDepositServiceImpl - initializing
```

As mybatis and production profiles are active, ProdDBConfiguration instance (refer example listing 7-28) is created by the Spring container and BankAppConfiguration's fixedDepositMyBatisDao method (refer example listing 7-30) is called by the Spring container.

The ch07-bankapp-profiles project also defines a BankAppWithoutProfile class whose main method doesn't set any active profile. If you run BankAppWithoutProfile's main method, you'll see the following output on the console:

```
INFO  .....DevDBConfiguration - initializing
INFO  .....BankAppConfiguration - creating FixedDepositHibernateDao. Database URL is - jdbc:mysql://localhost:3306/spring_bank_app_db
INFO  .....FixedDepositHibernateDao - initializing
INFO  .....FixedDepositServiceImpl - initializing
```

As no profile was set active, the default profile is considered active by Spring. For this reason, the above output shows that DevDBConfiguration (refer example listing 7-27) instance is created by the Spring container and BankAppConfiguration's fixedDepositHibernateDao (refer example listing 7-30) method is called by the Spring container.

In this section, we saw that @Profile annotation lets Spring conditionally include @Configuration classes and @Bean methods for processing by the Spring container. @Profile is meta-annotated with Spring's @Conditional annotation which specifies a Condition object that matches active profiles with profiles specified by @Profile annotation. If a match is found, the corresponding @Configuration class or @Bean method is included for processing by the Spring container.

If you want to define custom conditions (like availability of a particular bean in the Spring container, availability of the internet connection, and so on) based on which you want to include @Configuration classes and @Bean methods, then define those custom conditions by creating custom annotations that are meta-annotated with @Conditional (or directly use @Conditional) annotation.

Functional-style bean registration

AnnotationConfigApplicationContext's register method (refer listings 7-13 and 7-22) is used to register beans with the Spring container. In Spring 5, registerBean methods have been added to AnnotationConfigApplicationContext and GenericApplicationContext classes that allow functional-style bean registration.

IMPORT **chapter 7/ch07-functional-style** (This project shows functional-style registration of beans. To run the application, execute SampleApp class's main method.)

Example listing 7-32 – SampleApp – functional-style bean registration
Project – ch07-bankapp-profiles
Source location - src/main/java/sample/spring/chapter07/bankapp

```
package com.sample.functionalstyle;

.....
import org.springframework.beans.factory.config.BeanDefinition;
import org.springframework.context.annotation.AnnotationConfigApplicationContext;
.....
public class SampleApp {
    .....
    public static void main(String... args) {
        AnnotationConfigApplicationContext context =
           new AnnotationConfigApplicationContext();
        context.registerBean("primaryProfile", Profile.class,
                beanDefinition -> beanDefinition.setScope(BeanDefinition.SCOPE_PROTOTYPE),
                beanDefinition -> beanDefinition.setPrimary(true));

        context.registerBean("secondaryProfile", Profile.class,
                () -> new Profile("secondaryProfileName", "00"),
                beanDefinition -> beanDefinition.setScope(BeanDefinition.SCOPE_PROTOTYPE),
                beanDefinition -> beanDefinition.setPrimary(false));

        context.registerBean("personPrimary", Person.class);
        context.refresh();

        Profile profile = context.getBean(Person.class).getProfile();
        logger.info("Profile -> name: " + profile.getName()
              + ", age: " + profile.getAge());
        .....
    }
}
```

In the above listing, AnnotationConfigApplicationContext's registerBean method is used to register beans with names primaryProfile (of type Profile), secondaryProfile (of type Profile) and personPrimary (of type Person). Profile class defines a no-argument constructor and a constructor that accepts name and age arguments. When Profile class's no-argument constructor is called, it sets name to "defaultName" and age to "99".

The registerBean method that registers primaryProfile has the following signature:

```
void registerBean(@Nullable String beanName, Class<T> beanClass,
BeanDefinitionCustomizer... customizers)
```

here, beanName is the bean name, beanClass is the bean class, and BeanDefinitionCustomizer (new introduced in Spring 5) is a functional interface that accepts BeanDefinition as argument. You can customize the bean definition by calling BeanDefinition object's methods. Note that you can pass any number of BeanDefinitionCustomizer instances to the registerBean method. Also, @Nullable annotation on beanName argument means that you can pass null as the bean name.

In listing 7-32, registerBean method uses the no-argument constructor of Profile class for creating the Profile bean, and registers it with name primaryProfile. Lambda expressions are used to customize the bean definition. For instance, `setScope` method sets the bean scope to 'prototype', and `setPrimary` method sets the bean as the primary candidate for autowiring.

The `registerBean` method that registers `secondaryProfile` has the following signature:

```
void registerBean(@Nullable String beanName, Class<T> beanClass, @Nullable Supplier<T>
supplier, BeanDefinitionCustomizer... customizers)
```

here, `beanName` is the bean name, `beanClass` is the bean class, `Supplier` is a functional interface that creates the bean instance, and `BeanDefinitionCustomizer` is a functional interface that accepts `BeanDefinition` as argument. `@Nullable` annotation on `supplier` argument means that you can pass `null` as its value.

In listing 7-32, `registerBean` method uses the `() -> new Profile("secondaryProfileName", "00")` lambda expression to create a new `Profile` bean and registers it with name `secondaryProfile`. The bean definition is customized by calling the `setScope` and `setPrimary` methods of `BeanDefintion`.

As `Person` class's constructor accepts an argument of type `Profile`, the `primaryProfile` bean (the *primary* candidate for autowiring) is injected into the `Person` object. For this reason, if you execute `SampleApp`'s `main` method, it'll result in the following output:

```
Profile -> name: defaultName, age: 99
```

7-8 Summary

In this chapter, we looked at Java-based configuration approach to configuring Spring beans. We looked at various annotations (like `@Configuration`, `@Bean`, `@Profile`, and so on) that are used for configuration beans. We also looked at different approaches for performing dependency injection of beans, and how to use a mix of XML application context XML and Java-based configuration approach for developing Spring applications. The next chapter shows how Spring simplifies interacting with databases.

Chapter 8 - *Database interaction using Spring*

8-1 Introduction

Spring simplifies interaction with databases by providing a layer of abstraction on top of JDBC. Spring also simplifies using ORM (Object Relational Mapping) frameworks, like Hibernate (`http://www.hibernate.org/`) and MyBatis (`http://www.mybatis.org`), for database interaction. In this chapter, we'll look at examples that demonstrate how Spring simplifies developing applications that interact with databases.

> The support for Hibernate 4 is dropped in Spring 5. If you want to use Hibernate 4, then continue to use Spring 4.x.

We'll begin this chapter by looking at a sample application that uses Spring's JDBC abstraction to interact with MySQL database. After that, we we'll develop the same application using Spring's support for Hibernate framework. We'll wrap this chapter up by looking at Spring's support for programmatic and declarative transaction management.

Let's first look at the requirements of MyBank application discussed in this chapter.

8-2 MyBank application's requirements

MyBank application is an internet banking application that allows bank customers to check bank account details, generate bank statement, create fixed deposits, request check book, and so on. The following figure shows the `BANK_ACCOUNT_DETAILS` and `FIXED_DEPOSIT_DETAILS` tables in which MyBank application's data is stored:

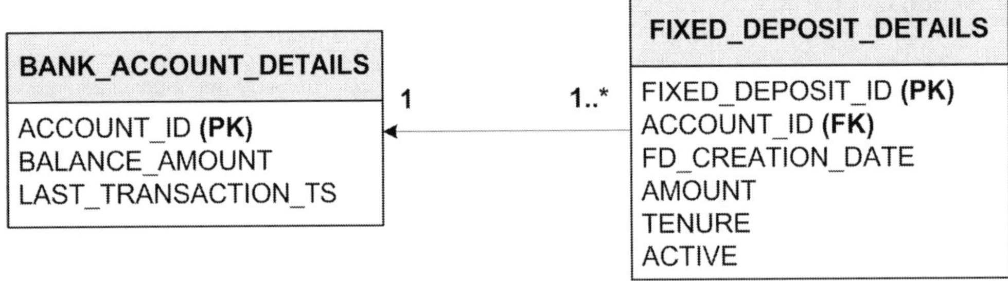

Figure 8-1 Database tables used by the MyBank application

`BANK_ACCOUNT_DETAILS` table contains information about bank accounts, and `FIXED_DEPOSIT_DETAILS` table contains information about fixed deposits. The above figure shows that there is many-to-one relationship between `FIXED_DEPOSIT_DETAILS` and `BANK_ACCOUNT_DETAILS` tables. When a bank customer opens a new fixed deposit, the fixed deposit amount is deducted from the `BANK_ACCOUNT_DETAILS` table's `BALANCE_AMOUNT` column, and the fixed deposit details are saved in the `FIXED_DEPOSIT_DETAILS` table.

The columns of BANK_ACCOUNT_DETAILS table are:

- `ACCOUNT_ID` – account identifier that uniquely identifies a customer's bank account.
- `BALANCE_AMOUNT` – holds the current balance in the bank account. When a customer requests for opening a fixed deposit, the fixed deposit amount is deducted from this column.
- `LAST_TRANSACTION_TS` – holds the date/time of the last transaction performed on this account.

The columns of `FIXED_DEPOSIT_DETAILS` table are:

- `FIXED_DEPOSIT_ID` – fixed deposit identifier that uniquely identifies a fixed deposit. When a customer opens a fixed deposit, a unique fixed deposit identifier is generated by MyBank application for future reference by the customer. The value of `FIXED_DEPOSIT_ID` column is auto-generated by MySQL database.

- `ACCOUNT_ID` – foreign key that identifies the bank account with which the fixed deposit is associated. Every quarter, interest earned on the fixed deposit is credited into the bank account identified by this column.

- `FD_CREATION_DATE` – the date on which the fixed deposit was created

- `AMOUNT` – fixed deposit amount

- `TENURE` – fixed deposit tenure (in months). Fixed deposit tenure must be greater than or equal to `12` months and less than or equal to `60` months.

- `ACTIVE` – indicates whether the fixed deposit is currently active or not. An active fixed deposit earns interest on the fixed deposit amount.

Let's now look at how the requirements of MyBank application can be met using Spring's JDBC module.

8-3 Developing the MyBank application using Spring's JDBC module

Spring's JDBC module simplifies interaction with data sources by taking care of lower level details of opening and closing connections, managing transactions, processing exceptions, and so on. In this section, we'll look at the MyBank application that is developed using Spring's JDBC module. For the sake of simplicity, we'll look only at the services and DAOs that form part of the MyBank application.

IMPORT **`chapter 8/ch08-bankapp-jdbc`** (This project shows the MyBank application that uses Spring's JDBC module to interact with the database. To run the application, execute the `main` method of the `BankApp` class of this project.)

> All the projects in this chapter require that you install MySQL database and execute the `spring_bank_app_db.sql` SQL script contained in the `sql` folder of the project. Executing `spring_bank_app_db.sql` script creates `SPRING_BANK_APP_DB` database and adds `BANK_ACCOUNT_DETAILS` and `FIXED_DEPOSIT_DETAILS` tables to the database. Also, you need to modify the `src/main/resources/META-INF/spring/database.properties` file to point to your MySQL installation.

To develop an application that uses Spring's JDBC module for database interaction, you need to do the following:

- configure a `javax.sql.DataSource` object that identifies the data source, and

- implement DAOs that use Spring's JDBC module classes for database interaction

Configuring a data source

If you are using Spring to develop a standalone application, you can configure the data source as a bean in the application context XML file. If you are developing an enterprise application, you can define a data source that is bound to the application server's JNDI, and use Spring's `jee` schema to retrieve the JNDI-bound data source and make it available as a bean. In the case of `ch08-bankapp-jdbc` project, the data source is configured in the application context XML file.

The following example listing shows how MyBank application's data source is configured in the application context XML file:

Example listing 8-1 – applicationContext.xml – data source configuration
Project – ch08-bankapp-jdbc
Source location - src/main/resources/META-INF/spring

```
<context:property-placeholder location="classpath*:META-INF/spring/database.properties" />

<bean id="dataSource" class="org.apache.commons.dbcp2.BasicDataSource"
     destroy-method="close" >
    <property name="driverClassName" value="${database.driverClassName}" />
    <property name="url" value="${database.url}" />
    <property name="username" value="${database.username}" />
    <property name="password" value="${database.password}" />
</bean>
```

In the above example listing, the <property-placeholder> element (refer section 5-4 of chapter 5 for more details) of Spring's context schema loads properties from the META-INF/spring/database.properties file and makes them available to bean definitions in the application context XML file. The dataSource bean represents a javax.sql.DataSource object that acts as a factory for creating connections to the data source. BasicDataSource class is an implementation of javax.sql.DataSource interface that supports connection pooling feature. BasicDataSource class is part of Apache Commons DBCP project (http://commons.apache.org/dbcp/). The values for driverClassName, url, username and password properties of BasicDataSource class come from the properties defined in the database.properties file. The close method of BasicDataSource class closes all idle connections in the pool. As the bean definition for the BasicDataSource class specifies value of destroy-method attribute as close, all idle connections in the pool are closed when the dataSource bean instance is destroyed by the Spring container.

Configuring a data source in Java EE environments

If you are developing an enterprise application that is deployed in an application server, you typically register javax.sql.DataSource object with application server's JNDI. In such scenarios, you can use Spring's jee schema's <jndi-lookup> element to make the JNDI-bound data source available as a Spring bean:

```
<jee:jndi-lookup jndi-name="java:comp/env/jdbc/bankAppDb" id="dataSource" />
```

here, jndi-name attribute specifies the JNDI name with which the javax.sql.DataSource object is bound to the JNDI, and id attribute specifies the name with which the javax.sql.DataSource object is registered as a bean in the ApplicationContext.

If you are using Java-based configuration approach, you can obtain the javax.sql.DataSource object from JNDI using Spring's JndiTemplate or JndiLocatorDelegate. The following example listing shows usage of JndiLocatorDelegate:

Example listing 8-2 – Obtaining JNDI-bound data source using Spring's JndiLocatorDelegate

```
@Bean(destroyMethod="")
public DataSource dataSource() throws NamingException {
    JndiLocatorDelegate delegate =
        JndiLocatorDelegate.createDefaultResourceRefLocator();
    return delegate.lookup("jdbc/bankAppDb", DataSource.class);
}
```

In the above example listing, JndiLocatorDelegate's createDefaultResourceRefLocator method specifies that all JNDI name lookups will be automatically prefixed with java:comp/env/. JndiLocatorDelegate's lookup method does the actual JNDI lookup for the given name. The second argument to the lookup method specifies the type of the object returned from JNDI lookup. Notice that we've set the destroyMethod attribute's value to "". As the JNDI-bound DataSource object's lifecycle is managed by the application server, the Spring container must *not* call the destruction method on the DataSource object when the Spring container is shutdown.

Let's now look at some of the Spring's JDBC module classes that you can use in your DAOs to interact with the database.

Creating DAOs that use Spring's JDBC module classes

Spring's JDBC module defines multiple classes that simplify database interaction. We'll first look at the JdbcTemplate class that is at the heart of Spring's JDBC module. The other classes that we'll discuss in this section are NamedParameterJdbcTemplate and SimpleJdbcInsert. To learn about other Spring's JDBC module classes, refer to Spring's reference documentation.

JdbcTemplate

JdbcTemplate class takes care of managing Connection, Statement and ResultSet objects, catching JDBC exceptions and translating them into easily understandable exceptions (like IncorrectResultSetColumnCountException and CannotGetJdbcConnectionException), performing batch operations, and so on. An application developer only needs to provide SQL to the JdbcTemplate class, and extract results after the SQL is executed.

As JdbcTemplate acts as a wrapper around javax.sql.DataSource object. A JdbcTemplate instance is typically initialized with reference to the javax.sql.DataSource object from which it obtains database connections, as shown in the following example listing:

Example listing 8-3 – applicationContext.xml – JdbcTemplate configuration
Project – ch08-bankapp-jdbc
Source location - src/main/resources/META-INF/spring

```
<bean id="jdbcTemplate" class="org.springframework.jdbc.core.JdbcTemplate">
    <property name="dataSource" ref="dataSource" />
</bean>

<bean id="dataSource" class="org.apache.commons.dbcp2.BasicDataSource".....>
   .....
</bean>
```

The above example listing shows that the JdbcTemplate class defines a dataSource property that refers to a javax.sql.DataSource object.

If your application uses a JNDI-bound data source, use the <jndi-lookup> element of jee schema to retrieve the JNDI-bound data source and register it as a bean with the Spring container. As shown in the following example listing, this approach makes the JNDI-bound data source accessible to JdbcTemplate as a bean:

Example listing 8-4 – JdbcTemplate configuration for JNDI-bound data source

```
<beans .....
      xmlns:jee="http://www.springframework.org/schema/jee"
      xsi:schemaLocation=".....
         http://www.springframework.org/schema/jee
         http://www.springframework.org/schema/jee/spring-jee.xsd">

   <bean id="jdbcTemplate" class="org.springframework.jdbc.core.JdbcTemplate">
```

```
        <property name="dataSource" ref="dataSource" />
    </bean>

    <jee:jndi-lookup jndi-name="java:comp/env/jdbc/bankAppDb" id="dataSource" />

  .....
</beans>
```

In the above example listing, reference to Spring's jee schema is included in the application context XML file. The <jndi-lookup> element retrieves javax.sql.DataSource object from JNDI and registers it as a bean named dataSource, which is referenced by the JdbcTemplate class.

A JdbcTemplate instance is thread-safe, which means multiple DAOs of your application can share the same instance of JdbcTemplate class to interact with the database. The following example listing shows FixedDepositDaoImpl's createFixedDeposit method that makes use of JdbcTemplate to save fixed deposit details in the database:

Example listing 8-5 – FixedDepositDaoImpl class – saving data using JdbcTemplate
Project – ch08-bankapp-jdbc
Source location - src/main/java/sample/spring/chapter08/bankapp/dao

```
package sample.spring.chapter08.bankapp.dao;

import java.sql.*;
import org.springframework.jdbc.core.JdbcTemplate;
import org.springframework.jdbc.core.PreparedStatementCreator;
import org.springframework.jdbc.support.GeneratedKeyHolder;
import org.springframework.jdbc.support.KeyHolder;
import org.springframework.stereotype.Repository;

@Repository(value = "fixedDepositDao")
public class FixedDepositDaoImpl implements FixedDepositDao {

    @Autowired
    private JdbcTemplate jdbcTemplate;
    .....
    public int createFixedDeposit(final FixedDepositDetails fixedDepositDetails) {
        final String sql =
            "insert into fixed_deposit_details(account_id, fixedDeposit_creation_date,
             amount, tenure, active) values(?, ?, ?, ?, ?)";

        KeyHolder keyHolder = new GeneratedKeyHolder();

        jdbcTemplate.update(new PreparedStatementCreator() {
            @Override
            public PreparedStatement createPreparedStatement(Connection con)
                    throws SQLException {
                PreparedStatement ps = con.prepareStatement(sql, new String[] {
                   "fixed_deposit_id" });
                ps.setInt(1, fixedDepositDetails.getBankAccountId());
                ps.setDate(2, new java.sql.Date(
                                 fixedDepositDetails.getFixedDepositCreationDate()
                                .getTime())
                        );
                .....
                return ps;
            }
```

```
        }, keyHolder);

        return keyHolder.getKey().intValue();
    }
    .....
}
```

In the above example listing, the FixedDepositDaoImpl class is annotated with Spring's @Repository annotation because the FixedDepositDaoImpl class represents a DAO. JdbcTemplate instance that we configured in the application context XML file (refer example listing 8-3) is autowired into FixedDepositDaoImpl instance. JdbcTemplate's update method is used to execute an insert, update or delete operation against the database. JdbcTemplate's update method accepts an instance of PreparedStatementCreator and an instance of KeyHolder. PreparedStatementCreator creates a java.sql.PreparedStatement given a Connection object. Spring's KeyHolder interface represents a holder for the keys that are auto-generated when insert SQL statements are executed. GeneratedKeyHolder class is the default implementation of KeyHolder interface.

Once the INSERT SQL statement is successfully executed, the auto-generated keys are added to the GeneratedKeyHolder instance. You can extract the auto-generated keys from the GeneratedKeyHolder by calling the getKey method. In example listing 8-5, the createFixedDeposit method inserts fixed deposit details into the FIXED_DEPOSIT_DETAILS table and returns the auto-generated key.

Example listing 8-5 shows that you don't need to worry about catching SQLException that may be thrown by the execution of PreparedStatement. This is because JdbcTemplate is responsible for handling SQLExceptions.

Let's now look at NamedParameterJdbcTemplate class.

NamedParameterJdbcTemplate

If the case of JdbcTemplate class, parameters are specified using **?** placeholders in the SQL statement (refer example listing 8-5). Spring's NamedParameterJdbcTemplate is a wrapper around JdbcTemplate instance that allows you to use named parameters instead of **?** in the SQL statement.

The following example listing shows how the NamedParameterJdbcTemplate class is configured in the application context XML file:

Example listing 8-6 – applicationContext.xml – NamedParameterJdbcTemplate configuration
Project – ch08-bankapp-jdbc
Source location - src/main/resources/META-INF/spring

```
<bean id="namedJdbcTemplate"
      class="org.springframework.jdbc.core.namedparam.NamedParameterJdbcTemplate">
    <constructor-arg ref="dataSource" />
</bean>

<bean id="dataSource" class="org.apache.commons.dbcp2.BasicDataSource".....>
    .....
</bean>
```

The above example listing shows that the NamedParameterJdbcTemplate class accepts javax.sql.DataSource object as constructor argument.

The following example listing shows the FixedDepositDaoImpl class that uses NamedParameterJdbcTemplate to fetch fixed deposit details from the FIXED_DEPOSIT_DETAILS table:

Example listing 8-7 – FixedDepositDaoImpl class – NamedParameterJdbcTemplate usage
Project – ch08-bankapp-jdbc
Source location - src/main/java/sample/spring/chapter08/bankapp/dao

```
package sample.spring.chapter08.bankapp.dao;

import java.sql.ResultSet;
import org.springframework.jdbc.core.RowMapper;
import org.springframework.jdbc.core.namedparam.MapSqlParameterSource;
import org.springframework.jdbc.core.namedparam.NamedParameterJdbcTemplate;
import org.springframework.jdbc.core.namedparam.SqlParameterSource;
.....
@Repository(value = "fixedDepositDao")
public class FixedDepositDaoImpl implements FixedDepositDao {
    .....
    @Autowired
    private NamedParameterJdbcTemplate namedParameterJdbcTemplate;
    .....
    public FixedDepositDetails getFixedDeposit(final int fixedDepositId) {
        final String sql = "select * from fixed_deposit_details where fixed_deposit_id
              = :fixedDepositId";

        SqlParameterSource namedParameters = new MapSqlParameterSource(
                "fixedDepositId", fixedDepositId);

        return namedParameterJdbcTemplate.queryForObject(sql, namedParameters,
                new RowMapper<FixedDepositDetails>() {
                    public FixedDepositDetails mapRow(ResultSet rs, int rowNum)
                           throws SQLException {
                        FixedDepositDetails fixedDepositDetails =
                            new FixedDepositDetails();
                        fixedDepositDetails.setActive(rs.getString("active"));
                        .....
                        return fixedDepositDetails;
                    }
                });
    }
}
```

NamedParameterJdbcTemplate instance that we configured in the application context XML file (refer example listing 8-6) is autowired into FixedDepositDaoImpl class. In the above example listing, the SQL query passed to NamedParameterJdbcTemplate's queryForObject method contains a named parameter fixedDepositId. The named parameter values are supplied via an implementation of Spring's SqlParameterSource interface. MapSqlParameterSource class is an implementation of SqlParameterSource interface that stores named parameters (and their values) in a java.util.Map. In the above example listing, MapSqlParameterSource instance holds value of fixedDepositId named parameter. NamedParameterJdbcTemplate's queryForObject method executes the supplied SQL query and returns a single object. Spring's RowMapper object is used for mapping each returned row to an object. In the above example listing, RowMapper maps the returned row in the ResultSet to a FixedDepositDetails object.

Let's now look at Spring's SimpleJdbcInsert class.

SimpleJdbcInsert

SimpleJdbcInsert class makes use of database metadata to simplify creating a basic SQL insert statement for a table.

The following example listing shows the BankAccountDaoImpl class that makes use of SimpleJdbcInsert to insert bank account details into BANK_ACCOUNT_DETAILS table:

Example listing 8-8 – BankAccountDaoImpl class – SimpleJdbcInsert usage
Project – ch08-bankapp-jdbc
Source location - src/main/java/sample/spring/chapter08/bankapp/dao

```
package sample.spring.chapter08.bankapp.dao;

import javax.sql.DataSource;
import org.springframework.jdbc.core.simple.SimpleJdbcInsert;
.....
@Repository(value = "bankAccountDao")
public class BankAccountDaoImpl implements BankAccountDao {
    private SimpleJdbcInsert insertBankAccountDetail;

    @Autowired
    private void setDataSource(DataSource dataSource) {
        this.insertBankAccountDetail = new SimpleJdbcInsert(dataSource)
                .withTableName("bank_account_details")
                .usingGeneratedKeyColumns("account_id");
    }

    @Override
    public int createBankAccount(final BankAccountDetails bankAccountDetails) {
        Map<String, Object> parameters = new HashMap<String, Object>(2);
        parameters.put("balance_amount", bankAccountDetails.getBalanceAmount());
        parameters.put("last_transaction_ts", new java.sql.Date(
                bankAccountDetails.getLastTransactionTimestamp().getTime()));

        Number key = insertBankAccountDetail.executeAndReturnKey(parameters);
        return key.intValue();
    }
    .....
}
```

As the setDataSource method is annotated with @Autowired annotation, javax.sql.DataSource object is passed as an argument to the setDataSource method. In the setDataSource method, an instance of SimpleJdbcInsert is created by passing reference to javax.sql.DataSource object to SimpleJdbcInsert's constructor.

SimpleJdbcInsert's withTableName method sets the name of the table into which you want to insert records. As we want to insert bank account details into BANK_ACCOUNT_DETAILS table, 'bank_account_details' string value is passed as an argument to the withTableName method. SimpleJdbcInsert's usingGeneratedKeyColumns method sets names of table columns that contain auto-generated keys. In the case of BANK_ACCOUNT_DETAILS table, ACCOUNT_ID column contains the auto-generated key; therefore, 'account_id' string value is passed to the usingGeneratedKeyColumns method. The actual insert operation is performed by calling SimpleJdbcInsert's executeAndReturnKey method. The executeAndReturnKey method accepts a java.util.Map type argument that contains table column names and corresponding values, and returns the generated key. You should note that the SimpleJdbcInsert class internally uses JdbcTemplate to execute the actual SQL insert operation.

If you look at BankAccountDaoImpl class of ch08-bankapp-jdbc project, you'll notice that it makes use of both SimpleJdbcInsert and JdbcTemplate classes to interact with the database. Similarly, FixedDepositDaoImpl class of ch08-bankapp-jdbc project uses both JdbcTemplate and

NamedParameterJdbcTemplate classes for database interaction. This shows that you can use a combination of Spring's JDBC module classes to interact with a database.

> As ch08-bankapp-jdbc project makes use of Spring's JDBC module and Spring's Transaction Management feature (explained in section 8-5), the pom.xml file of ch08-bankapp-jdbc project depends on spring-jdbc and spring-tx JAR files.

Let's now look at the BankApp class of ch08-bankapp-jdbc project that first creates a bank account and then opens a fixed deposit corresponding to it.

BankApp class

BankApp class of ch08-bankapp-jdbc project runs the MyBank application as a standalone Java application. BankApp's main method creates a bank account in the BANK_ACCOUNT_DETAILS table and creates a fixed deposit corresponding to it in the FIXED_DEPOSIT_DETAILS table.

The following example listing shows the BankApp class:

Example listing 8-9 – BankApp class
Project – ch08-bankapp-jdbc
Source location - src/main/java/sample/spring/chapter08/bankapp

```
package sample.spring.chapter08.bankapp;
.....
public class BankApp {
    private static Logger logger = LogManager.getLogger(BankApp.class);

    public static void main(String args[]) throws Exception {
        ConfigurableApplicationContext context = new ClassPathXmlApplicationContext(
                "classpath:META-INF/spring/applicationContext.xml");

        BankAccountService bankAccountService = context.getBean(BankAccountService.class);
        BankAccountDetails bankAccountDetails = new BankAccountDetails();
        .....
        int bankAccountId = bankAccountService.createBankAccount(bankAccountDetails);
        .....
        FixedDepositService fixedDepositService =
            context.getBean(FixedDepositService.class);
        FixedDepositDetails fixedDepositDetails = new FixedDepositDetails();
        .....
        int fixedDepositId = fixedDepositService.createFixedDeposit(fixedDepositDetails);
        .....
    }
}
```

In the above example listing, BankAccountService uses BankAccountDaoImpl (refer example listing 8-8) to create a bank account, and FixedDepositService uses FixedDepositDaoImpl (refer example listing 8-5 and 8-7) to open a fixed deposit corresponding to the newly created bank account. If you execute BankApp's main method, you'll find that a new record is inserted into both BANK_ACCOUNT_DETAILS and FIXED_DEPOSIT_DETAILS tables.

In this section, we looked at how Spring's JDBC module simplifies updating or fetching data from databases. Spring's JDBC module can also be used for the following purposes:

- executing stored procedures and functions. For instance, you can use Spring's SimpleJdbcCall class for executing stored procedures and functions.

- performing batch updates. For instance, you can use JdbcTemplate's batchUpdate method to batch multiple update calls on the same PreparedStatement.

- accessing relational databases in an object-oriented manner. For instance, you can extend Spring's MappingSqlQuery class to map each row in the returned ResultSet to an object.

- configuring an embedded database instance. For instance, you can Spring's jdbc schema to create an instance of HSQL, H2 or Derby databases, and register the database instance with the Spring container as a bean of type javax.sql.DataSource.

Let's now look at how we can use Spring's support for Hibernate ORM framework to interact with databases.

8-4 Developing the MyBank application using Hibernate

Spring's ORM module provides integration with Hibernate, Java Persistence API (JPA), and Java Data Objects (JDO). In this section, we'll see how Spring simplifies using Hibernate framework for database interaction. As Hibernate itself is a JPA provider, we'll use JPA annotations to map our persistent entity classes to database tables.

IMPORT **chapter 8/ch08-bankapp-hibernate** (This project shows the MyBank application that uses Hibernate to interact with the database. The version of Hibernate used by this project is 5.2.12.Final. To run the application, execute the main method of the BankApp class of this project.)

Let's first look at how to configure Hibernate's SessionFactory instance.

Configuring SessionFactory instance

SessionFactory is a factory for creating Hibernate's Session object. It is the Session object that is used by DAOs to perform create, read, delete and update operations on persistent entities. Spring's org.springframework.orm.hibernate5.LocalSessionFactoryBean (a FactoryBean implementation) creates a SessionFactory instance that is used by DAO classes for obtaining a Session instance.

> If you want to use JPA's EntityManager in your application's DAOs for database interaction, configure Spring's LocalContainerEntityManagerFactoryBean instead of org.springframework.orm.hibernate5.LocalSessionFactoryBean. Chapter 9 contains details on how to use JPA with Spring.

The following example listing shows how the LocalSessionFactoryBean class is configured in the application context XML file:

Example listing 8-10 – applicationContext.xml - LocalSessionFactoryBean configuration
Project – ch08-bankapp-hibernate
Source location - src/main/java/sample/spring/chapter08/bankapp

```
<bean id="sessionFactory"
        class=" org.springframework.orm.hibernate5.LocalSessionFactoryBean">
    <property name="dataSource" ref="dataSource" />
    <property name="packagesToScan" value="sample.spring" />
</bean>
```

The dataSource property specifies reference to a bean of type javax.sql.DataSource. The packagesToScan property specifies the package(s) under which Spring looks for persistent classes. For instance, the above example listing specifies that if a persistent class is annotated with JPA's @Entity annotation, and is located inside sample.spring package (or its sub-packages), it is automatically detected by org.springframework.orm.hibernate5. LocalSessionFactoryBean. An alternative to using packagesToScan property is to explicitly specify all the persistent classes using annotatedClasses property, as shown in the following example listing:

Example listing 8-11 LocalSessionFactoryBean's annotatedClasses property

```
<bean id="sessionFactory"
        class="org.springframework.orm.hibernate5.LocalSessionFactoryBean">
    <property name="dataSource" ref="dataSource" />
    <property name="annotatedClasses">
        <list>
            <value>sample.spring.chapter08.bankapp.domain.BankAccountDetails</value>
            <value>sample.spring.chapter08.bankapp.domain.FixedDepositDetails</value>
        </list>
    </property>
</bean>
```

In the above example listing, annotatedClasses property (of type java.util.List) lists down all the persistent classes in the application.

SessionFactory created by LocalSessionFactoryBean is used by DAOs to perform database operations. Let's look at how DAOs make use of SessionFactory.

Creating DAOs that use Hibernate API for database interaction

To interact with the database, DAOs need access to Hibernate's Session object. To access Hibernate's Session object, inject the SessionFactory instance created by LocalSessionFactoryBean bean (refer example listing 8-10) into DAOs, and use the injected SessionFactory instance to obtain a Session object.

The following example listing shows the FixedDepositDaoImpl class that uses Hibernate API for saving and retrieving the FixedDepositDetails persistent entity:

Example listing 8-12 – FixedDepositDaoImpl class - Hibernate API usage
Project – ch08-bankapp-hibernate
Source location - src/main/java/sample/spring/chapter08/bankapp/dao

```
package sample.spring.chapter08.bankapp.dao;

import org.hibernate.SessionFactory;
.....
@Repository(value = "fixedDepositDao")
public class FixedDepositDaoImpl implements FixedDepositDao {

    @Autowired
    private SessionFactory sessionFactory;

    public int createFixedDeposit(final FixedDepositDetails fixedDepositDetails) {
        sessionFactory.getCurrentSession().save(fixedDepositDetails);
        return fixedDepositDetails.getFixedDepositId();
    }

    public FixedDepositDetails getFixedDeposit(final int fixedDepositId) {
        String hql = "from FixedDepositDetails as fixedDepositDetails where "
                   + "fixedDepositDetails.fixedDepositId ="
                   + fixedDepositId;
        return (FixedDepositDetails) sessionFactory.getCurrentSession()
                .createQuery(hql).uniqueResult();
    }
```

```
}
```

The above example listing shows that an instance of `SessionFactory` is autowired into `FixedDepositDaoImpl` instance. `SessionFactory` is later used by `createFixedDeposit` and `getFixedDeposit` methods to save and retrieve `FixedDepositDetails` persistent entity.

As mentioned earlier, `SessionFactory` is created by `LocalSessionFactoryBean` – a `FactoryBean` implementation. Autowiring of `SessionFactory` instance shows that you can autowire an object created by a `FactoryBean` by simply defining the *type* created by the `FactoryBean` and annotating it with `@Autowired` annotation (refer section 3-9 of chapter 3 to know more about Spring's `FactoryBean` interface).

The `createFixedDeposit` and `getFixedDeposit` methods call `SessionFactory`'s `getCurrentSession` method to obtain an instance of `Session`. It is important to note that the call to `getCurrentSession` method returns the `Session` object associated with the *current transaction* or *thread*. Using `getCurrentSession` method is useful if you want Spring to manage transactions, which is the case in MyBank application.

Let's now look at Spring's programmatic and declarative transaction management feature.

8-5 Transaction management using Spring

Spring Framework supports both programmatic and declarative transaction management. In programmatic transaction management, Spring's transaction management abstraction is used to explicitly start, end and commit transactions. In declarative transaction management, you annotate methods that execute within a transaction with Spring's `@Transactional` annotation.

Let's first look at the transaction management requirement of MyBank application described in section 8-2.

MyBank's transaction management requirements

In section 8-2, it was mentioned that when a bank customer opens a new fixed deposit, the fixed deposit amount is deducted from the `BANK_ACCOUNT_DETAILS` table's `BALANCE_AMOUNT` column, and the fixed deposit details are saved in the `FIXED_DEPOSIT_DETAILS` table.

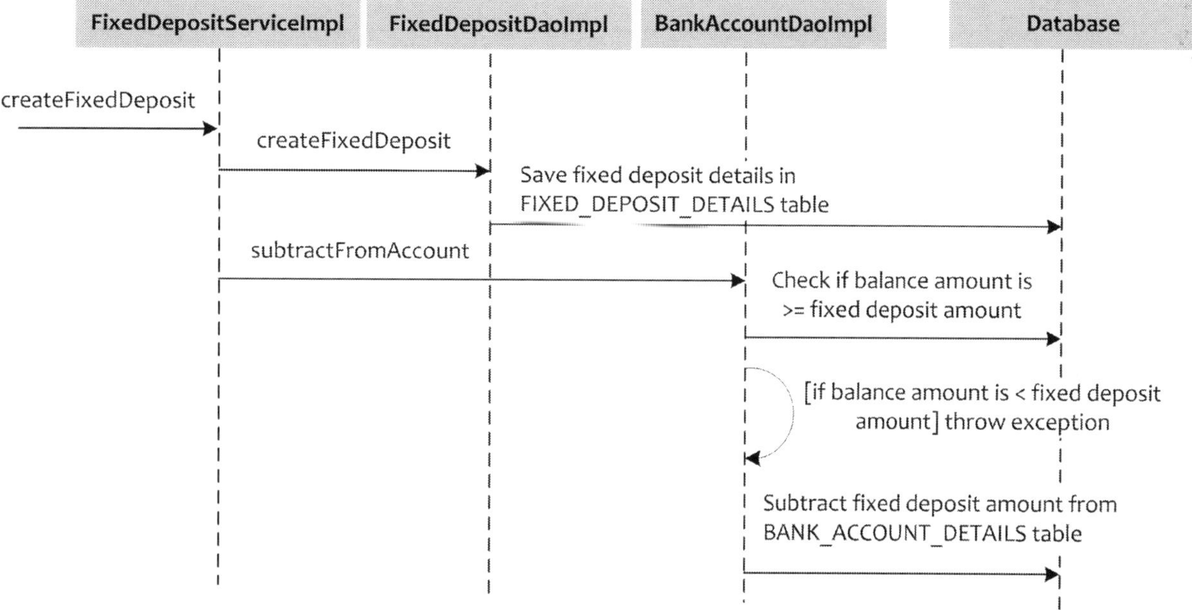

Figure 8-2 The sequence of actions performed by MyBank application when a customer opens a new fixed deposit

The above sequence diagram shows that the FixedDepositServiceImpl's createFixedDeposit method saves fixed deposit details in FIXED_DEPOSIT_DETAILS table and deducts the fixed deposit amount from the corresponding bank account in BANK_ACCOUNT_DETAILS table:

FixedDepositServiceImpl's createFixedDeposit method calls FixedDepositDaoImpl's createFixedDeposit method and BankAccountDaoImpl's subtractFromAccount method. FixedDepositDaoImpl's createFixedDeposit method saves the fixed deposit details in the FIXED_DEPOSIT_DETAILS table. BankAccountDaoImpl's subtractFromAccount method first checks that the customer's bank account contains sufficient balance to create the fixed deposit of the specified amount. If sufficient balance is available, subtractFromAccount method deducts the fixed deposit amount from the customer's bank account. If sufficient balance isn't available, an exception is thrown by BankAccountDaoImpl's subtractFromAccount method. If FixedDepositDaoImpl's createFixedDeposit or BankAccountDaoImpl's subtractFromAccount method fails for some reason, the system will be left in an inconsistent state; therefore, both the methods must be executed within a *transaction*.

Let's now look at how you can use Spring to programmatically manage transactions in the MyBank application.

Programmatic transaction management

You can programmatically manage transactions by using Spring's TransactionTemplate class or by using an implementation of Spring's PlatformTransactionManager interface. TransactionTemplate class simplifies transaction management by taking care of *initiating* and *committing* transactions. You only need to provide an implementation of Spring's TransactionCallback interface that contains the code to be executed within a transaction.

IMPORT **chapter 8/ch08-bankapp-tx-jdbc** (This project shows the MyBank application that uses Spring's TransactionTemplate class for programmatically managing transactions. To run the application, execute the main method of the BankApp class of this project. Create SPRING_BANK_APP_DB database, and BANK_ACCOUNT_DETAILS and FIXED_DEPOSIT_DETAILS tables as described for ch08-bankapp-jdbc project)

The following example listing shows how the TransactionTemplate class is configured in the application context XML file:

Example listing 8-13 – applicationContext.xml - TransactionTemplate configuration
Project – ch08-bankapp-tx-jdbc
Source location - src/main/resources/META-INF/spring

```
<bean id="dataSource" class="org.apache.commons.dbcp2.BasicDataSource".....>
    .....
</bean>

<bean id="txManager"
        class="org.springframework.jdbc.datasource.DataSourceTransactionManager">
    <property name="dataSource" ref="dataSource" />
</bean>

<bean id="transactionTemplate"
        class="org.springframework.transaction.support.TransactionTemplate">
    <property name="transactionManager" ref="txManager"/>
    <property name="isolationLevelName" value="ISOLATION_READ_UNCOMMITTED" />
    <property name="propagationBehaviorName" value="PROPAGATION_REQUIRED" />
</bean>
```

TransactionTemplate's transactionManager property refers to Spring's PlatformTransactionManager implementation that is responsible for managing transactions. TransactionTemplate's isolationLevelName property specifies the transaction isolation level to be set for the transactions managed by the transaction manager. The value of isolationLevelName property refers to a constant defined by Spring's TransactionDefinition interface. For instance, ISOLATION_READ_UNCOMMITTED is a constant defined by TransactionDefinition interface that indicates that *uncommitted* changes by a transaction *can* be read by other transactions.

TransactionTemplate's propagationBehaviorName property specifies the transaction propagation behavior. The value of propagationBehaviorName property refers to a constant defined by Spring's TransactionDefinition interface. For instance, PROPAGATION_REQUIRED is a constant defined by TransactionDefinition interface that indicates:

- if a method is *not* invoked within a transaction, the transaction manager starts a new transaction and executes the method in the newly created transaction
- if a method is invoked within a transaction, the transaction manager executes the method in the *same* transaction

Spring provides a couple of built-in PlatformTransactionManager implementations that you can choose from, depending upon the data access technology used by your application. For instance, DataSourceTransactionManager is appropriate for managing transactions in applications that use plain JDBC for interacting with a database, HibernateTransactionManager is appropriate when Hibernate's Session is used for database interaction and JpaTransactionManager when JPA's EntityManager is used for data access. HibernateTransactionManager and JpaTransactionManager also support using plain JDBC for database interaction.

In example listing 8-13, TransactionTemplate's transactionManager property refers to a DataSourceTransactionManager instance because the MyBank application of ch08-bankapp-tx-jdbc project uses plain JDBC for data access. The example listing 8-13 shows that DataSourceTransactionManager's dataSource property refers to a javax.sql.DataSource object that represents the database whose transactions are managed by the DataSourceTransactionManager instance.

The following example listing shows the FixedDepositServiceImpl class that uses TransactionTemplate instance for transaction management:

Example listing 8-14 – FixedDepositServiceImpl class that uses TransactionTemplate
Project – ch08-bankapp-tx-jdbc
Source location - src/main/java/sample/spring/chapter08/bankapp/service

```
package sample.spring.chapter08.bankapp.service;

import org.springframework.transaction.TransactionStatus;
import org.springframework.transaction.support.TransactionCallback;
import org.springframework.transaction.support.TransactionTemplate;
.....
@Service(value = "fixedDepositService")
public class FixedDepositServiceImpl implements FixedDepositService {

    @Autowired
    private TransactionTemplate transactionTemplate;
    .....
    @Override
    public int createFixedDeposit(final FixedDepositDetails fixedDepositDetails)
           throws Exception {
        transactionTemplate.execute(new TransactionCallback<FixedDepositDetails>() {
           public FixedDepositDetails doInTransaction(TransactionStatus status) {
```

```
                try {
                    myFixedDepositDao.createFixedDeposit(fixedDepositDetails);
                    bankAccountDao.subtractFromAccount(
                        fixedDepositDetails.getBankAccountId(),
                        fixedDepositDetails.getFixedDepositAmount()
                    );
                } catch (Exception e) {
                    status.setRollbackOnly();
                }
                return fixedDepositDetails;
            }
        });
        return fixedDepositDetails.getFixedDepositId();
    }
    .....
}
```

The above example listing shows FixedDepositServiceImpl's createFixedDeposit method (refer figure 8-2 for more details) that saves fixed deposit details in the FIXED_DEPOSIT_DETAILS table, and deducts the fixed deposit amount from the corresponding bank account in the BANK_ACCOUNT_DETAILS table.

TransactionCallback interface defines a doInTransaction method that you implement to provide the actions that should be executed within a transaction. TransactionCallback's doInTransaction method is invoked within a transaction by TransactionTemplate's execute method. The doInTransaction method accepts a TransactionStatus object that you can use to control the outcome of the transaction.

In example listing 8-14, TransactionCallback's doInTransaction method contains calls to FixedDepositDaoImpl's createFixedDeposit method and BankAccountDaoImpl's subtractFromAccount method because we want both the methods to be executed within a single transaction. As we'd want to roll back the transaction if either of the methods fails, the setRollbackOnly method of TransactionStatus is invoked in case of an exception. If you call TransactionStatus's setRollbackOnly method, the TransactionTemplate instance roll backs the transaction. A transaction will be automatically rolled back if the actions contained in the doInTransaction method result in a java.lang.RuntimeException.

TransactionCallback instance accepts a *generic type* argument which refers to the object type returned by the doInTransaction method. In example listing 8-14, a FixedDepositDetails object is returned by the doInTransaction method. If you don't want the doInTransaction method to return any object, use the TransactionCallbackWithoutResult abstract class that implements the TransactionCallback interface. The TransactionCallbackWithoutResult class allows you to create TransactionCallback implementations in which doInTransaction method doesn't return a value.

The following example listing shows the main method of BankApp class that calls BankAccountServiceImpl's createBankAccount method to create a bank account, and FixedDepositServiceImpl's createFixedDeposit method to create a fixed deposit corresponding to the newly created bank account:

Example listing 8-15 – BankApp class
Project – ch08-bankapp-tx-jdbc
Source location - src/main/java/sample/spring/chapter08/bankapp

```
package sample.spring.chapter08.bankapp;

public class BankApp {
    .....
    public static void main(String args[]) throws Exception {
        ConfigurableApplicationContext context = new ClassPathXmlApplicationContext(
```

```
            "classpath:META-INF/spring/applicationContext.xml");

        BankAccountService bankAccountService = context.getBean(BankAccountService.class);
        FixedDepositService fixedDepositService =
                context.getBean(FixedDepositService.class);

        BankAccountDetails bankAccountDetails = new BankAccountDetails();
        bankAccountDetails.setBalanceAmount(1000);
        .....
        int bankAccountId = bankAccountService.createBankAccount(bankAccountDetails);

        FixedDepositDetails fixedDepositDetails = new FixedDepositDetails();
        fixedDepositDetails.setFixedDepositAmount(1500);
        fixedDepositDetails.setBankAccountId(bankAccountId);
        .....
        int fixedDepositId = fixedDepositService.createFixedDeposit(fixedDepositDetails);
        .....
    }
}
```

The above example listing shows that a bank account is first created with a balance amount of 1000, followed by creating a fixed deposit of amount 1500. As fixed deposit amount is greater than the balance in the bank account, `BankAccountDaoImpl`'s `subtractFromAccount` method throws an exception (refer `BankAccountDaoImpl`'s `subtractFromAccount` method or figure 8-2). Exception thrown by `BankAccountDaoImpl`'s `subtractFromAccount` method is caught by `FixedDepositServiceImpl`'s `createFixedDeposit` method (refer example listing 8-14) and the transaction is marked for rollback by calling `TransactionStatus`'s `setRollbackOnly` method.

If you execute `BankApp`'s `main` method, you'll notice that the fixed deposit is *not* created in the `FIXED_DEPOSIT_DETAILS` table, and 1500 amount is *not* deducted from the `BANK_ACCOUNT_DETAILS` table. This shows that both `FixedDepositDaoImpl`'s `createFixedDeposit` and `BankAccountDaoImpl`'s `subtractFromAccount` are executed in the same transaction.

Instead of using `TransactionTemplate` class, you can directly use a `PlatformTransactionManager` implementation to programmatically manage transactions. When using `PlatformTransactionManager` implementation, you are required to explicitly initiate and commit (or rollback) transactions. For this reason, it is recommended to use `TransactionTemplate` instead of directly using a `PlatformTransactionManager` implementation.

Let's now look at declarative transaction management feature of Spring.

Declarative transaction management

Programmatic transaction management couples your application code with Spring-specific classes. On the other hand, declarative transaction management requires you to only annotate methods or classes with Spring's `@Transactional` annotation. If you want to execute a method within a transaction, annotate the method with `@Transactional` annotation. If you want to execute *all* the methods of a class within a transaction, annotate the class with `@Transactional` annotation.

> Instead of using `@Transactional` annotation for declarative transaction management, you can use Spring's `tx` schema elements to identify transactional methods. As using Spring's `tx` schema results in verbose application context XML file, we'll be only looking at using `@Transactional` annotation for declarative transaction management.

IMPORT **chapter 8/ch08-bankapp-jdbc** and **chapter 8/ch08-bankapp-hibernate** (The ch08-bankapp-jdbc project shows the MyBank application that uses Spring's JDBC module for database interaction (refer section 8-3 to learn more about ch08-bankapp-jdbc project). The ch08-bankapp-hibernate project shows the MyBank application that uses Hibernate to interact with the database (refer section 8-4 to learn more about ch08-bankapp-hibernate project).

You enable declarative transaction management using <annotation-driven> element of Spring's tx schema. The following example listing shows the <annotation-driven> element's usage in ch08-bankapp-jdbc project:

Example listing 8-16 – applicationContext.xml - <annotation-driven> element
Project – ch08-bankapp-jdbc
Source location - src/main/resources/META-INF/spring

```
<beans ..... xmlns:tx="http://www.springframework.org/schema/tx"
    xsi:schemaLocation=".....http://www.springframework.org/schema/tx
        http://www.springframework.org/schema/tx/spring-tx.xsd">
    .....
    <tx:annotation-driven transaction-manager="txManager" />

    <bean id="txManager"
          class="org.springframework.jdbc.datasource.DataSourceTransactionManager">
        <property name="dataSource" ref="dataSource" />
    </bean>
    .....
</beans>
```

In the above example listing, Spring's tx schema is included so that its elements are accessible in the application context XML file. The <annotation-driven> element enables declarative transaction management. The <annotation-driven> element's transaction-manager attribute specifies reference to the PlatformTransactionManager implementation to use for transaction management. The above example listing shows that the DataSourceTransactionManager is used as the transaction manager in ch08-bankapp-jdbc project.

The following example listing shows how you can use declarative transaction management in ch08-bankapp-hibernate project that uses Hibernate ORM for data access:

Example listing 8-17 – applicationContext.xml - <annotation-driven> element
Project – ch08-bankapp-hibernate
Source location - src/main/resources/META-INF/spring

```
<beans ..... xmlns:tx="http://www.springframework.org/schema/tx"
    xsi:schemaLocation=".....http://www.springframework.org/schema/tx
        http://www.springframework.org/schema/tx/spring-tx.xsd">
    .....
    <tx:annotation-driven transaction-manager="txManager" />

    <bean id="txManager"
          class="org.springframework.orm.hibernate5.HibernateTransactionManager">
        <property name="sessionFactory" ref="sessionFactory"/>
    </bean>
    .....
</beans>
```

If you compare the above example listing with 8-16, you'll notice that the only difference is in the PlatformTransactionManager implementation referenced by the transaction-manager attribute of

<annotation-driven> element. The above example listing shows that if Hibernate ORM is used for database interaction, the org.springframework.orm.hibernate5.HibernateTransactionManager implementation of PlatformTransactionManager is used for managing transactions.

The following example listing shows the FixedDepositServiceImpl class that makes use of declarative transaction management:

Example listing 8-18 – FixedDepositServiceImpl class - @Transactional annotation usage
Project – ch08-bankapp-jdbc
Source location - src/main/java/sample/spring/chapter08/bankapp/service

```
package sample.spring.chapter08.bankapp.service;

import org.springframework.transaction.annotation.Transactional;
.....
@Service(value = "fixedDepositService")
public class FixedDepositServiceImpl implements FixedDepositService {
    .....
    @Transactional
    public int createFixedDeposit(FixedDepositDetails fixedDepositDetails)
         throws Exception {
        bankAccountDao.subtractFromAccount(
            fixedDepositDetails.getBankAccountId(),
            fixedDepositDetails.getFixedDepositAmount()
        );
        return myFixedDepositDao.createFixedDeposit(fixedDepositDetails);
    }
    .....
}
```

In the above example listing, the createFixedDeposit method is annotated with @Transactional annotation. This means that the createFixedDeposit method is executed within a transaction. The transaction manager specified via the transaction-manager attribute of <annotation-driven> element (refer example listing 8-16 and 8-17) is used for managing the transaction. If a java.lang.RuntimeException is thrown during execution of createFixedDeposit method, the transaction is automatically rolled back.

@Transactional annotation defines attributes that you can use to configure the behavior of the transaction manager. For instance, you can use the rollbackFor attribute to specify exception classes that result in transaction rollback. The exception classes specified by rollbackFor attribute *must* be subclasses of java.lang.Throwable class. Similarly, you can use isolation attribute to specify the transaction isolation level.

In case your application defines multiple transaction managers, you can use @Transactional annotation's transactionManager attribute to specify the bean name of the PlatformTransactionManager implementation that you want to use for managing transactions. The following example listing shows two transaction managers, tx1 and tx2, defined in the application context XML file. The tx1 transaction manager is used by SomeServiceImpl's methodA and tx2 transaction manager is used by SomeServiceImpl's methodB:

Example listing 8-19 – @Transactional's transactionManager attribute usage

```
---------------------- SomeServiceImpl class -----------------------

@Service
public class SomeServiceImpl implements SomeService {
    .....
```

```
    @Transactional(transactionManager = "tx1")
    public int methodA() {.....}

    @Transactional(transactionManager = "tx2")
    public int methodB() {.....}
}
----------------------- application context XML file -----------------------

    <tx:annotation-driven />

    <bean id="tx1"
        class="org.springframework.orm.hibernate5.HibernateTransactionManager">
        <property name="sessionFactory1" ref="sessionFactory1"/>
    </bean>

    <bean id="tx2"
        class="org.springframework.jdbc.datasource.DataSourceTransactionManager">
        <property name="dataSource" ref="dataSource" />
    </bean>
```

In the above example listing, the `<annotation-driven>` element of Spring's `tx` schema doesn't specify the `transaction-manager` attribute because the transaction manager to use for managing transactions is specified by the `@Transactional` annotation itself. In the above example listing, `@Transactional` annotation's `transactionManager` attribute specifies the transaction manager to use for managing transactions. This means that `SomeServiceImpl`'s `methodA` executes under `tx1` transaction manager and `SomeServiceImpl`'s `methodB` executes under `tx2` transaction manager.

Let's now look at Spring's support for JTA (Java Transaction API) transactions.

Spring's support for JTA

In chapter 1, we discussed that when multiple transactional resources are involved in a transaction, JTA is used for transaction management. Spring provides a generic `JtaTransactionManager` class (a `PlatformTransactionManager` implementation) that you can use in applications to manage JTA transactions.

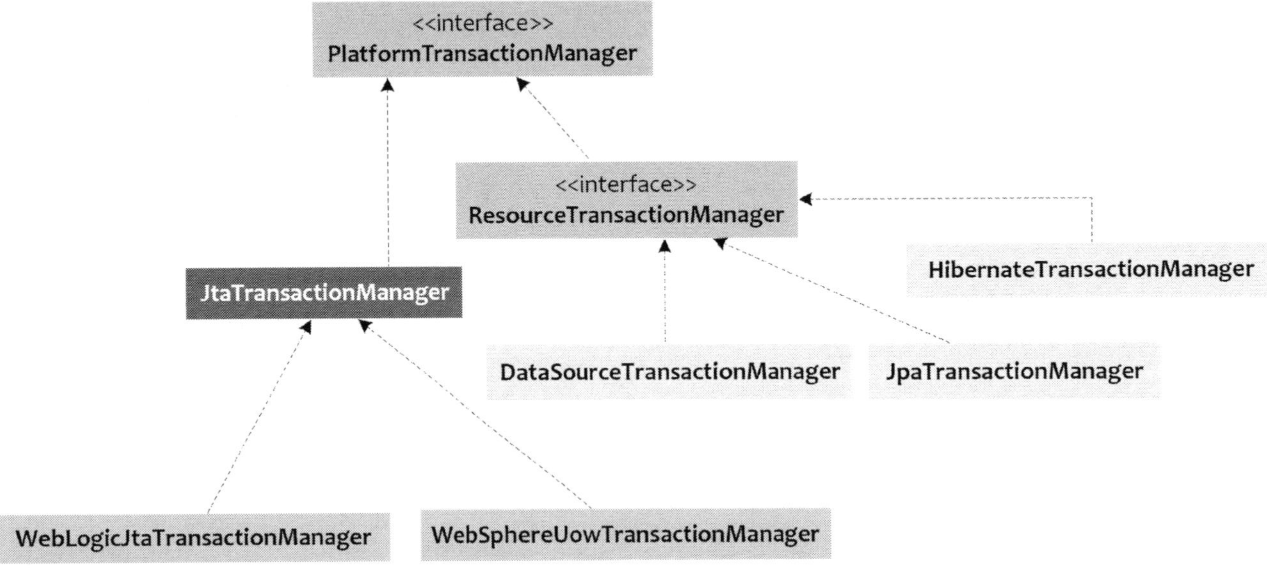

Figure 8-3 JTA transaction managers and resource-specific transaction managers implement `PlatformTransactionManager` interface

In most application server environments, the JtaTransactionManager will meet your requirements. But, Spring also provides vendor-specific JtaTransactionManager implementations that leverage application server-specific features to manage JTA transactions. The vendor-specific JTA transaction managers provided by Spring are: WebLogicJtaTransactionManager (for WebLogic application server), WebSphereUowTransactionManager (for WebSphere application server).

Figure 8-3 summarizes how JTA transaction managers and resource-specific transaction managers (like, DataSourceTransactionManager, HibernateTransactionManager, JmsTransactionManager, and so on) are related to the PlatformTransactionManager interface. The resource-specific transaction managers implement ResourceTransactionManager interface (a sub-interface of PlatformTransactionManager) and manage transactions associated with a single target resource. For instance, DataSourceTransactionManager, HibernateTransactionManager, and JpaTransactionManager manage transactions associated with a single DataSource, SessionFactory, and EntityManagerFactory, respectively.

Let's now look at how Spring simplifies configuring a JTA transaction manager in application context XML file.

Configuring a JTA transaction manager using <jta-transaction-manager> element

Spring's tx schema provides a <jta-transaction-manager> element that automatically detects the application server in which the application is deployed and configures an appropriate JTA transaction manager. This saves the effort for explicitly configuring an application server-specific JTA transaction manager in the application context XML file. For instance, if you deploy an application in WebSphere application server, the <jta-transaction-manager> element configures an instance of WebSphereUowTransactionManager instance. If the same application is deployed in WebLogic application server, the <jta-transaction-manager> element configures an instance of WebLogicJtaTransactionManager instance. If the application is deployed in any application server other than WebSphere or WebLogic, the <jta-transaction-manager> element configures an instance of JtaTransactionManager instance.

Let's now look at how to develop the MyBank application using Java-based configuration.

8-6 Developing the MyBank application using Java-based configuration

In the examples that we've seen so far, configurations related to javax.sql.DataSource, transactions, Hibernate, and so on, were specified in the application context XML file. In this section, we'll look at how to specify these configurations using Java-based configuration approach.

IMPORT **chapter 8/ch08-javaconfig-hibernate** (This project is a modified version of ch08-bankapp-hibernate project that uses Java-based configuration approach to configure application objects, javax.sql.DataSource, Hibernate's SessionFactory and declarative transaction management. To run the application, execute the main method of the BankApp class of this project.)

The ch08-javaconfig-hibernate project contains the following @Configuration classes:

- DatabaseConfig : configures javax.sql.DataSource, Hibernate's SessionFactory and declarative transaction management
- DaosConfig : configures DAOs in the application
- ServicesConfig : configures application services

Let's first look at the DatabaseConfig class that does the heavy lifting of configuring javax.sql.DataSource and Hibernate's SessionFactory, and adding support for using @Transactional annotation.

Configuring javax.sql.DataSource

The following example listing shows how a javax.sql.DataSource object is configured using Java-based configuration approach:

Example listing 8-20 – DatabaseConfig class - javax.sql.DataSource configuration
Project – ch08-javaconfig-hibernate
Source location - src/main/java/sample/spring/chapter08/bankapp

```
package sample.spring.chapter08.bankapp;

import javax.sql.DataSource;
import org.apache.commons.dbcp2.BasicDataSource;
import org.springframework.core.env.Environment;
.....
@Configuration
@PropertySource("classpath:/META-INF/database.properties")
.....
public class DatabaseConfig {
    @Autowired
    private Environment env;

    @Bean(destroyMethod = "close")
    public DataSource dataSource() {
        BasicDataSource dataSource = new BasicDataSource();
        dataSource.setDriverClassName(env.getProperty("database.driverClassName"));
        .....
        return dataSource;
    }
    .....
}
```

In the above example listing, @PropertySource adds properties defined in database.properties file to Spring's Environment object (refer section 7-7 of chapter 7 for more details). The database.properties file defines properties (like driver class, database URL, and so on) that are required for connecting to the database. The dataSource method creates an instance of BasicDataSource (an implementation of javax.sql.DataSource provided by Apache Commons DBCP project) using the properties read from the database.properties file.

Configuring Hibernate's SessionFactory

The following example listing shows how you can programmatically configure Hibernate's SessionFactory using Spring's LocalSessionFactoryBuilder class:

Example listing 8-21 – DatabaseConfig class – Hibernate's SessionFactory configuration
Project – ch08-javaconfig-hibernate
Source location - src/main/java/sample/spring/chapter08/bankapp

```
package sample.spring.chapter08.bankapp;
.....
import org.hibernate.SessionFactory;
import org.springframework.orm.hibernate5.LocalSessionFactoryBuilder;

@Configuration
.....
public class DatabaseConfig {
    .....
```

```
    @Bean
    public SessionFactory sessionFactory(DataSource dataSource) {
        LocalSessionFactoryBuilder builder = new LocalSessionFactoryBuilder(dataSource);
        builder.scanPackages("sample.spring");
        builder.setProperty("hibernate.show_sql", "true");
        builder.setProperty("hibernate.id.new_generator_mappings", "false");
        return builder.buildSessionFactory();
    }
    .....
}
```

In the above example listing, Spring's `LocalSessionFactoryBuilder` simplifies creation of Hibernate's `SessionFactory`. `LocalSessionFactoryBuilder` extends Hibernate's `Configuration` class that configures Hibernate. The `scanPackages` method looks for entity classes in the specified package (and its sub-packages) and registers them with Hibernate. The `setProperty` method sets a Hibernate property. For instance, we've set the `hibernate.id.new_generator_mappings` property as `false` (the default value is `true`). The `buildSessionFactory` method creates a `SessionFactory` instance based on the supplied configuration.

You should note that if the `hibernate.id.new_generator_mappings` property is set to `true`, new identifier generators are used by Hibernate for generating values for columns that use `AUTO` or `TABLE` or `SEQUENCE` strategy. In the case of `ch08-javaconfig-hibernate` project, if we set the value of `hibernate.id.new_generator_mappings` property to `true`, Hibernate will look for a `hibernate_sequence` table in MySQL with a single column `next_val` (of type `BIGINT`) for generating values. This is because the `FixedDepositDetails` and `BankAccountDetails` entities specify `AUTO` strategy for generating their primary keys.

Enabling @Transactional support

The following example listing shows how `@Transactional` support is enabled when using Java-based configuration approach:

Example listing 8-22 – `DatabaseConfig` class – enabling `@Transactional` support
Project – `ch08-javaconfig-hibernate`
Source location - `src/main/java/sample/spring/chapter08/bankapp`

```
package sample.spring.chapter08.bankapp;

import org.springframework.orm.hibernate5.HibernateTransactionManager;
import org.springframework.transaction.PlatformTransactionManager;
import org.springframework.transaction.annotation.EnableTransactionManagement;

@Configuration
@EnableTransactionManagement
.....
public class DatabaseConfig {
    .....
    @Bean
    public PlatformTransactionManager platformTransactionManager(
            SessionFactory sessionFactory) {
        return new HibernateTransactionManager(sessionFactory);
    }
}
```

In the above example listing, `@EnableTransactionManagement` annotation serves the same purpose as the `<annotation-driven>` element of Spring's `tx` schema (refer example listing 8-16); it enables `@Transactional` annotation support. `@Bean` annotated `platformTransactionManager` method returns an instance of `HibernateTransactionManager` that is used by Spring for transaction management.

If you run the BankApp's `main` method of `ch08-javaconfig-hibernate` project, you'll notice that it works the same way as BankApp's `main` method of `ch08-bankapp-hibernate` project.

8-7 Summary

In this chapter, we saw that Spring supports database interaction using plain JDBC and Hibernate. We also saw how we can use Spring to manage transactions programmatically and declaratively. In the next chapter, we'll look at how Spring simplifies interacting with relational and NoSQL databases using Spring Data.

Chapter 9 – *Spring Data*

9-1 Introduction

You may store data in relational data stores (like, MySQL, Oracle, and so on) or NoSQL data stores (like, MongoDB, Neo4j, Redis, and so on) or Big Data data stores (like, HDFS, Splunk, and so on). A lot of boilerplate code is required to implement the data access layer for these persistent stores. For instance, if you are using JPA for accessing a relational data store, you need to write queries for accessing entities, perform pagination and sorting of query results, and so on. Spring Data provides a level of abstraction on top of these distinct data stores that reduces the amount of boilerplate code required to implement the data access layer.

Spring Data consists of multiple projects, where each project focuses on a particular data store. The following table mentions some of the Spring Data projects:

Project	Description
Spring Data JPA	simplifies developing applications that use JPA for data access
Spring Data for Apache Solr	simplifies configuration and access to Apache Solr search server
Spring Data MongoDB	simplifies developing applications that use MongoDB
Spring Data Redis	simplifies developing applications that use Redis as the data store
Spring Data Elasticsearch	simplifies developing applications that interact with Elasticsearch

For a complete list of the supported data stores, please refer to the home page of Spring Data project (`http://projects.spring.io/spring-data/`). In this chapter, we'll look at how Spring Data JPA and Spring Data MongoDB projects simplify developing data access layer of applications that interact with relational databases and MongoDB.

Let's look at some of the core concepts and interfaces that are central to all Spring Data projects.

IMPORT **`chapter 9/ch09-javaconfig-jpa`** and **`chapter 9/ch09-springdata-jpa`** (The `ch09-javaconfig-jpa` project is a modified version of `ch08-javaconfig-hibernate` project that uses JPA's `EntityManager` (instead of Hibernate's `SessionFactory`) for database interaction. The `ch09-springdata-jpa` project uses Spring Data JPA (instead of plain JPA) for database interaction. To run the projects, execute the `main` method of the `BankApp` class.)

9-2 Core concepts and interfaces

When using Spring Data, you define a *repository* interface corresponding to each *domain entity* in your application. A repository contains methods for performing CRUD operations on the entity, and to paginate and sort entities. You can create a repository corresponding to a domain entity by extending the `Repository` or `CrudRepository` or `PagingAndSortingRepository` interface. `Repository` interface is a marker interface, that is, it doesn't define any methods. `CrudRepository` declares standard CRUD operations that can be performed on an entity. `PagingAndSortingRepository` declares methods that allow you to do pagination and sorting of entities.

The following class diagram shows that `Repository`, `CrudRepository` and `PagingAndSortingRepository` interfaces are related by inheritance:

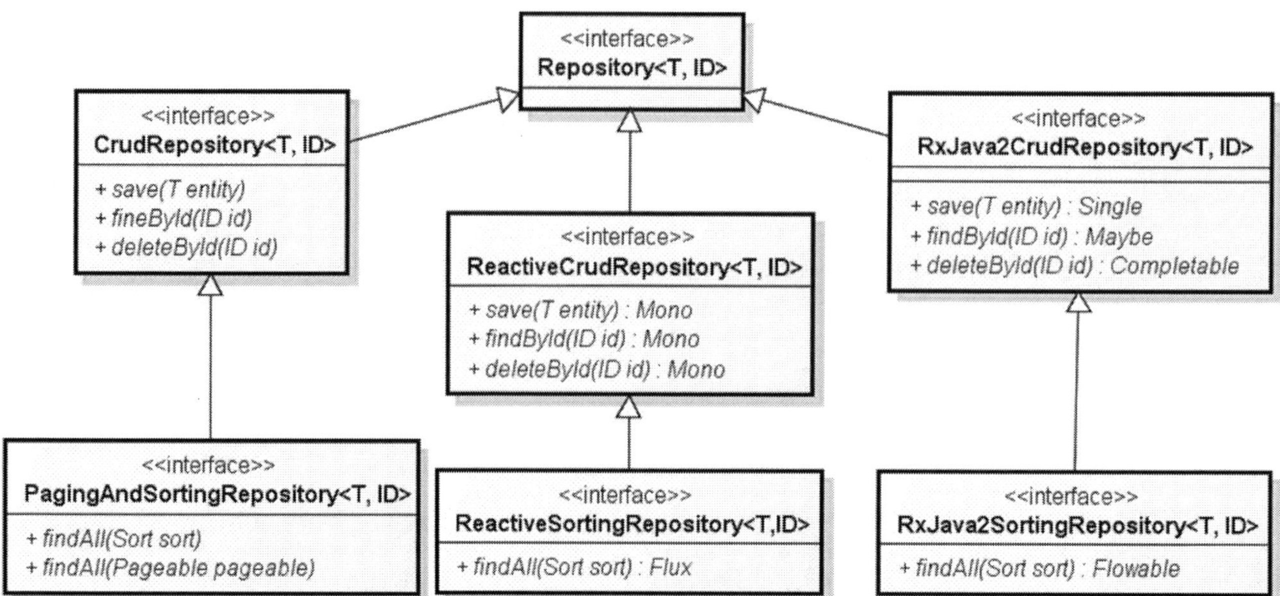

Figure 9-1 CrudRepository inherits from Repository, and PagingAndSortingRepository inherits from CrudRepository. Similar inheritance structure is followed by interfaces that provide support for developing *reactive applications*.

The above diagram also shows interfaces that Spring Data defines to support development of *reactive applications* (refer chapter 18). For instance, ReactiveCrudRepository and ReactiveSortingRepository interfaces are used for developing reactive applications using Reactor (refer chapter 19), and RxJava2CrudRepository and RxJava2SortingRepository interfaces are used for developing reactive applications using RxJava 2 (refer chapter 18). Chapter 19 shows how reactive applications are developed using these interfaces.

Spring Data uses the Repository interface (a marker interface) to discover repositories defined in the application. Repository interface accepts entity class (specified by T type) and its primary key type (specified by ID type) as type arguments. CrudRepository extends Repository and declares methods to perform CRUD operations on the entity. For instance, you can use the save method to save an entity instance into the data store, findById method to find an entity based on its primary key, and so on. PagingAndSortingRepository extends CrudRepository and adds pagination and sorting support. For instance, Spring Data uses the pagination information (specified by Pageable instance) passed to the findAll method to provide paginated access to entities.

The following example listing shows some of the methods declared in CrudRepository:

Example listing 9-1 – CrudRepository interface

```
package org.springframework.data.repository;
.....
public interface CrudRepository<T, ID extends Serializable> extends Repository<T, ID> {
    <S extends T> S save(S entity);
    T findById(ID id);
    Iterable<T> findAll();
    void deleteById(ID id);
    void delete(T entity);
    long count();
    .....
}
```

The above example listing shows that CrudRepository declares save, findById, findAll, deleteById, delete, count, and so on, methods. In some situations, you may want to restrict the methods exposed by a repository to its callers. For instance, you may *not* want the callers to access the deleteById method to delete an entity instance. You can achieve this requirement by using any of the following approaches for creating your custom repositories:

- create the repository by extending CrudRepository and declare only those methods in your repository interface that you want to make available to the callers, or
- create the repository by extending Repository interface and declare only those CrudRepository methods that you want to make available to the callers

The following example listing shows FixedDepositRepository interface that extends the Repository interface:

Example listing 9-2 – FixedDepositRepository interface
Project – ch09-springdata-jpa
Source location - src/main/java/sample/spring/chapter09/bankapp/repository

```
package sample.spring.chapter09.bankapp.repository;

import org.springframework.data.repository.Repository;
import sample.spring.chapter09.bankapp.domain.FixedDepositDetails;

public interface FixedDepositRepository extends Repository<FixedDepositDetails, Integer> ..
{
    FixedDepositDetails save(FixedDepositDetails entity);
    FixedDepositDetails findById(Integer id);
    .....
}
```

As the FixedDepositRepository manages FixedDepositDetails entity whose primary key is of type Integer, FixedDepositDetails and Integer types are passed as type arguments to the Repository interface. FixedDepositRepository exposes only save and findById methods to its callers. Notice that the signatures of save and findById methods matches the signatures of save and findById methods declared in the CrudRepository interface (refer example listing 9-1). The save method saves an instance of FixedDepositDetails entity into the data store, and the findById method returns an instance of FixedDepositDetails entity with the given primary key. You *don't* need to implement these methods because their implementation is provided by Spring Data.

Instead of extending Repository, CrudRepository or PagingAndSortingRepository interface, you can annotate an interface with @RepositoryDefinition to indicate that it represents a repository. The following example listing shows how FixedDepositRepository (refer example listing 9-2) can be rewritten using @RepositoryDefinition:

Example listing 9-3 – FixedDepositRepository interface - @RepositoryDefinition usage

```
package sample.spring.chapter09.bankapp.repository;

import org.springframework.data.repository.RepositoryDefinition;
.....
@RepositoryDefinition(domainClass=FixedDepositDetails.class, idClass=Integer.class)
public interface FixedDepositRepository {
    FixedDepositDetails save(FixedDepositDetails entity);
    FixedDepositDetails findById(Integer id);
    .....
```

```
}
```

In the above example listing, @RepositoryDefinition's domainClass attribute specifies the type of the domain entity managed by the repository, and the idClass attribute specifies the primary key type of the domain entity.

CrudRepository's count method returns the count of entities in the data store, and CrudRepository's delete method removes the given entity. You can declare variants of count and delete methods based on the fields defined by the entity. For instance, you can declare a countByTenure(int tenure) method in FixedDepositRepository to obtain count of FixedDepositDetails entities with the given tenure. The variants of count and delete methods have the following syntax:

```
countBy<field-name> or deleteBy<field-name>
```

here, <field-name> is a field defined by the entity.

If you declare a variant of delete method (like, deleteByTenure), it returns the count of deleted entities. If you want to access the deleted entities, declare removeBy... method instead of deleteBy... method in your custom repository.

As shown in the following example listing, FixedDepositRepository declares count, countByTenure, and removeByTenure methods:

Example listing 9-4 – FixedDepositRepository interface – declaring variants of count and delete methods
Project – ch09-springdata-jpa
Source location - src/main/java/sample/spring/chapter09/bankapp/repository

```
package sample.spring.chapter09.bankapp.repository;
.....
public interface FixedDepositRepository extends Repository<FixedDepositDetails, Integer>
.....
{
    .....
    long count();
    long countByTenure(int tenure);
    List<FixedDepositDetails> removeByTenure(int tenure);
}
```

In the above example listing, countByTenure returns the count of fixed deposits with the given tenure, removeByTenure deletes and returns fixed deposits with the given tenure, and the count method simply returns the total count of fixed deposits in the data store.

You can declare *query methods* in your custom repository interface to query the data store. Query method names have the following format: find...By, read...By, query...By, count...By, or get...By. Spring Data comes with a sophisticated query builder that builds queries specific to the data store based on the query methods declared in the repository. The following example listing shows the query methods declared in the FixedDepositRepository interface:

Example listing 9-5 – FixedDepositRepository interface – declaring query methods
Project – ch09-springdata-jpa
Source location - src/main/java/sample/spring/chapter09/bankapp/repository

```
package sample.spring.chapter09.bankapp.repository;
.....
public interface FixedDepositRepository extends Repository<FixedDepositDetails, Integer>
.....
```

```
{
    .....
    List<FixedDepositDetails> findByTenure(int tenure);
    List<FixedDepositDetails> findByTenureLessThan(int tenure);
    List<FixedDepositDetails> findByFdAmountGreaterThan(int fdAmount);
}
```

In the above example listing, `findByTenure`, `findByTenureLessThan` and `findByFdAmountGreaterThan` methods represent *query methods* whose implementations are provided by Spring Data. The keywords `LessThan` and `GreaterThan` are used by Spring Data's query builder to generate appropriate queries corresponding to query methods. For instance, `findByTenureLessThan` method will result in a query that returns `FixedDepositDetails` instances whose tenures are *less than* the given tenure.

In this section, we saw that Spring Data simplifies developing the data access layer of an application. A real world application's requirements are lot more complex than what we saw in this section. In the next section, we'll look at some more features offered by Spring Data in the context of Spring Data JPA project.

9-3 Spring Data JPA

`Repository`, `CrudRepository` and `PagingAndSortingRepository` interfaces are agnostic to the underlying data store, that is, you can't use them to take advantage of features specific to a data store. For this reason, each Spring Data project defines a data store specific repository interface that allows you to use features specific to that data store. For instance, Spring Data JPA defines a `JpaRepository` interface (a JPA-specific repository interface) and Spring Data MongoDB defines a `MongoRepository` interface (a MongoDB-specific interface). Both these interfaces extend `PagingAndSortingRepository` and `QueryByExampleExecutor` interfaces, and add features specific to the data store. Later in this chapter, we'll look at `QueryByExampleExecutor` that allows you to use a given entity instance as a search criteria for querying the data store.

> For using Spring Data JPA, `ch09-springdata-jpa` project's `pom.xml` includes dependency on version `2.0.1.RELEASE` of `spring-data-commons` and `spring-data-jpa` JAR.

So, how Spring Data really works? In the context of `FixedDepositRepository`, the following figure shows how Spring Data works:

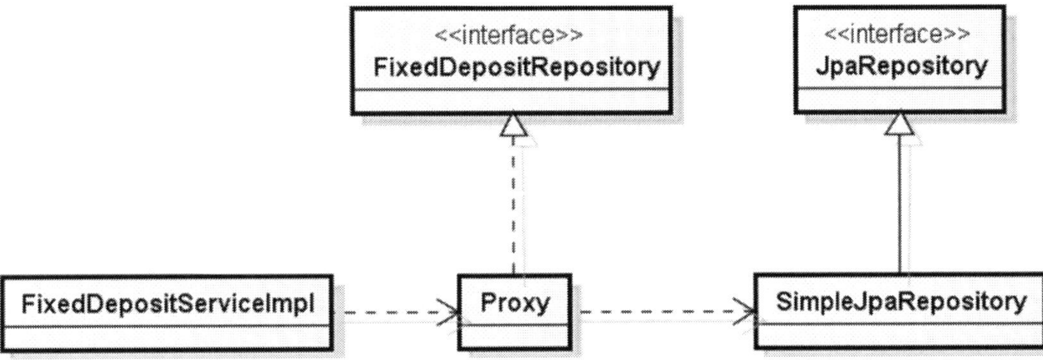

Figure 9-2 Spring Data creates a proxy corresponding to the repository that directs method calls to a default repository implementation

Spring Data creates a proxy corresponding to each repository interface that you define in your application. For instance, a proxy is created corresponding to the `FixedDepositRepository` interface. The proxy holds reference to a *default* repository implementation that is provided out-of-the-box by Spring Data. If you are using Spring Data JPA, the default repository implementation is an instance of `SimpleJpaRepository` class (an implementation of `JpaRepository` interface) that uses JPA for accessing relational data stores. Method calls to the `FixedDepositRepository` interface are intercepted by the proxy and delegated to

SimpleJpaRepository instance. For instance, when you call FixedDepositRepository's save method, proxy delegates the call to SimpleJpaRepository's save method.

Let's look at how you can plug-in a *custom* implementation for a repository method.

Substituting custom implementations for repository methods

In Spring Data, you substitute custom implementation for a repository method by defining the method in a class named *<your-repository-interface>*Impl. Here, *<your-repository-interface>* is the name of your custom repository whose method(s) you want to customize. This class must be located in the same package (or in one of its sub-packages) in which you have defined your custom repository interface.

Let's say that we want to override FixedDepositRepository's findByTenure method such that it throws a NoFixedDepositFoundException when no fixed deposits are found for the given tenure. To achieve this requirement, simply define a FixedDepositRepositoryImpl class (notice that the naming convention is *<your-repository-interface>*Impl) that contains the custom implementation for the findByTenure method:

Example listing 9-6 – FixedDepositRepositoryImpl – overriding findByTenure method
Project – ch09-springdata-jpa
Source location - src/main/java/sample/spring/chapter09/bankapp/repository

```
package sample.spring.chapter09.bankapp.repository;
.....
import javax.persistence.EntityManager;
import javax.persistence.PersistenceContext;
import sample.spring.chapter09.bankapp.exceptions.NoFixedDepositFoundException;
.....
public class FixedDepositRepositoryImpl {

    @PersistenceContext
    private EntityManager entityManager;

    public List<FixedDepositDetails> findByTenure(int tenure) {
        List<FixedDepositDetails> fds = entityManager
         .createQuery("SELECT details from FixedDepositDetails
                         details where details.tenure = :tenure",
         FixedDepositDetails.class).setParameter("tenure", tenure).getResultList();
        if (fds.isEmpty()) {
            throw new NoFixedDepositFoundException("No fixed deposits found");
        }
        return fds;
    }
}
```

The above example listing shows that the findByTenure method uses JPA's EntityManager to query the data store for fixed deposits. As FixedDepositRepositoryImpl is automatically picked up by Spring Data and treated like any other Spring bean, we've been able to use @PersistenceContext annotation to autowire an instance of EntityManager. At runtime, calls to FixedDepositRepository's findByTenure method are handled by FixedDepositRepositoryImpl's findByTenure method. The above example listing also shows that Spring Data JPA provides you the flexibility to directly use JPA in your application.

In some scenarios, you may want to add custom methods to your repository. Let's look at how you can add a custom method to your repository.

Adding custom methods to a repository

The following class diagram shows how `subtractFromAccount` custom method is added to `BankAccountRepository` in `ch09-springdata-jpa` project:

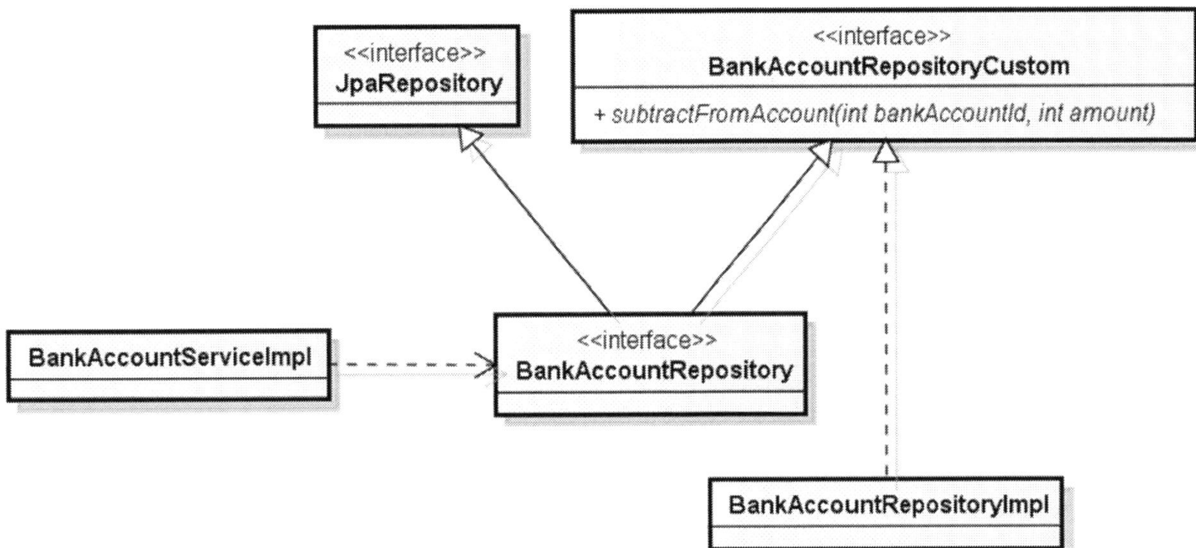

Figure 9-3 Adding `subtractFromAccount` custom method to `BankAccountRepository`

In the above figure, `BankAccountRepository` represents a repository that manages `BankAccountDetails` entities. `BankAccountRepository` extends `JpaRepository` interface (a JPA-specific repository interface provided by Spring Data JPA project). To add the `subtractFromAccount` method to `BankAccountRepository`:

- create `BankAccountRepositoryCustom` interface that declares the `subtractFromAccount` method
- add `subtractFromAccount` method to the `BankAccountRepository` by making `BankAccountRepository` a sub-interface of `BankAccountRepositoryCustom`
- create `BankAccountRepositoryImpl` class that implements the `BankAccountRepositoryCustom` interface. As the `BankAccountRepositoryImpl` class follows the *<your-repository-interface>*`Impl` naming convention, it is automatically picked-up by Spring Data.

At runtime, when `BankAccountRepository`'s `subtractFromAccount` method in called, the proxy corresponding to `BankAccountRepository` directs the call to `BankAccountRepositoryImpl`'s `subtractFromAccount` method.

The following example listing shows the `BankAccountRepositoryCustom` interface that declares the `subtractFromAccount` custom method:

Example listing 9-7 – `BankAccountRepositoryCustom` interface
Project – `ch09-springdata-jpa`
Source location - `src/main/java/sample/spring/chapter09/bankapp/repository`

```
package sample.spring.chapter09.bankapp.repository;

interface BankAccountRepositoryCustom {
    void subtractFromAccount(int bankAccountId, int amount);
}
```

The following example listing shows the `BankAccountRepositoryImpl` class that implements the `BankAccountRepositoryCustom` interface:

Example listing 9-8 – BankAccountRepositoryImpl class
Project – ch09-springdata-jpa
Source location - src/main/java/sample/spring/chapter09/bankapp/repository

```
package sample.spring.chapter09.bankapp.repository;
.....
public class BankAccountRepositoryImpl implements BankAccountRepositoryCustom {
    @PersistenceContext
    private EntityManager entityManager;

    @Override
    public void subtractFromAccount(int bankAccountId, int amount) {
        BankAccountDetails bankAccountDetails =
               entityManager.find(BankAccountDetails.class, bankAccountId);
        if (bankAccountDetails.getBalanceAmount() < amount) {
            throw new RuntimeException("Insufficient balance amount in bank account");
        }
        bankAccountDetails.setBalanceAmount(bankAccountDetails.getBalanceAmount()-amount);
        entityManager.merge(bankAccountDetails);
    }
}
```

BankAccountRepositoryImpl class uses JPA's EntityManager to implement the subtractFromAccount method.

The subtractFromAccount method is added to the BankAccountRepository interface by making it extend BankAccountRepositoryCustom interface:

Example listing 9-9 – BankAccountRepository interface
Project – ch09-springdata-jpa
Source location - src/main/java/sample/spring/chapter09/bankapp/repository

```
package sample.spring.chapter09.bankapp.repository;

import org.springframework.data.jpa.repository.JpaRepository;
.....
public interface BankAccountRepository extends JpaRepository<BankAccountDetails, Integer>,
   BankAccountRepositoryCustom { }
```

BankAccountRepository extends JpaRepository interface which defines JPA-specific methods also, like deleteInBatch and saveAndFlush.

Let's look at how to configure Spring Data JPA for your projects.

Configuring Spring Data JPA – Java-based configuration approach

You configure Spring Data JPA much like you configure JPA for any Spring application. The following example listing shows the DatabaseConfig class (an @Configuration class) that configures javax.sql.DataSource, LocalContainerEntityManagerFactoryBean and PlatformTransactionManager:

Example listing 9-10 – DatabaseConfig class
Project – ch09-springdata-jpa
Source location - src/main/java/sample/spring/chapter09/bankapp

```
package sample.spring.chapter09.bankapp;

import org.springframework.data.jpa.repository.config.EnableJpaRepositories;
.....
```

```
@Configuration
@PropertySource("classpath:/META-INF/database.properties")
@EnableTransactionManagement
@EnableJpaRepositories(basePackages = "sample.spring")
public class DatabaseConfig {

    @Bean(destroyMethod = "close")
    public DataSource dataSource() { ..... }

    @Bean
    public LocalContainerEntityManagerFactoryBean
              entityManagerFactory(DataSource dataSource) {

        LocalContainerEntityManagerFactoryBean entityManagerFactory
              = new LocalContainerEntityManagerFactoryBean();
        entityManagerFactory.setDataSource(dataSource);
        entityManagerFactory.setPackagesToScan("sample.spring");
        entityManagerFactory.setJpaVendorAdapter(new HibernateJpaVendorAdapter());

        Properties props = new Properties();
        props.put("hibernate.show_sql", "true");
        props.put("hibernate.id.new_generator_mappings", "false");

        entityManagerFactory.setJpaProperties(props);
        return entityManagerFactory;
    }

    @Bean(name = "transactionManager")
    public PlatformTransactionManager platformTransactionManager(
              EntityManagerFactory entityManagerFactory) {
        return new JpaTransactionManager(entityManagerFactory);
    }

    @Bean(name = "transactionTemplate")
    public TransactionTemplate transactionTemplate(
            PlatformTransactionManager platformTransactionManager) {
        return new TransactionTemplate(platformTransactionManager);
    }
}
```

Spring's `LocalContainerEntityManagerFactoryBean` is a `FactoryBean` implementation that configures JPA's `EntityManagerFactory`. The `setDataSource` method sets the `javax.sql.DataSource` object. The `setPackagesToScan` method specifies the packages that are scanned by Spring for JPA entities. All sub-packages under the specified packages are also scanned for JPA entities. The `setJpaVendorAdapter` method sets `HibernateJpaVendorAdapter` instance (an implementation of `JpaVendorAdapter`). `LocalContainerEntityManagerFactoryBean` uses the `JpaVendorAdapter` to determine the JPA's `javax.persistence.spi.PersistenceProvider` implementation to use for creating an `EntityManagerFactory` instance. The `setJpaProperties` method sets Hibernate-specific properties that are used while creating an `EntityManagerFactory`.

The `platformTransactionManager` method returns an instance of `JpaTransactionManager` (an implementation of Spring's `PlatformTransactionManager` interface) that is used by Spring for managing database transactions. `JpaTransactionManager` instance returned by `platformTransactionManager` method is registered as a bean named `transactionManager` because Spring Data JPA requires that a `PlatformTransactionManager` with name `transactionManager` is registered with the Spring container.

The transactionTemplate class returns an instance of TransactionTemplate that is used for programmatically managing transactions. Later in this chapter, we'll see that if a repository method returns a Stream type, then the data from the Stream *must* be consumed within a transaction. We'll use the TrasactionTemplate for executing the code that consumes data from the Stream within a transaction.

If you compare the DatabaseConfig class of ch09-springdata-jpa (a project that uses Spring Data JPA) with DatabaseConfig class of ch09-javaconfig-jpa (a project that uses plain JPA), you'll notice the following difference:

- DatabaseConfig's platformTransactionManager method of ch09-springdata-jpa sets the name of the returned JpaTransactionManager instance to transactionManager

- DatabaseConfig class of ch09-springdata-jpa is annotated with Spring Data JPA's @EnableJpaRepositories annotation

@EnableJpaRepositories annotation enables Spring Data JPA for the application. The basePackages attribute specifies the packages to be scanned for Spring Data repositories (that is, interfaces that extend the Repository interface). Spring Data creates proxies corresponding to repositories found in these packages. The other notable attributes defined by @EnableJpaRepositories are:

- repositoryImplementationPostfix – the postfix used by Spring Data to find custom repository implementations. The default value is Impl. We saw earlier that for adding custom methods to a repository or for customizing a repository method, we declared a repository implementation class whose name followed the *<your-repository-interface>*Impl naming convention.

- transactionManagerRef – specifies the name of the PlatformTransactionManager bean to be used for transaction management. The default value is transactionManager. This is the reason why in example listing 9-10, the JpaTransactionManager instance returned by the platformTransactionManager method was registered as a bean named transactionManager.

- queryLookupStrategy – specifies the strategy for resolving queries. We saw earlier that queries can be derived from query method names. For instance, Spring Data uses a query builder to derive the query corresponding to findByTenureLessThan method of FixedDepositRepository. If a query is quite complex, you can consider explicitly declaring the query using @Query annotation.

Configuring Spring Data JPA – XML-based configuration approach

The ch09-springdata-jpa project comes with an application context XML file that you can use, instead of DatabaseConfig class, for configuring the application. Let's look at how to enable support for Spring Data JPA and configure LocalContainerEntityManagerFactoryBean in application context XML file.

Enabling Spring Data JPA

Spring Data JPA includes spring-jpa schema whose <repositories> element enables support for Spring Data JPA. The following example listing shows usage of <repositories> element:

Example listing 9-11 – <repositories> element
Project – ch09-springdata-jpa
Source location - META-INF/spring/applicationContext.xml

```
<beans .....
    xmlns:jpa="http://www.springframework.org/schema/data/jpa"
    xsi:schemaLocation=".....http://www.springframework.org/schema/data/jpa
            http://www.springframework.org/schema/data/jpa/spring-jpa.xsd">

    <jpa:repositories base-package="sample.spring" />
```

```
    .....
</beans>
```

The <repositories> element of jpa namespace serves the same purpose as the @EnableJpaRepositories annotation. The base-package attribute specifies that the sample.spring package and its sub-packages are scanned for Spring Data JPA repositories.

Configuring LocalContainerEntityManagerFactoryBean

Example listing 9-12 – LocalContainerEntityManagerFactoryBean configuration
Project – ch09-springdata-jpa
Source location - META-INF/spring/applicationContext.xml

```
<beans .....>

    <bean id="entityManagerFactory"
          class="org.springframework.orm.jpa.LocalContainerEntityManagerFactoryBean">
        <property name="dataSource" ref="dataSource" />
        <property name="packagesToScan" value="sample.spring" />
        <property name="jpaVendorAdapter" ref="hibernateVendorAdapter" />
        <property name="jpaProperties" ref="props" />
    </bean>

    <bean class="org.apache.commons.dbcp2.BasicDataSource" destroy-method="close"
          id="dataSource">
        .....
    </bean>

    <bean id="hibernateVendorAdapter"
        class="org.springframework.orm.jpa.vendor.HibernateJpaVendorAdapter" />

    <util:properties id="props">
        <prop key="hibernate.show_sql">true</prop>
        <prop key="hibernate.id.new_generator_mappings">false</prop>
    </util:properties>
    ....
</beans>
```

The above example listing shows how dataSource, packagesToScan, jpaProperties and jpaVendorAdapter properties are set for LocalContainerEntityManagerFactoryBean. jpaProperties refers to a java.util.Properties instance created by <properties> element of Spring's util schema. jpaVendorAdapter refers to an instance of HibernateJpaVendorAdapter.

Configuring PlatformTransactionManager

Example listing 9-13 – PlatformTransactionManager configuration
Project – ch09-springdata-jpa
Source location - META-INF/spring/applicationContext.xml

```
<beans .....>
    .....
    <tx:annotation-driven transaction-manager="transactionManager" />

    <bean id="transactionManager"
          class="org.springframework.orm.jpa.JpaTransactionManager">
        <constructor-arg ref="entityManagerFactory" />
    </bean>
    .....
```

```
</beans>
```

The <annotation-driven> element of Spring's tx schema enables declarative transaction management.

Let's now take an in-depth look at different types of query methods that we can define in our repositories.

Query methods

We discussed earlier that the query method name is used by Spring Data to create the corresponding query. We also looked at some simple examples of query methods. In this section, we'll look at how you can define more complex query methods.

Limiting number of results

You can use the top or first keyword to limit the number of results returned by a query method. The following query method returns only two FixedDepositDetails objects:

```
List<FixedDepositDetails> findTop2ByTenure(int tenure);
```

In the above method, Top2 specifies that only top two results are returned by the method.

If you limit query results to only *one* entity instance, you can specify Java 8's Optional<T> as the return type of the query method. For instance, the following query method returns only one instance of FixedDepositDetails:

```
Optional<FixedDepositDetails> findTopByTenure(int tenure);
```

The Optional return type indicates that findTopByTenure method may not return any FixedDepositDetails instance.

Ordering results

You can use the OrderBy keyword followed by property name and sort direction (descending or ascending) to receive sorted results from a query method. For instance, the following method returns FixedDepositDetails in the descending order of fdCreationDate property:

```
List<FixedDepositDetails> findTop2ByOrderByFdCreationDateDesc();
```

In the above method, Desc means results are sorted in descending order. If you want results to be sorted in the ascending order, use Asc.

Querying based on multiple attributes

You can use And and Or keywords to query results based on multiple entity attributes. For instance, the following method returns FixedDepositDetails entities with given tenure and fixed deposit amount:

```
List<FixedDepositDetails> findByTenureAndFdAmount(int tenure, int fdAmount);
```

Adding pagination to queries

You can add Pageable argument to query methods for paginated access to entities. The following findByTenure method provides paginated access to FixedDepositDetails entities:

```
List<FixedDepositDetails> findByTenure(int tenure, Pageable pageable);
```

Pageable contains pagination details, like page number, page size, and so on. You create an instance of PageRequest object (an implementation of Pageable) containing information about the requested page, and pass it to the query method. For instance, this is how you can call the findByTenure method:

```
findByTenure(6, PageRequest.of(1, 10))
```

PageRequest's of method creates a PageRequest object. In the above code, we've created a PageRequest object with page number as 1 and page size as 10. Page numbers start from 0; therefore, the above call will return the second page and the page size will be 10.

Add sorting to queries

You can add Sort argument to query methods to add sorting to queries. The following findByTenure method returns sorted results:

```
List<FixedDepositDetails> findByTenure(int tenure, Sort sort)
```

The Sort argument specifies sorting details, which includes properties based on which sorting is performed and the sort order. This is how you can call the findByTenure method:

```
findByTenure(6, new Sort(Sort.Direction.ASC, "fdCreationDate"))
```

The Sort constructor accepts the sort order (specified by Sort.Direction.ASC constant) and the sort property (which is fdCreationDate) based on which query results are sorted.

Paginating through large result sets

If you want to paginate through a large result set, define Slice<T> or Page<T> as the return type of the query method. Both the methods provide paginated access to entities. The following methods show usage of Slice<T> and Page<T> as return types:

```
Page<FixedDepositDetails> findByFdAmountGreatherThan(int amount, Pageable pageable);
Slice<FixedDepositDetails> findByFdAmount(int amount, Pageable pageable);
```

A Page contains results returned by the query and the total number of entities in the data store. The downside of using Page<T> is that it results in execution of an extra query to find the total number of entities in the data store. As this query could be time consuming, you may only want to know whether there is a next page or not. You achieve this by using Slice<T> as the return type, which contains the results returned by the query and a flag that indicates if more entities are available in the data store.

The following example listing shows how Slice is used for paginated access to entities:

Example listing 9-14 – BankApp class – Slice usage
Project – ch09-springdata-jpa
Source location - src/main/java/sample/spring/chapter09/bankapp

```
package sample.spring.chapter09.bankapp;

import org.springframework.data.domain.Pageable;
import org.springframework.data.domain.Slice;
.....
public class BankApp {
    public static void main(String args[]) throws Exception {
        .....
        Slice<FixedDepositDetails> slice =
                    fixedDepositService.findByFdAmount(500, PageRequest.of(0, 2));
        if (slice.hasContent()) {
            logger.info("Slice has content");
            List<FixedDepositDetails> list = slice.getContent();
            for (FixedDepositDetails details : list) {
                logger.info("Fixed Deposit ID --> " + details.getFixedDepositId());
```

```
            }
        }
        if (slice.hasNext()) {
            Pageable pageable = slice.nextPageable();
            slice = fixedDepositService.findByFdAmount(500, pageable);
        }
        .....
    }
}
```

In the above example listing, we first call the findByFdAmount method to retrieve the first result page. Slice's hasContent method checks if there was any result returned by the query. Slice's getContent method is used to obtain the results returned by the query. Slice's hasNext method checks if more results are available. If more results are available, obtain the next Pageable object using Slice's nextPageable method and use it to call the query method again.

You should note that when using Slice<T> as the return type, Spring Data retrieves one more result than requested. For instance, call to findByFdAmount(500, PageRequest.of(0, 2)) method retrieves 3 FixedDepositDetails entities instead of 2 from the data store. If an extra result is returned by the query, hasNext method returns true.

Streaming query results

We saw earlier that we can use pagination to deal with large result sets. We can also use Stream<T> as the return type of the query method for handling large result sets. The following findAllByTenure method uses Stream<T> as the return type:

```
Stream<FixedDepositDetails> findAllByTenure(int tenure);
```

If you are using Stream<T> return type, the query method is *not* blocked until the complete result set is read into memory. The query method immediately returns after the first result is read from the data store. As JPA only provides query results as java.util.List, Spring Data JPA uses underlying persistence provider API to stream query results.

The following listing shows how data from a Stream is consumed:

Example listing 9-15 – BankApp class – consuming Stream data
Project – ch09-springdata-jpa
Source location - src/main/java/sample/spring/chapter09/bankapp

```
package sample.spring.chapter09.bankapp;

import java.util.stream.Stream;
import org.springframework.transaction.support.TransactionCallbackWithoutResult;
import org.springframework.transaction.support.TransactionTemplate;
.....
public class BankApp {
  .....
  public static void main(String args[]) throws Exception {
    AnnotationConfigApplicationContext context = new AnnotationConfigApplicationContext();
    .....
    logger.info("findAllByTenure : ");
    TransactionTemplate txTemplate = context.getBean(TransactionTemplate.class);
    txTemplate.execute(new TransactionCallbackWithoutResult() {
      @Override
      protected void doInTransactionWithoutResult(TransactionStatus status) {
        try (Stream<FixedDepositDetails> stream = fixedDepositService.findAllByTenure(6)) {
```

```
            logger.info("count from stream --> "
                            + stream.filter(t -> t.getActive().equals("Y")).count());
        }
      }
    });
    .....
  }
}
```

In the above listing, TransactionTemplate instance is obtained from the Spring container and is used to execute the following code within transaction:

```
        try (Stream<FixedDepositDetails> stream = fixedDepositService.findAllByTenure(6)) {
            logger.info("count from stream --> "
                            + stream.filter(t -> t.getActive().equals("Y")).count());
        }
```

This means the code that consumes data from Stream is executed within a transaction. The transaction ensures that the Stream is not closed until data is consumed from the Stream. If you don't execute the above code within a transaction, it'll result in org.springframework.dao.InvalidDataAccessApiUsageException.

Executing query methods asynchronously

You can execute a query method asynchronously by annotating it with Spring's @Async annotation, as shown here:

Example listing 9-16 – FixedDepositRepository – @Async query methods
Project – ch09-springdata-jpa
Source location - src/main/java/sample/spring/chapter09/bankapp/repository

```
package sample.spring.chapter09.bankapp.repository;

import java.util.concurrent.CompletableFuture;
import org.springframework.scheduling.annotation.Async;
.....
public  interface  FixedDepositRepository  extends  Repository<FixedDepositDetails,  Integer>
.....
{
    .....
    @Async
    CompletableFuture<List<FixedDepositDetails>> findAllByFdAmount(int fdAmount);
}
```

The possible return types of @Async annotated query methods are : Future<T>, ListenableFuture<T> and Java 8's CompletableFuture<T>. You enable support for @Async annotation by annotating your @Configuration class with @EnableAsync annotation. @Async and @EnableAsync annotations are covered in detail in chapter 10.

The following example listing shows @EnableAsync annotation usage in ch09-springdata-jpa project:

Example listing 9-17 – BankApp class – @EnableAsync annotation usage
Project – ch09-springdata-jpa
Source location - src/main/java/sample/spring/chapter09/bankapp

```
package sample.spring.chapter09.bankapp;

import org.springframework.scheduling.annotation.EnableAsync;
.....
@EnableAsync
```

```
public class DatabaseConfig { ..... }
```

In the following example listing, FixedDepositSerivce's findAllByFdAmount method calls @Async annotated FixedDepositRepository's findAllByFdAmount query method (refer example listing 9-16):

Example listing 9-18 – BankApp class – CompletableFuture usage
Project – ch09-springdata-jpa
Source location - src/main/java/sample/spring/chapter09/bankapp

```
package sample.spring.chapter09.bankapp;

import java.util.concurrent.CompletableFuture;
.....
public class BankApp {
    private static Logger logger = LogManager.getLogger(BankApp.class);

    public static void main(String args[]) throws Exception {
        AnnotationConfigApplicationContext context =
              new AnnotationConfigApplicationContext();
        .....
        FixedDepositService fixedDepositService =
              context.getBean(FixedDepositService.class);
        .....
        //-- async query method execution
        CompletableFuture<List<FixedDepositDetails>> future =
              fixedDepositService.findAllByFdAmount(500);
        while(!future.isDone()) {
            logger.info("Waiting for findAllByFdAmount method to complete .....");
        }
        logger.info(future.get());
        .....
    }
}
```

As FixedDepositRepository's findAllByFdAmount query method is executed asynchronously, the FixedDepositSerivce's findAllByFdAmount method call returns immediately. CompletableFuture's isDone method returns true only after the execution of FixedDepositRepository's findAllByFdAmount method is complete. When the execution of query method completes (that is, the isDone method returns true), the CompletableFuture's get method is called to retrieve the result.

Explicitly specifying queries using @Query annotation

If a query is quite complex, you can use @Query annotation to explicitly specify the query. In the following query method, we've explicitly specified the query using @Query annotation:

```
@Query("select fd from FixedDepositDetails fd where fd.tenure = ?1 and fd.fdAmount <= ?2
and fd.active = ?3")
List<FixedDepositDetails> findByCustomQuery(int tenure, int fdAmount, String active);
```

In the above example, @Query annotation specifies the JPQL query (a platform independent query language) to be executed. ?1, ?2 and ?3 refer to the arguments passed to the findByCustomQuery method.

@EnableJpaRepositories's queryLookupStrategy attribute specifies whether Spring Data JPA derives query from the query method name or directly uses the query specified by @Query annotation. By default, Spring Data JPA creates a query from the method name only if *no* @Query annotation is specified for the method.

Spring Data supports Querydsl – an open source project that simplifies creating queries.

9-4 Creating queries using Querydsl

Instead of using JPQL queries, you can create queries programmatically either by using JPA Criteria API or by using Querydsl. Unlike JPQL queries, the queries that you create using Criteria API and Querydsl are *type-safe*. In both the cases, you use a *metamodel generator* for creating *metamodel classes* that describe attributes of domain entities, and are used for creating queries. In this section, we'll only look at Querydsl as it is more compact and intuitive compared to JPA Criteria API.

> For using Querydsl, ch09-springdata-jpa project's pom.xml includes dependency on version 4.1.3 of querydsl-jpa and querydsl-apt JARs.

The querydsl-apt JAR contains an annotation processor, JPAAnnotationProcessor, which generates metamodel classes corresponding to domain entities in the application. In ch09-springdata-jpa project, JPAAnnotationProcessor is configured with Maven compiler plugin (https://maven.apache.org/plugins/maven-compiler-plugin/). So, when you compile the project using mvn clean compile command, the metamodel classes are generated.

The following example listing shows how Maven compiler Plugin is configured in ch09-springdata-jpa project's pom.xml file:

Example listing 9-19 – pom.xml – Maven compiler Plugin configuration
Project – ch09-springdata-jpa

```
<plugin>
  <groupId>org.apache.maven.plugins</groupId>
  <artifactId>maven-compiler-plugin</artifactId>
  <version>3.7.0</version>
  <configuration>
    .....
    <annotationProcessors>
      <annotationProcessor>
        com.querydsl.apt.jpa.JPAAnnotationProcessor
      </annotationProcessor>
    </annotationProcessors>
  </configuration>
</plugin>
```

The JPAAnnotationProcessor is the class responsible for creating metamodel classes at compile time. The metamodel classes are created in target/generated-sources/annotations directory when you compile the project. The naming convention followed by the generated metamodel classes is: Q*<domain-entity-name>*; where *<domain-entity-name>* is the simple name of the domain entity class. For instance, the metamodel class generated corresponding to FixedDepositDetails entity is QFixedDepositDetails.

> As the generated metamodel classes are annotated with JSR 250's @Generated annotation, ch09-springdata-jpa project's pom.xml file defines dependency on jsr250-api JAR file. Also, to ensure that the ch09-springdata-jpa project doesn't show compilation errors in Eclipse IDE, add target/generated-sources/annotations directory as a *source folder*.

Let's now look at how to use Querydsl with Spring Data.

Integrating Spring Data with Querydsl

Spring Data provides integration with Querydsl via QuerydslPredicateExecutor<T> interface. You can use Querydsl by making your custom repository interface extend QuerydslPredicateExecutor<T> interface.

The following example listing shows some of the methods declared by QuerydslPredicateExecutor<T> interface:

Example listing 9-20 – QuerydslPredicateExecutor<T> interface

```
public interface QuerydslPredicateExecutor<T> {
    T findOne(Predicate predicate);
    Iterable<T> findAll(Predicate predicate);
    Iterable<T> findAll(Predicate predicate, Sort sort);
    Page<T> findAll(Predicate predicate, Pageable pageable);
    long count(Predicate predicate);
    .....
}
```

In the above example listing, T type-parameter is the domain entity type. Predicate holds conditions that must be satisfied by the entities, which means that it represents the WHERE clause of the SQL query. The findOne method returns the entity that matches the conditions specified by the Predicate argument. The findAll method returns all the entities that satisfy the given Predicate. As findAll method can accept Pageable and Sort arguments, you can get paginated access to entities and also sort them. The count method returns the count of entities that satisfy the given Predicate.

The following example listing shows the FixedDepositRepository interface that extends QuerydslPredicateExecutor<T>:

Example listing 9-21 – FixedDepositRepository interface
Project – ch09-springdata-jpa
Source location - src/main/java/sample/spring/chapter09/bankapp/repository

```
package sample.spring.chapter09.bankapp.repository;

import org.springframework.data.querydsl.QuerydslPredicateExecutor;
.....
public interface FixedDepositRepository extends Repository<FixedDepositDetails, Integer>,
      QuerydslPredicateExecutor<FixedDepositDetails> {
    .....
}
```

You can now call the findOne(Predicate predicate), findAll(Predicate predicate), and so on, methods on FixedDepositRepository interface.

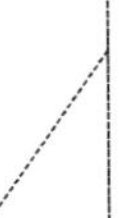

If your custom repository interface extends QuerydslPredicateExecutor<T> interface, the default repository implementation created by Spring Data JPA is QuerydslJpaRepository (an extension of SimpleJpaRepository) that implements the QuerydslPredicateExecutor<T> interface.

Constructing a Predicate

To construct a Predicate, you need to understand the structure of metamodel classes generated by Querydsl.

The following example listing shows the QFixedDepositDetails metamodel class that was generated corresponding to FixedDepositDetails entity:

Example listing 9-22 – `QFixedDepositDetails` class
Project – `ch09-springdata-jpa`
Source location – `target/generated-sources/annotations/sample/spring/chapter09/bankapp/domain`

```
package sample.spring.chapter09.bankapp.domain;
.....
public class QFixedDepositDetails extends EntityPathBase<FixedDepositDetails> {
    .....
    public static final QFixedDepositDetails fixedDepositDetails =
                new QFixedDepositDetails("fixedDepositDetails");
    public final NumberPath<Integer> fixedDepositId =
                createNumber("fixedDepositId", Integer.class);
    public final StringPath active = createString("active");
    public final NumberPath<Integer> fdAmount = createNumber("fdAmount", Integer.class);
    .....
}
```

Notice that the `QFixedDepositDetails` class defines attributes (like, `fixedDepositId`, `active`, `fdAmount`, and so on) whose names are same as the attributes defined in `FixedDepositDetails` entity. It also defines a static `fixedDepositDetails` field that provides access to an instance of `QFixedDepositDetails` instance itself.

To construct a `Predicate` for querying `FixedDepositDetails` entities, obtain an instance of `QFixedDepositDetails` and use its *attributes* to specify conditions that must be satisfied by the `FixedDepositDetails` entities. The following example listing shows how `FixedDepositServiceImpl`'s `getHighValueFds` method constructs a `Predicate` to fetch fixed deposits which are currently active (that is, the value is of active field is 'Y'), and the fixed deposit amount is greater than `1000`, and the tenure is between 6 and 12 months:

Example listing 9-23 – `FixedDepositServiceImpl` class – constructing `Predicate`
Project – `ch09-springdata-jpa`
Source location - `src/main/java/sample/spring/chapter09/bankapp/service`

```
package sample.spring.chapter09.bankapp.service;

import com.querydsl.core.types.Predicate;
import sample.spring.chapter09.bankapp.domain.QFixedDepositDetails;
import sample.spring.chapter09.bankapp.repository.FixedDepositRepository;
.....
@Service
public class FixedDepositServiceImpl implements FixedDepositService {
    @Autowired
    private FixedDepositRepository fixedDepositRepository;
    .....
    @Override
    public Iterable<FixedDepositDetails> getHighValueFds() {
        Predicate whereClause = QFixedDepositDetails.fixedDepositDetails.active.eq("Y")
                .and(QFixedDepositDetails.fixedDepositDetails.fdAmount.gt(1000))
                .and(QFixedDepositDetails.fixedDepositDetails.tenure.between(6, 12));
        return fixedDepositRepository.findAll(whereClause);
    }
}
```

In the above example listing, the `getHighValueFds` method obtains an instance of `QFixedDepositDetails` by accessing `QFixedDepositDetails`'s `fixedDepositDetails` field, and then sets conditions for `active`, `fdAmount` and `tenure` fields. For instance, the condition

QFixedDepositDetails.fixedDepositDetails.fdAmount.gt(1000) specifies that the fdAmount field must be greater than 1000. Each condition is represented by BooleanExpression type. You can combine multiple conditions using BooleanExpression's and and or methods. The WHERE clause constructed by JPA corresponding to the Predicate defined in the getHighValueFds method is:

```
select ..... from fixed_deposit_details fixeddepos0_ where fixeddepos0_.active='Y' and fixeddepos0_.amount> 1000 and (fixeddepos0_.tenure between 6 and 12)
```

This shows that the conditions specified in the Predicate are translated into the WHERE clause of the SQL query.

Let's now look at how you can use Query by Example technique for querying entities.

9-5 Query by Example (QBE)

In Query by Example, a populated entity instance is used by Spring Data to create the WHERE clause of the query for fetching entities. You add support for Query by Example by making your Spring Data repositories extend QueryByExampleExecutor<T> interface.

The following example listing shows some of the methods declared by QueryByExampleExecutor<T> interface:

Example listing 9-24 – QueryByExampleExecutor<T> interface

```
import org.springframework.data.domain.Example;
.....
public interface QueryByExampleExecutor<T> {
    <S extends T> S findOne(Example<S> example);
    <S extends T> Iterable<S> findAll(Example<S> example);
    <S extends T> Iterable<S> findAll(Example<S> example, Sort sort);
    <S extends T> Page<S> findAll(Example<S> example, Pageable pageable);
    .....
}
```

In the above example listing, T type-parameter is the domain entity type, and Example<S> consists of a populated entity instance and an ExampleMatcher object. The populated entity instance is used for creating the WHERE clause of the query, and ExampleMatcher is used for fine-tuning that WHERE clause.

The following example listing shows how to use Query by Example approach to query for FixedDepositDetails entities that are active, their fixed deposit amount is 500, and their tenure is 6 months:

Example listing 9-25 – FixedDepositServiceImpl class – Query By Example
Project – ch09-springdata-jpa
Source location - src/main/java/sample/spring/chapter09/bankapp/service

```
package sample.spring.chapter09.bankapp.service;
.....
import org.springframework.data.domain.Example;
import org.springframework.data.domain.ExampleMatcher;
.....
@Service
public class FixedDepositServiceImpl implements FixedDepositService {
    @Autowired
    private FixedDepositRepository fixedDepositRepository;
    .....
    //-- Query by Example
```

```
    @Override
    public Iterable<FixedDepositDetails> getAllFds() {
        FixedDepositDetails fd = new FixedDepositDetails();
        fd.setActive("Y");
        fd.setFdAmount(500);
        fd.setTenure(6);
        ExampleMatcher matcher =
                ExampleMatcher.matching().withIgnorePaths("fixedDepositId");
        Example<FixedDepositDetails> fdExample = Example.of(fd, matcher);
        return fixedDepositRepository.findAll(fdExample);
    }
}
```

In the above example listing, `FixedDepositServiceImpl`'s `getAllFds` method calls `FixedDepositRepository`'s `findAll(Example<FixedDepositDetails> example)` method to query `FixedDepositDetails` entities.

At first, we create an instance of `FixedDepositDetails` and populate its fields with values based on which we want to filter entities. As we want to filter `FixedDepositDetails` entities based on `active`, `fdAmount` and `tenure` fields, we've set values of these fields. The fields whose values you don't set are either set to their default value or `null`. This means, `fixedDepositId` field (of type `int`) is set to `0`, `fdCreationDate` field (of type `java.util.Date`) is set to `null`, and `bankAccountId` field (of type `BankAccountDetails`) is set to `null`.

As fields with `null` values are ignored while creating the query, you don't need to worry about `fdCreationDate` and `bankAccountId` fields. The `fixedDepositId` field's value is `0`; therefore, it'll automatically become part of the `WHERE` clause of the query. As we don't want `fixedDepositId` field to be part of the `WHERE` clause, we use the `ExampleMatcher` instance to specify that the `fixedDepositId` field is ignored during query creation. We use `Example`'s `of` method to create an instance of `Example` using the populated `FixedDepositDetails` instance and the `ExampleMatcher` instance. The `Example` instance is used by Spring Data to create the following SQL query:

```
select ..... from fixed_deposit_details fixeddepos0_ where fixeddepos0_.active=? and
fixeddepos0_.amount=500 and fixeddepos0_.tenure=6
```

It's quite easy to use Query By Example approach for querying entities, but it also has its limitations. For instance, the generated query always uses AND condition between field values for filtering entities. This means that you can't generate a query like this:

```
select ..... from fixed_deposit_details fixeddepos0_ where fixeddepos0_.active=? or
fixeddepos0_.amount=500 or fixeddepos0_.tenure=6
```

So far in this chapter we've looked at core concepts in Spring Data and how to use Spring Data JPA for developing an application that interacts with a relational database. Let's now look at Spring Data MongoDB project that simplifies developing applications that interact with MongoDB.

9-6 Spring Data MongoDB

MongoDB is a NoSQL database in which data is stored as *documents*. A document looks similar to a JSON (JavaScript Object Notation) string, as shown here:

Example listing 9-26 – An example MongoDB document

```
{
    _id : 5747d49f16e329249803bf47,
    balance : 1000,
    lastTransactionTimestamp : 2016-05-27 10:31:19
}
```

A MongoDB document consists of field-value pairs. A document is analogous to a record stored in a relational database table. Each document is associated with an _id field that represents the primary key of the document. The value of _id field is auto-generated by MongoDB. You create a *collection* (analogous to a relational database table) and store similar documents into it.

IMPORT **chapter 9/ch09-springdata-mongo** (The ch09-springdata-mongo project uses Spring Data MongoDB for database interaction. To run the project, execute the main method of the BankApp class. Refer to appendix A for instructions on how to download and install MongoDB database.)

> For using Spring Data MongoDB, ch09-springdata-mongo project's pom.xml includes dependency on version 2.0.1.RELEASE of spring-data-mongodb and spring-data-commons, and version 3.5.0 of mongo-java-driver.

Let's look at how domain entities are modeled in ch09-springdata-mongo project.

Modeling domain entities

The ch09-springdata-mongo project defines BankAccountDetails and FixedDepositDetails domain entities that are persisted in MongoDB. The following example listing shows the BankAccountDetails entity:

Example listing 9-27 – BankAccountDetails class
Project – ch09-springdata-mongo
Source location - src/main/java/sample/spring/chapter09/bankapp/domain

```
package sample.spring.chapter09.bankapp.domain;

import org.springframework.data.annotation.Id;
import org.springframework.data.mongodb.core.mapping.Document;
.....
@Document(collection = "bankaccounts")
public class BankAccountDetails {
    @Id
    private String accountId;
    private int balance;
    private Date lastTransactionTimestamp;
    private List<FixedDepositDetails> fixedDeposits;
    .....
}
```

@Document annotation specifies that BankAccountDetails objects are persisted into MongoDB. Spring Data MongoDB takes care of converting a domain object to a MongoDB document and vice versa. The collection attribute specifies the name of MongoDB collection into which the document is stored. This means, BankAccountDetails objects are stored into a collection named bankaccounts. @Id annotation identifies the field that acts as the primary key. The value of @Id annotated field is auto-generated by MongoDB, and is stored as a field named _id in the document. As a BankAccountDetails object is associated with one or more FixedDepositDetails object, we've defined a List<FixedDepositDetails> type attribute in the BankAccountDetails object.

As parent-child relationship exists between BankAccountDetails and FixedDepositDetails entities, FixedDepositDetails objects are stored as an *embedded document* inside BankAccountDetails document. The following example listing shows the FixedDepositDetails entity:

Example listing 9-28 – FixedDepositDetails class
Project – ch09-springdata-mongo
Source location - src/main/java/sample/spring/chapter09/bankapp/domain

```
package sample.spring.chapter09.bankapp.domain;
```

```
import org.bson.types.ObjectId;
import org.springframework.data.annotation.Id;
.....
public class FixedDepositDetails {
    @Id
    private ObjectId fixedDepositId;
    private int fdAmount;
    .....
    public FixedDepositDetails() {
        this.fixedDepositId = ObjectId.get();
    }
    .....
}
```

`FixedDepositDetails` is *not* annotated with `@Document` annotation because it is stored as an embedded document inside `BankAccountDetails` document. Even though the `fixedDepositId` is annotated with `@Id` annotation, its `_id` field is *not* set because it's an embedded document. As we want to uniquely identify fixed deposits by their `_id` values, we've explicitly set the `fixedDepositId` field by calling `ObjectId`'s get method. `ObjectId` provides a globally unique identifier for documents.

The following example listing shows a `BankAccountDetails` document that contains embedded `FixedDepositDetails` documents:

Example listing 9-29 – `BankAccountDetails` document with embedded `FixedDepositDetails`

```
{
    _id : 5747d5a316e32925ec26372c,
    _class : sample.spring.chapter09.bankapp.domain.BankAccountDetails,
    balance : 1000,
    lastTransactionTimestamp : 2016-05-27 05:05:39,
    fixedDeposits : [
        {
            _id : 5747d5a316e32925ec26372b,
            fdCreationDate : 2016-05-27 05:05:39,
            fdAmount : 500,
            tenure : 6,
            active : Y
        },
        {
            _id : 5747d5a316e32925ec26372d,
            fdCreationDate : 2016-05-27 05:05:39,
            fdAmount : 210000,
            tenure : 7,
            active : Y
        }
    ]
}
```

In the above example listing, the top-level document corresponds to `BankAccountDetails` entity. This is also indicated by the `_class` field, which contains the fully-qualified name of the domain entity. The `fixedDeposits` field contains two embedded `FixedDepositDetails` documents.

Let's now look at how you can configure Spring Data MongoDB for interacting with a MongoDB database.

Configuring Spring Data MongoDB – Java-based configuration

The following example listing shows the @Configuration annotated DatabaseConfig class that enables support for using Spring Data MongoDB in ch09-springdata-mongo project:

Example listing 9-30 – DatabaseConfig class
Project – ch09-springdata-mongo
Source location - src/main/java/sample/spring/chapter09/bankapp

```
package sample.spring.chapter09.bankapp;

import org.springframework.data.mongodb.MongoDbFactory;
import org.springframework.data.mongodb.core.MongoTemplate;
import org.springframework.data.mongodb.core.SimpleMongoDbFactory;
import org.springframework.data.mongodb.repository.config.EnableMongoRepositories;
import org.springframework.scheduling.annotation.EnableAsync;
import com.mongodb.MongoClient;

@Configuration
@EnableMongoRepositories(basePackages = "sample.spring")
@EnableAsync
public class DatabaseConfig {
    @Bean
    public MongoClient mongoClient() {
        return new MongoClient("localhost");
    }

    public MongoDbFactory mongoDbFactory() {
        return new SimpleMongoDbFactory(mongoClient(), "test");
    }

    @Bean
    public MongoTemplate mongoTemplate() {
        return new MongoTemplate(mongoDbFactory());
    }
}
```

@EnableMongoRepositories annotation enables Spring Data MongoDB for the application. The basePackages attribute specifies the packages to be scanned for Spring Data repositories. Spring Data creates proxies corresponding to repositories found in these packages. @EnableAsync annotation enables support for Spring's @Async annotation.

The @Bean annotated mongoClient method creates an instance of MongoClient that is used by the application for connecting to the MongoDB database. MongoClient's constructor accepts the name of the server on which MongoDB instance is running. As our MongoDB instance is running locally, we've passed localhost as an argument to the MongoClient's constructor. By default, it is assumed that MongoDB instance is listening for connections on port number 27017. If your MongoDB instance is running on a different port number, then pass port number also to MongoClient's constructor, as shown here:

```
new MongoClient("localhost", 27018);
```

The @Bean annotated mongoDbFactory method creates an instance of SimpleMongoDbFactory – a factory for creating the client-side representation of a database in MongoDB. SimpleMongoDbFactory's constructor accepts MongoClient instance and the name of the MongoDB database (which is test in our case) whose client-side representation we want to create. SimpleMongoDbFactory implements MongoDbFactory interface.

The @Bean annotated mongoTemplate method creates an instance of MongoTemplate that provides operations for interacting with a database in MongoDB. For instance, you can use MongoTemplate to perform CRUD operations on documents stored in a collection. MongoTemplate's constructor accepts an instance of MongoDbFactory that identifies the database with which MongoTemplate interacts. The MongoTemplate class implements MongoOperations interface, and uses a registered MongoConverter object for converting domain objects to MongoDB documents and vice versa.

Configuring Spring Data MongoDB – XML-based configuration

The ch09-springdata-mongo project comes with an application context XML file that you can use, instead of DatabaseConfig class, for configuring the application. The following example listing shows the application context XML file:

Example listing 9-31 –Spring Data MongoDB configuration
Project – ch09-springdata-mongo
Source location - META-INF/spring/applicationContext.xml

```
<beans .....
    xmlns:mongo="http://www.springframework.org/schema/data/mongo"
    xsi:schemaLocation="....http://www.springframework.org/schema/data/mongo
          http://www.springframework.org/schema/data/mongo/spring-mongo.xsd">

    <mongo:repositories base-package="sample.spring" />
    <mongo:mongo-client host="localhost" port="27017" />
    <mongo:db-factory dbname="test" mongo-ref="mongoClient" />
    <mongo:template db-factory-ref="mongoDbFactory"/>
    .....
</beans>
```

In the above example listing, the <repositories> element of Spring Data MongoDB's spring-mongo.xsd schema enables support for Spring Data MongoDB repositories. The <mongo-client> element creates an instance of MongoClient and registers it as a bean named mongoClient. The <db-factory> element creates an instance of MongoDbFactory and registers it as a bean named mongoDbFactory. The <template> element creates an instance of MongoTemplate for the given MongoDbFactory instance.

Let's now look at how to create custom Spring Data repositories for interacting with MongoDB database.

Creating custom repositories

To create custom repositories, you can either use database-agnostic repository interfaces (like Repository, CrudRepository and PagingAndSortingRepository) or you can use MongoDB-specific MongoRepository interface (provided by Spring Data MongoDB). Like JpaRepository interface, MongoRepository interface extends PagingAndSortingRepository and QueryByExampleExecutor interfaces.

The following example listing shows the BankAccountRepository interface that extends Spring Data's MongoRepository and QuerydslPredicateExecutor interfaces, and a custom BankAccountRepositoryCustom interface:

Example listing 9-32 – BankAccountRepository class
Project – ch09-springdata-mongo
Source location - src/main/java/sample/spring/chapter09/bankapp/repository

```
package sample.spring.chapter09.bankapp.repository;

import org.springframework.data.mongodb.repository.MongoRepository;
import org.springframework.data.mongodb.repository.Query;
import org.springframework.data.querydsl.QuerydslPredicateExecutor;
```

```
import org.springframework.scheduling.annotation.Async;
.....
public interface BankAccountRepository
        extends MongoRepository<BankAccountDetails, String>,
                QuerydslPredicateExecutor<BankAccountDetails>, BankAccountRepositoryCustom {
    .....
    List<BankAccountDetails> findByFixedDepositsTenureAndFixedDepositsFdAmount(int tenure,
            int fdAmount);
    @Async
    CompletableFuture<List<BankAccountDetails>> findAllByBalanceGreaterThan(int balance);

    @Query("{'balance' : {'$lte' : ?0} }")
    List<BankAccountDetails> findByCustomQuery(int balance);
}
```

The `BankAccountRepository` declares finder methods that return `BankAccountDetails` entities. A lot of similarities exists between repositories developed using Spring Data JPA and Spring Data MongoDB:

- you can annotate a query method with `@Async` annotation to execute it asynchronously. In the above example listing, `findAllByBalanceGreatherThan` method is executed asynchronously.
- you can annotate a query method with `@Query` to specify a custom query. In the above example listing, the query specified by `@Query` is executed when `findByCustomQuery` method is called.
- you can declare query methods that return `Stream<T>` type for streaming query results
- you can pass `Pageable` argument to query methods to get paginated access to documents
- you can pass `Sort` argument to query methods to add sorting to queries

As `BankAccountDetails` defines a `fixedDeposits` field that contains a list of `FixedDepositDetails`, the method `findByFixedDepositsTenureAndFixedDepositsFdAmount` is used to find `BankAccountDetails` based on `tenure` and `fdAmount` fields of *enclosing* `FixedDepositDetails`. This is an example of declaring finder methods that use *nested properties* for finding entities.

Let's now look at how we've added `subtractFromAccount` custom method to `BankAccountRepository`.

Adding custom methods to a repository

You can add custom methods to a MongoDB repository by following the same process that we followed for adding custom methods to JPA repositories (refer section 9-3). The steps followed for adding the `subtractFromAccount` method to `BankAccountRepository` are:

- created the `BankAccountRepositoryCustom` interface that declares the `subtractFromAccount` custom method
- provided implementation of `BankAccountRepositoryCustom` interface, and
- made the `BankAccountRepository` extend the `BankAccountRepositoryCustom` interface

The following example listing shows the `BankAccountRepositoryImpl` class that implements the `BankAccountRepositoryCustom` interface:

Example listing 9-33 – BankAccountRepositoryImpl class
Project – ch09-springdata-mongo
Source location - src/main/java/sample/spring/chapter09/bankapp/repository

```
package sample.spring.chapter09.bankapp.repository;

import org.springframework.data.mongodb.core.MongoOperations;
.....
public class BankAccountRepositoryImpl implements BankAccountRepositoryCustom {
    @Autowired
    private MongoOperations mongoOperations;

    @Override
    public void subtractFromAccount(String bankAccountId, int amount) {
        BankAccountDetails bankAccountDetails =
                mongoOperations.findById(bankAccountId, BankAccountDetails.class);
        if (bankAccountDetails.getBalance() < amount) {
            throw new RuntimeException("Insufficient balance amount in bank account");
        }
        bankAccountDetails.setBalance(bankAccountDetails.getBalance() - amount);
        mongoOperations.save(bankAccountDetails);
    }
}
```

BankAccountRepositoryImpl is automatically picked up by Spring Data and treated like any other Spring bean. The autowired MongoOperations that we configured earlier (refer example listing 9-30 and 9-31) is used for subtracting the fixed deposit amount from the BankAccountDetails's balance field. The above example shows that Spring Data MongoDB gives you the flexibility to directly use MongoOperations to interact with MongoDB.

Let's now look at how Querydsl is used for creating queries.

Creating queries using Querydsl

As in the case of Spring Data JPA, you can use Querydsl to create queries for fetching documents from MongoDB.

For using Querydsl, ch09-springdata-mongo project's pom.xml includes dependency on version 4.1.3 of querydsl-mongodb and querydsl-apt JARs.

The spring-data-mongodb JAR contains a MongoAnnotationProcessor class (an annotation processor) that generates metamodel classes corresponding to @Document annotated entities in the application. Maven compiler plugin (https://maven.apache.org/plugins/maven-compiler-plugin/) is responsible for executing the MongoAnnotationProcessor at compile-time to generate metamodel classes. You can refer to ch09-springdata-mongo project's pom.xml file to view the configuration of Maven compiler plugin.

As the generated metamodel classes are annotated with JSR 250's @Generated annotation, ch09-springdata-mongo project's pom.xml file defines dependency on jsr250-api JAR file. Also, to ensure that the ch09-springdata-mongo project doesn't show compilation errors in Eclipse IDE, add target/generated-sources/annotations directory as a *source folder*.

The following example listing shows BankAccountServiceImpl's getHighValueFds method that uses Querydsl to fetch fixed deposits that are currently active, and the fixed deposit amount is greater than 1000, and the tenure is between 6 and 12 months:

Example listing 9-34 – BankAccountServiceImpl's getHighValueFds method
Project – ch09-springdata-mongo
Source location - src/main/java/sample/spring/chapter09/bankapp/repository

```
public Iterable<BankAccountDetails> getHighValueFds() {
  Predicate whereClause =
      QBankAccountDetails.bankAccountDetails.fixedDeposits.any().active.eq("Y")
    .and(QBankAccountDetails.bankAccountDetails.fixedDeposits.any().fdAmount.gt(1000))
    .and(QBankAccountDetails.bankAccountDetails.fixedDeposits.any().tenure.between(6, 12));
  return bankAccountRepository.findAll(whereClause);
}
```

The QBankAccountDetails class is the metamodel class corresponding to BankAccountDetails entity. BankAccountDetails's fixedDeposits field refers to a list of FixedDepositDetails objects. As we want to query for BankAccountDetails based on the active, fdAmount and tenure fields of the *nested collection* of FixedDepositDetails objects, we've used the any() method to specify conditions that must be satisfied by one or more of the FixedDepositDetails objects in the nested collection.

Creating queries using Query by Example

As MongoRepository extends QueryByExampleExecutor interface, we can use Query by Example to query MongoDB documents. Let's look at how we can use Query by Example to fetch BankAccountDetails that are *not* associated with any FixedDepositDetails.

The following example listing shows the BankAccountDetails class:

Example listing 9-35 – BankAccountDetails class
Project – ch09-springdata-mongo
Source location - src/main/java/sample/spring/chapter09/bankapp/domain

```
package sample.spring.chapter09.bankapp.domain;
.....
@Document(collection = "bankaccounts")
public class BankAccountDetails {
    .....
    private List<FixedDepositDetails> fixedDeposits;

    public BankAccountDetails() {
        fixedDeposits = new ArrayList<>();
    }
    .....
}
```

BankAccountDetails defines a fixedDeposits field that contains a list of FixedDepositDetails object. You should note that the BankAccountDetails's constructor initializes the fixedDeposits field with an empty ArrayList.

The following example listing shows BankAccountServiceImpl's getAllBankAccountsWithoutFds method that fetches BankAccountDetails with no fixed deposits:

Example listing 9-36 – BankAccountServiceImpl's getAllBankAccountsWithoutFds method
Project – ch09-springdata-mongo
Source location - src/main/java/sample/spring/chapter09/bankapp/service

```
public Iterable<BankAccountDetails> getAllBankAccountsWithoutFds() {
    BankAccountDetails bankAccountDetails = new BankAccountDetails();
    ExampleMatcher matcher = ExampleMatcher.matching().withIgnorePaths("accountId",
        "balance", "lastTransactionTimestamp");
```

```
    Example<BankAccountDetails> example = Example.of(bankAccountDetails, matcher);
    return bankAccountRepository.findAll(example);
}
```

To fetch BankAccountDetails with *no* fixed deposits, we create an instance of BankAccountDetails with an *empty* fixedDeposits list, and use it for creating an Example. As we don't want accountId, balance and lastTransctionTimestamp fields of BankAccountDetails instance to be considered while querying for BankAccountDetails, we tell ExampleMatcher to ignore these fields.

9-7 Summary

This chapter looked at how you can use Spring Data JPA and Spring Data MongoDB projects to build repository layer of your applications. The core concepts covered in this chapter are followed in most (if not all) of the Spring Data projects. For instance, if you are using Neo4j graph database, you can use Spring Data Neo4j's GraphRepository interface to create a custom repository. If you are looking for a more in-depth coverage of Spring Data JPA and Spring Data MongoDB projects, then please refer to the reference documentation and the APIs of these projects.

Chapter 10 - *Messaging, emailing, asynchronous method execution, and caching using Spring*

10-1 Introduction

A real-world application goes a lot further than to interact with one or more databases to fetch or store data. This chapter covers features that are required by most real-world enterprise applications.

This chapter shows how Spring simplifies:

- sending and receiving JMS messages from a JMS provider, like ActiveMQ
- sending email messages
- asynchronously executing methods
- storing and retrieving data from cache

Let's first look at the MyBank application's requirements that we'll implement in this chapter.

10-2 MyBank application's requirements

MyBank application allows its customers to open fixed deposits and retrieve details of their existing fixed deposits. The following figure shows the sequence of events that occur when a customer requests for opening a new fixed deposit:

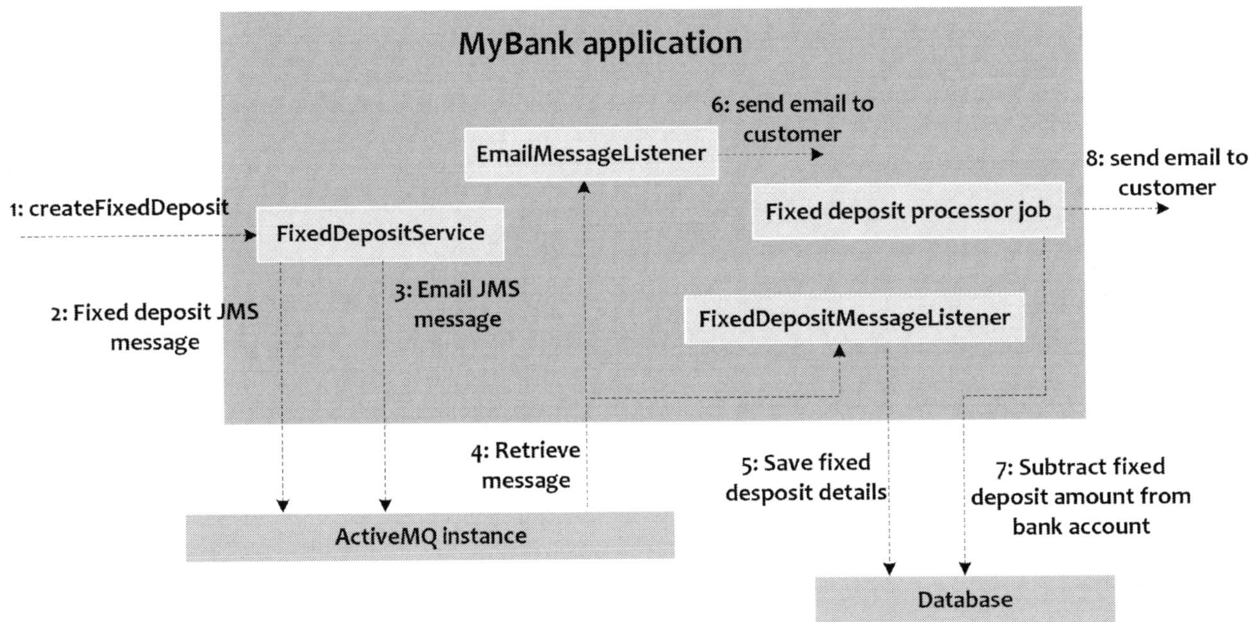

`Figure 10-1` MyBank application behavior when a customer requests for opening a new fixed deposit

First, `FixedDepositService`'s `createFixedDeposit` method is invoked that sends two JMS messages – a message containing customer's email id, and a message that contains fixed deposit details. `EmailMessageListener` retrieves the JMS message containing the email id of the customer and sends an email to the customer informing that the request for opening a fixed deposit has been received.

FixedDepositMessageListener retrieves the JMS message containing fixed deposit details and saves the fixed deposit details in the database.

A scheduled job runs every 5 seconds to check if any new fixed deposits have been created in the database. If the job finds any new fixed deposits, it subtracts the fixed deposit amount from the bank account of the customer and sends an email to the customer informing that the fixed deposit request has been successfully processed.

The following diagram shows the behavior of MyBank application when FixedDepositService's findFixedDepositsByBankAccount method is invoked to retrieve all fixed deposits corresponding to a bank account:

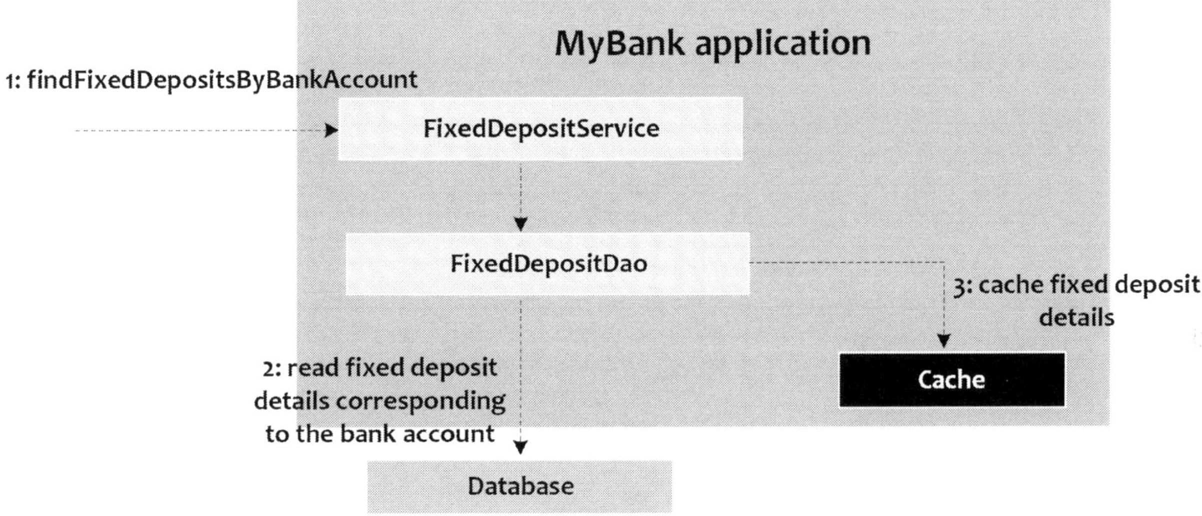

Figure 10-2 MyBank application behavior when a customer requests for the details of all his fixed deposits

The above figure shows that when FixedDepositService's findFixedDepositsByBankAccount method is invoked, the fixed deposit information is fetched from the database and cached into memory. If you call FixedDepositService's findFixedDepositsByBankAccount again, the fixed deposit information is fetched from the cache and *not* from the database.

Let's now look at how Spring is used in the MyBank application to send JMS messages to JMS destinations configured in ActiveMQ.

IMPORT **chapter 10/ch10-bankapp** and **chapter 10/ch10-bankapp-javaconfig** (The ch10-bankapp project implements the requirements discussed for the MyBank application in this chapter. The ch10-bankapp-javaconfig project is a modified version of ch10-bankapp project that uses Java-based configuration approach to configure the application.)

Instructions for setting up ch10-bankapp and ch10-bankapp-javaconfig projects: To get the most out of this chapter, install MySQL database and execute the spring_bank_app_db.sql SQL script contained in the sql folder of ch10-bankapp project. The spring_bank_app_db.sql script creates SPRING_BANK_APP_DB database and adds BANK_ACCOUNT_DETAILS and FIXED_DEPOSIT_DETAILS tables.

You need to modify the src/main/resources/META-INF/spring/database.properties file to point to your MySQL installation. To get the email feature working, modify src/main/resources/META-INF/spring/email.properties file to specify the email server and the email account that you want to use for sending emails. Also, modify the BankApp class to specify the email id of the customer to whom the emails are sent.

> If you want to use your Gmail account to send emails, then turn ON the 'Allow less secure apps' option by going to https://myaccount.google.com/lesssecureapps

10-3 Sending JMS messages

Spring simplifies interaction with JMS providers by providing a layer of abstraction on top of JMS API. In the context of MyBank application, this section shows how to *synchronously* and *asynchronously* send and receive messages from an ActiveMQ broker using Spring. For the sake of simplicity, the ActiveMQ broker is configured to run in *embedded* mode in ch10-bankapp project. To run ActiveMQ broker in embedded mode, the pom.xml file of ch10-bankapp project defines dependency on activemq-broker.jar and activemq-kahadb-store.jar files. In Spring, JMS support classes are defined in spring-jms module; therefore, pom.xml file also defines dependency on spring-jms.jar file to use Spring's support for JMS.

Configuring ActiveMQ broker to run in embedded mode

An embedded ActiveMQ broker runs in the *same* JVM as the application. You can use ActiveMQ's XML schema (activemq-core.xsd contained in activemq-spring.jar file) to configure an embedded ActiveMQ broker in a Spring application. The following example listing shows how ActiveMQ's XML schema is used to configure an embedded ActiveMQ broker in MyBank application:

Example listing 10-1 – applicationContext.xml – embedded ActiveMQ broker configuration
Project – ch10-bankapp
Source location - src/main/resources/META-INF/spring

```
<beans .....
    xmlns:amq="http://activemq.apache.org/schema/core"
    xsi:schemaLocation=".....http://activemq.apache.org/schema/core
         http://activemq.apache.org/schema/core/activemq-core.xsd.....">

    <amq:broker>
        <amq:transportConnectors>
            <amq:transportConnector uri="tcp://localhost:61616" />
        </amq:transportConnectors>
    </amq:broker>
    .....
</beans>
```

In the above example listing, the amq namespace refers to ActiveMQ's XML schema that allows you to configure an embedded ActiveMQ broker. The <broker> element configures an embedded ActiveMQ broker with name localhost. The <transportConnectors> element specifies the transport connectors on which the embedded ActiveMQ broker allows clients to connect. In the above example listing, the <transportConnector> sub-element of <transportConnectors> specifies that clients can connect to the embedded ActiveMQ broker on port number 61616 using a TCP socket.

> In Java-based configuration approach, you can configure an embedded ActiveMQ broker using ActiveMQ's BrokerService. For instance, the JmsConfig class of ch10-bankapp-javaconfig project defines a brokerService method that configures an embedded ActiveMQ broker using ActiveMQ's BrokerService class.

Let's now look at how to configure a JMS ConnectionFactory for creating connections to the embedded ActiveMQ instance.

Configuring a JMS ConnectionFactory

The following example listing shows how a JMS ConnectionFactory is configured in the application context XML file:

Example listing 10-2 – applicationContext.xml – JMS ConnectionFactory configuration
Project – ch10-bankapp
Source location - src/main/resources/META-INF/spring

```
<beans .....
    xmlns:amq="http://activemq.apache.org/schema/core"
    xsi:schemaLocation=".....http://activemq.apache.org/schema/core
         http://activemq.apache.org/schema/core/activemq-core.xsd.....">
    .....
    <amq:connectionFactory brokerURL="vm://localhost" id="jmsFactory">
        <amq:trustedPackages>
            <value>sample.spring.chapter10.bankapp.domain</value>
            <value>java.util</value>
        </amq:trustedPackages>
    </amq:connectionFactory>

    <bean class="org.springframework.jms.connection.CachingConnectionFactory"
         id="cachingConnectionFactory">
        <property name="targetConnectionFactory" ref="jmsFactory" />
    </bean>
    .....
</beans>
```

In the above example listing, the <connectionFactory> element of amq schema creates a JMS ConnectionFactory instance that is used for creating connections to the embedded ActiveMQ instance (refer example listing 10-1). The brokerURL attribute specifies the URL for connecting to the ActiveMQ broker. As we are using embedded ActiveMQ broker, the brokerURL specifies that VM protocol (specified by vm://) is used to connect to the ActiveMQ broker instance.

> In Java-based configuration approach, you can configure a ConnectionFactory for embedded ActiveMQ by using ActiveMQConnectionFactory. In ch10-bankapp-javaconfig project, JmsConfig's connectionFactory method configures an ActiveMQConnectionFactory.

In JMS, you can send and receive serializable objects using ObjectMessage. For security reasons, it is required (since ActiveMQ 5.12.2 and 5.13.0) that you explicitly specify the *packages* that contain objects trusted for exchange via JMS ObjectMessage. In ch10-bankapp project, FixedDepositDetails object contained in sample.spring.chapter10.bankapp.domain package is exchanged via ObjectMessage. Also, FixedDepositDetails class defines a java.util.Date type field. As both sample.spring.chapter10.bankapp.domain and java.util packages are not trusted by ActiveMQ, we've used the <trustedPackages> element to specify that both these packages contain objects that can be trusted for exchange via ObjectMessage.

Spring's CachingConnectionFactory is an adapter for the JMS ConnectionFactory (specified by the targetConnectionFactory property), that provides the additional feature of caching instances of JMS Session, MessageProducer and MessageConsumer.

Let's now look at how to use Spring's JmsTemplate class to send JMS messages.

Sending JMS messages using JmsTemplate

Spring's JmsTemplate class simplifies *synchronously* sending and receiving JMS messages. Like TransactionTemplate (refer section 8-5 of chapter 8) and JdbcTemplate (refer section 8-3 of chapter 8) classes, the JmsTemplate class provides a layer of abstraction so that you don't have to deal with lower-level JMS API.

The following example listing shows how the JmsTemplate class is configured in the application context XML file of ch10-bankapp project to send messages to the embedded ActiveMQ instance:

Example listing 10-3 – applicationContext.xml – JmsTemplate configuration
Project – ch10-bankapp
Source location - src/main/resources/META-INF/spring

```
<beans .....
    xmlns:amq="http://activemq.apache.org/schema/core"
    xsi:schemaLocation=".....http://activemq.apache.org/schema/core
        http://activemq.apache.org/schema/core/activemq-core.xsd.....">
    .....
    <bean class="org.springframework.jms.core.JmsTemplate" id="jmsTemplate">
        <property name="connectionFactory" ref="cachingConnectionFactory" />
        <property name="defaultDestination" ref="fixedDepositDestination" />
    </bean>

    <amq:queue id="fixedDepositDestination" physicalName="aQueueDestination" />
    <amq:queue id="emailQueueDestination" physicalName="emailQueueDestination" />
    .....
</beans>
```

JmsTemplate's connectionFactory property specifies the JMS ConnectionFactory that is used for creating a connection with the JMS provider. JmsTemplate's defaultDestination property refers to the default JMS destination to which the JmsTemplate sends JMS messages. In the above example listing, connectionFactory property refers to the CachingConnectionFactory instance (refer example listing 10-2), and defaultDestination property refers to the JMS queue destination created by amq schema's <queue> element.

The amq schema's <queue> element creates a JMS queue in ActiveMQ. In example listing 10-3, the first <queue> element creates a JMS queue named aQueueDestination, and the second <queue> element creates a JMS queue named emailQueueDestination. The physicalName attribute refers to the name with which the JMS queue is created in ActiveMQ, and the id attribute refers to the name with which the JMS queue is accessed by other beans in the Spring container. In example listing 10-3, JmsTemplate's defaultDestination property refers to the id attribute of the <queue> element that creates the aQueueDestination JMS destination; therefore, the aQueueDestination is the default JMS destination to which the JmsTemplate instance sends JMS messages.

JMS Session used by JmsTemplate has the acknowledgement mode set to *auto-acknowledge* and is *not* transactional in nature. You should consider using a transactional JMS Session if you want to send and/or receive a group of messages within a transaction. When a transaction is committed, all produced messages are *sent* and all consumed messages are *acknowledged*. A transaction rollback results in *destruction* of produced messages and *redelivery* of consumed messages. If you want JmsTemplate to use transactional Sessions, set JmsTemplate's transacted property to true.

Instead of setting JmsTemplate's transacted property to true for obtaining a transactional Session, you can use JmsTemplate with Spring's JmsTransactionManager. JmsTransactionManager ensures that you *always* get a transactional JMS Session. The primary benefit of using JmsTransactionManager is that by using it you can leverage Spring's transaction management abstraction.

Let's now look at how JmsTransactionManager is configured, and how JMS messages are sent by JmsTemplate within a transaction.

Sending JMS messages within a transaction

In chapter 8, we saw that Spring provides a couple of PlatformTransactionManager implementations that provide resource-specific transaction management. In your JMS applications, you can use Spring's JmsTransactionManager (an implementation of PlatformTransactionManager) class for managing transactions for a single JMS ConnectionFactory. As JmsTransactionManager implements PlatformTransactionManager, you can use TransactionTemplate for programmatically managing JMS transactions or you can use @Transactional annotation for declaratively managing JMS transactions.

The following example listing shows the configuration of Spring's JmsTransactionManager in application context XML file:

Example listing 10-4 – applicationContext.xml – JmsTransactionManager configuration
Project – ch10-bankapp
Source location - src/main/resources/META-INF/spring

```
<tx:annotation-driven />

<bean id="jmsTxManager"
      class="org.springframework.jms.connection.JmsTransactionManager">
    <property name="connectionFactory" ref="cachingConnectionFactory" />
</bean>
```

JmsTransactionManager's connectionFactory property specifies reference to the JMS ConnectionFactory for which the JmsTransactionManager manages transactions. In the above example listing, connectionFactory property refers to the CachingConnectionFactory bean (refer example listing 10-2). As the CachingConnectionFactory caches JMS Sessions, using CachingConnectionFactory with JmsTransactionManager results in reduced utilization of resources. The <annotation-driven> element of Spring's tx schema specifies that the application uses declarative transaction management. The <annotation-driven> element doesn't refer to the JmsTransactionManager bean because the application also uses a DataSourceTransactionManager for managing database transactions.

The following example listing shows the FixedDepositServiceImpl class that makes use of JmsTemplate to send messages to the embedded ActiveMQ broker:

Example listing 10-5 – FixedDepositServiceImpl class – send JMS messages using JmsTemplate
Project – ch10-bankapp
Source location - src/main/java/sample/spring/chapter10/bankapp/service

```
package sample.spring.chapter10.bankapp.service;

import javax.jms.*;
import org.springframework.jms.core.JmsTemplate;
import org.springframework.jms.core.MessageCreator;

@Service(value = "fixedDepositService")
public class FixedDepositServiceImpl implements FixedDepositService {
    @Autowired
    private JmsTemplate jmsTemplate;
    .....
```

```
    @Override
    @Transactional("jmsTxManager")
    public void createFixedDeposit(final FixedDepositDetails fixedDepositDetails)
            throws Exception {

        jmsTemplate.send("emailQueueDestination", new MessageCreator() {
            public Message createMessage(Session session) throws JMSException {
                TextMessage textMessage = session.createTextMessage();
                textMessage.setText(fixedDepositDetails.getEmail());
                return textMessage;
            }
        });

       // --this JMS message goes to the default destination configured for the JmsTemplate
        jmsTemplate.send(new MessageCreator() {
            public Message createMessage(Session session) throws JMSException {
                ObjectMessage objectMessage = session.createObjectMessage();
                objectMessage.setObject(fixedDepositDetails);
                return objectMessage;
            }
        });
    }
    .....
}
```

The above example listing shows that `JmsTemplate`'s `send` method is used to send messages to `emailQueueDestination` and `aQueueDestination` JMS destinations. Refer example listing 10-3 to see how these JMS destinations are configured in the application context XML file. The name of the JMS destination passed to `JmsTemplate`'s `send` method is resolved to the actual JMS `Destination` object by Spring's `DynamicDestinationResolver` instance (an implementation of Spring's `DestinationResolver` interface). If you have configured JMS destinations in the application context XML file using amq schema's <queue> (or <topic>) element, the JMS destination name passed to the `JmsTemplate`'s `send` message is the value of the `id` attribute of the <queue> (or <topic>) element. For instance, if we want to send message to `aQueueDestination` destination (refer example listing 10-3), then the destination name passed to the `send` method is `fixedDepositDestination`.

In example listing 10-5, the `FixedDepositServiceImpl`'s `createFixedDeposit` method is annotated with `@Transactional("jmsTxManager")`, which means that the `createFixedDeposit` method executes within a transaction, and the transaction is managed by `jmsTxManager` transaction manager (refer example listing 10-4 to see how `jmsTxManager` is configured). `JmsTemplate`'s `send` method accepts the name of the JMS destination and a `MessageCreator` instance. If you don't specify the JMS destination, the `send` method sends the message to the *default* destination that you configured for the `JmsTemplate` using `defaultDestination` property (refer example listing 10-3).

In `MessageCreator`'s `createMessage` method you create the JMS message that you want to send. You don't need to explicitly handle checked exceptions thrown by JMS API, as they are taken care by the `JmsTemplate` itself. Example listing 10-5 shows that if you are using `JmsTemplate`, you don't need to explicitly obtain `Connection` from `ConnectionFactory`, create `Session` from `Connection`, and so on, for sending JMS messages. This shows that by using `JmsTemplate` you don't have to deal with lower-level JMS API details.

In example listing 10-5, the `TextMessage` and `ObjectMessage` instances represent JMS messages. Both, `TextMessage` and `ObjectMessage` classes implement `javax.jms.Message` interface. In `ch10-bankapp` project, the `TextMessage` instance has been used to send the email id (a simple string value) of the customer requesting to open a fixed deposit, and the `ObjectMessage` instance has been used to send `FixedDepositDetails` object (a `Serializable` object) that contains fixed deposit information. As the

FixedDepositServiceImpl's createFixedDeposit method executes within a JMS transaction, either both the messages are sent to the ActiveMQ instance or none.

Instead of using @Transactional annotation, you can programmatically manage JMS transactions by using the TransactionTemplate class (refer section 8-5 of chapter 8). The following example listing shows how you can configure the TransactionTemplate class to use JmsTransactionManager for transaction management:

Example listing 10-6 – TransactionTemplate configuration

```
<bean id="jmsTxManager"
        class="org.springframework.jms.connection.JmsTransactionManager">
    <property name="connectionFactory" ref="cachingConnectionFactory" />
</bean>

<bean id="transactionTemplate"
        class="org.springframework.transaction.support.TransactionTemplate">
    <property name="transactionManager" ref="jmsTxManager" />
</bean>
```

In the above example listing, TransactionTemplate's transactionManager property refers to the JmsTransactionManager bean.

Once you have configured the TransactionTemplate class, you can use it to manage JMS transactions. The following example listing shows a variant of FixedDepositServiceImpl's createFixedDeposit method that uses TransactionTemplate for managing JMS transactions:

Example listing 10-7 – Programmatically managing JMS transactions using TransactionTemplate

```
package sample.spring.chapter10.bankapp.service;

import javax.jms.*;
import org.springframework.jms.core.JmsTemplate;
import org.springframework.jms.core.MessageCreator;

@Service(value = "fixedDepositService")
public class FixedDepositServiceImpl implements FixedDepositService {
    @Autowired
    private JmsTemplate jmsTemplate;

    @Autowired
    private TransactionTemplate transactionTemplate;
    .....
    public void createFixedDeposit(final FixedDepositDetails fixedDepositDetails)
           throws Exception {

        transactionTemplate.execute(new TransactionCallbackWithoutResult() {
            protected void doInTransactionWithoutResult(TransactionStatus status) {
                jmsTemplate.send("emailQueueDestination", new MessageCreator() { ..... });
                jmsTemplate.send(new MessageCreator() { ..... });
            }
        });
    }
    .....
}
```

The above example listing shows that JMS messages are sent from within the doInTransaction method of TransactionCallbackWithoutResult class so that they are in the same JMS transaction. This is similar to how we programmatically managed JDBC transactions (refer section 8-5 of chapter 8) using TransactionTemplate.

So far we have seen examples in which JmsTemplate is used to send messages to a *pre-configured* JMS destination. Let's now look at how to configure JmsTemplate class if an application uses *dynamic* JMS destinations.

Dynamic JMS destinations and JmsTemplate configuration

If your application uses dynamic JMS destinations (that is, JMS destinations are created by the application at runtime), you must specify the JMS destination type (queue or topic) using pubSubDomain property of JmsTemplate. The pubSubDomain property is used to determine the JMS destination type to which the JmsTemplate sends JMS messages. If you don't specify the pubSubDomain property, JMS queue is assumed to be the destination type.

The following example listing shows the JmsTemplate that sends messages to a dynamically created JMS topic:

Example listing 10-8 – Using JmsTemplate for sending messages to dynamic JMS topic destinations

```
------------- applicationContext.xml --------------

    <bean class="org.springframework.jms.core.JmsTemplate" id="jmsTemplate">
        <property name="connectionFactory" ref="cachingConnectionFactory" />
        <property name="defaultDestination" ref="fixedDepositDestination" />
        <property name="pubSubDomain" value="true" />
    </bean>

----------------- Dynamic topic creation -----------------

        jmsTemplate.send("dynamicTopic", new MessageCreator() {
            public Message createMessage(Session session) throws JMSException {
                session.createTopic("dynamicTopic");
                ObjectMessage objectMessage = session.createObjectMessage();
                objectMessage.setObject(someObject);
                return objectMessage;
            }
        });
```

In the above example listing, JmsTemplate's pubSubDomain property is set to true, which means that when dynamic destinations are used, Spring resolves a dynamic destination's name to a JMS *topic*. Notice that the name of the JMS destination passed to JmsTemplate's send method is dynamicTopic, and a JMS topic with the same name is created by MessageCreator's createMessage method. As no dynamicTopic destination is configured in the application context XML file, Spring doesn't know whether the dynamicTopic destination is a queue or a topic. As JmsTemplate's pubSubDomain property is set to true, Spring's DynamicDestinationResolver resolves dynamicTopic destination name to the dynamicTopic JMS topic created at runtime by MessageCreator's createMessage method. If you had *not* set JmsTemplate's pubSubDomain property, Spring's DynamicDestinationResolver would have tried resolving dynamicTopic destination name to a JMS *queue* named dynamicTopic.

Let's now look at how JmsTemplate simplifies sending Java objects as JMS messages.

JmsTemplate and message conversion

JmsTemplate defines multiple convertAndSend methods that convert and send a Java object as a JMS message. By default, JmsTemplate is configured with a SimpleMessageConverter instance (an implementation of Spring's MessageConverter interface) that converts Java objects to JMS messages, and vice versa.

MessageConverter interface defines the following methods:

- Object toMessage(Object object, Session session) – converts the Java object (represented by object argument) to a JMS Message using the supplied JMS Session (represented by session argument)
- Object fromMessage(Message message) - converts Message argument to Java object

Spring's SimpleMessageConverter class provides conversion between String and JMS TextMessage, byte[] and JMS BytesMessage, Map and JMS MapMessage, and between Serializable object and JMS ObjectMessage. If you want to modify the JMS Message created by JmsTemplate's convertAndSend method, you can use a MessagePostProcessor implementation to make modifications.

The following example listing shows a scenario in which a MessagePostProcessor implementation is used to modify the JMS message created by JmsTemplate's convertAndSend method:

Example listing 10-9 – JmsTemplate's convertAndSend method usage

```
jmsTemplate.convertAndSend("aDestination", "Hello, World !!",
    new MessagePostProcessor() {
        public Message postProcessMessage(Message message) throws JMSException {
            message.setBooleanProperty("printOnConsole", true);
            return message;
        }
    }
);
```

In the above example listing, 'Hello, World !!' string is passed to the convertAndSend method. The convertAndSend method creates a JMS TextMessage instance and makes it available to the MessagePostProcessor implementation to post-process the message *before* it is sent. In the above example listing, MessagePostProcessor's postProcessMessage method sets a printOnConsole boolean type property on the JMS message before it is sent to aDestination.

So far we have seen how to send JMS messages to JMS destinations using JmsTemplate. Let's now look at how to receive JMS messages from JMS destinations using JmsTemplate and Spring's *message listener containers*.

10-4 Receiving JMS messages

You can receive JMS messages *synchronously* using JmsTemplate and *asynchronously* using Spring's message listener containers.

Synchronously receiving JMS messages using JmsTemplate

JmsTemplate defines multiple receive methods that you can use to *synchronously* receive JMS messages. It is important to note that call to JmsTemplate's receive method causes the calling thread to block until a JMS message is obtained from the JMS destination. To ensure that the calling thread is not blocked indefinitely, you must specify an appropriate value for JmsTemplate's receiveTimeout property. The receiveTimeout property specifies the amount of time (in milliseconds) the calling thread should wait before giving up.

`JmsTemplate` also defines multiple `receiveAndConvert` methods that automatically convert the received JMS message to a Java object. By default, `JmsTemplate` uses `SimpleMessageConverter` for performing conversions.

Asynchronously receiving JMS messages using message listener containers

You can use Spring's message listener containers to *asynchronously* receive JMS messages. As a message listener container takes care of transaction and resource management aspects, you can focus on writing the message processing logic.

A message listener container receives messages from JMS destinations and dispatches them to JMS `MessageListener` implementations for processing. In the following example listing, the `<listener-container>` element of Spring's `jms` schema creates a `JmsListenerContainerFactory` instance that holds the configuration of message listener containers created for each `<listener>` sub-element:

Example listing 10-10 – applicationContext.xml – message listener container configuration
Project – ch10-bankapp
Source location - src/main/resources/META-INF/spring

```
<beans ..... xmlns:jms="http://www.springframework.org/schema/jms"
          xsi:schemaLocation=".....
                    http://www.springframework.org/schema/jms
                    http://www.springframework.org/schema/jms/spring-jms.xsd">
    .....
    <jms:listener-container connection-factory="cachingConnectionFactory"
        destination-type="queue"  transaction-manager="jmsTxManager">

        <jms:listener destination="aQueueDestination" ref="fixedDepositMessageListener" />
        <jms:listener destination="emailQueueDestination" ref="emailMessageListener" />
    </jms:listener-container>

    <bean class="sample.spring.chapter10.bankapp.jms.EmailMessageListener"
          id="emailMessageListener" />

    <bean class="sample.spring.chapter10.bankapp.jms.FixedDepositMessageListener"
          id="fixedDepositMessageListener" />
    .....
</beans>
```

In the above example listing, Spring's `jms` schema is included so that its elements are available in the application context XML file. The `<listener-container>` element configures a message listener container for *each* of the `MessageListeners` defined by `<listener>` sub-elements.

The `connection-factory` attribute refers to the JMS `ConnectionFactory` bean that the message listener container uses to obtain connections to the JMS provider. As we are using Spring's `CachingConnectionFactory` in the MyBank application, the `connection-factory` attribute refers to the `cachingConnectionFactory` bean (refer example listing 10-2).

The `destination-type` attribute specifies the JMS destination type with which the message listener container is associated with. The possible values that the `destination-type` attribute can accept are: `queue`, `topic` and `durableTopic`.

The `transaction-manager` attribute specifies a `PlatformTransactionManager` implementation that ensures JMS message *reception* and message *processing* by `MessageListeners` occur within a transaction. In the above example listing, the `transaction-manager` attribute refers to the `JmsTransactionManager` bean (refer example listing 10-4). If a `MessageListener` implementation interacts with other transactional resources also, consider using Spring's JtaTransactionManager instead of JmsTransactionManager. In a standalone application, you can use embedded transaction managers, like Atomikos (http://www.atomikos.com/), to perform JTA transactions in your application.

> The <listener-container> element creates an instance of Spring's DefaultJmsListenerContainerFactory (implementation of JmsListenerContainerFactory interface) that creates an instance of DefaultMessageListenerContainer corresponding to each JMS MessageListeners specified by <listener> sub-elements.

A <listener> element specifies a JMS MessageListener that is invoked *asynchronously* by the message listener container. The <listener> element's destination attribute specifies the JMS destination name from which MessageListener receives messages. The <listener> element's ref attribute refers to the MessageListener responsible for processing JMS messages received from the destination. Example listing 10-10 shows that the FixedDepositMessageListener (a MessageListener implementation) is responsible for processing messages received from aQueueDestination destination, and the EmailMessageListener (a MessageListener implementation) is responsible for processing messages received from emailQueueDestination destination.

MessageListener interface defines an onMessage method that is *asynchronously* invoked by the message listener container. The message listener container passes the JMS Message received from the JMS destination to the onMessage method. The onMessage method is responsible for processing the received JMS message.

The following example listing shows implementation of FixedDepositMessageListener class whose onMessage method retrieves FixedDepositDetails object from the JMS Message, and then saves the fixed deposit information into the database:

Example listing 10-11 – FixedDepositMessageListener class – processing JMS message
Project – ch10-bankapp
Source location - src/main/java/sample/spring/chapter10/bankapp/jms

```
package sample.spring.chapter10.bankapp.jms;

import javax.jms.MessageListener;
import javax.jms.ObjectMessage;
import sample.spring.chapter10.bankapp.domain.FixedDepositDetails;
.....
public class FixedDepositMessageListener implements MessageListener {
    @Autowired
    @Qualifier(value = "fixedDepositDao")
    private FixedDepositDao myFixedDepositDao;

    @Autowired
    private BankAccountDao bankAccountDao;

    @Transactional("dbTxManager")
    public int createFixedDeposit(FixedDepositDetails fixedDepositDetails) {
        bankAccountDao.subtractFromAccount(fixedDepositDetails.getBankAccountId(),
                        fixedDepositDetails.getFixedDepositAmount());
        return myFixedDepositDao.createFixedDeposit(fixedDepositDetails);
    }

    @Override
    public void onMessage(Message message) {
        ObjectMessage objectMessage = (ObjectMessage) message;
        FixedDepositDetails fixedDepositDetails = null;
```

```
        try {
            fixedDepositDetails = (FixedDepositDetails) objectMessage.getObject();
        } catch (JMSException e) {
            e.printStackTrace();
        }
        if (fixedDepositDetails != null) {
            createFixedDeposit(fixedDepositDetails);
        }
    }
}
```

The above example listing shows that the `FixedDepositMessageListener's createFixedDeposit` method is responsible for saving the fixed deposit information into the database. As the `createFixedDeposit` method is annotated with `@Transactional("dbTxManager")` annotation, it is executed under the transaction managed by `dbTxManager` (a `DataSourceTransactionManager`). The message listener container receives the JMS message and executes `FixedDepositMessageListener's onMessage` method under the transaction managed by `JmsTransactionManager` (refer example listing 10-10).

As `onMessage` and `createFixedDeposit` methods execute under different transaction managers, the database update is *not* rolled back if the JMS transaction fails for some reason, and the JMS message is *not* redelivered to the `MessageListener` if the database update fails for some reason. If you want JMS message reception (and processing) and the database update to be part of the same transaction, you should use JTA transactions.

Let's look at how we can simplify configuration of JMS `MessageListeners` by using `@JmsListener` annotation.

Registering JMS listener endpoints using @JmsListener

Instead of creating `javax.jms.MessageListener` implementations (like `EmailMessageListener` and `FixedDepositMessageListener` classes of `ch10-bankapp` project), you can use `@JmsListener` annotation to designate a Spring bean method as a message listener.

You enable use of `@JmsListener` annotation by using `<annotation-driven>` element of Spring's `jms` schema, as shown here:

```
<jms:annotation-driven />
```

> If you are using Java-based configuration, you can use `@EnableJms` annotation (refer `@Configuration` annotated `JmsConfig` class of `ch10-bankapp-javaconfig` project) to enable support for `@JmsListener` annotation.

The `ch10-bankapp` project contains a `MyAnnotatedJmsListener` class that defines `@JmsListener` annotated `processEmailMessage` and `processFixedDeposit` methods. The `processEmailMessage` serves the same purpose as the `EmailMessageListener's onMessage` method, and the `processFixedDeposit` method serves the same purpose as the `FixedDepositMessageListener's onMessage` method. The following example listing shows the `MyAnnotatedJmsListener` class:

Example listing 10-12 – `MyAnnotatedJmsListener` class - `@JmsListener` annotation usage
Project – `ch10-bankapp`
Source location - `src/main/java/sample/spring/chapter10/bankapp/jms`

```
package sample.spring.chapter10.bankapp.jms;

import org.springframework.jms.annotation.JmsListener;
import javax.jms.Message;
.....
```

```
@Component
public class MyAnnotatedJmsListener {
    @Autowired
    private transient MailSender mailSender;
    .....
    @JmsListener(destination = "emailQueueDestination")
    public void processEmailMessage(Message message) { ..... }

    @JmsListener(destination = "aQueueDestination")
    public void processFixedDeposit(Message message) { ..... }
    .....
}
```

In the above example listing, @JmsListener's destination attribute specifies the JMS destination from which the method receives JMS messages. For instance, messages sent to emailQueueDestination are received and processed by processEmailMessage method.

As we don't create javax.jms.MessageListener implementations when using @JmsListener annotation, we need to modify the JMS message listener container configuration accordingly:

Example listing 10-13 – Message listener container configuration for using @JmsListener

```
    <jms:listener-container connection-factory="cachingConnectionFactory"
        destination-type="queue" transaction-manager="jmsTxManager"
        factory-id="jmsListenerContainerFactory" />
```

We've specified the factory-id attribute of <listener-container> element to expose the message container listener configuration as a bean named jmsListenerContainerFactory. By default, Spring looks for a bean named jmsListenerContainerFactory to create message listener containers for @JmsListener annotated methods.

Let's look at how we can use spring-messaging module to build JMS-based applications.

Messaging using spring-messaging module

Spring provides a spring-messaging module that abstracts key concepts required in developing messaging applications. Instead of using JMS-specific objects, you can use abstractions defined in spring-messaging module to build your JMS applications. To use spring-messaging module's abstractions for building JMS applications, you need to make following changes in your code:

- use JmsMessagingTemplate instead of JmsTemplate for sending and receiving JMS messages. JmsMessagingTemplate is a wrapper around JmsTemplate instance that uses messaging abstractions provided by spring-messaging module.

- use org.springframework.messaging.Message instead of javax.jms.Message to represent a JMS message. org.springframework.messaging.Message is the spring-messaging module's abstraction for javax.jms.Message.

- use MessageBuilder instead of MessageCreator. MessageBuilder is the spring-messaging module's abstraction for MessageCreator.

- use @JmsListener instead of implementing MessageListener interface. @JmsListener methods can have flexible signatures. For instance, you can pass JMS Session, message headers, and so on, to a @JmsListener annotated method.

The ch10-bankapp-javaconfig project uses spring-messaging module's abstraction for sending and receiving JMS messages. The following example listing shows the @Configuration annotated class that configures an instance of JmsMessagingTemplate for sending messages:

Example listing 10-14 – JmsConfig class – configuring JmsMessagingTemplate
Project – ch10-bankapp-javaconfig
Source location - src/main/java/sample/spring/chapter10/bankapp

```
package sample.spring.chapter10.bankapp;

import org.springframework.jms.annotation.EnableJms;
import org.springframework.jms.core.JmsMessagingTemplate;
.....
@ImportResource(locations = "classpath:META-INF/spring/applicationContext.xml")
@Configuration
@EnableJms
public class JmsConfig {
    .....
    @Bean
    public CachingConnectionFactory cachingConnectionFactory(
                ActiveMQConnectionFactory activeMQConnectionFactory) { ..... }
    .....
    @Bean

    public JmsMessagingTemplate jmsMessagingTemplate(
                CachingConnectionFactory cachingConnectionFactory) {
        JmsMessagingTemplate jmsMessagingTemplate =
            new JmsMessagingTemplate(cachingConnectionFactory);
        jmsMessagingTemplate.setDefaultDestinationName("fixedDepositDestination");
        return jmsMessagingTemplate;
    }
}
```

In the above example listing, @EnableJms annotation enables use of @JmsListener annotation for specifying JMS listener endpoints. The jmsMessagingTemplate method creates an instance of JmsMessagingTemplate using the supplied CachingConnectionFactory. The JmsMessagingTemplate creates an instance of JmsTemplate from the given CachingConnectionFactory instance. If you want to use JmsTemplate configuration (like, default destination), pass an instance of JmsTemplate instance to JmsMessagingTemplate's constructor.

The following example listing shows the FixedDepositServiceImpl class that uses JmsMessagingTemplate for sending messages to the embedded ActiveMQ:

Example listing 10-15 – FixedDepositServiceImpl class – JmsMessagingTemplate usage
Project – ch10-bankapp-javaconfig
Source location - src/main/java/sample/spring/chapter10/bankapp/service

```
package sample.spring.chapter10.bankapp.service;

import org.springframework.jms.core.JmsMessagingTemplate;
import org.springframework.messaging.support.MessageBuilder;
.....
@Service(value = "fixedDepositService")
public class FixedDepositServiceImpl implements FixedDepositService {
    @Autowired
    private JmsMessagingTemplate jmsMessagingTemplate;
    .....
```

```
    @Transactional(transactionManager = "jmsTxManager")
    public void createFixedDeposit(final FixedDepositDetails fdd) throws Exception {
        jmsMessagingTemplate.send("emailQueueDestination",
             MessageBuilder.withPayload(fdd.getEmail()).build());
        jmsMessagingTemplate.send(MessageBuilder.withPayload(fdd).build());
    }
    .....
}
```

In the above example listing, FixedDepositServiceImpl's createFixedDeposit method uses JmsMessagingTemplate's send method to send messages to embedded ActiveMQ. The send method accepts the JMS destination name and the message (an instance of org.springframework.messaging.Message) to send. MessageBuilder class defines static methods that simplify creating a message. The withPayload method specifies the message payload.

The following example listing shows MyAnnotatedJmsListener class that defines @JmsListener annotated methods that asynchronously receive messages from the embedded ActiveMQ:

Example listing 10-16 – MyAnnotatedJmsListener – processing JMS messages
Project – ch10-bankapp-javaconfig
Source location - src/main/java/sample/spring/chapter10/bankapp/jms

```
package sample.spring.chapter10.bankapp.jms;

import org.springframework.mail.MailSender;
import org.springframework.messaging.Message;
.....
@Component
public class MyAnnotatedJmsListener {
    .....
    private transient SimpleMailMessage simpleMailMessage;

    @JmsListener(destination = "emailQueueDestination")
    public void processEmailMessage(Message<String> message) {
        simpleMailMessage.setTo(message.getPayload());
        .....
    }

    @JmsListener(destination = "fixedDepositDestination")
    public void processFixedDeposit(Message<FixedDepositDetails> message) {
        FixedDepositDetails fdd = message.getPayload();
        .....
    }
    .....
}
```

In the above example listing, the processEmailMessage and processFixedDeposit methods accept an argument of type org.springframework.messaging.Message representing the JMS message received from ActiveMQ. The Message's getPayload method returns the message payload.

In this section, we looked at how to send and receive JMS messages using Spring. Let's now look at how Spring simplifies sending emails.

10-5 Sending emails

Spring simplifies sending emails from an application by providing a layer of abstraction on top of JavaMail API. Spring takes care of resource management and exception handling aspects, so that you can focus on writing the necessary logic required to prepare the email message.

To send emails using Spring, you first need to configure Spring's `JavaMailSenderImpl` class in your application context XML file. The `JavaMailSenderImpl` class acts as a wrapper around JavaMail API. The following example listing shows how `JavaMailSenderImpl` class is configured in MyBank application:

Example listing 10-17 – applicationContext.xml – JavaMailSenderImpl class configuration
Project – ch10-bankapp
Source location - src/main/resources/META-INF/spring

```
<bean id="mailSender" class="org.springframework.mail.javamail.JavaMailSenderImpl">
    <property name="host" value="${email.host}" />
    <property name="protocol" value="${email.protocol}" />
    .....
    <property name="javaMailProperties">
        <props>
            <prop key="mail.smtp.auth">true</prop>
            <prop key="mail.smtp.starttls.enable">true</prop>
        </props>
    </property>
</bean>
```

`JavaMailSenderImpl` class defines properties, like `host`, `port`, `protocol`, and so on, that provide information about the mail server. The `javaMailProperties` property specifies configuration information that is used by `JavaMailSenderImpl` instance for creating a JavaMail `Session` object. The `mail.smtp.auth` property value is set to `true`, which means that SMTP (Simple Mail Transfer Protocol) is used for authentication with the mail server. The `mail.smtp.starttls.enable` property value is set to `true`, which means TLS-protected connection is used for authenticating with the mail server.

Example listing 10-17 shows that the values of some of the properties of `JavaMailSenderImpl` class are specified using property placeholders. For instance, `host` property value is specified as `${email.host}` and `protocol` property value as `${email.protocol}`. The value of these property placeholders are specified in `email.properties` file (located in `src/main/resources/META-INF/spring` directory). The following example listing shows the contents of `email.properties` file:

Example listing 10-18 – email.properties
Project – ch10-bankapp
Source location - src/main/resources/META-INF/spring

```
email.host=smtp.gmail.com
email.port=587
email.protocol=smtp
email.username=<enter-email-id>
email.password=<enter-email-password>
```

The above example listing shows that `email.properties` file contains mail server information, communication protocol information, and the mail account to use for connecting to the mail server. The properties specified in the `email.properties` file are used to configure the `JavaMailSenderImpl` instance (refer example listing 10-17).

> The classes that provide abstraction on top of JavaMail API are defined in spring-context-support JAR file. So, to use Spring's support for sending emails, you must define that your application depends on spring-context-support JAR file.

Spring's SimpleMailMessage class represents a simple email message. SimpleMailMessage defines properties, like to, cc, subject, text, and so on, that you can set to construct the email message that you want to send from your application.

The following example listing shows the MyBank's application context XML file that configures two SimpleMailMessage instances corresponding to the two email messages that we send from the MyBank application:

Example listing 10-19 – applicationContext.xml – SimpleMailMessage configuration
Project – ch10-bankapp
Source location - src/main/resources/META-INF/spring

```
<bean class="org.springframework.mail.SimpleMailMessage" id="requestReceivedTemplate">
    <property name="subject" value="${email.subject.request.received}" />
    <property name="text" value="${email.text.request.received}" />
</bean>

<bean class="org.springframework.mail.SimpleMailMessage" id="requestProcessedTemplate">
    <property name="subject" value="${email.subject.request.processed}" />
    <property name="text" value="${email.text.request.processed}" />
</bean>
```

In the above example listing, the requestReceivedTemplate bean represents the email message that is sent to the customer informing that the request for opening a fixed deposit has been received, and the requestProcessedTemplate bean represents the email message that is sent to the customer informing that the request for opening the fixed deposit has been successfully processed. SimpleMailMessage's subject property specifies the subject line of the email, and the text property specifies the body of the email. The values for these properties are defined in the emailtemplate.properties file, as shown in the following example listing:

Example listing 10-20 – emailtemplate.properties
Project – ch10-bankapp
Source location - src/main/resources/META-INF/spring

```
email.subject.request.received=Fixed deposit request received
email.text.request.received=Your request for creating the fixed deposit has been received

email.subject.request.processed=Fixed deposit request processed
email.text.request.processed=Your request for creating the fixed deposit has been processed
```

We have so far seen how to configure JavaMailSenderImpl and SimpleMailMessage classes in the application context XML file. Let's now look at how to send email messages.

The following example listing shows the MyBank application's EmailMessageListener class (a JMS MessageListener implementation) that retrieves customer's email address from the JMS message and sends an email to the customer informing that the request for opening a fixed deposit has been received:

Example listing 10-21 – EmailMessageListener class – sending emails using MailSender
Project – ch10-bankapp
Source location - src/main/java/sample/spring/chapter10/bankapp/jms

```
package sample.spring.chapter10.bankapp.jms;

import org.springframework.mail.MailSender;
import org.springframework.mail.SimpleMailMessage;
.....
public class EmailMessageListener implements MessageListener {
    @Autowired
    private transient MailSender mailSender;

    @Autowired
    @Qualifier("requestReceivedTemplate")
    private transient SimpleMailMessage simpleMailMessage;

    public void sendEmail() {
        mailSender.send(simpleMailMessage);
    }

    public void onMessage(Message message) {
        TextMessage textMessage = (TextMessage) message;
        try {
            simpleMailMessage.setTo(textMessage.getText());
        } catch (Exception e) {
            e.printStackTrace();
        }
        sendEmail();
    }
}
```

As JavaMailSenderImpl class implements Spring's MailSender interface, the JavaMailSenderImpl instance (refer example listing 10-17) is autowired. SimpleMailMessage instance named requestReceivedTemplate (refer example listing 10-19) is also autowired. As SimpleMailMessage's to property identifies the email recipient, the onMessage method retrieves the email id of the customer from the JMS message and sets it as the value of to property. The onMessage method calls sendEmail method that uses MailSender's send method to send the email message represented by the SimpleMailMessage instance.

Spring's MailSender interface represents a generic interface that is independent of JavaMail API, and is suited for sending simple email messages. Spring's JavaMailSender interface (a sub-interface of MailSender) is dependent on JavaMail API, and defines the functionality for sending MIME messages. A MIME message is used if you want to send emails containing inline images, attachments, and so on. A MIME message is represented by a MimeMessage class in JavaMail API. Spring provides a MimeMessageHelper class and a MimeMessagePreparator callback interface that you can use to create and populate a MimeMessage instance.

Preparing MIME messages using MimeMessageHelper

The following example listing shows the MyBank application's FixedDepositProcessorJob class that subtracts the fixed deposit amount from the customer's bank account and sends an email to the customer informing that the request for opening the fixed deposit has been processed:

Example listing 10-22 – FixedDepositProcessorJob class – JavaMailSender usage
Project – ch10-bankapp
Source location - src/main/java/sample/spring/chapter10/bankapp/job

```
package sample.spring.chapter10.bankapp.job;

import javax.mail.internet.MimeMessage;
import org.springframework.mail.javamail.JavaMailSender;

public class FixedDepositProcessorJob {
    .....
    @Autowired
    private transient JavaMailSender mailSender;

    @Autowired
    @Qualifier("requestProcessedTemplate")
    private transient SimpleMailMessage simpleMailMessage;

    private List<FixedDepositDetails> getInactiveFixedDeposits() {
        return myFixedDepositDao.getInactiveFixedDeposits();
    }

    public void sendEmail() throws AddressException, MessagingException {
        List<FixedDepositDetails> inactiveFixedDeposits = getInactiveFixedDeposits();

        for (FixedDepositDetails fixedDeposit : inactiveFixedDeposits) {
            MimeMessage mimeMessage = mailSender.createMimeMessage();
            MimeMessageHelper mimeMessageHelper = new MimeMessageHelper(mimeMessage);
            mimeMessageHelper.setTo(fixedDeposit.getEmail());
            mimeMessageHelper.setSubject(simpleMailMessage.getSubject());
            mimeMessageHelper.setText(simpleMailMessage.getText());
            mailSender.send(mimeMessage);
        }
        myFixedDepositDao.setFixedDepositsAsActive(inactiveFixedDeposits);
    }
}
```

In the above example listing, JavaMailSender's send method is used to send a MIME message. JavaMailSenderImpl and SimpleMailMessage named requestProcessedTemplate (refer example listing 10-19) are autowired into FixedDepositProcessorJob. The mailSender instance variable is defined of type JavaMailSender (and not MailSender) because the FixedDepositProcessorJob creates and sends MIME messages. FixedDepositProcessorJob's sendEmail method creates an instance of a MimeMessage using JavaMailSender's createMimeMessage method. Spring's MimeMessageHelper is then used to populate the MimeMessage instance with to, subject and text properties.

Preparing MIME messages using MimeMessagePreparator

The following example listing shows how the FixedDepositProcessorJob's sendEmail method can be rewritten using Spring's MimeMessagePreparator callback interface instead of MimeMessageHelper:

Example listing 10-23 – MimeMessagePreparator usage

```
import javax.mail.Message;
import javax.mail.internet.InternetAddress;
import org.springframework.mail.javamail.MimeMessagePreparator;

public class FixedDepositProcessorJob {
```

```
.....
public void sendEmail_() throws AddressException, MessagingException {
    List<FixedDepositDetails> inactiveFixedDeposits = getInactiveFixedDeposits();
    for (final FixedDepositDetails fixedDeposit : inactiveFixedDeposits) {
        mailSender.send(new MimeMessagePreparator() {
            @Override
            public void prepare(MimeMessage mimeMessage) throws Exception {
                mimeMessage.setRecipient(Message.RecipientType.TO,
                        new InternetAddress(fixedDeposit.getEmail()));
                mimeMessage.setSubject(simpleMailMessage.getText());
                mimeMessage.setText(simpleMailMessage.getText());
            }
        });
    }
    myFixedDepositDao.setFixedDepositsAsActive(inactiveFixedDeposits);
}
}
```

In the above example listing, an instance of MimeMessagePreparator is passed to JavaMailSender's send method to prepare a MimeMessage instance for sending. MimeMessagePreparator's prepare method provides a new instance of MimeMessage that you need to populate. In the above example listing, notice that setting the MimeMessage's recipient property requires you to deal with lower-level JavaMail API. On the other hand, in example listing 10-22, MimeMessageHelper's setTo method simply accepted an email id string to set the MimeMessage's recipient property. For this reason, you should consider using MimeMessageHelper to populate the MimeMessage instance passed to the prepare method of MimeMessagePreparator.

Let's now look at how you can use Spring to execute a task asynchronously, and to schedule execution of a task in the future.

10-6 Task scheduling and asynchronous execution

You can asynchronously execute java.lang.Runnable tasks using Spring's TaskExecutor, and you can schedule execution of java.lang.Runnable tasks using Spring's TaskScheduler. Instead of directly using TaskExecutor and TaskScheduler, you can use Spring's @Async and @Scheduled annotations to execute a method asynchronously and to schedule execution of a method, respectively.

Let's first look at TaskExecutor and TaskScheduler interfaces.

TaskExecutor interface

Java 5 introduced the concept of *executors* for executing java.lang.Runnable tasks. An executor implements java.util.concurrent.Executor interface that defines a single method, execute(Runnable runnable). Spring's TaskExecutor extends java.util.concurrent.Executor interface. Spring provides a couple of TaskExecutor implementations that you can choose from depending upon your application's requirements. For instance, ThreadPoolTaskExecutor asynchronously executes tasks using a thread from a thread pool, SyncTaskExecutor executes tasks synchronously, SimpleAsyncTaskExecutor asynchronously executes each task in a new thread, WorkManagerTaskExecutor uses CommonJ WorkManager for executing tasks, and so on.

ThreadPoolTaskExecutor is the most commonly used TaskExecutor implementation that uses Java 5's ThreadPoolExecutor to execute tasks. The following example listing shows how to configure a ThreadPoolTaskExecutor instance in the application context XML file:

Example listing 10-24 –ThreadPoolTaskExecutor configuration

```
<bean id="myTaskExecutor"
      class="org.springframework.scheduling.concurrent.ThreadPoolTaskExecutor">
    <property name="corePoolSize" value="5" />
    <property name="maxPoolSize" value="10" />
    <property name="queueCapacity" value="15" />
    <property name="rejectedExecutionHandler" ref="abortPolicy"/>
</bean>

<bean id="abortPolicy" class="java.util.concurrent.ThreadPoolExecutor.AbortPolicy"/>
```

The corePoolSize property specifies the minimum number of threads in the thread pool. The maxPoolSize property specifies the maximum number of threads that can be accommodated in the thread pool. The queueCapacity property specifies the maximum number of tasks that can wait in the queue if all the threads in the thread pool are busy executing tasks. The rejectedExecutionHandler property specifies a handler for tasks rejected by the ThreadPoolTaskExecutor. A task is rejected by ThreadPoolTaskExecutor if the queue is full and there is no thread available in the thread pool for executing the submitted task. The rejectedExecutionHandler property refers to an instance of java.util.concurrent.RejectedExecutionHandler object.

In example listing 10-24, the rejectedExecutionHandler property refers to java.util.concurrent.ThreadPoolExecutor.AbortPolicy handler that always throws RejectedExecutionException. The other possible handlers for rejected tasks are: java.util.concurrent.ThreadPoolExecutor.CallerRunsPolicy (the rejected task is executed in caller's thread), java.util.concurrent.ThreadPoolExecutor.DiscardOldestPolicy (the handler discards the oldest task from the queue and retries executing the rejected task), and java.util.concurrent.ThreadPoolExecutor.DiscardPolicy (the handler simply discards the rejected task).

The <executor> element of Spring's task schema simplifies configuring a ThreadPoolTaskExecutor instance, as shown in the following example listing:

Example listing 10-25 –ThreadPoolTaskExecutor configuration using Spring's task schema

```
<beans ..... xmlns:task="http://www.springframework.org/schema/task"
    xsi:schemaLocation=".....http://www.springframework.org/schema/task
        http://www.springframework.org/schema/task/spring-task.xsd">

    <task:executor id=" myTaskExecutor" pool-size="5-10"
        queue-capacity="15" rejection-policy="ABORT" />
</beans>
```

In the above example listing, the <executor> element configures a ThreadPoolTaskExecutor instance. The pool-size attribute specifies the core pool size and the maximum pool size. In the above example listing, 5 is the core pool size and 10 is the maximum pool size. The queue-capacity attribute sets the queueCapacity property, and rejection-policy attribute specifies the handler for rejected tasks. The possible values for rejection-policy attribute are ABORT, CALLER_RUNS, DISCARD_OLDEST, and DISCARD.

Once you have configured a ThreadPoolTaskExecutor instance by explicitly defining it as a Spring bean (refer example listing 10-24) or by using Spring's task schema (refer example listing 10-25), you can inject the ThreadPoolTaskExecutor instance into beans that want to asynchronously execute java.lang.Runnable tasks, as shown in the following example listing:

Example listing 10-26 – Executing tasks using ThreadPoolTaskExecutor

```
import org.springframework.core.task.TaskExecutor;

@Component
public class Sample {
    @Autowired
    private TaskExecutor taskExecutor;

    public void executeTask(Runnable task) {
        taskExecutor.execute(task);
    }
}
```

In the above example listing, an instance of ThreadPoolTaskExecutor is autowired into the Sample class, and is later used by Sample's executeTask method to execute a java.lang.Runnable task.

TaskExecutor executes a java.lang.Runnable task immediately after it is submitted, and the task is executed only *once*. If you want to schedule execution of a java.lang.Runnable task, and you want the task to be executed periodically, you should use a TaskScheduler implementation.

TaskScheduler interface

Spring's TaskScheduler interface provides the abstraction to schedule execution of java.lang.Runnable tasks. Spring's Trigger interface abstracts the time when a java.lang.Runnable task is executed. You associate a TaskScheduler instance with a Trigger instance to schedule execution of java.lang.Runnable tasks. PeriodicTrigger (an implementation of Trigger interface) is used if you want *periodic* execution of tasks. CronTrigger (another implementation of Trigger interface) accepts a *cron expression* that indicates the date/time when the task is executed.

ThreadPoolTaskScheduler is one of the most commonly used implementations of TaskScheduler that internally uses Java 5's ScheduledThreadPoolExecutor to schedule task execution. You can configure a ThreadPoolTaskScheduler implementation and associate it with a Trigger implementation to schedule task execution. The following example listing shows how ThreadPoolTaskScheduler is configured and used:

Example listing 10-27 –ThreadPoolTaskExecutor configuration and usage

```
----------- ThreadPoolTaskScheduler configuration --------------------

    <bean id="myScheduler"
          class="org.springframework.scheduling.concurrent.ThreadPoolTaskScheduler">
        <property name="poolSize" value="5"/>
    </bean>

-------------- ThreadPoolTaskScheduler usage --------------------

import org.springframework.scheduling.TaskScheduler;
import org.springframework.scheduling.support.PeriodicTrigger;

@Component
public class Sample {
    @Autowired
    @Qualifier("myScheduler")
    private TaskScheduler taskScheduler;

    public void executeTask(Runnable task) {
```

```
        taskScheduler.schedule(task, new PeriodicTrigger(5000));
    }
}
```

In the above example listing, ThreadPoolTaskScheduler's poolSize property specifies the number of threads in the thread pool. To schedule a task for execution, ThreadPoolTaskScheduler's schedule method is called, passing the java.lang.Runnable task and a Trigger instance. In the above example listing, PeriodicTrigger instance is passed to ThreadPoolTaskScheduler's schedule method. The argument to the PeriodicTrigger constructor specifies the time interval (in milliseconds) between task executions.

Instead of explicitly defining a ThreadPoolTaskScheduler bean in the application context XML file, you can use <scheduler> element of Spring's task schema to configure a ThreadPoolTaskScheduler instance, as shown here:

```
<task:scheduler id="myScheduler" pool-size="5" />
```

Let's now look at how you can schedule execution of bean methods using <schedule-tasks> element of Spring's task schema.

Scheduling execution of bean methods

The ThreadPoolTaskScheduler instance created by the <scheduler> element can be used by the <scheduled-tasks> element of Spring's task schema to schedule execution of *bean methods*. The following example listing shows how <scheduler> and <scheduled-tasks> elements are used by MyBank application to execute FixedDepositProcessorJob's sendEmail method every 5 seconds:

Example listing 10-28 –<scheduler> and <scheduled-tasks> elements
Project – ch10-bankapp
Source location - src/main/java/sample/spring/chapter10/bankapp/job

```
<task:scheduler id="emailScheduler" pool-size="10" />

<task:scheduled-tasks scheduler="emailScheduler">
    <task:scheduled ref="fixedDepositProcessorJob" method="sendEmail" fixed-rate="5000" />
</task:scheduled-tasks>

<bean id="fixedDepositProcessorJob"
      class="sample.spring.chapter10.bankapp.job.FixedDepositProcessorJob" />
```

In the above example listing, the <scheduler> element configures a ThreadPoolTaskScheduler instance. The id attribute of the <scheduler> element specifies the name with which the ThreadPoolTaskScheduler instance is accessed by other beans in the Spring container. The <scheduled-tasks> element's scheduler attribute refers to the ThreadPoolTaskScheduler instance that is used for scheduling execution of bean methods. In the above example listing, the ThreadPoolTaskScheduler instance created by the <scheduler> element is referenced by the <scheduled-tasks> element's scheduled attribute.

The <scheduled-tasks> element contains one or more <scheduled> elements. The <scheduled> element contains information about the bean method to be executed and the trigger for executing that bean method. The ref attribute specifies reference to the Spring bean, the method attribute specifies the bean's method, and the fixed-rate attribute (an interval-based trigger) specifies the time interval between successive executions. In example listing 10-28, the <scheduled> element specifies that FixedDepositProcessorJob's sendEmail method is executed every 5 seconds.

Instead of using fixed-rate attribute of the <scheduled> element, you can use fixed-delay (an interval-based trigger) or cron (a cron-based trigger) or trigger (reference to a Trigger implementation) attribute, to specify a trigger for the bean method execution.

Let's now look at Spring's @Async and @Scheduled annotations for executing bean methods.

@Async and @Scheduled annotations

If you annotate a bean method with Spring's @Async annotation, it is asynchronously executed by Spring. If you annotate a bean method with Spring's @Scheduled annotation, it is scheduled for execution by Spring.

Use of @Async and @Scheduled annotations is enabled by <annotation-driven> element of Spring's task schema, as shown in the following example listing:

Example listing 10-29 – Enabling @Async and @Scheduled annotations

```
<task:annotation-driven executor="anExecutor" scheduler="aScheduler"/>

<task:executor id="anExecutor"/>

<task:scheduled-tasks scheduler="aScheduler">
    <task:scheduled ref="sampleJob" method="doSomething" fixed-rate="5000" />
</task:scheduled-tasks>
```

The <annotation-driven> element's executor attribute specifies reference to a Spring's TaskExecutor (or Java 5's Executor) instance that is used for executing @Async annotated methods. The scheduler attribute specifies reference to a Spring's TaskScheduler instance that is used for executing @Scheduled annotated methods.

> In Java-based configuration approach, you can enable use of @Async annotation using @EnableAsync, and enable use of @Scheduled annotation using @EnableScheduling annotation. Refer to ch10-bankapp-javaconfig project's TaskConfig class to see usage of @EnableScheduling annotation.

Let's now look at @Async annotation in detail.

@Async annotation

The following example listing highlights some of the important points that you need to know when using @Async annotation:

Example listing 10-30 –@Async annotation usage

```
import java.util.concurrent.Future;
import org.springframework.scheduling.annotation.Async;
import org.springframework.scheduling.annotation.AsyncResult;
import org.springframework.stereotype.Component;

@Component
public class Sample {
    @Async
    public void doA() { ..... }

    @Async(value="someExecutor")
    public void doB(String str) { ..... }

    @Async
    public Future<String> doC() {
        return new AsyncResult<String>("Hello");
    }
```

```
}
```

@Async annotation's value attribute specifies the Spring's TaskExecutor (or Java 5's Executor) instance to use for asynchronously executing the method. As the @Async annotation on the doA method doesn't specify the executor to use, Spring's SimpleAsyncTaskExecutor is used for asynchronously executing the doA method. @Async annotation on the doB method specifies the value attribute's value as someExecutor, which means the bean named someExecutor (of type TaskExecutor or Java 5's Executor) is used for asynchronously executing the doB method.

@Async annotated methods can accept arguments, like the doB method in the above example listing. @Async annotated methods can either return void (like the doA and doB methods) or a Future instance (like the doC method). To return a Future instance, you'll need to wrap the value that you want to return into an AsyncResult object, and return the AsyncResult object.

Let's now look at @Scheduled annotation in detail.

@Scheduled annotation

The following example listing highlights some of the important points that you need to know when using @Scheduled annotation:

Example listing 10-31 –@Scheduled annotation usage

```
import org.springframework.scheduling.annotation.Scheduled;

@Component
public class Sample {
    @Scheduled(cron="0 0 9-17 * * MON-FRI")
    public void doA() { ..... }

    @Scheduled(fixedRate = 5000)
    public void doB() { ..... }
}
```

A method annotated with @Scheduled annotation *must* return void and *must not* be defined to accept any arguments. You *must* specify cron, fixedRate or fixedDelay attribute of @Scheduled annotation.

> If you want to use the Quartz Scheduler (http://quartz-scheduler.org/) in your Spring application, you can use the integration classes provided by Spring that simplify using the Quartz Scheduler.

Spring simplifies using caching in an application by providing an abstraction on top of existing caching solutions.

10-7 Caching

If you want to use caching in your application, you can consider using Spring's cache abstraction. Spring's cache abstraction shields developers from directly dealing with the underlying caching implementation's API. As of Spring 5, cache abstraction is available out-of-the-box for java.util.concurrent.ConcurrentMap, Ehcache, Caffeine, Guava, GemFire, and for caching solutions that implement JSR 107 – Java Temporary Caching API (referred to as JCACHE).

If you are using a caching solution which is *not* currently supported by Spring's cache abstraction, you have the option to either directly use the API of the caching solution or create adapters that map Spring's cache abstraction to the caching solution.

`CacheManager` and `Cache` interfaces are central to Spring's cache abstraction. A `CacheManager` instance acts as a wrapper around the cache manager provided by the underlying caching solution, and is responsible for managing a collection of `Cache` instances. For instance, `EhCacheCacheManager` is a wrapper around Ehcache's `net.sf.ehcache.CacheManager`, `JCacheCacheManager` is a wrapper around JSR 107 provider's `javax.cache.CacheManager` implementation, and so on. A `Cache` instance is a wrapper around the underlying cache, and it provides methods for interacting with the underlying cache. For instance, `EhCacheCache` (a `Cache` implementation) is a wrapper around `net.sf.ehcache.Ehcache`, and `JCacheCache` (a `Cache` implementation) is a wrapper around JSR 107 provider's `javax.cache.Cache` instance.

Spring also provides a `ConcurrentMapCacheManager` that you can use if you want to use `java.util.concurrent.ConcurrentMap` as the underlying cache. The `Cache` instance managed by `ConcurrentMapCacheManager` is a `ConcurrentMapCache`. The following diagram summarizes relationship between `CacheManager` and `Cache` interfaces provided by Spring's caching abstraction:

If you want to use Spring's caching abstraction for a caching solution that is *not* currently supported by Spring's caching abstraction, all you need to do is to provide `CacheManager` and `Cache` implementations for the caching solution.

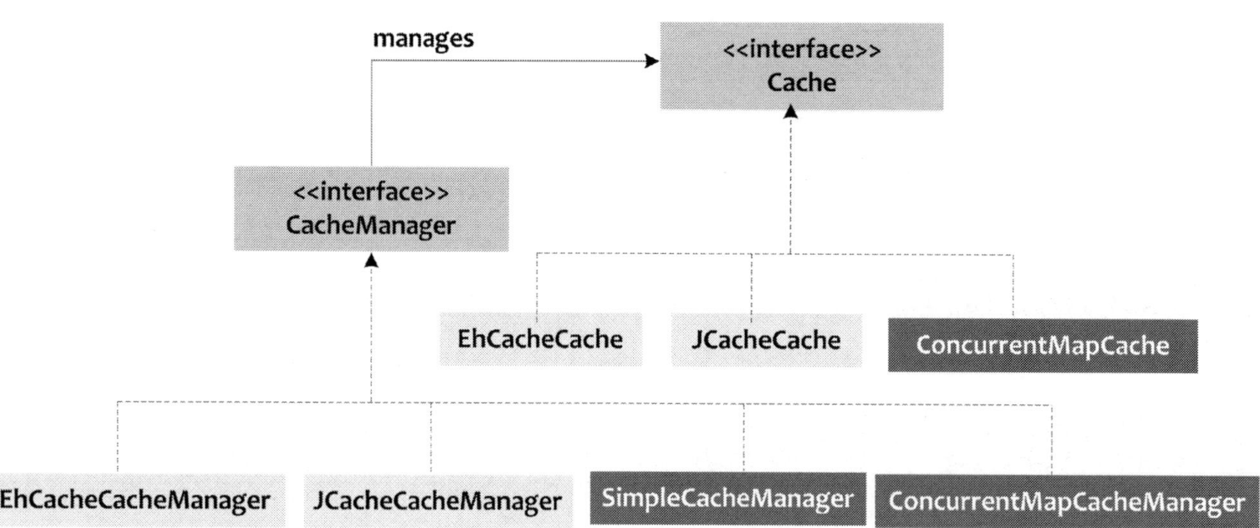

Figure 10-3 A `CacheManager` implementation acts as wrapper around the cache manager of the underlying caching solution, and a `Cache` implementation provides operations to interact with the underlying cache.

The above figure shows that a `CacheManager` manages `Cache` instances. `EhCacheCacheManager` manages `EhCacheCache` instances (underlying cache store is Ehcache), `JCacheCacheManager` manages `JCacheCache` instances (underlying cache store is a caching solution that implements JSR 107), `ConcurrentMapCacheManager` manages `ConcurrentMapCache` instances (underlying cache store is `java.util.concurrent.ConcurrentMap`), and so on.

Figure 10-3 shows a `SimpleCacheManager` class that implements `CacheManager` interface. `SimpleCacheManager` is useful for simple caching scenarios and for testing purposes. For instance, if you want to use java.util.concurrent.ConcurrentMap as the underlying cache store, you can use SimpleCacheManager, instead of ConcurrentMapCacheManager, to manage the cache.

Let's now look at how a CacheManager is configured in the application context XML file.

Configuring a CacheManager

In MyBank application, a collection of java.util.concurrent.ConcurrentMap instances are used as the underlying cache store; therefore, SimpleCacheManager is used to manage the cache.

The following example listing shows how a SimpleCacheManager instance is configured in MyBank application:

Example listing 10-32 – SimpleCacheManager configuration
Project – ch10-bankapp
Source location - src/main/resources/META-INF/spring/

```
<bean id="myCacheManager"
      class="org.springframework.cache.support.SimpleCacheManager">
    <property name="caches">
        <set>
            <bean
               class="org.springframework.cache.concurrent.ConcurrentMapCacheFactoryBean">
                <property name="name" value="fixedDepositList" />
            </bean>
            <bean
               class="org.springframework.cache.concurrent.ConcurrentMapCacheFactoryBean">
                <property name="name" value="fixedDeposit" />
            </bean>
        </set>
    </property>
</bean>
```

SimpleCacheManager's caches property specifies a collection of caches managed by the SimpleCacheManager instance. ConcurrentMapCacheFactoryBean (a FactoryBean) simplifies configuring a ConcurrentMapCache instance - a Cache instance that uses a java.util.concurrent.ConcurrentHashMap instance (an implementation of java.util.concurrent.ConcurrentMap interface) as the underlying cache store. ConcurrentMapCacheFactoryBean's name property specifies a name for the cache. In the above example listing, the fixedDepositList and fixedDeposit caches are managed by the SimpleCacheManager instance.

After you have configured an appropriate CacheManager for your application, you need to choose how you want to use Spring's cache abstraction. You can use Spring's cache abstraction either by using caching annotations (like @Cacheable, @CacheEvict and @CachePut) or by using Spring's cache schema.

Let's look at how to use Spring's caching annotations in applications.

Caching annotations - @Cacheable, @CacheEvict and @CachePut

To use caching annotations, you need to configure <annotation-driven> element of Spring's cache schema, as shown here for the MyBank application:

Example listing 10-33 – Enable caching annotations using <annotation-driven>
Project – ch10-bankapp
Source location - src/main/resources/META-INF/spring/

```
<beans .....xmlns:cache="http://www.springframework.org/schema/cache"
            xsi:schemaLocation=".....
```

```
                    http://www.springframework.org/schema/cache
                    http://www.springframework.org/schema/cache/spring-cache.xsd">

    <cache:annotation-driven cache-manager="myCacheManager"/>
  .....
</beans>
```

In the above example listing, Spring's cache schema is included so that its elements are accessible in the application context XML file. The <annotation-driven> element's cache-manager attribute refers to the CacheManager bean that is used for managing the cache. You don't need to specify the cache-manager attribute if the CacheManager bean is named cacheManager.

> If you are using Java-based configuration approach, you can use @EnableCaching annotation to enable use of caching annotations. Refer to ch10-bankapp-javaconfig project's CacheConfig class to see usage of @EnableScheduling annotation.

Now that we have enabled caching annotations, let's look at different caching annotations.

@Cacheable

@Cacheable annotation on a method indicates that the value returned by the method is cached. @Cacheable's key attribute specifies the key with which the returned value is stored in cache.

If you don't specify the key attribute, Spring's SimpleKeyGenerator class (an implementation of KeyGenerator interface) is used *by default* to generate the key with which the method's return value is stored in the cache. SimpleKeyGenerator uses the method signature and its arguments to compute the key. You can change the default key generator by specifying your custom KeyGenerator implementation as the value of key-generator attribute of <annotation-driven> element.

The following example listing shows the usage of @Cacheable annotation to cache the value returned by FixedDepositService's findFixedDepositsByBankAccount method in the MyBank application:

Example listing 10-34 – @Cacheable annotation
Project – ch10-bankapp
Source location - src/main/java/sample/spring/chapter10/bankapp/service

```
package sample.spring.chapter10.bankapp.service;

import org.springframework.cache.annotation.Cacheable;
.....
@Service(value = "fixedDepositService")
public class FixedDepositServiceImpl implements FixedDepositService {
    .....
    @Cacheable(cacheNames = { "fixedDepositList" } )
    public List<FixedDepositDetails> findFixedDepositsByBankAccount(int bankAccountId) {
        logger.info("findFixedDepositsByBankAccount method invoked");
        return myFixedDepositDao.findFixedDepositsByBankAccount(bankAccountId);
    }
}
```

@Cacheable annotation's cacheNames attribute specifies the cache regions into which the returned value is cached. In listing 10-32, we created a cache region named fixedDepositList for the MyBank application. In the above example listing, the @Cacheable annotation specifies that the value returned by the findFixedDepositsByBankAccount method is stored in the fixedDepositList cache. As no key attribute is specified, the default SimpleKeyGenerator uses the value of bankAccountId method argument as the key.

When an @Cacheable method is called, the configured KeyGenerator is used to compute the key. If the key exists in the cache, the @Cacheable method is *not* invoked. If the key doesn't exist in the cache, the @Cacheable method is invoked and the returned value is cached with the computed key. In the case of SimpleKeyGenerator, the @Cacheable annotated method is *not* invoked if the same set of argument values are passed to the method. But, @Cacheable annotated method is invoked if you pass a different value for at least one of the arguments.

@CacheEvict

If you want to evict data from the cache when a method is called, annotate the method with the @CacheEvict annotation. In the MyBank application, when a new fixed deposit is created, the fixed deposit details cached by FixedDepositServiceImpl's findFixedDepositsByBankAccount method *must* be evicted from the cache. This ensures that when the next time findFixedDepositsByBankAccount method is invoked, the newly created fixed deposit is also fetched from the database. The following example listing shows usage of @CacheEvict annotation:

Example listing 10-35 – @CacheEvict annotation
Project – ch10-bankapp
Source location - src/main/java/sample/spring/chapter10/bankapp/service

```
package sample.spring.chapter10.bankapp.service;

import org.springframework.cache.annotation.CacheEvict;
.....
@Service(value = "fixedDepositService")
public class FixedDepositServiceImpl implements FixedDepositService {
    .....
    @Transactional("jmsTxManager")
    @CacheEvict(cacheNames = { "fixedDepositList" }, allEntries=true,
        beforeInvocation = true)
    public void createFixedDeposit(final FixedDepositDetails fixedDepositDetails)
            throws Exception {
        .....
    }
    .....
}
```

In the above example listing, the @CacheEvict annotation on the createFixedDeposit method instructs Spring to remove all the cached entries from the cache region named fixedDepositList. The cacheNames attribute specifies the cache regions from which to evict the cached item, and allEntries attribute specifies whether or not all entries from the specified cache regions are evicted.

If you want to evict a particular cached item, use the key attribute to specify the key with which the item is cached. You can also specify conditional eviction of items by using the condition attribute. The condition and key attributes support specifying values using SpEL (refer section 6-8 of chapter 6 for more details), making it possible to perform sophisticated cache evictions.

The beforeInvocation attribute specifies whether the cache eviction is performed *before* or after the method execution. As the value of beforeInvocation attribute is set to true, cache is evicted before the createFixedDeposit method is invoked.

@CachePut

Spring also provides a @CachePut annotation that indicates that a method is *always* invoked, and the value returned by the method is put into the cache. @CachePut annotation is different from the @Cacheable annotation in the sense that @Cacheable annotation instructs Spring to skip the method invocation if the computed key already exists in the cache.

The following example listing shows usage of @CachePut annotation by FixedDepositServiceImpl class of MyBank application:

Example listing 10-36 – @CachePut annotation
Project – ch10-bankapp
Source location - src/main/java/sample/spring/chapter10/bankapp/service

```
package sample.spring.chapter10.bankapp.service;

import org.springframework.cache.annotation.CachePut;
import org.springframework.cache.annotation.Cacheable;
.....
@Service(value = "fixedDepositService")
public class FixedDepositServiceImpl implements FixedDepositService {
    .....
    @CachePut(cacheNames = {"fixedDeposit"}, key="#fixedDepositId")
    public FixedDepositDetails getFixedDeposit(int fixedDepositId) {
        logger.info("getFixedDeposit method invoked with fixedDepositId "
                    + fixedDepositId);
        return myFixedDepositDao.getFixedDeposit(fixedDepositId);
    }

    @Cacheable(cacheNames = { "fixedDeposit" }, key="#fixedDepositId")
    public FixedDepositDetails getFixedDepositFromCache(int fixedDepositId) {
        logger.info("getFixedDepositFromCache method invoked with fixedDepositId "
                    + fixedDepositId);
        throw new RuntimeException("This method throws exception because "
                    + "FixedDepositDetails object must come from the cache");
    }
    .....
}
```

In the above example listing, the getFixedDeposit method is annotated with @CachePut annotation, which means that the getFixedDeposit method is always invoked, and the returned FixedDepositDetails object is stored into the cache named fixedDeposit. The cacheNames attribute specifies names of the caches into which the returned FixedDepositDetails object is stored. The key attribute specifies the key to be used for storing the returned FixedDepositDetails object. The key attribute makes use of SpEL to specify the key. The #fixedDepositId value of key attribute refers to the fixedDepositId argument passed to the getFixedDeposit method. This means that the FixedDepositDetails object returned by the getFixedDeposit method is stored in the cache named fixedDeposit, and the value of fixedDepositId method argument is used as the key.

In example listing 10-36, FixedDepositServiceImpl's getFixedDepositFromCache method retrieves the FixedDepositDetails object from the cache based on the key attribute value specified by the @Cacheable annotation. Notice that the body of the getFixedDepositFromCache method does nothing but throw a RuntimeException. The key attribute value refers to the fixedDepositId argument passed to the getFixedDepositFromCache method. If the FixedDepositDetails object is not found in the cache, the getFixedDepositFromCache method is invoked, which will result in RuntimeException.

Cache configuration using Spring's cache schema

Instead of using annotations, you can use Spring's cache schema to configure caching for your application. The following example listing shows how cache schema's <advice> element specifies the caching behavior of methods defined in FixedDepositServiceImpl class:

Example listing 10-37 – applicationContext.xml - caching configuration using cache schema
Project – ch10-bankapp
Source location - src/main/resources/spring/applicationContext.xml

```
<beans .....
    xmlns:cache="http://www.springframework.org/schema/cache"
    xsi:schemaLocation=".....
         http://www.springframework.org/schema/cache/spring-cache.xsd">

    <cache:advice id="cacheAdvice" cache-manager="myCacheManager">
        <cache:caching cache="fixedDepositList">
            <cache:cache-evict method="createFixedDeposit" all-entries="true"
                 before-invocation="true" />
            <cache:cacheable method="findFixedDepositsByBankAccount" />
        </cache:caching>
        <cache:caching cache="fixedDeposit">
            <cache:cache-put method="getFixedDeposit" key="#fixedDepositId" />
            <cache:cacheable method="getFixedDepositFromCache" key="#fixedDepositId" />
        </cache:caching>
    </cache:advice>

    <bean id="myCacheManager" class="org.springframework.cache.support.SimpleCacheManager">
    .....
</beans>
```

The <advice> element's cache-manager attribute specifies the CacheManager bean to use for managing the cache. The <caching> element describes the cache behavior for the cache region(s) specified by the cache attribute. The <cache-evict>, <cache-put>, and <cacheable> elements are equivalent to @CacheEvict, @CachePut and @Cacheable annotations, respectively. The method attribute of <cache-evict>, <cache-put> and <cacheable> elements specifies the bean method to which the element applies. And, the key attribute specifies the key with which the method's returned value is stored in the cache.

The following example listing shows how Spring's aop schema's <config> element is used for applying the caching behavior defined in example listing 10-37 to methods defined by FixedDepositService interface:

Example listing 10-38 – applicationContext.xml – applying caching behavior
Project – ch10-bankapp
Source location - src/main/resources/spring/applicationContext.xml

```
<beans .....
    xmlns:aop="http://www.springframework.org/schema/aop"
    xsi:schemaLocation=".....http://www.springframework.org/schema/aop
                        http://www.springframework.org/schema/aop/spring-aop.xsd">

    <aop:config>
      <aop:advisor advice-ref="cacheAdvice" pointcut=
        "execution(* sample.spring.chapter10.bankapp.service.FixedDepositService.*(..))" />
    </aop:config>
```

In the above example listing, <advisor> element's advice-ref attribute refers to the <advice> element that defines the caching behavior (a *cross-cutting concern*), and the pointcut attribute specifies the methods on which the caching behavior applies. You'll learn more about `<config>` element and AOP (Aspect-oriented programming) in chapter 11.

Let's now look at what happens when you run the MyBank application of `ch10-bankapp` project.

10-8 Running the MyBank application

`BankApp` class of MyBank application defines the `main` method of the application. The `main` method accesses methods of `FixedDepositService` and `BankAccountService` instances to demonstrate different features that we discussed in this chapter.

The following example listing shows the MyBank application's `BankApp` class:

Example listing 10-39 – BankApp class
Project – ch10-bankapp
Source location - src/main/java/sample/spring/chapter10/bankapp

```
package sample.spring.chapter10.bankapp;
.....
public class BankApp {
    public static void main(String args[]) throws Exception {
        ConfigurableApplicationContext context = new ClassPathXmlApplicationContext(
                "classpath:META-INF/spring/applicationContext.xml");

        BankAccountService bankAccountService = context.getBean(BankAccountService.class);
        BankAccountDetails bankAccountDetails = new BankAccountDetails();
        .....
        int bankAccountId = bankAccountService.createBankAccount(bankAccountDetails);

        FixedDepositService fixedDepositService =
              context.getBean(FixedDepositService.class);
        FixedDepositDetails fixedDepositDetails = new FixedDepositDetails();
        .....
        fixedDepositDetails.setEmail("someUser@someDomain.com");
        fixedDepositService.createFixedDeposit(fixedDepositDetails);
        .....
        fixedDepositService.findFixedDepositsByBankAccount(bankAccountId);
        logger.info("Invoking FixedDepositService's findFixedDepositsByBankAccount again");
        fixedDepositService.findFixedDepositsByBankAccount(bankAccountId);

        fixedDepositService.createFixedDeposit(fixedDepositDetails);
        .....
        logger.info("Invoking FixedDepositService's findFixedDepositsByBankAccount after
                        creating a new fixed deposit");
        List<FixedDepositDetails> fixedDepositDetailsList = fixedDepositService
                .findFixedDepositsByBankAccount(bankAccountId);

        for (FixedDepositDetails detail : fixedDepositDetailsList) {
            fixedDepositService.getFixedDeposit(detail.getFixedDepositId());
        }

        for (FixedDepositDetails detail : fixedDepositDetailsList) {
            fixedDepositService.getFixedDepositFromCache(detail.getFixedDepositId());
        }
        .....
    }
```

```
}
```

In the above example listing, following sequence of actions are performed by the main method:

Step 1. First, a bank account is created in the BANK_ACCOUNT_DETAILS table by calling BankAccountService's createBankAccount method.

Step 2. Corresponding to the newly created bank account, a fixed deposit is created in the FIXED_DEPOSIT_DETAILS table by calling FixedDepositService's createFixedDeposit method.

You should make sure that email property of FixedDepositDetails object is set to the email id where you can check the emails. The FixedDepositService's createFixedDeposit method sends *two* JMS messages (refer example listing 10-5). One JMS message contains the email id specified by the FixedDepositDetails object's email attribute, and is processed by EmailMessageListener (refer example listing 10-21) that sends an email to the customer. The other JMS message is processed by FixedDepositMessageListener (refer example listing 10-11) that saves the fixed deposit details in the FIXED_DEPOSIT_DETAILS table.

You should note that FixedDepositServiceImpl's createFixedDeposit method is annotated with @CacheEvict annotation (refer example listing 10-35) that results in removing all the items cached in fixedDepositList cache.

Step 3. FixedDepositService's findFixedDepositsByBankAccount method is invoked that retrieves fixed deposits corresponding to the bank account that we created in Step 1. As the findFixedDepositsByBankAccount method is annotated with @Cacheable annotation (refer example listing 10-34), fixed deposits returned by the findFixedDepositsByBankAccount method are stored in the cache named fixedDepositList.

Listing 10-34 showed that findFixedDepositsByBankAccount method writes the following message to the console 'findFixedDepositsByBankAccount method invoked'. In the above example listing, the findFixedDepositsByBankAccount is called twice for the same bankAccountId argument, but you'll notice that only once 'findFixedDepositsByBankAccount method invoked' is written to the console. This is because the second call to the findFixedDepositsByBankAccount results in retrieving fixed deposit details from the cache named fixedDepositList, and the findFixedDepositsByBankAccount method is *not* executed.

Step 4. Corresponding to the bank account created in Step 1, another fixed deposit is created in the FIXED_DEPOSIT_DETAILS table by calling FixedDepositService's createFixedDeposit method. Now, the FixedDepositServiceImpl's createFixedDeposit method is annotated with @CacheEvict annotation (refer example listing 10-35) that results in removing all the items cached in fixedDepositList cache.

Step 5. FixedDepositService's findFixedDepositsByBankAccount method is invoked once again. This time findFixedDepositsByBankAccount is executed because the previous call to createFixedDeposit method (refer Step 4) resulted in evicting all the items from the fixedDepositList cache. At this time, you'll once again see 'findFixedDepositsByBankAccount method invoked' message written on the console. The fixed deposits returned by the findFixedDepositsByBankAccount method are cached in fixedDepositList cache because the method is annotated with @Cacheable annotation.

Step 6. For each fixed deposit retrieved in Step 5, FixedDepositService's getFixedDeposit method (refer example listing 10-36) is invoked. The getFixedDeposit method accepts the fixed deposit identifier and fetches the fixed deposit details from the database. The getFixedDeposit method is annotated with @CachePut, which means it is *always* invoked. The fixed deposit returned by the getFixedDeposit method is cached in the fixedDeposit cache.

Step 7. For each fixed deposit retrieved in Step 5, FixedDepositService's getFixedDepositFromCache method (refer example listing 10-36) is invoked. The getFixedDepositFromCache method accepts the fixed deposit identifier and throws a RuntimeException on execution. The getFixedDepositFromCache method is annotated with @Cacheable, and is executed only when the fixed deposit is not found in the fixedDeposit cache. As all the fixed deposits were cached by the getFixedDeposit method in Step 6, the getFixedDepositFromCache method is never executed.

Step 8. Every 5 seconds, the FixedDepositProcessorJob (refer example listing 10-22) checks if any new fixed deposits have been created in the database. If new fixed deposits are found in the database, the FixedDepositProcessorJob activates the fixed deposit and sends an email to the customer, confirming that the fixed deposit request has been successfully processed.

10-9 Summary

In this chapter, we touched upon some of the frequently used features of Spring. We saw that Spring simplifies sending and receiving JMS messages, sending emails, asynchronously invoking bean methods, scheduling bean methods for execution, and caching data. In the next chapter, we'll look at Spring's support for AOP (Aspect-oriented programming).

Chapter 11 - *Aspect-oriented programming*

11-1 Introduction

Aspect-oriented programming (AOP) is a programming approach in which responsibilities that are distributed across multiple classes are encapsulated into a separate class, referred to as an 'aspect'. The responsibilities that are distributed across multiple classes are referred to as 'cross-cutting concerns'. Logging, transaction management, caching, security, and so on, are examples of cross-cutting concerns.

Spring provides an AOP framework that is used internally by Spring for implementing declarative services, like transaction management (refer chapter 8), caching (refer chapter 10), security (refer chapter 16), and so on. Instead of using Spring AOP framework, you can consider using AspectJ (`http://www.eclipse.org/aspectj/`) as the AOP framework for your application. As Spring AOP framework is sufficient for most AOP scenarios, and provides integration with the Spring container, this chapter focuses on Spring AOP framework.

Let's begin this chapter by looking at an example usage of AOP.

11-2 A simple AOP example

Let's say that for auditing purposes we want to capture the arguments passed to the methods of classes defined in the service layer of MyBank application. A simple approach to log details of method arguments is to write the logging logic inside each method. But, this would mean that each method is *additionally* responsible for logging details of method arguments. As the responsibility to log details of method arguments is distributed across multiple classes and methods, it represents a *cross-cutting concern*.

To address a cross-cutting concern using AOP, you need to follow these steps:

- create a Java class (referred to as an *aspect*), and add implementation of the cross-cutting concern to that Java class
- use a regular expression to specify the methods to which the cross-cutting concern applies

In terms of AOP terminology, the method of an aspect that implements the cross-cutting concern is referred to as an *advice*. And, each advice is associated with a *pointcut* that identifies the methods to which the advice applies. The methods to which an advice applies are referred to as *join points*.

In Spring AOP, you have the option to develop an aspect using AspectJ *annotation-style* or XML *schema-style*. In AspectJ annotation-style, AspectJ annotations, like `@Aspect`, `@Pointcut`, `@Before`, and so on, are used to develop an aspect. In XML schema-style, elements of Spring's aop schema are used to configure a Spring bean as an aspect.

IMPORT **`chapter 11/ch11-simple-aop`** (The `ch11-simple-aop` project shows the MyBank application that uses Spring AOP to log details of arguments passed to the methods defined by the classes in the service layer. To run the application, execute the `main` method of the `BankApp` class of this project.)

The following example listing shows the logging aspect that logs arguments passed to the methods defined by the classes in the service layer of MyBank application:

Example listing 11-1 – LoggingAspect class
Project – ch11-simple-aop
Source location - src/main/java/sample/spring/chapter11/bankapp/aspects

```
package sample.spring.chapter11.bankapp.aspects;

import org.aspectj.lang.JoinPoint;
import org.aspectj.lang.annotation.Aspect;
import org.aspectj.lang.annotation.Before;
import org.springframework.stereotype.Component;

@Aspect
@Component
public class LoggingAspect {
    private Logger logger = LogManager.getLogger(LoggingAspect.class);

    @Before(value = "execution(* sample.spring.chapter11.bankapp.service.*Service.*(..))")
    public void log(JoinPoint joinPoint) {
        logger.info("Entering "
                + joinPoint.getTarget().getClass().getSimpleName() + "'s "
                + joinPoint.getSignature().getName());

        Object[] args = joinPoint.getArgs();
        for (int i = 0; i < args.length; i++) {
            logger.info("args[" + i + "] -->" + args[i]);
        }
    }
}
```

In example listing 11-1:

- AspectJ's @Aspect type-level annotation specifies that the LoggingAspect class is an AOP *aspect*
- AspectJ's @Before method-level annotation specifies that the log method represents an *advice* that is applied *before* the methods matched by the value attribute are executed. Refer section 11-5 to learn about different advice types that you can create.
- @Before annotation's value attribute specifies a *pointcut expression* that is used by Spring AOP framework to identify methods (referred to as *target methods*) to which an advice applies. In section 11-4, we'll take an in-depth look at pointcut expressions. For now, you can assume that the pointcut expression execution(* sample.spring.chapter11.bankapp.service.*Service.*(..)) specifies that LoggingAspect's log method is applied to *all* the public methods defined by classes (or interfaces) in sample.spring.chapter11.bankapp.service package, and whose names end with Service.
- The log method's JoinPoint argument represents the target method to which the advice is being applied. The log method uses JoinPoint instance to retrieve information about the arguments passed to the target method. In example listing 11-1, JoinPoint's getArgs method is invoked to retrieve the method arguments being passed to the target method.

You need to register an aspect with the Spring container so that the Spring AOP framework is made aware of the aspect. In example listing 11-1, the LoggingAspect class is annotated with Spring's @Component annotation so that it is automatically registered with the Spring container.

The following example listing shows the BankApp class that invokes methods of BankAccountServiceImpl (implements BankAccountService interface) and FixedDepositServiceImpl (implements FixedDepositService interface) classes of MyBank application:

Example listing 11-2 – BankApp class
Project – ch11-simple-aop
Source location - src/main/java/sample/spring/chapter11/bankapp

```
package sample.spring.chapter11.bankapp;
.....
public class BankApp {
    public static void main(String args[]) throws Exception {
        ConfigurableApplicationContext context = new ClassPathXmlApplicationContext(
                "classpath:META-INF/spring/applicationContext.xml");

        BankAccountService bankAccountService = context.getBean(BankAccountService.class);
        BankAccountDetails bankAccountDetails = new BankAccountDetails();
        bankAccountDetails.setBalanceAmount(1000);
        bankAccountDetails.setLastTransactionTimestamp(new Date());
        bankAccountService.createBankAccount(bankAccountDetails);

        FixedDepositService fixedDepositService =
            context.getBean(FixedDepositService.class);
        fixedDepositService.createFixedDeposit(new FixedDepositDetails(1, 1000, 12,
            "someemail@somedomain.com"));
    }
}
```

In the above example listing, BankAccountService's createBankAccount and FixedDepositService's createFixedDeposit methods are invoked by BankApp's main method. If you execute BankApp's main method, you'll see the following output on the console:

```
INFO  LoggingAspect - Entering BankAccountServiceImpl's createBankAccount
INFO  LoggingAspect - args[0] -->BankAccountDetails [accountId=0, balanceAmount=1000,
lastTransactionTimestamp=Sat Oct 27 16:48:11 IST 2012]
INFO  BankAccountServiceImpl - createBankAccount method invoked
INFO  LoggingAspect - Entering FixedDepositServiceImpl's createFixedDeposit
INFO  LoggingAspect - args[0] -->id :1, deposit amount : 1000.0, tenure : 12, email :
someemail@somedomain.com
INFO  FixedDepositServiceImpl - createFixedDeposit method invoked
```

The above output shows that LoggingAspect's log method is executed before the execution of BankAccountService's createBankAccount and FixedDepositService's createFixedDeposit method.

In the context of LoggingAspect, let's look at how Spring AOP framework works.

> To use AspectJ annotation-style aspects, ch11-simple-aop project defines dependency on spring-aop, aopalliance, aspectjrt and aspectjweaver JAR files. Please refer to the pom.xml file of ch11-simple-aop project for details.

11-3 Spring AOP framework

Spring AOP framework is *proxy-based*; a *proxy object* is created for objects that are target of an advice. A proxy is an intermediary object, introduced by the AOP framework, between the calling object and the target object. At runtime, calls to the target object are intercepted by the proxy, and advices that apply to the target method are executed by the proxy. In Spring AOP, a target object is a bean instance registered with the Spring container.

The following diagram shows how the LoggingAspect's log method (refer example listing 11-1) is applied to the methods of BankAccountService and FixedDepositService objects (refer example listing 11-2):

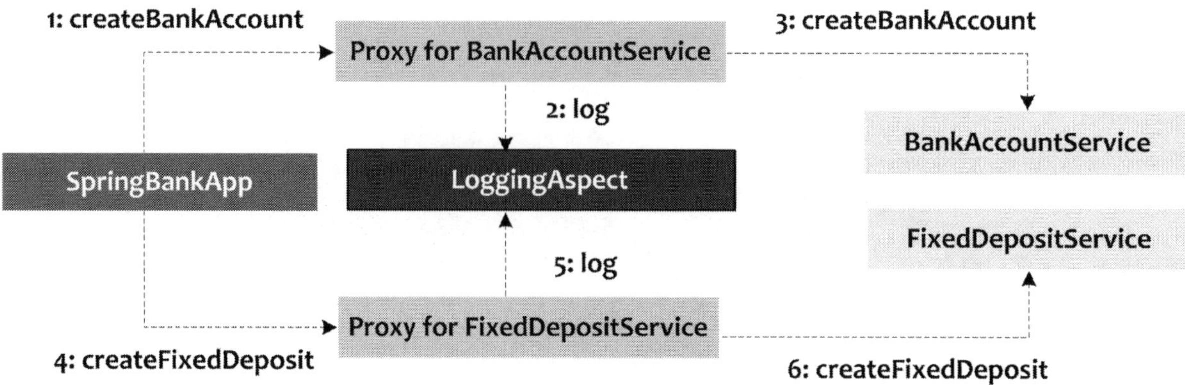

Figure 11-1 The proxy object is responsible for intercepting method calls to the target object and executing the advices that apply to the target method.

The above diagram shows that a proxy is created for both BankAccountService and FixedDepositService objects. The proxy for BankAccountService intercepts the call to BankAccountService's createBankAccount method, and the proxy for FixedDepositService intercepts the call to FixedDepositService's createFixedDeposit method. The proxy for BankAccountService first executes LoggingAspect's log method, followed by BankAccountService's createBankAccount method invocation. Similarly, the proxy for FixedDepositService first executes LoggingAspect's log method, followed by FixedDepositService's createFixedDeposit method invocation.

The timing of the execution of an advice (like the log method of LoggingAspect aspect) depends on the *type* of the advice. In AspectJ annotation-style, type of an advice is specified by the AspectJ annotation on the advice. For instance, AspectJ's @Before annotation specifies that the advice is executed *before* the invocation of the target method, @After annotation specifies that the advice is executed *after* the invocation of the target method, @Around annotation specifies that the advice is executed both *before* and *after* the execution of the target method, and so on. As LoggingAspect's log method is annotated with @Before annotation, log method is executed *before* the execution of the target object's method.

Let's now look at how Spring AOP framework creates a proxy object.

Proxy creation

When using Spring AOP, you have the option to explicitly create AOP proxies via Spring's ProxyFactoryBean (refer to org.springframework.aop.framework package) or you can let Spring automatically create AOP proxies. The automatic generation of AOP proxies by Spring AOP is referred to as *autoproxying*.

If you want to use AspectJ annotation-style for creating aspects, you need to enable support for using AspectJ annotation-style by specifying Spring aop schema's <aspectj-autoproxy> element. The <aspectj-autoproxy> element also instructs Spring AOP framework to automatically create AOP proxies for target objects. The following example listing shows usage of <aspectj-autoproxy> element in ch11-simple-aop project:

Example listing 11-3 – applicationContext.xml - <aspectj-autoproxy> element
Project – ch11-simple-aop
Source location - src/main/resources/META-INF/spring

```
<beans .....
    xmlns:context="http://www.springframework.org/schema/context"
```

```
    xmlns:aop="http://www.springframework.org/schema/aop"
    xsi:schemaLocation=".....http://www.springframework.org/schema/aop
          http://www.springframework.org/schema/aop/spring-aop.xsd">

    <context:component-scan base-package="sample.spring" />
    <aop:aspectj-autoproxy proxy-target-class="false" expose-proxy="true"/>

</beans>
```

The `<aspectj-autoproxy>` element's `proxy-target-class` attribute specifies whether JavaSE- or CGLIB-based proxies are created for target objects, and `expose-proxy` attribute specifies whether the AOP proxy itself is available to the target object. If `expose-proxy`'s value is set to `true`, the target object's method can access the AOP proxy by calling `AopContext`'s `currentProxy` static method.

In Java-based configuration approach, the `@EnableAspectJAutoProxy` annotation serves the same purpose as the `<aspectj-autoproxy>` element.

Spring AOP framework creates a CGLIB- or JavaSE-based proxy. If the target object doesn't implement any interface, Spring AOP creates a CGLIB-based proxy. If the target object implements one or more interfaces, Spring AOP creates a JavaSE-based proxy. If the value of `<aspectj-autoproxy>` element's `proxy-target-class` attribute is set to `false`, it instructs Spring AOP to create a JavaSE-based proxy if the target object implements one or more interface. If you set `proxy-target-class` attribute's value to `true`, it instructs Spring AOP to create CGLIB-based proxies even if a target object implements one or more interfaces.

Let's now look at a scenario in which you'd prefer to set `expose-proxy` attribute of `<aspectj-autoproxy>` element to `true`.

IMPORT **chapter 11/ch11-aop-proxy** (The `ch11-aop-proxy` project shows the MyBank application in which `AopContext`'s `currentProxy` method is used by a target method to retrieve the AOP proxy object created by Spring AOP framework. To run the application, execute the `main` method of the `BankApp` class of this project.)

expose-proxy attribute

The following example listing shows a modified `BankAccountServiceImpl` class in which the `createBankAccount` method invokes the `isDuplicateAccount` method to check if a bank account with same details already exists in the system:

Example listing 11-4 – `BankAccountServiceImpl` class

```
@Service(value = "bankAccountService")
public class BankAccountServiceImpl implements BankAccountService {
    @Autowired
    private BankAccountDao bankAccountDao;

    @Override
    public int createBankAccount(BankAccountDetails bankAccountDetails) {
        if(!isDuplicateAccount(bankAccountDetails)) {
            return bankAccountDao.createBankAccount(bankAccountDetails);
        } else {
            throw new BankAccountAlreadyExistsException("Bank account already exists");
        }
    }

    @Override
    public boolean isDuplicateAccount(BankAccountDetails bankAccountDetails) { ..... }
```

```
}
```

The above example listing shows that the createBankAccount method invokes the isDuplicateAccount method to check if the bank account already exists in the system.

Now, the question arises that whether the LoggingAspect's log method (refer example listing 11-1) will be executed when the isDuplicateAccount method is invoked by the createBankAccount method? Even though the isDuplicateAccount method matches the pointcut expression specified by @Before annotation on the LoggingAspect's log method (refer example listing 11-1), the LoggingAspect's log method is *not* invoked. This is because methods invoked by the target object on itself are *not* proxied by the AOP proxy. As the method invocation doesn't go through the AOP proxy object, any advice that is associated with the target method is *not* executed.

To ensure that the call to isDuplicateAccount method goes to the target object through the AOP proxy, retrieve the AOP proxy object in the createBankAccount method and invoke the isDuplicateAccount method on the AOP proxy object. The following example listing shows how to retrieve AOP proxy object inside the createBankAccount method:

Example listing 11-5 – BankAccountServiceImpl class
Project – ch11-aop-proxy
Source location - src/main/java/sample/spring/chapter11/bankapp/service

```
package sample.spring.chapter11.bankapp.service;

import org.springframework.aop.framework.AopContext;
.....
@Service(value = "bankAccountService")
public class BankAccountServiceImpl implements BankAccountService {
    .....
    @Override
    public int createBankAccount(BankAccountDetails bankAccountDetails) {
        //-- obtain the proxy and invoke the isDuplicateAccount method via proxy
        boolean isDuplicateAccount =
             ((BankAccountService)AopContext.currentProxy())
                 .isDuplicateAccount(bankAccountDetails);

        if(!isDuplicateAccount) { ..... }
        .....
    }

    @Override
    public boolean isDuplicateAccount(BankAccountDetails bankAccountDetails) { ..... }
}
```

In the above example listing, call to AopContext's currentProxy method returns the AOP proxy that made the call to the createBankAccount method. If the createBankAccount method is not invoked through Spring AOP framework, or if the value of expose-proxy attribute of <aspectj-autoproxy> element is false, call to the currentProxy method will result in throwing java.lang.IllegalStateException. As the AOP proxy implements the same interface as the target object, the above example listing shows that the AOP proxy returned by the currentProxy method is first cast to BankAccountService type and then BankAccountService's isDuplicateAccount method is invoked.

If you now go to ch11-aop-proxy project and execute BankApp's main method, you'll notice that LoggingAspect's log method is executed when isDuplicateAccount method is invoked by the createBankAccount method.

Let's now take at an in-depth look at pointcut expressions.

11-4 Pointcut expressions

When using Spring AOP, a pointcut expression identifies the *join points* to which an advice is applied. In Spring AOP, join points are *always* bean methods. If you want to apply an advice to fields, constructors, non-public methods, and to objects that are not Spring beans, you need to use AspectJ instead of Spring AOP framework. If you develop aspects using AspectJ annotation-style, you can specify a pointcut expression using AspectJ's `@Pointcut` annotation or by using AspectJ's `@Before`, `@After`, and so on, annotations that specify the advice type.

Pointcut expressions use *pointcut designators*, like `execution`, `args`, `within`, `this`, and so on, to find methods to which the advice is applied. For instance, in example listing 11-1, `@Before` annotation made use of `execution` pointcut designator to find methods to which the `LoggingAspect`'s `log` method is applied.

Let's now look at how pointcut expressions are specified using `@Pointcut` annotation.

IMPORT **chapter 11/ch11-aop-pointcuts** (The `ch11-aop-pointcuts` project shows the MyBank application that uses AspectJ's `@Pointcut` annotation to specify a pointcut expression. To run the application, execute the `main` method of the `BankApp` class of this project.)

@Pointcut annotation

`@Pointcut` annotation's `value` attribute specifies the pointcut expression. To use `@Pointcut` annotation, create an *empty* method and annotate it with `@Pointcut` annotation. The empty method *must* be defined to return void. An advice that refers to the `@Pointcut` annotated method is applied to the methods matched by the pointcut expression specified by the `@Pointcut` annotation.

Using `@Pointcut` annotation is particularly useful if a pointcut expression is shared by multiple advices in the same or different aspects.

The following example listing shows a modified version of `LoggingAspect` (refer example listing 11-1) class that uses `@Pointcut` annotation:

Example listing 11-6 – `LoggingAspect` class
Project – `ch11-aop-pointcuts`
Source location - `src/main/java/sample/spring/chapter11/bankapp/aspects`

```
package sample.spring.chapter11.bankapp.aspects;

import org.aspectj.lang.annotation.Before;
import org.aspectj.lang.annotation.Pointcut;

@Aspect
@Component
public class LoggingAspect {
    @Pointcut(value =
            "execution(* sample.spring.chapter11.bankapp.service.*Service.*(..))")
    private void invokeServiceMethods() { }

    @Before(value = "invokeServiceMethods()")
    public void log(JoinPoint joinPoint) {
        logger.info("Entering " + joinPoint.getTarget().getClass().getSimpleName() + "'s "
              + joinPoint.getSignature().getName());
        .....
```

```
    }
}
```

In the above example listing, the invokeServiceMethods method is annotated with @Pointcut, and the log method's @Before annotation refers to the invokeServiceMethods method. This means that the log method is applied to methods that match the pointcut expression specified by the @Pointcut annotation on the invokeServiceMethods method.

As the execution and args pointcut designators are mostly used when specifying pointcut expressions, let's look at execution and args pointcut designators in detail.

execution and args pointcut designators

The execution pointcut designator has the following format:

execution(*<access-modifier-pattern>* *<return-type-pattern>* *<declaring-type-pattern>* *<method-name-pattern>*(*<method-param-pattern>*) *<throws-pattern>*)

If you compare an execution expression to a method declaration, you'll notice that an execution expression is similar to a method declaration. The following figure shows that the different parts of an execution expression map to a method declaration:

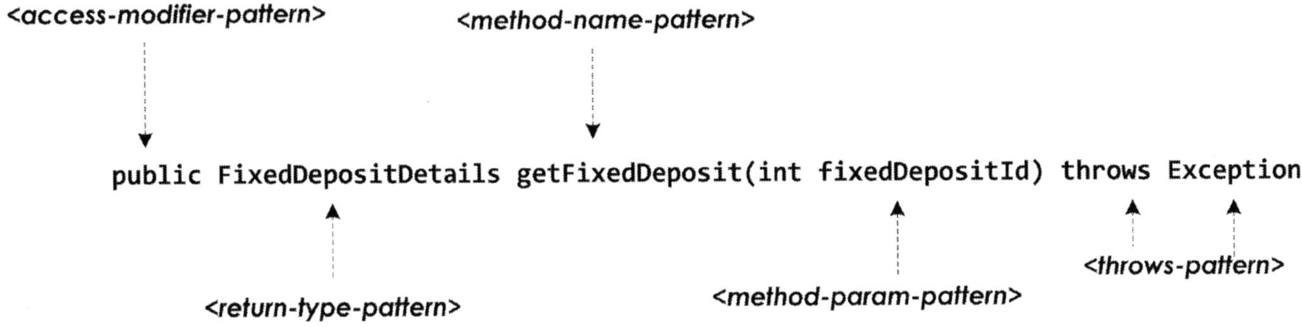

Figure 11-2 Different parts of an execution expression map to different parts of a method declaration.

Spring AOP framework matches different parts of an execution expression with different parts of a method declaration to find the methods to which an advice is applied. The *<declaring-type-pattern>* is not shown in the above figure because *<declaring-type-pattern>* is only used when you want to refer to methods contained in a particular type or package.

The following table describes different parts of an execution expression:

Expression part	Description
access-modifier-pattern	specifies the access modifier of the target method. In Spring AOP, the only value that can be specified for this expression part is public. This part of execution expression is *optional*.
return-type-pattern	specifies the fully-qualified name of the return type of the target method. A value of * means that the return type of a method doesn't matter.
declaring-type-pattern	specifies the fully-qualified name of the type that contains the target method. This part of execution expression is *optional*. A value of * means that all types (classes and interfaces) in the application are considered by the pointcut expression.

method-name-pattern	specifies the method name pattern. For instance, a value of `save*` means that the methods whose names begin with `save` are target of advice.
method-param-pattern	specifies the method parameter pattern. If the value is `(..)`, it means that the target method can contain any number of arguments or no arguments at all.
throws-pattern	specifies the exception(s) thrown by the target method. This part of `execution` expression is *optional*.

The `args` pointcut designator specifies the arguments that must be accepted by the target method *at runtime*. For instance, if you want the pointcut expression to locate methods that accept an instance of `java.util.List` at runtime, then the `args` expression looks like: `args(java.util.List)`. Later in this section, we'll see how an advice can access method arguments passed to the target method by using `args` pointcut designator.

Let's now look at some pointcut expressions that use `execution` and `args` pointcut designators:

Example 1

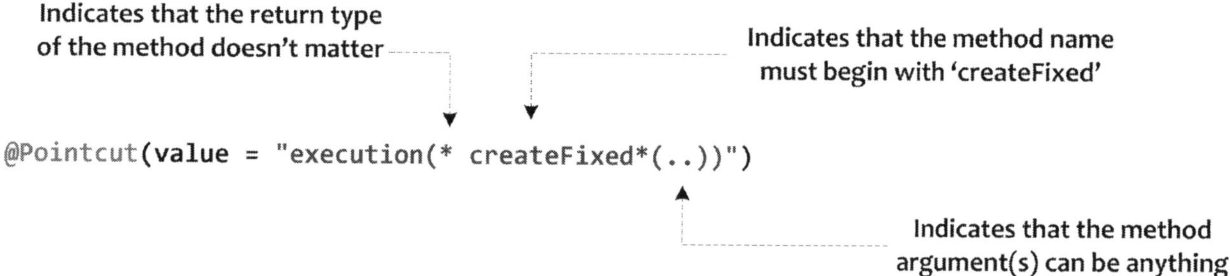

Figure 11-3 `execution` expression that uses a method name pattern

The methods matched by the above pointcut expression are the methods whose names start with `createFixed`. The return type is specified as `*`, which means the target method may return any type. The `(..)` specifies that the target method may accept zero or more arguments.

Example 2

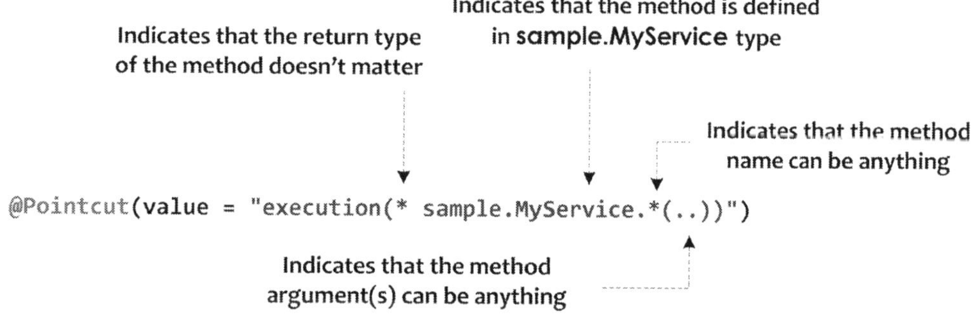

Figure 11-4 `execution` expression that specifies the *type* (class or interface) containing the target method(s)

The methods matched by the above pointcut expression are the methods defined by the `MyService` type in `sample` package.

Example 3

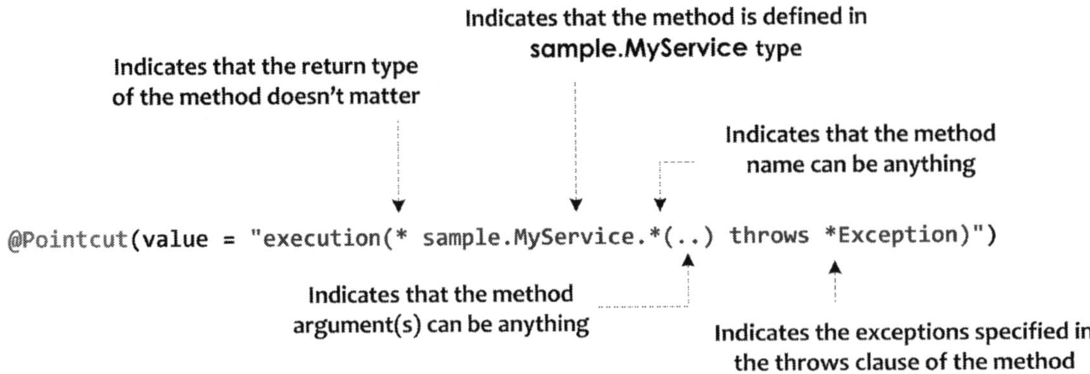

Figure 11-5 `execution` expression that specifies an exception pattern for the method

The methods matched by the above pointcut expression are the methods of `sample.MyService` type that specify a `throws` clause.

Example 4

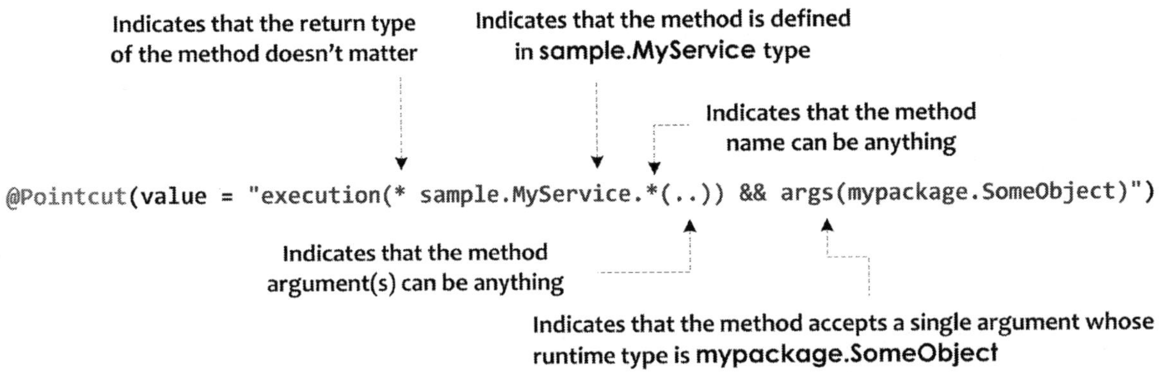

Figure 11-6 `args` pointcut designator specifies the object *instance* passed to the target method

In the above pointcut expression, combinations of `execution` and `args` pointcut designators have been used. You can combine pointcut designators using && and|| operators to create complex pointcut expressions. The methods matched by the above pointcut expression are the methods defined in `sample.MyService` type that accept an instance of `SomeObject` at runtime. The && in the above pointcut expression specifies that the target method *must* match the expressions specified by the `execution` and `args` pointcut designators.

If you want an advice to have access to one or more method arguments passed to the target method, specify names of the method arguments in the `args` expression, as shown here:

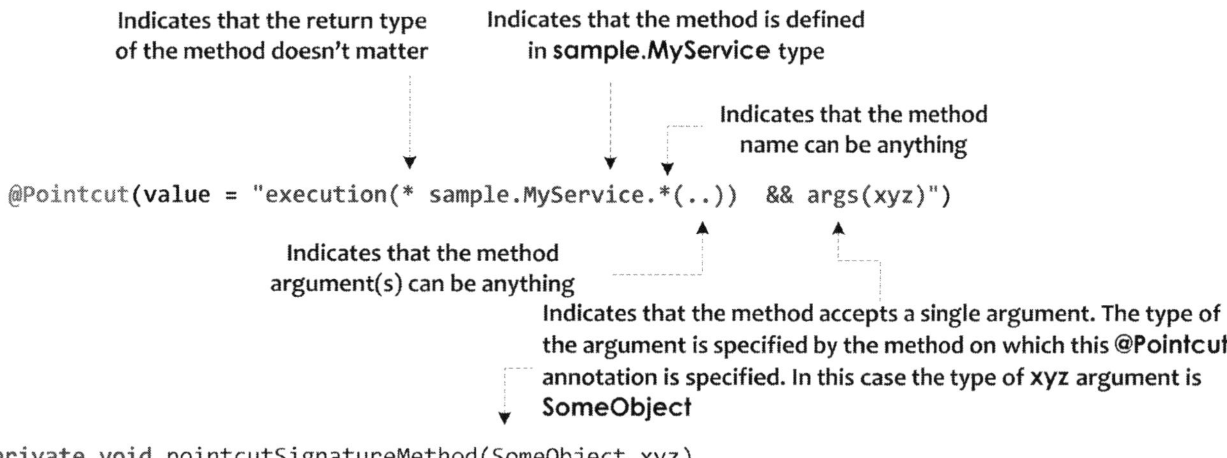

Figure 11-7 args pointcut designator specifies the target method's argument(s) that *must* be made available to the advice

In the above pointcut expression, args expression specifies that the target method *must* accept an argument of type SomeObject, and that argument is available to advice via xyz parameter. Let's see, a real example that makes use of this feature to pass arguments to the advice.

Passing target method's arguments to an advice

The following example listing shows a modified version of LoggingAspect in which log method is executed only if the method argument passed to the target method is an instance of FixedDepositDetails, and that FixedDepositDetails instance is also made available to the log method:

Example listing 11-7 – LoggingAspect class – passing target method's arguments to an advice

```
import org.aspectj.lang.annotation.Before;
import org.aspectj.lang.annotation.Pointcut;

@Aspect
@Component
public class LoggingAspect {
    .....
    @Pointcut(value =
     "execution(* sample.spring.chapter11.bankapp.service.*Service.*(..))
          && args(fixedDepositDetails)")
    private void invokeServiceMethods(FixedDepositDetails fixedDepositDetails) { }

    @Before(value = "invokeServiceMethods(fixedDepositDetails)")
    public void log(JoinPoint joinPoint, FixedDepositDetails fixedDepositDetails) {
        .....
    }
}
```

In the above example listing, the args expression specifies that the FixedDepositDetails instance passed to the target method is available to log method (an advice) via fixedDepositDetails parameter. As the args expression provides log method with an instance of FixedDepositDetails object, the log method has been modified to accept an additional argument of type FixedDepositDetails.

Pointcut designators, like execution, args, within, this, target, and so on, are defined by AspectJ. Spring AOP defines a bean pointcut designator that is specific to Spring AOP framework. Let's take a quick look at bean pointcut designator.

bean pointcut designator

The bean pointcut designator is for limiting the target methods to the specified bean id (or name). You can specify the exact bean id or name, or you can specify a pattern. Let's look at a few examples of bean pointcut designator:

Example 1

Name or id of the bean whose methods are target of the advice

```
@Pointcut(value = "bean(someBean)")
```

Figure 11-8 bean pointcut designator specifies the bean id or name whose methods are target of the advice

The methods matched by the above pointcut expression are the methods defined by the bean named someBean.

Example 2

Advice is applied to methods of beans whose names or ids begin with someBean

```
@Pointcut(value = "bean(someBean*)")
```

Figure 11-9 bean pointcut designator specifies that advice is applied to methods of beans whose ids or names begin with someBean.

In the above pointcut expression, bean pointcut designator specifies that advice is applied to methods of beans whose ids or names begin with someBean.

Like any other pointcut designator, you can combine bean pointcut designator with other pointcut designators using && and ||operators to form complex pointcut expressions.

Let's now look at pointcut designators that perform matching based on annotations.

Annotations-based pointcut designators

AspectJ also provides pointcut designators, like @annotation, @target, @within and @args that you can use with Spring AOP to find target methods. Let's look at couple of examples that show usage of these pointcut designators:

Example 1

Advice is applied to methods that are annotated with Spring's @Cacheable annotation

```
@Pointcut(value = "@annotation(org.springframework.cache.annotation.Cacheable)")
```

Figure 11-10 `@annotation` pointcut designator specifies that advice is applied to methods annotated with Spring's `Cacheable` annotation

The methods matched by the above pointcut expression are the methods annotated with Spring's `@Cacheable` annotation.

Example 2

Advice is applied to methods that are contained in an object annotated with Spring's @Component annotation

```
@Pointcut(value = "@target(org.springframework.stereotype.Component)")
```

Figure 11-11 `@target` pointcut designator specifies that advice is applied to the methods of objects annotated with Spring's `@Component` annotation

The methods matched by the above pointcut expression are the methods contained in an object annotated with Spring's `@Component` annotation.

In this section, we looked at some of the pointcut designators defined by AspectJ. It is important to note that *not* all pointcut designators defined by AspectJ are supported by Spring AOP framework. If you use an unsupported pointcut designator in pointcut expressions, Spring AOP framework throws a `java.lang.IllegalArgumentException`. For instance, if you use `call`, `set` and `get` pointcut designators in pointcut expressions, Spring AOP will throw `java.lang.IllegalArgumentException`.

Let's now look at different advice types and how to create them.

11-5 Advice types

So far in this chapter, we've seen examples of *before* advice type. A before advice type is created by annotating a method of an aspect with `@Before` annotation (refer listing 11-1, 11-6 and 11-7). The other advice types that you can create are *after*, *after returning*, *after throwing*, *after* and *around*.

IMPORT **`chapter 11/ch11-aop-advices`** (The `ch11-aop-advices` project contains a `SampleAspect` class that defines different advice types. To run the application, execute the `main` method of the `BankApp` class of this project.)

Let's now look at salient features of various advice types, and how to create them.

Before advice

A *before* advice is executed before the target method is executed. If a *before* advice doesn't throw an exception, the target method will *always* be invoked. You can control whether the target method is executed or not, by using an *around* advice (explained later in this section). As discussed earlier, AspectJ's @Before annotation indicates that an advice is a *before* advice.

@Before annotated method may define its first argument to be of type JoinPoint. You can use the JoinPoint argument inside the advice to retrieve information about the target method. For instance, in example listing 11-1, the JoinPoint argument was used to obtain the class name of the target object and the arguments passed to the target method.

After returning advice

An *after returning* advice is executed *after* the target method returns. You should note that an *after returning* advice is not executed if the target method throws an exception. An *after returning* advice is annotated with AspectJ's @AfterReturning annotation. An *after returning* advice can access the value returned by the target method, and modify it before it is returned to the caller.

The following example listing shows an *after returning* advice that prints the value returned by BankAccountService's createBankAccount method:

Example listing 11-8 – SampleAspect class – *after returning* advice
Project – ch11-aop-advices
Source location - src/main/java/sample/spring/chapter11/bankapp/aspects

```
package sample.spring.chapter11.bankapp.aspects;

import org.aspectj.lang.annotation.AfterReturning;
.....
@Aspect
public class SampleAspect {
    .....
    @Pointcut(value =
               "execution(* sample.spring..BankAccountService.createBankAccount(..))")
    private void createBankAccountMethod() {}

    @AfterReturning(value = "createBankAccountMethod()", returning = "aValue")
    public void afterReturningAdvice(JoinPoint joinPoint, int aValue) {
        logger.info("Value returned by " + joinPoint.getSignature().getName()
              + " method is " + aValue);
    }
    .....
}
```

In the above example listing, afterReturningAdvice method represents an *after returning* advice. The pointcut expression specified by the @Pointcut annotation limits the join point to BankAccountService's createBankAccount method. The .. in the execution expression specifies that the sample.spring package and its sub-packages are searched to find the BankAccountService type.

In example listing 11-8, SampleAspect's afterReturningAdvice method is invoked after the invocation of BankAccountService's createBankAccount method. @AfterReturning's returning attribute specifies the name with which the target method's return value is available to the advice. In the above example listing, the value returned by the createBankAccount method is made available to the afterReturningAdvice method via aValue argument. The type of the aValue argument has been specified as int because the createBankAccount method returns an int value.

You should note that if you specify the returning attribute, the advice is applied only to methods that return the specified type. For instance, in example listing 11-8, if we specify the type of aValue argument as java.util.List, then the afterReturningAdvice is applied only to methods that return an object of type java.util.List. If you apply afterReturningAdvice to methods that return different types (including void), and you want to access the returned value of these methods, then specify Object as the type of aValue argument.

As shown in example listing 11-8, a @AfterReturning annotated method can access target method information by defining JoinPoint as its first argument.

After throwing advice

An *after throwing* advice is executed when the target method throws an exception. An *after throwing* advice can access the exception thrown by the target method. An *after throwing* advice is annotated with AspectJ's @AfterThrowing annotation.

The following example listing shows an *after throwing* advice that is executed when an exception is thrown by target methods:

Example listing 11-9 – SampleAspect class – *after throwing* advice
Project – ch11-aop-advices
Source location - src/main/java/sample/spring/chapter11/bankapp/aspects

```
package sample.spring.chapter11.bankapp.aspects;

import org.aspectj.lang.annotation.AfterThrowing;
.....
@Aspect
public class SampleAspect {
    .....
    @Pointcut(value = " execution(* sample.spring..FixedDepositService.*(..)) ")
    private void exceptionMethods() {}
    .....
    @AfterThrowing(value = "exceptionMethods()", throwing = "exception")
    public void afterThrowingAdvice(JoinPoint joinPoint, Throwable exception) {
        logger.info("Exception thrown by " + joinPoint.getSignature().getName()
                + " Exception type is : " + exception);
    }
}
```

In the above example listing, afterThrowingAdvice method represents an *after throwing* advice. The afterThrowingAdvice method is executed when an exception is thrown by any of the FixedDepositService object's methods. In the above example listing, the throwing attribute of @AfterThrowing annotation specifies the name with which the exception thrown by the target method is made available to the afterThrowingAdvice method. As the throwing attribute's value is exception, the exception is passed to the afterThrowingAdvice method via argument named exception. Notice that the type of the exception argument is java.lang.Throwable, which means that the afterThrowingAdvice method is executed for all exceptions thrown by the target method.

If you want afterThrowingAdvice method is executed only when a specific exception type is thrown by the target method, change the type of the exception argument. For instance, if you want the afterThrowingAdvice method is executed only when the target method throws java.lang.IllegalStateException, specify java.lang.IllegalStateException as the type of the exception argument.

As shown in example listing 11-9, `@AfterThrowing` annotated method can access target method information by defining `JoinPoint` as its first argument.

After advice

An *after* advice is executed after the target method is executed, irrespective of whether the target method completes normally or throws an exception. An *after* advice is annotated with AspectJ's `@After` annotation.

The following example listing shows an *after* advice that is executed for `BankAccountService`'s `createBankAccount` method, and for the methods defined by the `FixedDepositService` interface:

Example listing 11-10 – `SampleAspect` class – *after* advice
Project – `ch11-aop-advices`
Source location - `src/main/java/sample/spring/chapter11/bankapp/aspects`

```
package sample.spring.chapter11.bankapp.aspects;

import org.aspectj.lang.annotation.After;
.....
@Aspect
public class SampleAspect {
    .....
    @Pointcut(value =
           "execution(* sample.spring..BankAccountService.createBankAccount(..))")
    private void createBankAccountMethod() {}

    @Pointcut(value = "execution(* sample.spring..FixedDepositService.*(..))")
    private void exceptionMethods() {}
    .....
    @After(value = "exceptionMethods() || createBankAccountMethod()")
    public void afterAdvice(JoinPoint joinPoint) {
        logger.info("After advice executed for " + joinPoint.getSignature().getName());
    }
}
```

In the above example listing, `afterAdvice` method represents an *after* advice. The `afterAdvice` method is executed after the target method is executed. Notice that the `@After` annotation's `value` attribute uses `||` operator to combine pointcut expressions represented by `createBankAccountMethod` and `exceptionMethods` methods to form a new pointcut expression.

Example listing 11-10 shows that an `@After` annotated method can access target method information by defining `JoinPoint` as its first argument.

Around advice

An *around* advice is executed both *before* and *after* the execution of the target method. Unlike other advices, an *around* advice can control whether the target method is executed or not. An *around* advice is annotated with AspectJ's @Around annotation.

The following example listing shows an *around* advice:

Example listing 11-11 – `SampleAspect` class – *around* advice
Project – `ch11-aop-advices`
Source location - `src/main/java/sample/spring/chapter11/bankapp/aspects`

```
package sample.spring.chapter11.bankapp.aspects;
```

```
import org.aspectj.lang.ProceedingJoinPoint;
import org.aspectj.lang.annotation.Around;
import org.springframework.util.StopWatch;
.....
@Aspect
public class SampleAspect {
    .....
    @Around(value = "execution(* sample.spring..*Service.*(..))")
    public Object aroundAdvice(ProceedingJoinPoint pjp) {
        Object obj = null;
        StopWatch watch = new StopWatch();
        watch.start();
        try {
            obj = pjp.proceed();
        } catch (Throwable throwable) {
            // -- perform any action that you want
        }
        watch.stop();
        logger.info(watch.prettyPrint());
        return obj;
    }
}
```

In the above example listing, the `aroundAdvice` method represents an *around* advice. The `ProceedingJoinPoint` argument to the `aroundAdvice` method is meant for controlling the invocation of the target method. It is important to note that `ProceedingJoinPoint` argument *must* be the first argument passed to an *around* advice. When you invoke `ProceedingJoinPoint`'s `proceed` method, the target method is invoked. This means that if you don't invoke the `ProceedingJoinPoint`'s `proceed` method, the target method is *not* invoked. If you pass an `Object[]` to the `proceed` method, the values contained in the `Object[]` are passed as arguments to the target method. If an around advice chooses *not* to invoke the target method, the around advice may itself return a value.

As the target method is invoked only when you call `ProceedingJoinPoint`'s `proceed` method, around advice allows you to perform actions *before* and *after* the invocation of the target method, and to share information between these action. In example listing 11-11, the `aroundAdvice` method records the time taken for the target method to execute. The `aroundAdvice` method starts a stop watch (represented by Spring's `StopWatch` object) before calling `ProceedingJoinPoint`'s `proceed` method, and stops the stop watch after calling `ProceedingJoinPoint`'s `proceed` method. `StopWatch`'s `prettyPrint` method is then used to print the time taken by the target method to execute.

If you want to modify the value returned by the target method, cast the returned value of `ProceedingJoinPoint`'s `proceed` method to the return type of the target method and modify it. A calling method sees the value returned by the around advice; therefore, you *must* define the return type of an advice method as `Object` or the type that is returned by the target method. An advice method has the option to return the value returned by the target method, or to return a different value altogether. For instance, instead of invoking the target method, an around advice may inspect the argument(s) being passed to the target method and return a value from the cache if a cache entry exists for the same set of arguments.

Creating advices by implementing special interfaces

Instead of using annotations, you can use special interfaces provided by Spring for creating various advice types. For instance, you can create a *before* advice by implementing Spring's `MethodBeforeAdvice` interface, and you can create an *after returning* advice by implementing Spring's `AfterReturningAdvice` interface, and so on.

The following example listing shows a *before* advice that is created by implementing MethodBeforeAdvice:

Example listing 11-12 – MethodBeforeAdvice interface

```
import java.lang.reflect.Method;
import org.springframework.aop.MethodBeforeAdvice;

public class MyBeforeAdvice implements MethodBeforeAdvice {
    @Override
    public void before(Method method, Object[] args, Object target) throws Throwable {
        .....
    }
}
```

In the above example listing, MyBeforeAdvice class implements the MethodBeforeAdvice interface. MethodBeforeAdvice interface defines a before method that contains the logic that you want to execute before the target method is invoked.

An advice created by implementing a special interface is configured using Spring aop schema's <config> element (explained in the next section).

So far we have looked at examples that showed how to use AspectJ annotation-style to create aspects. Let's now look at how to use a regular Spring bean as an AOP aspect.

11-6 Spring AOP - XML schema-style

In XML schema-style, a regular Spring bean acts as an aspect. A method defined in an aspect is associated with an advice type and a pointcut expression using Spring's aop schema.

IMPORT **chapter 11/ch11-aop-xml-schema** (The ch11-aop-xml-schema project is same as ch11-aop-advices project, except that ch11-aop-xml-schema's SampleAspect class is a simple Java class that doesn't use AspectJ's annotations.)

The following example listing shows the SampleAspect class of ch11-aop-xml-schema project that defines advices:

Example listing 11-13 – SampleAspect class
Project – ch11-aop-xml-schema
Source location - src/main/java/sample/spring/chapter11/bankapp/aspects

```
package sample.spring.chapter11.bankapp.aspects;
.....
public class SampleAspect {
    .....
    public void afterReturningAdvice(JoinPoint joinPoint, int aValue) {
        logger.info("Value returned by " + joinPoint.getSignature().getName()
                + " method is " + aValue);
    }
    public void afterThrowingAdvice(JoinPoint joinPoint, Throwable exception) {
        logger.info("Exception thrown by " + joinPoint.getSignature().getName()
                + " Exception type is : " + exception);
    }
    .....
}
```

The above example listing shows that the SampleAspect class defines methods that represent AOP advices. Notice that the SampleAspect class is *not* annotated with @Aspect annotation and the methods are *not* annotated with @After, @AfterReturning, and so on, annotations.

Let's now look at how <config> element of Spring's aop schema is used to configure a regular Spring bean as an AOP aspect.

Configuring an AOP aspect

In XML schema-style, the <config> element specifies AOP-specific configurations, and the enclosing <aspect> sub-elements configure AOP aspects.

The following example listing shows how the SampleAspect class is configured as an aspect using <aspect> sub-element of <config> element:

Example listing 11-14 – applicationContext.xml – Spring's aop schema usage
Project – ch11-aop-xml-schema
Source location - src/main/resources/META-INF/spring

```
<beans ..... xmlns:aop="http://www.springframework.org/schema/aop" ..... >
    .....
    <bean id="sampleAspect" class="sample.spring.chapter11.bankapp.aspects.SampleAspect" />

    <aop:config proxy-target-class="false" expose-proxy="true">
        <aop:aspect id="sampleAspect" ref="sampleAspect">
            .....
        </aop:aspect>
    </aop:config>
</beans>
```

As the <config> element relies on autoproxying, the <config> element defines proxy-target-class and expose-proxy attributes. If you remember, the same attributes were defined by <aspectj-autoproxy> element of Spring's aop schema. Refer section 11-3 to know more about proxy-target-class and expose-proxy attributes.

In example listing 11-14, the sampleAspect bean definition defines SampleAspect class as a bean. The <aspect> element configures the sampleAspect bean as an AOP aspect. The <aspect> element's id attribute specifies a unique identifier for an aspect, and the ref attribute specifies the Spring bean that you want to configure as an AOP aspect.

> The <config> element can contain an <advisor> sub-element for associating an advice (specified by the advice-ref attribute) with the pointcut expression (specified by the pointcut attribute). An advice referenced by advice-ref attribute is a Spring bean that implements the sppecial interface (like, MethodBeforeAdvice, AfterReturningAdvice, and so on) provided by Spring for creating an advice. Refer example listing 10-38 of chapter 10 to see usage of <advisor> element.

Now that we have configured an AOP aspect, let's look at how to map methods defined in an AOP aspect to different advice types and pointcut expressions.

Configuring an advice

You configure an advice using one of the following sub-elements of <aspect> element: <before> (for configuring a *before* advice type), <after-returning> (for configuring an *after returning* advice type),

<after-throwing> (for configuring an *after throwing* advice type), <after> (for configuring an *after* advice type) and <around> (for configuring an *around* advice type).

Let's now look at how the advices defined in the SampleAspect class of ch11-aop-xml-schema project are configured in the application context XML file.

Configuring an *after returning* advice

The following figure shows how the SampleAspect's afterReturningAdvice method is configured as an *after returning* advice using <after-returning> element:

```
public void afterReturningAdvice(JoinPoint joinPoint, int aValue) {
        logger.info("Value returned by " + joinPoint.getSignature().getName()
                        + " method is " + aValue);
}

<aop:after-returning method="afterReturningAdvice" returning="aValue"
pointcut="execution(*sample.spring..BankAccountService.createBankAccount(..))" />
```

Figure 11-12 afterReturningAdvice method of SampleAspect class is configured as an *after returning* advice using <after-returning> element of Spring's aop schema

The <after-returning> element's method attribute specifies the name of the bean method which you want to configure as an *after returning* advice. The returning attribute serves the same purpose as the @AfterReturning annotation's returning attribute; it makes the returned value from the target method available to the advice. The pointcut attribute specifies the pointcut expression used for finding the methods to which the advice is applied.

Configuring an *after throwing* advice

The following figure shows how the SampleAspect's afterThrowingAdvice method is configured as an *after throwing* advice using <after-throwing> element:

```
public void afterThrowingAdvice(JoinPoint joinPoint, Throwable exception) {
        logger.info("Exception thrown by " + joinPoint.getSignature().getName()
                        + " Exception type is : " + exception);
}

<aop:after-throwing method="afterThrowingAdvice" throwing="exception"
pointcut="execution(* sample.spring..FixedDepositService.*(..))" />
```

Figure 11-13 afterThrowingAdvice method of SampleAspect class is configured as an *after throwing* advice using <after-throwing> element of Spring's aop schema

The <after-throwing> element's method attribute specifies the name of the bean method which you want to configure as an *after throwing* advice. The throwing attribute serves the same purpose as the @AfterThrowing annotation's throwing attribute; it makes the exception thrown by the target method available to the advice. The pointcut attribute specifies the pointcut expression used for finding the methods to which the advice is applied.

The other advice types (*before*, *after* and *around*) are configured the same way as the *after returning* and *after throwing* advices that we just saw. Refer to applicationContext.xml file of ch11-aop-xml-schema project to see how afterAdvice and aroundAdvice methods of SampleAspect class have been configured as *after* and *around* advices, respectively.

Let's now look at different ways in which you can associate a pointcut expression with an advice.

Associating a pointcut expression with an advice

The <after>, <after-returning>, <after-throwing>, <before> and <around> elements of Spring's aop schema define a pointcut attribute that you can use to specify the pointcut expression associated with the advice. If you want to share pointcut expressions between different advices, you can use the <pointcut> sub-element of the <config> element to define pointcut expressions.

The following example listing uses <pointcut> element for defining pointcut expressions:

Example listing 11-15 – application context XML - <pointcut> element

```
<beans ..... xmlns:aop="http://www.springframework.org/schema/aop" ..... >
    .....
    <bean id="sampleAspect"
       class="sample.spring.chapter11.bankapp.aspects.SampleAspect" />

    <aop:config proxy-target-class="false" expose-proxy="true">
       <aop:pointcut expression=
                 "execution(* sample.spring..*Service.*(..))" id="services" />

        <aop:aspect id="sampleAspect" ref="sampleAspect">
            <aop:after method="afterAdvice" pointcut-ref="services" />
            <aop:around method="aroundAdvice" pointcut-ref="services"/>
        </aop:aspect>
    </aop:config>
</beans>
```

In the above example listing, the <pointcut> element specifies a pointcut expression. The expression attribute specifies the pointcut expression, and the id attribute specifies a unique identifier for the pointcut expression. The pointcut expression defined by a <pointcut> element can be referenced by <after>, <after-returning>, and so on, advice type elements using pointcut-ref attribute. For instance, in the above example listing, <after> and <around> elements use pointcut-ref attribute to refer to the services pointcut expressions.

11-7 Summary

In this chapter, we looked at AOP concepts and how Spring AOP is used to address cross-cutting concerns in Spring applications. We saw how to create aspects using AspectJ annotation-style and XML schema-style. We also discussed how to create and configure different advice types. We touched upon the pointcut expressions that you can create to find matching methods in the application. For a more comprehensive coverage of Spring AOP please refer to Spring reference documentation. In the next chapter, we'll look at how to develop web applications using Spring Web MVC module of Spring Framework.

Chapter 12 – *Spring Web MVC basics*

12-1 Introduction

The Spring Web MVC module of Spring Framework provides an MVC (Model-View-Controller) framework that you can use for developing servlet-based web applications. Spring Web MVC is a *non-intrusive* framework that provides a clear *separation of concerns* between application objects that form the web layer. For instance, a *controller* object is used for processing the request, a *validator* object is used for performing validation, and a *model attribute* object is used for storing form data, and so on. It is important to note that none of these application objects implement or extend from any Spring-specific interface or class.

In this chapter, we'll first look at the directory structure that will be followed by all the sample *web* projects discussed in this chapter. We'll then look at a simple 'Hello World' web application developed using Spring Web MVC. In the rest of this chapter, we'll look at some of the Spring Web MVC annotations in the context of our MyBank web application. This chapter sets the stage for discussing more advanced Spring Web MVC features in the next chapter.

IMPORT **`chapter 12/ch12-helloworld`** (This project shows a simple 'Hello World' web application that uses Spring Web MVC. Refer appendix B to learn how to deploy sample web projects on Tomcat server. Once you have deployed the application, go to the following URL: `http://localhost:8080/ch12-helloworld/helloworld/sayhello`. If the application is deployed successfully, it will show you '`Hello World !!`' message.)

12-2 Directory structure of sample web projects

Figure 12-1 describes the important directories of `ch12-helloworld` web project. Some of the important points that you need to remember are:

- The `src/main/resources/META-INF/spring` folder contains the *root web application context XML* file that defines beans that are shared by all the servlets and filters of the web application. The root web application context XML file typically defines data sources, services, DAOs, transaction managers, and so on. The root web application context XML file is loaded by Spring's `ContextLoaderListener` (a `javax.servlet.ServletContextListener` implementation). Refer section 12-10 to learn about how `ContextLoaderListener` is configured in `web.xml` file.

- The `src/main/webapp/WEB-INF/spring` folder contains the *web application context XML* file (also referred to as *child* web application context XML file) that defines beans that form part of the *web* layer of the application. The web application context XML file typically defines *controllers* (also referred to as *handlers*), *handler mappings*, *view resolvers*, *exception resolvers*, and so on. We'll learn about these objects later in this chapter.

  - The beans defined in the root web application context XML file are *available* to the beans defined in the child web application context XML file. This means, a bean defined in the child web application context XML file can be dependent on a bean defined in the root web application context XML file, but *not* the other way round.

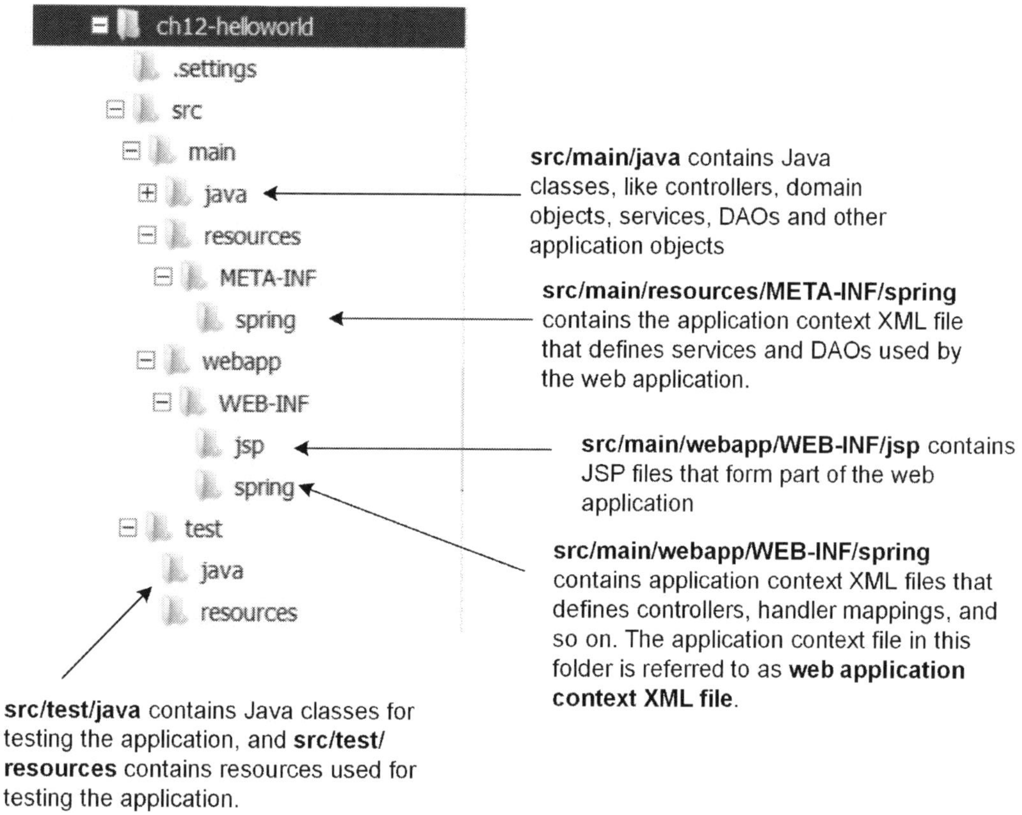

Figure 12-1 Directory structure of `ch12-helloworld` project

Let's now look at the configuration files and the classes that form the `ch12-helloworld` project.

12-3 Understanding the 'Hello World' web application

If you right-click on the `ch12-helloworld` project in your Eclipse IDE and select `Build Path` → `Configure Build Path` option, you'll notice that the project depends on `spring-beans`, `spring-context`, `spring-core`, `spring-expression`, `spring-web` and `spring-webmvc` JAR files. These JAR files are required for building a basic Spring Web MVC application.

The following table describes the configuration files and the Java source files that constitute the `ch12-helloworld` project. Later in this section, we'll take a closer look at these files and classes.

Configuration file or Java source file	Description
`HelloWorldController.java`	Spring Web MVC *controller* that is responsible for request handling. You'll find this file inside `sample.spring.chapter12.web` package of `src/main/java` folder.
`helloworld.jsp`	JSP file that shows the 'Hello World !!' message You'll find this file inside `src/main/webapp/WEB-INF/jsp` folder
`myapp-config.xml`	Web application context XML file that contains bean definitions for controllers, handler mappings, and so on. You'll find this file inside `src/main/webapp/WEB-INF/spring` folder

web.xml	Web application deployment descriptor You'll find this file inside src/main/webapp/WEB-INF folder

Apart from the files shown in the above table, the ch12-helloworld project also contains log4j2.properties file that contains Log4j 2 configuration, and pom.xml file that goes as input to the maven build tool. To know more about these files refer to Log4j 2 (http://logging.apache.org/log4j/2.x/) and Maven (http://maven.apache.org/) documentation.

Let's now take a closer look at each of the files described in the above table.

HelloWorldController.java – Hello World web application's controller class

In Spring Web MVC applications, the request handling logic is contained in controller classes. The following example listing shows the HelloWorldController controller class of ch12-helloworld project:

Example listing 12-1 – HelloWorldController class
Project – ch12-helloworld
Source location - src/main/java/sample/spring/chapter12/web

```
package sample.spring.chapter12.web;

import org.springframework.web.servlet.ModelAndView;
import org.springframework.web.servlet.mvc.Controller;
.....
public class HelloWorldController implements Controller {

    @Override
    public ModelAndView handleRequest(HttpServletRequest request,
           HttpServletResponse response) throws Exception {

        Map<String, String> modelData = new HashMap<String, String>();

        modelData.put("msg", "Hello World !!");
        return new ModelAndView("helloworld", modelData);
    }
}
```

The above example listing shows that the HelloWorldController class implements Spring's Controller interface. The Controller interface defines a handleRequest method, which you need to implement to provide the request handling logic. The handleRequest method returns a ModelAndView object that contains the following information:

- the data (referred to as *model* data) to be shown to the user, and
- logical name of the JSP page (referred to as *view*) that shows the model data

The model data is usually represented as a java.util.Map type object, and each entry in the java.util.Map object represents a *model attribute*. The name of the view (the JSP page) to be shown to the user is specified as a String value.

Example listing 12-1 shows that the HelloWorldController's handleRequest method returns a ModelAndView object that contains helloworld (a String value) as the view name and modelData (a java.util.Map type object) as the model data. The modelData contains a msg model attribute whose value is the 'Hello World !!' message. We'll soon see that the msg model attribute is used by the helloworld view (a JSP page) to show the 'Hello World !!' message to the users.

Figure 12-2 summarizes how `HelloWorldController`'s `handleRequest` method renders a JSP page. The figure shows that the Spring Web MVC framework intercepts an incoming HTTP request and invokes the `HelloWorldController`'s `handleRequest` method. The `handleRequest` method returns a `ModelAndView` object that contains the model data and the view information. After receiving the `ModelAndView` object from the `handleRequest` method, the Spring Web MVC framework dispatches the HTTP request to the `helloworld.jsp` page and makes the model attributes available to the `helloworld.jsp` page as *request attributes*.

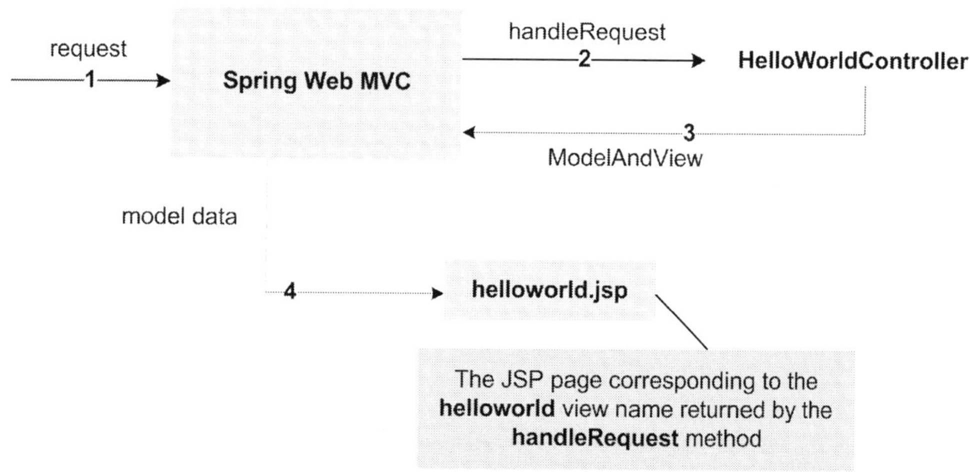

Figure 12-2 Spring Web MVC framework invokes the `HelloWorldController`'s `handleRequest` method and uses the returned `ModelAndView` object to render the `helloworld.jsp` page

> Spring Web MVC makes the model attributes available to the view technology (like JSP and Velocity) in a format that is suitable for the view technology. For instance, if you are using JSP as the view technology, model attributes are made available to the JSP pages as request attributes.

`helloworld.jsp` – JSP page that shows the 'Hello World !!' message

The following example listing shows the `helloworld.jsp` page of `ch12-helloworld` project:

Example listing 12-2 – `helloworld.jsp` JSP page
Project – `ch12-helloworld`
Source location - `src/main/webapp/WEB-INF/jsp`

```
<%@taglib uri="http://java.sun.com/jsp/jstl/core" prefix="c" %>

<c:out value="${msg}"/>
```

In the above example listing, `<c:out>` prints the value of `msg` request attribute. The `msg` request attribute refers to the `msg` model attribute returned by `HelloWorldController`'s `handleRequest` method (refer example listing 12-1). As the value of `msg` model attribute is 'Hello World !!', `helloworld.jsp` JSP page shows 'Hello World !!' message.

`myapp-config.xml` – Web application context XML file

The following example listing shows the beans configured in `myapp-config.xml` file of `ch12-helloworld` project:

Example listing 12-3 – myapp-config.xml
Project – ch12-helloworld
Source location - src/main/webapp/WEB-INF/spring

```
<beans xmlns="http://www.springframework.org/schema/beans"
       xmlns:xsi="http://www.w3.org/2001/XMLSchema-instance"
       xsi:schemaLocation="http://www.springframework.org/schema/beans
   http://www.springframework.org/schema/beans/spring-beans.xsd">

    <bean name="helloWorldController"
           class="sample.spring.chapter12.web.HelloWorldController" />

    <bean id="handlerMapping"
         class="org.springframework.web.servlet.handler.SimpleUrlHandlerMapping">
        <property name="urlMap">
            <map>
                <entry key="/sayhello" value-ref="helloWorldController" />
            </map>
        </property>
    </bean>

    <bean id="viewResolver"
          class="org.springframework.web.servlet.view.InternalResourceViewResolver">
        <property name="prefix" value="/WEB-INF/jsp/" />
        <property name="suffix" value=".jsp" />
    </bean>
</beans>
```

The above example listing shows that apart from the HelloWorldController, Spring's SimpleUrlHandlerMapping and InternalResourceViewResolver beans are also configured in the myapp-config.xml file.

SimpleUrlHandlerMapping bean (an implementation of Spring's HandlerMapping interface) maps an incoming HTTP request to the controller responsible for handling the request. SimpleUrlHandlerMapping bean uses the URL path to map a request to a controller. The urlMap property (of type java.util.Map) specifies URL path to controller bean mapping. In example listing 12-3, the "/sayhello" URL path (specified by the key attribute) is mapped to the HelloWorldController bean (specified by the value-ref attribute). You should note that the URL path specified by the key attribute is *relative* to the URL path to which Spring's DispatcherServlet (a servlet) is mapped in the web application deployment descriptor. DispatcherServlet is discussed later in this section.

InternalResourceViewResolver bean (an implementation of Spring's ViewResolver interface) locates the actual view (like, JSP or servlet) based on the view name contained in the ModelAndView object. The actual view is located by *prepending* the value of prefix property and *appending* the value of suffix property to the view name. The example listing 12-3 shows that the value of prefix property is /WEB-INF/jsp, and the value of suffix property is .jsp. As the HelloWorldController's handleRequest method returns a ModelAndView object which contains helloworld as the view name, the actual view is /WEB-INF/jsp/helloworld.jsp (a string that is obtained by prepending /WEB-INF/jsp and appending .jsp to the helloworld view name).

The following figure shows the role played by SimpleUrlHandlerMapping and InternalResourceViewResolver beans in the 'Hello World' web application:

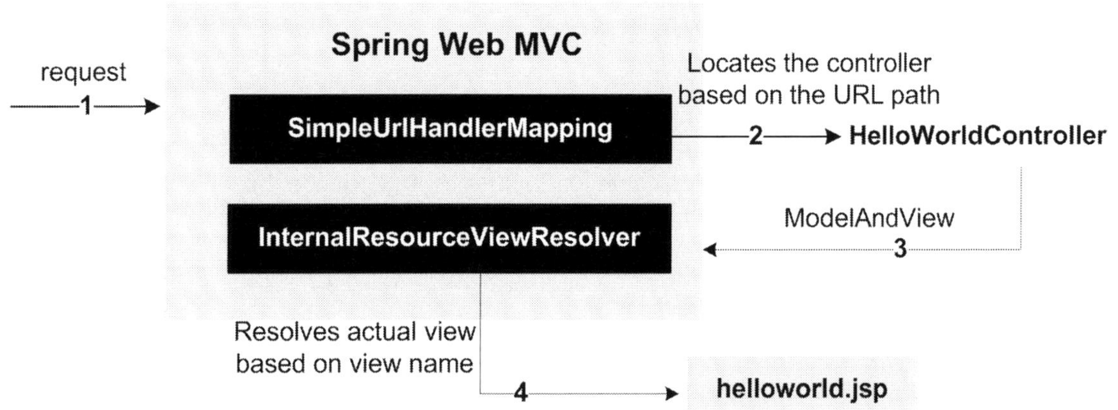

Figure 12-3 SimpleUrlHandlerMapping locates the controller to be invoked and InternalResourceViewResolver resolves the actual view based on the view name

SimpleUrlHandlerMapping and InternalResourceViewResolver beans are *automatically* detected by Spring Web MVC and used for finding the controller for request handling and resolving views, respectively.

web.xml – Web application deployment descriptor

In Spring Web MVC based applications, requests are intercepted by a DispatcherServlet (a servlet provided by Spring Web MVC) that is responsible for dispatching requests to the appropriate controller.

The following example listing shows the configuration of DispatcherServlet in web.xml file of ch12-helloworld project:

Example listing 12-4 – web.xml – DispatcherServlet configuration
Project – ch12-helloworld
Source location - src/main/webapp/WEB-INF/spring

```
<web-app xmlns="java.sun.com/xml/ns/javaee"
    xmlns:xsi="w3.org/2001/XMLSchema-instance"
    xsi:schemaLocation="java.sun.com/xml/ns/javaee
                        java.sun.com/xml/ns/javaee/web-app_3_0.xsd"
    version="3.0">

    <servlet>
        <servlet-name>hello</servlet-name>
        <servlet-class>org.springframework.web.servlet.DispatcherServlet</servlet-class>
        <init-param>
            <param-name>contextConfigLocation</param-name>
            <param-value>/WEB-INF/spring/myapp-config.xml</param-value>
        </init-param>
        <load-on-startup>1</load-on-startup>
    </servlet>

    <servlet-mapping>
        <servlet-name>hello</servlet-name>
        <url-pattern>/helloworld/*</url-pattern>
    </servlet-mapping>
</web-app>
```

A DispatcherServlet is associated with a web application context XML file which is identified by the contextConfigLocation servlet initialization parameter. In the above example listing, the contextConfigLocation initialization parameter refers to the myapp-config.xml file (refer example listing 12-3).

If you don't specify the contextConfigLocation parameter, the DispatcherServlet looks for the web application context XML file named <name-of-DispatcherServlet>-servlet.xml file in the WEB-INF directory of the web application. Here, the value of <name-of-DispatcherServlet> is the servlet name specified by the <servlet-name> sub-element of <servlet> that configures the DispatcherServlet. For instance, if we had *not* specified the contextConfigLocation parameter in example listing 12-3, the DispatcherServlet would have looked for a file named hello-servlet.xml in the WEB-INF directory.

The HandlerMapping and ViewResolver beans defined in the web application context XML file are used by the DispatcherServlet for request processing. DispatcherServlet uses the HandlerMapping implementation for finding the appropriate controller for the request, and uses the ViewResolver implementation for resolving the actual view based on the view name returned by the controller.

In the context of 'Hello World' web application, the following figure summarizes the role played by the DispatcherServlet servlet in request processing:

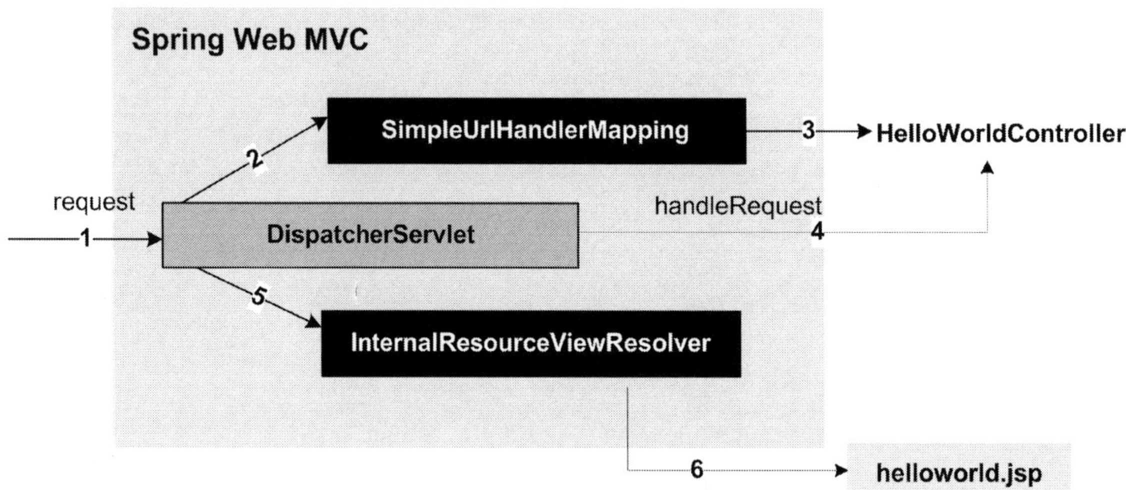

Figure 12-4 DispatcherServlet uses HandlerMapping and ViewResolver beans for request processing.

The above figure shows that the following sequence of activities are performed by Spring Web MVC during request processing:

- request is first intercepted by the DispatcherServlet servlet
- DispatcherServlet uses the HandlerMapping bean (which is SimpleUrlHandlerMapping bean in the case of 'Hello World' web application) to find an appropriate controller for handling the request
- DispatcherServlet calls the request handling method of the controller (which is HelloWorldController's handleRequest method in the case of 'Hello World' web application)
- DispatcherServlet sends the view name returned by the controller to the ViewResolver bean (which is InternalResourceViewResolver bean in the case of 'Hello World' web application) to find the actual view (JSP or servlet) to be rendered
- DispatcherServlet dispatches the request to the actual view (JSP or servlet). The model data returned by the controller are made available to the view as request attributes.

The DispatcherServlet of 'Hello World' web application is mapped to /helloworld/* pattern (refer example listing 12-4), and SimpleUrlHandlerMapping maps /sayhello URL path to HelloWorldController bean (refer example listing 12-3). If you access the URL http://localhost:8080/ch12-helloworld/helloworld/sayhello, it results in invocation of handleRequest method of HelloWorldController controller. The following figure shows how Spring Web MVC maps the URL http://localhost:8080/ch12-helloworld/helloworld/sayhello to the HelloWorldController controller:

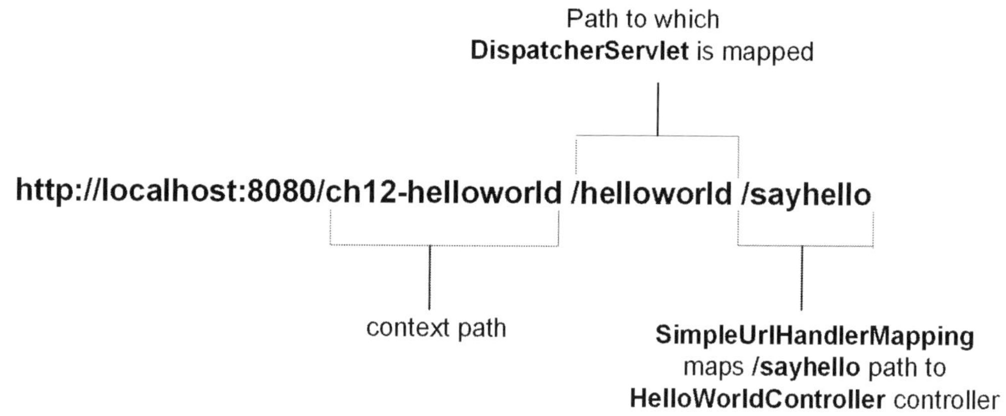

Figure 12-5 How the URL path http://localhost:8080/ch12-helloworld/helloworld/sayhello is mapped to the HelloWorldController by Spring Web MVC

In the above figure, the /ch12-helloworld part of the URL represents the context path of the 'Hello World' web application, the /helloworld part of the URL maps to the DispatcherServlet servlet (refer example listing 12-4), and the /sayhello part of the URL maps to the HelloWorldController controller (refer example listing 12-3).

In this section, we saw how a simple 'Hello World' web application is developed using Spring Web MVC. Let's now take a closer look at the DispatcherServlet servlet that acts a *front controller* in a Spring Web MVC application.

12-4 DispatcherServlet – the front controller

In the previous section, we saw that the DispatcherServlet acts as a *front controller* that interacts with the HandlerMapping and ViewResolver beans defined in the web application context XML file to process requests. In this section, we'll look at how DispatcherServlet works behind the scenes.

At the time of initialization, a DispatcherServlet loads the corresponding web application context XML file (which could be specified via contextConfigLocation initialization parameter, or is named as <name-of-DispatcherServlet>-servlet.xml file and placed in the WEB-INF directory), and creates an instance of Spring's WebApplicationContext object. WebApplicationContext is a sub-interface of ApplicationContext interface that provides features that are specific to web applications. For instance, beans in the WebApplicationContext can have additional scopes, like request and session. You can think of WebApplicationContext object as an object that represents a Spring container instance in Spring Web MVC applications.

The following table describes the additional scopes that you can specify for beans configured in the web application context XML file:

Bean scope	Description
`request`	Spring container creates a *new* bean instance for every HTTP request. The bean instance is destroyed by the Spring container when the HTTP request completes. This scope is valid only for `ApplicationContext` implementations that are applicable in web application scenarios. For instance, if you are using `XmlWebApplicationContext` or `AnnotationConfigWebApplicationContext`, only then you can specify the `request` scope for a bean.
`session`	Spring container creates a *new* bean instance when an HTTP `Session` is created. The bean instance is destroyed by the Spring container when the HTTP `Session` is destroyed. This scope is valid only for `ApplicationContext` implementations that are applicable in web application scenarios.
`application`	Spring container creates a *new* bean instance when the `ServletContext` is created, and destroys it when the `ServletContext` is destroyed. This scope is valid only for `ApplicationContext` implementations that are applicable in web application scenarios.
`websocket`	Spring container creates a *new* bean instance when the WebSocket session is created, and is destroyed when the WebSocket session is destroyed. This scope is valid only for `ApplicationContext` implementations that are applicable in web application scenarios.

If your web application consists of multiple modules, you may define a `DispatcherServlet` for each of the modules in the `web.xml` file. In such a scenario, each `DispatcherServlet` has its own web application context XML file that contains beans (like controllers, view resolvers, and so on) specific to that module. You should note that these beans are *not* shared between `DispatcherServlet` instances. The beans that are shared between `DispatcherServlet` instances are defined in the *root* web application context XML file. As mentioned earlier, the *root* web application context XML file defines data sources, services and DAOs, and so on, that are typically shared by different modules of a web application. Refer to section 12-10 to learn how the root web application context XML file is loaded.

The following figure shows relationship between beans defined by the web application context XML file associated with a `DispatcherServlet` and the beans defined by the root web application context XML file:

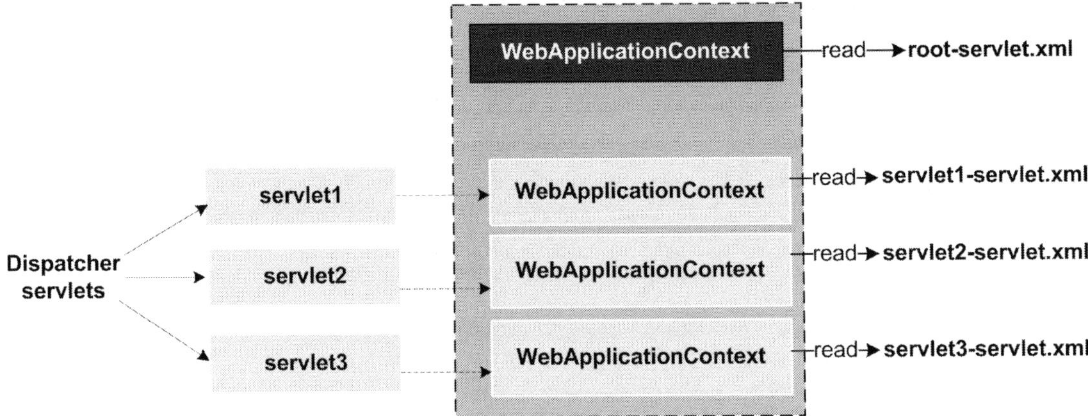

Figure 12-6 Beans in the root `WebApplicationContext` are inherited by the `WebApplicationContext` instance associated with a `DispatcherServlet`

In the above figure, servlet1, servlet2 and servlet3 are the names of DispatcherServlet instances configured in the web.xml file. And, servlet1-servlet.xml, servlet2-servlet.xml and servlet3-servlet.xml are web application context XML files that are loaded by servlet1, servlet2 and servlet3, respectively. When DispatcherServlet instances are initialized, an instance of WebApplicationContext is created corresponding to each servlet1-servlet.xml, servlet2-servlet.xml and servlet3-servlet.xml files and associated with the DispatcherServlet instance. A WebApplicationContext instance is also created corresponding to the *root* web application context XML file, root-servlet.xml. The beans contained in the root WebApplicationContext instance are available to all the WebApplicationContext instances associated with DispatcherServlets.

Let's now look at how a controller or any other Spring bean defined in a web application context XML file can access ServletContext and ServletConfig objects.

Accessing ServletContext and ServletConfig objects

In some scenarios, beans defined in the web application context XML file may require access to the ServletContext or ServletConfig object associated with the web application.

ServletContext is a Servlet API object that a bean can use to communicate with the servlet container. For instance, you can use it to get and set context attributes, obtain context initialization parameters, and so on. If a bean class implements Spring's ServletContextAware interface (a callback interface), the Spring container provides the bean instance with an instance of ServletContext object.

ServletConfig is a Servlet API object that a bean can use to obtain configuration information about the DispatcherServlet that intercepted the request. For instance, you can use it to obtain initialization parameters passed to the DispatcherServlet and the name with which the DispatcherServlet is configured in web.xml. If a bean class implements Spring's ServletConfigAware interface (a callback interface), the Spring container provides the bean instance with an instance of ServletConfig object.

The following example listing shows a bean class that implements both ServletContextAware and ServletConfigAware interfaces:

Example listing 12-5 – ServletContextAware and ServletConfigAware usage

```
import javax.servlet.ServletConfig;
import javax.servlet.ServletContext;
import org.springframework.web.context.ServletConfigAware;
import org.springframework.web.context.ServletContextAware;

public class ABean implements ServletContextAware, ServletConfigAware {
    private ServletContext servletContext;
    private ServletConfig servletConfig;

    @Override
    public void setServletContext(ServletContext servletContext) {
        this.servletContext = servletContext;
    }

    @Override
    public void setServletConfig(ServletConfig servletConfig) {
        this.servletConfig = servletConfig;
    }

    public void doSomething() {
        //--use ServletContext and ServletConfig objects
    }
```

```
}
```

The above example listing shows that the ABean class implements ServletContextAware and ServletConfigAware interfaces. The ServletContextAware interface defines a setServletContext method which is invoked by the Spring container to provide ABean instance with an instance of ServletContext object. The ServletConfigAware interface defines a setServletConfig method which is invoked by the Spring container to provide ABean instance with an instance of ServletConfig object.

We saw earlier that you can create a controller by implementing the Controller interface. Let's now look at @Controller and @RequestMapping annotations that simplify developing controllers.

12-5 Developing controllers using @Controller and @RequestMapping annotations

Spring Web MVC provides classes, like MultiActionController, UrlFilenameViewController, AbstractController, and so on, that you can extend to create your controllers. If you extend a Spring-specific class or implement a Spring-specific interface to create a controller, the controller class becomes tightly coupled with Spring. Spring defines annotations like @Controller, @RequestMapping, @ModelAttribute, and so on, that allow you to create controllers with flexible method signatures. In this section, we'll look at different Spring Web MVC annotations for developing *annotated* controllers.

Let's first look at a 'Hello World' web application that uses an annotated controller to show the 'Hello World !!' message.

IMPORT **chapter 12/ch12-annotation-helloworld** (This project shows a simple 'Hello World' web application that uses an annotated controller to show 'Hello World !!' message. If you deploy the project on Tomcat server and access the URL http://localhost:8080/ch12-annotation-helloworld/helloworld/saySomething/sayhello, you'll see the 'Hello World !!' message.)

Developing a 'Hello World' web application using an annotated controller

The ch12-annotation-helloworld project is similar to ch12-helloworld, except that the ch12-annotation-helloworld project uses an annotated controller to show 'Hello World !!' message. The web.xml and helloworld.jsp files in both the projects are exactly the same, but HelloWorldController.java and myapp-config.xml files are different. For this reason, we'll restrict our discussion to HelloWorldController.java and myapp-config.xml files in this section.

Let's first look at how to create a controller using @Controller and @RequestMapping annotations.

@Controller and @RequestMapping annotations

You designate a particular class as a Spring Web MVC controller by annotating it with @Controller annotation. And, you use @RequestMapping annotation to map an incoming request to the appropriate method of a controller.

The following example listing shows the HelloWorldController class that uses @Controller and @RequestMapping annotations:

Example listing 12-6 – HelloWorldController class - @Controller and @RequestMapping usage
Project – ch12-annotation-helloworld
Source location - src/main/java/sample/spring/chapter12/web

```
package sample.spring.chapter12.web;

import org.springframework.stereotype.Controller;
```

```
import org.springframework.web.bind.annotation.RequestMapping;
import org.springframework.web.servlet.ModelAndView;
.....
@Controller(value="sayHelloController")
@RequestMapping("/saySomething")
public class HelloWorldController {

    @RequestMapping("/sayhello")
    public ModelAndView sayHello() {
        Map<String, String> modelData = new HashMap<String, String>();
        modelData.put("msg", "Hello World !!");
        return new ModelAndView("helloworld", modelData);
    }
}
```

In the above example listing, the `HelloWorldController` class is annotated with `@Controller` and `@RequestMapping` annotations, and the `sayHello` method is annotated with `@RequestMapping` annotation. `@Controller` annotation is a specialized form of `@Component` annotation (refer chapter 6) that indicates that the `HelloWorldController` is a controller component.

Like `@Service` (refer chapter 6) and `@Repository` (refer chapter 8) annotated classes, `@Controller` annotated classes are automatically registered with the Spring container; you don't need to explicitly define a `@Controller` annotated class in the web application context XML file. The `value` attribute of `@Controller` annotation specifies the name with which the class is registered with the Spring container. The `value` attribute serves the same purpose as the `<bean>` element's `id` attribute. If the `value` attribute is not specified, the name (beginning with lowercase first letter) of the class is used to register the class with the Spring container.

`@RequestMapping` annotation maps incoming web requests to appropriate controllers and/or controller methods. `@RequestMapping` annotation at the type-level maps a request to the appropriate controller. For instance, `@RequestMapping("/saySomething")` on `HelloWorldController` class indicates that all requests to `/saySomething` request path are handled by the `HelloWorldController` controller.

`@RequestMapping` at the method-level narrows down the `@RequestMapping` at the type-level to a specific method in the controller class. For instance, `@RequestMapping("/sayhello")` annotation on `sayHello` method in example listing 12-6 specifies that the `sayHello` method is invoked when the request path is `/saySomething/sayhello`. Notice that the `HelloWorldController`'s `sayHello` method doesn't accept any arguments and returns a `ModelAndView` object. This is possible because annotated controllers can have flexible method signatures. In section 12-7, we'll look at possible arguments and return types `@RequestMapping` annotated methods can define.

`@RequestMapping` annotation at the type level usually specifies a request path or a path pattern. And, `@RequestMapping` annotation at the method-level usually specifies an HTTP method or a request parameter to further narrow down the mapping specified by the type-level `@RequestMapping` annotation. The following figure shows how `http://localhost:8080/ch12-annotation-helloworld/helloworld/saySomething/sayhello` URL will result in invocation of `HelloWorldController`'s `sayHello` method by Spring Web MVC:

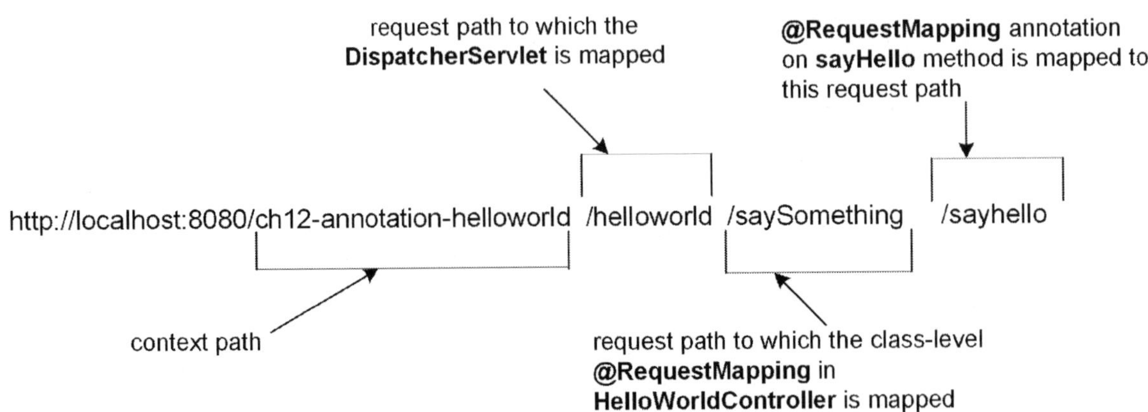

Figure 12-7 How a request URL is mapped to an appropriate `@RequestMapping` annotated method of a controller

The above figure shows how a particular request URL results in invocation of `HelloWorldController`'s `sayHello` method.

Let's now look at how annotation-driven development of Spring Web MVC controllers is enabled in an application.

Enabling Spring Web MVC annotations

To use annotated controllers in your Spring Web MVC application, you need to enable Spring Web MVC annotations using `<annotation-driven>` element of Spring's `mvc` schema, as shown in the following example listing:

Example listing 12-7 – myapp-config.xml
Project – ch12-annotation-helloworld
Source location - src/main/webapp/WEB-INF/spring

```
<beans .....
   xmlns:mvc="http://www.springframework.org/schema/mvc"
    xsi:schemaLocation=".....http://www.springframework.org/schema/mvc
                          http://www.springframework.org/schema/mvc/spring-mvc.xsd.....">

   <mvc:annotation-driven />
   <context:component-scan base-package="sample.spring.chapter12.web" />

    <bean id="viewResolver"
          class="org.springframework.web.servlet.view.InternalResourceViewResolver">
        <property name="prefix" value="/WEB-INF/jsp/" />
        <property name="suffix" value=".jsp" />
    </bean>
</beans>
```

In the above example listing, `<mvc:annotation-driven>` element of Spring's `mvc` schema enables use of Spring Web MVC annotations in implementing controllers. Also, `<component-scan>` element (refer section 6-2 of chapter 6 for more details) of context schema is used to automatically register `@Controller` annotated classes with the Spring container.

> In Java-based configuration approach, the `@EnableWebMvc` annotation serves the same purpose as the `<annotation-driven>` element of Spring's `mvc` schema.

In this section, we saw how to develop a simple 'Hello World' web application using `@Controller` and `@RequestMapping` annotations. Let's now look at the requirements of the MyBank web application that we'll develop in this chapter using Spring Web MVC annotations.

12-6 MyBank web application's requirements

Figure 12-8 shows the home page of MyBank web application that displays a list of currently active fixed deposits in the system. In figure 12-8, the `ID` column shows the unique identifier for a fixed deposit. The `ID` value is automatically assigned to a fixed deposit when it is created by a user. `Close` and `Edit` hyperlinks allow a user to remove and edit details of a fixed deposit, respectively.

ID	Deposit amount	Tenure	Email	Action
1	10000	24	a1email@somedomain.com	Close Edit
2	20000	36	a2email@somedomain.com	Close Edit
3	30000	36	a3email@somedomain.com	Close Edit
4	50000	36	a4email@somedomain.com	Close Edit
5	15000	36	a5email@somedomain.com	Close Edit

Create new Fixed Deposit

Figure 12-8 MyBank web application's home page shows fixed deposit details. The web page provides the option to close, edit and create a fixed deposit.

The `Create new Fixed Deposit` button shows the '`Open fixed deposit`' form for entering details of the fixed deposit to be opened, as shown in the following figure:

Open fixed deposit

Amount (in USD): 100 must be greater than or equal to 1000

Tenure (in months): 6 must be greater than or equal to 12

Email: xyz not a well-formed email address

Save Go Back

Figure 12-9 '`Open fixed deposit`' form for opening fixed deposits. `Amount`, `Tenure` and `Email` fields are mandatory.

In the above figure, clicking the `Save` button saves the fixed deposit details in the data store, and `Go Back` hyperlink takes the user back to the web page that shows the fixed deposit list (refer figure 12-8). The above figure shows that appropriate error messages are displayed if the entered data doesn't meet the constraints set on `Amount`, `Tenure` and `Email` fields.

When you click the Edit hyperlink in figure 12-8, a form similar to figure 12-9 is shown for modifying details of the selected fixed deposit. And, clicking the Close hyperlink in figure 12-8 removes the selected fixed deposit from the list of fixed deposits.

Now that we know the MyBank web application requirements, let's look at how we implement it using Spring Web MVC annotations.

12-7 Spring Web MVC annotations - @RequestMapping and @RequestParam

In section 12-5, we saw that we can use @Controller and @RequestMapping annotations to develop a simple controller. In this section, we'll take a closer look at @RequestMapping and other Spring Web MVC annotations that simplify developing annotated controllers.

IMPORT **chapter 12/ch12-bankapp** (This project shows the MyBank web application that allows its user to manage fixed deposits. If you deploy the project on Tomcat server and access the URL http://localhost:8080/ch12-bankapp, you'll see the list of fixed deposits (as shown in figure 12-8) in the system.)

Let's begin by looking at the @RequestMapping annotation.

Mapping requests to controllers or controller methods using @RequestMapping

In section 12-5, we saw that the @RequestMapping annotation is used at the *type* and *method*-level to map requests to controllers and its methods. In this section, we'll first look at how Spring Web MVC maps a web request to a particular controller method that uses @RequestMapping annotation. We'll then look at the attributes of @RequestMapping annotation, and the arguments and return types that @RequestMapping annotated methods can have.

@RequestMapping annotation and RequestMappingHandlerMapping

The following example listing shows @RequestMapping annotation usage in SomeController (a Spring Web MVC controller) class:

Example listing 12-8 – SomeController class - @RequestMapping usage

```
@Controller
@RequestMapping("/type_Level_Url")
public class SomeController {

    @RequestMapping("/methodA_Url")
    public ModelAndView methodA() { ..... }

    @RequestMapping("/methodB_Url")
    public ModelAndView methodB() { ..... }
}
```

The <annotation-driven> element of Spring's mvc schema creates an instance of RequestMappingHandlerMapping (a HandlerMapping implementation) that is responsible for mapping a web request to an appropriate @RequestMapping annotated method. RequestMappingHandlerMapping considers controller methods as endpoints, and is responsible for *uniquely* mapping a request to a controller method based on the @RequestMapping annotations at type- and method-level. In the case of SomeController, if the request path is /type_Level_Url/methodA_Url, methodA is invoked, and if the request path is /type_Level_Url/methodB_Url, methodB is invoked. You should note that if a request cannot be mapped uniquely to a controller method, then a HTTP 404 (which means, resource not found) status code is returned.

The attributes of @RequestMapping annotation are used to narrow down the mapping of a request to a particular controller or a controller method. You can specify these attributes at both type- and method-level @RequestMapping annotations. Let's now look at the attributes of @RequestMapping annotation.

Mapping requests based on request path

@RequestMapping's path attribute (alias for value attribute) specifies the request path to which a controller or controller method is mapped. You can specify the request path without explicitly specifying the path attribute in the @RequestMapping annotation. For instance, you can specify @RequestMapping(path = "/type_Level_Url") as @RequestMapping("/type_Level_Url").

You can also specify Ant-style path patterns as the value of path attribute. For instance, you can specify patterns, like /myUrl/*, /myUrl/** and /myUrl/*.do, as the value of path attribute. The following example listing shows a @RequestMapping annotation that specifies /myUrl/** as the path pattern:

Example listing 12-9 – SomeController class – Ant-style request path pattern usage

```
@Controller
@RequestMapping("/myUrl/**")
public class SomeController { ..... }
```

In the above example listing, @RequestMapping("/myUrl/**") annotation at the type-level specifies that the SomeController controller handles all requests that begin with /myUrl path. For instance, requests to /myUrl/abc, /myUrl/xyz and /myUrl/123/something paths are handled by SomeController controller.

Mapping requests based on HTTP methods

@RequestMapping's method attribute specifies the HTTP method that is handled by the controller or controller method. So, if the method attribute specifies an HTTP GET method, the controller or the controller method handles *only* HTTP GET requests.

The following example listing shows the FixedDepositController's listFixedDeposits method that is responsible for rendering the list of fixed deposits in the system:

Example listing 12-10 – @RequestMapping's method attribute usage
Project – ch12-bankapp
Source location - src/main/java/sample/spring/chapter12/web

```
package sample.spring.chapter12.web;

import org.springframework.web.bind.annotation.RequestMethod;
.....
@Controller
@RequestMapping(path="/fixedDeposit")
public class FixedDepositController {
    .....
    @RequestMapping(path = "/list", method = RequestMethod.GET)
    public ModelAndView listFixedDeposits() { ..... }
    .....
}
```

In the above example listing, @RequestMapping annotation on the listFixedDeposits method specifies value of method attribute as RequestMethod.GET. The RequestMethod is an enum that defines HTTP request methods, like GET, POST, PUT, DELETE, and so on. As the value of the method attribute is RequestMethod.GET, the listFixedDeposits method is invoked only if an HTTP GET request is sent to /fixedDeposit/list path.

For instance, if you send an HTTP POST request to /fixedDeposit/list path, application will return an HTTP 405 (which means, the HTTP method is not supported) status code.

You can also specify an array of HTTP methods as the value of method attribute, as shown in the following example listing:

Example listing 12-11 – Specifying multiple HTTP methods as the value of method attribute

```
@Controller
@RequestMapping(path="/sample")
public class MyController {

    @RequestMapping(path = "/action" method={ RequestMethod.GET, RequestMethod.POST })
    public ModelAndView action() { ..... }
}
```

In the above example listing, the action method is annotated with @RequestMapping annotation whose method attribute's value is { RequestMethod.GET, RequestMethod.POST }. This means that the action method is invoked if an HTTP GET or POST request is sent to /sample/action path.

Instead of using the generic @RequestMapping annotation, you can use HTTP method-specific annotations, like @GetMapping, @PostMapping, @PutMapping, and so on. In chapter 6, we saw how you can create a custom qualifier annotation by using @Qualifier as a meta-annotation. Similarly, these HTTP method-specific annotations are created by using @RequestMapping as a meta-annotation.

> Custom annotations that are created by using existing annotations as meta-annotations are referred to as *composed annotations*. The HTTP method-specific annotations, like @GetMapping, @PostMapping, and so on, are examples of composed annotations.

The following example listing shows how the @GetMapping annotation is defined:

Example listing 12-12 – @GetMapping annotation

```
@Target(ElementType.METHOD)
@Retention(RetentionPolicy.RUNTIME)
@Documented
@RequestMapping(method = RequestMethod.GET)
public @interface GetMapping {
.....
}
```

Notice that the @GetMapping annotation is meta-annotated with @RequestMapping annotation and the method attribute is explicitly set to RequestMethod.GET.

Mapping requests based on request parameters

@RequestMapping's params attribute typically specifies the name and value of the request parameter that *must* be present in the request. The following example listing shows the FixedDepositController's showOpenFixedDepositForm method that is responsible for showing the form for creating a fixed deposit:

Example listing 12-13 – @RequestMapping's params attribute usage
Project – ch12-bankapp
Source location - src/main/java/sample/spring/chapter12/web

```
package sample.spring.chapter12.web;

import org.springframework.web.bind.annotation.RequestMethod;
```

```
.....
@Controller
@RequestMapping(path="/fixedDeposit")
public class FixedDepositController {
    .....
    @RequestMapping(params = "fdAction=createFDForm", method = RequestMethod.POST)
    public ModelAndView showOpenFixedDepositForm() { ..... }
    .....
}
```

In the above example listing, `@RequestMapping` annotation on the `showOpenFixedDepositForm` method specifies the value of params attribute as `fdAction=createFDForm`. As the `FixedDepositController` is mapped to `/fixedDeposit` path, the `showOpenFixedDepositForm` method is invoked if an HTTP POST request containing request parameter named `fdAction` with value `createFDForm` is sent to `/fixedDeposit` path.

If you want to map requests to a controller or controller method based on the values of multiple request parameters, you can specify an array of request parameter name-value pairs as the value of `params` attribute, as shown in the following example listing:

Example listing 12-14 – Specifying multiple request parameter name-value pairs as the value of `params` attribute

```
    @RequestMapping(params = { "x=a", "y=b" })
    public void perform() { ..... }
```

In the above example listing, the `perform` method is invoked only if the request contains parameters named x and y with values a and b, respectively.

You can also map requests to a controller or controller method based on the existence of a request parameter in the request. All you need to do is to simply specify the name of the request parameter as the value of `params` attribute. For instance, the `perform` method shown here is invoked irrespective of the value of request parameter x:

Example listing 12-15 – `perform` method is invoked if request parameter x is found

```
    @RequestMapping(params = "x")
    public void perform() { ..... }
```

To map requests to a controller or controller method if a request parameter does *not* exist, use the ! operator. For example, the following `perform` method is invoked if request parameter named x is *not* found in the request:

Example listing 12-16 – `perform` method is invoked if request parameter x is *not* found

```
    @RequestMapping(params = "!x")
    public void perform() { ..... }
```

You can use != operator to map requests to a controller or controller method if the value of a request parameter is *not* equal to the specified value, as shown here:

Example listing 12-17 – `perform` method is invoked if the value of request parameter x is *not equal* to a

```
    @RequestMapping(params = "x != a")
    public void perform() { ..... }
```

In the above example listing, `perform` method is invoked only if the request contains a request parameter named x, and the value of x is *not equal* to a.

Mapping requests based on the MIME type of the request

The Content-Type request header specifies the MIME type of the request. @RequestMapping's consumes attribute specifies the MIME type of the request that a controller or a controller method handles. So, if the value of consumes attribute matches the value of the Content-Type request header, the request is mapped to that particular controller or controller method.

The following example listing shows that the perform method is invoked if the Content-Type request header's value is application/json:

Example listing 12-18 – perform method is invoked if the value of Content-Type header is application/json

```
@RequestMapping(consumes = "application/json")
public void perform() { ..... }
```

As with the params attribute, you can use ! operator to specify the condition that a Content-Type header value is *not* present. For instance, the following perform method is invoked if the Content-Type header's value is *not* application/json:

Example listing 12-19 – perform method is invoked if the value of Content-Type header is *not* application/json

```
@RequestMapping(consumes = "!application/json")
public void perform() { ..... }
```

You can specify an array of values in the consumes attribute, in which case the request is mapped to the controller or the controller method if the Content-Type value matches one of the values specified by the consumes attribute. In the following example listing, the perform method is invoked if the Content-Type is application/json or text/plain:

Example listing 12-20 – perform method is invoked if Content-Type is application/json or text/plain

```
@RequestMapping(consumes = { "application/json", "text/plain")
public void perform() { ..... }
```

Mapping requests based on the acceptable MIME type of the response

The Accept request header specifies the acceptable MIME type of the response. @RequestMapping's produces attribute specifies the acceptable MIME type of the response. So, if the value of produces attribute value matches the Accept request header, the request is mapped to that particular controller or controller method.

The following example listing shows that the perform method is invoked if the Accept request header's value is application/json:

Example listing 12-21 – perform method is invoked if the value of Accept header is application/json

```
@RequestMapping(produces = "application/json")
public void perform() { ..... }
```

As with the consumes attribute, you can use ! operator to specify the condition that an Accept header value is *not* present in the request. If you specify an array of values for the produces attribute, request is mapped to the controller or the controller method if the Accept header value matches one of the values specified by the produces attribute.

Mapping requests based on a request header value

To map requests based on request headers, you can use @RequestMapping's headers attribute. The following example listing shows that the request is mapped to the perform method if the value of Content-Type header is text/plain:

Example listing 12-22 – perform method is invoked if the value of Content-Type header is text/plain

```
@RequestMapping(headers = "Content-Type=text/plain")
public void perform() { ..... }
```

As with the params attribute, you can use ! and != operators while specifying value of headers attribute. For instance, the following example listing shows that the request is mapped to the perform method if the value of Content-Type header is *not equal* to application/json, the Cache-Control header *doesn't exist* in the request, and the From header *exists* in the request with any value:

Example listing 12-23 – Using ! and != operators for specifying value of headers attribute

```
@RequestMapping(headers = { "Content-Type != application/json",
                            "!Cache-Control", "From"} )
public void perform() { ..... }
```

Now that we have looked at the attributes of @RequestMapping annotation, let's look at the arguments that you can pass to @RequestMapping annotated methods.

@RequestMapping annotated methods arguments

@RequestMapping annotated methods can have flexible method signatures. The argument types that can be passed to @RequestMapping annotated methods include HttpServletRequest, HttpSession, java.security.Principal, org.springframework.validation.BindingResult, org.springframework.web.bind.support.SessionStatus, org.springframework.ui.Model, and so on. To view a complete list of arguments that can be passed to @RequestMapping annotated method, please refer to @RequestMapping Javadoc.

As we discuss different Spring Web MVC features in this book, we'll come across scenarios which require us to pass different argument types to @RequestMapping annotated methods. For now, we'll look at a scenario in which we need to send HttpServletRequest object as an argument.

The following example listing shows the FixedDepositController's viewFixedDepositDetails method that accepts an argument of type HttpServletRequest:

Example listing 12-24 – FixedDepositController class - passing HttpServletRequest argument
Project – ch12-bankapp
Source location - src/main/java/sample/spring/chapter12/web

```
package sample.spring.chapter12.web;

import javax.servlet.http.HttpServletRequest;
.....
public class FixedDepositController {
  .....
  @RequestMapping(params = "fdAction=view", method = RequestMethod.GET)
  public ModelAndView viewFixedDepositDetails(HttpServletRequest request) {
     FixedDepositDetails fixedDepositDetails = fixedDepositService
           .getFixedDeposit(Integer.parseInt(request.getParameter("fixedDepositId")));
     .....
  }
```

```
    .....
}
```

The viewFixedDepositDetails method is invoked when you click the Edit hyperlink corresponding to a fixed deposit (refer figure 12-8). HttpServletRequest is used by the viewFixedDepositDetails method to obtain the fixedDepositId request parameter that uniquely identifies a fixed deposit in the system.

Let's now look at the return types that are supported for @RequestMapping annotated methods.

@RequestMapping annotated methods return types

The supported return types for @RequestMapping annotated methods include ModelAndView, org.springframework.web.servlet.View, String, java.util.concurrent.Callable, void, ListenableFuture, and so on. To view a complete list of return types supported for @RequestMapping annotated methods, please refer to @RequestMapping Javadoc.

As we discuss different Spring Web MVC features in this book, we'll come across scenarios which require @RequestMapping annotated methods to have different return types. In this section, we'll only look at examples that show methods that have String or ModelAndView as return types.

The following example listing shows FixedDepositController's showOpenFixedDepositForm method that renders the HTML form for opening a new fixed deposit (refer figure 12-9):

Example listing 12-25 – FixedDepositController class - ModelAndView return type example
Project – ch12-bankapp
Source location - src/main/java/sample/spring/chapter12/web

```
package sample.spring.chapter12.web;

import org.springframework.ui.ModelMap;
.....
public class FixedDepositController {
    .....
    @RequestMapping(params = "fdAction=createFDForm", method = RequestMethod.POST)
    public ModelAndView showOpenFixedDepositForm() {
        FixedDepositDetails fixedDepositDetails = new FixedDepositDetails();
        fixedDepositDetails.setEmail("You must enter a valid email");

        ModelMap modelData = new ModelMap();
        modelData.addAttribute(fixedDepositDetails);
        return new ModelAndView("createFixedDepositForm", modelData);
    }
    .....
}
```

The showOpenFixedDepositForm method returns a ModelAndView object that contains an instance of FixedDepositDetails as a model attribute and createFixedDepositForm string value as the view name.

If you compare the above example listing with 12-1 and 12-6, you'll notice that the showOpenFixedDepositForm method uses Spring's ModelMap object instead of java.util.Map to store model attributes. ModelMap is an implementation of java.util.Map interface that allows you to store model attributes without explicitly specifying their names. ModelMap automatically generates the name of the model attribute based on a pre-defined strategy. For instance, if you add a custom Java object as a model attribute, the name (beginning with lowercase first letter) of the object's class is used as the name of the model attribute. In the above example listing, when an instance of FixedDepositDetails is added to the ModelMap, it is stored in the ModelMap with the name fixedDepositDetails.

When a @RequestMapping annotated method returns a string value, it is considered as the name of the view that is resolved to an actual view (like, JSP page or servlet) by the ViewResolver configured for the web application. The following example listing shows the configuration of InternalResourceViewResolver in ch12-bankapp project:

Example listing 12-26 – bankapp-config.xml – ViewResolver configuration
Project – ch12-bankapp
Source location - src/main/webapp/WEB-INF/spring

```
<bean id="viewResolver"
      class="org.springframework.web.servlet.view.InternalResourceViewResolver">
    <property name="prefix" value="/WEB-INF/jsp/" />
    <property name="suffix" value=".jsp" />
</bean>
```

The above configuration suggests that when a string value xyz is returned, it is resolved to /WEB-INF/jsp/xyz.jsp. Refer section 12-3 to learn more about the InternalResourceViewResolver configuration shown above.

If the string value returned by the @RequestMapping annotated method has the prefix redirect:, it is treated as a redirect URL and *not* as a view name. The following example listing shows FixedDepositController's closeFixedDeposit method that is responsible for closing a fixed deposit when a user clicks the Close button (refer figure 12-9):

Example listing 12-27 – FixedDepositController class - String return type example
Project – ch12-bankapp
Source location - src/main/java/sample/spring/chapter12/web

```
@RequestMapping(params = "fdAction=close", method = RequestMethod.GET)
public String closeFixedDeposit(..... int fdId) {
    fixedDepositService.closeFixedDeposit(fdId);
    return "redirect:/fixedDeposit/list";
}
```

FixedDepositController's closeFixedDeposit method closes the fixed deposit identified by the fdId argument and returns redirect:/fixedDeposit/list string value. As the returned string value is prefixed with redirect:, the user is redirected to the /fixedDeposit/list URL that shows the list of fixed deposits (refer figure 12-8).

Let's now look at the @RequestParam annotation that allows you to assign a request parameter value to a controller method argument.

Passing request parameters to controller methods using @RequestParam

We saw in example listing 12-24 that we can pass HttpServletRequest object to a controller method and use it to retrieve request parameters. Instead of passing HttpServletRequest object to a controller method, you can annotate a method argument with @RequestParam annotation to assign value of a request parameter to the method argument.

You should note that the @RequestParam annotation can only be used if the method is annotated with @RequestMapping or @ModelAttribute (explained in chapter 13) annotation.

The following example listing shows FixedDepositController's closeFixedDeposit method that is invoked when a user clicks the Close button (refer figure 12-8) to close a fixed deposit:

Example listing 12-28 – FixedDepositController class - @RequestParam usage
Project – ch12-bankapp
Source location - src/main/java/sample/spring/chapter12/web

```
package sample.spring.chapter12.web;

import org.springframework.web.bind.annotation.RequestParam;
.....
public class FixedDepositController {
    .....
    @RequestMapping(params = "fdAction=close", method = RequestMethod.GET)
    public String closeFixedDeposit(@RequestParam(value = "fixedDepositId") int fdId) {
        fixedDepositService.closeFixedDeposit(fdId);
        return "redirect:/fixedDeposit/list";
    }
    .....
}
```

@RequestParam's name (alias for value attribute) attribute specifies the name of the request parameter whose value is assigned to the method argument. In the above example listing, @RequestParam annotation is used to assign the value of fixedDepositId request parameter to fdId method argument. As the type of the fdId argument is int, Spring is responsible for converting the fixedDepositId request parameter to int type. By default, Spring automatically provides type conversion for simple Java types, like int, long, java.util.Date, and so on. To convert request parameters to custom Java types (like Address), you need to register custom PropertyEditors with Spring's WebDataBinder instance or org.springframework.format.Formatters with Spring's FormattingConversionService instance. We'll learn more about WebDataBinder in chapter 13, and Formatter and FormattingConversionService in chapter 15.

Let's now look at how you can access all the request parameters in a controller method.

Passing all the request parameters to a controller method

To pass *all* the request parameters to a controller method, define an argument of type Map<String, String> or MultiValueMap<String, String> (an object provided by Spring that implements java.util.Map interface) and annotate it with @RequestParam annotation.

The following example listing shows FixedDepositController's openFixedDeposit method that creates a fixed deposit when a user enters fixed deposit details and clicks the Save button on the 'Open fixed deposit' form for opening fixed deposits (refer figure 12-9):

Example listing 12-29 – FixedDepositController class – accessing all request parameters
Project – ch12-bankapp
Source location - src/main/java/sample/spring/chapter12/web

```
package sample.spring.chapter12.web;

import java.util.Map;
.....
@RequestMapping(path = "/fixedDeposit")
public class FixedDepositController {
    .....
    @RequestMapping(params = "fdAction=create", method = RequestMethod.POST)
    public ModelAndView openFixedDeposit(@RequestParam Map<String, String> params) {
```

```
        String depositAmount = params.get("depositAmount");
        String tenure = params.get("tenure");
        .....
    }
}
```

In the above example listing, params argument of type Map<String, String> is annotated with @RequestParam annotation. Notice that the name attribute of @RequestParam annotation is *not* specified. If @RequestParam's name attribute is not specified and the type of the method argument is Map<String, String> or MultiValueMap<String, String>, Spring copies all the requests parameters into the method argument. Each request parameter's value is stored in the Map (or MultiValueMap) with the name of the request parameter as the key.

The following example listing shows FixedDepositController's editFixedDeposit method that is responsible for making changes to an existing fixed deposit:

Example listing 12-30 – FixedDepositController class – accessing all request parameters
Project – ch12-bankapp
Source location - src/main/java/sample/spring/chapter12/web

```
package sample.spring.chapter12.web;

import org.springframework.util.MultiValueMap;
.....
public class FixedDepositController {
    .....
    @RequestMapping(params = "fdAction=edit", method = RequestMethod.POST)
    public ModelAndView editFixedDeposit(
            @RequestParam MultiValueMap<String, String> params) {
        String depositAmount = params.get("depositAmount").get(0);
        String tenure = params.get("tenure").get(0);
        .....
    }
}
```

In the above example listing, editFixedDeposit's params argument is of type MultiValueMap<String, String>, and is annotated with @RequestParam annotation. If an object is of type MultiValueMap<K, V>, then it means that K is the type of the key and List<V> is the type of the value. As the params argument is of type MultiValueMap<String, String>, it means that the key is of type String and the value is of type List<String>. When storing request parameters in MultiValueMap<String, String> type, Spring uses request parameter's name as key and the value of the request parameter is added to the List<String> value. MultiValueMap is particularly useful if you have multiple request parameters with the same name.

As the value corresponding to a request parameter is of type List<String>, calling params.get(String key) returns a List<String> type. For this reason, get(0) is called on the returned List<String> to get the value of request parameters depositAmount, tenure, and so on. Alternatively, you can use getFirst(String key) method of MultiValueMap to obtain the first element from the List<String> value.

Let's now take a closer look at the various attributes of @RequestParam annotation.

Specifying request parameter name using name attribute

We saw earlier that @RequestParam's name attribute specifies the name of the request parameter whose value is assigned to the method argument. If you don't specify the name of a request parameter, method argument name is considered as the name of the request parameter name. For instance, in the following example listing, value of request parameter named param is assigned to the param argument:

Example listing 12-31 – @RequestParam usage - unspecified request parameter name

```
@RequestMapping(.....)
public String doSomething(@RequestParam String param) { ..... }
```

In the above example listing, @RequestParam doesn't specify the name of the request parameter whose value is assigned to the param argument; therefore, param is considered as the name of the request parameter.

Specifying request parameter is optional or mandatory by using required attribute

By default, request parameter specified by the @RequestParam annotation is mandatory; if the specified request parameter is not found in the request, an exception is thrown. You can specify that the request parameter is optional by setting the value of required attribute to false, as shown here:

Example listing 12-32 – @RequestParam's required attribute

```
@RequestMapping(.....)
public String perform(@RequestParam(name = "myparam", required = false) String param) {
    .....
}
```

In the above example listing, @RequestParam's required attribute value is set to false, which means that the myparam request parameter is optional. Now, if the myparam request parameter is not found in the request, it'll *not* result in an exception. Instead, a null value is assigned to the param method argument.

Instead of using the required attribute to specify that a request parameter is optional, you can use Java 8's Optional type (discussed earlier in section 6-5 of chapter 6). The following example listing shows the perform method that uses Java 8's Optional type:

Example listing 12-33 – @RequestParam – using Java 8's Optional type

```
@RequestMapping(.....)
public String perform(@RequestParam(name = "myparam") Optional<String> param) { ..... }
```

As the type of the param argument is Optional<String>, no exception is thrown if a request parameter named myparam is not found in the request.

Specifying default value for a request parameter using defaultValue attribute

@RequestParam's defaultValue attribute specifies the default value for a request parameter. If the request parameter specified by @RequestParam's name attribute is not found in the request, the value specified by the defaultValue attribute is assigned to the method argument. The following example listing shows usage of defaultValue attribute:

Example listing 12-34 – @RequestParam's defaultValue attribute

```
@RequestMapping(.....)
public String perform(@RequestParam(value = "location", defaultValue = "earth")
                            String param) {
     .....
}
```

In the above example listing, if request parameter named location is not found in the request, the value earth is assigned to the param method argument.

In this section, we looked at @RequestMapping and @RequestParam annotations to create the FixedDepositController of MyBank application. Let's now look at how validation of form data is performed in the FixedDepositController class.

12-8 Validation

We saw earlier that FixedDepositController's showOpenFixedDepositForm method (refer example listing 12-25) renders createFixedDepositForm.jsp JSP page that shows the form for opening a new fixed deposit. When the form is submitted, the data entered in the form is validated by FixedDepositController's openFixedDeposit method (refer example listing 12-29). If errors are reported during validation, the createFixedDepositForm.jsp JSP page is rendered again with validation error messages and the original form data that was entered by the user (refer figure 12-9).

The following example listing shows the <form> element of createFixedDepositForm.jsp JSP page:

Example listing 12-35 – createFixedDepositForm.jsp – <form> element
Project – ch12-bankapp
Source location - src/main/webapp/WEB-INF/jsp

```
<form name="createFixedDepositForm" method="POST"
      action="${pageContext.request.contextPath}/fixedDeposit?fdAction=create">
    .....
    <input type="submit" value="Save" />
</form>
```

In the above example listing, <form> element's method attribute specifies POST as the HTTP method, and action attribute specifies /fixedDeposit?fdAction=create as the URL to which the form is submitted when the user clicks the Save button. Submission of the form results in the invocation of FixedDepositController's openFixedDeposit method.

The following example listing shows how the validation is performed by the openFixedDeposit method, and how the original form data entered by the user is shown again in case of validation errors:

Example listing 12-36 – FixedDepositController's openFixedDeposit method
Project – ch12-bankapp
Source location - src/main/java/sample/spring/chapter12/web

```
package sample.spring.chapter12.web;
.....
import org.apache.commons.lang3.math.NumberUtils;
@RequestMapping(path = "/fixedDeposit")
public class FixedDepositController {
    .....
    @RequestMapping(params = "fdAction=create", method = RequestMethod.POST)
    public ModelAndView openFixedDeposit(@RequestParam Map<String, String> params) {
        String depositAmount = params.get("depositAmount");
        .....
        Map<String, Object> modelData = new HashMap<String, Object>();

        if (!NumberUtils.isNumber(depositAmount)) {
            modelData.put("error.depositAmount", "enter a valid number");
        } else if (NumberUtils.toInt(depositAmount) < 1000) {
            modelData.put("error.depositAmount", "must be greater than or equal to 1000");
        }
        .....
        FixedDepositDetails fixedDepositDetails = new FixedDepositDetails();
```

```
        fixedDepositDetails.setDepositAmount(depositAmount);
        .....
        if (modelData.size() > 0) { // --this means there are validation errors
            modelData.put("fixedDepositDetails", fixedDepositDetails);
            return new ModelAndView("createFixedDepositForm", modelData);
        } else {
            fixedDepositService.saveFixedDeposit(fixedDepositDetails);
            return new ModelAndView("redirect:/fixedDeposit/list");
        }
    }
    .....
}
```

The openFixedDeposit method validates deposit amount, tenure and email information entered by the user. Notice that to simplify validation of data, NumberUtils class of Apache Commons Lang (http://commons.apache.org/proper/commons-lang/) library has been used. The modelData variable is a java.util.Map object that stores model attributes that we want to pass to the createFixedDepositForm.jsp JSP page in case of validation errors.

As we want to show validation error messages and the original form data if validation fails, the validation error messages and the original form data are stored in modelData. For instance, if the deposit amount entered by the user fails validation, an appropriate validation error message is stored in the modelData with name error.depositAmount. The values entered by the user are set on a new instance of FixedDepositDetails object. If validation errors are reported, the newly created FixedDepositDetails instance is added to the modelData with name fixedDepositDetails, and the createFixedDepositForm.jsp JSP page is rendered. Alternatively, if no validation errors are reported, the newly created FixedDepositDetails object is saved in the data source, and the page that shows the complete list of fixed deposits is rendered.

As we are using FixedDepositDetails object to store the original form data entered by the user, all the attributes of FixedDepositDetails have been defined of type String, as shown here:

Example listing 12-37 – FixedDepositDetails class
Project – ch12-bankapp
Source location - src/main/java/sample/spring/chapter12/domain

```
package sample.spring.chapter12.domain;

public class FixedDepositDetails {
    private long id; //-- id value is set by the system
    private String depositAmount;
    private String tenure;
    private String email;

    //--getters and setters for fields
    .....
}
```

As depositAmount and tenure fields are defined of type String, we had to write extra logic to convert them into numeric values for performing numerical comparisons. In chapter 13, we'll look at how Spring Web MVC simplifies binding form data to *form backing* objects (like FixedDepositDetails) and re-displaying the original form data in case of validation errors.

The following fragments from the createFixedDepositForm.jsp JSP page demonstrate how validation error messages and the original form data are displayed in the MyBank application:

Example listing 12-38 – createFixedDepositForm.jsp
Project – ch12-bankapp
Source location - src/main/webapp/WEB-INF/jsp

```
<%@taglib uri="http://java.sun.com/jsp/jstl/core" prefix="c"%>

<form name="createFixedDepositForm" method="POST"
    action="${pageContext.request.contextPath}/fixedDeposit?fdAction=create">
  .....
      <td class="td"><b>Amount (in USD):</b></td>
      <td class="td">
          <input type="text" name="depositAmount"
                 value="${requestScope.fixedDepositDetails.depositAmount}"/>
          <font style="color: #C11B17;">
              <c:out value="${requestScope['error.depositAmount']}"/>
          </font>
       </td>
       .....
    <input type="submit" value="Save" />
</form>
```

In the above example listing, the value of depositAmount form field is specified as ${requestScope.fixedDepositDetails.depositAmount}. In the openFixedDeposit method (refer example listing 12-36), we added a FixedDepositDetails instance as a model attribute named fixedDepositDetails; therefore, the ${requestScope.fixedDepositDetails.depositAmount} expression shows the original value that the user entered for the depositAmount field.

The expression ${requestScope['error.depositAmount']} refers to the error.depositAmount request attribute. In the openFixedDeposit method (refer example listing 12-36), we saw that the error.depositAmount contains validation error message corresponding to the fixed deposit amount entered by the user; therefore, the <c:out value= "${requestScope['error.depositAmount']}"/> element shows the validation error message corresponding to the fixed deposit amount entered by the user.

Let's now look at how to handle exceptions in Spring Web MVC applications.

12-9 Handling exceptions using @ExceptionHandler annotation

@ExceptionHandler annotation is used in an annotated controller to identify the method responsible for handling exceptions thrown by the controller. Spring's HandlerExceptionResolver is responsible for mapping an exception to an appropriate controller method responsible for handling the exception. You should note that the <annotation-driven> element of Spring's mvc schema configures an instance of ExceptionHandlerExceptionResolver (a HandlerExceptionResolver implementation) that maps an exception to an appropriate @ExceptionHandler annotated method.

The following example listing shows usage of @ExceptionHandler annotation in ch12-bankapp project:

Example listing 12-39 – @ExceptionHandler annotation usage
Project – ch12-bankapp
Source location - src/main/java/sample/spring/chapter12/web

```
package sample.spring.chapter12.web;

import org.springframework.web.bind.annotation.ExceptionHandler;
.....
@Controller
@RequestMapping(path = "/fixedDeposit")
```

```
public class FixedDepositController {
    .....
    @ExceptionHandler
    public String handleException(Exception  ex) {
        return "error";
    }
}
```

The above example listing shows that the FixedDepositController's handleException method is annotated with @ExceptionHandler annotation. This means that the handleException method is invoked by Spring Web MVC to handle exceptions thrown during execution of FixedDepositController controller. @ExceptionHandler methods typically render an error page containing error details. An @ExceptionHandler annotation's value attribute specifies the list of exceptions that the @ExceptionHandler annotated method handles. If the value attribute is *not* specified, the exception types specified as method arguments are handled by the @ExceptionHandler annotated method. In the above example listing, the handleException method handles exceptions of type java.lang.Exception.

Like @RequestMapping methods, @ExceptionHandler methods can have flexible method signatures. The return types supported for @ExceptionHandler methods include ModelAndView, View, String, void, Model, and so on. The argument types supported for @ExceptionHandler methods include HttpServletRequest, HttpServletResponse, HttpSession, and so on. Refer to @ExceptionHandler Javadoc for the complete list of supported arguments and return types.

The view information returned by an @ExceptionHandler annotated method is used by the DispatcherServlet to render an appropriate error page. For instance, in example listing 12-39, the error string value returned by the handleException method is used by the DispatcherServlet to render /WEB-INF/jsp/error.jsp page. If the @ExceptionHandler method doesn't return any view information (that is, the return type is void or Model), Spring's RequestToViewNameTranslator class (refer section 13-2 of chapter 13 for details) is used to determine the view to be rendered.

You can define multiple @ExceptionHandler annotated methods in your controller class for handling different exception types. The value attribute of @ExceptionHandler annotation allows you to specify the exception types that are handled by the method. The following example listing shows that the myExceptionHandler method handles exceptions of type IOException and FileNotFoundException, and myOtherExceptionHandler method handles exceptions of type TimeoutException:

Example listing 12-40 – Specifying the type of exceptions handled by an @ExceptionHandler method

```
@Controller
.....
public class MyController {
    .....
    @ExceptionHandler(value = {IOException.class, FileNotFoundException.class})
    public String myExceptionHandler() {
        return "someError";
    }

    @ExceptionHandler(value = TimeoutException.class)
    public String myOtherExceptionHandler() {
        return "otherError";
    }
}
```

If MyController throws an exception of type IOException or FileNotFoundException (or an exception that is a subtype of IOException or FileNotFoundException), the myExceptionHandler method is invoked to handle the exception. If MyController throws an exception of type TimeoutException (or an exception that is a subtype of TimeoutException), the myOtherExceptionHandler method is invoked to handle the exception.

Let's now look at how Spring's ContextLoaderListener is used to load root web application context XML file(s).

12-10 Loading root web application context XML file(s)

As mentioned at the beginning of this chapter, the root web application context file defines beans that are shared by all the servlets and filters of the web application. The following example listing shows the configuration of ContextLoaderListener:

Example listing 12-41 – ContextLoaderListener configuration
Project – ch12-bankapp
Source location - src/main/webapp/WEB-INF/web.xml

```
<context-param>
    <param-name>contextConfigLocation</param-name>
    <param-value>classpath*:/META-INF/spring/applicationContext.xml</param-value>
</context-param>

<listener>
   <listener-class>org.springframework.web.context.ContextLoaderListener</listener-class>
</listener>
```

In the above example listing, <listener> element configures the ContextLoaderListener (a ServletContextListener) that is responsible for loading the root web application context XML file(s) specified by the contextConfigLocation servlet context initialization parameter. The <context-param> element specifies the contextConfigLocation servlet context initialization parameter. ContextLoaderListener creates an instance of the root WebApplicationContext with which the beans loaded from the root web application context XML file(s) are registered.

In the above example listing, contextConfigLocation parameter specifies /META-INF/spring/applicationContext.xml file as the root web application context XML file. You can specify multiple application context XML files separated by comma or newline or whitespace or semicolon. If you don't specify the contextConfigLocation parameter, the ContextLoaderListener treats /WEB-INF/applicationContext.xml file as the root web application context XML file.

12-11 Summary

In this chapter, we looked at some of the important objects of a simple Spring Web MVC application. We also looked at how to use @Controller, @RequestMapping, @RequestParam and @ExceptionHandler annotations to create annotated controllers. In the next chapter, we'll look at how Spring transparently *binds* request parameters to form backing objects and performs validation.

Chapter 13 – *Validation and data binding in Spring Web MVC*

13-1 Introduction

In the previous chapter, we looked at the MyBank web application that was developed using `@Controller`, `@RequestMapping` and `@RequestParam` annotations. We saw that the form data was retrieved from the request (refer example listing 12-24, 12-29 and 12-30) and *explicitly* set on the form backing object (which was `FixedDepositDetails` object). Also, the validation logic was written in the controller method itself (refer example listing 12-36).

In this chapter, we'll discuss:

- `@ModelAttribute` and `@SessionAttributes` annotations that are useful when dealing with model attributes
- how Spring's `WebDataBinder` simplifies binding form data to form backing objects
- validating form backing objects using Spring Validation API and JSR 380's constraint annotations
- Spring's `form` tag library that simplifies writing JSP pages

Let's first look at the `@ModelAttribute` annotation that is used for adding and retrieving model attributes to and from Spring's `Model` object.

13-2 Adding and retrieving model attributes using `@ModelAttribute` annotation

In the previous chapter, we saw that a `@RequestMapping` method stores model attributes in a `HashMap` (or `ModelMap`) instance and returns these model attributes via `ModelAndView` object. The model attributes returned by a `@RequestMapping` method are stored in Spring's `Model` object.

A model attribute may represent a form backing object or a *reference data*. `FixedDepositDetails` object in the MyBank web application is an example of a form backing object; when the form for opening a new fixed deposit is submitted, the information contained in the form is stored in the `FixedDepositDetails` object. Typically, *domain* objects or entities in an application are used as form backing objects. *Reference data* refers to the additional information (other than the form backing object) required by the view. For instance, if you add a user category (like military personnel, senior citizen, and so on) to each fixed deposit, the form for opening new fixed deposits would need to show a combo box displaying the list of categories. The list of categories would be the *reference data* needed for displaying the form for opening new fixed deposits.

`@ModelAttribute` annotation is used on methods and method arguments to store and retrieve model attributes from Spring's `Model` object, respectively. `@ModelAttribute` annotation on a method indicates that the method adds one or more model attributes to the `Model` object. And, `@ModelAttribute` annotation on a method argument is used to retrieve a model attribute from the `Model` object and assign it to the method argument.

IMPORT **`chapter 13/ch13-bankapp`** (This project shows the MyBank web application that uses `@ModelAttribute` annotation and Spring's `form` tag library. The MyBank web application functionality offered by `ch13-bankapp` and `ch12-bankapp` projects is the same. If you deploy the project on Tomcat server and access the URL `http://localhost:8080/ch13-bankapp`, you'll see the list of fixed deposits in the system.)

Let's first look at `@ModelAttribute` annotated methods.

Adding model attributes using method-level @ModelAttribute annotation

The following example listing shows FixedDepositController's getNewFixedDepositDetails method that is annotated with @ModelAttribute annotation:

Example listing 13-1 – @ModelAttribute annotation usage at method level
Project – ch13-bankapp
Source location - src/main/java/sample/spring/chapter13/web

```
package sample.spring.chapter13.web;

import org.springframework.web.bind.annotation.ModelAttribute;
import sample.spring.chapter13.domain.FixedDepositDetails;
.....
@Controller
@RequestMapping(path = "/fixedDeposit")
.....
public class FixedDepositController {
    private static Logger logger = LogManager.getLogger(FixedDepositController.class);
    .....
    @ModelAttribute(name = "newFixedDepositDetails")
    public FixedDepositDetails getNewFixedDepositDetails() {
        FixedDepositDetails fixedDepositDetails = new FixedDepositDetails();
        fixedDepositDetails.setEmail("You must enter a valid email");
        logger.info("getNewFixedDepositDetails() method: Returning a new instance of
                FixedDepositDetails");
        return fixedDepositDetails;
    }
    .....
}
```

The getNewFixedDepositDetails method creates and returns a new instance of FixedDepositDetails object. As the getNewFixedDepositDetails method is annotated with @ModelAttribute annotation, the returned FixedDepositDetails instance is added to the Model object. @ModelAttribute's name attribute (alias for value attribute) specifies that the returned FixedDepositDetails object is stored with name newFixedDepositDetails in the Model object. Notice that the getNewFixedDepositDetails method logs the following message - 'getNewFixedDepositDetails() method: Returning a new instance of FixedDepositDetails'.

> You should note that the scope of model attributes is *request*. This means that the model attributes are lost when a request completes, or if a request is *redirected*.

Later in this section, we'll see how the createFixedDepositForm.jsp JSP page (refer src/main/webapp/WEB-INF/jsp/createFixedDepositForm.jsp file) of ch13-bankapp project uses Spring's form tag library to access the FixedDepositDetails object named newFixedDepositDetails from the Model object.

If you don't specify @ModelAttribute's name attribute, the returned object is stored in the Model object using the simple name of the returned object's *type*. In the following example listing, the Sample object returned by the getSample method is stored with name sample in the Model object:

Example listing 13-2 – @ModelAttribute usage – name attribute is *not* specified

```
import org.springframework.ui.Model;
.....
```

```
public class SampleController {

    @ModelAttribute
    public Sample getSample() {
        return new Sample();
    }
}
```

A @ModelAttribute annotated method accepts same types of arguments as a @RequestMapping method. The following example listing shows a @ModelAttribute annotated method that accepts an argument of type HttpServletRequest:

Example listing 13-3 – @ModelAttribute annotated method that accepts HttpServletRequest as argument

```
    @ModelAttribute(name = "myObject")
    public SomeObject doSomething(HttpServletRequest request) { ..... }
```

In chapter 12, we saw that the @RequestParam annotation is used to pass request parameters to a @RequestMapping annotated method. @RequestParam annotation can also be used to pass request parameters to a @ModelAttribute annotated method, as shown in the following example listing:

Example listing 13-4 – Passing request parameters to a @ModelAttribute annotated method

```
    @ModelAttribute(name = "myObject")
    public SomeObject doSomething(@RequestParam("someArg") String myarg) { ..... }
```

As @RequestMapping and @ModelAttribute annotated methods can accept Model objects as argument, you can *directly* add model attributes to the Model object in a @ModelAttribute or @RequestMapping annotated method. The following example listing shows a @ModelAttribute method that directly adds model attributes to the Model object:

Example listing 13-5 – Adding model attributes directly to Model object

```
import org.springframework.ui.Model;
.....
public class SampleWebController {

    @ModelAttribute
    public void doSomething(Model model) {
        model.addAttribute("myobject", new MyObject());
        model.addAttribute("otherobject", new OtherObject());
    }
}
```

In the above example listing, the Model object is passed as an argument to doSomething method that directly adds model attributes to the Model object. As the doSomething method adds model attributes directly to the Model object, the doSomething method's return type is specified as void, and the @ModelAttribute's name attribute is *not* specified.

It is possible to have a single method annotated with both @RequestMapping and @ModelAttribute annotations. The following example listing shows FixedDepositController's listFixedDeposits method that is annotated with both @RequestMapping and @ModelAttribute annotations:

Example listing 13-6 – @ModelAttribute and @RequestMapping annotations on the same method
Project – ch13-bankapp
Source location - src/main/java/sample/spring/chapter13/web

```
package sample.spring.chapter13.web;
.....
@Controller
@RequestMapping(path = "/fixedDeposit")
.....
public class FixedDepositController {
    private static Logger logger = LogManager.getLogger(FixedDepositController.class);

    @RequestMapping(path = "/list", method = RequestMethod.GET)
    @ModelAttribute(name = "fdList")
    public List<FixedDepositDetails> listFixedDeposits() {
        logger.info("listFixedDeposits() method: Getting list of fixed deposits");
        return fixedDepositService.getFixedDeposits();
    }
    .....
}
```

The listFixedDeposits method renders the list.jsp JSP page (refer src/main/webapp/WEB-INF/jsp/fixedDeposit/list.jsp file of ch13-bankapp project) that shows the list of fixed deposits in the system. When a method is annotated with both @RequestMapping and @ModelAttribute annotations, the value returned by the method is considered as a model attribute, and *not* as a view name. In such a scenario, view name is determined by Spring's RequestToViewNameTranslator class that determines the view to render based on the request URI of the incoming request. Later in this chapter, we'll discuss RequestToViewNameTranslator in detail. In example listing 13-6, notice that the listFixedDeposits method logs the following message – 'listFixedDeposits() method: Getting list of fixed deposits'.

It is important to note that you can define multiple methods annotated with @ModelAttribute annotation in a controller. When a request is dispatched to a @RequestMapping annotated method of a controller, *all* the @ModelAttribute annotated methods of that controller are invoked *before* the @RequestMapping annotated method is invoked. The following example listing shows a controller that defines @RequestMapping and @ModelAttribute annotated methods:

Example listing 13-7 – @RequestMapping method is invoked after all the @ModelAttribute methods are invoked

```
@RequestMapping("/mycontroller")
public class MyController {

    @RequestMapping("/perform")
    public String perform() { ..... }

    @ModelAttribute(name = "a")
    public A getA() { ..... }

    @ModelAttribute(name = "b")
    public B getB() { ..... }
}
```

In the above example listing, if a request is mapped to MyController's perform method, Spring Web MVC will first invoke getA and getB methods, followed by invoking the perform method.

If a method is annotated with both @RequestMapping and @ModelAttribute annotations, the method is invoked only *once* for processing the request. The following example listing shows a controller that defines a method that is annotated with both @RequestMapping and @ModelAttribute annotations:

Example listing 13-8 – Method annotated with both @RequestMapping and @ModelAttribute annotations is invoked only *once* for processing the request

```
@RequestMapping("/mycontroller")
public class MyController {

    @RequestMapping("/perform")
    @ModelAttribute
    public String perform() { ..... }

    @ModelAttribute(name = "a")
    public A getA() { ..... }

    @ModelAttribute(name = "b")
    public B getB() { ..... }
}
```

In the above example listing, if a request is mapped to MyController's perform method, Spring Web MVC will first invoke getA and getB methods, followed by invoking the perform method. As the perform method is annotated with both @RequestMapping and @ModelAttribute annotations, Spring's RequestToViewNameTranslator class is used for determining the name of the view to render after the perform method is executed.

If you now deploy the ch13-bankapp project on Tomcat and go to http://localhost:8080/ch13-bankapp/fixedDeposit/list URL, you'll see a web page showing the list of fixed deposits. Also, you'll see the following sequence of messages on the console:

```
INFO  sample.spring.chapter13.web.FixedDepositController - getNewFixedDepositDetails()
method: Returning a new instance of FixedDepositDetails
INFO  sample.spring.chapter13.web.FixedDepositController - listFixedDeposits() method:
Getting list of fixed deposits
```

The above output shows that the getNewFixedDepositDetails method (which is annotated with @ModelAttribute annotation) is invoked first, followed by the listFixedDeposits (which is annotated with both @ModelAttribute and @RequestMapping annotation).

Let's now look at how model attributes are retrieved from the Model object using @ModelAttribute annotation on a method argument.

Retrieving model attributes using @ModelAttribute annotation

You can use @ModelAttribute annotation on arguments of a @RequestMapping annotated method to retrieve model attributes from the Model object.

The following example listing shows FixedDepositController's openFixedDeposit method that uses @ModelAttribute annotation to retrieve newFixedDepositDetails object from the Model object:

Example listing 13-9 – @ModelAttribute annotation on a method argument
Project – ch13-bankapp
Source location - src/main/java/sample/spring/chapter13/web

```
package sample.spring.chapter13.web;
.....
```

```
@Controller
@RequestMapping(path = "/fixedDeposit")
.....
public class FixedDepositController {
    .....
    @ModelAttribute(name = "newFixedDepositDetails")
    public FixedDepositDetails getNewFixedDepositDetails() {
        .....
        logger.info("getNewFixedDepositDetails() method: Returning a new instance of
           FixedDepositDetails");
        .....
    }
    .....
    @RequestMapping(params = "fdAction=create", method = RequestMethod.POST)
    public String openFixedDeposit(
         @ModelAttribute(name = "newFixedDepositDetails")
                  FixedDepositDetails fixedDepositDetails,.....) {
        .....
        fixedDepositService.saveFixedDeposit(fixedDepositDetails);
        logger.info("openFixedDeposit() method: Fixed deposit details successfully saved.
                 Redirecting to show the list of fixed deposits.");
            .....
        }
    }
    .....
}
```

In the above example listing, @ModelAttribute annotated getNewFixedDepositDetails method is invoked *before* @RequestMapping annotated openFixedDeposit method. When the getNewFixedDepositDetails method is invoked, the returned FixedDepositDetails instance is stored in the Model object with name newFixedDepositDetails. Now, the openFixedDeposit method's fixedDepositDetails argument is annotated with @ModelAttribute(name="newFixedDepositDetails"); therefore, the newFixedDepositDetails object is obtained from the Model object and assigned to the fixedDepositDetails argument.

If you look at the FixedDepositController's openFixedDeposit method, you'll notice that we have *not* written any logic to obtain values of tenure, amount and email fields from the request and populate the newFixedDepositDetails instance. This is because the Spring's WebDataBinder object (explained later in this chapter) is responsible for transparently retrieving request parameters from the request and populating the fields (with matching names) of newFixedDepositDetails instance. For instance, if a request parameter named tenure is found in the request, WebDataBinder sets the value of tenure field of newFixedDepositDetails instance to the value of tenure request parameter.

Figure 13-1 summarizes the sequence of actions that are performed by Spring when a request is dispatched to FixedDepositController's openFixedDeposit method. In figure 13-1, the RequestMappingHandlerAdapter object of Spring Web MVC is responsible for invoking @ModelAttribute and @RequestMapping annotated methods of a controller. At first, the getNewFixedDepositDetails method is invoked and the returned FixedDepositDetails instance is stored in the Model object with name newFixedDepositDetails. Next, the newFixedDepositDetails instance is retrieved from the Model and passed as an argument to the openFixedDeposit method.

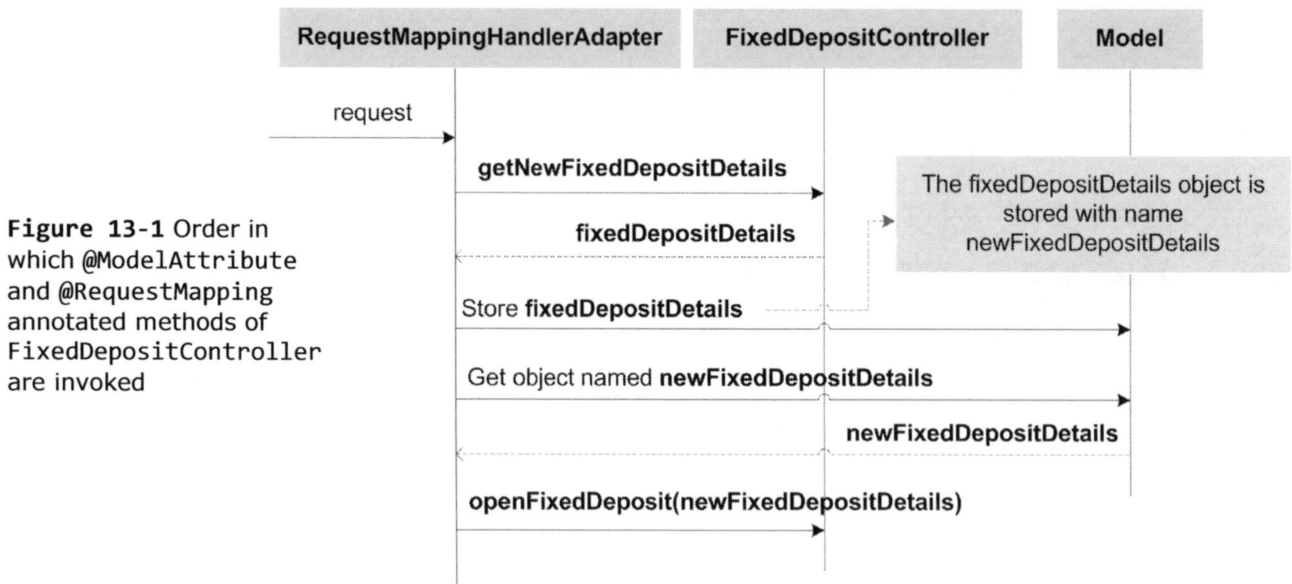

Figure 13-1 Order in which `@ModelAttribute` and `@RequestMapping` annotated methods of `FixedDepositController` are invoked

Let's now look at what times during the processing of a request a `@ModelAttribute` annotated method is invoked.

Request processing and @ModelAttribute annotated methods

In example listing 13-6, we saw that the execution of `listFixedDeposits` method logs the following message:

```
listFixedDeposits() method: Getting list of fixed deposits
```

In example listing 13-9, we saw that the execution of `getNewFixedDepositDetails` method logs the following message:

```
getNewFixedDepositDetails() method: Returning a new instance of FixedDepositDetails
```

And, the `openFixedDeposit` method logs the following message:

```
openFixedDeposit() method: Fixed deposit details successfully saved. Redirecting to show the list of fixed deposits
```

To see the order in which the `listFixedDeposits`, `getNewFixedDepositDetails` and `openFixedDeposit` methods are invoked, deploy the `ch13-bankapp` project and follow these steps:

1. Go to `http://localhost:8080/ch13-bankapp/fixedDeposit/list` URL. You'll see the list of fixed deposits in the system and the `'Create new Fixed Deposit'` button (refer figure 12-8 of chapter 12).

2. Click the `'Create new Fixed Deposit'` button that shows the HTML form for opening a new fixed deposit (refer figure 12-9 of chapter 12).

3. Enter fixed deposit details and click the `'Save'` button. If no validation errors are found in the entered data, the fixed deposit details are successfully saved and the list of fixed deposits in the system (which includes the newly created fixed deposit) is displayed once again.

The following table describes the actions performed by you and the corresponding messages that are printed by the MyBank application on the console:

Action	Messages printed on the console
Go to `http://localhost:8080/ch13-bankapp/fixedDeposit/list` URL	**`getNewFixedDepositDetails()`** `method: Returning a new instance of FixedDepositDetails` **`listFixedDeposits()`** `method: Getting list of fixed deposits`
Click the 'Create new Fixed Deposit' button	**`getNewFixedDepositDetails()`** `method: Returning a new instance of FixedDepositDetails` **`showOpenFixedDepositForm()`** `method: Showing form for opening a new fixed deposit`
Enter fixed deposit details and click the 'Save' button	**`getNewFixedDepositDetails()`** `method: Returning a new instance of FixedDepositDetails` **`openFixedDeposit()`** `method: Fixed deposit details successfully saved. Redirecting to show the list of fixed deposits.` **`getNewFixedDepositDetails()`** `method: Returning a new instance of FixedDepositDetails` **`listFixedDeposits()`** `method: Getting list of fixed deposits`

The above table shows that the `@ModelAttribute` annotated `getNewFixedDepositDetails` method is called *before each* invocation of `@RequestMapping` annotated method of the `FixedDepositController` class. As the `getNewFixedDepositDetails` method creates a new instance of `FixedDepositDetails` object, a new instance of `FixedDepositDetails` object is created each time a request is handled by the `FixedDepositController`.

If a `@ModelAttribute` annotated method fires SQL queries or invokes an external web service to populate the model attribute returned by the method, multiple invocations of `@ModelAttribute` annotated method will adversely affect the performance of the application. Later in this chapter, we'll see that you can use `@SessionAttributes` annotation to avoid multiple invocations of a `@ModelAttribute` annotated method. `@SessionAttributes` annotation instructs Spring to cache the object returned by the `@ModelAttribute` annotated method.

Let's now look at a scenario in which the model attribute referred by the `@ModelAttribute` annotated method argument is *not* found in the `Model` object.

Behavior of `@ModelAttribute` annotated method arguments

We saw earlier that the `@ModelAttribute` annotation can be used on a method argument to retrieve a model attribute from the `Model` object. If the model attribute specified by the `@ModelAttribute` annotation is *not* found in the `Model`, Spring automatically creates a new instance of the method argument type, assigns it to the method argument and also puts it into the `Model` object. To allow Spring to create an instance of the method argument type, the Java class of the method argument type *must* provide a no-argument constructor.

Let's consider the following `SomeController` controller that defines a single `@RequestMapping` method, `doSomething`:

Example listing 13-10 – @ModelAttribute argument is *not* available in the Model object

```
@Controller
@RequestMapping(path = "/some")
public class SomeController {
    .....
    @RequestMapping("/do")
    public void doSomething(@ModelAttribute("myObj") MyObject myObject) {
        logger.info(myObject);
        .....
    }
}
```

The above example listing shows that the SomeController class doesn't define any @ModelAttribute annotated method that adds an object named myObj of type MyObject in the Model. For this reason, when a request for doSomething method is received, Spring creates an instance of MyObject, assigns it to the myObject argument and also puts the newly created MyObject instance into the Model object.

Let's now look at Spring's RequestToViewNameTranslator object.

RequestToViewNameTranslator

RequestToViewNameTranslator determines the view to be rendered when a @RequestMapping annotated method doesn't explicitly specify the view to be rendered.

We saw earlier that when a @RequestMapping method is also annotated with @ModelAttribute annotation, the value returned by the method is considered as a model attribute. In such a situation, the RequestToViewNameTranslator object is responsible for determining the view to be rendered based on the incoming web request. Similarly, if a @RequestMapping annotated method returns void, org.springframework.ui.Model or java.util.Map, the RequestToViewNameTranslator object determines the view to be rendered.

DefaultRequestToViewNameTranslator is an implementation of RequestToViewNameTranslator that is used by default by DispatcherServlet to determine the view to be rendered when no view is explicitly returned by a @RequestMapping method. DefaultRequestToViewNameTranslator uses the request URI to determine the name of the logical view to render. DefaultRequestToViewNameTranslator removes the leading and trailing slashes and the file extension from the URI to determine the view name. For instance, if the URL is http://localhost:8080/doSomething.htm, the view name becomes doSomething.

In the case of MyBank web application, the FixedDepositController's listFixedDeposits method (refer example listing 13-6 or FixedDepositController.java file of ch13-bankapp project) is annotated with both @RequestMapping and @ModelAttribute; therefore, RequestToViewNameTranslator is used by the DispatcherServlet to determine the view to render. As the listFixedDeposits method is mapped to request URI /fixedDeposit/list, RequestToViewNameTranslator returns /fixedDeposit/list as the view name. The ViewResolver configured in the web application context XML file of MyBank web application (refer bankapp-config.xml file of ch13-bankapp project) maps /fixedDeposit/list view name to /WEB-INF/jsp/fixedDeposit/list.jsp JSP view.

Let's now look at @SessionAttributes annotation.

13-3 Caching model attributes using @SessionAttributes annotation

In the previous section, we saw that *all* the @ModelAttribute annotated methods of a controller are *always* invoked before the @RequestMapping annotated method. This behavior may not be acceptable in situations in which @ModelAttribute methods obtain data from the database or from an external web service to populate the model attribute. In such scenarios, you can annotate your controller class with @SessionAttributes annotation that specifies the model attributes that are stored in HttpSession between requests.

If @SessionAttributes annotation is used, a @ModelAttribute annotated method is invoked only if the model attribute specified by the @ModelAttribute annotation is *not* found in the HttpSession. Also, @ModelAttribute annotation on a method argument will result in creation of a new instance of model attribute only if the model attribute is not found in the HttpSession.

IMPORT **chapter 13/ch13-session-attributes** (This project shows a modified version of ch13-bankapp project that uses @SessionAttributes annotation to temporarily store model attributes in HttpSession. The MyBank web application functionality offered by ch13-session-attributes and ch12-bankapp projects are the same. If you deploy the project on Tomcat server and access the URL http://localhost:8080/ch13-session-attributes, you'll see the list of fixed deposits in the system.)

The following example listing shows usage of @SessionAttributes annotation in ch13-session-attributes project to temporarily store newFixedDepositDetails and editableFixedDepositDetails model attributes in HttpSession:

Example listing 13-11 – @SessionAttributes annotation usage
Project – ch13-session-attributes
Source location - src/main/java/sample/spring/chapter13/web

```
package sample.spring.chapter13.web;

import org.springframework.web.bind.annotation.SessionAttributes;
.....
@SessionAttributes(names = { "newFixedDepositDetails", "editableFixedDepositDetails" })
public class FixedDepositController {
    .....
    @ModelAttribute(name = "newFixedDepositDetails")
    public FixedDepositDetails getNewFixedDepositDetails() {
        FixedDepositDetails fixedDepositDetails = new FixedDepositDetails();
        fixedDepositDetails.setEmail("You must enter a valid email");
        return fixedDepositDetails;
    }
    .....
    @RequestMapping(params = "fdAction=create", method = RequestMethod.POST)
    public String openFixedDeposit(
          @ModelAttribute(name = "newFixedDepositDetails")
             FixedDepositDetails fixedDepositDetails,.....) { ..... }
    .....

    @RequestMapping(params = "fdAction=view", method = RequestMethod.GET)
    public ModelAndView viewFixedDepositDetails(
          @RequestParam(name = "fixedDepositId") int fixedDepositId) {
        FixedDepositDetails fixedDepositDetails = fixedDepositService
            .getFixedDeposit(fixedDepositId);
        Map<String, Object> modelMap = new HashMap<String, Object>();
        modelMap.put("editableFixedDepositDetails", fixedDepositDetails);
        .....
        return new ModelAndView("editFixedDepositForm", modelMap);
    }
}
```

@SessionAttributes annotation's names attribute (alias for value attribute) specifies *names* of the model attributes that are temporarily stored in HttpSession. In the above example listing, model attributes named newFixedDepositDetails and editableFixedDepositDetails are stored in HttpSession between requests. The newFixedDepositDetails model attribute is returned by @ModelAttribute annotated getNewFixedDepositDetails method, and the editableFixedDepositDetails model attribute is returned by the @RequestMapping annotated viewFixedDepositDetails method.

A controller contributes model attributes via @ModelAttribute annotated methods, @RequestMapping methods (that return ModelAndView, Model or Map), and by directly adding model attributes to the Model object. The model attributes contributed by the controller through *any* approach are candidate for storage in the HttpSession by @SessionAttributes annotation.

When using @SessionAttributes annotation, you should ensure that the model attributes stored in the HttpSession are removed when they are no longer required. For instance, the newFixedDepositDetails model attribute represents an instance of FixedDepositDetails that is used by the 'Open fixed deposit' form to show the default value(s) of Email form field as 'You must enter a valid email' (refer getNewFixedDepositDetails method in example listing 13-11). Also, when the user clicks the 'Save' button on the 'Open fixed deposit' form, the fixed deposit details entered by the user are set on the newFixedDepositDetails instance (refer openFixedDeposit method in example listing 13-11). After the fixed deposit is successfully created, the newFixedDepositDetails instance is no longer required; therefore, it must be removed from the HttpSession. Similarly, editableFixedDepositDetails model attribute is not required after you have successfully modified details of a fixed deposit.

You can instruct Spring to remove *all* the model attributes stored in HttpSession by calling setComplete method of Spring's SessionStatus object. The following example listing shows FixedDepositController's openFixedDeposit and editFixedDeposit methods that invoke SessionStatus's setComplete method after a fixed deposit is successfully created or modified:

Example listing 13-12 – Removing model attributes from HttpSession using SessionStatus object
Project – ch13-session-attributes
Source location - src/main/java/sample/spring/chapter13/web

```
package sample.spring.chapter13.web;

import org.springframework.web.bind.support.SessionStatus;
.....
@SessionAttributes(names = { "newFixedDepositDetails", "editableFixedDepositDetails" })
public class FixedDepositController {
    .....
    @RequestMapping(params = "fdAction=create", method = RequestMethod.POST)
    public String openFixedDeposit(
       @ModelAttribute(name = "newFixedDepositDetails")
         FixedDepositDetails fixedDepositDetails,....., SessionStatus sessionStatus) {

        fixedDepositService.saveFixedDeposit(fixedDepositDetails);
        sessionStatus.setComplete();
    }

    @RequestMapping(params = "fdAction=edit", method = RequestMethod.POST)
    public String editFixedDeposit(
            @ModelAttribute("editableFixedDepositDetails")
              FixedDepositDetails fixedDepositDetails,....., SessionStatus sessionStatus) {
        fixedDepositService.editFixedDeposit(fixedDepositDetails);
        sessionStatus.setComplete();
        .....
    }
    .....
```

```
}
```

The above example listing shows that both openFixedDeposit and editFixedDeposit methods are defined to accept an argument of type SessionStatus. When a @RequestMapping annotated method specifies an argument of type SessionStatus, Spring supplies an instance of SessionStatus to the method. The call to setComplete method instructs Spring to remove the *current* controller's model attributes from the HttpSession object.

In example listing 13-11 and 13-12, we saw that the @SessionAttributes's names attribute specifies the names of model attributes that are temporarily stored in HttpSession. If you want that only certain *types* of model attributes are stored in HttpSession, you can use @SessionAttributes's types attribute. For instance, the following @SessionAttributes annotation specifies that attributes named x and y, and *all* model attributes that are of type MyObject, are temporarily stored in HttpSession:

```
@SessionAttributes(value = { "x", "y" }, types = { MyObject.class })
```

You can see the order in which listFixedDeposits, getNewFixedDepositDetails and openFixedDeposit methods are invoked by deploying ch13-session-attributes project and perform the actions described in the following table:

Action	Messages printed on the console
Go to http://localhost:8080/ch13-session-attributes/fixedDeposit/list URL	**getNewFixedDepositDetails() method:** Returning a new instance of FixedDepositDetails **listFixedDeposits() method:** Getting list of fixed deposits
Click the 'Create new Fixed Deposit' button	**showOpenFixedDepositForm()** method: Showing form for opening a new fixed deposit
Enter fixed deposit details and click the 'Save' button	**openFixedDeposit()** method: Fixed deposit details successfully saved. Redirecting to show the list of fixed deposits. **getNewFixedDepositDetails()** method: Returning a new instance of FixedDepositDetails **listFixedDeposits()** method: Getting list of fixed deposits

In ch13-bankapp project, we saw that the @ModelAttribute annotated getNewFixedDepositDetails method of FixedDepositController was invoked each time a request was dispatched to FixedDepositController. The above table shows that the getNewFixedDepositDetails method is invoked when request is handled by the FixedDepositController for the first time. As the openFixedDeposit method removes the model attributes stored in the HttpSession, request to listFixedDeposits method results in invocation of getNewFixedDepositDetails method once again.

Now that we have seen how to use @ModelAttribute and @SessionAttributes annotations, let's look at how *data binding* is performed in Spring Web MVC applications.

13-4 Data binding support in Spring

When a form is submitted in a Spring Web MVC application, request parameters contained in the request are *automatically* set on the *model attribute* that acts as the form backing object. This process of setting request parameters on the form backing object is referred to as *data binding*. In this section, we'll look at Spring's WebDataBinder instance that binds request parameters to form backing objects.

IMPORT **chapter 13/ch13-data-binding** (This project shows a modified version of ch13-session-attributes project that shows how to register PropertyEditor implementations with Spring container. If you deploy the project on Tomcat server and access the URL http://localhost:8080/ch13-data-binding, you'll see the list of fixed deposits in the system.)

The following example listing shows the FixedDepositDetails class of ch13-data-binding project:

Example listing 13-13 – FixedDepositDetails class
Project – ch13-data-binding
Source location - src/main/java/sample/spring/chapter13/web

```
package sample.spring.chapter13.domain;

import java.util.Date;

public class FixedDepositDetails {
    .....
    private long depositAmount;
    private Date maturityDate;
    .....
    public void setDepositAmount(long depositAmount) {
        this.depositAmount = depositAmount;
    }
    public void setMaturityDate(Date maturityDate) {
        this.maturityDate = maturityDate;
    }
    .....
}
```

The above example listing shows that the depositAmount and maturityDate fields are of type long and java.util.Date, respectively. The values of depositAmount and maturityDate fields are set when the 'Open fixed deposit' form of ch13-data-binding project is submitted. The following figure shows the 'Open fixed deposit' form of ch13-data-binding project that is used for opening new fixed deposits:

Open fixed deposit

Amount (in USD): 1200

Maturity date: 01-27-2013

Email: mail@somedomain.com

Save Go Back

Figure 13-2 'Open fixed deposit' form for opening new fixed deposits

In the above figure, 'Amount(in USD)' and 'Maturity date' form fields correspond to depositAmount and maturityDate fields of FixedDepositDetails class (refer example listing 13-13). One of the important things to note is that the 'Maturity date' field accepts a date in the format 'MM-dd-yyyy', like 01-27-2013. As depositAmount field is of type long, and maturityDate is of type java.util.Date, Spring's data binding mechanism is responsible for doing the type conversion from `String` to the type defined by the `FixedDepositDetails` instance.

The following example listing shows `FixedDepositController`'s `openFixedDeposit` method that is invoked when a user fills the 'Open fixed deposit' form and clicks the 'Save' button (refer figure 13-2):

Example listing 13-14 – `FixedDepositController` - automatic data binding example
Project – ch13-data-binding
Source location - src/main/java/sample/spring/chapter13/web

```
package sample.spring.chapter13.web;

@Controller
.....
public class FixedDepositController {
    .....
    @RequestMapping(params = "fdAction=create", method = RequestMethod.POST)
    public String openFixedDeposit(
         @ModelAttribute(name = "newFixedDepositDetails")
             FixedDepositDetails fixedDepositDetails, BindingResult bindingResult,
             SessionStatus sessionStatus) {
        ....
    }
    .....
}
```

In the above example listing, the `@ModelAttribute` annotated `FixedDepositDetails` argument represents the form backing object on which the request parameters are set when the 'Open fixed deposit' form is submitted. Spring's `WebDataBinder` instance binds request parameters to the `FixedDepositDetails` instance.

Let's now look at how `WebDataBinder` performs data binding.

WebDataBinder – data binder for web request parameters

`WebDataBinder` uses the request parameter name to find the corresponding JavaBean-style setter method on the form backing object. If a JavaBean-style setter method is found, `WebDataBinder` invokes the setter method and passes the request parameter value as an argument to the setter method. If the setter method is defined to accept a non-`String` type argument, `WebDataBinder` uses an appropriate `PropertyEditor` to perform the type conversion.

The following example listing shows the `MyObject` class that acts as a form backing object in an application:

Example listing 13-15 – `MyObject` class – a form backing object

```
public class MyObject {
    private String x;
    private N y;
    .....
    public void setX(String x) {
        this.x = x;
    }
    public void setY(N y) {
        this.y = y;
    }
}
```

The above example listing shows that the `MyObject` class defines properties named `x` and `y` of type `String` and `N`, respectively.

The following figure shows how `WebDataBinder` binds request parameters named `x` and `y` to `x` and `y` properties of `MyObject` instance:

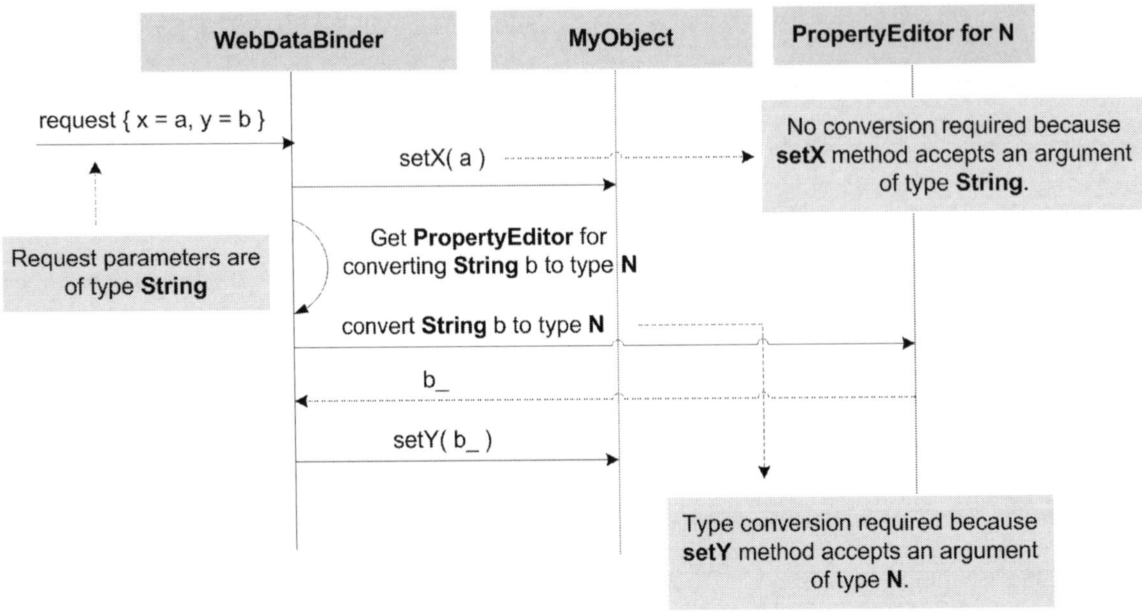

Figure 13-3 `WebDataBinder` performs data binding by using registered `PropertyEditors` to perform type conversion

The above figure shows that the `WebDataBinder` uses a `PropertyEditor` to convert `String` value `b` to type `N`, before calling the `setY` method of `MyObject` instance.

Spring provides a couple of built-in `PropertyEditor` implementations that are used by `WebDataBinder` for converting `String` type request parameter value to the type defined by the form backing object. For instance, `CustomNumberEditor`, `FileEditor` and `CustomDateEditor` are some of the built-in `PropertyEditors` provided by Spring. For a complete list of built-in `PropertyEditors`, refer to `org.springframework.beans.propertyeditors` package.

`CustomNumberEditor` is used for converting a `String` value to a `java.lang.Number` type, like `Integer`, `Long`, `Double`, and so on. `CustomDateEditor` is used for converting a `String` value to a `java.util.Date` type. You can pass a `java.text.DateFormat` instance to `CustomDateEditor` to specify the date format to be used for parsing and rendering dates. Both these `PropertyEditors` are required in `ch13-data-binding` project because we need to convert request parameter values to `depositAmount` (which is of type `long`) and `maturityDate` (which is of type `java.util.Date`). `CustomNumberEditor` is *pre-registered* with the `WebDataBinder` instance but you need to explicitly register `CustomDateEditor`.

Let's now look at how you can configure a `WebDataBinder` instance and register a `PropertyEditor` implementation with it.

Configuring a `WebDataBinder` instance

You can configure a `WebDataBinder` instance by:

- defining an `@InitBinder` annotated method in the controller class
- configuring a `WebBindingInitializer` implementation in the web application context XML file

- defining an @InitBinder annotated method in a @ControllerAdvice annotated class

Let's look at each of the above mentioned approach for configuring a WebDataBinder instance and registering a PropertyEditor with it.

Defining an @InitBinder annotated method in the controller class

An @InitBinder annotated method in a controller class specifies that the method initializes an instance of WebDataBinder that will be used by the controller during data binding. The value attribute of @InitBinder annotation specifies the name(s) of the model attribute to which the initialized WebDataBinder instance applies.

The following example listing shows FixedDepositController's initBinder_New method that is annotated with @InitBinder:

Example listing 13-16 – FixedDepositController - @InitBinder annotation usage
Project – ch13-data-binding
Source location - src/main/java/sample/spring/chapter13/web

```
package sample.spring.chapter13.web;

import java.text.SimpleDateFormat;
import org.springframework.beans.propertyeditors.CustomDateEditor;
import org.springframework.web.bind.WebDataBinder;
import org.springframework.web.bind.annotation.InitBinder;

@Controller
.....
public class FixedDepositController {
    .....
    @ModelAttribute(name = "newFixedDepositDetails")
    public FixedDepositDetails getNewFixedDepositDetails() { ..... }

    @InitBinder(value = "newFixedDepositDetails")
    public void initBinder_New(WebDataBinder webDataBinder) {
        webDataBinder.registerCustomEditor(Date.class,
             new CustomDateEditor(new SimpleDateFormat("MM-dd-yyyy"), false));
    }
    .....
}
```

In the above example listing, the @InitBinder annotation's value attribute is set to newFixedDepositDetails, which means that the WebDataBinder initialized by the initBinder_New method applies *only* to the newFixedDepositDetails model attribute. An @InitBinder annotated method can accept same set of arguments (like HttpServletRequest, SessionStatus, and so on) that can be passed to a @RequestMapping annotated method. But, an @InitBinder annotated method can't be defined to accept model attributes and BindingResult (or Errors) objects as arguments. Typically, WebDataBinder instance, along with Spring's WebRequest or java.util.Locale instance, is passed to an @InitBinder method. You should note that the return type of an @InitBinder method must be void.

WebDataBinder's registerCustomEditor method is used for registering a PropertyEditor with the WebDataBinder instance. In example listing 13-16, initBinder_New method registers CustomDateEditor (a PropertyEditor) with the WebDataBinder instance.

You can define an `@InitBinder` annotated method for each model attribute of a controller, or you can define a single `@InitBinder` annotated method that applies to all the model attributes of the controller. If you don't specify the value attribute of `@InitBinder` annotation, the `WebDataBinder` instance initialized by the method is applicable to *all* the model attributes of the controller.

Configuring a `WebBindingInitializer` implementation

A `WebDataBinder` instance is first initialized by `RequestMappingHandlerAdapter`, followed by further initialization by `WebBindingInitializer` and `@InitBinder` methods.

The `<annotation-driven>` element of Spring's `mvc` schema creates an instance of Spring's `RequestMappingHandlerAdapter` that initializes the `WebDataBinder`. You can supply an implementation of Spring's `WebBindingInitializer` interface to `RequestMappingHandlerAdapter` to further initialize `WebDataBinder` instances. You can additionally use `@InitBinder` methods in a controller class to further initialize `WebDataBinder` instances.

The following figure shows the sequence in which `RequestMappingHandlerAdapter`, `WebBindingInitializer` and `@InitBinder` methods initialize a `WebDataBinder` instance:

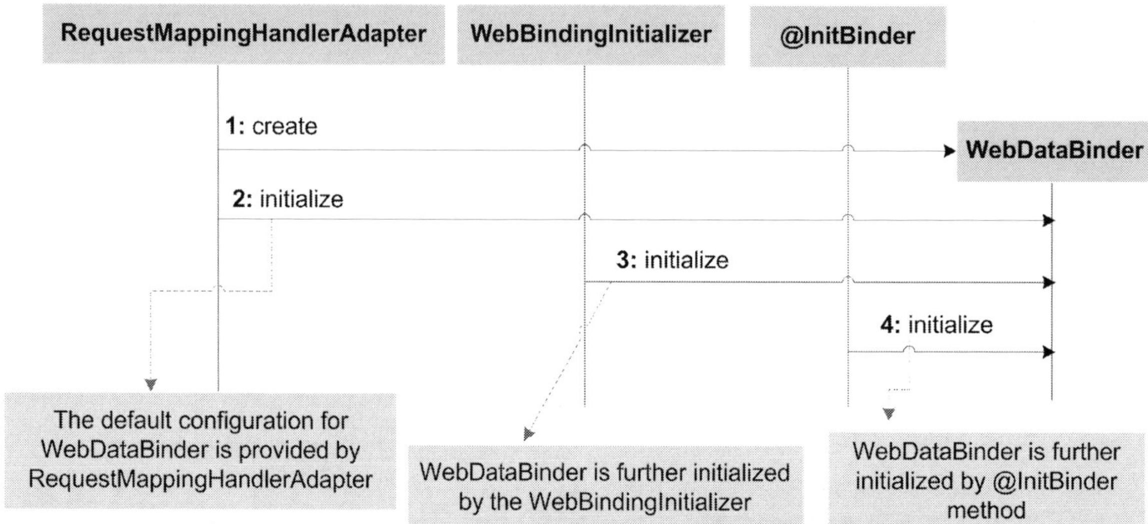

Figure 13-4 The sequence in which a `WebDataBinder` instance is initialized by `RequestMappingHandlerAdapter`, `WebBindingInitializer` and `@InitBinder` methods of a controller class

`WebDataBinder` initialization by an `@InitBinder` method of a controller class is applicable only to that controller's model attributes. For instance, if you use an `@InitBinder` method in controller `X` to set the `CustomDateEditor` property editor on the `WebDataBinder` instance, then the `CustomDateEditor` property editor will be available only to the model attributes of controller `X` during data binding. In MyBank application, the `CustomDateEditor` was required only by the model attributes of the `FixedDepositController`; therefore, we used `@InitBinder` annotated methods in the `FixedDepositController` class to register `CustomDateEditor` with `WebDataBinder` instance.

Spring's `WebBindingInitializer` is a callback interface whose implementation is responsible for initializing a `WebDataBinder` with the configuration that applies to *all* the controllers (and thereby to all the model attributes) in the application. Let's look at how to configure a custom `WebBindingInitializer` when using `<annotation-driven>` element of Spring's `mvc` schema.

The `<annotation-driven>` element of Spring's `mvc` schema creates and registers `RequestMappingHandlerAdapter` and `RequestMappingHandlerMapping` objects with the Spring container.

The other objects that are configured by <annotation-driven> element are LocalValidatorFactoryBean (explained in section 13-5) and FormattingConversionServiceFactoryBean (explained in section 13-5). The <annotation-driven> element provides couple of attributes that help you customize RequestMappingHandlerAdapter and RequestMappingHandlerMapping objects. If the customization you want to make to RequestMappingHandlerAdapter or RequestMappingHandlerMapping object is not provided by the <annotation-driven> element, the only option is to remove <annotation-driven> element and explicitly configure RequestMappingHandlerAdapter and RequestMappingHandlerMapping objects in the web application context XML file. As <annotation-driven> element doesn't provide any option to supply a custom WebBindingInitializer instance to the RequestMappingHandlerAdapter object, you'll have to explicitly configure RequestMappingHandlerAdapter and RequestMappingHandlerMapping objects in the web application context XML file.

The following example listing shows how you can use Spring's ConfigurableWebBindingInitializer (an implementation of WebBindingInitializer) to make CustomDateEditor property editor available to all the controllers in the MyBank application:

Example listing 13-17 – WebBindingInitializer configuration

```
<bean id="handlerAdapter" class=
     "org.springframework.web.servlet.mvc.method.annotation.RequestMappingHandlerAdapter">
    <property name="webBindingInitializer" ref="myInitializer" />
</bean>

<bean id="handlerMapping" class=
    "org.springframework.web.servlet.mvc.method.annotation.RequestMappingHandlerMapping" />

<bean id="myInitializer"
      class="org.springframework.web.bind.support.ConfigurableWebBindingInitializer">
    <property name="propertyEditorRegistrars">
        <list>
            <bean class="mypackage.MyPropertyEditorRegistrar" />
        </list>
    </property>
</bean>
```

The above example listing shows that RequestMappingHandlerAdapter and RequestMappingHandlerMapping beans are *explicitly* defined in the web application context XML file. The RequestMappingHandlerAdapter's webBindingInitializer property refers to the ConfigurableWebBindingInitializer bean that implements WebBindingInitializer interface. ConfigurableWebBindingInitializer's propertyEditorRegistrars property specifies classes that register one or more PropertyEditors with WebDataBinder. The following example listing shows how MyPropertyEditorRegistrar class registers CustomDateEditor property editor with WebDataBinder:

Example listing 13-18 – MyPropertyEditorRegistrar class

```
import org.springframework.beans.PropertyEditorRegistrar;
import org.springframework.beans.PropertyEditorRegistry;
import org.springframework.beans.propertyeditors.CustomDateEditor;

public class MyPropertyEditorRegistrar implements PropertyEditorRegistrar {

    @Override
    public void registerCustomEditors(PropertyEditorRegistry registry) {
        registry.registerCustomEditor(Date.class, new CustomDateEditor(
                new SimpleDateFormat("MM-dd-yyyy"), false));
    }
```

```
}
```

The above example listing shows that the MyPropertyEditorRegistrar class implements Spring's PropertyEditorRegistrar interface, and provides implementation for registerCustomEditors method defined in the PropertyEditorRegistrar interface. The PropertyEditorRegistry instance passed to the registerCustomEditors method is used for registering property editors. PropertyEditorRegistry's registerCustomEditor method is used for registering a PropertyEditor implementation with the WebDataBinder. In the above example listing, PropertyEditorRegistry's registerCustomEditor is used for registering the CustomDateEditor property editor with the WebDataBinder.

As we saw, using WebBindingInitializer for initializing WebDataBinder is quite an involved task. A simpler alternative to using WebBindingInitializer is to define @InitBinder annotated methods in a @ControllerAdvice annotated class.

Defining an @InitBinder method in a @ControllerAdvice annotated class

Like @Service, @Controller and @Repository annotations, @ControllerAdvice annotation is a specialized form of @Component annotation. The @ControllerAdvice annotation on a class indicates that the class provides support to controllers. You can define @InitBinder, @ModelAttribute and @ExceptionHandler annotated methods in the @ControllerAdvice annotated class, and these annotated methods apply to *all* the annotated controllers in the application. As with @Service, @Controller and @Repository annotations, <component-scan> element of Spring's context schema automatically detects and registers @ControllerAdvice annotated classes with the Spring container.

If you notice that you are duplicating @InitBinder, @ModelAttribute and @ExceptionHandler methods in multiple controllers, then consider defining such methods in a @ControllerAdvice annotated class. For instance, if you want to initialize the WebDataBinder with the configuration that applies to multiple controllers in the application, then define an @InitBinder method in a @ControllerAdvice annotated class instead of defining an @InitBinder method in multiple controller classes.

The following table summarizes the three approaches that we discussed for initializing WebDataBinder:

@InitBinder method in controller class	WebBindingInitializer	@InitBinder method in @ControllerAdvice class
Requires defining an @InitBinder method in a controller	Requires explicitly configuring RequestMappingHandlerAdapter in the web application context XML file	Requires defining an @InitBinder method in a @ControllerAdvice annotated class
WebDataBinder initialization applies only to the controller that contains the @InitBinder method	WebDataBinder initialization applies to all the annotated controllers in the application	WebDataBinder initialization applies to all the annotated controllers in the application

Let's now look at how you can allow or disallow fields of a model attribute from participating in the data binding process.

Allowing or disallowing fields from data binding process

WebDataBinder allows you to specify fields of a model attribute that are allowed or disallowed from participating in the data binding process. It is strongly recommended that you specify the fields of a model attribute that are allowed or disallowed from the data binding processes, as failing to do so may compromise the *security* of your application. Let's look at a scenario in which we would like to allow or disallow fields from data binding.

In MyBank application, when a user selects a fixed deposit for editing, the details of the selected fixed deposit are loaded from the data store and temporarily cached in the HttpSession. The user makes changes to the fixed deposit and saves the changes. The following example listing shows the @RequestMapping methods that are responsible for loading the selected fixed deposit and saving the updated fixed deposit information:

Example listing 13-19 – FixedDepositController
Project – ch13-data-binding
Source location - src/main/java/sample/spring/chapter13/web

```
package sample.spring.chapter13.web;
.....
@SessionAttributes(names = { "newFixedDepositDetails", "editableFixedDepositDetails" })
public class FixedDepositController {
    .....
    @RequestMapping(params = "fdAction=view", method = RequestMethod.GET)
    public ModelAndView viewFixedDepositDetails(
            @RequestParam(name = "fixedDepositId") int fixedDepositId) {
        FixedDepositDetails fixedDepositDetails = fixedDepositService
              .getFixedDeposit(fixedDepositId);
        Map<String, Object> modelMap = new HashMap<String, Object>();
        modelMap.put("editableFixedDepositDetails", fixedDepositDetails);
        .....
        return new ModelAndView("editFixedDepositForm", modelMap);
    }
    .....
    @RequestMapping(params = "fdAction=edit", method = RequestMethod.POST)
    public String editFixedDeposit(
       @ModelAttribute("editableFixedDepositDetails")
          FixedDepositDetails fixedDepositDetails, BindingResult bindingResult,
                 SessionStatus status) {
        .....
    }
}
```

In MyBank application, a fixed deposit is uniquely identified by the id field of FixedDepositDetails object (refer FixedDepositDetails class of ch13-data-binding project). When a user selects a fixed deposit for editing, the id field value is passed to the viewFixedDepositDetails method via the fixedDepositId request parameter. The viewFixedDepositDetails method uses the value of fixedDepositId request parameter to load fixed deposit details and show them on the 'Edit fixed deposit' form, as shown in figure 13-5.

As the id value (that corresponds to id attribute of FixedDepositDetails object) uniquely identifies a fixed deposit in the system, the 'Edit fixed deposit' form doesn't provide any mechanism to change it. When the user clicks the 'Save' button, the FixedDepositController's editFixedDeposit method is invoked. The editFixedDeposit method saves the changes to the fixed deposit detail.

When FixedDepositController's editFixedDeposit method is invoked, the WebDataBinder instance binds request parameter values to the fields of editableFixedDepositDetails model attribute – the FixedDepositDetails object that was loaded by viewFixedDepositDetails method and temporarily stored in HttpSession (refer @SessionAttributes annotation in example listing 13-19). If a malicious user sends a request parameter named id with value 10, then the WebDataBinder will blindly go ahead and set the id attribute of FixedDepositDetails object to 10 during data binding. This is *not* desirable because changing id attribute of a FixedDepositDetails object will compromise application data.

Edit fixed deposit

Id: 4 → read-only field

Amount (in USD): 50000

Maturity date: 05-22-2013

Email: a4email@somedomain.co

Save Go Back

Figure 13-5 'Edit fixed deposit' form for editing an existing fixed deposit

WebDataBinder provides setAllowedFields and setDisallowedFields methods that you can use to set the names of model attribute fields that can and cannot participate in the data binding process. The following example listing shows the FixedDepositController's initBinder_Edit method that specifies that the id field of editableFixedDepositDetails model attribute must *not* participate in the data binding process:

Example listing 13-20 – FixedDepositController – WebDataBinder's setDisallowedFields method
Project – ch13-data-binding
Source location - src/main/java/sample/spring/chapter13/web

```
package sample.spring.chapter13.web;
.....
public class FixedDepositController {
    .....
    @RequestMapping(params = "fdAction=edit", method = RequestMethod.POST)
    public String editFixedDeposit(@ModelAttribute("editableFixedDepositDetails")
          FixedDepositDetails fixedDepositDetails, .....) {
        .....
    }
    .....
    @InitBinder(value = "editableFixedDepositDetails")
    public void initBinder_Edit(WebDataBinder webDataBinder) {
        webDataBinder.registerCustomEditor(Date.class, new CustomDateEditor(
                new SimpleDateFormat("MM-dd-yyyy"), false));
        webDataBinder.setDisallowedFields("id");
    }
}
```

In the above example listing, the initBinder_Edit method initializes WebDataBinder instance for the editableFixedDepositDetails model attribute. As the setDisallowedFields method specifies that the id field of editableFixedDepositDetails model attribute is disallowed to participate in the binding process, the id field is *not* set even if a request parameter named id is contained in the request.

Let's now look at Spring's BindingResult object that exposes errors that occur during data binding and validation.

Inspecting data binding and validation errors using BindingResult object

Spring's BindingResult object provides a controller method with the results of binding request parameters to the model attribute's fields. For instance, if any type conversion error occurs during data binding, they are reported by the BindingResult object.

The following example listing shows FixedDepositController's openFixedDeposit method that creates a fixed deposit only if no errors are reported by the BindingResult object:

Example listing 13-21 – FixedDepositController – checking for binding and validation errors using BindingResult
Project – ch13-data-binding
Source location - src/main/java/sample/spring/chapter13/web

```
package sample.spring.chapter13.web;

import org.springframework.validation.BindingResult;
import org.springframework.web.bind.annotation.ModelAttribute;
.....
public class FixedDepositController {
    .....
    @RequestMapping(params = "fdAction=create", method = RequestMethod.POST)
    public String openFixedDeposit(@ModelAttribute(name = "newFixedDepositDetails")
            FixedDepositDetails fixedDepositDetails,
            BindingResult bindingResult, SessionStatus sessionStatus) {
        .....
        if (bindingResult.hasErrors()) {
            return "createFixedDepositForm";
        } else {
            fixedDepositService.saveFixedDeposit(fixedDepositDetails);
            sessionStatus.setComplete();
            return "redirect:/fixedDeposit/list";
        }
    }
    .....
}
```

In the above example listing, the BindingResult's hasErrors method returns true if the BindingResult object holds one or more data binding or validation errors. In section 13-5, we'll see how validation errors are stored in the BindingResult object. If errors are reported by the BindingResult object, the openFixedDeposit method renders the 'Create fixed deposit' form with appropriate error messages. If no errors are reported, the fixed deposit details are saved in the data store.

You should note that the BindingResult argument must immediately follow the model attribute argument whose BindingResult object you want to access in the controller method. For instance, in example listing 13-21, the BindingResult argument immediately follows the newFixedDepositDetails model attribute. The following example listing shows an incorrect ordering of the model attribute and the BindingResult object for the openFixedDeposit method:

Example listing 13-22 – Incorrect ordering of the model attribute and the BindingResult object

```
.....
public class FixedDepositController {
    .....
    @RequestMapping(params = "fdAction=create", method = RequestMethod.POST)
    public String openFixedDeposit(@ModelAttribute(name = "newFixedDepositDetails")
```

```
        FixedDepositDetails fixedDepositDetails, SessionStatus sessionStatus,
        BindingResult bindingResult) {
      .....
    }
    .....
}
```

In the above example listing, the ordering of the newFixedDepositDetails model attribute and the BindingResult object is incorrect because the SessionStatus argument is defined between them.

If a controller method accepts multiple model attributes, the BindingResult object corresponding to each model attribute is specified immediately after each model attribute argument, as shown in the following example listing:

Example listing 13-23 – Multiple model attributes and their BindingResult objects

```
@RequestMapping
public String doSomething(
    @ModelAttribute(name = "a") AObject aObj,BindingResult bindingResultA,
    @ModelAttribute(name = "b") BObject bObj,BindingResult bindingResultB,) {
      .....
}
```

The above example listing shows that both model attributes a and b are immediately followed by their corresponding BindingResult objects.

Now that we have seen the data binding process, let's look at how validation is performed in Spring Web MVC applications.

13-5 Validation support in Spring

In the previous section, we saw that the WebDataBinder binds request parameters to model attributes. The next step in request processing is to validate model attributes. In Spring Web MVC applications, you can validate model attributes using Spring Validation API (discussed in section 6-9 of chapter 6) or by specifying JSR 380 (Bean Validation 2.0) constraints (discussed in section 6-10 of chapter 6) on fields of model attributes.

> In this chapter, Spring Validation API and JSR 380 (Bean Validation 2.0) have been used to validate form backing objects (which are model attributes) in the web layer of the application. You should note that both JSR 380 (Bean Validation 2.0) and Spring Validation API can be used to validate objects in *any* application layer.

Let's first look at how to validate model attributes using Spring Validation API's Validator interface.

Validating model attributes using Spring's Validator interface

The following example listing shows the FixedDepositDetailsValidator class of MyBank application that validates FixedDepositDetails object:

Example listing 13-24 – FixedDepositDetailsValidator – Spring's Validator interface usage
Project – ch13-data-binding
Source location - src/main/java/sample/spring/chapter13/web

```
package sample.spring.chapter13.web;

import org.springframework.validation.*;
```

```
import sample.spring.chapter13.domain.FixedDepositDetails;

public class FixedDepositDetailsValidator implements Validator {

    public boolean supports(Class<?> clazz) {
        return FixedDepositDetails.class.isAssignableFrom(clazz);
    }

    public void validate(Object target, Errors errors) {
        FixedDepositDetails fixedDepositDetails = (FixedDepositDetails) target;
        long depositAmount = fixedDepositDetails.getDepositAmount();
        .....
        if (depositAmount < 1000) {
            errors.rejectValue("depositAmount", "error.depositAmount.less",
                    "must be greater than or equal to 1000");
        }
         if (email == null || "".equalsIgnoreCase(email)) {
            ValidationUtils.rejectIfEmptyOrWhitespace(errors, "email", "error.email.blank",
                    "must not be blank");
        }
        .....
    }
}
```

Spring's `Validator` interface defines `supports` and `validate` methods. The `supports` method checks if the supplied object instance (represented by the `clazz` attribute) can be validated. If the `supports` method returns `true`, the `validate` method is used to validate the object. In the above example listing, the `FixedDepositDetailsValidator`'s `supports` method checks if the supplied object instance is of type `FixedDepositDetails`. If the `supports` method returns `true`, the `FixedDepositDetailsValidator`'s `validate` method validates the object. The `validate` method accepts the object instance to be validated, and an `Errors` instance. `Errors` instance stores and exposes errors that occur during validation. `Errors` instance provides multiple `reject` and `rejectValue` methods to register errors with the `Errors` instance. The `rejectValue` methods are used to report field-level errors, and `reject` methods are used to report errors that apply to the object being validated. Spring's `ValidationUtils` class is a utility class that provides convenience methods to invoke a `Validator`, and for rejecting empty fields.

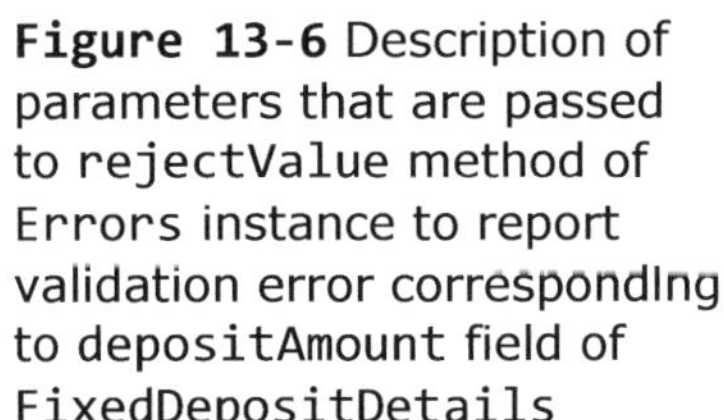

Figure 13-6 Description of parameters that are passed to `rejectValue` method of `Errors` instance to report validation error corresponding to `depositAmount` field of `FixedDepositDetails`

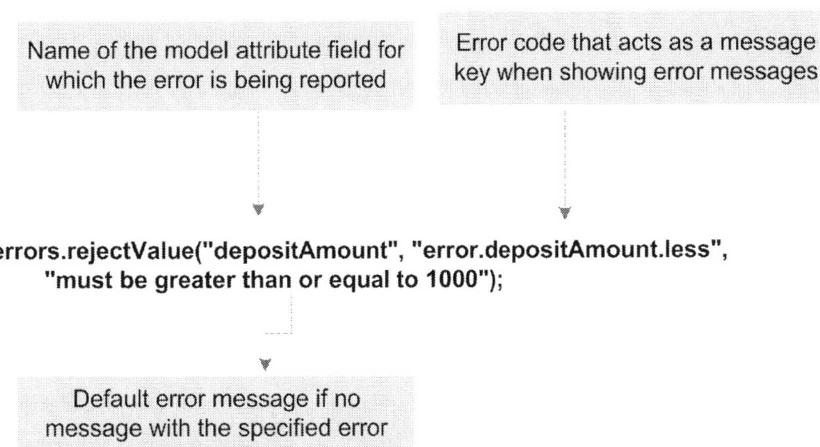

Figure 13-6 describes the parameters that were passed to the `rejectValue` method in example listing 13-24 to report validation errors corresponding to `FixedDepositDetails`'s `depositAmount` field. The figure shows that field name, error code (which is basically a message key) and a default error message are passed to the rejectValue method. In chapter 15, we'll see how message keys are used by JSP pages to show messages from resource bundles.

You can validate model attributes by:

- explicitly invoking validate method on Validator implementation
- setting Validator implementation on WebDataBinder, and annotating the model attribute argument in the @RequestMapping method with JSR 380's @Valid annotation

Let's look at each of the above mentioned approaches in detail.

Validating model attributes by explicitly calling validate method

The following example listing shows the FixedDepositController's openFixedDeposit method that uses FixedDepositDetailsValidator (refer example listing 13-24) to validate FixedDepositDetails model attribute:

Example listing 13-25 – FixedDepositController – validation by explicitly invoking FixedDepositDetailsValidator's validate method
Project – ch13-data-binding
Source location - src/main/java/sample/spring/chapter13/web

```
package sample.spring.chapter13.web;
.....
public class FixedDepositController {
    .....
    @RequestMapping(params = "fdAction=create", method = RequestMethod.POST)
    public String openFixedDeposit(@ModelAttribute(name = "newFixedDepositDetails")
        FixedDepositDetails fixedDepositDetails,
        BindingResult bindingResult, SessionStatus sessionStatus) {

        new FixedDepositDetailsValidator().validate(fixedDepositDetails,bindingResult);
        if (bindingResult.hasErrors()) {
            logger.info("openFixedDeposit() method: Validation errors
                 - re-displaying form for opening a new fixed deposit");
            return "createFixedDepositForm";
        }
        .....
    }
}
```

The above example listing shows that the openFixedDeposit method creates an instance of FixedDepositDetailsValidator and invokes its validate method. As BindingResult is a sub-interface of Errors, you can pass a BindingResult object where Errors object is expected. The openFixedDeposit method passes the fixedDepositDetails model attribute and the BindingResult object to the validate method. As BindingResult already contains data binding errors, passing BindingResult object to validate method adds validation errors also to the BindingResult object.

Invoking model attributes validation using JSR 380's @Valid annotation

You can instruct Spring to automatically validate a model attribute argument passed to a @RequestMapping method by adding JSR 380's @Valid annotation to the model attribute argument, and setting the validator for the model attribute on the WebDataBinder instance.

The following example listing shows how FixedDepositController's openFixedDeposit method can use @Valid annotation to validate FixedDepositDetails model attribute:

Example listing 13-26 – FixedDepositController – invoking validation using @Valid annotation

```
import javax.validation.Valid;
.....
public class FixedDepositController {
    .....
    @RequestMapping(params = "fdAction=create", method = RequestMethod.POST)
    public String openFixedDeposit(
            @Valid @ModelAttribute(value = "newFixedDepositDetails") FixedDepositDetails
               fixedDepositDetails, BindingResult bindingResult,
               SessionStatus sessionStatus) {

        if (bindingResult.hasErrors()) {
            logger.info("openFixedDeposit() method:
                 Validation errors - re-displaying form for opening a new fixed deposit");
            return "createFixedDepositForm";
        }
        .....
    }
    .....
    @InitBinder(value = "newFixedDepositDetails")
    public void initBinder_New(WebDataBinder webDataBinder) {
        webDataBinder.registerCustomEditor(Date.class, new CustomDateEditor(
                new SimpleDateFormat("MM-dd-yyyy"), false));
        webDataBinder.setValidator(new FixedDepositDetailsValidator());
    }
    .....
}
```

In the above example listing, the initBinder_New method calls WebDataBinder's setValidator method to set FixedDepositDetailsValidator as the validator for newFixedDepositDetails model attribute, and in the openFixedDeposit method the newFixedDepositDetails model attribute is annotated with JSR 380's @Valid annotation. When the openFixedDeposit method is invoked, both data binding *and* validation are performed on the newFixedDepositDetails model attribute, and the results of data binding and validation are made available via the BindingResult argument.

It is important to note that if @InitBinder annotation specifies name of the model attribute, the validator set on the WebDataBinder applies only to that particular model attribute. For instance, in example listing 13-26, the FixedDepositDetailsValidator applies only to the newFixedDepositDetails model attribute. If a validator applies to multiple controllers in the application, consider defining an @InitBinder method inside a @ControllerAdvice annotated class (or use WebBindingInitializer) to set a validator on the WebDataBinder.

Let's now look at how constraints are specified on properties of JavaBeans component using JSR 380 annotations.

Specifying constraints using JSR 380 annotations

JSR 380 (Bean Validation 2.0) defines annotations that you can use to specify constraints on properties of JavaBeans components.

IMPORT **chapter 13/ch13-jsr380-validation** (This project shows a modified version of ch13-data-binding project that uses JSR 380 annotations to specify constraints on FixedDepositDetails object. If you deploy the project on Tomcat server and access the URL http://localhost:8080/ch13-jsr380-validation, you'll see the list of fixed deposits in the system.)

The following example listing shows the FixedDepositDetails class that uses JSR 380 annotations to specify constraints on its fields:

Example listing 13-27 – FixedDepositDetails – specifying JSR 380 constraints
Project – ch13-jsr380-validation
Source location - src/main/java/sample/spring/chapter13/domain

```
package sample.spring.chapter13.domain;

import javax.validation.constraints.*;

public class FixedDepositDetails {
    private long id;

    @Min(1000)
    @Max(500000)
    private long depositAmount;

    @Email
    @Size(min=10, max=25)
    private String email;

    @NotNull
    private Date maturityDate;
    .....
}
```

@Min, @Max, @Email, @Size, and @NotNull are some of the annotations defined by JSR 380. The above example listing shows that by using JSR 380 annotations FixedDepositDetails class clearly specifies the constraints that apply on its fields. On the other hand, if you are using Spring's Validator implementation to validate an object, constraints are contained in the Validator implementation (refer example listing 13-24).

The following table describes the constraints enforced by JSR 380 annotations on the FixedDepositDetails object shown in example listing 13-27:

JSR 380 annotation	Constraint description
@NotNull	The annotated field must not be null. For instance, maturityDate field must not be null.
@Min	The annotated field's value must be greater than or equal to the specified minimum value. For instance, @Min(1000) annotation on depositAmount field of FixedDepositDetails object means that depositAmount's value must be greater than or equal to 1000.
@Max	The annotated field's value must be less than or equal to the specified value. For instance, @Max(500000) annotation on depositAmount field of FixedDepositDetails object means that the depositAmount's value must be less than or equal to 500000.
@Size	The annotated field's size must be between the specified min and max attributes. For instance, @Size(min=10, max=25) annotation on email field of FixedDepositDetails object means that the size of the email field must be greater than or equal to 10 and less than or equal to 25.

@Email	The annotated field's value must be a well-formed email address. For instance, @Email annotation on the email field of FixedDepositDetails object means that the email field's value must be a well-formed email address.

To use JSR 380 annotations, ch13-jsr380-validation project specifies dependency on JSR 380 API JAR file (validation-api-2.0.0.FINAL) and Hibernate Validator framework (hibernate-validation-6.0.4.Final). The Hibernate Validator framework provides the reference implementation for JSR 380. The Hibernate Validator framework provides additional constraint annotations that you can use along with JSR 380 annotations. For instance, you can use Hibernate Validator's @CreditCardNumber annotation to specify that a field's value must be a valid credit card number.

It is important to note that JSR 380 also allows you to create custom constraints and use them in your application. For instance, you can create a @MyConstraint custom constraint and a corresponding validator to enforce that constraint on objects.

Now that we have specified JSR 380 constraints on FixedDepositDetails class, let's look at how to validate FixedDepositDetails object.

Validating objects that use JSR 380 annotations

If a JSR 380 provider (like Hibernate Validator) is found in the application's classpath, and you have specified <annotation-driven> element of Spring's mvc schema in the web application context XML file, then Spring automatically enables support for JSR 380. Behind the scenes, the <annotation-driven> element configures an instance of Spring's LocalValidatorFactoryBean class that is responsible for detecting the presence of a JSR 380 provider (like Hibernate Validator) in the application's classpath and initializing it.

LocalValidatorFactoryBean implements JSR 380's Validator and ValidatorFactory interfaces, and also Spring's Validator interface. For this reason, you can choose to validate an object by calling validate method of Spring's Validator interface or by calling validate method of JSR 380's Validator. As discussed earlier, you can also instruct Spring to automatically validate a model attribute argument passed to a @RequestMapping method by simply adding @Valid annotation on the model attribute argument.

Validating model attributes by explicitly calling validate method

The following example listing shows the FixedDepositController class that uses Spring's Validator to validate the FixedDepositDetails object (refer example listing 13-27) that uses JSR 380's constraints:

Example listing 13-28 – FixedDepositController – validating FixedDepositDetails using Spring Validation API
Project – ch13-jsr380-validation
Source location - src/main/java/sample/spring/chapter13/web

```
package sample.spring.chapter13.web;

import org.springframework.validation.Validator;
import javax.validation.Valid;
.....
public class FixedDepositController {
    .....

    @Autowired
    private Validator validator;
    .....
    @RequestMapping(params = "fdAction=create", method = RequestMethod.POST)
    public String openFixedDeposit(@ModelAttribute(name = "newFixedDepositDetails")
```

```
            FixedDepositDetails fixedDepositDetails,
            BindingResult bindingResult, SessionStatus sessionStatus) {
        validator.validate(fixedDepositDetails, bindingResult);

        if (bindingResult.hasErrors()) { ..... }
        .....
    }
    .....
}
```

In the above example listing, the LocalValidatorFactoryBean (that implements Spring's Validator interface) is autowired into FixedDepositController's validator instance variable. In the openFixedDeposit method, call to Validator's validate method results in invocation of LocalValidatorFactoryBean's validate(Object, Errors) method to validate the FixedDepositDetails instance. The BindingResult object is passed to the validate method to hold the validation errors. An important point to notice in the above example listing is that the FixedDepositController doesn't directly deal with JSR 380-specific API to validate FixedDepositDetails object. Instead, Spring Validation API is used to validate FixedDepositDetails object.

The following example listing shows an alternate version of FixedDepositController that uses JSR 380-specific API to validate FixedDepositDetails object:

Example listing 13-29 – FixedDepositController – validating FixedDepositDetails using JSR 380-specific API

```
import javax.validation.ConstraintViolation;
import javax.validation.Validator;
import java.util.Set;
.....
public class FixedDepositController {
    .....
    @Autowired
    private Validator validator;
    .....
    @RequestMapping(params = "fdAction=create", method = RequestMethod.POST)
    public String openFixedDeposit(@ModelAttribute(name = "newFixedDepositDetails")
            FixedDepositDetails fixedDepositDetails,
            BindingResult bindingResult, SessionStatus sessionStatus) {

        Set<ConstraintViolation<FixedDepositDetails>> violations =
                validator.validate(fixedDepositDetails);
        Iterator<ConstraintViolation<FixedDepositDetails>> itr = violations.iterator();

        if(itr.hasNext()) { ..... }
        .....
    }
    .....
}
```

In the above example listing, the LocalValidatorFactoryBean (that implements JSR 380's Validator interface) is autowired into FixedDepositController's validator instance variable. In the openFixedDeposit method, call to Validator's validate method results in invocation of LocalValidatorFactoryBean's validate(T) method to validate the FixedDepositDetails instance. The validate method returns a java.util.Set object that contains the constraint violations reported by the JSR 380 provider. You can check the java.util.Set object returned by the validate method to find if any constraint violations were reported.

Invoking model attributes validation using JSR 380's @Valid annotation

You can instruct Spring to automatically validate a model attribute argument passed to a @RequestMapping method by adding JSR 380's @Valid annotation to the model attribute argument. The following example listing shows FixedDepositController's editFixedDeposit method that uses @Valid annotation to validate editableFixedDepositDetails model attribute:

Example listing 13-30 – FixedDepositController – invoking validation using @Valid annotation
Project – ch13-jsr380-validation
Source location - src/main/java/sample/spring/chapter13/web

```
package sample.spring.chapter13.web;

import javax.validation.Valid;
.....
public class FixedDepositController {
    .....
    @RequestMapping(params = "fdAction=edit", method = RequestMethod.POST)
    public String editFixedDeposit(@Valid @ModelAttribute("editableFixedDepositDetails")
            FixedDepositDetails fixedDepositDetails,
            BindingResult bindingResult, SessionStatus sessionStatus) {

        if (bindingResult.hasErrors()) { ..... }
        .....
    }
    .....
}
```

In the above example listing, @Valid annotation on editableFixedDepositDetails model attribute results in its automatic validation by Spring. The constraint violations reported during validation are added to the BindingResult object along with any data binding errors.

Let's now look at how Spring's form tag library simplifies writing forms in JSP pages.

13-6 Spring's form tag library

Spring's form tag library provides tags that simplify creating JSP pages for Spring Web MVC applications. The Spring's form tag library provides tags to render various input form elements and for binding form data to form backing objects.

The following example listing shows the createFixedDepositForm.jsp JSP page of ch13-jsr380-validation project that uses Spring's form tag library tags:

Example listing 13-31 – createFixedDepositForm.jsp – Spring's form tag library usage
Project – ch13-jsr380-validation
Source location - src/main/webapp/WEB-INF/jsp

```
<%@taglib uri="http://java.sun.com/jsp/jstl/core" prefix="c"%>
<%@taglib prefix="form" uri="http://www.springframework.org/tags/form"%>

<html>
.....
    <form:form modelAttribute="newFixedDepositDetails"
        name="createFixedDepositForm" method="POST"
        action="${pageContext.request.contextPath}/fixedDeposit?fdAction=create">
        .....
```

```
        <tr>
            <td class="td"><b>Amount (in USD):</b></td>
            <td class="td">
                <form:input path="depositAmount" />
                <font style="color: #C11B17;">
                    <form:errors path="depositAmount"/>
                </font>
            </td>
        </tr>
        <tr>
            <td class="td"><b>Maturity date:</b></td>
            <td class="td">
                <form:input path="maturityDate" />
                <font style="color: #C11B17;">
                    <form:errors path="maturityDate"/>
                </font>
            </td>
        </tr>
        .....
            <td class="td">
                <input type="submit" value="Save" />
        .....
    </form:form>
</html>
```

In the above example listing, the following taglib directive makes the Spring's form tag library tags accessible to the JSP page:

```
<%@taglib prefix="form" uri="http://www.springframework.org/tags/form"%>
```

Spring's form tag library's <form> tag renders an HTML form that binds form fields to the properties of model attribute identified by the modelAttribute attribute. The <form> tag contains <input> tags that correspond to the properties of the model attribute specified by the modelAttribute attribute. When the form is rendered, properties are read from the model attribute and displayed by <input> tags. And, when the form is submitted, the field values in the form are bound to the corresponding properties of the model attribute.

> Prior to Spring 5, <form> tag's commandName attribute was used to specify the model attribute name to which the form fields are bound. As of Spring 5, commandName attribute is replaced by modelAttribute attribute. If you use commandName attribute with Spring 5, it'll result in an exception at runtime.

In example listing 13-31, the <form> tag renders an HTML form for opening a fixed deposit. The modelAttribute attribute's value is newFixedDepositDetails, which means that the form fields are mapped to the properties of the newFixedDepositDetails model attribute. The name attribute specifies the name of the HTML form rendered by the <form> tag. The method attribute specifies the HTTP method to use for sending form data when the form is submitted. The action attribute specifies the URL to which the form data is sent when the form is submitted. The URL specified by the action attribute must map to a unique @RequestMapping annotated method in your Spring Web MVC application. In example listing 13-31, the URL ${pageContext.request.contextPath}/fixedDeposit?fdAction=create maps to FixedDepositController's openFixedDeposit method (refer FixedDepositController.java file of ch13-jsr380-validation project). You should note that the expression ${pageContext.request.contextPath} returns the *context path* of the web application.

The <input> tag of Spring's form tag library renders an HTML <input> element with type attribute set to text. The path attribute specifies the property of the model attribute to which the field is mapped. When the form is rendered, the value of the property is displayed by the input field. And, when the form is submitted, the value of the property is set to the value entered by the user in the input field.

The `<errors>` tag of Spring's `form` tag library shows data binding and validation error messages that were added to the `BindingResult` during data binding and validation. If you want to display error messages corresponding to a particular property, specify the name of the property as the value of the `path` attribute. If you want to display all the error messages stored in the `BindingResult` object, specify value of `path` attribute as `*`.

The `createFixedDepositForm.jsp` page uses only a subset of Spring's `form` tag library tags. The following table shows the other tags that Spring's `form` tag library offers:

Tag	Description
`<checkbox>`	Renders an HTML checkbox (that is, `<input type="checkbox" />`) As the value of an HTML checkbox is *not* sent to the server if the checkbox is unchecked, the `<checkbox>` tag additionally renders a hidden field corresponding to each checkbox to allow sending the state of the checkbox to the server. Example: `<form:checkbox path="myProperty" />` The `path` attribute specifies the name of the property to which the checkbox value is bound.
`<checkboxes>`	Renders multiple HTML checkboxes. Example: `<form:checkboxes path="myPropertyList" items="${someList}"/>` The `path` attribute specifies the name of the property to which the selected checkboxes values are bound. The `items` attribute specifies the name of the model attribute that contains the list of options to show as checkboxes.
`<radiobutton>`	Renders an HTML radio button (that is, `<input type="radio" />`) Example: `<form:radiobutton path="myProperty" value="myValue"/>` The `path` attribute specifies the name of the property to which the radio button is bound, and the `value` attribute specifies the value assigned to the radio button.
`<radiobuttons>`	Renders multiple HTML radio buttons. Example: `<form:radiobuttons path="myProperty" items="${myValues}"/>` The `items` attribute specifies the list of options to show as radio buttons, and the `path` attribute specifies the property to which the selected radio buttons values are bound.
`<password>`	Renders an HTML password field (that is, `<input type="password"/>`)
`<select>`	Renders an HTML `<select>` element. Example: `<form:select path="book" items="${books}"/>` The `items` attribute specifies the model attribute property that contains the list of options to display in the HTML `<select>` element. The `path` attribute specifies the property to which the selected option is bound.
`<option>`	Renders an HTML `<option>` element. Example: `<form:select path="book">`

	`<form:option value="Getting started with Spring Framework"/>` `<form:option value="Getting started with Spring Web MVC"/>` `</form:select>`
<options>	Renders multiple HTML <option> elements.
<textarea>	Renders an HTML <textarea> element.
<hidden>	Renders an HTML hidden input field (that is, <input type="hidden" />)

Let's now look at HTML5 support in Spring's form tag library.

HTML5 support in Spring's form tag library

The form tag library allows you to use HTML5-specific attributes in the tags. For instance, the following <textarea> tag uses HTML5's required attribute:

```
<form:textarea path="myProperty" required="required"/>
```

The required="required" attribute specifies that it is mandatory for the user to enter information in the textarea. The use of required attribute saves the effort to write the JavaScript code to perform client-side validation for mandatory fields. If the user doesn't enter any information in the textarea and attempts to submit the form, the web browser shows a message saying that the textarea is required and must not be left blank.

In HTML5 you can specify type attribute's value as email, datetime, date, month, week, time, range, color, reset, and so on. For instance, the following <input> tag specifies type attribute's value as email:

```
<form:input path="myProperty" type="email"/>
```

When a user attempts to submit the form containing a field of type email, the web browser checks that the email type field contains a valid email address. If the email type field doesn't contain a valid email address, the web browser shows a message indicating that the field doesn't contain a valid email address. As the web browser performs the validation, you don't need to write the JavaScript code to validate the email address.

Let's now look at how we can configure a Spring Web MVC application without using XML files.

13-7 Configuring web applications using Java-based configuration

In the web application examples that we've seen so far, Spring beans were defined in root web application context XML (loaded by ContextLoaderListener) and child web application context XML (loaded by DispatcherServlet), and the web.xml configured DispatcherServlet and ContextLoaderListener. In this section, we'll see how to configure a Spring Web MVC application using Java-based configuration approach.

IMPORT **chapter 13/ch13-jsr380-validation-javaconfig** (This project is a modified version of ch13-jsr380-validation project that uses Java-based configuration approach. If you deploy the project on Tomcat server and access the URL http://localhost:8080/ch13-jsr380-validation-javaconfig, you'll see the list of fixed deposits in the system.)

As root and child web application context beans are treated differently, you need to define different @Configuration annotated classes corresponding to root and child web application contexts. The following example listing shows @Configuration annotated RootContextConfig class that configures beans that belong to the *root* web application context:

Example listing 13-32 – RootContextConfig
Project – ch13-jsr380-validation-javaconfig
Source location - src/main/java/sample/spring/chapter13

```
package sample.spring.chapter13;
.....
@Configuration
@ComponentScan(basePackages = { "sample.spring.chapter13.domain",
                    "sample.spring.chapter13.dao", "sample.spring.chapter13.service" })
public class RootContextConfig { ..... }
```

As shown above, the RootContextConfig class makes use of @ComponentScan to register domain entities, DAOs and services. The RootContextConfig class is equivalent to applicationContext.xml file (located in src/main/resources/META-INF/spring/) of ch13-jsr380-validation project.

The following example listing shows @Configuration annotated WebContextConfig class that configures beans belonging to the web layer of the application:

Example listing 13-33 – WebContextConfig
Project – ch13-jsr380-validation-javaconfig
Source location - src/main/java/sample/spring/chapter13

```
package sample.spring.chapter13;

import org.springframework.web.servlet.config.annotation.EnableWebMvc;
import org.springframework.web.servlet.config.annotation.ViewResolverRegistry;
import org.springframework.web.servlet.config.annotation.WebMvcConfigurer;
import org.springframework.web.servlet.view.InternalResourceViewResolver;

@EnableWebMvc
@Configuration
@ComponentScan("sample.spring.chapter13.web")
public class WebContextConfig implements WebMvcConfigurer {

    @Override
    public void configureViewResolvers(ViewResolverRegistry registry) {
        InternalResourceViewResolver viewResolver = new InternalResourceViewResolver();
        viewResolver.setPrefix("/WEB-INF/jsp/");
        viewResolver.setSuffix(".jsp");
        registry.viewResolver(viewResolver);
    }
}
```

@EnableWebMvc annotation serves the same purpose as the <annotation-driven> element of Spring's mvc schema; it configures objects that are required for developing Spring Web MVC applications. To override default configurations, implement the WebMvcConfigurer interface class that defines *default* methods for different configurations. In the above example listing, WebContextConfig implements WebMvcConfigurer class and overrides configureViewResolvers method to register an InternalResourceViewResolver that resolves views to JSP pages located in /WEB-INF/jsp folder.

Instead of using a web.xml file, you can use Spring's AbstractAnnotationConfigDispatcherServletInitializer class (an implementation of Spring's WebApplicationInitializer) to programmatically configure the ServletContext, and to register a DispatcherServlet and a ContextLoaderListener with the ServletContext. The following example listing shows the BankAppInitializer class that extends AbstractAnnotationConfigDispatcherServletInitializer class:

Example listing 13-34 – BankAppInitializer
Project – ch13-jsr380-validation-javaconfig
Source location - src/main/java/sample/spring/chapter13

```
package sample.spring.chapter13;

import org.springframework.web.servlet.support.*;

public class BankAppInitializer extends
        AbstractAnnotationConfigDispatcherServletInitializer {

    @Override
    protected Class<?>[] getRootConfigClasses() {
        return new Class[] { RootContextConfig.class };
    }

    @Override
    protected Class<?>[] getServletConfigClasses() {
        return new Class[] { WebContextConfig.class };
    }

    @Override
    protected String[] getServletMappings() {
        return new String[] { "/" };
    }
}
```

In the above example listing, getRootConfigClasses method returns @Configuration (or @Component) annotated classes that we want to register with the root web application context. As the RootContextConfig class configures beans that form part of the root web application context, the getRootConfigClasses method returns the RootContextConfig class. AbstractAnnotationConfigDispatcherServletInitializer supplies the root web application context to an instance of ContextLoaderListener.

The getServletConfigClasses method returns @Configuration (or @Component) annotated classes that we want to register with the *child* web application context. As the WebContextConfig class configures beans that form part of the web layer, the getServletConfigClasses method returns the WebContextConfig class. AbstractAnnotationConfigDispatcherServletInitializer supplies the child web application context to an instance of DispatcherServlet.

The getServletMappings method specifies the servlet mappings for the DispatcherServlet.

This is all you need to do to create a Spring Web MVC application that doesn't use web.xml and application context XML files.

13-8 Summary

We looked at many core features of Spring Web MVC in this chapter. We looked at @ModelAttribute and @SessionAttributes annotations which are most commonly used in developing annotated controllers. We also took an in-depth look at how Spring performs data binding and validation. In the next chapter, we'll look at how to develop RESTful web services using Spring Web MVC.

Chapter 14 –*Developing RESTful web services using Spring Web MVC*

14-1 Introduction

Representational State Transfer (also referred to as *REST*) is an architectural-style in which an application defines *resources* that are *uniquely* identified by URIs (*Uniform Resource Identifier*). The clients of a REST-style application interact with a resource by sending HTTP GET, POST, PUT and DELETE method requests to the URI to which the resource is mapped. The following figure shows a REST-style application that is accessed by its clients:

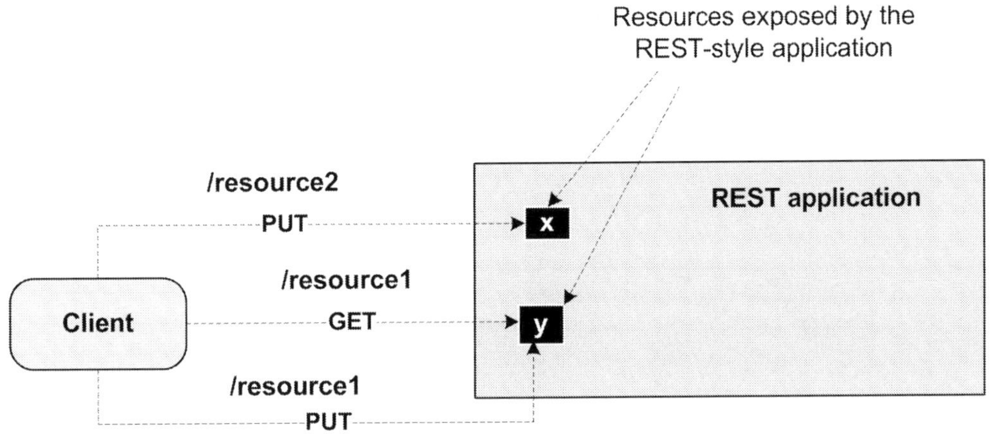

Figure 14-1 REST-style application defines x and y resources that are uniquely identified by /resource2 and /resource1 URIs, respectively.

The above figure shows a REST-style application that consists of two resources – x and y. The resource x is mapped to /resource2 URI and the y resource is mapped to /resource1 URI. A client can interact with resource x by sending HTTP requests to /resource2 URI, and can interact with resource y by sending HTTP requests to /resource1 URI.

If a web service follows the REST architectural-style, it is referred to as a *RESTful web service*. In the context of RESTful web services, you can think of a resource as the *data* exposed by the web service. The client can perform CRUD (CREATE, READ, UPDATE and DELETE) operations on the exposed data by sending HTTP requests to the RESTful web service. The client and the RESTful web service exchange *representation* of the data, which could be in XML, JSON (JavaScript Object Notation) format, or a simple string, or any other MIME type supported by the HTTP protocol.

RESTful web services are simpler to implement and are more scalable compared to SOAP-based web services. In SOAP-based web services, requests and responses are always in XML format. In RESTful web services, you can use JSON (JavaScript Object Notation), XML, plain text, and so on, for requests and responses. In this chapter, we'll look at how Spring Web MVC simplifies developing and accessing RESTful web services.

Let's begin by looking at the requirements of a RESTful web service that we'll implement using Spring Web MVC.

14-2 Fixed deposit web service

We saw earlier that the MyBank web application provides the functionality to display a list of fixed deposits, and to create, edit and close fixed deposits. As the fixed deposit related functionality may also be accessed by other applications, the fixed deposit related functionality needs to be taken out from the MyBank web application and deployed as a RESTful web service. Let's call this new RESTful web service as FixedDepositWS.

The following figure shows that the FixedDepositWS web service is accessed by MyBank and Settlement applications:

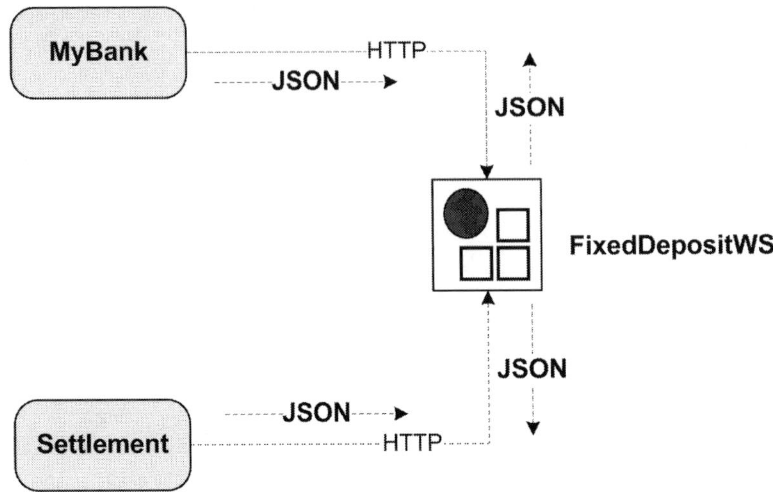

`Figure 14-2` MyBank and Settlement applications access FixedDepositWS web service

The above figure shows that MyBank and Settlement web applications interact with FixedDepositWS web service by exchanging data in JSON format. We'll soon see that JSON represents a simpler alternative to XML for exchanging data between applications.

Let's now look at how to implement FixedDepositWS web service as a RESTful web service using Spring Web MVC.

14-3 Implementing a RESTful web service using Spring Web MVC

To develop a RESTful web service, you need to do the following:

- identify resources that are exposed by the web service
- specify URIs corresponding to the identified resources
- identify operations that can be performed on the resources
- map HTTP methods to the identified operations

In the case of FixedDepositWS web service, fixed deposit data represents the resource exposed by the web service. If the FixedDepositWS web service maps fixed deposits in the system to `/fixedDeposits` URI, a FixedDepositWS web service client can perform actions on fixed deposits by sending HTTP requests to `/fixedDeposits` URI.

In RESTful web services, the HTTP method used by clients for interacting with a resource indicates the operation to be performed on the resource. `GET` retrieves the resource state, `POST` creates a new resource, `PUT` modifies the resource state and `DELETE` deletes the resource. The following figures shows the actions performed by the FixedDepositWS web service when a client sends `GET`, `POST`, `PUT` and `DELETE` HTTP requests to the `/fixedDeposits` URI:

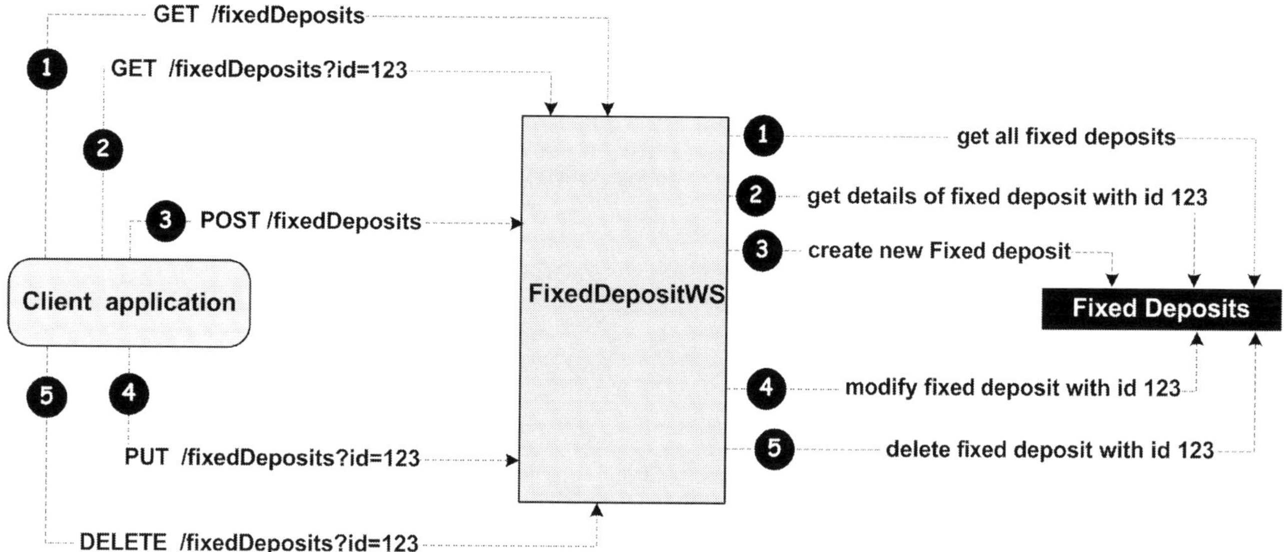

Figure 14-3 HTTP requests are sent by the FixedDepositWS's client to `/fixedDeposits` URI to interact with the fixed deposit data

The above figure shows that the client of FixedDepositWS web service sends `GET`, `POST`, `PUT` and `DELETE` HTTP requests to `/fixedDeposits` URI to interact with the fixed deposit data. The `id` query string parameter uniquely identifies a fixed deposit in the system. The following table defines the purpose of each request shown in the above figure:

HTTP method	URI	Purpose
`GET`	`/fixedDeposits`	Retrieve details of all the fixed deposits in the system. The FixedDepositWS web service sends the response in JSON format.
`GET`	`/fixedDeposits?id=123`	Retrieve details of the fixed deposit whose `id` is `123`. The FixedDepositWS web service sends the response in JSON format.
`POST`	`/fixedDeposits`	Create a new fixed deposit in the system. The web service client sends the details of the fixed deposit to be created in JSON format.
`PUT`	`/fixedDeposits?id=123`	Modifies the fixed deposit whose `id` is `123`. The web service client sends the modified details of the fixed deposit in JSON format.
`DELETE`	`/fixedDeposits?id=123`	Removes the fixed deposit whose id is 123.

The above table shows that the FixedDepositWS and its clients exchange information in JSON format. Before delving into the details of how to implement FixedDepositWS, let's look at how the data looks like in JSON format.

JSON (JavaScript Object Notation)

JSON is a text-based data format that is used by applications for exchanging *structured* data. As JSON representation of data is more compact compared to XML, JSON serves as a simpler alternative to XML. To simplify conversion of Java objects to JSON and vice versa, you can use JSON libraries like FlexJson (`http://flexjson.sourceforge.net/`) and Jackson (`https://github.com/FasterXML/jackson`).

Let's say a `Person` class defines `firstName` and `lastName` attributes. If you create an instance of `Person` object and set `firstName` to `Myfirstname` and `lastName` to `Mylastname`, the representation of the `Person` object in JSON format would look like this:

Example listing 14-1 – Person object representation in JSON format

```
{
    "firstName" : "Myfirstname",
    "lastName" : "Mylastname"
}
```

The above example listing shows that each attribute of `Person` object is represented as `<attribute-name> : <attribute-value>` in JSON format.

You can also represent a collection of Java objects in JSON format. The following example listing shows how you can represent a collection of `Person` objects in JSON format:

Example listing 14-2 – Collection of `Person` objects represented in JSON format

```
[
    {
        "firstName" : "Myfirstname",
        "lastName" : "Mylastname"
    },
    {
        "firstName" : "Yourfirstname",
        "lastName" : "Yourlastname"
    }
]
```

You don't need to write code to convert an object into JSON representation and vice versa. Instead, the RESTful web service and its clients can make use of FlexJson or Jackson library to perform conversion. As we'll soon see, Spring Web MVC uses Jackson for converting JSON to Java objects and vice versa.

Let's now look at the implementation of FixedDepositWS web service using Spring Web MVC.

IMPORT **chapter 14/ch14-webservice** (This project shows the implementation of FixedDepositWS RESTful web service using Spring Web MVC. Later in this chapter, we'll see how FixedDepositWS web service is accessed by its clients.)

FixedDepositWS web service implementation

Spring Web MVC annotations, like `@Controller`, `@RequestMapping`, `@RequestParam`, `@PathVariable` `@ResponseBody`, `@RequestBody`, and so on, support building RESTful web services. In this section, we'll look at usage of some of these annotations in developing the FixedDepositWS web service.

In FixedDepositWS web service, the `FixedDepositController` (a Spring Web MVC controller) is responsible for handling web service requests. `FixedDepositController` is like any other Spring Web MVC controller with the exception that its `@RequestMapping` methods *don't* render views. The following example listing shows that

@Controller and @RequestMapping annotations are used to map web requests to appropriate methods of FixedDepositController class:

Example listing 14-3 – FixedDepositController – web service request handler
Project – ch14-webservice
Source location - src/main/java/sample/spring/chapter14/web

```
package sample.spring.chapter14.web;

import org.springframework.http.ResponseEntity;
.....
@Controller
@RequestMapping(path = "/fixedDeposits")
public class FixedDepositController {
    .....
    @RequestMapping(method = RequestMethod.GET)
    public ResponseEntity<List<FixedDepositDetails>> getFixedDepositList() { ..... }

    @RequestMapping(method = RequestMethod.GET, params = "id")
    public ResponseEntity<FixedDepositDetails> getFixedDeposit(@RequestParam("id") int id)
{ ..... }
    .....
}
```

The getFixedDepositList method returns the list of fixed deposits in the system, and the getFixedDeposit method returns details of the fixed deposit identified by the id argument. The above example listing shows that the @RequestMapping annotation is used at the class- and method-level to map requests to getFixedDepositList and getFixedDeposit methods. The getFixedDepositList method is invoked when a client application sends an HTTP GET request to /fixedDeposits URI, and the getFixedDeposit method is invoked when a client application sends an HTTP GET request containing id request parameter to /fixedDeposits URI. So, if the request URI is /fixedDeposits?id=123, the getFixedDeposit method is invoked.

The following table summarizes the mapping of request URIs and HTTP methods to the methods defined in the FixedDepositController class:

HTTP method	URI	FixedDepositController method
GET	/fixedDeposits	getFixedDepositList
GET	/fixedDeposits?id=123	getFixedDeposit
POST	/fixedDeposits	openFixedDeposit
PUT	/fixedDeposits?id=123	editFixedDeposit
DELETE	/fixedDeposits?id=123	closeFixedDeposit

We saw in chapter 12 and 13 that @RequestMapping annotated methods return view information that is used by the DispatcherServlet to render a view (like JSP or servlet). In RESTful web services, @RequestMapping methods return data (and *not* the view information) to the client applications. For this reason, the getFixedDepositList and getFixedDeposit methods have been defined to return objects of type ResponseEntity. Let's now look at the usage of ResponseEntity object in the FixedDepositController class.

Specifying HTTP response using ResponseEntity

ResponseEntity represents an HTTP response consisting of headers, body and status code. The object that you set as *body* on the ResponseEntity object is written to the HTTP response body by Spring Web MVC.

The following example listing shows how the ResponseEntity object is created by FixedDepositController's getFixedDepositList method:

Example listing 14-4 – FixedDepositController – creating ResponseEntity instance
Project – ch14-webservice
Source location - src/main/java/sample/spring/chapter14/web

```
package sample.spring.chapter14.web;

import org.springframework.http.HttpStatus;
import org.springframework.http.ResponseEntity;
.....
public class FixedDepositController {
    .....
    @RequestMapping(method = RequestMethod.GET)
    public ResponseEntity<List<FixedDepositDetails>> getFixedDepositList() {
        .....
        return new ResponseEntity<List<FixedDepositDetails>>(
                fixedDepositService.getFixedDeposits(), HttpStatus.OK);
    }
    .....
}
```

In the above example listing, the fixed deposit list passed to the ResponseEntity constructor is written to the HTTP response body. The HttpStatus is an enum type that defines HTTP status codes. The constant OK refers to the HTTP status code 200. Notice that the return type of the getFixedDepositList method is ResponseEntity<List<FixedDepositDetails>>, which means that an object of type List<FixedDepositDetails> is written to the HTTP response body. Spring Web MVC uses an appropriate HttpMessageConverter (explained in section 14-5) to convert the List<FixedDepositDetails> object into the format expected by the client application.

> Later in this chapter, we'll see that client applications can use Spring's RestTemplate to invoke methods defined in the FixedDepositController and to retrieve the objects written to the HTTP response body.

All the @RequestMapping annotated methods of FixedDepositController class define ResponseEntity as their return type. If you *don't* need to send HTTP status code in the response, you can use Spring's HttpEntity class instead of ResponseEntity. HttpEntity represents an HTTP request or response containing headers and body. RequestEntity and ResponseEntity subclasses represent HTTP request and HTTP response, respectively. ResponseEntity adds response status code, and RequestEntity adds HTTP method and URI to HttpEntity.

The following example listing shows a modified version of getFixedDepositList method that creates and returns an instance of HttpEntity:

Example listing 14-5 – FixedDepositController – using HttpEntity instead of ResponseEntity

```
import org.springframework.http.HttpStatus;
import org.springframework.http.HttpEntity;
.....
public class FixedDepositController {
```

```
    .....
    @RequestMapping(method = RequestMethod.GET)
    public HttpEntity<List<FixedDepositDetails>> getFixedDepositList() {
       .....
       return
         new HttpEntity<List<FixedDepositDetails>>(fixedDepositService.getFixedDeposits());
    }
    .....
}
```

The above example listing shows that the fixed deposits found in the system are passed to the HttpEntity constructor. As in the case of ResponseEntity (refer example listing 14-4), fixed deposits passed to the HttpEntity are written to the HTTP response body.

To send response headers, you can use HttpHeaders object. The following example listing shows a scenario in which some-header header is set on the HTTP response:

Example listing 14-6 – HttpHeaders usage

```
import org.springframework.http.HttpHeaders;
.....
    @RequestMapping(method = RequestMethod.GET)
    public HttpEntity<String> doSomething() {
        HttpHeaders responseHeaders = new HttpHeaders();
        responseHeaders.set("some-header", "some-value");

        return new HttpEntity<String>("Hello world !", responseHeaders);
    }
.....
```

Spring's HttpHeaders object is used to set HTTP request and response headers. In the above example listing, HttpHeaders's set method sets some-header response header (with value some-value). When the doSomething method is invoked, the 'Hello world !' string is written to the response body, and some-header header is written to the HTTP response.

As @RequestMapping methods can be defined to accept HttpServletResponse object as argument, let's look at how you can directly set response body and headers on the HttpServletResponse object.

Specifying HTTP response using HttpServletResponse

The following example listing shows a @RequestMapping method which writes directly to the HttpServletResponse object:

Example listing 14-7 – Setting response on HttpServletResponse

```
import javax.servlet.http.HttpServletResponse;
.....
    @RequestMapping(method = RequestMethod.GET)
    public void doSomething(HttpServletResponse response) throws IOException {
        response.setHeader("some-header", "some-value");
        response.setStatus(200);
        response.getWriter().write("Hello world !");
    }
.....
```

Instead of directly writing response to HttpServletResponse, you should use ResponseEntity (or HttpEntity) object to improve the testability of the controllers.

Let's now look at Spring's @ResponseBody method-level annotation that writes the return value of the method to HTTP response body.

> Since Spring 4.0, @ResponseBody annotation can also be specified at the class level. If @ResponseBody annotation is specified at the class level, it is inherited by the @RequestMapping methods of the controller.

Binding returned value of a method to HTTP response body using @ResponseBody

The following example listing shows usage of @ResponseBody annotation:

Example listing 14-8 – @ResponseBody annotation usage

```
import org.springframework.web.bind.annotation.ResponseBody;
.....
    @RequestMapping(method = RequestMethod.GET)
    @ResponseBody
    public String doSomething() {
        return "Hello world !";
    }
.....
```

In the above example listing, the 'Hello world !' string value returned by the doSomething method is written to the HTTP response body. In section 12-7 of chapter 12, we discussed that if the return type of a @RequestMapping annotated method is String, the returned value is treated as the name of the *view* to render. In the above example listing, the @ResponseBody annotation on the doSomething method instructs Spring Web MVC to write the string value to the HTTP response body instead of treating the string value as the view name. You should note that Spring uses an appropriate HttpMessageConverter (explained in section 14-5) implementation to write the value returned by the @ResponseBody annotated method to the HTTP response body.

> Instead of using both @RequestMapping and @ResponseBody annotations, you can use @RestController *composed* annotation that combines both @RequestMapping and @ResponseBody annotations.

Now that we have seen different ways in which a @RequestMapping method can write to the HTTP response, let's look at how a @RequestMapping method can read information from the HTTP request body using @RequestBody annotation.

Binding HTTP request body to a method parameter using @RequestBody

A @RequestMapping annotated method can use @RequestBody method-parameter level annotation to bind HTTP request body to the method parameter. Spring Web MVC uses an appropriate HttpMessageConverter (explained in section 14-5) implementation to convert the HTTP request body to the method parameter type. The following example listing shows usage of @RequestBody annotation in MyBank application's FixedDepositController:

Example listing 14-9 – @RequestBody annotation usage
Project – ch14-webservice
Source location - src/main/java/sample/spring/chapter14/web

```
package sample.spring.chapter14.web;
.....
```

```
import org.springframework.web.bind.annotation.RequestBody;
.....
@Controller
@RequestMapping(path = "/fixedDeposits")
public class FixedDepositController {
    .....
    @RequestMapping(method = RequestMethod.POST)
    public ResponseEntity<FixedDepositDetails> openFixedDeposit(
            @RequestBody FixedDepositDetails fixedDepositDetails,
            BindingResult bindingResult) {
        new FixedDepositDetailsValidator().validate(fixedDepositDetails, bindingResult);
        .....
    }
    .....
}
```

In the above example listing, the FixedDepositDetails type method argument is annotated with @RequestBody annotation. Spring Web MVC is responsible for converting the HTTP request body to FixedDepositDetails type object. In the above example listing, FixedDepositDetailsValidator class is an implementation of Spring's Validator interface that validates the FixedDepositDetails object before the fixed deposit is created.

An alternative to using @RequestBody annotation is to directly read HTTP request body from the HttpServletRequest object and convert the request body content to the Java type required by the method. Spring's @RequestBody annotation simplifies the conversion because it uses an appropriate HttpMessageConverter implementation to convert HTTP request body to the object type expected by the @RequestMapping method.

Let's now look at the @ResponseStatus annotation that allows you to set HTTP response status.

Setting HTTP response status using @ResponseStatus

You can use the @ResponseStatus annotation to specify the HTTP response status returned by a @RequestMapping method. The following example listing shows usage of @ResponseStatus annotation:

Example listing 14-10 – @ResponseStatus annotation usage

```
import org.springframework.web.bind.annotation.ResponseStatus;

public class SomeController {

    @RequestMapping(method = RequestMethod.GET)
    @ResponseStatus(code = HttpStatus.OK)
    @ResponseBody
    public SomeObject doSomething() {
        .....
    }
}
```

As the doSomething method is annotated with @ResponseBody annotation, the SomeObject returned by the doSomething method is written to the HTTP response body. And, the @ResponseStatus annotation sets the HTTP response status code to 200 (represented by HttpStatus.OK constant).

Let's now look at how the @ExceptionHandler annotation is used in FixedDepositWS web service to handle exceptions.

Handling exceptions using @ExceptionHandler

In section 12-9 of chapter 12, we saw that the @ExceptionHandler annotation identifies a controller method that is responsible for handling exceptions. Like @RequestMapping methods, @ExceptionHandler methods in RESTful web services are annotated with @ResponseBody annotation or the return type is defined as ResponseEntity (or HttpEntity).

The following example listing shows usage of @ExceptionHandler annotation in FixedDepositController class of ch14-webservice project:

Example listing 14-11 – @ExceptionHandler annotation usage
Project – ch14-webservice
Source location - src/main/java/sample/spring/chapter14/web

```
package sample.spring.chapter14.web;

import sample.spring.chapter14.exception.ValidationException;
.....
public class FixedDepositController {
    .....
    @ExceptionHandler(ValidationException.class)
    @ResponseBody
    @ResponseStatus(code = HttpStatus.BAD_REQUEST)
    public String handleException(Exception ex) {
        logger.info("handling ValidationException " + ex.getMessage());
        return ex.getMessage();
    }
}
```

@ExceptionHandler annotation on handleException method indicates that the handleException method is invoked when ValidationException is thrown by the FixedDepositController during request processing. As the handleException method is also annotated with @ResponseBody annotation, the exception message returned by the handleException method is written to the HTTP response body. @ResponseStatus on the handleException method results in setting the HTTP response status code to 400 (represented by HttpStatus.BAD_REQUEST constant).

In this section, we saw how to implement FixedDepositWS web service using Spring Web MVC. Let's now look at how to access FixedDepositWS web service using Spring's RestTemplate.

14-4 Accessing RESTful web services using RestTemplate and WebClient

Spring's RestTemplate (for *synchronous* access) and WebClient (for asynchronous access) classes simplify accessing RESTful web services by taking care of managing HTTP connections and handling HTTP errors.

IMPORT **chapter 14/ch14-webservice-client** (This project represents a standalone Java application that accesses FixedDepositWS RESTful web service using Spring's RestTemplate (for *synchronously* accessing the web service) and WebClient (for *asynchronously* accessing the web service) classes. The ch14-webservice-client project assumes that the ch14-webservice project representing the FixedDepositWS RESTful web service is deployed at http://localhost:8080/ch14-webservice URL.)

RestTemplate configuration

The following example listing shows how RestTemplate is configured in the application context XML file of ch14-webservice-client project:

Example listing 14-12 – applicationContext.xml - RestTemplate configuration
Project – ch14-webservice-client
Source location - src/main/resources/META-INF/spring

```
<beans .....>
    <bean id="restTemplate" class="org.springframework.web.client.RestTemplate">
        <property name="errorHandler" ref="errorHandler" />
    </bean>

    <bean id="errorHandler" class="sample.spring.chapter14.MyErrorHandler" />
    .....
</beans>
```

RestTemplate's errorHandler property refers to an implementation of Spring's ResponseErrorHandler interface that inspects the HTTP response for errors and handles the response in case of errors. DefaultResponseErrorHandler is the default implementation of ResponseErrorHandler interface that is provided out-of-the-box by Spring. If you don't specify the errorHandler property, Spring uses the DefaultResponseErrorHandler implementation. The above example listing shows that the RestTemplate uses a custom response error handler, MyErrorHandler.

The following example listing shows the implementation of MyErrorHandler class:

Example listing 14-13 – MyErrorHandler class – HTTP response error handler
Project – ch14-webservice-client
Source location - src/main/java/sample/spring/chapter14

```
package sample.spring.chapter14;

import org.apache.commons.io.IOUtils;
import org.springframework.http.client.ClientHttpResponse;
import org.springframework.web.client.DefaultResponseErrorHandler;

public class MyErrorHandler extends DefaultResponseErrorHandler {
    private static Logger logger = LogManager.getLogger(MyErrorHandler.class);

    @Override
    public void handleError(ClientHttpResponse response) throws IOException {
        logger.info("Status code received from the web service : "
            + response.getStatusCode());
        String body = IOUtils.toString(response.getBody());
        logger.info("Response body: " + body);
        super.handleError(response);
    }
}
```

The above example listing shows that the MyErrorHandler class extends DefaultResponseErrorHandler class and overrides the handleError method. If the HTTP response's status code indicates an error, the handleError method is responsible for handling the response. The ClientHttpResponse argument to the handleError method represents the HTTP response received from calling the RESTful web service. The call to ClientHttpResponse's getBody method returns the body of HTTP response as an InputStream object. MyErrorHandler's handleError method logs information about the status code and the body of the HTTP response, and delegates handling of the error to DefaultResponseErrorHandler's handleError method. The above example listing shows that the MyErrorHandler class uses Apache Commons IO's IOUtils class to get the content of the HTTP response body as a String.

Now that we have seen how a RestTemplate class is configured, let's look at how RestTemplate is used by client applications to access RESTful web services.

Accessing FixedDepositWS web service using RestTemplate

The following example listing shows the FixedDepositWSClient class that uses RestTemplate to access FixedDepositWS web service:

Example listing 14-14 – FixedDepositWSClient class – RestTemplate usage
Project – ch14-webservice-client
Source location - src/main/java/sample/spring/chapter14

```
package sample.spring.chapter14;
.....
import org.springframework.web.client.RestTemplate;

public class FixedDepositWSClient {
    private static ApplicationContext context;

    public static void main(String args[]) {
        context = new ClassPathXmlApplicationContext(
                "classpath:META-INF/spring/applicationContext.xml");
        getFixedDepositList(context.getBean(RestTemplate.class));
        getFixedDeposit(context.getBean(RestTemplate.class));
        .....
    }

    private static void getFixedDepositList(RestTemplate restTemplate) { ..... }
    .....
}
```

The above example listing shows that the FixedDepositWSClient's main method performs the following actions:

- bootstraps the Spring container (represented by the ApplicationContext object)
- calls getFixedDepositList, getFixedDeposit, and so on, methods. These methods accept an instance of RestTemplate, and are responsible for calling the FixedDepositWS web service.

The following example listing shows the implementation of FixedDepositWSClient's getFixedDepositList method that calls the FixedDepositWS web service deployed at http://localhost:8080/ch14-webservice to obtain the list of fixed deposits in the system:

Example listing 14-15 – FixedDepositWSClient's getFixedDepositList method
Project – ch14-webservice-client
Source location - src/main/java/sample/spring/chapter14

```
package sample.spring.chapter14;
.....
import org.springframework.core.ParameterizedTypeReference;
import org.springframework.http.*;
import org.springframework.web.client.RestTemplate;

public class FixedDepositWSClient {
    .....
    private static void getFixedDepositList(RestTemplate restTemplate) {
        HttpHeaders headers = new HttpHeaders();
```

```
        headers.add("Accept", "application/json");

        HttpEntity<String> requestEntity = new HttpEntity<String>(headers);

        ParameterizedTypeReference<List<FixedDepositDetails>> typeRef =
              new ParameterizedTypeReference<List<FixedDepositDetails>>() { };

        ResponseEntity<List<FixedDepositDetails>> responseEntity = restTemplate
              .exchange("http://localhost:8080/ch14-webservice/fixedDeposits",
                     HttpMethod.GET, requestEntity, typeRef);

        List<FixedDepositDetails> fixedDepositDetails = responseEntity.getBody();
        logger.info("List of fixed deposit details: \n" + fixedDepositDetails);
    }
    .....
}
```

In the above example listing, RestTemplate's exchange method has been used to send HTTP GET request to http://localhost:8080/ch14-webservice/fixedDeposits URL. As the FixedDepositWS web service is deployed at http://localhost:8080/ch14-webservice URL, sending HTTP GET request to http://localhost:8080/ch14-webservice/fixedDeposits URL results in invocation of FixedDepositController's getFixedDepositList method. This is because the FixedDepositController's getFixedDepositList method is mapped to /fixedDeposits URI (refer example listing 14-3 or FixedDepositController class of ch14-webservice project).

In example listing 14-15, the HttpEntity object represents the request sent to the web service, the HttpHeaders object represents the request headers in the request, and the ParameterizedTypeReference object represents the *generic* type of the response received from the web service. The Accept request header's value has been set to application/json to specify that the response from the FixedDepositWS web service is expected in JSON format.

On the web service-side, the value of Accept header is used by Spring Web MVC to choose an appropriate HttpMessageConverter to convert the value returned by the @ResponseBody annotated method into the format specified by the Accept header. For instance, if the Accept header value is application/json, Spring Web MVC uses MappingJackson2HttpMessageConverter (an implementation of HttpMessageConverter) to convert the value returned by the @ResponseBody annotated method into JSON format. The FixedDepositWSClient's getFixedDepositList method specifies the value of Accept header as application/json; therefore, the value returned by FixedDepositController's getFixedDepositList method is converted to JSON format.

The RestTemplate's exchange method returns an instance of ResponseEntity which represents the response returned by the web service. As the generic type of the response received from invocation of FixedDepositController's getFixedDepositList is List<FixedDepositDetails>, an instance of ParameterizedTypeReference<List<FixedDepositDetails>> is created and passed to the exchange method. You can call ResponseEntity's getBody method to retrieve the response returned by the web service. In example listing 14-15, ResponseEntity's getBody method returns an object of type List<FixedDepositDetails> that represents the list of fixed deposits returned by the FixedDepositWS web service.

The following figure shows the role played by MappingJackson2HttpMessageConverter when FixedDepositWSClient invokes FixedDepositController's getFixedDepositList method:

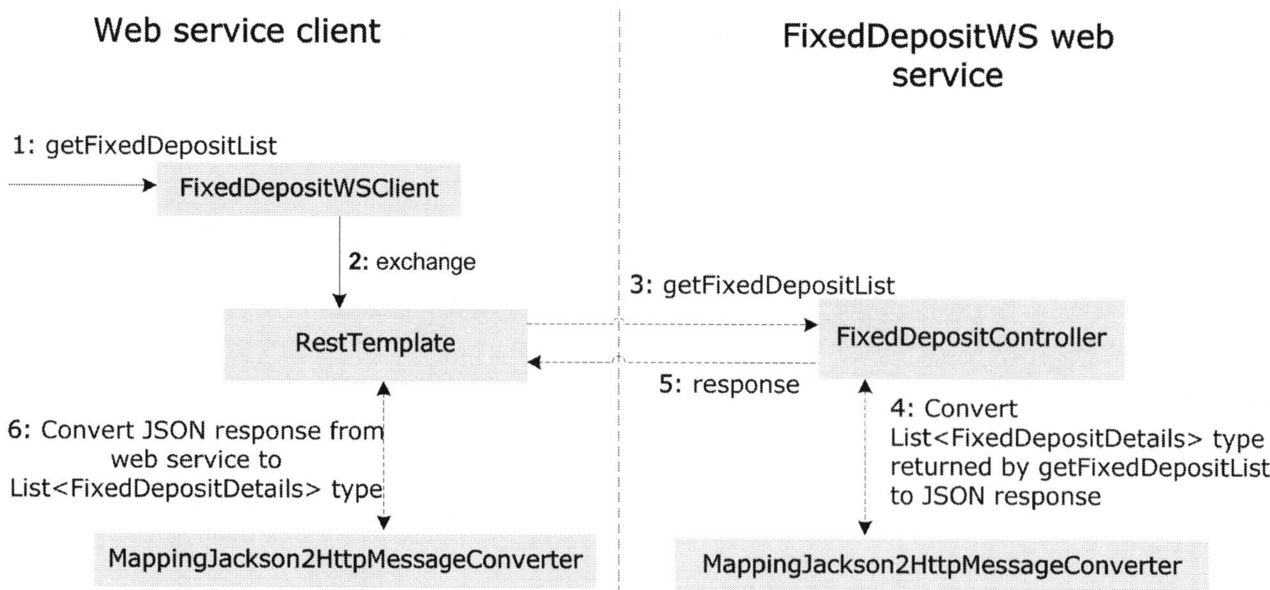

Figure 14-4 FixedDepositWSClient's getFixedDepositList method uses RestTemplate to send a web request to FixedDepositWS web service

The above figure shows that MappingJackson2HttpMessageConverter is used to convert the return value of FixedDepositController's getFixedDepositList method into JSON format. Also, MappingJackson2HttpMessageConverter is used by the RestTemplate to convert the JSON response received from the FixedDepositController to a Java object of type List<FixedDepositDetails>.

In example listing 14-15, RestTemplate's exchange method was used to send an HTTP GET request to FixedDepositWS web service. The exchange method is typically used if the HTTP response from the web service needs to be converted to a Java generic type, and to send HTTP request headers. RestTemplate also defines HTTP method-specific methods that simplify writing RESTful clients. For instance, you can use getForEntity method to send HTTP GET request, postForEntity to send HTTP POST request, delete to send HTTP DELETE request, and so on.

The following example listing shows FixedDepositWSClient's openFixedDeposit method that sends an HTTP POST request to FixedDepositWS web service to create a new fixed deposit:

Example listing 14-16 – FixedDepositWSClient's openFixedDeposit method
Project – ch14-webservice-client
Source location - src/main/java/sample/spring/chapter14

```
package sample.spring.chapter14;

import org.springframework.http.ResponseEntity;
import org.springframework.web.client.RestTemplate;
.....
public class FixedDepositWSClient {
    .....
    private static void openFixedDeposit(RestTemplate restTemplate) {
        FixedDepositDetails fdd = new FixedDepositDetails();
        fdd.setDepositAmount("9999");
        .....
        ResponseEntity<FixedDepositDetails> responseEntity = restTemplate
                .postForEntity("http://localhost:8080/ch14-webservice/fixedDeposits",
                                    fdd, FixedDepositDetails.class);
```

```
        FixedDepositDetails fixedDepositDetails = responseEntity.getBody();
        .....
    }
}
```

FixedDepositWSClient's openFixedDeposit method sends details of the fixed deposit to be created to the FixedDepositWS web service. If the fixed deposit is created successfully, FixedDepositWS returns the newly created FixedDepositDetails object containing the unique identifier assigned to it. The above example listing shows that RestTemplate's postForEntity method accepts web service URL, object to be POSTed (which is FixedDepositDetails object), and the HTTP response type (which is FixedDepositDetails.class). Sending HTTP POST request to http://localhost:8080/ch14-webservice/fixedDeposits URL results in invocation of FixedDepositController's openFixedDeposit method (refer example listing 14-9 or FixedDepositController class of ch14-webservice project).

FixedDepositController's openFixedDeposit method validates details of the fixed deposit before attempting to create the fixed deposit. FixedDepositDetailsValidator is responsible for validating the fixed deposit details. If the fixed deposit amount is less than 1000 or tenure is less than 12 months or if the email id specified is not well-formed, an exception is thrown by the openFixedDeposit method. The following example listing shows openFixedDeposit and handleException methods of FixedDepositController:

Example listing 14-17 FixedDepositController - openFixedDeposit and handleException methods
Project – ch14-webservice
Source location - src/main/java/sample/spring/chapter14/web

```
package sample.spring.chapter14.web;

import org.springframework.validation.BindingResult;
import org.springframework.web.bind.annotation.ExceptionHandler;
import sample.spring.chapter14.exception.ValidationException;
.....
@Controller
@RequestMapping(path = "/fixedDeposits")
public class FixedDepositController {
    .....
    @RequestMapping(method = RequestMethod.POST)
    public ResponseEntity<FixedDepositDetails> openFixedDeposit(
            @RequestBody FixedDepositDetails fixedDepositDetails,
            BindingResult bindingResult) {

        new FixedDepositDetailsValidator().validate(fixedDepositDetails, bindingResult);

        if (bindingResult.hasErrors()) {
            throw new ValidationException("Validation errors occurred");
        } else {
            fixedDepositService.saveFixedDeposit(fixedDepositDetails);
            .....
        }

        @ExceptionHandler(ValidationException.class)
        @ResponseBody
        @ResponseStatus(value = HttpStatus.BAD_REQUEST)
        public String handleException(Exception ex) {
            return ex.getMessage();
        }
    }
    .....
```

```
}
```

The above example listing shows that the openFixedDeposit method throws ValidationException if fixed deposit fails validation. As the handleException method is annotated with @ExceptionHandler(ValidationException.class), the ValidationException thrown by the openFixedDeposit method is handled by the handleException method. @ResponseBody and @ResponseStatus(code=HttpStatus.BAD_REQUEST) annotations specify that the exception message returned by the handleException method is written to the response body and the status code is set to HttpStatus.BAD_REQUEST constant (which corresponds to HTTP status code 400).

FixedDepositWSClient's openInvalidFixedDeposit method attempts to create a fixed deposit with deposit amount 100, as shown here:

Example listing 14-18 – FixedDepositWSClient - openInvalidFixedDeposit method
Project – ch14-webservice-client
Source location - src/main/java/sample/spring/chapter14

```
    private static void openInvalidFixedDeposit(RestTemplate restTemplate) {
        FixedDepositDetails fdd = new FixedDepositDetails();
        fdd.setDepositAmount("100");
        fdd.setEmail("99@somedomain.com");
        fdd.setTenure("12");

        ResponseEntity<FixedDepositDetails> responseEntity = restTemplate
                .postForEntity("http://localhost:8080/ch14-webservice/fixedDeposits",
                        fdd, FixedDepositDetails.class);

        FixedDepositDetails fixedDepositDetails = responseEntity.getBody();
        logger.info("Details of the newly created fixed deposit: "
                + fixedDepositDetails);
    }
```

The openInvalidFixedDeposit method uses RestTemplate to send request to FixedDepositController's openFixedDeposit method. As the fixed deposit amount is specified as 100, FixedDepositController's openFixedDeposit method throws ValidationException (refer example listing 14-17). FixedDepositController's handleException method (refer example listing 14-17) handles the ValidationException and sets the HTTP response status to 400. As the response status code received by RestTemplate is 400, the handling of response is delegated to the MyErrorHandler implementation (refer example listing 14-12 and 14-13) that we configured for the RestTemplate.

RestTemplate allows clients to *synchronously* access RESTful web services. Let's now look at how to *asynchronously* access RESTful web services using Spring's WebClient.

Asynchronously accessing RESTful web services using WebClient

To allow clients to asynchronously access RESTful web services, Spring provides WebClient class. WebClient class is part of spring-webflux module (explained in chapter 19) that provides *functional* (explained in chapter 17) and *reactive* (explained in chapter 18) style access to RESTful web services. WebClient class is covered in detail in chapter 19.

The following example listing shows the FixedDepositWSWebClient class that uses WebClient to access FixedDepositWS web service:

Example listing 14-19 – FixedDepositWSWebClient - openFixedDeposit method
Project – ch14-webservice-client
Source location - src/main/java/sample/spring/chapter14

```
package sample.spring.chapter14;

import org.springframework.http.HttpEntity;
import org.springframework.http.MediaType;
import org.springframework.web.reactive.function.BodyInserters;
import org.springframework.web.reactive.function.client.WebClient;
.....
public class FixedDepositWSWebClient {
    .....
    public static void main(String args[]) throws InterruptedException {
        .....
        WebClient webClient = WebClient.create("http://localhost:8080/ch14-webservice");
        try {
            .....
            openFixedDeposit(webClient);
        } catch (Exception e) {
            e.printStackTrace();
        }
        Thread.sleep(10000);
    }

    private static void openFixedDeposit(WebClient webClient) {
        FixedDepositDetails fdd = new FixedDepositDetails();
        fdd.setDepositAmount("9999");
        .....
        webClient.post().uri("/fixedDeposits")
                        .accept(MediaType.APPLICATION_JSON)
                        .body(BodyInserters.fromObject(fdd))
                        .retrieve().bodyToMono(FixedDepositDetails.class)
                        .subscribe(fixedDeposit -> logger
                                .info("createFixedDeposit method. returned id is -> "
                                          + fixedDeposit.getId()));
    }
}
```

The above example listing shows that the openFixedDeposit method uses WebClient to send a request to FixedDepositWS web service. In the main method, WebClient's create method creates an instance of WebClient with base URL, host and port information. WebClient instance is passed to openFixedDeposit method so that it can be used to send requests to FixedDepositWS web service. The post method creates an HTTP POST request, the uri method specifies the URI for the request, accept method specifies values for the Accept request header, body method specifies the request body (which is the FixedDepositDetails object in our example), retrieve method sends the request and receives the response from the web service, and the subscribe method processes the response body. As the response body contains the newly persisted FixedDepositDetails object, the subscribe method writes the id of the received FixedDepositDetails object.

Let's now look at the purpose served by HttpMessageConverters in Spring Web MVC.

14-5 Converting Java objects to HTTP requests and responses and vice versa using `HttpMessageConverter`

`HttpMessageConverters` are used by Spring in the following scenarios to perform conversion:

- if a method argument is annotated with `@RequestBody` annotation, Spring converts HTTP request body to the Java type of the method argument
- if a method is annotated with `@ResponseBody` annotation, Spring converts the returned Java object from the method to HTTP response body
- if the return type of a method is `HttpEntity` or `ResponseEntity`, Spring converts the object returned by the method to the HTTP response body
- objects passed to and returned from the methods of `RestTemplate` class (like `getForEntity`, `postForEntity`, `exchange`, and so on) are converted to HTTP request body and HTTP response body, respectively

The following table describes some of the `HttpMessageConverter` implementations that are provided out-of-the-box by Spring Web MVC:

`HttpMessageConverter` implementation	Description
`StringHttpMessageConverter`	converts to/from strings
`FormHttpMessageConverter`	converts form data to/from `MultiValueMap<String, String>` type. This `HttpMessageConverter` is used by Spring when dealing with form data and file uploads.
`MappingJackson2HttpMessageConverter`	converts to/from JSON
`MarshallingHttpMessageConverter`	converts to/from XML

`MappingJackson2HttpMessageConverter`, `StringHttpMessageConverter` and `FormHttpMessageConverter` are automatically registered with the Spring container by the `<annotation-driven>` element of Spring's `mvc` schema. To use `MarshallingHttpMessageConverter` you need to explicitly register it with the Spring container. To view the complete list of `HttpMessageConverters` that are registered by default by `<annotation-driven>` element, refer to the Spring Framework reference documentation.

Let's now look at `@PathVariable` and `@MatrixVariable` annotations that further simplify developing RESTful web services using Spring Web MVC.

14-6 `@PathVariable` and `@MatrixVariable` annotations

Instead of specifying the actual URI, a `@RequestMapping` annotation may specify a *URI template* to access specific parts of the request URI. A URI template contains *variable names* (specified within braces) whose values are derived from the actual request URI. For example, the URI template `http://www.somebank.com/fd/{fixeddeposit}` contains the variable name `fixeddeposit`. If the actual request URI is `http://www.somebank.com/fd/123`, the value of `{fixeddeposit}` URI template variable becomes `123`.

`@PathVariable` is a method argument level annotation that is used by `@RequestMapping` methods to assign value of a *URI template variable* to the method argument.

IMPORT **chapter 14/ch14-webservice-uritemplates** and **chapter 14/ch14-webservice-client-uritemplates** (ch14-webservice-uritemplates project is a modified version of ch14-webservice project that shows the implementation of FixedDepositWS RESTful web service using @PathVariable annotation. ch14-webservice-client-uritemplates is a modified version of ch14-webservice-client project that accesses the FixedDepositWS web service represented by ch14-webservice-uritemplates project.)

The following example listing shows usage of @PathVariable annotation in FixedDepositController of ch14-webservice-uritemplates project:

Example listing 14-20 – FixedDepositController - @PathVariable usage
Project – ch14-webservice-uritemplates
Source location - src/main/java/sample/spring/chapter14/web

```
package sample.spring.chapter14.web;

import org.springframework.web.bind.annotation.PathVariable;
.....
@Controller
public class FixedDepositController {
    .....
    @RequestMapping(path="/fixedDeposits/{fixedDepositId}", method = RequestMethod.GET)
    public ResponseEntity<FixedDepositDetails> getFixedDeposit(
            @PathVariable("fixedDepositId") int id) {
        return new ResponseEntity<FixedDepositDetails>(
                fixedDepositService.getFixedDeposit(id), HttpStatus.OK);
    }
    .....
}
```

Instead of specifying the actual URI, @RequestMapping annotation in the above example listing specifies /fixedDeposits/{fixedDepositId} URI template. Now, if the incoming request URI is /fixedDeposits/1, the value of fixedDepositId URI template variable is set to 1. As the @PathVariable annotation specifies fixedDepositId as the name of the URI template variable, value 1 is assigned to the id argument of the getFixedDeposit method.

If a URI template defines multiple variables, the @RequestMapping method can define multiple @PathVariable annotated arguments, as shown in the following example listing:

Example listing 14-21 – Multiple URI template variables

```
@Controller
public class SomeController {
    .....
    @RequestMapping(path="/users/{userId}/bankstatements/{statementId}", .....)
    public void getBankStatementForUser(
            @PathVariable("userId") String user,
        @PathVariable("statementId") String statement) {
        .....
    }
}
```

In the above example listing, the URI template defines userId and statementId variables. If the incoming request URI is /users/me/bankstatements/123, value me is assigned to the user argument and value 123 is assigned to the statement argument.

If you want to assign all the URI template variables and their values to a method argument, you can use @PathVariable annotation on a Map<String, String> argument type, as shown in the following example listing:

Example listing 14-22 – Accessing all URI template variables and their values

```
@Controller
public class SomeController {
    .....
    @RequestMapping(path="/users/{userId}/bankstatements/{statementId}", .....)
    public void getBankStatementForUser(
            @PathVariable Map<String, String> allVariables) {
        .....
    }
}
```

In the above example listing, URI template variables (userId and statementId) and their values (me and 123) are assigned to the allVariables method argument.

You should note that URI template can also be specified by class level @RequestMapping annotation, as shown here:

Example listing 14-23 – URI template specified at both class and method level @RequestMapping annotations

```
@Controller
@RequestMapping(path="/service/{serviceId}", .....)
public class SomeController {
    .....
    @RequestMapping(path="/users/{userId}/bankstatements/{statementId}", .....)
    public void getBankStatementForUser(@PathVariable Map<String, String> allVariables) {
        .....
    }
}
```

In the above example listing, URI template /service/{serviceId} is specified by the class level @RequestMapping annotation, and /users/{userId}/bankstatements/{statementId} is specified by the method level @RequestMapping annotation. If the request URI is /service/bankingService/users/me/bankstatements/123, the allVariables argument contains details of serviceId, userId and statementId URI template variables.

The scenarios in which you may want to have fine-grained control over what to extract from the request URI, you can use regular expressions in URI templates. The following example listing shows usage of regular expressions to extract 123.json value from /bankstatements/123.json request URI:

Example listing 14-24 – URI templates – regular expressions usage

```
@Controller
public class SomeController {
    .....
    @RequestMapping(path="/bankstatements/{statementId:[\\d\\d\\d]}.{responseType:[a-z]}",
..)
    public void getBankStatementForUser(@PathVariable ("statementId") String statement,
         @PathVariable("responseType") String responseTypeExtension) {
        .....
    }
}
```

Regular expressions in URI templates are specified in the following format: {variable-name:regular-expression}. If the request URI is /bankstatements/123.json, statementId variable is assigned the value 123 and responseType is assigned the value json.

> You can also use Ant-style patterns in URI templates. For instance, you can specify patterns, like /myUrl/*/{myId} and /myUrl/**/{myId} as URI templates.

So far in this section we have seen examples of how to use @PathVariable to selectively extract information from the request URI path. Let's now look at @MatrixVariable annotation that is used to extract *name-value pairs* from path segments.

Matrix variables appear as name-value pairs in the request URI, and you can assign value of these variables to method arguments. For instance, in the request URI /bankstatement/123;responseType=json, the responseType variable represents a matrix variable whose value is json.

> You should note that by default Spring *removes* matrix variables from the URL. To ensure that matrix variables are not removed, set the enable-matrix-variables attribute of <annotation-driven> element of Spring mvc schema to true. When using matrix variables, the path segments that contain matrix variables must be represented by URI template variables.

The following example listing shows usage of @MatrixVariable annotation:

Example listing 14-25 – @MatrixVariable annotation

```
@Controller
public class SomeController {
    .....
    @RequestMapping(path="/bankestatement/{statementId}", ..)
    public void getBankStatementForUser(@PathVariable("statementId") String statement,
                @MatrixVariable("responseType") String responseTypeExtension) {
        .....
    }
}
```

In the above example listing, if the request URI is /bankstatement/123;responseType=json, the value json is assigned to responseTypeExtension argument. The above example listing also shows a scenario in which both @PathVariable and @MatrixVariable annotations are used to retrieve information from the request URI.

As matrix variables can appear in any path segment of the request URI, you should specify the path segment from which the matrix variable should be retrieved. The following example listing shows a scenario in which two matrix variables with the same name are present in different path segments:

Example listing 14-26 – @MatrixVariable annotation – multiple matrix variables with the same name

```
@Controller
public class SomeController {
     .....
     @RequestMapping(path="/bankestatement/{statementId}/user/{userId}", ..)
     public void getBankStatementForUser(
               @MatrixVariable(name = "id", pathVar = "statementId") int someId,
               @MatrixVariable(name= "id", pathVar = "userId") int someOtherId) {
          .....
     }
}
```

The pathVar attribute of @MatrixVariable annotation specifies the name of the URI template variable that contains the matrix variable. So, if the request URI is /bankstatement/123;**id=555**/user/me;**id=777**, the value 555 is assigned to someId, and the value 777 is assigned to someOtherId argument.

As in the case of @PathVariable annotation, you can annotate a method argument type of Map<String, String> with @MatrixVariable to assign all the matrix variables to the method argument. Unlike @PathVariable annotation, @MatrixVariable annotation allows you to specify a default value for the matrix variable using defaultValue attribute. Also, you can set required attribute of @MatrixVariable annotation to false to indicate that the matrix variable is *optional*. By default, the value of required attribute is set to true. If the required attribute is set to true, and the matrix variable is not found in the request, then an exception is thrown.

14-7 Summary

In this chapter, we looked at how to develop RESTful web services and access them. We looked at how to use URI templates along with @PathVariable and @MatrixVariable annotations to access information from the request URI. We also looked at how to access RESTful web services synchronously using RestTemplate and asynchronously using WebClient.

Chapter 15 – *More Spring Web MVC – internationalization, file upload and asynchronous request processing*

15-1 Introduction

In earlier chapters, we saw that Spring Web MVC simplifies creating web applications and RESTful web services. In this chapter, we'll look at some more features offered by Spring Web MVC framework that you may require in your web applications. We'll particularly look at:

- pre- and post-processing requests using *handler interceptors*
- internationalizing Spring Web MVC applications
- *asynchronously* processing requests
- performing type conversion and formatting, and
- uploading files

IMPORT **chapter 15/ch15-bankapp** (This project is a variant of ch12-bankapp project that demonstrates how to incorporate internationalization in MyBank web application, and how to use handler interceptors.)

Let's begin by looking at how to pre- and post-process requests using handler interceptors.

15-2 Pre- and post-processing requests using handler interceptors

Handler interceptors allow you to pre- and post-process requests. The concept of handler interceptors is similar to that of servlet filters. Handler interceptors implement Spring's HandlerInterceptor interface. A handler interceptor contains the pre- and post-processing logic that is required by multiple controllers. For instance, you can use handler interceptors for logging, security checks, changing locale, and so on.

Let's now look at how to implement and configure handler interceptors.

Implementing and configuring a handler interceptor

You can create handler interceptors by implementing HandlerInterceptor interface. HandlerInterceptor interface defines the following methods:

- preHandle – this method is executed *before* the controller processes the request. If the preHandle method returns true, the controller is invoked by Spring to process the request. If the preHandle method returns false, the controller is *not* invoked.
- postHandle – this method is executed *after* the controller processes the request, but *before* the view is rendered by the DispatcherServlet.
- afterCompletion – this method is invoked *after* the completion of request processing (that is, after the view is rendered by the DispatcherServlet) to do any cleanup, if required.

The following example listing shows MyRequestHandlerInterceptor class of ch15-bankapp that implements HandlerInterceptor interface:

Example listing 15-1 – MyRequestHandlerInterceptor
Project – ch15-bankapp
Source location - src/main/java/sample/spring/chapter15/web

```
package sample.spring.chapter15.web;

import org.springframework.web.servlet.HandlerInterceptor;
.....
public class MyRequestHandlerInterceptor implements HandlerInterceptor {
    .....
    public boolean preHandle(HttpServletRequest request, HttpServletResponse response,
                             Object handler) throws Exception {
        logger.info("HTTP method --> " + request.getMethod());
        Enumeration<String> requestNames = request.getParameterNames();
        .....
        return true;
    }

    public void postHandle(HttpServletRequest request, HttpServletResponse response,
                           Object handler, ModelAndView modelAndView) throws Exception {
        logger.info("Status code --> " + response.getStatus());
    }

    public void afterCompletion(HttpServletRequest request, HttpServletResponse response,
                                Object handler, Exception ex) throws Exception {
        logger.info("Request processing complete");
    }
}
```

In the above example listing, the preHandle method inspects each incoming request and logs the HTTP method associated with the request and the request parameters contained in the request. The preHandle method returns true, which means that the request will be processed by the controller. The postHandle method logs the HTTP response status code. The afterCompletion method logs the message that the request was successfully processed.

> Instead of directly implementing the HandlerInterceptor interface, you can extend the *abstract* HandlerInterceptorAdapter class that provides empty implementations for postHandle and afterCompletion methods, and the preHandle method is defined to simply return true.

The following example listing shows how handler interceptors are configured in the web application context XML file:

Example listing 15-2 – MyRequestHandlerInterceptor
Project – ch15-bankapp
Source location - src/main/webapp/WEB-INF/spring/bankapp-config.xml

```
<beans .....xmlns:mvc="http://www.springframework.org/schema/mvc".....>

    <mvc:annotation-driven />
    <mvc:interceptors>
        .....
        <bean class="sample.spring.chapter15.web.MyRequestHandlerInterceptor" />
    </mvc:interceptors>
</beans>
```

The above example listing shows that the <interceptors> element of Spring's mvc schema is used for configuring handler interceptors. The <interceptors> element can have the following sub-elements:

- <bean> element of Spring's beans schema - specifies a Spring bean that implements the HandlerInterceptor interface. A handler interceptor specified using <bean> element applies to all requests.

- <ref> element of Spring's beans schema - refers to a Spring bean that implements the HandlerInterceptor interface. A handler interceptor specified using <ref> element applies to all requests.

- <interceptor> element of Spring's mvc schema – specifies a Spring bean that implements the HandlerInterceptor interface, and the request URIs to which that HandlerInterceptor applies.

The following example listing shows a scenario in which MyRequestHandlerInterceptor is mapped to /audit/** request URI:

Example listing 15-3 – <mvc:interceptor> usage

```
<beans .....xmlns:mvc="http://www.springframework.org/schema/mvc".....>
    <mvc:annotation-driven />
    <mvc:interceptors>
        <mvc:interceptor>
            <mvc:mapping path="/audit/**"/>
            <bean class="sample.spring.chapter15.web.MyRequestHandlerInterceptor" />
        </mvc:interceptor>
    </mvc:interceptors>
</beans>
```

In the above example listing, <interceptor> element of Spring's mvc schema is used for mapping MyRequestHandlerInterceptor to /audit/** URI pattern. The <mapping> element of Spring's mvc schema specifies the request URI pattern to which the handler interceptor specified by the <bean> element applies.

> If you are using Java-based configuration approach, you can override WebMvcConfigurer's addInterceptors(InterceptorRegistry registry) method to register HandlerInterceptors for web controllers.

Let's now look at how to internationalize a Spring Web MVC application.

15-3 Internationalizing using resource bundles

Before delving into the details of how to internationalize Spring Web MVC applications, let's look at the internationalization and localization requirements of the MyBank web application.

MyBank web application's requirements

It is required that the MyBank web application supports English (en_US and en_CA locales) and German (de_DE locale) languages. Figure 15-1 shows one of the web pages of MyBank web application in de_DE locale. Figure 15-1 shows that a user can choose one of the following languages: English(US), German, or English(Canada). If a user chooses German language option, the web pages are displayed in de_DE locale. If a user chooses English(US) language option, the web pages are displayed in en_US locale. If a user chooses English(Canada) language option, the web pages are displayed in en_CA locale.

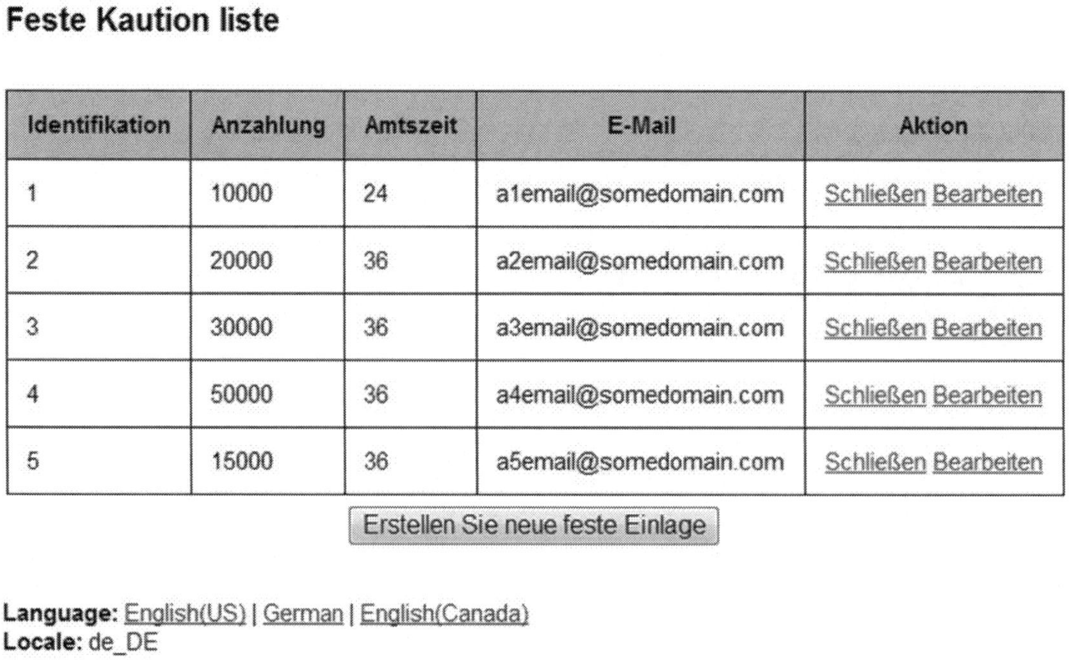

Feste Kaution liste

Identifikation	Anzahlung	Amtszeit	E-Mail	Aktion
1	10000	24	a1email@somedomain.com	Schließen Bearbeiten
2	20000	36	a2email@somedomain.com	Schließen Bearbeiten
3	30000	36	a3email@somedomain.com	Schließen Bearbeiten
4	50000	36	a4email@somedomain.com	Schließen Bearbeiten
5	15000	36	a5email@somedomain.com	Schließen Bearbeiten

Erstellen Sie neue feste Einlage

Language: English(US) | German | English(Canada)
Locale: de_DE

Figure 15-1 Web page that shows the list of fixed deposits in de_DE locale. A user can select a locale from the given options.

Let's now look at how to address internationalization and localization requirements of MyBank web application.

Internationalizing and localizing MyBank web application

In Spring Web MVC, the `DispatcherServlet` uses a `LocaleResolver` for automatically resolving messages based on the user's locale. To support internationalization, you need to configure the following beans in your web application context XML file:

- `LocaleResolver` – resolves the current locale of the user
- `MessageSource` – resolves messages from resource bundles based on the current locale of the user
- `LocaleChangeInterceptor` – allows changing current locale on every request based on a configurable request parameter

The following example listing shows configuration of `LocaleResolver`, `LocaleChangeInterceptor` and `MessageSource` beans in the web application context XML file of `ch15-bankapp` project:

Example listing 15-4 – `bankapp-config.xml`
Project – `ch15-bankapp`
Source location - `src/main/webapp/WEB-INF/spring`

```
<beans .....>
    <bean class="org.springframework.web.servlet.i18n.CookieLocaleResolver"
          id="localeResolver">
        <property name="cookieName" value="mylocale" />
    </bean>

    <bean
          class="org.springframework.context.support.ReloadableResourceBundleMessageSource"
          id="messageSource">
        <property name="basenames" value="WEB-INF/i18n/messages" />
```

```
    </bean>

    <mvc:interceptors>
        .....
        <bean class="org.springframework.web.servlet.i18n.LocaleChangeInterceptor">
            <property name="paramName" value="lang" />
        </bean>
    </mvc:interceptors>
    .....
</beans>
```

In the above example listing, CookieLocaleResolver (an implementation of LocaleResolver interface) has been configured for locale resolution. If the locale information is stored in a cookie by the web application, CookieLocaleResolver is used for locale resolution. CookieLocaleResolver's cookieName property specifies the name of the cookie that contains the locale information. If the cookie is not found in the request, CookieLocaleResolver determines the locale either by looking at the default locale (configured using defaultLocale property of CookieLocaleResolver) or by inspecting the Accept-Language request header. Spring additionally provides the following built-in LocaleResolver implementations that you can use: AcceptHeaderLocaleResolver (returns the locale specified by the Accept-Language request header), SessionLocaleResolver (returns the locale information stored in the HttpSession of the user) and FixedLocaleResolver (always returns a fixed default locale).

In addition to knowing user's locale, you may also want to know user's time zone to convert date and time in user's time zone. LocaleContextResolver (introduced in Spring 4.0) not only provides the locale information but also the time zone information of the user. CookieLocaleResolver, SessionLocaleResolver and FixedLocaleResolver implement the LocaleContextResolver interface; therefore, if you are using any of these resolvers you can obtain user's time zone in your controllers using getTimeZone method of LocaleContextHolder (or RequestContextUtils) class. If you only want to obtain the locale information in your controllers, you can use getLocale method of LocaleContextHolder (or RequestContextUtils) class.

Spring provides a LocaleChangeInterceptor (a HandlerInterceptor) that uses a configurable request parameter (specified by paramName property) to change the current locale on every request. In example listing 15-4, the paramName property is set to lang. LocaleResolver defines a setLocale method that is used by the LocaleChangeInterceptor to change the current locale. If you don't want to use LocaleChangeInterceptor, then you can change the user's locale in your controller by calling setLocale method of LocaleContextHolder (or RequestContextUtils) class.

Once the user's locale is resolved, Spring uses the configured MessageSource implementation to resolve messages. Spring provides the following built-in implementations of MessageSource interface:

- ResourceBundleMessageSource – a MessageSource implementation that accesses resource bundles using the specified *basenames*
- ReloadableResourceBundleMessageSource – similar to ResourceBundleMessageSource implementation. This implementation supports *reloading* of resource bundles.

Example listing 15-4 shows that the MyBank web application uses ReloadableResourceBundleMessageSource. The basenames property is set to WEB-INF/i18n/messages, which means that the ReloadableResourceBundleMessageSource looks for resource bundles named messages inside WEB-INF/i18n folder. So, if the user's locale is resolved to en_US, the ReloadableResourceBundleMessageSource will resolve messages from the messages_en_US.properties file.

If you look at /src/main/webapp/WEB-INF/i18n folder of ch15-bankapp project, you'll find the following properties files: messages.properties, messages_en_US.properties and messages_de_DE.properties.

The messages_de_DE.properties file contains messages and labels for de_DE locale, messages_en_US.properties contains messages and labels for en_US locale, and messages.properties contains messages and labels that are shown when *no* locale-specific resource bundles are found. As there is no messages_en_CA.properties file corresponding to en_CA locale, selecting the English(Canada) option (refer figure 15-1) shows messages from the messages.properties file.

In figure 15-1, we saw that we can change the language of the MyBank web application by selecting English(US), English(Canada) and German language options. We saw earlier that the LocaleChangeInterceptor can change the locale of the MyBank web application if the locale information is contained in a request parameter named lang. To simplify changing the locale, lang request parameter is appended to the hyperlinks shown by English(US), English(Canada) and German language options, as shown here:

Example listing 15-5 – fixedDepositList.jsp
Project – ch15-bankapp
Source location - src/main/webapp/WEB-INF/jsp

```
<b>Language:</b>
<a href="${pageContext.request.contextPath}/fixedDeposit/list?lang=en_US">English(US)</a> |
<a href="${pageContext.request.contextPath}/fixedDeposit/list?lang=de_DE">German</a> |
<a href="${pageContext.request.contextPath}/fixedDeposit/list?lang=en_CA">English(Canada)
</a>
```

Let's now look at how you can asynchronously process requests in Spring Web MVC applications.

15-4 Asynchronously processing requests

A @RequestMapping annotated method that returns a java.util.concurrent.Callable or Spring's DeferredResult object processes web requests *asynchronously*. If a @RequestMapping method returns Callable, Spring Web MVC takes care of processing the Callable in an application thread (and *not* the Servlet container thread) to produce the result. If a @RequestMapping method returns DeferredResult, it is application's responsibility to process the DeferredResult in an application thread (and *not* the Servlet container thread) to produce the result. Before delving into the detail of how Callable and DeferredResult return values are processed, let's look at how to configure a Spring Web MVC application to support asynchronous request processing.

IMPORT **chapter 15/ch15-async-bankapp** (This project is a variant of ch12-bankapp project that asynchronously processes requests. @RequestMapping methods defined in the FixedDepositController of this project return Callable. You should deploy and run the ch15-async-bankapp project to see asynchronous request processing in action.)

Asynchronous request processing configuration

As asynchronous request processing in Spring Web MVC is based on Servlet 3, web.xml must refer to Servlet 3 XML schema. Also, <async-supported> element must be added to the DispatcherServlet definition in web.xml file to indicate that it supports asynchronous request processing. The following example listing shows the web.xml file of ch15-async-bankapp project:

Example listing 15-6 – web.xml – asynchronous request processing configuration
Project – ch15-async-bankapp
Source location - src/main/webapp/WEB-INF

```
<web-app .....
    xsi:schemaLocation="java.sun.com/xml/ns/javaee
```

```
                    java.sun.com/xml/ns/javaee/webapp_3_0.xsd"
                    version="3.0">
  .....
  <servlet>
      <servlet-name>bankapp</servlet-name>
      <servlet-class>org.springframework.web.servlet.DispatcherServlet</servlet-class>
      .....
      <async-supported>true</async-supported>
  </servlet>
  .....
</web-app>
```

The above example listing shows that the bankapp servlet is configured to support asynchronous request processing. Now, the bankapp servlet can asynchronously process web requests.

> If you are using Spring's AbstractAnnotationConfigDispatcherServletInitializer to programmatically configure the ServletContext, you can override the isAsyncSupported method to enable or disable async request processing by the DispatcherServlet. By default, the isAsyncSupported method returns true, which means that by default DispatcherServlet supports asynchronous request processing.

Returning Callable from @RequestMapping methods

The following example listing shows the FixedDepositController whose @RequestMapping methods return Callable:

Example listing 15-7 – FixedDepositController – returning Callable from @RequestMapping methods
Project – ch15-async-bankapp
Source location - src/main/java/sample/spring/chapter15/web

```
package sample.spring.chapter15.web;

import java.util.concurrent.Callable;
.....
public class FixedDepositController {
    .....
    @RequestMapping(path = "/list", method = RequestMethod.GET)
    public Callable<ModelAndView> listFixedDeposits() {
        return new Callable<ModelAndView>() {

            @Override
            public ModelAndView call() throws Exception {
                Thread.sleep(5000);
                Map<String, List<FixedDepositDetails>> modelData =
                      new HashMap<String, List<FixedDepositDetails>>();
                modelData.put("fdList", fixedDepositService.getFixedDeposits());
                return new ModelAndView("fixedDepositList", modelData);
            }
        };
    }
    .....
}
```

The above example listing shows that the listFixedDeposits method returns a Callable<T> object, where T is the type of the result that is asynchronously computed. The Callable's call method contains the logic that needs to be executed asynchronously to produce the result. The call method shown in the above example listing invokes FixedDepositService's getFixedDeposits method, and returns a ModelAndView object containing the model and view information. The Thread.sleep method is invoked in the beginning of call method to simulate a scenario in which the request processing takes time.

If an exception is thrown during the execution of the Callable returned from the controller, the @ExceptionHandler method (or the configured HandlerExceptionResolver bean) of the controller is responsible for handling the exception. For more information on @ExceptionHandler annotation, refer to section 12-9 of chapter 12.

Example listing 15-7 shows that to switch from synchronous request processing approach to asynchronous request processing, move the logic from the @RequestMapping method to the call method of Callable, and change the return type of the @RequestMapping method to Callable<T>.

Let's now look at how requests are asynchronously processed when a @RequestMapping method returns a DeferredResult object.

IMPORT **chapter 15/ch15-async-webservice** and **ch15-async-webservice-client** (The ch15-async-webservice project is a variant of FixedDepositWS web service (refer ch14-webservice project of chapter 14) that asynchronously processes web service requests. @RequestMapping methods defined in the FixedDepositController of this project return an instance of DeferredResult object. The ch15-async-webservice-client project is same as the FixedDepositWS web service client (refer ch14-webservice-client project of chapter 14) that assumes that the web service is deployed at http://localhost:8080/ch15-async-webservice.)

Returning DeferredResult from @RequestMapping methods

A DeferredResult instance represents a result that is asynchronously computed. You set the result on the DeferredResult instance by calling its setResult method. Typically, a @RequestMapping method stores a DeferredResult instance in a Queue or a Map or any other data structure, and a separate thread is responsible for computing the result and setting the result on the DeferredResult instance.

Let's first look at @RequestMapping methods that return DeferredResult type.

@RequestMapping method implementation

The following example listing shows the FixedDepositController whose @RequestMapping methods return DeferredResult objects:

Example listing 15-8 – FixedDepositController – returning DeferredResult from @RequestMapping methods
Project – ch15-async-webservice
Source location - src/main/java/sample/spring/chapter15/web

```
package sample.spring.chapter15.web;

import java.util.Queue;
import java.util.concurrent.ConcurrentLinkedQueue;
import org.springframework.web.context.request.async.DeferredResult;
.....
@Controller
@RequestMapping(path = "/fixedDeposits")
public class FixedDepositController {
    private static final String LIST_METHOD = "getFixedDepositList";
    private static final String GET_FD_METHOD = "getFixedDeposit";
    .....
    private final Queue<ResultContext> deferredResultQueue =
```

```
                        new ConcurrentLinkedQueue<ResultContext>();
    .....
    @RequestMapping(method = RequestMethod.GET)
    public DeferredResult<ResponseEntity<List<FixedDepositDetails>>>
      getFixedDepositList() {
        DeferredResult<ResponseEntity<List<FixedDepositDetails>>> dr =
                new DeferredResult<ResponseEntity<List<FixedDepositDetails>>>();

        ResultContext<ResponseEntity<List<FixedDepositDetails>>> resultContext =
          new ResultContext<ResponseEntity<List<FixedDepositDetails>>>();
        resultContext.setDeferredResult(dr);
        resultContext.setMethodToInvoke(LIST_METHOD);
        resultContext.setArgs(new HashMap<String, Object>());

        deferredResultQueue.add(resultContext);
        return dr;
    }
    .....
}
```

Each @RequestMapping method of FixedDepositController performs these steps:

Step 1 - creates an instance of DeferredResult<T> object, where T represents the *type* of the result that is asynchronously computed. As the type of the result computed for the getFixedDepositList method is ResponseEntity<List<FixedDepositDetails>>, an instance of DeferredResult<ResponseEntity<List<FixedDepositDetails>>> is created.

Step 2 - creates an instance of ResultContext object. ResultContext object holds DeferredResult instance that we created in Step 1, and other details that are required to asynchronously compute the result for the DeferredResult object. In the case of FixedDepositController's getFixedDepositList method, result is represented by the list of fixed deposits obtained by invoking FixedDepositService's getFixedDeposits method.

The following example listing shows the ResultContext class:

Example listing 15-9 – ResultContext class for storing DeferredResult and other information
Project – ch15-async-webservice
Source location - src/main/java/sample/spring/chapter15/web

```
package sample.spring.chapter15.web;

import java.util.Map;
import org.springframework.web.context.request.async.DeferredResult;

public class ResultContext<T> {
    private String methodToInvoke;
    private DeferredResult<T> deferredResult;
    private Map<String, Object> args;

    public void setDeferredResult(DeferredResult<T> deferredResult) {
        this. deferredResult = deferredResult;
    }
    .....
}
```

The deferredResult property refers to an instance of DeferredResult, the methodToInvoke property specifies the name of the FixedDepositService method that is invoked to compute the result for the

DeferredResult object, and args property (of type java.util.Map) specifies the arguments to be passed to the FixedDepositService method. A separate thread (as explained later in this section) uses the methodToInvoke and args properties to invoke the specified FixedDepositService method, and sets the returned result on the DeferredResult instance.

As the LIST_METHOD, GET_FD_METHOD, and so on, constants in the FixedDepositController class refer to the names of the FixedDepositService methods (refer example listing 15-8), the methodToInvoke property is set to one of these constants. In example listing 15-8, FixedDepositController's getFixedDepositList method sets the methodToInvoke property to LIST_METHOD constant (whose value is getFixedDeposits) because FixedDepositService's getFixedDeposits method needs to be invoked to obtain the result for the DeferredResult object.

Step 3 - stores the ResultContext instance created in Step 2 into a Queue (refer to deferredResultQueue instance variable in example listing 15-8)

Step 4 - returns the DeferredResult object created in Step 1

The above sequence of steps suggests that for each web request an instance of ResultContext is stored in the deferredResultQueue. The following figure summarizes the actions that are performed by FixedDepositController's getFixedDepositList method.

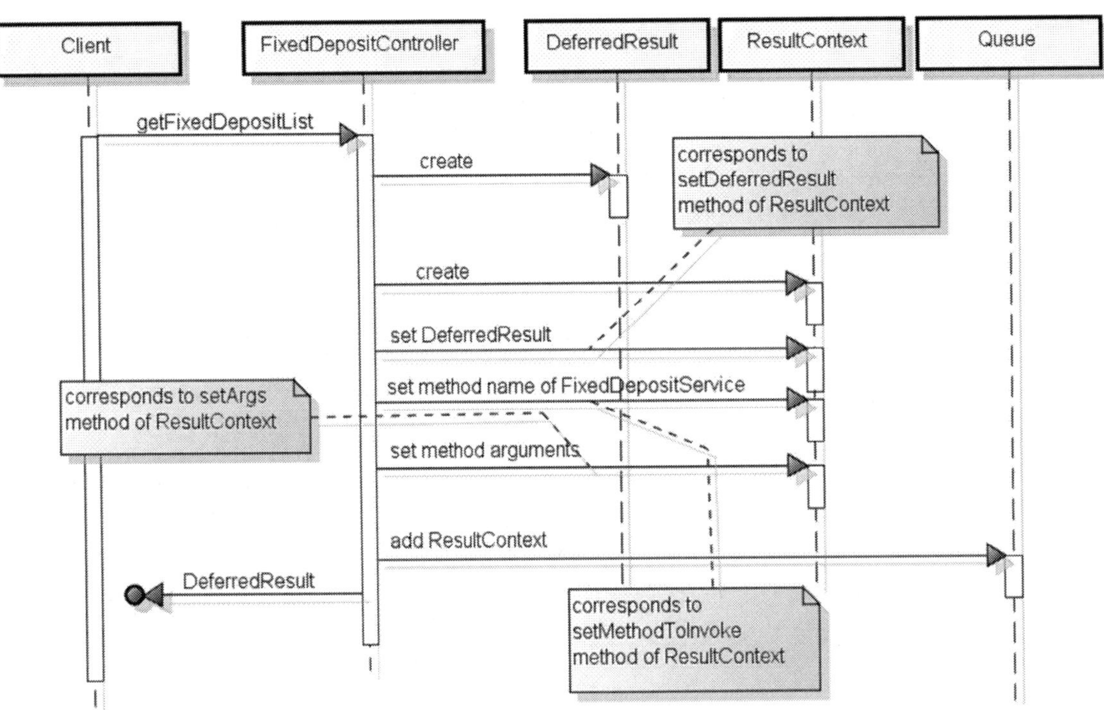

Figure 15-2 FixedDepositController's getFixedDepositList method adds a ResultContext object to the queue and returns a DeferredResult object

Let's now look at how the result is computed for the DeferredResult instance contained inside the ResultContext object.

Computing result for a DeferredResult instance

FixedDepositController's processResults method is responsible for iterating over the ResultContext objects stored in the deferredResultQueue (refer example listing 15-8), computing the result for each

DeferredResult object, and setting the result on the DeferredResult object. The following example listing shows the processResults method:

Example listing 15-10 – processResults method – computing and setting results on DeferredResult objects
Project – ch15-async-webservice
Source location - src/main/java/sample/spring/chapter15/web

```
package sample.spring.chapter15.web;

import org.springframework.scheduling.annotation.Scheduled;
import org.springframework.web.context.request.async.DeferredResult;

@Controller
@RequestMapping(path = "/fixedDeposits")
public class FixedDepositController {
    private static final String LIST_METHOD = "getFixedDepositList";
    .....
    private final Queue<ResultContext> deferredResultQueue =
                    new ConcurrentLinkedQueue<ResultContext>();
    @Autowired
    private FixedDepositService fixedDepositService;
    .....
    @Scheduled(fixedRate = 10000)
    public void processResults() {
        for (ResultContext resultContext : deferredResultQueue) {
            if (resultContext.getMethodToInvoke() == LIST_METHOD) {
                resultContext.getDeferredResult().setResult(
                        new ResponseEntity<List<FixedDepositDetails>>(
                                fixedDepositService.getFixedDeposits(), HttpStatus.OK));
            }
            .....
            deferredResultQueue.remove(resultContext);
        }
    }
}
```

@Scheduled annotation (refer section 10-6 of chapter 10 for more details) on processResults method specifies that every 10 seconds an application thread is responsible for executing the processResults method. The processResults method uses the method name and argument information stored in the ResultContext instance to invoke the appropriate FixedDepositService's method. The processResults method then sets the result on the DeferredResult instance by calling its setResult method. In the end, the processResults method removes the ResultContext instance from the Queue. After processing a ResultContext instance, the processResults method removes the ResultContext instance from the Queue so that it is not re-processed by the processResults method when it executes again after 10 seconds.

Figure 15-3 summarizes the actions performed by FixedDepositController's processResults method to compute the result and set it on the DeferredResult instance.

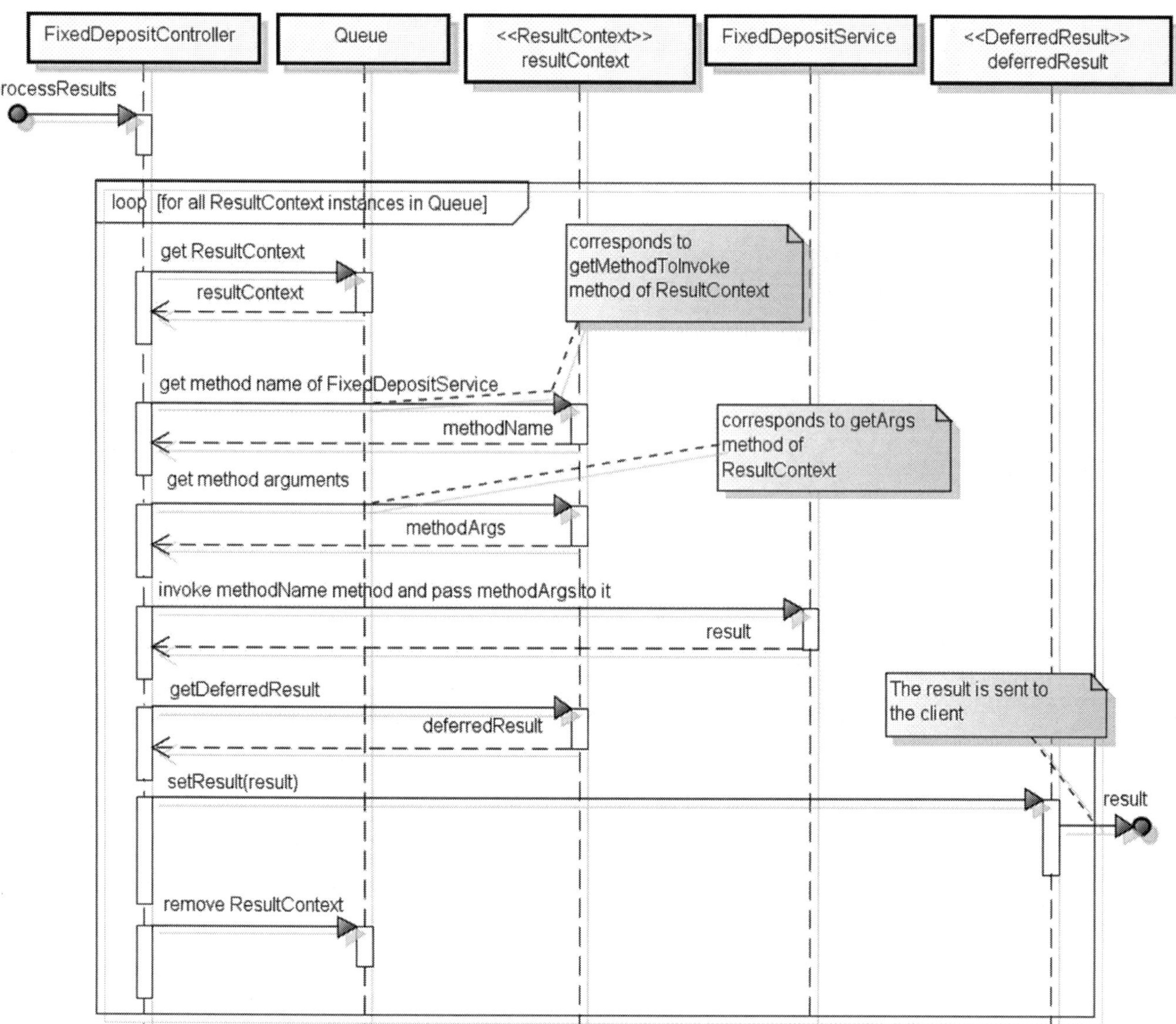

Figure 15-3 The `processResults` method reads method name and argument information from the `ResultContext` object to compute the result for the `DeferredResult` instance

Let's now look at how exceptions are handled when a `@RequestMapping` method returns a `DeferredResult` instance.

Exception Handling

If you set an object of type `java.lang.Exception` using `DeferredResult`'s `setErrorResult` method, the result is handled by `@ExceptionHandler` annotated method of the controller (or by the configured `HandlerExceptionResolver` bean). For more information on `@ExceptionHandler` annotation, refer to section 12-9 of chapter 12.

The following example listing shows `FixedDepositController`'s `openFixedDeposit` method that opens a new fixed deposit:

Example listing 15-11 – FixedDepositController's openFixedDeposit method
Project – ch15-async-webservice
Source location - src/main/java/sample/spring/chapter15/web

```
package sample.spring.chapter15.web;

@Controller
@RequestMapping(path = "/fixedDeposits")
public class FixedDepositController {
    private static final String OPEN_FD_METHOD = "openFixedDeposit";
    .....
    private final Queue<ResultContext> deferredResultQueue =
                        new ConcurrentLinkedQueue<ResultContext>();

    @RequestMapping(method = RequestMethod.POST)
    public DeferredResult<ResponseEntity<FixedDepositDetails>> openFixedDeposit(
            @RequestBody FixedDepositDetails fixedDepositDetails,
            BindingResult bindingResult) {

        DeferredResult<ResponseEntity<FixedDepositDetails>> dr =
             new DeferredResult<ResponseEntity<FixedDepositDetails>>();

        ResultContext<ResponseEntity<FixedDepositDetails>> resultContext =
              new ResultContext<ResponseEntity<FixedDepositDetails>>();
        resultContext.setDeferredResult(dr);
        resultContext.setMethodToInvoke(OPEN_FD_METHOD);

        Map<String, Object> args = new HashMap<String, Object>();
        args.put("fixedDepositDetails", fixedDepositDetails);
        args.put("bindingResult", bindingResult);
        resultContext.setArgs(args);

        deferredResultQueue.add(resultContext);
        return dr;
    }
    .....
}
```

The above example listing shows that the arguments (fixedDepositDetails and bindingResult) passed to the openFixedDeposit method are set on the ResultContext instance so that these arguments are available when the processResults method executes the logic for opening a new fixed deposit. The fixedDepositDetails argument contains the details of the fixed deposit to be opened and the bindingResult argument contains the results of data binding.

The following example listing shows how the processResults method executes the logic for opening a new fixed deposit:

Example listing 15-12 – FixedDepositController's processResults method
Project – ch15-async-webservice
Source location - src/main/java/sample/spring/chapter15/web

```
package sample.spring.chapter15.web;

@Controller
@RequestMapping(path = "/fixedDeposits")
public class FixedDepositController {
    private static final String OPEN_FD_METHOD = "openFixedDeposit";
```

```
    .....
    private final Queue<ResultContext> deferredResultQueue =
            new ConcurrentLinkedQueue<ResultContext>();

    @Autowired
    private FixedDepositService fixedDepositService;
    .....
    @ExceptionHandler(ValidationException.class)
    @ResponseBody
    @ResponseStatus(code = HttpStatus.BAD_REQUEST)
    public String handleException(Exception ex) {
        logger.info("handling ValidationException " + ex.getMessage());
        return ex.getMessage();
    }

    @Scheduled(fixedRate = 10000)
    public void processResults() {
        for (ResultContext resultContext : deferredResultQueue) {
            .....
            if (resultContext.getMethodToInvoke() == OPEN_FD_METHOD) {
                FixedDepositDetails fixedDepositDetails =
                  (FixedDepositDetails) resultContext.getArgs().get("fixedDepositDetails");
                BindingResult bindingResult =
                  (BindingResult) resultContext.getArgs().get("bindingResult");

                new FixedDepositDetailsValidator().validate(fixedDepositDetails,
                       bindingResult);

                if (bindingResult.hasErrors()) {
                    logger.info("openFixedDeposit() method: Validation errors occurred");
                    resultContext.getDeferredResult()
                           .setErrorResult(new ValidationException(
                                       "Validation errors occurred"));
                } else {
                    fixedDepositService.saveFixedDeposit(fixedDepositDetails);
                    resultContext.getDeferredResult().setResult(
                         new ResponseEntity<FixedDepositDetails>(fixedDepositDetails,
                              HttpStatus.CREATED));
                }
            }
            .....
        }
    }
}
```

The above example listing shows the @ExceptionHandler annotated handleException method that handles exceptions of type ValidationException. The handleException method logs that a validation exception has occurred and returns the exception message.

To open a new fixed deposit, the processResults method retrieves the fixedDepositDetails (of type FixedDepositDetails) and bindingResult (of type BindingResult) arguments from the ResultContext and validates the fixedDepositDetails object by calling FixedDepositValidator's validate method. If validation errors are reported, the processResults method invokes DeferredResult's setErrorResult method to set ValidationException (of type java.lang.Exception) as the result. Setting the ValidationException using DeferredResult's setErrorResult method will cause handling of the result by FixedDepositController's handleException method.

It is recommended that you deploy the ch15-async-webservice project (which represents the FixedDepositWS RESTful web service) and access it by running the main method of FixedDepositWSClient of ch15-async-webservice-client project (which represents a client of FixedDepositWS RESTful web service). The FixedDepositWSClient's openInvalidFixedDeposit method invokes FixedDepositController's openFixedDeposit web service method such that it results in ValidationException. You can check the logs to verify that the FixedDepositController's handleException method handles the result when processResults method sets ValidationException on the DeferredResult object by calling DeferredResult's setErrorResult method.

Let's now look at how to set default timeout value for asynchronous requests.

Setting default timeout value

You can set the default timeout value of asynchronous requests by using default-timeout attribute of Spring mvc schema's <async-support> element, as shown here:

Example listing 15-13 – Setting default timeout for asynchronous requests
Project – ch15-async-webservice
Source location – src/main/webapp/WEB-INF/spring/webservice-config.xml

```
<mvc:annotation-driven>
    <mvc:async-support default-timeout="10000" >
        .....
    </mvc:async-support>
</mvc:annotation-driven>
```

In the above example listing, default timeout for asynchronous requests is set to 10 seconds. If you don't specify the default timeout, the timeout for asynchronous requests depends on the Servlet container on which you deployed your web application.

Let's now look at how you can intercept asynchronous requests using CallableProcessingInterceptor and DeferredResultProcessingInterceptor.

Intercepting asynchronous requests

If you are using Callable to asynchronously process requests, you can use Spring's CallableProcessingInterceptor callback interface to intercept asynchronous request processing. For instance, the CallableProcessingInterceptor's postProcess method is called after the Callable has produced the result, and the CallableProcessingInterceptor's preProcess method is called before the Callable task is executed. Similarly, if you are using DeferredResult to asynchronously process requests, you can use Spring's DeferredResultProcessingInterceptor callback interface to intercept asynchronous request processing.

You can configure a CallableProcessingInterceptor using <callable-interceptors> element of Spring's mvc schema. And, you can configure a DeferredResultProcessingInterceptor using <deferred-result-interceptors> element of Spring's mvc schema. The following example listing shows configuration of MyDeferredResultInterceptor (a DeferredResultProcessingInterceptor implementation):

Example listing 15-14 – Configuring a DeferredResultProcessingInterceptor implementation
Project – ch15-async-webservice
Source location – src/main/webapp/WEB-INF/spring/webservice-config.xml

```
<mvc:annotation-driven>
    <mvc:async-support default-timeout="10000">
        <mvc:deferred-result-interceptors>
            <bean class="sample.spring.chapter15.web.MyDeferredResultInterceptor"/>
```

```
            </mvc:deferred-result-interceptors>
        </mvc:async-support>
    </mvc:annotation-driven>
```

If you are using Java-based configuration approach, you can override WebMvcConfigurer's configureAsyncSupport(AsyncSupportConfigurer configurer) method and use AsyncSupportConfigurer's setDefaultTimeout method to configure default timeout value for asynchronous requests. You can also use AsyncSupportConfigurer's registerCallableInterceptors and registerDeferredResultInterceptors methods to register CallableProcessingInterceptors and DeferredResultProcessingInterceptors, respectively.

Let's now look at Spring's support for type conversion and formatting.

15-5 Type conversion and formatting support in Spring

Spring's Converter interface simplifies converting an object type to another object type. And, Spring's Formatter interface is useful when converting an object type to its *localized* String representation, and vice versa. You can find a number of built-in Converter implementations in the org.springframework.core.convert.support package of spring-core JAR file. Spring also provides built-in Formatters for java.lang.Number and java.util.Date types that you can find in org.springframework.format.number and org.springframework.format.datetime packages, respectively.

IMPORT **chapter 15/ch15-converter-formatter-bankapp** (This project is a variant of ch15-bankapp project that shows how to create custom Converters and Formatters)

Let's first look at how to create a custom Converter.

Creating a custom Converter

A converter implements Spring's Converter<S, T> interface, where S (referred to as the *source* type) is the type of the object given to the converter, and T (referred to as the *target* type) is the type of the object to which S is converted by the converter. Converter interface defines a convert method that provides the conversion logic.

The following example listing shows the IdToFixedDepositDetailsConverter that converts an object of type String (representing the fixed deposit ID) to an object of type FixedDepositDetails (representing the fixed deposit corresponding to the fixed deposit ID):

Example listing 15-15 – Converter implementation
Project – ch15-converter-formatter-bankapp
Source location – src/main/java/sample/spring/chapter15/converter

```
package sample.spring.chapter15.converter;

import org.springframework.core.convert.converter.Converter;
.....
public class IdToFixedDepositDetailsConverter implements
                 Converter<String, FixedDepositDetails> {

    @Autowired
    private FixedDepositService fixedDepositService;

    @Override
    public FixedDepositDetails convert(String source) {
        return fixedDepositService.getFixedDeposit(Integer.parseInt(source));
```

```
    }
}
```

IdToFixedDepositDetailsConverter implements Converter<String, FixedDepositDetails> interface, where String is the source type and FixedDepositDetails is the target type. IdToFixedDepositDetailsConverter's convert method uses FixedDepositService's getFixedDeposit method to retrieve the FixedDepositDetails object corresponding to the fixed deposit ID.

Let's now look at how to configure and use a custom converter.

Configuring and using a custom Converter

To use a custom converter, you need to register the custom converter with Spring's ConversionService. A ConversionService acts as a registry of Converters and Formatters, and Spring delegates type conversion responsibility to the registered ConversionService. By default, the <annotation-driven> element of Spring's mvc schema automatically registers Spring's FormattingConversionService (an implementation of ConversionService) with the Spring container. Spring comes with a couple of built-in converters and formatters that are automatically registered with the FormattingConversionService. If you want to substitute a different implementation of ConversionService, you can do so by using conversion-service attribute of <annotation-driven> element.

To register custom converters with the FormattingConversionService instance, configure Spring's FormattingConversionServiceFactoryBean (a FactoryBean implementation that creates and configures a FormattingConversionService instance) and specify custom converters as part of the configuration, as shown in the following example listing:

Example listing 15-16 – Registering a custom Converter with FormattingConversionService
Project – ch15-converter-formatter-bankapp
Source location – src/main/webapp/WEB-INF/spring

```
<mvc:annotation-driven conversion-service="myConversionService" />

<bean id="myConversionService"
      class="org.springframework.format.support.FormattingConversionServiceFactoryBean">
    <property name="converters">
      <set>
        <bean class="sample.spring.chapter15.converter.IdToFixedDepositDetailsConverter" />
      </set>
    </property>
    .....
</bean>
```

By default, FormattingConversionServiceFactoryBean registers only the built-in converters and formatters with the FormattingConversionService instance. You register custom converters and formatters using FormattingConversionServiceFactoryBean's converters and formatters properties. As we want our Spring application to use FormattingConversionService instance created by the FormattingConversionServiceFactoryBean, the conversion-service attribute of <annotation-driven> element refers to the FormattingConversionServiceFactoryBean.

The converters and formatters registered with the FormattingConversionService are used by the Spring container to perform type conversion during *data binding*. In the following example listing, FixedDepositController's viewFixedDepositDetails method shows a scenario in which the Spring container uses IdToFixedDepositDetailsConverter<String, FixedDepositDetails> to convert fixed deposit ID (of type String) to FixedDepositDetails instance:

Example listing 15-17 – FixedDepositController's viewFixedDepositDetails method
Project – ch15-converter-formatter-bankapp
Source location – src/main/java/sample/spring/chapter15/web

```
package sample.spring.chapter15.web;
.....
public class FixedDepositController {
    .....
    @RequestMapping(params = "fdAction=view", method = RequestMethod.GET)
    public ModelAndView viewFixedDepositDetails(
          @RequestParam(name = "fixedDepositId") FixedDepositDetails fixedDepositDetails) {
        .....
    }
}
```

@RequestParam annotation specifies that the value of fixedDepositId request parameter is assigned to the fixedDepositDetails method argument. The fixedDepositId request parameter uniquely identifies a fixed deposit. As the fixedDepositId request parameter is of type String and method argument type is FixedDepositDetails, Spring uses IdToFixedDepositDetailsConverter<String, FixedDepositDetails> to perform the type conversion.

The use of ConversionService is not limited to the web layer. You can use ConversionService to programmatically perform type conversion in any layer of your application. The following example listing shows a variant of FixedDepositController's viewFixedDepositDetails method that uses ConversionService directly for performing type conversion:

Example listing 15-18 – Performing type conversion programmatically

```
import org.springframework.core.convert.ConversionService;
.....
public class FixedDepositController {
    @Autowired
    private ConversionService conversionService;
    .....
    @RequestMapping(params = "fdAction=view", method = RequestMethod.GET)
    public ModelAndView viewFixedDepositDetails(HttpServletRequest request) {
        String fixedDepositId = request.getParameter("fixedDepositId");
        FixedDepositDetails fixedDepositDetails =
             conversionService.convert(fixedDepositId, FixedDepositDetails.class);
        .....
    }
}
```

In the above example listing, ConversionService instance that is registered with the Spring container is autowired into the FixedDepositController. The viewFixedDepositDetails method uses ConversionService's convert method to convert fixedDepositId (of type String) to FixedDepositDetails. Behind the scenes, ConversionService makes use of the IdToFixedDepositDetailsConverter<String, FixedDepositDetails> converter registered with it to perform the type conversion.

Now that we have seen how to create and use a custom Converter, let's now look at how to create and use a custom Formatter.

Creating a custom Formatter

A formatter converts an object of type T to a String value for display purposes, and parses a String value to the object type T. A formatter implements Spring's Formatter<T > interface, where T is the type of the object that the formatter formats. This may sound similar to what PropertyEditors do in web applications. As we'll see in this chapter, Formatters offer a more robust alternative to PropertyEditors.

Spring's tag library tags use the formatters registered with the FormattingConversionService to perform type conversion during data binding and rendering.

The following example listing shows the AmountFormatter that is used by the MyBank application to display fixed deposit amount in the currency that applies to the user's locale, and to parse the fixed deposit amount entered by the user. For simplicity's sake, currency conversion is not applied on the fixed deposit amount; the currency symbol that applies to the user's locale is simply appended to the fixed deposit amount.

Example listing 15-19 – AmountFormatter - a Formatter implementation
Project – ch15-converter-formatter-bankapp
Source location – src/main/java/sample/spring/chapter15/formatter

```
package sample.spring.chapter15.formatter;

import java.text.ParseException;
import java.util.Locale;
import org.springframework.format.Formatter;

public class AmountFormatter implements Formatter<Long>{

    @Override
    public String print(Long object, Locale locale) {
        String returnStr = object.toString() + " USD";
        if(locale.getLanguage().equals(new Locale("de").getLanguage())) {
            returnStr = object.toString() + " EURO";
        }
        return returnStr;
    }

    @Override
    public Long parse(String text, Locale locale) throws ParseException {
        String str[] = text.split(" ");
        return Long.parseLong(str[0]);
    }
}
```

AmountFormatter implements Formatter<Long> interface, which means that the AmountFormatter applies to Long type objects. The print method converts the Long type object (representing the fixed deposit amount) to a String value that is displayed to the user. Based on the language code obtained from the locale, the print method simply appends USD (for en language code) or EURO (for de language code) to the fixed deposit amount. For instance, if the fixed deposit amount is 1000 and the language code is de, the print method returns '1000 EURO'. The parse method takes the fixed deposit amount entered by the user (like, '1000 EURO') and converts it into a Long type object by simply extracting the fixed deposit amount from the user entered value.

Let's now look at how to configure a custom formatter.

Configuring a custom Formatter

You can register custom formatters with the FormattingConversionService using the formatters property of FormattingConversionServiceFactoryBean, as shown here:

Example listing 15-20 – Registering a custom Formatter with FormattingConversionService

```
<beans .....>
    .....
    <mvc:annotation-driven conversion-service="myConversionService" />
    .....
    <bean id="myConversionService"
         class="org.springframework.format.support.FormattingConversionServiceFactoryBean">
        <property name="formatters">
            <set>
                <bean class="sample.spring.chapter15.formatter.AmountFormatter" />
            </set>
        </property>
    </bean>
</beans>
```

AmountFormatter registered with the FormattingConversionService is applied to *all* the Long type fields during data binding and rendering.

> If you are using Java-based configuration approach, you can override WebMvcConfigurer's addFormatters(FormatterRegistry registry) method to register custom formatters and converters with the Spring container. For instance, you can call FormatterRegistry's addFormatter method to register a formatter, and call FormatterRegistry's addConverter method to register a converter.

You can control the fields on which a Formatter applies by using Spring's AnnotationFormatterFactory. An AnnotationFormatterFactory implementation creates formatters for fields that are annotated with a particular *annotation*. Let's see how we can use AnnotationFormatterFactory to format only the Long type fields annotated with @AmountFormat annotation.

Creating AnnotationFormatterFactory to format only @AmountFormat annotated fields

The following example listing shows the definition of @AmountFormat annotation:

Example listing 15-21 – AmountFormat annotation
Project – ch15-converter-formatter-bankapp
Source location – src/main/java/sample/spring/chapter15/formatter

```
package sample.spring.chapter15.formatter;
.....
@Target(value={ElementType.FIELD})
@Retention(RetentionPolicy.RUNTIME)
@Documented
public @interface AmountFormat { }
```

In the above example listing, the @Target annotation specifies that the @AmountFormat annotation can only appear on fields.

The following example listing shows the implementation of AnnotationFormatterFactory that creates formatters for fields annotated with @AmountFormat annotation:

Example listing 15-22 – AmountFormatAnnotationFormatterFactory class
Project – ch15-converter-formatter-bankapp
Source location – src/main/java/sample/spring/chapter15/formatter

```
package sample.spring.chapter15.formatter;

import org.springframework.format.AnnotationFormatterFactory;
```

```
import org.springframework.format.Parser;
import org.springframework.format.Printer;

public class AmountFormatAnnotationFormatterFactory implements
        AnnotationFormatterFactory<AmountFormat> {

    public Set<Class<?>> getFieldTypes() {
        Set<Class<?>> fieldTypes = new HashSet<Class<?>>(1, 1);
        fieldTypes.add(Long.class);
        return fieldTypes;
    }

    public Parser<?> getParser(AmountFormat annotation, Class<?> fieldType) {
        return new AmountFormatter();
    }

    public Printer<?> getPrinter(AmountFormat annotation, Class<?> fieldType) {
        return new AmountFormatter();
    }
}
```

In the above example listing, AmountFormatAnnotationFormatterFactory implements AnnotationFormatterFactory<AmountFormat> interface, which means that the AmountFormatAnnotationFormatterFactory creates formatters for fields annotated with @AmountFormat annotation.

The getFieldTypes method returns the field types that may be annotated with @AmountFormat annotation. The getFieldTypes method in the above example listing returns a single type, Long type. This means that only a Long type field annotated with @AmountFormat annotation is considered for formatting by the formatters created by the AmountFormatAnnotationFormatterFactory. The getParser and getPrinter methods return formatters for fields that are annotated with @AmountFormat annotation. You should note that the Formatter interface is a sub-interface of Parser and Printer interfaces.

Configuring AnnotationFormatterFactory implementation

As in the case of Formatters configuration, an AnnotationFormatterFactory implementation is registered with FormattingConversionService via formatters property of FormattingConversionServiceFactoryBean:

Example listing 15-23 – AmountFormatAnnotationFormatterFactory configuration
Project – ch15-converter-formatter-bankapp
Source location – src/main/webapp/WEB-INF/spring

```
<beans .....>
    .....
    <mvc:annotation-driven conversion-service="myConversionService" />
    .....
    <bean id="myConversionService"
        class="org.springframework.format.support.FormattingConversionServiceFactoryBean">
        <property name="formatters">
           <set>
              <bean class=
               "sample.spring.chapter15.formatter.AmountFormatAnnotationFormatterFactory"/>
           </set>
        </property>
    </bean>
</beans>
```

Now that we have seen how to use `AnnotationFormatterFactory` to enable formatting of fields that are annotated with a specific annotation, let's look at how it is used in `ch15-converter-formatter-bankapp` project.

The following figure shows the web page of `ch15-converter-formatter-bankapp` project that shows the lists of fixed deposits:

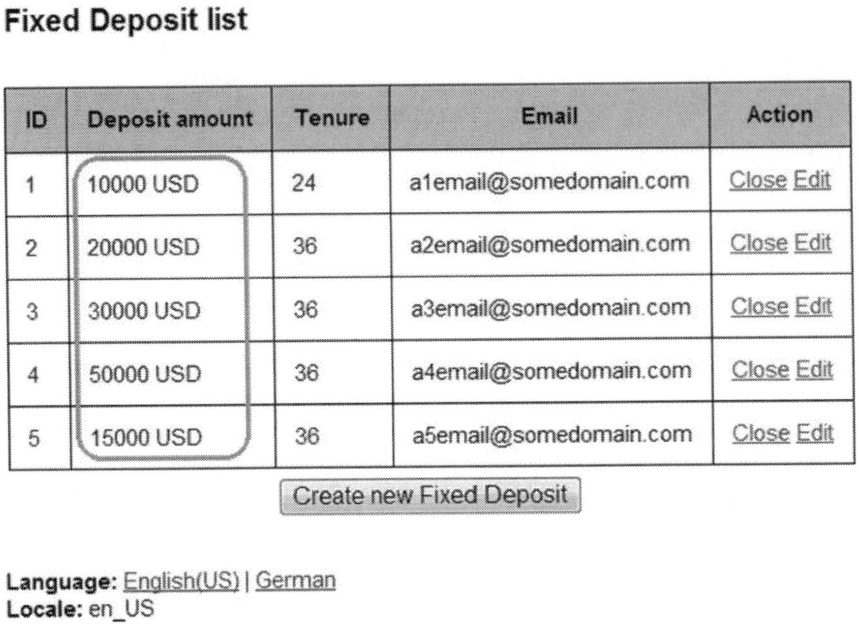

Fixed Deposit list

ID	Deposit amount	Tenure	Email	Action
1	10000 USD	24	a1email@somedomain.com	Close Edit
2	20000 USD	36	a2email@somedomain.com	Close Edit
3	30000 USD	36	a3email@somedomain.com	Close Edit
4	50000 USD	36	a4email@somedomain.com	Close Edit
5	15000 USD	36	a5email@somedomain.com	Close Edit

Create new Fixed Deposit

Language: English(US) | German
Locale: en_US

Figure 15-4 - The 'Deposit amount' column shows USD or EURO depending upon the language code obtained from the user's current locale

The above figure shows that USD is appended to the fixed deposit amount if the language chosen by the user is English. If you switch the language to German, the USD will be replaced by EURO. In example listing 15-19, we saw that the `AmountFormatter` contained the logic to show USD or EURO depending upon the language code obtained from the user's current locale.

To ensure that the formatters configured with the `FormattingConversionService` are invoked during page rendering and form submission, Spring's tag library tags (like, <eval> and <input>) have been used in the JSP pages of `ch15-converter-formatter-bankapp` project.

> If you are using Java-based configuration approach, you can override `WebMvcConfigurer`'s `addFormatters(FormatterRegistry registry)` method and call `FormatterRegistry`'s `addFormatterForFieldAnnotation(AnnotationFormatterFactory factory)` method to configure an `AnnotationFormatterFactory` implementation.

Let's now look at how Spring Web MVC simplifies uploading files.

15-6 File upload support in Spring Web MVC

You can handle multipart requests in your Spring Web MVC applications by configuring a `MultipartResolver`. Spring provides the following out-of-the-box implementations of `MultipartResolver` interface that you can use in your web applications:

- `CommonsMultipartResolver` – based on `Apache Commons FileUpload` library

- StandardServletMultipartResolver – based on Servlet 3.0 Part API

When a multipart request is received, DispatcherServlet uses the configured MultipartResolver to wrap the HttpServletRequest into a MultipartHttpServletRequest instance. In Spring Web MVC, an uploaded file is represented by the MultipartFile object. The controller responsible for handling file uploads accesses the uploaded file using methods defined by the MultipartHttpServletRequest or by directly accessing the MultipartFile object.

Let's first look at a sample web application that uses CommonsMultipartResolver for uploading files.

IMPORT **chapter 15/ch15-commons-file-upload** (This project shows how to use CommonsMultipartResolver to upload files. As CommonsMultipartResolver uses Apache Commons FileUpload library, the project is dependent on commons-fileupload JAR file.)

Uploading files using CommonsMultipartResolver

The following example listing shows the file upload form that is displayed by ch15-commons-file-upload project:

Example listing 15-24 – uploadForm.jsp – shows the upload form
Project – ch15-commons-file-upload
Source location – src/main/webapp/WEB-INF/jsp

```
.....
    <form method="post" action="/ch15-commons-file-upload/uploadFile"
            enctype="multipart/form-data">
        <table style="padding-left: 200px;">
            <tr>
                <td colspan="2"><c:out value="${uploadMessage}" /></td>
            </tr>
            <tr>
                <td><b>Select the file to be uploaded:  </b></td>
                <td><input type="file" name="myFileField" /></td>
            </tr>
            <tr>
                <td colspan="2" align="center"><input type="button"
                    value="Upload file" onclick="document.forms[0].submit();" /></td>
            </tr>
        </table>
    </form>
.....
```

The above example listing shows that the enctype attribute of <form> element is set to multipart/form-data, which means that the form submission results in sending multipart request to the server. The uploadMessage request attribute shows the success or failure message after the user selects a file and clicks the 'Upload file' button.

The following example listing shows the configuration of CommonsMultipartResolver that resolves multipart requests:

Example listing 15-25 – fileupload-config.xml – CommonsMultipartResolver configuration
Project – ch15-commons-file-upload
Source location – src/main/webapp/WEB-INF/spring

```
    <bean id="multipartResolver"
        class="org.springframework.web.multipart.commons.CommonsMultipartResolver">
        <property name="maxUploadSize" value="100000" />
```

```
        <property name="resolveLazily" value="true" />
    </bean>
```

It is important to note that the MultipartResolver implementation must be configured with id as multipartResolver in the web application context XML file. The maxUploadSize property specifies the maximum size (in bytes) of the file that can be uploaded. If you attempt to upload a file whose size is greater than 100 KB, the CommonsMultipartResolver shown in the above example listing will throw an exception. If an exception is thrown by the CommonsMultipartResolver instance, the controller responsible for handling the file upload doesn't get the opportunity to handle the exception. For this reason, the resolveLazily property is set to true. If the resolveLazily property is set to true, the multipart request is resolved only when the uploaded file is accessed by the controller. This gives the opportunity to the controller to handle exceptions that occur during multipart request resolution.

The following example listing shows the FileUploadController that handles file uploads:

Example listing 15-26 – FileUploadController
Project – ch15-commons-file-upload
Source location – src/main/java/sample/spring/chapter15/web

```
package sample.spring.chapter15.web;

import org.springframework.web.multipart.MultipartFile;
.....
public class FileUploadController {
    .....
    @RequestMapping(path = "/uploadFile", method = RequestMethod.POST)
    public ModelAndView handleFileUpload(
            @RequestParam("myFileField") MultipartFile file) throws IOException {
        ModelMap modelData = new ModelMap();

        if (!file.isEmpty()) {
            // -- save the uploaded file on the filesystem
            String successMessage = "File successfully uploaded";
            modelData.put("uploadMessage", successMessage);
            return new ModelAndView("uploadForm", modelData);
        }
        .....
    }

    @ExceptionHandler(value = Exception.class)
    public ModelAndView handleException() {
        .....
    }
}
```

FileUploadController's handleFileUpload method accepts an argument of type MultipartFile which identifies the uploaded file. Notice that the @RequestParam annotation specifies name of the <input type="file" .....> field in the uploadForm.jsp page (refer example listing 15-24). If the file is successfully uploaded, the handleFileUpload method sets a success message which is shown to the user. @ExceptionHandler method shows an error message in case an exception occurs during file upload process. For instance, if the file size is greater than 100 KB, an error message is shown to the user.

Now that we have seen how to use CommonsMultipartResolver to upload files, let's look at how to upload files using StandardServletMultipartResolver.

IMPORT **chapter 15/ch15-servlet3-file-upload** (This project shows how to use StandardServletMultipartResolver to upload files.)

Uploading files using StandardServletMultipartResolver

The support for handling multipart request is provided out-of-the-box in Servlet 3. If you want to use the multipart support provided by Servlet 3, enable multipart request handling by specifying <multipart-config> element in the DispatcherServlet configuration, and configure StandardServletMultipartResolver in the web application context XML file. Unlike, CommonsMultipartResolver, StandardMultipartResolver doesn't define any properties.

The following example listing shows the DispatcherServlet configuration in web.xml file:

Example listing 15-27 – web.xml
Project – ch15-servlet3-file-upload
Source location – src/main/webapp

```
<servlet>
    <servlet-name>fileupload</servlet-name>
    <servlet-class>org.springframework.web.servlet.DispatcherServlet</servlet-class>
    .....
    <multipart-config>
        <max-file-size>100000</max-file-size>
    </multipart-config>
</servlet>
```

As the <multipart-config> element is specified, the fileupload servlet can handle multipart requests. The <max-file-size> element specifies the maximum file size that can be uploaded. Notice that the maximum file size is now specified as part of <multipart-config> element.

15-7 Summary

In this chapter, we looked at some of the important features of Spring Web MVC framework that simplify developing web applications. In the next chapter, we'll look at how to secure Spring applications using Spring Security framework.

Chapter 16 – *Securing applications using Spring Security*

16-1 Introduction

Security is an important aspect of any application. Spring Security is built on top of Spring Framework, and provides a comprehensive framework for securing Spring-based applications. In this chapter, we'll look at how to use Spring Security framework to:

- authenticate users
- implement web request security
- implement method-level security
- secure domain objects using ACL (Access Control List) based security

Let's begin by looking at the MyBank web application's security requirements that we'll address using Spring Security.

16-2 Security requirements of the MyBank web application

The users of the MyBank web application are *customers* and *administrators* that manage fixed deposits in the system. A customer can open and edit fixed deposits but *can't* close them. An administrator *can't* create or edit fixed deposits but can close fixed deposits of customers.

As only authenticated users can access the MyBank web application, a login form is displayed to unauthenticated users:

Login with Username and Password

User: cust1

Password: •••••

Remember me on this computer.

Login

`Figure 16-1` - Login form that is displayed to unauthenticated users

The above figure shows the login form that is displayed to unauthenticated users. If the user selects the `'Remember me on this computer'` checkbox, the MyBank web application remembers the credentials entered by the user and uses it for automatic authentication of the user in future visits.

When a *customer* logs in, details of the fixed deposits associated with the customer are displayed, as shown here:

Logout

Username: cust1

Fixed deposit list

ID	Deposit amount	Tenure	Email	Action
0	10000	24	cust1@somedomain.com	Edit

Create new Fixed Deposit

Figure 16-2 - Fixed deposits of the customer are displayed after authentication

The above figure shows a `Logout` hyperlink that the customer can click to logout from the MyBank web application. A customer can edit details of a fixed deposit by clicking the `Edit` hyperlink corresponding to that fixed deposit. A customer can view the form for opening a new fixed deposit by clicking the `Create new Fixed Deposit` button. Notice that the username of the authenticated user is displayed below the `Logout` hyperlink.

When an administrator logs in, details of *all* the fixed deposits in the system are displayed by the MyBank web application, as shown here:

Logout

Username: admin

Fixed deposit list

ID	Customer	Deposit amount	Tenure	Email	Action
0	cust1	10000	24	cust1@somedomain.com	Close
1	cust2	10000	24	cust2@somedomain.com	Close

Create new Fixed Deposit

Figure 16-3 - Fixed deposits of *all* the customers are displayed when an administrator logs in

In the above figure, an administrator can choose to close a fixed deposit by clicking the `Close` hyperlink corresponding to that fixed deposit. As in the case of customers, the `Create new Fixed Deposit` button is visible to an administrator also, but an attempt to save details of the new fixed deposit will result in a security exception thrown by the application.

Let's now look at how to address the security requirements of MyBank web application using Spring Security.

IMPORT **`chapter 16/ch16-bankapp-simple-security`** (This project represents the MyBank web application that uses Spring Security framework for addressing security requirements described in section 16-2.)

16-3 Securing MyBank web application using Spring Security

Spring Security framework consists of multiple modules that address various security aspects of applications. The following table describes some of the important modules of Spring Security:

Module	Description
spring-security-core	defines the core classes and interfaces of Spring Security framework. This module is required by any application that uses Spring Security.
spring-security-web	provides support for securing web applications
spring-security-config	provides support for configuring Spring Security using security schema and Java-based configuration approach
spring-security-taglibs	defines tags that you can use to access security information and to secure the content displayed by JSP pages
spring-security-acl	enables use of ACLs (Access Control List) to secure instances of domain objects in applications

In this section, we'll look at usage of spring-security-core, spring-security-web, spring-security-config and spring-security-taglibs modules to secure the MyBank web application. Later in this chapter, we'll look at how to use spring-security-acl module to secure domain object instances.

Let's begin by looking at how web request security is configured.

Web request security configuration

You can add web request security to an application by:

- configuring Spring's DelegatingFilterProxy filter in the web.xml file, and
- enabling web request security provided by the Spring Security framework

Let's first look at how to configure DelegatingFilterProxy filter.

DelegatingFilterProxy filter configuration

Spring Framework's *web* module (represented by spring-web-5.0.1.RELEASE.jar file) defines the DelegatingFilterProxy class that implements Servlet API's Filter interface. The following example listing shows the configuration of DelegatingFilterProxy filter in the web.xml file:

Example listing 16-1 – web.xml - DelegatingFilterProxy filter configuration
Project – ch16-bankapp-simple-security
Source location - src/main/webapp/WEB-INF

```
<filter>
    <filter-name>springSecurityFilterChain</filter-name>
    <filter-class>org.springframework.web.filter.DelegatingFilterProxy</filter-class>
</filter>

<filter-mapping>
    <filter-name>springSecurityFilterChain</filter-name>
    <url-pattern>/*</url-pattern>
</filter-mapping>
```

The <filter-mapping> element specifies that the DelegatingFilterProxy filter is mapped to all incoming web requests. The filter name specified by the <filter-name> element carries a special significance in the context of DelegatingFilterProxy filter. DelegatingFilterProxy filter delegates request processing to the Spring bean whose name matches the value of <filter-name> element. In the above example listing, web requests received by the DelegatingFilterProxy filter are delegated to the Spring bean named springSecurityFilterChain in the *root* application context. We'll soon see that the springSecurityFilterChain bean is created by the Spring Security framework.

Now that we have configured the DelegatingFilterProxy filter, let's look at how to configure web request security.

Configuring web request security

The following example listing shows the application context file that uses <http> element of security schema to configure web request security:

Example listing 16-2 – applicationContext-security.xml – web security configuration
Project – ch16-bankapp-simple-security
Source location - src/main/resources/META-INF/spring

```
<beans:beans xmlns="http://www.springframework.org/schema/security"
    xmlns:beans="http://www.springframework.org/schema/beans"
    xsi:schemaLocation=".....
       http://www.springframework.org/schema/security
           http://www.springframework.org/schema/security/spring-security.xsd">

    <http>
        <intercept-url  pattern="/**" access="hasAnyRole('ROLE_CUSTOMER', 'ROLE_ADMIN')" />
        <form-login />
        <logout />
        <remember-me />
        <headers>
            <cache-control/>
            <xss-protection/>
        </headers>
    </http>
    .....
</beans:beans>
```

The above example listing shows that the spring-security.xsd schema is referenced by the application context XML file. The spring-security.xsd schema is contained in the org.springframework.security.config package of spring-security-config-4.1.0.RELEASE.jar file.

The <http> element contains the web request security configuration for the application. Spring Security framework parses the <http> element and registers a bean named springSecurityFilterChain with the Spring container. The springSecurityFilterChain bean is responsible for handling web request security. The DelegatingFilterProxy filter that we configured earlier (refer example listing 16-1) delegates web request handling to the springSecurityFilterChain bean. The springSecurityFilterChain bean represents an instance of FilterChainProxy bean (refer Spring Security docs for more information) that contains a chain of Servlet filters that are added to the chain by the sub-elements of <http> element.

The <intercept-url> element's access attribute specifies a Spring EL expression that evaluates to a boolean value. If the Spring EL expression returns true, the URLs matched by the pattern attribute are accessible to the user. If the Spring EL expression returns false, access is denied to the URLs matched by the pattern attribute. Spring Security framework provides a couple of built-in expressions, like hasRole, hasAnyRole, isAnonymous, and so on.

In example listing 16-2, the hasAnyRole('ROLE_CUSTOMER', 'ROLE_ADMIN') expression returns true if the authenticated user has ROLE_CUSTOMER or ROLE_ADMIN role. In MyBank web application, the ROLE_CUSTOMER role is assigned to a customer and the ROLE_ADMIN role is assigned to an administrator. As the pattern /*

matches all URLs, the `<intercept-url>` element in example listing 16-2 specifies that only a user with role `ROLE_CUSTOMER` or `ROLE_ADMIN` can access the MyBank web application.

The `<form-login>` element configures a login page that is used to authenticate users. You can use various attributes of `<form-login>` element, like `login-page`, `default-target-url`, and so on, to customize the login page. The `login-page` attribute specifies the URL that is used to render the login page. If the `login-page` attribute is not specified, a login page is automatically rendered at the `/login` URL.

The `<logout>` element configures the logout processing feature of Spring Security framework. You can use various attributes of `<logout>` element, like `logout-url`, `delete-cookies`, `invalidate-session`, and so on, to configure the logout functionality. For instance, you can use the `delete-cookies` attribute to specify comma-separated names of cookies that should be deleted when the user logs out of the application. The `logout-url` attribute allows you to configure the URL that performs the logout processing. If you don't specify the `logout-url` attribute, the `logout-url` attribute value is set to `/logout` by default.

The `<remember-me>` element configures the 'remember-me' authentication in which the web application remembers the identity of the authenticated user between sessions. When a user is successfully authenticated, Spring Security framework generates a unique token that can either be stored in a persistent store or sent to the user in a cookie. In example listing 16-2, `<remember-me>` element configures a cookie-based remember-me authentication service. When the user revisits the web application, the token is retrieved from the cookie and is automatically authenticated.

The `<headers>` element specifies the security headers that are added to the HTTP response by the Spring Security framework. For instance, in example listing 16-2, the `<cache-control>` element adds `Cache-Control`, `Pragma` and `Expires` response headers, and the `<xss-protection>` element adds `X-XSS-Protection` header.

When an unauthenticated user accesses the MyBank web application, Spring Security displays the login page (refer figure 16-1) configured by the `<form-login>` element to the user. Let's now look at how authentication is performed when the user enters his credentials and clicks the `Login` button.

Authentication configuration

When a user enters his credentials and submits the login page, Spring Security's `AuthenticationManager` is responsible for processing the authentication request. An `AuthenticationManager` is configured with one or more `AuthenticationProvider`s against which the `AuthenticationManager` attempts to authenticate users. For instance, if you want to authenticate users against an LDAP server, you can configure an `LdapAuthenticationProvider` (an implementation of `AuthenticationProvider`) that authenticates users against an LDAP server.

The `security` schema simplifies configuration of `AuthenticationManager` and `AuthenticationProvider` objects, as shown in the following example listing:

Example listing 16-3 – applicationContext-security.xml
Project – ch16-bankapp-simple-security
Source location - src/main/resources/META-INF/spring

```
<authentication-manager>
    <authentication-provider>
        <password-encoder hash="bcrypt" />
        <user-service>
            <user name="admin" password="<bcrypt-encoded-pwd>"
                      authorities="ROLE_ADMIN" />
            <user name="cust1" password="<bcrypt-encoded pwd>"
                       authorities="ROLE_CUSTOMER" />
```

```
            <user name="cust2" password="<bcrypt-encoded pwd>"
                        authorities="ROLE_CUSTOMER" />
        </user-service>
    </authentication-provider>
</authentication-manager>
```

The <authentication-manager> element configures an AuthenticationManager instance. The <authentication-provider> element configures an AuthenticationProvider instance. By default, the <authentication-provider> element configures a DaoAuthenticationProvider (an implementation of AuthenticationProvider) that uses Spring's UserDetailsService as a DAO to load user details.

DaoAuthenticationProvider uses the configured UserDetailsService to load user details from the user repository based on the supplied username. DaoAuthenticationProvider performs authentication by comparing the login credentials supplied by the user with the user details loaded by the configured UserDetailsService. You should note that a UserDetailsService may load user details from a data source, a flat file or any other user repository.

The <password-encoder> element specifies the password encoder that is used by the AuthenticationProvider for converting the submitted passwords to their hashed form. The <password-encoder> element's hash attribute specifies the encoding strategy. The hash attribute value is "bcrypt", which means that BCrypt hashing function is used for password encoding.

The <user-service> sub-element of <authentication-provider> configures an *in-memory* UserDetailsService that loads users defined by the <user> elements. In example listing 16-3, the <user-service> element defines that the application has three users: admin (ROLE_ADMIN role), cust1 (ROLE_CUSTOMER role) and cust2 (ROLE_CUSTOMER role). The name attribute specifies the username assigned to the user, the password attribute specifies the *encoded* password assigned to the user, and authorities attribute specifies the role(s) assigned to the user. For the sake of simplicity, the password assigned to a user is same as the user's username. For instance, if cust1 is the username then the corresponding password is also cust1.

> ch16-bankapp-simple-security project contains a PwdEncoder utility class (in package password.encoder) that you can use to convert any plain-text password into its BCrypt hash version. We've used PwdEncoder to encode passwords for cust1, cust2 and admin users, and pasted them as the value of <user> element's password attribute.

Now, if you deploy the ch16-bankapp-simple-security project and access it by going to the http://localhost:8080/ch16-bankapp-simple-security URL, the login page (refer figure 16-1) of the web application is displayed. If you authenticate by entering username as cust1 and password as cust1, the web application will display fixed deposits associated with cust1 (refer figure 16-2) user. Similarly, if you login with username as cust2 and password as cust2, the web application will display fixed deposits associated with cust2 user. If you login with username as admin and password as admin, the web application will display fixed deposits of both cust1 and cust2 users.

Let's now look at how to use Spring Security's JSP tag library to access security information and to apply security constraints on the content displayed by JSP pages.

Securing JSP content using Spring Security's JSP tab library

One of the requirements of MyBank web application is that the option to edit a fixed deposit (refer figure 16-2) is available only to users with role ROLE_CUSTOMER. And, the option to close a fixed deposit (refer figure 16-3) is available only to users with role ROLE_ADMIN. As we need to secure Edit and Close hyperlinks based on the authenticated user's role, the MyBank web application uses Spring Security's JSP tag library to secure JSP content.

The following example listing shows usage of Spring Security's JSP tag library to access authenticated user's username, and to secure JSP content based on the role of the logged in user:

Example listing 16-4 – fixedDepositList.jsp
Project – ch16-bankapp-simple-security
Source location - src/main/webapp/WEB-INF/jsp

```
<%@ taglib uri="http://www.springframework.org/security/tags" prefix="security"%>
.....
<body>
    <form id="logoutForm" method="POST" action="${pageContext.request.contextPath}/logout">
        <security:csrfInput/>
    </form>
    .....
    <td style="font-family: 'arial'; font-size: 12px; font-weight: bold" align="right">
        <input type="button" class="button" value="Logout"
             onclick="document.getElementById('logoutForm').submit();"/>
        <p>
            Username: <security:authentication property="principal.username" />
        </p>
    </td>
    .....
    <td class="td">
        <security:authorize access="hasRole('ROLE_CUSTOMER')">
           <a href="${pageContext.request.contextPath}/fixedDeposit?....." >Edit</a>
        </security:authorize>
        <security:authorize access="hasRole('ROLE_ADMIN')">
           <a href="${pageContext.request.contextPath}/fixedDeposit.....">Close</a>
        </security:authorize>
    </td>
</body>
</html>
```

The above example listing shows that clicking the Logout button (which is displayed as a hyperlink using button CSS class) submits the logoutForm form to ${pageContext.request.contextPath}/**logout** URL. As mentioned earlier, if you don't specify the logout-url attribute of <logout> element, the logout-url value is set to /logout. So, when a user clicks the Logout button, the user is logged out of the MyBank web application.

It might look a little odd to you that we are submitting the logoutForm when the Logout button is clicked. If CSRF (Cross Site Request Forgery) protection is enabled, Spring Security requires that logout occurs only using HTTP POST request. As CSRF protection is enabled by default, you need to send an HTTP POST request to /logout URL to logout a user. For this reason, the logoutForm is submitted to /logout URL when the Logout button is clicked. As CSRF token is required when sending PATCH, POST, PUT and DELETE requests, we need to send CSRF token along with the POST request to /logout URL. This is achieved by using <csrfInput> tag of Spring Security's JSP tag library (included via taglib directive) . The <csrfInput> tag adds a CSRF token to the logoutForm, as shown here:

```
<input type="hidden" name="_csrf" value="1dfa0939-982f-4efb-9f13-9d19210bb078" />
```

Spring Security's Authentication object contains information about the authenticated user. For instance, it contains information about authenticated user's role(s) and username that the user used for authentication. The <authentication> tag prints the specified property of the Authentication object. In the above example listing, the principal.username property refers to the username property of the authenticated user.

The <authorize> tag secures the enclosed JSP content based on the result of evaluation of the security expression specified by the access attribute. If the security expression evaluates to true, the enclosed content is rendered, otherwise the enclosed content is not rendered. In the above example listing, the hasRole('ROLE_CUSTOMER') expression returns true if the authenticated user has ROLE_CUSTOMER role, and the hasRole('ROLE_ADMIN') expression returns true if the authenticated user has ROLE_ADMIN role. In the above example listing, the hasRole expression has been used such that the Edit option is displayed only to a user with ROLE_CUSTOMER role and the Close option is displayed only to a user with ROLE_ADMIN role.

Let's now look at how to incorporate method-level security using Spring Security.

Securing methods

One of the requirements of MyBank application is that a user with ROLE_ADMIN role can view the 'Create new Fixed Deposit' button (refer figure 16-3) but an attempt to save details of the new fixed deposit will result in a security exception. This is an example in which we want to secure the FixedDepositService's saveFixedDeposit method such that only a user with ROLE_CUSTOMER role can invoke it.

We also want to secure other methods of the FixedDepositService so that it is not invoked by unauthorized users. For instance, cust1 user logged in with ROLE_CUSTOMER can invoke the FixedDepositService's closeFixedDeposit method to close an existing fixed deposit by entering the following URL in the browser:

```
http://localhost:8080/ch16-bankapp-simple-security/fixedDeposit?fdAction=close
     &fixedDepositId=<fixed-deposit-id>
```

The <fixed-deposit-id> in the above URL is the id of the fixed deposit that you want to close, as highlighted in the following figure:

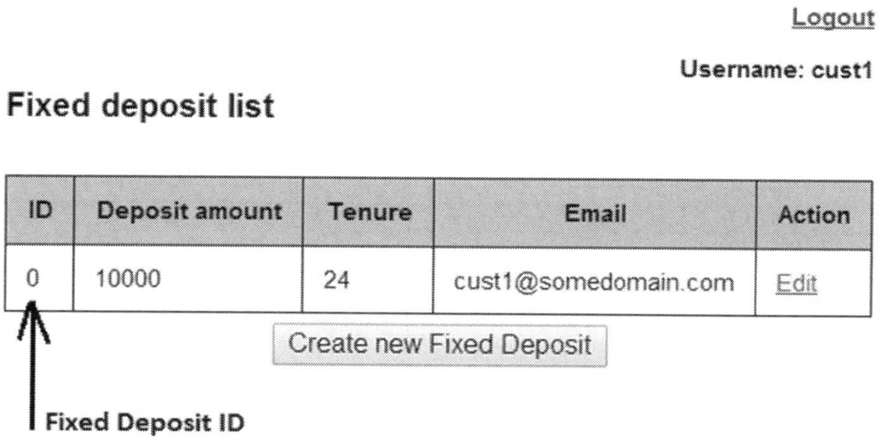

Logout

Username: cust1

Fixed deposit list

ID	Deposit amount	Tenure	Email	Action
0	10000	24	cust1@somedomain.com	Edit

Create new Fixed Deposit

Fixed Deposit ID

Figure 16-4 – Fixed deposit ID of a fixed deposit is displayed in the ID column

As only a user with role ROLE_ADMIN is allowed to close a fixed deposit, the FixedDepositService's closeFixedDeposit method must *not* be invoked if a user with role ROLE_CUSTOMER enters the above URL in the web browser.

To add method-level security to your application, you need to do the following:

- configure method-level security for your application by using <global-method-security> element of security schema
- add @Secured annotations to the methods that you want to secure against unauthorized access

Let's first look at the <global-method-security> element.

Configuring method-level security using <global-method-security> element

The following example listing shows usage of <global-method-security> element:

Example listing 16-5 – applicationContext-security.xml
Project – ch16-bankapp-simple-security
Source location - src/main/resources/META-INF/spring

```
<beans:beans xmlns="http://www.springframework.org/schema/security" .....>
    .....
    <global-method-security secured-annotations="enabled" />
</beans:beans>
```

The <global-method-security> element configures method-level security. The <global-method-security> element is applicable only to the application context in which it is defined. For instance, if the <global-method-security> element is defined in the *root* web application context XML file, then it is applicable only to the beans registered with the root WebApplicationContext instance. In ch16-bankapp-simple-security project, the applicationContext-security.xml (shown in the above example listing) and the applicationContext.xml (that defines services and DAOs) files constitute the root web application context XML files (refer web.xml file of ch16-bankapp-simple-security project); therefore, the <global-method-security> element applies only to the beans defined in these application context XML files.

The <global-method-security> element's secured-annotations attribute specifies whether the use of Spring's @Secured annotation should be enabled or disabled for the beans registered with the Spring container. As the value is set to enabled, you can use Spring's @Secured annotation to specify the bean methods that are secured.

If you want to secure controller methods, then define the <global-method-security> element in the web application context XML file instead of the root web application context XML file.

Let's now look at how to secure methods using Spring's @Secured annotation.

Specifying security constraints on bean methods using @Secured annotation

The following example listing shows usage of Spring's @Secured annotation to define security constraints on methods:

Example listing 16-6 – FixedDepositService interface
Project – ch16-bankapp-simple-security
Source location - src/main/java/sample/spring/chapter16/service

```
package sample.spring.chapter16.service;

import org.springframework.security.access.annotation.Secured;
.....
public interface FixedDepositService {
    .....
    @Secured("ROLE_CUSTOMER")
    void saveFixedDeposit(FixedDepositDetails fixedDepositDetails);
    .....
    @Secured("ROLE_ADMIN")
    void closeFixedDeposit(int fixedDepositId);

    @Secured("ROLE_CUSTOMER")
    void editFixedDeposit(FixedDepositDetails fixedDepositDetails);
}
```

The above example listing shows the `FixedDepositService` interface that defines methods that operate on fixed deposits. `@Secured("ROLE_CUSTOMER")` annotation on the `saveFixedDeposit` and `editFixedDeposit` methods specifies that these methods can only be invoked by a user whose role is `ROLE_CUSTOMER`. `@Secured("ROLE_ADMIN")` annotation on the `closeFixedDeposit` method specifies that the method can only be invoked by a user whose role is `ROLE_ADMIN`.

> By default, method-level security is based on Spring AOP. If you want to use AspectJ instead of Spring AOP, set `mode` attribute of `<global-method-security>` element to `aspectj`. Also, add `spring-security-aspects` Spring module to your project, and specify `@Secured` annotations on the class instead of the interface.

Instead of using `@Secured` annotation, you can use Spring's `@PreAuthorize` annotation to apply security constraints on methods. Unlike `@Secured` annotation, `@PreAuthorize` annotation accepts security expressions, like `hasRole`, `hasAnyRole`, and so on. To enable use of `@PreAuthorize` annotation, set `pre-post-annotations` attribute of `<global-method-security>` element to `enabled`. The following example listing shows usage of `@PreAuthorize` annotation:

Example listing 16-6 – `@PreAuthorize` annotation

```
import org.springframework.security.access.prepost.PreAuthorize;
.....
public interface SomeService {
    .....
    @PreAuthorize("hasRole('ROLE_XYZ')")
    void doSomething(.....);
    .....
}
```

In the above example listing, `@PreAuthorize` annotation specifies that the `doSomething` method is accessible only to users with role `ROLE_XYZ`.

Spring Security also supports security annotations, like `@RolesAllowed`, `@DenyAll`, `@PermitAll`, and so on, defined by JSR-250 – Common Annotations. To enable use of JSR-250 security annotations, set `jsr250-annotations` attribute of `<global-method-security>` to `enabled`. The following example listing shows usage of `@RolesAllowed` annotation:

Example listing 16-7 – `@RolesAllowed` annotation

```
import javax.annotation.security.RolesAllowed;
.....
public interface SomeService {
    .....
    @RolesAllowed("ROLE_XYZ")
    void doSomething(.....);
    .....
}
```

In the above example listing, `@RolesAllowed` annotation specifies that the `doSomething` method is accessible only to users with role `ROLE_XYZ`.

> To use `@RolesAllowed`, `@PermitAll`, and so on, security annotations defined by JSR 250, you need to include `jsr250-api` JAR file in your project.

In this section, we looked at how to use Spring Security to authenticate users, secure web requests and implement method-level security. Let's now look at Spring Security's ACL module for securing domain object instances.

IMPORT **chapter 16/ch16-bankapp-db-security** (This project represents the MyBank web application that uses Spring Security's ACL module for securing FixedDepositDetails instances.)

16-4 MyBank web application - securing FixedDepositDetails instances using Spring Security's ACL module

The ch16-bankapp-db-security project represents a variant of MyBank web application that uses Spring Security's ACL module to secure FixedDepositDetails instances.

Let's look at how to deploy and use ch16-bankapp-db-security project.

Deploying and using ch16-bankapp-db-security project

The ch16-bankapp-db-security project uses MySQL database to store application users, fixed deposit details and ACL information. Before deploying the ch16-bankapp-db-security project, create a database named securitydb in MySQL and execute the bankapp.sql script located in scripts folder of ch16-bankapp-db-security project. Also, change the src/main/resources/META-INF/database.properties file to point to your MySQL installation.

The execution of bankapp.sql script creates the following tables: ACL_CLASS, ACL_ENTRY, ACL_OBJECT_IDENTITY, ACL_SID, FIXED_DEPOSIT_DETAILS, AUTHORITIES, and USERS. Tables whose names begin with ACL_ store ACL related information (more on these tables later in this chapter). FIXED_DEPOSIT_DETAILS table contains fixed deposit details. USERS and AUTHORITIES tables contain user and role information, respectively. The bankapp.sql script also inserts setup data into USERS, AUTHORITIES, ACL_CLASS and ACL_SID tables.

Now that you have setup the database for ch16-bankapp-db-security project, deploy the project on Tomcat 9 server (refer appendix B for more information on how to deploy web projects on Tomcat 9 server). Once the project is successfully deployed, go to http://localhost:8080/ch16-bankapp-db-security URL. You should see the login page, as shown below:

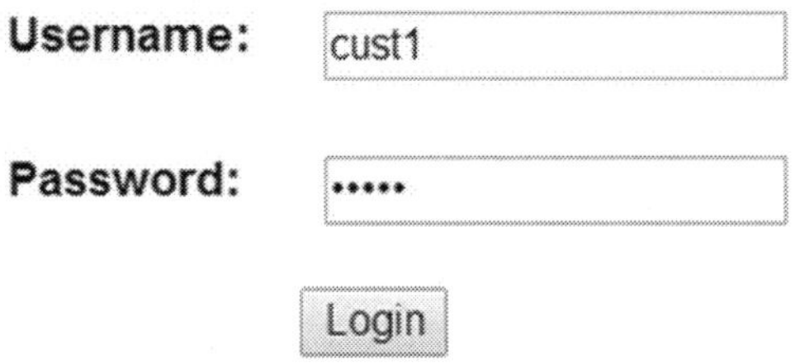

Username: cust1

Password: •••••

Login

Figure 16-5 – Login page of MyBank web application

By default, the following three users are configured for the MyBank web application: cust1 (ROLE_CUSTOMER role), cust2 (ROLE_CUSTOMER role), and admin (ROLE_ADMIN role). When you login with username cust1 and password as cust1, you'll see the fixed deposits associated with cust1 customer, as shown in the following figure:

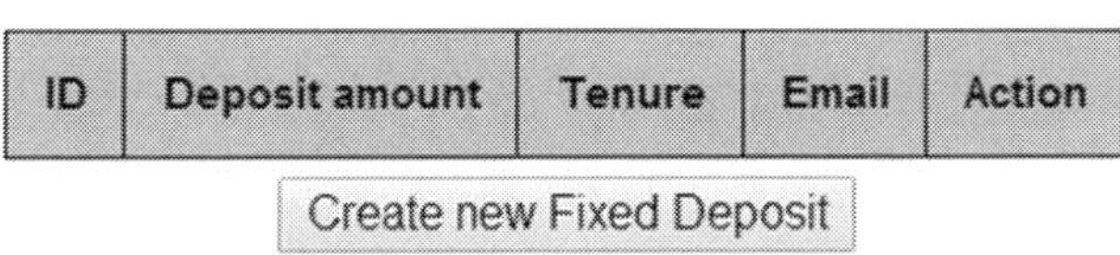

Figure 16-6 – List of fixed deposits associated with customer `cust1`

As no fixed deposits are currently associated with cust1, the above figure shows an empty list of fixed deposits. Clicking the 'Create new Fixed Deposit' button opens the form for creating a new fixed deposit. If you create a new fixed deposit, it'll appear in the list of fixed deposits, as shown here:

Logout

Username: cust1

Fixed deposit list

ID	Deposit amount	Tenure	Email	Action
14	1200	12	cust1@somedomain.com	Edit Provide access to admin

Create new Fixed Deposit

Figure 16-7 – A customer can edit fixed deposits or make them accessible to the admin user.

In the above figure, the 'Edit' option allows the customer to edit fixed deposit details, and the 'Provide access to admin' option makes the fixed deposit accessible to the admin user. The admin user can only view fixed deposits that are made accessible by customers. Click the 'Provide access to admin' hyperlink to make the fixed deposit accessible to the admin user.

Now, logout from the MyBank web application, and login using admin username and admin as password. The admin user can view all the fixed deposits that were made accessible by customers, as shown here:

Logout

Username: admin

Fixed deposit list

ID	Customer	Deposit amount	Tenure	Email	Action
14	cust1	1200	12	cust1@somedomain.com	Close

Create new Fixed Deposit

Figure 16-8 – The admin user can close a fixed deposit by selecting the 'Close' option

The above figure shows that the admin user can choose the 'Close' option to close the fixed deposit. Closing a fixed deposit deletes the fixed deposit from the FIXED_DEPOSIT_DETAILS table.

To summarize, you can login using cust1/cust1, cust2/cust2 and admin/admin credentials to see the following features of the MyBank web application:

- only cust1 (ROLE_CUSTOMER role) and cust2 (ROLE_CUSTOMER role) users can create fixed deposits
- cust1 and cust2 can only edit fixed deposits that they own. For instance, cust1 can't edit a fixed deposit created by cust2.
- cust1 and cust2 can make only their own fixed deposits accessible to the admin user. For instance, cust1 can't make a fixed deposit created by cust2 accessible to the admin user.
- admin user (ROLE_ADMIN role) can only view fixed deposits that are made accessible by cust1 and cust2 users
- only the admin user can close fixed deposits

Before delving into the implementation details of MyBank web application, let's look at the standard database tables required by Spring Security to store ACL and user information.

Database tables to store ACL and user information

Spring Security's ACL module provides domain object instance security. MyBank web application uses Spring Security's ACL module to secure instances of FixedDepositDetails. Spring Security tables (ACL_CLASS, ACL_ENTRY, ACL_OBJECT_IDENTITY and ACL_SID) contain permissions that apply to fixed deposits stored in the FIXED_DEPOSIT_DETAILS table. When a FixedDepositDetails instance is accessed, Spring Security's ACL module verifies that the authenticated user has the necessary permissions to operate on the FixedDepositDetails instance.

Let's look at each of the Spring Security tables that are used to store ACL information.

ACL_CLASS table

ACL_CLASS table contains fully-qualified name of domain classes whose instances we want to secure in our application. In the case of MyBank web application, the ACL_CLASS table contains the fully-qualified name of the FixedDepositDetails class, as shown here:

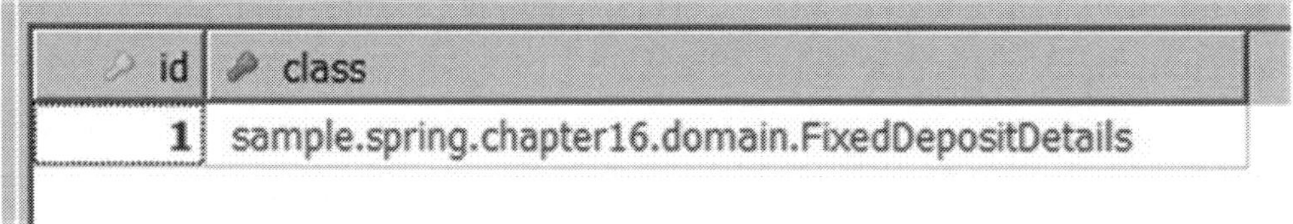

id	class
1	sample.spring.chapter16.domain.FixedDepositDetails

Figure 16-9 ACL_CLASS table

Table column description

id – contains the primary key

class – fully-qualified name of the domain class whose instances we want to secure

ACL_SID table

ACL_SID table (SID means 'security identity') contains the principals (that is, usernames) or authorities (that is, roles) in the system. In the case of MyBank web application, ACL_SID table contains admin, cust1 and cust2 usernames, as shown here:

id	principal	sid
1	true	cust1
2	true	cus
3	true	adr

Figure 14-10 ACL_SID table

Table column description

id – contains the primary key

principal – specifies whether the sid column stores role or username. The value true specifies that the sid column stores username. The value false specifies that the sid column stores role.

sid – contains username or role

ACL_OBJECT_IDENTITY table

ACL_OBJECT_IDENTITY table contains identities of domain objects that we want to secure. In the case of MyBank web application, the ACL_OBJECT_IDENTITY table contains identities of fixed deposits stored in FIXED_DEPOSIT_DETAILS table, as shown here:

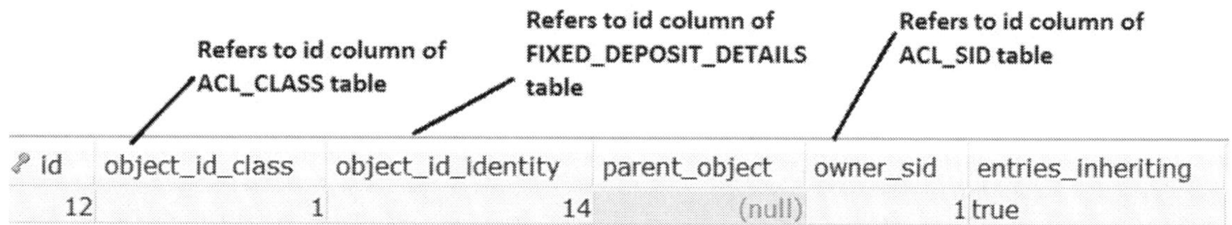

id	object_id_class	object_id_identity	parent_object	owner_sid	entries_inheriting
12	1	14	(null)	1	true

Figure 16-11 ACL_OBJECT_IDENTITY table

In the above figure, the object_id_identity column contains identities of fixed deposits stored in the FIXED_DEPOSIT_DETAILS table.

Table column description

id – contains the primary key

object_id_class – refers to the domain class defined in the ACL_CLASS table

object_id_identity – refers to the domain object instance stored in the FIXED_DEPOSIT_DETAILS table

parent_object – if a parent object exists for the domain object referenced by the object_id_identity column, this column refers to the identity of the parent object

owner_sid – refers to the user or role that owns the domain object instance

entries_inheriting – flag that indicates whether the object inherits ACL entries from any parent ACL entry or not

ACL_ENTRY table

ACL_ENTRY table contains permissions (read, write, create, and so on) assigned to users on domain objects. In the case of MyBank web application, the ACL_ENTRY table contains permissions assigned to users on fixed deposits stored in the FIXED_DEPOSIT_DETAILS table, as shown here:

Refers to id column of ACL_OBJECT_IDENTITY table

Refers to id column of ACL_SID table

Specifies the permission (read, write, and so on) assigned to the user

id	acl_object_identity	ace_order	sid	mask	granting	audit_success	audit_failure
768	12	0	1	1	true	false	false
769	12	1	1	2	true	false	false
770	12	2	3	1	true	false	false
771	12	3	3	16	true	false	false
772	12	4	3	8	true	false	false

Figure 16-12 ACL_ENTRY table

In the above figure, the acl_object_identity, mask and sid columns determine the permissions assigned to a user (or role) on a domain object instance. You should note that an entry in the ACL_ENTRY table is commonly referred to as ACE (**A**ccess **C**ontrol **E**ntry).

Table column description

id – contains the primary key

acl_object_identity – refers to the id column of the ACL_OBJECT_IDENTITY table, which in turn identifies the domain object instance

ace_order – specifies the ordering of the access control entries

sid – refers to the id column of ACL_SID table, which in turn identifies the user (or role)

mask – specifies the permissions (read, write, create, and so on) assigned to the user (or role). 1 means read, 2 means write, 8 means delete and 16 means administration permission.

granting – flag that indicates whether the entry in the mask column identifies as granting access or denying access. For instance, if the value in the mask column is 1 and granting column is true, it means that the corresponding SID has read access. But, if the value in the mask column is 1 and granting column is false, it means that the corresponding SID *doesn't* have read access.

audit_success – flag that indicates whether to audit successful permissions or not. Later in this chapter, we'll see that Spring Security's ConsoleAuditLogger can be used to log successful permissions.

audit_failure - flag that indicates whether to audit failed permissions or not. Later in this chapter, we'll see that Spring Security's ConsoleAuditLogger can be used to log failed permissions.

Figure 16-13 summarizes relationship between ACL tables. The arrows in the figure represent foreign key references from a table. For instance, the ACL_OBJECT_IDENTITY table contains foreign keys that refer to ACL_CLASS, ACL_SID and FIXED_DEPOSIT_DETAILS tables.

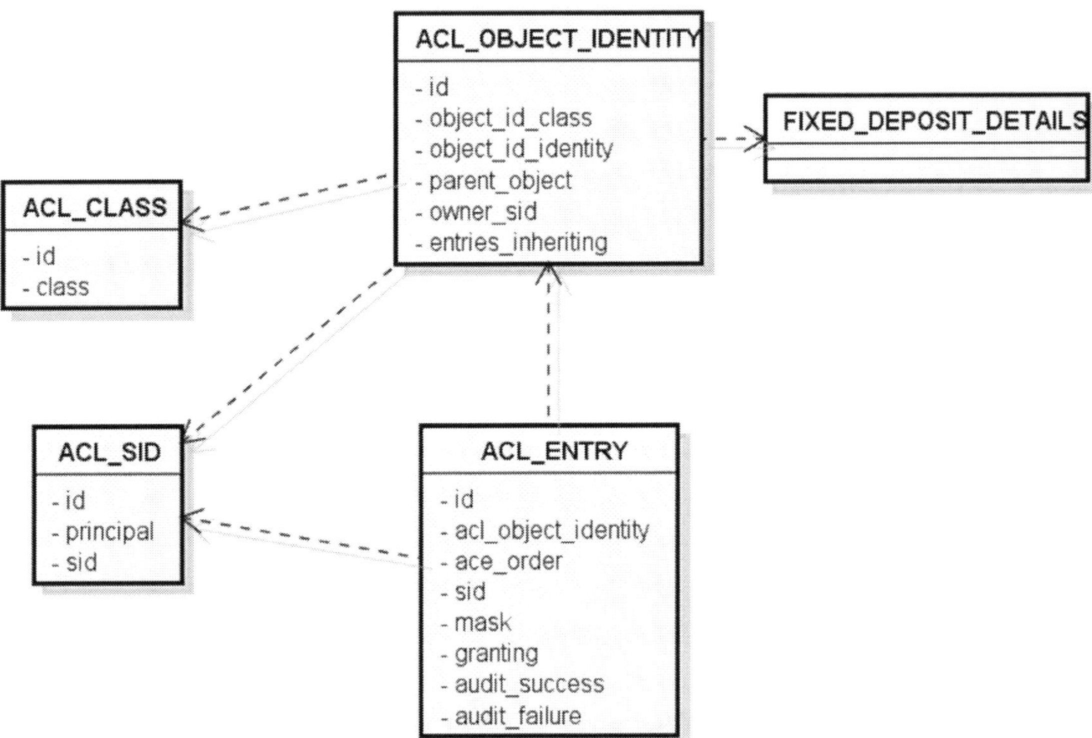

Figure 16-13 ACL tables and their relationships. The arrows represent foreign key references from a table.

Now that we have seen the ACL tables required to store ACL information, let's now look at the Spring Security tables that store users and their roles information.

USERS table

USERS table stores credentials of users, as shown here:

username	password	enabled
admin	admin	true
cust1	cust1	true
cust2	cust2	true

Figure 16-14 USERS table

Table column description

username – username of the user

password – the *encoded* password of the user

enabled – flag that indicates whether the user is enabled or disabled

AUTHORITIES table

AUTHORITIES table contains the role assigned to each user defined in the USERS table

Table column description

username – username of the user

authority – role assigned to the user

username	authority
admin	ROLE_ADMIN
cust1	ROLE_CUSTOMER
cust2	ROLE_CUSTOMER

Figure 16-15 AUTHORITIES table

Let's now look at how the users are authenticated in MyBank web application.

User authentication

MyBank web application explicitly configures the UserDetailsService to load user details from the USERS and AUTHORITIES database tables, as shown in the following example listing:

Example listing 16-8 – applicationContext-security.xml
Project – ch16-bankapp-db-security
Source location - src/main/resources/META-INF/spring

```
<authentication-manager>
    <authentication-provider user-service-ref="userDetailsService">
        <password-encoder hash="bcrypt"/>
    </authentication-provider>
</authentication-manager>

<beans:bean id="userDetailsService"
            class="org.springframework.security.core.userdetails.jdbc.JdbcDaoImpl">
    <beans:property name="dataSource" ref="dataSource" />
</beans:bean>
```

In the above example listing, the user-service-ref attribute of <authentication-provider> element refers to an implementation of UserDetailsService that is responsible for loading user (and their authorities) details based on the supplied username. JdbcDaoImpl is an implementation of UserDetailsService that loads user (and their authorities) details from the data source (specified by the dataSource property) using JDBC queries. Refer to the applicationContext.xml file of ch16-bankapp-db-security project to view the dataSource bean definition. By default, JdbcDaoImpl loads user details from the USERS (refer figure 16-14) table and authorities information from the AUTHORITIES (refer figure 16-15) table. If you already have custom database tables that contain user and authorities details, then set the usersByUsernameQuery and authoritiesByUsernameQuery properties of JdbcDaoImpl to retrieve user details and their authorities from these custom tables.

The usersByUsernameQuery property specifies the SQL query to retrieve user details based on the given username. If user details are stored in a table named MY_USERS that contains USERNAME and PASSWORD columns, you can set the following SQL query as the value of usersByUsernameQuery property to retrieve user details:

```
select USERNAME, PASSWORD, 'true' as ENABLED from MY_USERS where USERNAME = ?
```

You should note that the columns returned by the SQL query must be USERNAME, PASSWORD and ENABLED. If a particular column (like, ENABLED) doesn't exist in your database table, then return a default value (like, 'true') for that column.

The authoritiesByUsernameQuery property specifies the SQL query to retrieve authorities based on the given username. If authority details are stored in a table named MY_ AUTHORITIES that contains USER and

ROLE columns, you can set the following SQL query as the value of authoritiesByUsernameQuery property to retrieve authorities:

```
select USER AS USERNAME, ROLE AS AUTHORITY from MY_AUTHORITIES where USER = ?
```

You should note that the columns returned by the SQL query must be USERNAME and AUTHORITY.

As our application stores encoded passwords in the database, the <password-encoder> sub-element of <authentication-provider> element (refer listing 16-8) is used to specify the password encoder (an implementation of Spring's PasswordEncoder interface) to be used to convert the submitted passwords into their encoded form. BCryptPasswordEncoder is a concrete implementation of PasswordEncoder that uses BCrypt hashing algorithm (http://en.wikipedia.org/wiki/Bcrypt). AuthenticationProvider uses the configured password encoder to encode the submitted password and compare it with the password loaded by the UserDetailsService.

Let's now look at the web request security configuration in the MyBank web application.

Web request security

The following example listing shows how web request security is configured for the MyBank web application:

Example listing 16-9 – applicationContext-security.xml – web security configuration
Project – ch16-bankapp-db-security
Source location - src/main/resources/META-INF/spring

```
<http>
    <access-denied-handler error-page="/access-denied" />
    <intercept-url pattern="/fixedDeposit/*"
                   access="hasAnyRole('ROLE_CUSTOMER', 'ROLE_ADMIN')" />
    <form-login login-page="/login"
                authentication-failure-handler-ref="authFailureHandler" />
    <logout />
    ....
</http>

<beans:bean id="authFailureHandler"
        class="sample.spring.chapter16.security.MyAuthFailureHandler" />
```

If you compare the web request security configuration shown above with the one we saw in ch16-bankapp-simple-security project (refer example listing 16-2), you'll notice that we have added some additional configuration information.

The <access-denied-handler> element's error-page attribute specifies the error page (refer to scr/main/webapp/WEB-INF/jsp/access-denied.jsp page) to which an authenticated user is redirected in case the user attempts to access an unauthorized web page. The <form-login> element's login-page attribute specifies the URL that renders the login page. The value /login URL is mapped to LoginController (refer to LoginController class of ch16-bankapp-db-security project) that renders the login page (refer to scr/main/webapp/WEB-INF/jsp/login.jsp page). The authentication-failure-handler-ref attribute refers to an AuthenticationFailureHandler bean that handles authentication failures. As the above example listing shows, MyAuthFailureHandler (an implementation of AuthenticationFailureHandler) is responsible for handling authentication failures in MyBank web application. The following example listing shows the implementation of MyAuthFailureHandler class:

Example listing 16-10 – MyAuthFailureHandler class
Project – ch16-bankapp-db-security
Source location - src/main/java/sample/spring/chatper16/security

```
package sample.spring.chapter16.security;
.....
import org.springframework.security.core.AuthenticationException;
import org.springframework.security.web.authentication.AuthenticationFailureHandler;

public class MyAuthFailureHandler implements AuthenticationFailureHandler {

    @Override
    public void onAuthenticationFailure(HttpServletRequest request,
                HttpServletResponse response, AuthenticationException exception)
                throws IOException, ServletException {
        request.setAttribute("exceptionMsg", exception.getMessage());
        response.sendRedirect(request.getContextPath() + "/login?exceptionMsg=" +
            exception.getMessage());
    }
}
```

AuthenticationFailureHandler interface defines an onAuthenticationFailure method which is invoked when authentication fails. The onAuthenticationFailure method accepts an instance of AuthenticationException that represents an authentication failure. In the above example listing, the onAuthenticationFailure method redirects the user to the login page and passes the exception message as a query string parameter. If you enter wrong credentials (or enter credentials of a user who is disabled in the system) on the login page of MyBank web application, you'll notice that the MyAuthFailureHandler's onAuthenticationFailure method is invoked. For instance, if you enter wrong credentials, you'll see the message 'Bad credentials'.

Let's now look at ACL-specific configuration in MyBank web application.

JdbcMutableAclService configuration

As ACL permissions are stored in database tables, the MyBank web application uses Spring's JdbcMutableAclService to perform CRUD (**C**reate **R**ead **U**pdate **D**elete) operations on ACLs in the tables. The following example listing shows the configuration of JdbcMutableAclService:

Example listing 16-11 – applicationContext-security.xml – JdbcMutableAclService configuration
Project – ch16-bankapp-db-security
Source location - src/main/resources/META-INF/spring

```
<beans:bean id="aclService"
        class="org.springframework.security.acls.jdbc.JdbcMutableAclService">
    <beans:constructor-arg ref="dataSource" />
    <beans:constructor-arg ref="lookupStrategy" />
    <beans:constructor-arg ref="aclCache" />
</beans:bean>
```

The above example listing shows references to dataSource, lookupStrategy and aclCache beans are passed to the JdbcMutableAclService's constructor. Let's now look at how dependencies (dataSource, lookupStrategy and aclCache) of JdbcMutableAclService are configured.

The dataSource bean identifies the javax.sql.DataSource that holds the ACL tables (refer to the dataSource bean definition in the applicationContext.xml file for more details).

The lookupStrategy bean represents an implementation of Spring's LookupStrategy interface that is responsible for looking up ACL information. The following example listing shows the lookupStrategy bean definition:

Example listing 16-12 – applicationContext-security.xml – LookupStrategy configuration
Project – ch16-bankapp-db-security
Source location - src/main/resources/META-INF/spring

```
<beans:bean id="lookupStrategy"
    class="org.springframework.security.acls.jdbc.BasicLookupStrategy">

    <beans:constructor-arg ref="dataSource" />
    <beans:constructor-arg ref="aclCache" />
    <beans:constructor-arg ref="aclAuthorizationStrategy" />
    <beans:constructor-arg ref="permissionGrantingStrategy" />
</beans:bean>

<beans:bean id="aclAuthorizationStrategy"
        class="org.springframework.security.acls.domain.AclAuthorizationStrategyImpl">
    <beans:constructor-arg>
        <beans:bean
            class="org.springframework.security.core.authority.SimpleGrantedAuthority">
            <beans:constructor-arg value="ROLE_CUSTOMER" />
        </beans:bean>
    </beans:constructor-arg>
</beans:bean>

<beans:bean id="permissionGrantingStrategy"
        class="org.springframework.security.acls.domain.DefaultPermissionGrantingStrategy">
    <beans:constructor-arg>
        <beans:bean
            class="org.springframework.security.acls.domain.ConsoleAuditLogger" />
    </beans:constructor-arg>
</beans:bean>
```

In the above example listing, Spring's BasicLookupStrategy (an implementation of LookupStrategy interface) uses JDBC queries to fetch ACL details from standard ACL tables (ACL_CLASS, ACL_ENTRY, ACL_SID and ACL_OBJECT_IDENTITY). If the ACL information is stored in custom database tables, then you can customize the JDBC queries by setting selectClause, lookupPrimaryKeysWhereClause, lookupObjectIdentitiesWhereClause and orderByClause properties of BasicLookupStrategy. For more details on these properties, please refer to the API documentation of Spring Security.

BasicLookupStrategy's constructor accepts arguments of types DataSource (represents the database that contains the ACL tables), AclCache (represents the ACL caching layer), AclAuthorizationStrategy (represents the strategy to determine if a SID has the permissions to perform administrative actions on the ACL entries of a domain object instance), and PermissionGrantingStrategy (strategy to grant or deny access to secured objects depending on the permissions assigned to SIDs).

In the above example listing, the AclAuthorizationStrategyImpl class implements AclAuthorizationStrategy. The AclAuthorizationStrategyImpl's constructor accepts an instance of GrantedAuthority that specifies the role that can perform administrative actions (like, changing ownership of an ACL entry) on the ACL entries (represented by an object of type MutableAcl) of a domain object instance. In the above example listing, ROLE_ADMIN role is passed to the AclAuthorizationStrategyImpl, which means that a user with ROLE_ADMIN role can perform administrative actions on ACL entries. Later in this chapter, we'll see that the AclAuthorizationStrategy secures the MutableAcl instance from unauthorized modification.

In the above example listing, the DefaultPermissionGrantingStrategy implements PermissionGrantingStrategy. The DefaultPermissionGrantingStrategy's constructor accepts an instance of AuditLogger that logs success and/or failure in granting permissions for an ACL entry in the ACL_ENTRY table. In the above example listing, the ConsoleAuditLogger (an implementation of AuditLogger that writes on the console) logs successful permissions if audit_success column's value is set to true (that is, 1), and logs failed permissions if audit_failure column's value is set to true (that is, 1). For instance, the following message shows output from the ConsoleAuditLogger on successful permission to an ACL entry:

```
GRANTED due to ACE: AccessControlEntryImpl[id: 1037; granting: true; sid:
PrincipalSid[cust1]; permission: BasePermission[..............................R=1];
auditSuccess: true; auditFailure: true]
```

BasicLookupStrategy accepts an instance of AclCache object (represented by the aclCache bean in example listing 16-12) that represents a cache for ACLs. The following example listing shows the aclCache bean definition that is used by BasicLookupStrategy to cache ACLs:

Example listing 16-13 – applicationContext-security.xml – Cache configuration
Project – ch16-bankapp-db-security
Source location - src/main/resources/META-INF/spring

```
<beans:bean id="aclCache"
          class="org.springframework.security.acls.domain.EhCacheBasedAclCache">
    <beans:constructor-arg>
        <beans:bean class="org.springframework.cache.ehcache.EhCacheFactoryBean">
            <beans:property name="cacheManager">
                <beans:bean
                     class="org.springframework.cache.ehcache.EhCacheManagerFactoryBean" />
            </beans:property>
            <beans:property name="cacheName" value="aclCache" />
        </beans:bean>
    </beans:constructor-arg>
    <beans:constructor-arg ref="aclAuthorizationStrategy" />
    <beans:constructor-arg ref="permissionGrantingStrategy" />
</beans:bean>
```

EhCacheBasedAclCache is an implementation of AclCache that uses EhCache (http://ehcache.org/) for caching ACLs. EhCacheFactoryBean is an implementation of Spring's FactoryBean that creates an instance of net.sf.ehcache.EhCache. The cacheManager property of EhCacheFactoryBean specifies the net.sf.ehcache.CacheManager instance that is responsible for managing the cache. In the above example listing, EhCacheManagerFactoryBean is an implementation of Spring's FactoryBean that creates an instance of net.sf.ehcache.CacheManager. The EhCacheFactoryBean's cacheName property refers to the cache region to be created in EhCache for storing ACLs. Notice that the EhCacheBasedAclCache accepts the same AclAuthorizationStrategy and PermissionGrantingStrategy instances that were passed to BasicLookupStrategy bean.

Now that we have configured JdbcMutableAclService to perform CRUD operations on ACLs, let's look at the method-level security configuration that uses ACLs loaded by JdbcMutableAclService for authorization purposes.

Method-level security configuration

The following example listing shows method-level security configuration in the MyBank web application:

Example listing 16-14 – applicationContext-security.xml – Method-level security configuration
Project – ch16-bankapp-db-security
Source location - src/main/resources/META-INF/spring

```
<global-method-security pre-post-annotations="enabled">
    <expression-handler ref="expressionHandler" />
</global-method-security>
```

The `<global-method-security>` element's `pre-post-annotations` attribute value is set to enabled, which enables use of `@PreAuthorize` (explained earlier in this chapter), `@PostAuthorize`, `@PostFilter` and `@PostAuthorize` annotations. In the above example listing, the `<expression-handler>` element refers to the `expressionHandler` bean that configures a `SecurityExpressionHandler` instance.

A `SecurityExpressionHandler` is used by Spring Security to evaluate security expressions, like `hasRole`, `hasAnyRole`, `hasPermission`, and so on. The following example listing shows the `expressionHandler` bean definition that configures a `DefaultMethodSecurityExpressionHandler` (a `SecurityExpressionHandler` implementation) instance:

Example listing 16-15 – applicationContext-security.xml – SecurityExpressionHandler configuration
Project – ch16-bankapp-db-security
Source location - src/main/resources/META-INF/spring

```
<beans:bean id="expressionHandler"
        class="org.springframework.security.access.expression.method.
            DefaultMethodSecurityExpressionHandler">
    <beans:property name="permissionEvaluator" ref="permissionEvaluator" />
    <beans:property name="permissionCacheOptimizer">
        <beans:bean class="org.springframework.security.acls.AclPermissionCacheOptimizer">
            <beans:constructor-arg ref="aclService" />
        </beans:bean>
    </beans:property>
</beans:bean>

<beans:bean id="permissionEvaluator"
        class="org.springframework.security.acls.AclPermissionEvaluator">
    <beans:constructor-arg ref="aclService" />
</beans:bean>
```

In the above example listing, the `permissionEvaluator` property refers to an instance of `AclPermissionEvaluator` instance that uses ACLs to evaluate security expressions. The `permissionCacheOptimzer` property refers to an instance of `AclPermissionCacheOptimizer` that loads ACLs in batches to optimize performance.

Let's now look at how domain object instance security is achieved in the MyBank web application.

Domain object instance security

We saw earlier that the `@PreAuthorize` annotation specifies role-based security constraints on the methods. If a `@PreAuthorize` annotated method accepts a domain object instance as an argument, the `@PreAuthorize` annotation can specify the ACL permissions that the authenticated user must have on the domain object instance to invoke the method. The following example listing shows the `@PreAuthorize` annotation that specifies ACL permissions:

Example listing 16-16 – FixedDepositService interface – @PreAuthorize annotation with ACL permissions
Project – ch16-bankapp-db-security
Source location - src/main/java/sample/spring/chatper16/service

```
package sample.spring.chapter16.service;
```

```
import org.springframework.security.access.prepost.PreAuthorize;
import sample.spring.chapter16.domain.FixedDepositDetails;
.....
public interface FixedDepositService {
    .....
    @PreAuthorize("hasPermission(#fixedDepositDetails, write)")
    void editFixedDeposit(FixedDepositDetails fixedDepositDetails);
}
```

In the above example listing, the FixedDepositService's editFixedDeposit method accepts an instance of FixedDepositDetails. In the hasPermission expression, #fixedDepositDetails represents an expression variable that refers to the FixedDepositDetails instance passed to the editFixedDeposit method. The hasPermission expression evaluates to true if the authenticated user has write permission on the FixedDepositDetails instance passed to the editFixedDeposit method. At runtime, the hasPermission expression is evaluated by the configured AclPermissionEvaluator (refer example listing 16-15). If the hasPermission evaluates to true, the editFixedDeposit method is invoked.

If a method accepts a domain object *identifier* (instead of the actual domain object instance) as an argument, you can still specify ACL permissions that apply to the domain object instance referred by the identifier. The following example listing shows the provideAccessToAdmin method that accepts fixedDepositId (which uniquely identifies a FixedDepositDetails instance) as argument:

Example listing 16-17 – FixedDepositService interface – @PreAuthorize annotation usage
Project – ch16-bankapp-db-security
Source location - src/main/java/sample/spring/chatper16/service

```
package sample.spring.chapter16.service;

import org.springframework.security.access.prepost.PreAuthorize;
.....
public interface FixedDepositService {
    .....
    @PreAuthorize("hasPermission(#fixedDepositId,
                'sample.spring.chapter16.domain.FixedDepositDetails', write)")
    void provideAccessToAdmin(int fixedDepositId);
}
```

In the above example listing, #fixedDepositId expression variable refers to the fixedDepositId argument passed to the provideAccessToAdmin method. As the fixedDepositId argument identifies an instance of FixedDepositDetails object, the fully-qualified name of the FixedDepositDetails class is specified as the second argument of hasPermission expression. The hasPermission(#fixedDepositId, 'sample.spring.chapter16.domain.FixedDepositDetails', write) evaluates to true if the authenticated user has write permission on the FixedDepositDetails instance identified by the fixedDepositId argument passed to the provideAccessToAdmin method.

It is also possible to combine multiple security expressions to form a more complex security expression, as shown in the following example listing:

Example listing 16-18 – FixedDepositService interface – @PreAuthorize annotation usage
Project – ch16-bankapp-db-security
Source location - src/main/java/sample/spring/chatper16/service

```
package sample.spring.chapter16.service;

import org.springframework.security.access.prepost.PreAuthorize;
.....
public interface FixedDepositService {
```

```
    .....
    @PreAuthorize("hasPermission(#fixedDepositId,
           'sample.spring.chapter16.domain.FixedDepositDetails', read) or "
            + "hasPermission(#fixedDepositId,
           'sample.spring.chapter16.domain.FixedDepositDetails', admin)")
    FixedDepositDetails getFixedDeposit(int fixedDepositId);
    .....
}
```

In the above example listing, the two `hasPermission` expressions have been combined using or operator to form a more sophisticated security expression. The `getFixedDeposit` method will be invoked only if the authenticated user has `read` or `admin` permission on the `FixedDepositDetails` instance identified by the `fixedDepositId` argument.

If a method returns a list of domain object instances, you can filter the results by using `@PostFilter` annotation. The following example listing shows usage of `@PostFilter` annotation:

Example listing 16-19 – FixedDepositService interface – `@PostFilter` annotation usage
Project – ch16-bankapp-db-security
Source location - src/main/java/sample/spring/chatper16/service

```
package sample.spring.chapter16.service;

import org.springframework.security.access.prepost.PostFilter;
.....
public interface FixedDepositService {
    .....
    @PreAuthorize("hasRole('ROLE_ADMIN')")
    @PostFilter("hasPermission(filterObject, read) or hasPermission(filterObject, admin)")
    List<FixedDepositDetails> getAllFixedDeposits();
    .....
}
```

Like `@PreAuthorize` annotation, `@PostFilter` specifies a security expression. If a method is annotated with `@PostFilter` annotation, Spring Security iterates over the collection returned by the method and removes the elements for which the specified security expression returns `false`. In the above example listing, Spring Security iterates over the collection of `FixedDepositDetails` instances returned by the `getAllFixedDeposits` method and removes the instances for which the authenticated user doesn't have `read` or `admin` permission. The term `filterObject` in the `hasPermission` expression of `@PostFilter` annotation refers to the current object in the collection. Notice that the `getAllFixedDeposits` method is also annotated with `@PreAuthorize` annotation, which indicates that the `getAllFixedDeposits` method is only invoked if the authenticated user has `ROLE_ADMIN` role.

We saw earlier that a customer (`ROLE_CUSTOMER` role) makes a fixed deposit available to the `admin` user (`ROLE_ADMIN` role) by clicking the '`Provide access to admin`' hyperlink (refer figure 16-7). When the customer clicks the '`Provide access to admin`', application grants `read`, `admin` and `delete` permissions on the fixed deposit to the `admin` user. We'll see later in this chapter how this is done programmatically. The `FixedDepositService`'s `getAllFixedDeposits` method is invoked when a user with `ROLE_ADMIN` role visits the web page that shows lists of fixed deposits (refer figure 16-8). As the `admin` user should only be able to see fixed deposits for which customers have granted permissions, the `getAllFixedDeposits` method is annotated with `@PostFilter` annotation to remove fixed deposits on which the `admin` user doesn't have `read` or `admin` permission.

Let's now look at how to programmatically manage ACL entries.

Managing ACL entries programmatically

You can manage ACL entries programmatically by using the JdbcMutableAclService that was configured in the application context XML file (refer example listing 16-11).

When a customer creates a new fixed deposit, read and write permissions on the newly created fixed deposit are granted to the customer. When a customer clicks the 'Provide access to admin' hyperlink corresponding to a fixed deposit, the MyBank web application grants read, admin and delete permissions on the fixed deposit to the admin user.

The following example listing shows the FixedDepositServiceImpl's provideAccessToAdmin method that is invoked when the 'Provide access to admin' hyperlink is clicked:

Example listing 16-20 – FixedDepositServiceImpl class – adding ACL permissions
Project – ch16-bankapp-db-security
Source location - src/main/java/sample/spring/chatper16/service

```
package sample.spring.chapter16.service;

import org.springframework.security.acls.domain.*;
import org.springframework.security.acls.model.*;
.....
@Service
public class FixedDepositServiceImpl implements FixedDepositService {
    .....
    @Autowired
    private MutableAclService mutableAclService;

    @Override
    public void provideAccessToAdmin(int fixedDepositId) {
        addPermission(fixedDepositId, new PrincipalSid("admin"), BasePermission.READ);
        addPermission(fixedDepositId, new PrincipalSid("admin"),
                    BasePermission.ADMINISTRATION);
        addPermission(fixedDepositId, new PrincipalSid("admin"), BasePermission.DELETE);
    }

    private void addPermission(long fixedDepositId, Sid recipient, Permission permission) {
        .....
    }
}
```

In the above example listing, the provideAccessToAdmin method uses the addPermission method to grant read, admin and delete permissions to the admin user. The following arguments are passed to the addPermission method:

- fixedDepositId – uniquely identifies the FixedDepositDetails instance on whom we want to grant permissions
- PrincipalSid object - represents the SID (that is, the user or role) whom we want to grant permissions. The PrincipalSid class implements Spring Security's Sid interface.
- permission to grant – The BasePermission class defines constants, like READ, ADMINISTRATION, DELETE, and so on, representing standard permissions that we can grant to PrincipalSid. The BasePermission class implements Spring Security's Permission interface.

The following example listing shows the implementation of addPermission method:

Example listing 16-21 – FixedDepositServiceImpl class – adding ACL permissions
Project – ch16-bankapp-db-security
Source location - src/main/java/sample/spring/chatper16/service

```
package sample.spring.chapter16.service;

import org.springframework.security.acls.domain.*;
import org.springframework.security.acls.model.*;
.....
@Service
public class FixedDepositServiceImpl implements FixedDepositService {
    .....
    @Autowired
    private MutableAclService mutableAclService;
    .....
    private void addPermission(long fixedDepositId, Sid recipient, Permission permission) {
        MutableAcl acl;
        ObjectIdentity oid =
            new ObjectIdentityImpl(FixedDepositDetails.class, fixedDepositId);

        try {
            acl = (MutableAcl) mutableAclService.readAclById(oid);
        } catch (NotFoundException nfe) {
            acl = mutableAclService.createAcl(oid);
        }
        acl.insertAce(acl.getEntries().size(), permission, recipient, true);
        mutableAclService.updateAcl(acl);
    }
    .....
}
```

As JdbcMutableAclService class implements MutableAclService interface, JdbcMutableAclService instance is autowired into the FixedDepositServiceImpl class.

To grant permissions, the addPermission method follows these steps:

1) declares an object of type MutableAcl. A MutableAcl object represents ACL entries of a domain object instance. MutableAcl defines methods that you can use to modify ACL entries.

2) creates an instance of ObjectIdentityImpl by passing domain object type (which is FixedDepositDetails.class) and identity (which is fixedDepositId) as arguments to the constructor

3) retrieves the ACL entries for the domain object instance by calling MutableAclService's readAclById method. If no ACL entries are found, the readAclById method throws NotFoundException.

    - If NotFoundException is thrown, MutableAclService's createAcl method is used to create an empty instance of MutableAcl that doesn't contain any ACL entries. This is equivalent to creating an entry in the ACL_OBJECT_IDENTITY table (refer figure 16-11).

4) adds ACL entries to the MutableAcl instance using insertAce method. The ACL entries added to MutableAcl are eventually persisted into the ACL_ENTRY table (refer figure 16-12). The arguments passed to the insertAce method are - the index location where the ACL entry is to be added (corresponds to the ACE_ORDER column), the permission to be added (corresponds to the MASK column), the SID for whom the permission is to be added (corresponds to the SID column), and the flag indicating that the ACL entry is for granting or denying permission (corresponds to the GRANTING column).

5) persists changes made to the MutableAcl instance using MutableAclService's updateAcl method.

The following example listing shows FixedDepositServiceImpl's closeFixedDeposit method that is invoked when the admin user clicks the 'Close' hyperlink to close a fixed deposit (refer figure 16-8):

Example listing 16-22 – FixedDepositServiceImpl class – removing ACLs
Project – ch16-bankapp-db-security
Source location - src/main/java/sample/spring/chatper16/service

```
package sample.spring.chapter16.service;

import org.springframework.security.acls.domain.ObjectIdentityImpl;
import org.springframework.security.acls.model.MutableAclService;
import org.springframework.security.acls.model.ObjectIdentity;
.....
@Service
public class FixedDepositServiceImpl implements FixedDepositService {
    .....
    @Autowired
    private MutableAclService mutableAclService;
    .....
    @Override
    public void closeFixedDeposit(int fixedDepositId) {
        fixedDepositDao.closeFixedDeposit(fixedDepositId);
        ObjectIdentity oid =
              new ObjectIdentityImpl(FixedDepositDetails.class, fixedDepositId);
        mutableAclService.deleteAcl(oid, false);
    }
    .....
}
```

In the above example listing, MutableAclService's deleteAcl method is used to delete ACL entries of the fixed deposit identified by the ObjectIdentity instance. For instance, if the fixedDepositId is 101, deleteAcl method deletes all ACL entries of fixed deposit 101 from ACL_ENTRY (refer figure 16-12) and ACL_OBJECT_IDENTITY (refer figure 16-11) tables.

Let's now look at how MutableAcl instance is secured from unauthorized modifications.

MutableAcl and security

Spring Security's MutableAcl interface defines methods for modifying ACL entries of a domain object instance. We saw that the MyBank web application uses MutableAcl's insertAce method to add an ACL entry for a domain object instance (refer example listing 16-21). The AclAuthorizationStrategyImpl instance that we supplied to the BasicLookupStrategy (refer example listing 16-12) is used behind the scenes to ensure that the authenticated user has appropriate permissions to modify ACL entries.

An authenticated user can modify ACL entries of a domain object instance if at least one of the following conditions is true:

- if the authenticated user owns the domain object instance, the user can modify the ACL entries of that domain object instance
- if the authenticated user holds the authority that was passed to AclAuthorizationStrategyImpl's constructor. In example listing 16-12, the ROLE_ADMIN role was passed to AclAuthorizationStrategyImpl's constructor; therefore, a user with ROLE_ADMIN role can make changes to ACL entries of any domain object instance.

- if the authenticated user has BasePermission's ADMINISTRATION permission on the domain object instance.

Let's now look at how you can use Java-based configuration approach to configure Spring Security for your web application.

16-5 Configuring Spring Security using Java-based configuration approach

To configure Spring Security for your web application using Java-based configuration approach, you need to do the following:

- create an @Configuration annotated class that extends Spring Security's WebSecurityConfigurerAdapter class. This class is responsible for configuring the web request security.
- create an @Configuration annotated class that extends Spring Security's GlobalMethodSecurityConfiguration class. This class is responsible for configuring method-level security.
- create a class that extends Spring Security's AbstractSecurityWebApplicationInitializer class. This class is responsible for registering Spring's DelegatingFilterProxy filter (named springSecurityFilterChain) with the ServletContext.
- create a class that extends Spring's AbstractAnnotationConfigDispatcherServletInitializer class. This class is responsible for registering a DispatcherServlet and a ContextLoaderListener with the ServletContext.

IMPORT **chapter 16/ch16-javaconfig-simple-security** (This project is a modified version of ch16-bankapp-simple-security project that uses Java-based configuration approach to configure Spring Security.)

Let's look at each of the classes mentioned above in the context of ch16-javaconfig-simple-security project.

Configuring web request security using WebSecurityConfigurerAdapter class

The following example listing shows the @Configuration annotated WebRequestSecurityConfig class that extends WebSecurityConfigurerAdapter class to configure web request security:

Example listing 16-23 – WebRequestSecurityConfig class – configuring web request security
Project – ch16-javaconfig-simple-security
Source location - src/main/java/sample/spring/chatper16

```
package sample.spring.chapter16;

import org.springframework.security.config.annotation.web.builders.HttpSecurity;
import org.springframework.security.config.annotation.web.configuration.EnableWebSecurity;
import org.springframework.security.config.annotation.web.configuration
        .WebSecurityConfigurerAdapter;
.....
@Configuration
@EnableWebSecurity
public class WebRequestSecurityConfig extends WebSecurityConfigurerAdapter {

    protected void configure(HttpSecurity http) throws Exception {
        http.authorizeRequests().antMatchers("/**")
```

```
            .hasAnyAuthority("ROLE_CUSTOMER", "ROLE_ADMIN").and()
            .formLogin().and().logout().and().rememberMe().and().headers()
            .cacheControl().and().xssProtection();
    }

    protected void configure(AuthenticationManagerBuilder auth) throws Exception {
        auth.inMemoryAuthentication()
            .passwordEncoder(new BCryptPasswordEncoder())
            .withUser("admin").password(<bcrypt-encoded-password>)
            .authorities("ROLE_ADMIN").and().withUser("cust1")
            .password(<bcrypt-encoded-password>).authorities("ROLE_CUSTOMER").and()
            .withUser("cust2").password(<bcrypt-encoded-password>)
            .authorities("ROLE_CUSTOMER");
    }

    @Bean
    @Override
    public AuthenticationManager authenticationManagerBean() throws Exception {
        return super.authenticationManagerBean();
    }
}
```

WebRequestSecurityConfig class is annotated with @EnableWebSecurity annotation, which is required for any class that extends WebSecurityConfigurerAdapter class. The WebSecurityConfigurerAdapter class defines methods that you can override to configure web request security. In the above example listing, the configure(HttpSecurity http) method serves the same purpose as the <http> element of security schema. The code http.authorizeRequests().antMatchers("/**"). hasAnyAuthority("ROLE_CUSTOMER","ROLE_ADMIN") specifies that URLs matched by antMatchers method are accessible only to users with role ROLE_CUSTOMER or ROLE_ADMIN. The and method is provided so that we can use method chaining approach to configure web security. The formLogin method serves the same purpose as <form-login>, rememberMe method serves the same purpose as <remember-me>, and so on. The configure(HttpSecurity http) method in the above example listing has the same effect as the <http> element used in the applicationContext-security.xml file of ch16-bankapp-simple-security project.

The configure(AuthenticationManagerBuilder auth) method is used to configure the AuthenticationManager for the application. This method serves the same purpose as the <authentication-manager> element of security schema. AuthenticationManagerBuilder's inMemoryAuthentication method configures in-memory authentication based on the specified users. The configure(AuthenticationManagerBuilder auth) method in the above example listing has the same effect as the <authentication-manager> element used in the applicationContext-security.xml file of ch16-bankapp-simple-security project.

You must also override the authenticationManagerBean method to expose the AuthenticationManager configured by AuthenticationManagerBuilder as a Spring bean. The call to super.authenticationManagerBean method returns the AuthenticationManager instance that we configured in the configure(AuthenticationManagerBuilder auth) method.

Configuring method-level security using GlobalMethodSecurityConfiguration class

The following example listing shows the @Configuration annotated MethodSecurityConfig class that extends GlobalMethodSecurityConfiguration class to configure method-level security:

Example listing 16-24 – MethodSecurityConfig class – configuring method-level security
Project – ch16-javaconfig-simple-security
Source location - src/main/java/sample/spring/chatper16

```
package sample.spring.chapter16;

import org.springframework.security.config.annotation.method.configuration.*;

@EnableGlobalMethodSecurity(securedEnabled = true)
public class MethodSecurityConfig extends GlobalMethodSecurityConfiguration  { }
```

MethodSecurityConfig class is annotated with @EnableGlobalMethodSecurity annotation, which is required for any class that extends GlobalMethodSecurityConfiguration class. The securedEnabled attribute specifies whether @Secured annotation is enabled or not. As the securedEnabled attribute's value is set to true, @Secured annotation is enabled. You can override protected methods defined in the GlobalMethodSecurityConfiguration to further customize method-level security configuration. MethodSecurityConfig class in the above example listing has the same effect as the <global-security-element> element used in the applicationContext-security.xml file of ch16-bankapp-simple-security project.

Registering DelegatingFilterProxy filter with ServletContext

The following example listing shows the SecurityWebApplicationInitializer class that extends Spring Security's AbstractSecurityWebApplicationInitializer class (an implementation of Spring's WebApplicationInitializer) to programmatically register DelegatingFilterProxy filter with the ServletContext:

Example listing 16-25 – SecurityWebApplicationInitializer class – registering DelegatingFilterProxy filter
Project – ch16-javaconfig-simple-security
Source location - src/main/java/sample/spring/chatper16

```
package sample.spring.chapter16;

import org.springframework.security.web.context.AbstractSecurityWebApplicationInitializer;

public class SecurityWebApplicationInitializer extends
AbstractSecurityWebApplicationInitializer { }
```

SecurityWebApplicationInitializer registers DelegatingFilterProxy filter with ServletContext with name springSecurityFilterChain.

Registering DispatcherServlet and ContextLoaderListener with ServletContext

We saw in section 13-7 of chapter 13 that AbstractAnnotationConfigDispatcherServletInitializer (an implementation of Spring's WebApplicationInitializer) is used to programmatically register DispatcherServlet and ContextLoaderListener with the ServletContext. The following example listing shows the BankInitializer class that extends AbstractAnnotationConfigDispatcherServletInitializer class:

Example listing 16-26 – BankInitializer – registering DispatcherServlet and ContextLoaderListener
Project – ch16-javaconfig-simple-security
Source location - src/main/java/sample/spring/chatper16

```
package sample.spring.chapter16;
.....
```

```
public class BankAppInitializer extends
        AbstractAnnotationConfigDispatcherServletInitializer {

    @Override
    protected Class<?>[] getRootConfigClasses() {
        return new Class[] {
                  RootContextConfig.class, WebRequestSecurityConfig.class,
                  MethodSecurityConfig.class
        };
    }

    @Override
    protected Class<?>[] getServletConfigClasses() {
        return new Class[] { WebContextConfig.class };
    }

    @Override
    protected String[] getServletMappings() {
        return new String[] { "/" };
    }
}
```

As Spring Security related beans are registered with the root web application context, the `getRootConigClasses` method returns `WebRequestSecurityConfig` (refer example listing 16-23) and `MethodSecurityConfig` (refer example listing 16-24) classes along with `RootContextConfig` (that defines DAOs and Services) class.

This is all you need to do to configure Spring Security using Java-based configuration approach.

16-6 Summary

In this chapter, we looked at how to use Spring Security framework to secure Spring applications. We looked at how to incorporate web request security, method-level security, and domain object instance security. In the next chapter, we'll look at Java constructs that support *functional* style of programming.

Chapter 17 – *Functional programming with Java*

17-1 Introduction

Java 8 added support for *functional* style of programming in the Java programming language. In this chapter, we'll look at the new language constructs and features in Java 8 that support functional style of programming. This chapter sets the stage for the next chapter on *reactive* programming.

This chapter covers:

- imperative vs functional style of programming
- lambda expressions
- higher-order functions
- `Stream` API
- method references

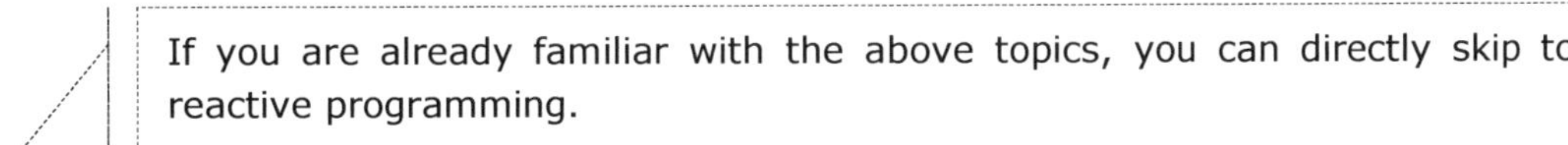

If you are already familiar with the above topics, you can directly skip to the next chapter on reactive programming.

Let's begin by looking at how imperative style of programming is different from functional style.

17-2 Imperative vs functional style

Prior to Java 8 release, the Java programming language supported only the *imperative* style of programming. A program written in the imperative style has the following characteristics:

- the program is written as a sequence of instructions that *must* be executed in a particular order
- the program instructions typically change (or read) *mutable* variables
- the program not only tells 'what' to do but *also* 'how' to do things to solve a problem

Java 8 introduced language constructs (like lambda expressions, method references, and so on) and features (like `Stream` API) that support *functional* style of programming. A program that follows the functional style has the following characteristics:

- the program is written as a set of *functions* such that each function solves a part of the problem
- the functions don't change (or read) *mutable* variables
- the program uses functions to tell 'what' to do to solve a problem. This makes programs written in the functional style more intuitive in nature.

Later in this chapter, we'll look at examples that show how a Java program written in the functional style is different from a Java program written in the imperative style.

Lambda expressions are at the heart of functional style of programming in Java. Let's look at what lambda expressions are and how they simplify writing Java programs.

17-3 Lambda expressions

Java 8 introduced the concept of *functional interfaces* – interfaces that define a *single* abstract method. A functional interface may define multiple static and default methods but they must define only one abstract method. For instance, java.lang.Runnable interface defines a single abstract method run; therefore, java.lang.Runnable interface is an example of a functional interface. Similarly, java.util.concurrent.Callable is a functional interface because it defines a single abstract method call.

A lambda expression represents an *anonymous function* that can be passed to a method that accepts a functional interface type. For instance, you can pass lambda expression to a method that accepts a java.lang.Runnable or java.util.concurrent.Callable type or any other functional interface type.

The syntax of a lambda expression is:

```
(<arg1>, <arg2>, ...) -> { <method-body> }
```

here, *<arg1>*, *<arg2>*, and so on, refer to the arguments accepted by the abstract method of the functional interface, and *<method-body>* is the implementation of the abstract method

IMPORT **chapter 17/ch17-lambdas** (This project contains examples that show how lambda expressions simplify writing Java programs)

The following example listing shows the Sample class that executes a Callable task:

Example listing 17-1 Sample – executing a Callable task
Project – ch17-lambdas
Source location - src/main/java/sample/lambdas

```
package sample.lambdas;

import java.util.concurrent.*;

public class Sample {
    public static void main(String args[]) throws Exception {
      System.out.println(executeTask().get());
    }

    private static Future<String> executeTask() throws Exception {
        ExecutorService executorService = Executors.newSingleThreadExecutor();

        Future<String> future = executorService.submit(new Callable<String>() {
            public String call() throws Exception {
                return "did something successfully";
            }
        });
        return future;
    }
}
```

Sample's executeTask method passes an anonymous implementation of Callable interface to ExecutorService's submit method. Notice that Callable's call method doesn't accept any arguments and it contains a single statement: return "did something successfully".

The following example listing shows a variant of Sample class that passes a lambda expression (instead of an anonymous implementation of Callable interface) to ExecutorService's submit method:

Example listing 17-2 SampleWithLambda – executing a Callable task
Project – ch17-lambdas
Source location - src/main/java/sample/lambdas

```
package sample.lambdas;

import java.util.concurrent.*;

public class SampleWithLambda {
    .....
    private static Future<String> executeTask() throws Exception {
        ExecutorService executorService = Executors.newSingleThreadExecutor();

        Future<String> future = executorService.submit(() -> {
            return "did something successfully";
        });
        return future;
    }
}
```

The above listing shows that the following lambda expression is passed to ExecutorService's service method:

```
    () -> { return "did something successfully"; }
```

As Callable's call method doesn't accept any arguments, empty brackets () have been used. And, the call method's body is specified within opening { and closing } braces. This shows that using lambda expressions results in a more concise program.

If the body of a lambda expression consists of a single statement, you can remove the braces and replace the return statement with an expression. The following listing shows a more simplified SampleWithLambda class:

Example listing 17-3 SampleWithLambda – a more simplified lambda expression

```
package sample.lambdas;

import java.util.concurrent.*;

public class SampleWithLambda {
    .....
    private static Future<String> executeTask() throws Exception {
        ExecutorService executorService = Executors.newSingleThreadExecutor();
        Future<String> future = executorService.submit(() ->
            "did something successfully"
        );
        return future;
    }
}
```

In the above listing, the lambda expression is simply:

```
    () -> "did something successfully"
```

We've removed braces and replaced the return "did something successfully" statement with the expression "did something successfully". When you replace the return statement with an expression, the Java compiler infers the return type from the type of expression.

The following example listing shows SortCars class that uses java.util.Comparator (a functional interface) to sort Car objects based on their top speeds:

Example listing 17-4 SortCars – sorting a list of Car objects
Project – ch17-lambdas
Source location - src/main/java/sample/lambdas

```
package sample.lambdas;

import java.util.*;

public class SortCars {
    public static void main(String args[]) {
        List<Car> cars = new ArrayList<Car>();
        cars.add(new Car(10));
        cars.add(new Car(7));
        cars.add(new Car(5));

        cars.sort(new Comparator<Car>() {
            public int compare(Car o1, Car o2) {
                if (o1.getTopSpeed() == o2.getTopSpeed())
                    return 0;
                else if (o1.getTopSpeed() > o2.getTopSpeed())
                    return 1;
                else
                    return -1;
            }
        });
    }
}
```

We first create a List and add Car objects to it. The argument to Car's constructor is the top speed that the car can attain. We pass a Comparator implementation to List's sort method to sort Car objects based on their top speed.

The following example listing shows the SortCarsWithLambda class that passes a lambda expression (instead of a Comparator implementation) to List's sort method to sort Car objects:

Example listing 17-5 SortCarsWithLambda – use lambda expression instead of Comparator
Project – ch17-lambdas
Source location - src/main/java/sample/lambdas

```
package sample.lambdas;

import java.util.*;

public class SortCarsWithLambda {
    public static void main(String args[]) {
        List<Car> cars = new ArrayList<Car>();
        cars.add(new Car(10));
        .....
        cars.sort((Car o1, Car o2) -> {
            if (o1.getTopSpeed() == o2.getTopSpeed())
                return 0;f
            else if (o1.getTopSpeed() > o2.getTopSpeed())
                return 1;
            else
                return -1;
        });
    }
}
```

In the above listing, we pass the following lambda expression to List's sort method:

```
(Car o1, Car o2) -> {
      if (o1.getTopSpeed() == o2.getTopSpeed())
          return 0;
      else if (o1.getTopSpeed() > o2.getTopSpeed())
          return 1;
      else
          return -1;
    }
```

As Comparator's compare method accepts two Car objects for comparison, (Car o1, Car o2) specifies arguments to the compare method. And, the compare method's body is specified between opening { and closing } braces.

As the *type* of a method argument can be inferred by the compiler, we can rewrite the lambda expression as:

```
(o1, o2) -> {
      if (o1.getTopSpeed() == o2.getTopSpeed())
          return 0;
      else if (o1.getTopSpeed() > o2.getTopSpeed())
          return 1;
      else
          return -1;
    }
```

As reading a multiline lambda expression is a bit difficult, we can move the method body to a separate method and call that method from the lambda expression. The following listing shows a more simplified version of SortCarsWithLambda class:

Example listing 17-6 SimplifiedSortCarsWithLambda – a simplified lambda expression
Project – ch17-lambdas
Source location - src/main/java/sample/lambdas

```
package sample.lambdas;

import java.util.ArrayList;
import java.util.List;

public class SimplifiedSortCarsWithLambda {
    public static void main(String args[]) {
        List<Car> cars = new ArrayList<Car>();
        cars.add(new Car(10));
        .....
        cars.sort((o1, o2) -> compareCars(o1, o2));
    }

    private static int compareCars(Car o1, Car o2) {
        if (o1.getTopSpeed() == o2.getTopSpeed())
            return 0;
        .....
    }
}
```

In the above listing, we've defined a separate compareCars method that does the comparison of Car objects. This results in a simplified lambda expression passed to List's sort method:

```
    (o1, o2) -> compareCars(o1, o2)
```

In functional programming, you can create *higher-order functions* - functions that take one or more functions as input parameters or return a function. Let's look at how you can create higher-order functions in Java.

17-4 Creating simple functions and higher-order functions

In the previous section, we saw that we can pass a lambda expression to a method that accepts a functional interface type. This means that we can assign a lambda expression to a functional interface type variable, as shown here:

```
Callable<String> callable = () -> "did something successfully";
```

and,

```
Comparator<Car> comparator = (o1, o2) -> compareCars(o1, o2);
```

The `java.util.function` package defines functional interfaces that help with creating higher-order functions. The following table describes some of these functional interfaces that we'll be using shortly for creating higher-order functions:

Functional interface	Description
Function<T,R>	represents a function that accepts an argument of type T and returns a result of type R
BiFunction<T,U,R>	represents a function that takes arguments of types T and U, and returns a result of type R
Consumer<T>	represents a function that takes an argument of type T and returns nothing
BiConsumer<T,U>	represents a function that takes arguments of types T and U, and returns nothing

Let's first look at an example that shows how the above mentioned functional interfaces are used for creating functions.

IMPORT **chapter 17/ch17-functions** (This project contains examples that show how to write higher-order functions in Java)

Example: Given two `String`s (let's say `prefix` and `suffix`), perform the following operations:

- concatenate `prefix` and `suffix` to create a new `String`
- calculate the hash code of the concatenated `String`
- print the calculated hash code to the output

Let's first look at how to write a program that uses simple functions to perform the above set of operations.

Simple functions

The following example listing shows the `MyFunctions` class that defines simple functions to perform the above mentioned operations:

Example listing 17-7 MyFunctions – creating simple functions
Project – ch17-functions
Source location - src/main/java/sample/higherorder

```
package sample.higherorder;

import java.util.function.*;

public class MyFunctions {
    private static BiFunction<String, String, String> concatFn = (prefix,suffix) ->
            prefix + " " + suffix;

    private static Function<String, Integer> hashFn = input -> input.hashCode();

    private static Consumer<Object> printFn = input -> System.out.println(input);

    public static void main(String args[]) {
        printFn.accept(concatAndHash("Welcome", "Java 8"));
    }

    private static int concatAndHash(String prefix, String suffix) {
        return hashFn.apply(concatFn.apply(prefix, suffix));
    }
}
```

The following functions are defined by MyFunctions class: concatFn, hashFn and printFn. Let's look at each of these functions in detail.

concatFn:

```
    private static BiFunction<String, String, String> concatFn =  (prefix, suffix) ->
            prefix + " " + suffix;
```

As concatFn variable is of type BiFunction<String, String, String>, it means that the concatFn function accepts *two* String type arguments and returns a String type value. concatFn function concatenates prefix and suffix string arguments and returns the concatenated string.

hashFn:

```
    private static Function<String, Integer> hashFn = input -> input.hashCode();
```

As hashFn variable is of type Function<String, Integer>, it means that the hashFn function accepts a String type argument and returns an Integer type value. hashFn function returns the hash code (of type Integer) by calling the hashCode method of the input argument.

printFn:

```
    private static Consumer<Object> printFn = input -> System.out.println(input);
```

As printFn variable is of type Consumer<Object>, it means that the printFn function accepts an Object type argument and returns *nothing*. printFn function uses the System.out.println method to write the value of the argument (identified by input variable) to the output.

Both Function and BiFunction interfaces define an apply method that executes the function for the given argument(s). MyFunctions's concatAndHash method executes both concatFn and hashFn functions by calling their apply methods, as shown here:

```
    private static int concatAndHash(String prefix, String suffix) {
        return hashFn.apply(concatFn.apply(prefix, suffix));
```

```
    }
```

MyFunctions's main method calls the concatAndHash method with arguments "Welcome" (the value of prefix argument) and "Java 8" (the value of suffix argument):

```
    public static void main(String args[]) {
        printFn.accept(concatAndHash("Welcome", "Java 8"));
    }
```

As the value of prefix is "Welcome" and suffix is "Java 8", the following things happen in the concatAndHash method:

- concatFn's apply method concatenates "Welcome" and "Java 8" to return "Welcome Java 8"
- the output of concatFn function is passed to hashFn's apply method. The hashFn function returns the hash code of "Welcome Java 8" string

Consumer interface defines an accept method that executes the function with the given argument. As the hash code returned by the concatAndHash method is passed to printFn's accept method, it simply writes the hash code to the output.

Let's now look at how we could have rewritten the MyFunctions class using higher-order functions.

Higher-order functions

The following example listing shows a modified version of MyFunctions class that uses higher-order functions to write hash code of "Welcome Java 8" string to the output:

Example listing 17-8 MyHigherOrderFunctions – creating higher-order functions
Project – ch17-functions
Source location - src/main/java/sample/higherorder

```
package sample.higherorder;

import java.util.function.*;

public class MyHigherOrderFunctions {
  private static Function<String, Function<String, String>> concatFn =
      prefix -> {
          Function<String, String> addSuffixFn = suffix -> {
             return prefix + " " + suffix;
          };
          return addSuffixFn;
      };

  private static Function<String, Integer> hashFn = input -> input.hashCode();

  private static BiConsumer<String, Function<String, Integer>> hashAndPrintFn =
      (input, hashFn) -> {
           System.out.println(hashFn.apply(input));
      };

  public static void main(String args[]) {
      Function<String, String> prefix = concatFn.apply("Welcome");
      String string = prefix.apply("Java 8");
      hashAndPrintFn.accept(string, hashFn);
  }
}
```

MyHigherOrderFunctions class defines the following functions: concatFn, hashFn and hashAndPrintFn. Let's look at each of these functions in detail.

concatFn:

```
private static Function<String, Function<String, String>> concatFn =
    prefix -> {
        Function<String, String> addSuffixFn = suffix -> {
           return prefix + " " + suffix;
        };
        return addSuffixFn;
    };
```

As concatFn function is of type Function<String, Function<String, String>>, it means that concatFn accepts a String argument and returns a function of type Function<String, String>. The concatFn function uses the prefix argument to build and return addSuffixFn function that accepts a suffix argument. The addSuffixFn concatenates prefix and suffix strings and returns the concatenated string. As concatFn returns another function, it is an example of a higher-order function.

hashFn:

```
private static Function<String, Integer> hashFn = input -> input.hashCode();
```

hashFn takes a String argument and returns its hash code value.

hashAndPrintFn:

```
private static BiConsumer<String, Function<String, Integer>>
    hashAndPrintFn = (input, hashFn) -> {
         System.out.println(hashFn.apply(input));
    };
```

As hashAndPrintFn function is of type BiConsumer<String, Function<String, Integer>>, it means that hashAndPrintFn accepts arguments of types String (the input argument) and Function<String, Integer> (the hashFn argument). hashAndPrintFn function uses the hashFn function to calculate hash code of input string and writes the hash code to the output using System.out.println method. As hashAndPrintFn accepts another function as argument, it is an example of a higher-order function.

The main method of MyHigherOrderFunctions class uses the concatFn and hashAndPrintFn functions to write hash code value of "Welcome Java 8" string to the output:

```
public static void main(String args[]) {
    Function<String, String> suffixFn = concatFn.apply("Welcome");
    String string = suffixFn.apply("Java 8");
    hashAndPrintFn.accept(string, hashFn);
}
```

The main method follows the following sequence of steps:

→ concatFn's apply method is called with "Welcome" argument, which returns the following function:

```
Function<String, String> addSuffixFn = suffix -> {
    return "Welcome" + " " + suffix;
};
```

Notice that the prefix variable in the returned function is set to "Welcome" string that was passed to the concatFn function. The reference to the returned function is stored in the suffixFn variable of main method.

→ suffixFn function's apply method is called with argument "Java 8". The suffixFn function returns the concatenated string "Welcome Java 8".

→ hashAndPrintFn function's accept method is called with the following arguments: "Welcome Java 8" string and hashFn function. hashAndPrintFn calculates the hash code of "Welcome Java 8" using the hashFn function and writes the hash code to the output.

In this section, we saw how to create higher-order functions in Java. Let's now look at Stream API that provides a functional-style interaction with Java collections.

17-5 Stream API

Stream API allows you to work with a *stream* of elements from a *stream source*. A stream source can be:

- a data structure (like collection, array, and so on)
- an I/O source (like files)
- a *generator function* that generates elements for consumption by a stream

> An object stream is represented by java.util.Stream<T> type, where T is the type of objects in the stream. java.util.IntStream, java.util.LongStream and java.util.DoubleStream represent streams of int, long and double primitive types, respectively.

IMPORT **chapter 17/ch17-streams** (This project contains examples that show how Stream API can be used to process data obtained from a stream source)

A stream does *not* store data; it is a *pipeline* of operations that processes each element from the stream source. The following example listing shows how streams can be used to calculate sum of *odd* numbers in a given array:

Example listing 17-9 SumOfOddNumbers – using Stream API
Project – ch17-streams
Source location - src/main/java/sample/streams

```
package sample.streams;

import java.util.Arrays;
import java.util.stream.IntStream;

public class SumOfOddNumbers {
    public static void main(String args[]) {
        int[] numbers = { 1, 2, 3, 4, 5, 6, 7, 8, 9, 10 };
        IntStream intStream = Arrays.stream(numbers);
        int sum = intStream
                .filter(n -> n % 2 != 0)
                .sum();
        System.out.println("Sum of odd numbers in numbers array is : " + sum);
    }
}
```

In the above listing, we first define a numbers array that contains integers from 1 to 10. We then pass the numbers array to Arrays's stream method that returns an IntStream. This makes the numbers array as the stream source. The following sequence of methods are then called on the returned stream to calculate the sum of odd numbers:

- filter – returns another stream (of type IntStream) containing elements that match the given predicate (a boolean-valued function). In the lambda expression n -> n % 2 != 0, n is the stream element and n % 2 != 0 expression returns true only if n is an odd number. This means, call to filter(n -> n % 2 != 0) returns a new stream that consists of odd numbers.
- sum – returns the sum of all the elements in the stream. As the filter(n -> n % 2 != 0) method returned a stream of odd numbers, the sum method returns sum of 1, 3, 5, 7 and 9 (that is, 25).

Instead of using streams, we can use the for loop (or the forEach method of collection) to calculate sum of odd numbers. The following listing shows the SumUsingForLoop class that uses the for loop instead of streams:

Example listing 17-10 SumUsingForLoop – using for loop for calculating sum
Project – ch17-streams
Source location - src/main/java/sample/streams

```
package sample.streams;

import java.util.*;

public class SumUsingForLoop {
    public static void main(String args[]) {
        List<Integer> numbers = Arrays.asList(1, 2, 3, 4, 5, 6, 7, 8, 9, 10);
        int sum = 0;
        for(int n : numbers) {
            if(n % 2 != 0) {
                sum = sum + n;
            }
        }
        System.out.println("Sum of odd numbers in numbers array is : " + sum);
    }
}
```

In the above listing, a for loop iterates over the numbers list and adds odd numbers found in the numbers list to the sum variable.

The above listing shows that using the for loop requires you to write details on *how* the sum of odd numbers is calculated – an *imperative* style of programming. On the other hand, a code written using streams uses the *functional* style of programming. The code written using streams describes *what* to do and not how to do; it abstracts the lower level details from the developers. This makes the code written using streams much easier to read and maintain. For instance, the following piece of code (refer example listing 17-9) clearly specifies - first *filter* the stream to return only odd numbers, and then *sum* them up:

```
    intStream.filter(n -> n % 2 != 0).sum()
```

Let's now look at different operation types in a stream pipeline.

Intermediate and terminal operations

A stream pipeline consists of one or more *intermediate* operations and a *terminal* operation. An intermediate operation produces a *stream*, and a terminal operation produces a *value* or *side-effect*. For instance, filter is an intermediate operation because it produces a stream and sum is a terminal operation because it produces a value.

We saw earlier how IntSream's filter and sum operations can used to filter and calculate sum of numbers. Let's look at a few more examples that show usage of additional operations defined by streams.

mapToInt

The following example listing uses streams to calculate sum of the ages of Student objects (with attributes age and name) in a list:

Example listing 17-11 SumOfStudentsAges – calculate sum of ages of Student objects
Project – ch17-streams
Source location - src/main/java/sample/streams

```
package sample.streams;

import java.util.*;

public class SumOfStudentsAges {
    public static void main(String args[]) {
        List<Student> students = new ArrayList<>();
        students.add(new Student("A", 15));
        students.add(new Student("B", 12));
        students.add(new Student("C", 13));

        int sumOfAges = students
                        .stream()
                        .mapToInt(s -> s.getAge())
                        .sum();
        System.out.println("sum of ages is: " + sumOfAges);
    }
}
```

In the above listing, we create and add multiple Student objects to the students list. We create a Student object by passing student's name and age to the constructor. Student class defines getName and getAge methods to retrieve name and age of a student, respectively.

We obtain a stream of Student objects from students list by calling the stream method. You should note that calling stream method on students list returns a stream of type Stream<Student> - a stream that contains Student objects as its elements.

> In Java 8, stream default method was added to the java.util.Collection interface. For this reason, the stream method is available to all the sub-interfaces (like java.util.List, java.util.Set, and so on) of java.util.Collection.

The mapToInt method accepts a lambda expression that is applied to the stream elements. The lambda expression passed to the mapToInt method *must* evaluate to an integer value. The mapToInt method returns an IntStream that consists of results of applying the lambda expression to the stream elements. For instance, applying s -> s.getAge() expression on the stream of Student objects returns an IntStream consisting of their ages. As mapToInt method returns a stream, it is an intermediate operation.

The sum method on the IntStream returned by mapToInt method calculates the sum of the ages in the IntStream.

map, collect and forEach

The following example listing uses streams to create a list of student names from a list of Student objects and to write the student names to the output:

Example listing 17-12 NamesOfStudentsList – print names of students
Project – ch17-streams
Source location - src/main/java/sample/streams

```
package sample.streams;

import java.util.*;
import java.util.stream.Collectors;

public class NamesOfStudentsList {
    public static void main(String args[]) {
        List<Student> students = new ArrayList<>();
        students.add(new Student("A", 15));
        .....
        List<String> names = students.stream()
                                .map(s -> s.getName())
                                .collect(Collectors.toList());

        names.stream()
            .forEach(name -> System.out.println("Name is: " + name));
    }
}
```

At first, the stream method is called on the students list to obtain a stream of Student objects. Next, Stream's map method is called to get a stream of student names. The map method is similar to mapToInt in the sense that it applies the given lambda expression to the stream elements. As the map method returns a stream, it is an intermediate operation. In the end, the collect method accumulates the student names in the stream into a java.util.List type (specified by Collectors.toList() argument), which is then assigned to the names variable. As the collect method doesn't return a stream, it is a terminal operation.

To stream student names, we call the stream method on the names list returned by the collect method. We then use Stream's forEach method to print names of the students in the stream. The forEach method accepts the name -> System.out.println("Name is: " + name) lambda expression that prints the names of students to the output. Notice that the forEach method doesn't return any value but has the side-effect of writing the names of students to the output.

reduce

The following example listing uses streams to create a string that contains student names (separated by commas) obtained from a list of Student objects:

Example listing 17-13 ConcatenatedStudentNames – concatenate names of students
Project – ch17-streams
Source location - src/main/java/sample/streams

```
package sample.streams;

import java.util.*;

public class ConcatenatedStudentNames {
    public static void main(String args[]) {
        List<Student> students = new ArrayList<>();
        students.add(new Student("A", 15));
        students.add(new Student("B", 12));

        String combinedNames = students.stream()
                                .map(s -> s.getName())
```

```
                          .reduce("", (combinedNamesStr, name) ->
                                    combinedNamesStr.concat(name + ","));

        System.out.println("student names " + combinedNames);
    }
}
```

In the above listing, the map method returns a stream consisting of student names ("A" and "B"), and the reduce method returns a string containing comma-separated student names.

The reduce method accepts the following arguments:

- a BinaryOperator function (a specialized form of BiFunction whose arguments and return types are *same*) – a function that accepts two arguments. The first argument is the value that was returned by applying the function to the *previous* stream element, and the second argument is the *current* stream element. The reduce method returns the result of applying this function to stream elements.

- an identity element – an element that represents the initial result of the function or the default value of the function if no stream elements are found

In the above example, empty string argument "" is the identity element that acts as the initial or default value returned by the BinaryOperator function. And, the following lambda expression represents the BinaryOperator function:

```
(combinedNamesStr, name) -> combinedNamesStr.concat(name + ",")
```

here, combinedNamesStr is the result of applying the above function to the *previous* stream element and name is the *current* stream element.

When the first stream element "A" is processed by the reduce method, the combinedNamesStr value is empty string "" because it is the initial value of the BinaryOperator function (specified by the identity element's value). The function returns "".concat("A", + ","), which means "A," is returned as the result.

When the second stream element "B" (which is also the last element in the stream) is processed by the reduce method, the combinedNamesStr value is "A," (the result from processing the previous "A" element). For this reason, the function returns "A,".concat("B", + ","), which means "A,B," is returned as the result.

Let's now look at stream's support for *lazy-evaluation*.

Lazy evaluation

In a stream pipeline, intermediate operations are lazily-evaluated; they are *not* executed until terminal operation is invoked.

The following listing shows the Person class that represents a person:

Example listing 17-14 Person class
Project – ch17-lazy-evaluation
Source location – src/main/java/sample/streams

```
package sample.streams;

public class Person {
    private String name;
    private int age;
```

```
    public Person(String name, int age) {
        this.name = name;
        this.age = age;
    }
    .....
    public String getName() {
        System.out.println("getName method --> age of " + name + " is " + age);
        return name;
    }

    public int getAge() {
        System.out.println("getAge method --> age of " + name + " is " + age);
        return age;
    }
    .....
}
```

Person class defines age and name attributes. Notice that when getName and getAge methods are called, they print the name and age of the person.

The following listing shows the LazyEval class whose main method goes through a list of Person objects and prints the age of the *first* person named "Sam":

Example listing 17-15 LazyEval class – lazy-evaluation of intermediate operations
Project – ch17-lazy-evaluation
Source location - src/main/java/sample/streams

```
package sample.streams;

import java.util.*;
import java.util.stream.IntStream;

public class LazyEval {
    public static void main(String args[]) {
        List<Person> persons = new ArrayList<>();

        persons.add(new Person("Tom", 15));
        persons.add(new Person("Sam", 30));
        persons.add(new Person("Bob", 25));
        persons.add(new Person("Sam", 18));
        persons.add(new Person("Tim", 25));

        IntStream ageStream = persons.stream()
                              .filter(p -> p.getName().equals("Sam"))
                              .mapToInt(p -> p.getAge());

        System.out.println("main method --> Calling findFirst operation");
        ageStream.findFirst()
                .ifPresent(e -> System.out.println("output --> Sam's age is : " + e));
    }
}
```

In the above listing, the persons variable holds a list of Person objects. The list contains two persons named "Sam". As we want to print the age of the *first* person named "Sam", we create an IntStream representing ages of persons named "Sam":

```
IntStream ageStream = persons.stream()
                        .filter(p -> p.getName().equals("Sam"))
                        .mapToInt(p -> p.getAge());
```

`filter` returns a stream of persons named `"Sam"` and `mapToInt` returns a stream of ages of those persons.

`IntStream`'s `findFirst` method returns an `Optional` containing the first element of the stream, or an empty `Optional` if the stream is empty. As `ageStream` stream represents ages of persons named `"Sam"`, calling `findFirst` method returns the age of the first person named `"Sam"`:

```
ageStream.findFirst()
        .ifPresent(e -> System.out.println("output --> Sam's age is : " + e));
```

If you run `LazyEval`'s `main` method, you'll get the following output:

```
main method --> Calling findFirst operation
getName method --> age of Tom is 15
getName method --> age of Sam is 30
getAge method --> age of Sam is 30
output --> Sam's age is : 30
```

The output shows that intermediate stream operations (`filter` and `mapToInt`) are not executed until the terminal operation (that is, `findFirst`) is called on the stream. This shows that the intermediate operations are *lazily-evaluated*.

The output also shows that not all `Person` objects are looked at to find the age of the first person named `"Sam"`. The stream processing ends when the first person named `"Sam"` is found in the stream. This means, Java runtime optimizes the stream processing based on what you are trying to do.

In the examples that we've seen so far, we obtained a *sequential* stream from a stream source. We can also obtain a *parallel* stream from a stream source for executing operations in parallel. Let's look at how a parallel stream is obtained from a stream source and how operations are executed in parallel.

Sequential and parallel streams

In a sequential stream, elements are processed sequentially by a *single* thread. And, in a parallel stream, elements are processed in parallel by *multiple* threads. If a `java.util.Collection` implementation is the stream source, you can use `java.util.Collection`'s `parallelStream` method to obtain a parallel stream.

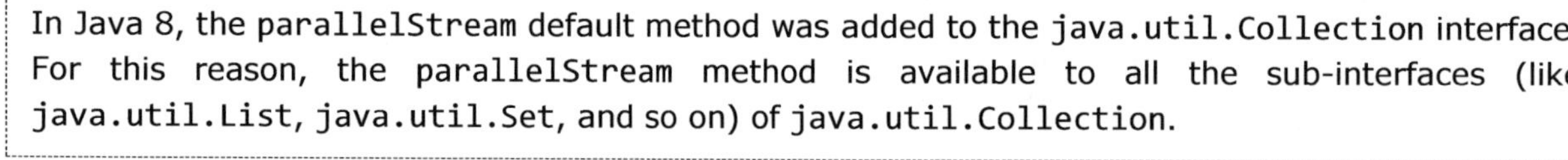

In Java 8, the `parallelStream` default method was added to the `java.util.Collection` interface. For this reason, the `parallelStream` method is available to all the sub-interfaces (like `java.util.List`, `java.util.Set`, and so on) of `java.util.Collection`.

The following example listing uses both sequential and parallel streams to print individual names in a given `List`:

Example listing 17-16 `PrintNames` – print names using sequential and parallel streams
Project – `ch17-streams`
Source location - `src/main/java/sample/streams/parallel`

```
package sample.streams.parallel;

import java.util.*;

public class PrintNames {

    public static void main(String args[]) {
```

```
        List<String> names = Arrays.asList("James", "John", "Robert",
                                           "Michael", "Mary");

        System.out.println("Serial stream result:");
        names.stream()
            .forEach(e -> System.out.println(">" + e));

        System.out.println("\nParallel stream result:");
        names.parallelStream()
            .forEach(e -> System.out.println(">" + e));
    }
}
```

The names variable holds a list of names. We first obtain both sequential and parallel streams using names as the stream source. Then, the forEach method prints each name in the stream. If you run PrintNames's main method, you'll get an output like this:

```
Serial stream result:
>James
>John
>Robert
>Michael
>Mary

Parallel stream result:
>Robert
>Mary
>John
>James
>Michael
```

Notice that in the case of sequential stream, the names are printed in the order they are defined in the names list. On the other hand, in the case of parallel stream, the names are printed out of order. The difference in output is because the behavior of forEach method is *non-deterministic* for parallel streams. This means, in the case of parallel streams, each execution of forEach method may generate a *different* result for the *same* input. For instance, if you re-execute PrintNames's main method, the names may be printed in a different order for the parallel stream.

The following listing shows ConcatNames class that uses both sequential and parallel streams to concatenate names in a given List:

Example listing 17-17 ConcatNames – concatenate names using sequential and parallel streams
Project – ch17-streams
Source location - src/main/java/sample/streams/parallel

```
package sample.streams.parallel;

import java.util.*;
import java.util.function.BinaryOperator;

public class ConcatNames {
    private static BinaryOperator<String> concatFn =
        (combinedNamesStr, name) -> combinedNamesStr.concat(name);

    public static void main(String args[]) {
        List<String> names = Arrays.asList("James", "John", "Robert",
                                           "Michael", "Mary");
```

```
        String sequentialStream = names.stream()
                                      .reduce("", concatFn);
        System.out.println("Serial concat : " + sequentialStream);

        String parallelStream = names.parallelStream()
                                      .reduce("", concatFn);
        System.out.println("Parallel concat : " + parallelStream);
    }
}
```

In the above listing, concatFn function (a BinaryOperator function) concatenates the two String types passed as arguments. The names variable holds a list of names. A sequential and a parallel stream are obtained using names as the stream source. The reduce method is called on both the streams with "" as the identity element and concatFn as the function for concatenating names.

If you run ConcatNames's main method, you'll get the following output:

```
Serial concat : JamesJohnRobertMichaelMary
Parallel concat : JamesJohnRobertMichaelMary
```

Notice that irrespective of whether the stream is a sequential or parallel stream, the result is the same - 'JamesJohnRobertMichaelMary'. This is because reduce is a *deterministic* method – a method that gives the same result irrespective of whether the stream is sequential or parallel.

Let's now look at how *method references* simplify writing lambda expressions.

17-6 Method references

A *method reference* represents a reference to a method or a constructor. If a lambda expression simply calls a method or a constructor, you can replace the expression by a method reference.

The following syntax is used to represent a reference to a method:

```
<object-or-class>::<method-name>
```

here, *<object-or-class>* is the object or class whose method we want to reference, and *<method-name>* is the method name.

The following syntax is used to represent a reference to a constructor:

```
<class>::new
```

here, *<class>* is the class whose constructor we want to reference

> The only limitation with method references is that you can't *explicitly* pass arguments to the referenced method or constructor

IMPORT **chapter 17/ch17-method-references** (This project contains an example that shows how method references can be used to replace lambda expressions)

The following listing shows the MethodRefs class that sorts a given list of Car objects based on their top speeds and then prints their top speeds:

Example listing 17-18 MethodRefs
Project – ch17-method-references
Source location - src/main/java/sample/methodref

```
package sample.methodref;

import java.util.*;

public class MethodRefs {
    public static void main(String args[]) {
        List<Car> cars = new ArrayList<Car>();
        cars.add(new Car(10));
        cars.add(new Car(7));
        cars.add(new Car(5));

        cars.sort((o1, o2) -> MyUtils.compareCars(o1, o2));
        cars.stream().mapToInt(car -> car.getTopSpeed())
                    .forEach(e -> System.out.println(e));
    }
}
```

In the above listing, cars variable holds a list of Car objects that are sorted by calling MyUtils's compareCars static method. The top speeds of the cars are then printed using the Stream's forEach method.

As the lambda expression (o1, o2) -> MyUtils.compareCars(o1, o2) simply calls the MyUtils's compareCars(o1, o2) static method, we can replace it with a method reference:

```
    cars.sort(MyUtils::compareCars);
```

here, MyUtils::compareCars is the method reference

You can also rewrite the code for printing top speeds of cars using a method reference:

```
    cars.stream()
        .mapToInt(car -> car.getTopSpeed())
        .forEach(System.out::println);
```

here, System.out::println is the method reference

17-7 Summary

This chapter covered features that support functional-style of programming in Java. The concepts covered in this chapter will help us better understand *reactive programming* paradigm covered in the next chapter.

Chapter 18 – *Reactive programming with RxJava 2*

18-1 Introduction

With the advent of mobile phones, IoT (Internet of Things) and cloud infrastructure, the application requirements have changed drastically in the last few years. We now expect the applications to respond in milliseconds, store petabytes of data, have 100% uptime, scale to varying load, remain responsive even when failures occur, and so on. These new age application requirements can be addressed by following *reactive* design principles. An application built using reactive design principles is highly-responsive, scalable and resilient.

> Applications built using reactive design principles are referred to as *reactive applications*, and the programming paradigm for developing reactive applications is referrred to as *reactive programming*.

Reactive applications have the following characteristics:

- `responsive`: application's ability to respond to requests in a timely manner
- `resilient`: application's ability to stay responsive in an event of failure
- `elastic`: application's ability to stay responsive even under varying load
- `message driven`: different application components communicate asynchronously with each other using messages

The key characteristic that differentiates reactive applications from others is that they are 'message driven'. This asynchronous message-based interaction between components results in *loose-coupling* between components. This loose-coupling helps a reactive application achieve *responsiveness*, *resilience* and *elasticity*.

You can create a *responsive* application by asynchronously executing requests in a separate thread. But, it is extremely difficult to develop a multi-threaded application that is also *resilient* and *elastic*. Also, if a multi-threaded application contains *blocking* code (like file I/O or database access), then irrespective of the number of processors you use, the performance of the application is limited by the duration for which executing threads are blocked. When an executing thread is blocked, the processor executing that thread is not available to other application threads. Unlike typical multi-threaded applications, reactive applications are fundamentally *non-blocking* in nature, resulting in efficient utilization of processors.

Reactive application development is simplified by using *reactive libraries* that abstract lower-level details of messaging between components and provide functional-style approach to compose results. `RxJava` (`https://github.com/ReactiveX/RxJava`) and `Reactor` (`https://projectreactor.io/`) are examples of reactive libraries that you can use to develop reactive applications. `RxJava 2.x` and `Reactor 3.x` implement the Reactive Streams (`http://www.reactive-streams.org/`) specification that standardizes how reactive components interact asynchronously with each other using streams of messages. Spring 5 supports using both `RxJava 2.x` and `Reactor 3.x` for developing reactive applications.

> Developing reactive applications in Java doesn't require that your application is built using Java 8 or 9. For instance, you can develop reactive applications using `RxJava 1.x`, which requires Java 6 and above. You should note that `RxJava 1.x` doesn't implement the Reactive Streams specification, and `RxJava 2.x` implements the Reactive Streams specification.

In this chapter, we'll look at:

- core interfaces and concepts defined by Reactive Streams specification
- building simple reactive applications using RxJava 2

Let's begin by looking at Reactive Streams specification.

18-2 Reactive Streams

Reactive Streams specification defines the standard for asynchronous interaction between components of a reactive application. Reactive Streams specification has been adopted as part of Java 9 and is represented by the `java.util.concurrent.Flow` class.

The following interfaces defined in the `java.util.concurrent.Flow` class correspond to the interfaces defined by the Reactive Streams specification:

`Publisher<T>` – `Publisher<T>` interface is implemented by the component that *produces* a stream of elements of type `T`. `Publisher` interface defines the following method:

- `void subscribe(Subscriber<? Super T>)` – adds a subscriber (represented by the `Subscriber` argument) for the publisher.

`Subscriber<T>` – `Subscriber` interface is implemented by subscribers that receive elements of type `T`. `Subscriber` interface defines the following methods:

- `void onSubscribe(Subscription)` – this method is called when a subscriber is successfully subscribed to a `Publisher` by calling `Publisher's subscribe` method. `Subscription` argument represents an object that is used to control flow of elements from the `Publisher` to the `Subscriber`.
- `void onNext(T)` – this method is called when an element (of type `T`) is received from the `Publisher`
- `void onError(Throwable)` – this method is called when an unrecoverable error is encountered by the `Publisher` or `Subscription`
- `void onComplete()` – this method is called when the `Publisher` informs its subscribers that it has completed sending data

`Subscription` – `Subscription` links a `Subscriber` to a `Publisher`, and is used to control flow of events from the `Publisher` to the `Subscriber`. `Subscription` interface defines the following methods:

- `void request(int n)` – this method is called to request `n` elements (specified as argument) from the `Publisher` associated with this subscription
- `void cancel()` – this method is to inform the `Publisher` that the `Subscriber` is no longer interested in receiving data from the `Publisher`

`Processor<T,R>` – `Processor` represents a component that acts both as a `Publisher` and a `Subscriber`. `T` is the type of elements published by the `Processor`, and `R` represents the type of elements consumed by the `Processor`.

Figure 18-1 shows how a `Publisher` and a `Subscriber` interact with each other. The figure shows that the `Publisher` sends data to the `Subscriber` only when the `Subscriber` requests for it by calling `Subscription's request` method. The `onComplete` method is invoked when `Publisher` informs the `Subscriber` that it has completed sending data.

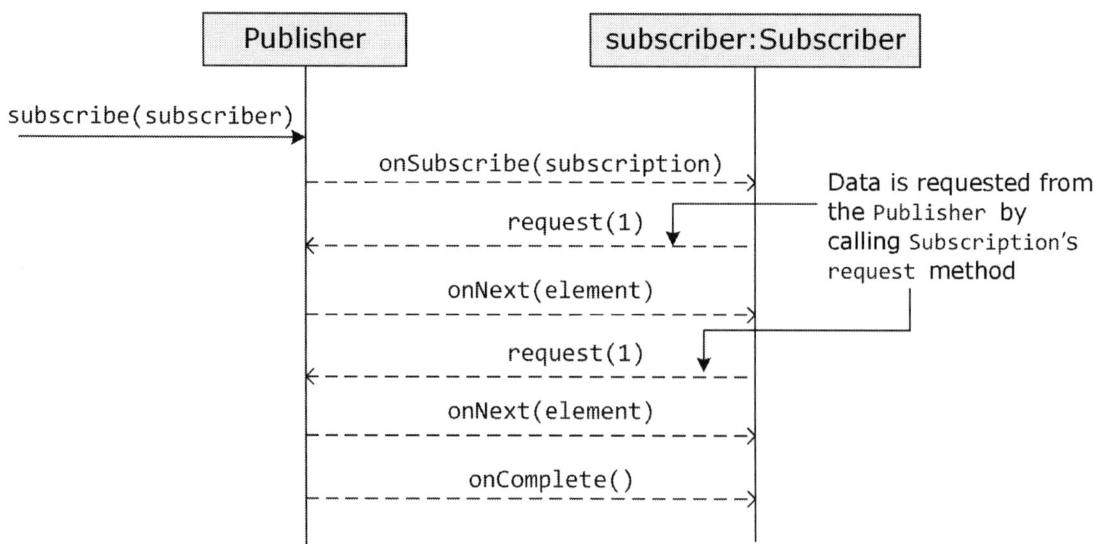

Figure 18-1 Publisher and Subscriber interact with each by asynchronously exchanging messages

Let's look at a heartbeat monitoring application built using RxJava 2 that demonstrates concepts of Publisher, Subscriber and Subscription.

Heartbeat monitoring application

The heartbeat monitoring application monitors the heartbeat rate and alerts when the heartbeat rate crosses a preconfigured limit. The heartbeat application consists of following components:

- HeartbeatPublisher – this component publishes the heartbeat rate
- HeartbeatSubscriber – this component receives the heartbeat rate published by the HeartbeatPublisher and raises an alarm when the rate crosses a preconfigured limit

> In this chapter, we'll develop the Heartbeat monitoring application as a standalone Java application. But, in the real world, this application can be developed as a mobile or smart watch app that uses some mechanism to receive heartbeat rate of the person and issues an alert when the heartbeat rate reaches a preconfigured limit.

IMPORT **chapter 18/ch18-reactiveapp** (This project contains the source code for the Heartbeat monitoring application. To run the application, execute HeartbeatPublisher class's main method.)

The following listing shows the HeartbeatPublisher class that publishes observed heartbeat rate:

Example listing 18-1 HeartbeatPublisher – publishes heartbeat rate
Project – ch18-reactiveapp
Source location - src/main/java/sample/reactiveapp

```
package sample.reactiveapp;

import io.reactivex.BackpressureStrategy;
import io.reactivex.Flowable;

public class HeartbeatPublisher {

    public static void main(String[] args) {
        Flowable.<Integer> create(flowableOnSubscribe,
                BackpressureStrategy.ERROR).subscribe(new HeartbeatSubscriber(120));
```

```
    }

    public static FlowableOnSubscribe<Integer> flowableOnSubscribe =
            new FlowableOnSubscribe<Integer>() {
        @Override
        public void subscribe(FlowableEmitter<Integer> emitter)
                throws Exception {
            for (int i = 90; i < 150; i++) {
                emitter.onNext(i);
            }
            emitter.onComplete();
        }
    };
}
```

The following are the important points to note in the above listing:

- io.reactivex package belongs to RxJava 2 library. The pom.xml file of ch18-reactiveapp project defines dependency on RxJava 2 library, as shown here:

```
<dependency>
    <groupId>io.reactivex.rxjava2</groupId>
    <artifactId>rxjava</artifactId>
    <version>2.1.3</version>
</dependency>
```

- io.reactivex.Flowable implements Reactive Streams specification's Publisher interface. Flowable's create static method is used to create an instance of Flowable. The create method accepts objects of types FlowableOnSubscribe<T> and BackpressureStrategy.

- FlowableOnSubscribe<T> is a functional interface that defines a subscribe method that accepts a FlowableEmitter<T> object. When a Subscriber subscribes by calling Flowable's subscribe method, the FlowableOnSubscribe's subscribe method is called that uses the FlowableEmitter<T> object for sending elements of type T to the Subscriber. As HeartbeatPublisher sends heartbeat rate (of type Integer), T is specified as Integer in the above listing.

- FlowableEmitter<T> defines the following methods for sending data to the Subscriber:

    - void onNext(T) – this method sends an element of type T to the subscribers

    - void onError(Throwable) – this method sends an error to the subscribers

    - void onComplete() – this method signals subscribers that the data publishing is complete and no more data will be sent by the publisher

  FlowableEmitter<T> defines a few more methods that we'll cover later in this chapter.

The following code in listing 18-1 creates a Flowable instance and adds a HeartbeatSubscriber (an implementation of Reactive Streams specification's Subscriber interface) to it:

```
    Flowable.<Integer> create(flowableOnSubscribe,
        BackpressureStrategy.ERROR).subscribe(new HeartbeatSubscriber(120));
```

In listing 18-1, FlowableOnSubscribe's subscribe method uses FlowableEmitter to send *fixed* heartbeat rates from 90 to 149 to the subscribers:

```
    public void subscribe(FlowableEmitter<Integer> emitter) throws Exception {
        for (int i = 90; i < 150; i++) {
```

```
            emitter.onNext(i);
        }
        emitter.onComplete();
    }
```

FlowableEmitter's onNext method is called inside the for loop to send the heartbeat rates. In a real world application, the observed heartbeat rates will be sent to the subscribers. FlowableEmitter's onComplete method is called in the end to communicate to the subscribers that no more data will be sent to them.

The following listing shows the HeartbeatSubscriber class that implements RxJava 2's FlowableSubscriber<T> interface:

Example listing 18-2 HeartbeatSubscriber – subscribes to heartbeat rate published by HeartbeatPublisher
Project – ch18-reactiveapp
Source location - src/main/java/sample/reactiveapp

```
package sample.reactiveapp;

import io.reactivex.FlowableSubscriber;
import org.reactivestreams.Subscription;

public class HeartbeatSubscriber implements FlowableSubscriber<Integer> {
    private final int targetHeartbeatRate;
    private Subscription subscription;

    public HeartbeatSubscriber(int targetHeartbeatRate) {
        this.targetHeartbeatRate = targetHeartbeatRate;
    }

    public void onSubscribe(Subscription subscription) {.....}

    public void onNext(Integer t) {.....}

    public void onError(Throwable t) {.....}

    public void onComplete() {.....}
}
```

The important points to note in the above listing are:

- FlowableSubscriber<T> is a sub-interface of Subscriber<T> interface defined by the Reactive Streams specification. This means that the HeartbeatSubscriber represents a data subscriber. T represents the type of elements consumed by the subscriber. As HeartbeatPublisher (refer listing 18-1) sends heartbeat rates of type Integer, T is specified as an Integer.

- The targetHeartbeatRate instance variable specifies the upper limit for the heartbeat rate at which the subscriber issues an alert. The value for targetHeartbeatRate is supplied as a constructor argument.

- The subscription instance variable holds the Subscription object that links the Subscriber to the Publisher. Notice that the Subscription interface belongs to org.reactivestreams package. The org.reactivestreams package belongs to Reactive Streams API JAR file (reactive-streams-1.x.jar) that gets included into the classpath by RxJava 2 library.

- As the Subscriber interface defines onSubscribe, onNext, onError and onComplete methods, their implementations are provided by the HeartbeatSubscriber class.

Let's look at the implementations of onSubscribe, onNext, onError and onComplete methods in the HeartbeatSubscriber class:

onSubscribe method

```
public void onSubscribe(Subscription subscription) {
    this.subscription = subscription;
    subscription.request(1);
}
```

- the onSubscribe method receives a Subscription object that we store in the subscription instance variable for later use.
- Subscription's request method is used by the subscriber to request the publisher to send more data. The request method accepts the number of elements that the publisher should send to the subscriber. In the above code, request(1) method call means that the subscriber is requesting 1 element from the publisher.

onNext method

```
public void onNext(Integer t) {
    logger.info("Heartbeat --> " + t);
    if (t >= targetHeartbeatRate) {
        logger.info("Alert !! " + t);
        subscription.cancel();
    }
    subscription.request(1);
}
```

The argument t represents the heartbeat rate received from the HeartbeatPublisher. If the value of t is >= targetHeartbeatRate, an alert is issued and the subscription is cancelled by calling Subscription's cancel method. Once Subscription's cancel method is called, the request for more elements by calling Subscription's request method are ignored. If the value of t is *not* >= targetHeartbeatRate, request for 1 more element is sent to the HeartbeatPublisher by calling Subscription's request method.

We saw in the HeartbeatPublisher class that we create an instance of HeartbeatSubscriber and pass it to Flowable's subscribe method, as shown here:

```
Flowable.<Integer> create(flowableOnSubscribe,
    BackpressureStrategy.ERROR).subscribe(new HeartbeatSubscriber(120));
```

As we pass 120 as argument to HeartbeatSubscriber's constructor, the value of targetHeartbeatRate variable is set to 120.

onError and **onComplete** methods

```
public void onError(Throwable t) {
    logger.info("Error " + t);
}

public void onComplete() {
   logger.info("Processing complete");
}
```

The onError method prints the Throwable argument, and the onComplete method prints the message 'Processing complete'.

If you run HeartbeatPublisher's main method, you'll get the following output on the console:

```
Heartbeat --> 90
Heartbeat --> 91
.....
.....
Heartbeat --> 120
Alert !! 120
```

Notice that when the heartbeat rate reaches 120, the HeartbeatSubscriber stops receiving more data from the HeartbeatPublisher, and the message 'Alert !! 120' is written. This is because the HeartbeatSubscriber's onNext method calls Subscription's cancel method when the received heartbeat rate is >= 120, resulting in no more data sent to the HeartbeatSubscriber.

Let's look at what happens if HeartbeatPublisher doesn't call Subscription's cancel method or doesn't request data by calling Subscription's request method.

Case 1: Subscription's cancel method is *not* called from HeartbeatSubscriber's onNext method

As the HeartbeatSubscriber cancelled the subscription before HeartbeatPublisher could send the end of data signal by calling FlowableEmitter's onComplete method (refer listing 18-1), the HeartbeatSubscriber's onComplete method is *never* invoked.

If you remove the call to Subscription's cancel method from HeartbeatSubscriber's onNext method, then running HeartbeatPublisher's main method will show the following output:

```
Heartbeat --> 90
Heartbeat --> 91
.....
Heartbeat --> 120
Alert !! 120
Heartbeat --> 121
Alert !! 121
.....
Heartbeat --> 149
Alert !! 149
Processing complete
```

As the HeartbeatSubscriber no longer calls Subscription's cancel method when the heartbeat rate is >= 120 is received from the publisher the alert is continuously raised by HeartbeatSubscriber after the heartbeat rate reaches 120. When the end of data signal is received from the HeartbeatPublisher, it results in invocation of HeartbeatSubscriber's onComplete method. For this reason, the 'Processing Complete' message is written to the output in the end.

Case 2: Subscription's request method is *not* called from HeartbeatSubscriber's onNext method

We saw in figure 18-1 that the Publisher doesn't send data to the Subscriber unless the Subscriber requests it by calling Subscription's request method. If you remove the call to Subscription's request method from HeartbeatSubscriber's onNext method and run HeartbeatPublisher's main method, you'll get the following output:

```
Heartbeat --> 90
Error io.reactivex.exceptions.MissingBackpressureException: create: could not emit value due to lack of requests
```

The output shows that HeartbeatPublisher first sends a value of 90 (corresponding to Subscription's request method call from HeartbeatSubscriber's onSubscribe method) followed by an error signal that results in invocation of HeartbeatSubscriber's onError method. The error signal was sent by the

`HeartbeatPublisher` because there were items that it could have sent but the `HeartbeatSubscriber` *never* requested them.

Let's look at what are *hot* and *cold* publishers.

18-3 Hot and cold publishers

A *cold* publisher doesn't start emitting data unless a subscriber subscribes to the publisher. When a subscriber attaches to a cold publisher, the cold publisher emits the complete data *once again* to the subscriber. So, a subscriber of a cold publisher *never* misses any data that was emitted *before* the subscriber attached to the publisher.

Some of the examples of cold publishers are:

- a publisher that emits movies released in the last year
- a publisher that emits stock symbols of companies trading at a stock exchange

As the consumers of such data would not like to miss any movie or stock symbol, the publishers of such data should be modelled as cold publishers.

The following figure summarizes how a cold publisher works:

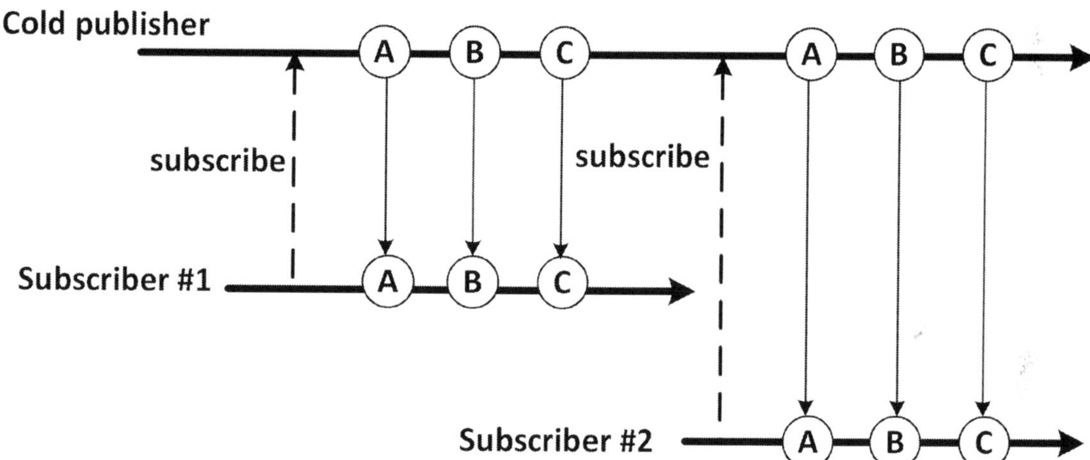

Figure 18-2 `Subscriber #1` and `Subscriber #2` receive the same data from the cold publisher

The thick right-arrowed lines in the above figure represent time. The above figure shows that both `Subscriber #1` and `Subscriber #2` get same set of elements `A`, `B` and `C` from the cold publisher irrespective of when they subscribed to the publisher. In RxJava 2, `Flowable` represents a cold publisher.

> You should note that when multiple subscribers subscribe to a `Flowable` (that is, a cold publisher), each subscriber effectively gets its *own* instance of `Flowable` that re-executes the data publishing logic contained in the `FlowableOnSubscribe`'s `subscribe` method.

A *hot* publisher publishes data even if there are no subscribers attached to the publisher. A subscriber of a hot publisher only receives the data that was published *after* the subscriber was added to the publisher. This means, there is effectively a *single* hot publisher for all the subscribers.

Some of the examples of hot publishers are:

- a publisher that emits video stream of live performances
- a publisher that emits stock quotes of companies trading at a stock exchange

As the consumers of such data will be fine with not receiving data that was emitted before they subscribed, the publishers of such data should be modelled as hot publishers.

The following figure summarizes how a hot publisher works:

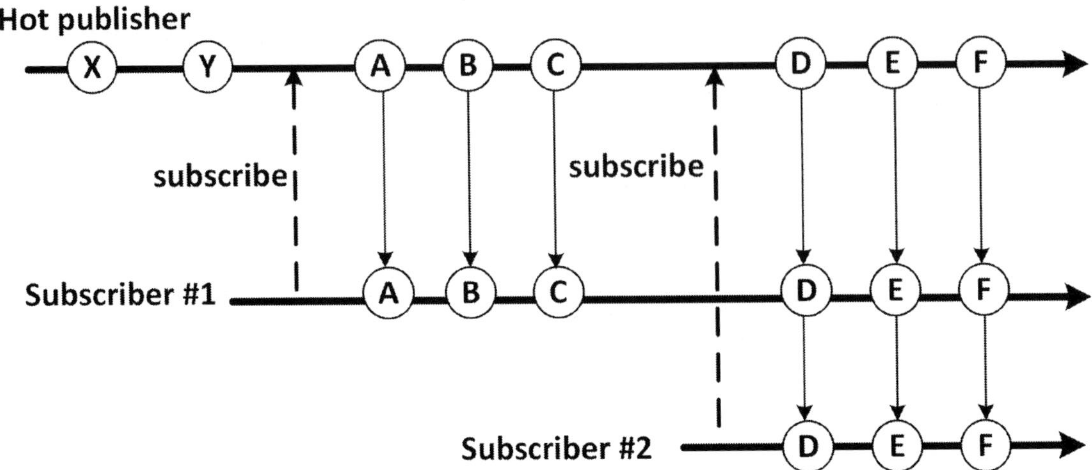

Figure 18-3 `Subscriber #1` and `Subscriber #2` only receive the elements that are emitted after they subscribe to the hot publisher

The thick right-arrowed lines in the above figure represent time. The figure shows that the elements `X` and `Y` are emitted by the hot publisher even though no subscriber has subscribed to the publisher. `Subscriber #1` receives elements `A`, `B`, `C`, `D`, `E` and `F` that are emitted after `Subscriber #1` subscribes to the publisher. `Subscriber #2` receives elements `D`, `E` and `F` that are emitted after `Subscriber #2` subscribes to the publisher. In RxJava 2, `ConnectableFlowable` represents a hot publisher.

Let's look at a StockQuote application that uses both hot and cold publishers to emit stock quotes.

IMPORT **`chapter 18/ch18-stockquote`** (This project contains the source code for the StockQuote application)

StockQuote application

In the StockQuote application, a stock quote publisher emits stock quotes for *multiple* stocks in real-time and each subscriber subscribes for the stock quotes of a *single* stock. When a stock reaches a pre-defined target price, the corresponding subscriber sells a pre-defined quantity of that stock. We'll look at the StockQuote application behavior when the stock quote publisher is modelled as a cold or hot publisher.

The following `StockQuote` class holds the stock symbol and its current price:

Example listing 18-3 StockQuote
Project – `ch18-stockquote`
Source location - `src/main/java/sample/reactiveapp/hotcold`

```
package sample.reactiveapp.hotcold;

public class StockQuote {
    private String symbol;
    private float price;
```

```
    public StockQuote(String symbol, float price) {
        this.symbol = symbol;
        this.price = price;
    }
    .....
}
```

StockQuote class defines symbol and price variables that represent the stock symbol and current price, respectively.

The following StockQuoteSupplier class represents a utility class that provides stock prices:

Example listing 18-4 StockQuoteSupplier – provides stock quotes
Project – ch18-stockquote
Source location - src/main/java/sample/reactiveapp/hotcold

```
package sample.reactiveapp.hotcold;

import java.util.*;

public class StockQuoteSupplier {
    private static Map<String, StockQuote> stockQuotes = new HashMap<String, StockQuote>();

    static {
        stockQuotes.put("XX", new StockQuote("XX", 10));
        stockQuotes.put("YY", new StockQuote("YY", 50));
        stockQuotes.put("ZZ", new StockQuote("ZZ", 100));
    }

    public static StockQuote getStockQuote(String symbol) {
        StockQuote stockQuote = stockQuotes.get(symbol);
        stockQuote.setPrice(stockQuote.getPrice() + 5);
        return new StockQuote(symbol, stockQuote.getPrice());
    }
}
```

The stockQuotes variable (of type java.util.Map<String,StockQuote>) holds mapping of stock symbols (of type String) to StockQuote objects. The static block initializes the stockQuotes variable with initial stock quotes for XX, YY and ZZ stocks. The getStockQuote method returns the stock quote for the requested stock symbol. To simulate a near real-world stock quote supplier, getStockQuote method adds 5 to the stock price before returning it. Notice that the initial price of "XX", "YY" and "ZZ" stocks is 10, 50 and 100. This means, when you call getStockQuote method for the first time for "XX", "YY" and "ZZ" stock symbols, you'll get 15, 55 and 105 as their prices, respectively.

The following listing shows the StockQuoteSubscriber that consumes stock quotes specific to a stock symbol:

Example listing 18-5 StockQuoteSubscriber – consumer of stock quotes
Project – ch18-stockquote
Source location - src/main/java/sample/reactiveapp/hotcold

```
package sample.reactiveapp.hotcold;

import io.reactivex.FlowableSubscriber;
import org.reactivestreams.Subscription;

public class StockQuoteSubscriber implements FlowableSubscriber<StockQuote> {
    private final String symbol;
```

```
    private final float targetPrice;
    private int quantityToSell;
    private Subscription subscription;
    private String uniqueSubscriberId;
    .....
    public void onSubscribe(Subscription subscription) {
        logger.info("onSubscribe called for " + symbol);
        this.subscription = subscription;
        subscription.request(1);
    }

    public void onNext(StockQuote t) {
        if(t.getSymbol().equalsIgnoreCase(symbol)) {
            logger.info(uniqueSubscriberId + ":" + t.getSymbol() + ": --> "
                    + t.getPrice());
            if(t.getPrice() >= targetPrice) {
                logger.info(uniqueSubscriberId + ":"
                   + "Selling " + quantityToSell + " stocks of "
                   + t.getSymbol() + " at " + t.getPrice());
                subscription.cancel();
            }
        }
        subscription.request(1);
    }

    public void onError(Throwable t) {
        logger.info("Error " + t);
    }

    public void onComplete() {
        logger.info("Processing complete");
    }
}
```

StockQuoteSubscriber class implements FlowableSubscriber<StockQuote> interface, which means that StockQuoteSubscriber consumes elements of type StockQuote.

The following instance variables are defined by StockQuoteSubscriber:

- symbol – the stock symbol in which the subscriber in interested
- targetPrice – the price at which the subscriber wants to sell the stock
- quantityToSell – the quantity of stock that the subscriber wants to sell
- subscription – Subscription that links the subscriber to the publisher
- uniqueSubscriberId – a unique identifier for the subscriber

StockQuoteSubscriber provides following implementations for the methods defined in the FlowableSubscriber interface:

- onSubscribe(Subscription) – this method writes "onSubscribe called for <symbol>" on the output, assigns the Subscription type argument to subscription instance variable, and requests 1 element from the publisher by calling Subscription's request method

- `onNext(StockQuote)` – this method receives stock quotes from the publisher. It sells the stock (specified by the `symbol` instance variable) when the price of the stock reaches the target price (specified by the `targetPrice` instance variable).

  As the onNext method will receive *all* the stock quotes from the publisher, the method first checks if the symbol of the received stock quote (obtained by calling `StockQuote`'s `getSymbol` method) is same as the symbol in which the subscriber is interested (represented by `symbol` instance variable). If the symbols match, the method writes "`<uniqueSubscriberId> : <symbol> : --> <price>`" on the output. This output tells which *subscriber* got which *stock symbol* data and what was the *price* of that stock. The `onNext` method also checks if the stock price is `>= targetPrice`. If stock price is `>= targetPrice`, the subscriber writes the message ""`<uniqueSubscriberId>`:`Selling <quantity> stocks of <symbol> at <price>`" and cancels the subscription by calling `Subscription`'s `cancel` method.

- `onError(Throwable)` – writes the `Throwable` argument to the output

- `onComplete()` – writes the message "`Processing complete`" to the output

The following listing shows the `ColdStockQuotePublisher` class's `main` method that fetches stock quotes from `StockQuoteSupplier` and creates a cold publisher:

Example listing 18-6 `ColdStockQuotePublisher` – publishes stock quotes using `Flowable`
Project – `ch18-stockquote`
Source location - `src/main/java/sample/reactiveapp/hotcold`

```
package sample.reactiveapp.hotcold;

import io.reactivex.Flowable;
import io.reactivex.schedulers.Schedulers;
import java.util.*;

public class ColdStockQuotePublisher {
    private static Flowable<StockQuote> flowable;

    public static void main(String[] args) throws InterruptedException {
        List<StockQuote> stockQuoteList = new ArrayList<StockQuote>();

        for (int i = 0; i < 100; i++) {
            stockQuoteList.add(StockQuoteSupplier.getStockQuote("XX"));
            stockQuoteList.add(StockQuoteSupplier.getStockQuote("YY"));
            stockQuoteList.add(StockQuoteSupplier.getStockQuote("ZZ"));
        }

        flowable = Flowable.fromIterable(stockQuoteList)
                        .doAfterNext(t -> Thread.sleep(100))
                        .subscribeOn(Schedulers.io(), false);

        logger.info("adding XX subscriber");
        addSubscriber(new StockQuoteSubscriber("XX", 40, 10, "XX subscriber"));

        logger.info("adding YY subscriber");
        addSubscriber(new StockQuoteSubscriber("YY", 100, 10, "YY subscriber"));

        logger.info("adding ZZ subscriber");
        addSubscriberLater(new StockQuoteSubscriber("ZZ", 200, 10, "ZZ subscriber"));

        Thread.sleep(100000);
```

```
    }
    .....
}
```

The following are the important points to note in the above listing:

- ColdStockQuotePublisher's main method uses a for loop to get 100 stock quotes from StockQuoteSupplier for each "XX", "YY" and "ZZ" stock symbols. The stock quotes are stored in stockQuoteList (a java.util.List) variable. Flowable's fromIterable method accepts an argument of type java.lang.Iterable whose data is emitted by Flowable. As the stockQuoteList is passed to Flowable's fromIterable method, Flowable emits stock quotes stored in the stockQuoteList.

- Flowable's doAfterNext method allows you to perform some action after an element is emitted. As we want to have 100 milliseconds gap between emission of consecutive stock quotes, we've passed t -> Thread.sleep(100) lambda expression to the doAfterNext method.

- If you don't specify any thread pool, subscribers are added *synchronously* to Flowable in the main thread. Flowable's subscribeOn method uses the thread pool created by calling Schedulers.io() to *asynchronously* add subscribers. You should note that the same thread pool is used by subscribers for receiving data from the Flowable. If the observeOn method (explained later in this chapter) is also specified, the thread pool specified by the observeOn method is used by subscribers for receiving data.

- addSubscriber method adds subscribers for "XX" and "YY" stock symbols to Flowable. The target selling price of "XX" is 40, quantity to sell is 10, and subscriber Id is "XX subscriber". Similarly, target selling price of "YY" is 100, quantity to sell is 10, and subscriber Id is "YY subscriber".

- addSubscriberLater method is a variant of addSubscriber method that adds a subscriber to the Flowable after a delay of 10 seconds. This means, the subscriber for "ZZ" stock symbol is added to the Flowable after 10 seconds. The target selling price of "ZZ" is 200, quantity to sell is 10, and subscriber Id is "ZZ subscriber".

- At the end of the main method, Thread.sleep method is called to make the main thread sleep for 100 seconds. This is done to ensure that the main thread doesn't terminate before child threads of the application are terminated.

> Most of the the methods (also referred to as *operators*) defined by Flowable return a new Flowable instance. Once a Flowable instance is created, subsequent operators add functionality to the Flowable returned by the previous operator. Flowable defines methods like doOnEach, doAfterNext, filter, and so on, that process each item emitted by Flowable before it is sent to the subscriber(s).

If you run ColdStockQuotePublisher's main method, you'll get the following output:

```
adding XX subscriber
XX subscriber: onSubscribe called for XX

adding YY subscriber
YY subscriber: onSubscribe called for YY

adding ZZ subscriber
XX subscriber:XX: --> 15.0
YY subscriber:YY: --> 55.0
.....
```

```
XX subscriber:XX: --> 40.0
XX subscriber:Selling 10 stocks of XX at 40.0
YY subscriber:YY: --> 80.0
.....
YY subscriber:YY: --> 100.0
YY subscriber:Selling 10 stocks of YY at 100.0
ZZ subscriber: onSubscribe called for ZZ
ZZ subscriber:ZZ: --> 105.0
ZZ subscriber:ZZ: --> 110.0
.....
ZZ subscriber:ZZ: --> 200.0
ZZ subscriber:Selling 10 stocks of ZZ at 200.0
```

The output shows:

- the subscribers for "XX" and "YY" stock symbols are immediately added to `Flowable` when `addSubscriber` method is called
- the subscriber for "ZZ" stock symbol is added to `Flowable` after `10` seconds
- as soon as a subscriber is added, `Flowable` starts emitting stock quotes from `stockQuoteList`
- subscribers for "XX", "YY" and "ZZ" stock symbols start receiving stock quotes only after they have subscribed to the `Flowable`
- when the stock price of "XX" is `>= 40`, the "`XX subscriber`" sells the "XX" stock
- when the stock price of "YY" is `>= 100`, the "`YY subscriber`" sells the "YY" stock
- when the stock price of "ZZ" is `>= 200`, the "`ZZ subscriber`" sells the "ZZ" stock

As `Flowable` represents a cold publisher, each of the subscribers get *all* the stock quotes right from the beginning. For instance, notice that the first quote received by "`ZZ subscriber`" for "ZZ" stock is `105.0` even though it subscribed `10` seconds *after* the `Flowable` started emitting stock quote data. This shows that when a subscriber is added to `Flowable`, the subscriber gets its own copy of `Flowable` that provides the subscriber with all the data by re-executing the data publishing logic.

Let's now look at how the StockQuote application behaves if we replace the cold publisher with a hot publisher. The following listing shows the `HotStockQuotePublisher` that uses `ConnectableFlowable` (instead of `Flowable`) to publish stock quotes:

Example listing 18-7 `HotStockQuotePublisher` – publishes stock quotes using `ConnectableFlowable`
Project – `ch18-stockquote`
Source location - `src/main/java/sample/reactiveapp/hotcold`

```
package sample.reactiveapp.hotcold;

import io.reactivex.flowables.ConnectableFlowable;
.....
public class HotStockQuotePublisher {
    private static ConnectableFlowable<StockQuote> flowable;

    public static void main(String[] args) throws InterruptedException {
        List<StockQuote> stockQuoteList = new ArrayList<StockQuote>();

        for (int i = 0; i < 100; i++) {
            stockQuoteList.add(StockQuoteSupplier.getStockQuote("XX"));
            .....
```

```
        }

        flowable = Flowable.fromIterable(stockQuoteList)
                        .doAfterNext(t -> Thread.sleep(100))
                        .subscribeOn(Schedulers.io(), false).publish();

        logger.info("adding XX subscriber");
        addSubscriber("XX", 40, 10, "XX subscriber");

        logger.info("adding YY subscriber");
        addSubscriber("YY", 100, 10, "YY subscriber");

        logger.info("adding ZZ subscriber");
        addSubscriberLater("ZZ", 200, 10, "ZZ subscriber");

        flowable.connect();
        Thread.sleep(100000);
    }
    .....
}
```

HotStockQuotePublisher uses RxJava 2's ConnectableFlowable for publishing stock quotes. The call to Flowable's publish method returns an instance of ConnectableFlowable – a hot publisher. The subscribers for "XX" and "YY" stock symbols are added to ConnectableFlowable using addSubscriber method. The subscriber for "ZZ" stock symbol is added using addSubscriberLater method. ConnectableFlowable's connect method is called to instruct ConnectableFlowable to start emitting stock data.

> A Flowable starts emitting data as soon as a subscriber is added to it, and a ConnectableFlowable starts emitting data only *after* its connect method is called.

If you run HotStockQuotePublisher's main method, you'll get the following output:

```
adding XX subscriber
XX subscriber: onSubscribe called for XX
adding YY subscriber
YY subscriber: onSubscribe called for YY
adding ZZ subscriber
XX subscriber:XX: --> 15.0
YY subscriber:YY: --> 55.0
....
XX subscriber:Selling 10 stocks of XX at 40.0
YY subscriber:YY: --> 80.0
YY subscriber:YY: --> 85.0
....
YY subscriber:Selling 10 stocks of YY at 100.0
ZZ subscriber: onSubscribe called for ZZ
ZZ subscriber:ZZ: --> 270.0
ZZ subscriber:Selling 10 stocks of ZZ at 270.0
```

The above output shows:

- As data emission from the ConnectableFlowable is guaranteed to start after the connect method is called, subscribers for "XX" and "YY" stock symbols will *not* miss any data emitted by ConnectableFlowable.
- As the subscriber for "ZZ" stock symbol is added 10 seconds later to ConnectableFlowable, it receives data that is emitted *after* subscription. The output shows that the *first* price of "ZZ" stock

received by the subscriber is 270.0 (and not 105.0), which means that the ConnectableFlowable was emitting data for "ZZ" stock earlier also but is no longer available to "ZZ" stock subscriber.

We mentioned earlier that a cold publisher starts emitting data only after a subscriber is added and a hot publisher continues to emit data regardless of whether there is any subscriber or not. You can verify this behavior of Flowable (the cold publisher) or ConnectableFlowable (the hot publisher) by using the doOnEach method. The doOnEach method is invoked for each item emitted by the publisher.

The following code shows modified configuration of Flowable in HotStockQuotePublisher class that uses doOnEach method to print "Emitting data" message:

Modified HotStockQuotePublisher that prints "Emitting data" message after an item is emitted

```
flowable = Flowable.fromIterable(stockQuoteList)
                    .doAfterNext((t) -> Thread.sleep(100))
                    .doOnEach(t -> logger.info("Emitting data"))
                    .subscribeOn(Schedulers.io(), false).publish();
```

If you now run HotStockQuotePublisher's main method, you'll notice that "Emitting data" message is printed even after the subscriber for "ZZ" symbol has cancelled the subscription.

The following code shows modified configuration of Flowable in ColdStockQuotePublisher class that uses doOnEach method to print "Emitting data" message:

Modified ColdStockQuotePublisher that prints "Emitting data" message after an item is emitted

```
flowable = Flowable.fromIterable(stockQuoteList)
                    .doAfterNext(t -> Thread.sleep(100))
                    .doOnEach(t -> logger.info("Emitting data"))
                    .subscribeOn(Schedulers.io(), false);
```

If you now run ColdStockQuotePublisher's main method, you'll notice that "Emitting data" message is *not* printed after the subscriber for "ZZ" symbol has cancelled the subscription. This shows that a cold subscriber stops publishing data if there are no active subscribers.

Let's look at the concept of *backpressure* as defined in Reactive Streams specification.

18-4 Backpressure

If the subscriber cannot handle the rate at which the publisher is sending data, the subscriber will eventually fail. In such cases, the subscriber informs the publisher to slow down the rate at which the data is being sent. This mechanism of informing the publisher to slow down is referred to as 'backpressure'. The concept of backpressure is central to developing resilient reactive applications. Applying backpressure adversely impacts application's throughput but ensures that the application is resilient under heavy load.

Let's look at a simple example that demonstrates how backpressure works in reactive applications.

The following listing shows the NumberPublisher class that uses a while loop to emit even numbers between 1 and Integer.MAX_VALUE:

Example listing 18-8 NumberPublisher – publishes even numbers between 1 and Integer.MAX_VALUE
Project – ch18-backpressure
Source location - src/main/java/sample/reactiveapp/backpressure

```
package sample.reactiveapp.backpressure;

import io.reactivex.*;
import io.reactivex.schedulers.Schedulers;
```

```
public class NumberPublisher {
    private static final Logger logger = LogManager.getLogger(NumberPublisher.class);

    public static void main(String args[]) throws InterruptedException {

        Flowable.create(flowableOnSubscribe, BackpressureStrategy.ERROR)
                .subscribeOn(Schedulers.computation())
                .doOnEach(t -> logger.info("emitting -> " + t.getValue()))
                .observeOn(Schedulers.computation(), true)
                .filter(t -> {
                    logger.info("--> filter operation called");
                    return t % 2 == 0;
                 })
                .subscribe(new NumberSubscriber());
        Thread.sleep(100000);
    }

    private static FlowableOnSubscribe<Integer> flowableOnSubscribe
          = new FlowableOnSubscribe<Integer>() {
        public void subscribe(FlowableEmitter<Integer> emitter) {
            logger.info("FlowableOnSubscriber's subscribe method called");

            int count = 1;
            while (count < Integer.MAX_VALUE) {
                emitter.onNext(count++);
            }
        }
    };
}
```

The following are the important points to note in the above listing:

- Flowable's create method accepts an argument of type BackpressureStrategy (an enum). BackpressureStrategy defines different backpressure strategies that can be applied when a publisher emits data at a rate higher than the subscriber can process. In the above listing, the backpressure strategy of BackpressureStrategy.ERROR is passed as an argument to Flowable's create method. When BackpressureStrategy.ERROR is specified, no backpressure is applied on the publisher to slow down the rate at which data is published. Instead, MissingBackpressureException is sent by the publisher to the subscriber if the subscriber is not able to keep up with the publisher. So, if there is no pending request for data from the subscriber when the publisher is ready to emit the data, publisher sends MissingBackpressureException to the subscriber.

- FlowableOnSubscribe's subscribe method uses a while loop to emit integers from 1 to Integer.MAX_VALUE

- Flowable's subscribeOn method specifies the thread pool (obtained by calling Schedulers.computation() method) used for adding subscribers and for processing data received by subscribers from Flowable

- Flowable's doOnEach method is called for each emitted items. The method writes "emitting -> " + <emitted-value> to the output.

- Flowable's observeOn method specifies the thread pool (obtained by calling Schedulers.computation() method) used by operations or methods that come after the observeOn method. You should note that the same thread pool is used by subscribers for receiving data.

- Flowable's filter method filters odd numbers from the emission. The filter method writes the message "--> filter operation called" to the output. Notice that the filter method comes *after* the observeOn method.

- Flowable's subscribe method is used to add a NumberSubscriber (an implementation of FlowableSubscriber interface) to Flowable

The following listing shows the NumberSubscriber class that implements FlowableSubscriber interface:

Example listing 18-9 NumberSubscriber
Project – ch18-backpressure
Source location - src/main/java/sample/reactiveapp/backpressure

```
package sample.reactiveapp.backpressure;

import org.reactivestreams.*;

public class NumberSubscriber implements FlowableSubscriber<Integer> {
    private static final Logger logger = LogManager.getLogger(NumberSubscriber.class);

    private Subscription subscription;

    @Override
    public void onNext(Integer t) {
        logger.info("onNext -> " + t);
        subscription.request(1);
    }

    @Override
    public void onError(Throwable t) {
        logger.info("onError -> " + t);
    }

    @Override
    public void onComplete() {
        logger.info("onComplete -> Processing complete");
    }

    @Override
    public void onSubscribe(Subscription subscription) {
        logger.info("onSubscribe -> onSubscribe called");
        this.subscription = subscription;
        subscription.request(1);
    }
}
```

NumberSubscriber's onNext, onError, onComplete and onSubscribe methods write messages to the console.

If you run NumberPublisher's main method, you'll see an output similar to this:

```
[main] INFO ..NumberSubscriber  - onSubscribe -> onSubscribe called
[RxComputationThreadPool-2] INFO ..NumberPublisher  - FlowableOnSubscribe's subscribe
method called
[RxComputationThreadPool-2] INFO ..NumberPublisher  - emitting -> 1
[RxComputationThreadPool-2] INFO ..NumberPublisher  - emitting -> 2
[RxComputationThreadPool-2] INFO ..NumberPublisher  - emitting -> 3
[RxComputationThreadPool-1] INFO ..NumberPublisher  - --> filter operation called
```

```
[RxComputationThreadPool-2] INFO ..NumberPublisher  - emitting -> 4
[RxComputationThreadPool-1] INFO ..NumberPublisher  - --> filter operation called
.....
[RxComputationThreadPool-1] INFO ..NumberSubscriber  - onNext -> 2
[RxComputationThreadPool-1] INFO ..NumberSubscriber  - onNext -> 4
.....
[RxComputationThreadPool-2] INFO ..NumberPublisher  - emitting -> null
.....
[RxComputationThreadPool-1] INFO ..NumberSubscriber  - onError ->
io.reactivex.exceptions.MissingBackpressureException: create: could not emit value due to
lack of requests
```

In the above output, each line contains the name of the thread or the thread pool that was used by NumberPublisher and NumberSubscriber objects. The following are the important points to note in the above output:

- NumberSubscriber's onSubscribe method is executed on the main thread. This is because Flowable's subscribe method is called on the main thread, which results in invocation of NumberSubscriber's onSubscribe method on the main thread.
- As odd numbers are filtered by the filter operator (refer listing 18-8), only even numbers are received by NumberSubscriber.
- When subscribeOn method is executed, RxComputationThreadPool-2 thread pool (obtained via Schedulers.computation()) is used for adding subscribers to Flowable and for sending data to subscribers. For this reason, FlowableOnSubscribe's subscribe and Flowable's doOnEach methods are executed on a thread from RxComputationThreadPool-2 thread pool.
- When observeOn method is executed, RxComputationThreadPool-1 thread pool (obtained via Schedulers.computation()) is used for processing the operations that come *after* observeOn. For this reason, filter method is executed on a thread from RxComputationThreadPool-1 thread pool.
- As the observeOn method uses RxComputationThreadPool-1 thread pool, the subscribers will now receive data on RxComputationThreadPool-1 thread pool. For this reason, NumberSubscriber's onNext, onError and onComplete methods execute on a thread from RxComputationThreadPool-1 thread pool.
- io.reactivex.exceptions.MissingBackpressureException is sent in the end by Flowable. The exception is thrown because NumberPublisher sends data at a faster rate than NumberSubscriber can process.
- Flowable stops sending data to the subscriber after MissingBackpressureException is sent. Infact, if you request items using Subscription's request method from the NumberSubscriber's onError method, Flowable will *not* send any data.

> If you remove observeOn method in listing 18-8, then FlowableOnSubscribe's subscribe method, Flowable's doOnEach and filter methods, and NumberSubscriber's onNext, onError and onComplete methods are executed using the same thread pool.

Figure 18-4 summarizes which Flowable operator uses which thread pool for execution. As subscribeOn uses RxComputationThreadPool-2, the same thread pool is used by doOnEach operator. The observeOn operator uses RxComputationThreadPool-1 thread pool. As the filter operator comes *after* the observeOn operator, filter operator uses RxComputationThreadPool-1 thread pool. The subscriber also receives data on RxComputationThreadPool-1 thread pool.

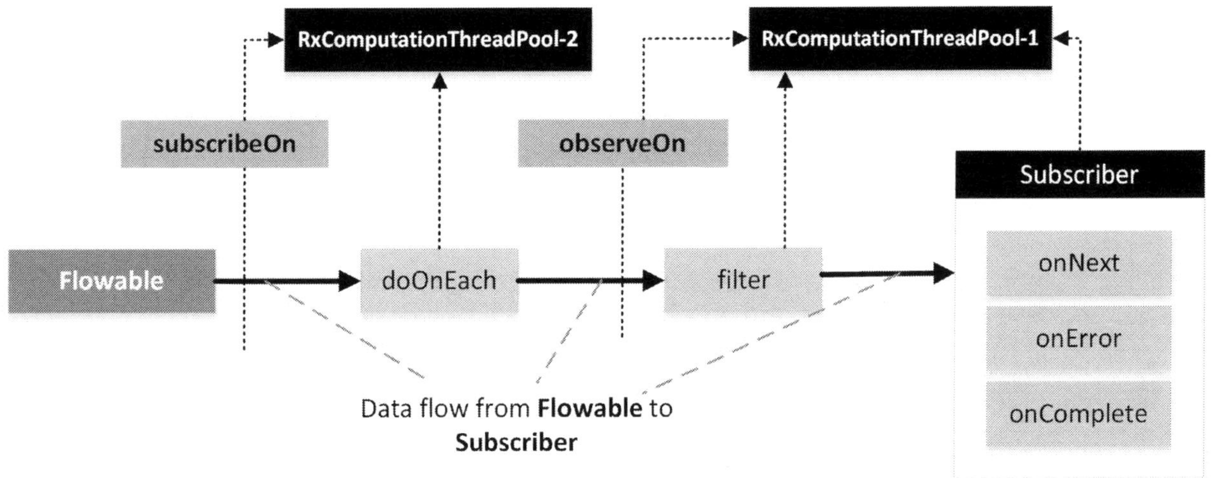

Figure 18-4 Thread pools used by different operators of `Flowable` in `NumberPublisher` (refer listing 18-8)

The following listing shows the `NumberPublisherDropOnBackpressure` class (a variant of `NumberPublisher`) that creates a `Flowable` that drops items if the subscriber is not able to keep up with the rate at which the items are published:

Example listing 18-10 `NumberPublisherDropOnBackpressure` – defines a publisher that drops items on backpressure
Project – ch18-backpressure
Source location - src/main/java/sample/reactiveapp/backpressure

```
package sample.reactiveapp.backpressure;

import io.reactivex.*;
import io.reactivex.schedulers.Schedulers;

public class NumberPublisherDropOnBackpressure {
    private static final Logger logger = LoggerFactory
                .getLogger(NumberPublisherDropOnBackpressure.class);

    public static void main(String args[]) throws InterruptedException {
        Flowable.create(flowableOnSubscribe, BackpressureStrategy.MISSING)
                .subscribeOn(Schedulers.computation())
                .doOnEach(t -> Thread.sleep(50))
                .onBackpressureDrop(t -> logger.info("---------------> Dropped " + t))
                .observeOn(Schedulers.computation(), true)
                .filter(t -> t % 2 == 0).subscribe(new NumberSubscriber());
        Thread.sleep(100000);
    }

    private static FlowableOnSubscribe<Integer> flowableOnSubscribe
            = new FlowableOnSubscribe<Integer>() {
        .....
    };
}
```

The following are the important points to note in the above listing:

- `BackpressureStrategy.MISSING` backpressure strategy means that *no* backpressure strategy is defined for the publisher. In such scenarios, an onBackpressureXXX operator is used to specify how the backpressure is handled by the publisher.

- onBackpressureDrop operator instructs the publisher to drop items if the subscriber is not able to keep up with the publisher. onBackpressureDrop operator accepts the dropped item as an argument. In the above listing, onBackpressureDrop operator simply prints the item that was dropped.

- Thread.sleep method is called from doOnEach operator to make the publisher thread sleep for 50 ms after each item is emitted. Thread.sleep slows down the publisher so that you can view the items being dropped in the output.

As we've added a sleep of 50 ms to Flowable, we need to make NumberSubscriber process items slower so that the backpressure is applied on Flowable. To achieve this, add sleep of 500 ms to the onNext method of NumberSubscriber class:

```
public class NumberSubscriber implements FlowableSubscriber<Integer>{
    .....
    @Override
    public void onNext(Integer t) {
        logger.info("onNext -> " + t);
        try {
            Thread.sleep(500);
        } catch (InterruptedException e) { e.printStackTrace(); }
        subscription.request(1);
    }
    .....
}
```

Now, the NumberSubscriber's onNext method will appear to take at least 500 ms to process each item received from the publisher.

If you now run NumberPublisherDropOnBackpressure's main method, you'll see an output similar to this:

```
sample.reactiveapp.backpressure.NumberSubscriber  - onSubscribe -> onSubscribe called
sample.reactiveapp.backpressure.NumberPublisherDropOnBackpressure  - FlowableOnSubscriber's subscribe method called
sample.reactiveapp.backpressure.NumberSubscriber  - onNext -> 2
sample.reactiveapp.backpressure.NumberSubscriber  - onNext -> 4
.....
sample.reactiveapp.backpressure.NumberPublisherDropOnBackpressure  --------> Dropped 129
sample.reactiveapp.backpressure.NumberPublisherDropOnBackpressure  --------> Dropped 130
.....
sample.reactiveapp.backpressure.NumberSubscriber  - onNext -> 128
.....
sample.reactiveapp.backpressure.NumberSubscriber  - onNext -> 390
sample.reactiveapp.backpressure.NumberPublisherDropOnBackpressure  --------> Dropped 520
.....
sample.reactiveapp.backpressure.NumberSubscriber  - onNext -> 392
```

The above output shows:

- the publisher started dropping numbers from 129 onwards

- NumberSubscriber received even numbers till 128, and then the next number it received from the publisher is 390. This shows that numbers from 129 and 389 are dropped by the publisher because the subscriber was not able to keep up with the rate at which the publisher was emitting numbers.

In addition to ERROR and MISSING, BackpressureStrategy class offers BUFFER, DROP and LATEST backpressure strategies. You can choose the backpressure strategy that best suits your application requirements. For instance, if you want the publisher to buffer *all* items until they are consumed by the subscriber, you can use `BUFFER` backpressure strategy. If you want better control on what to do when backpressure is applied, use `MISSING` backpressure strategy along with an appropriate `onBackpressureXXX` method to handle the backpressure.

18-5 Summary

This chapter covered reactive design principles, and the core concepts and APIs defined by Reactive Streams specification. We also looked at how you can use RxJava 2 library to develop reactive applications. In the next chapter, we'll look at how you can develop real-world reactive applications using MongoDB's reactive JDBC driver, Spring Data, Spring Security, and Spring WebFlux.

Chapter 19 – *Developing reactive RESTful web services using Spring WebFlux, Spring Data and Spring Security*

19-1 Introduction

The reactive design principles can also be applied to develop reactive web applications and RESTful web services. Spring 5's WebFlux module simplifies developing reactive web applications and RESTful web services. In this chapter, we'll develop a reactive RESTful web service that uses:

- Spring WebFlux for developing the web layer
- MongoDB as the data store

  We've chosen to use MongoDB as the data store because a reactive Java driver is available for MongoDB (`https://mongodb.github.io/mongo-java-driver-reactivestreams/`), and the Spring Data MongoDB 2.0 project (`https://projects.spring.io/spring-data-mongodb/`) provides reactive support for MongoDB. We'll use the reactive driver for MongoDB database so that the database calls are *not* blocked.

- Spring Data MongoDB 2.0 for interacting with MongoDB
- Spring Security 5 for securing the web service

  Spring Security 5 supports securing reactive web applications and RESTful web services that use Spring WebFlux

Let's begin by looking at *reactive types* defined by Reactor (the library that internally powers Spring 5's support for developing reactive applications) and RxJava 2.

IMPORT **`chapter 19/ch19-reactor3-webservice`** **and** **`chapter 19/ch19-rxjava2-webservice`** (`ch19-reactor3-webservice` project represents a RESTful web service that uses Spring's Reactor 3.x, and `ch19-rxjava2-webservice` represents the same RESTful web service that uses RxJava 2. These web services store and retrieve `BankAccountDetails` entities to and from MongoDB database.)

19-2 Reactive types defined by Reactor and RxJava 2

Reactor (`https://projectreactor.io/`), like RxJava 2, is an implementation of Reactive Streams specification. When developing reactive applications, the return type of a method is specified as a *reactive type* – a type that represents a data publisher. Spring 5 supports building reactive applications using *reactive types* defined by both RxJava 2 and Reactor.

In the examples that we've seen so far, the methods defined in the data access layer typically return either a `java.util.List`, a POJO or simply void. For instance, the following listing shows some of the data access methods defined by `BankAccountRepository` interface (a Spring Data repository) of `ch09-springdata-mongo` project:

`Example listing 19-1` `BankAccountRepository` – a repository for managing `BankAccountDetails` entities
`Project` – `ch09-springdata-mongo`
`Source location` - `src/main/java/sample/spring/chapter09/bankapp/repository`

```
package sample.spring.chapter09.bankapp.repository;
.....
public interface BankAccountRepository
```

```
        extends MongoRepository<BankAccountDetails, String ..... {

    long countByBalance(int balance);
    List<BankAccountDetails> removeByBalance(int balance);
    .....
    @Query("{'balance' : {'$lte' : ?0} }")
    List<BankAccountDetails> findByCustomQuery(int balance);
}
```

Notice that the countByBalance method returns a long type, and removeByBalance and findByCustomQuery methods return List<BankAccountDetails> type.

The following listing shows the BankAccountRxJava2Repository interface (a reactive version of BankAccountRepository of ch09-springdata-mongo project) of ch19-rxjava2-webservice project whose methods return reactive types defined by RxJava 2:

Example listing 19-2 BankAccountRxJava2Repository – a reactive Spring Data repository
Project – ch19-rxjava2-webservice
Source location - src/main/java/sample/spring/chapter19/bankapp/repository

```
package sample.spring.chapter19.bankapp.repository;

import io.reactivex.Flowable;
import io.reactivex.Single;
import org.springframework.data.mongodb.repository.ReactiveMongoRepository;
.....
public interface BankAccountRxJava2Repository extends
        ReactiveMongoRepository<BankAccountDetails, String> ..... {

    Single<Long> countByBalance(int balance);

    Flowable<BankAccountDetails> removeByBalance(int balance);
    .....
    @Query("{'balance' : {'$lte' : ?0} }")
    Flowable<BankAccountDetails> findByCustomQuery(int balance);
}
```

The above listing shows that BankAccountRxJava2Repository extends Spring Data MongoDB's ReactiveMongoRepository interface instead of the non-reactive MongoRepository interface. Notice that the methods return Single or Flowable type – the reactive types defined by RxJava 2. As Flowable (discussed in the previous chapter) represents a publisher that emits 0 to N items, we've replaced List<BankAccountDetails> return type of removeByBalance and findByCustomQuery methods with Flowable<BankAccountDetails> type. As Single represents a publisher that emits a *single* item, we've replaced the long return type of countByBalance method with Single<Long> type.

If a method's return type is void, you can replace it with RxJava 2's Completable reactive type. Completable represents a publisher that doesn't emit any item; it only emits the successful completion of the task or an error. And, if a method's return type is Optional, you can replace it with RxJava 2's Maybe reactive type. Maybe represents a publisher that emits 0 or 1 item or an error. This means, Maybe reactive type is a union of Completable and Single types.

Instead of using RxJava 2's reactive types, you can use Reactor's reactive types when developing reactive applications using Spring. The following listing shows BankAccountReactorRepository interface of ch19-reactor3-webservice project whose methods return reactive types (Flux and Mono) defined by Reactor:

Example listing 19-3 BankAccountReactorRepository – a reactive Spring Data repository
Project – ch19-reactor3-webservice
Source location - src/main/java/sample/spring/chapter19/bankapp/repository

```
package sample.spring.chapter19.bankapp.repository;

import reactor.core.publisher.Flux;
import reactor.core.publisher.Mono;
.....
public interface BankAccountReactorRepository
        extends ReactiveMongoRepository<BankAccountDetails, String> ..... {

    Mono<Long> countByBalance(int balance);
    Flux<BankAccountDetails> removeByBalance(int balance);
    .....
    @Query("{'balance' : {'$lte' : ?0} }")
    Flux<BankAccountDetails> findByCustomQuery(int balance);
}
```

Flux is equivalent to RxJava 2's Flowable type; it represents a publisher that emits 0 to N items. Mono represents a publisher that emits 0 or 1 item or an error. Mono<T> (where T is the element type emitted by Mono) is equivalent to RxJava 2's Maybe and Single types. Mono<Void> is equivalent to RxJava 2's Completable reactive type; it only emits successful completion of a task or an error.

Let's look at how to develop the data access layer of a reactive application that interacts with MongoDB database.

19-3 Developing the data access layer using Spring Data

The traditional database drivers are non-reactive (or blocking) in nature. To develop a reactive application that interacts with a database, use a reactive (or non-blocking) database driver. At the time of writing this book, reactive database drivers are available for MongoDB, Apache Cassandra and Redis. And, for this reason, Spring Data now supports reactive access to these databases.

> ch19-reactor3-webservice and ch19-rxjava2-webservice projects use the reactive MongoDB driver available from here: https://mongodb.github.io/mongo-java-driver-reactivestreams/. This driver implements the Reactive Streams specification.

Let's look at how the reactive data access layer of ch19-reactor3-webservice project is developed using Spring Data MongoDB repositories that use Reactor's reactive types.

Reactor

To use Reactor's reactive types with Spring Data MongoDB repositories, ch19-reactor3-webservice project's pom.xml file defines dependencies on reactor-core, spring-data-commons and spring-data-mongodb JAR files.

Defining the reactive repository

If you want to use Reactor reactive types for developing the data access layer, your repository interface must extend ReactiveMongoRepository (refer listing 19-3), and the methods must return reactive types defined by Reactor.

You can also create a custom reactive repository that contains methods that return reactive types defined by Reactor. For instance, the following listing shows the BankAccountReactorRepositoryCustom repository that defines an addFixedDeposit method:

Example listing 19-4 BankAccountReactorRepositoryCustom – a custom reactive repository
Project – ch19-reactor3-webservice
Source location - src/main/java/sample/spring/chapter19/bankapp/repository

```
package sample.spring.chapter19.bankapp.repository;

import reactor.core.publisher.Mono;

interface BankAccountReactorRepositoryCustom {
    Mono<Void> addFixedDeposit(String bankAccountId, int amount);
}
```

BankAccountReactorRepositoryCustom's addFixedDeposit method returns Mono<Void>. The addFixedDeposit method adds a fixed deposit of given amount (specified by the amount argument) to the bank account (identified by the bankAccountId argument).

The following listing shows the class that implements BankAccountReactorRepositoryCustom interface:

Example listing 19-5 BankAccountReactorRepositoryCustomImpl – custom repository implementation
Project – ch19-reactor3-webservice
Source location - src/main/java/sample/spring/chapter19/bankapp/repository

```
package sample.spring.chapter19.bankapp.repository;

import org.springframework.data.mongodb.core.ReactiveMongoTemplate;
import reactor.core.publisher.Mono;
.....
public class BankAccountReactorRepositoryCustomImpl implements
        BankAccountReactorRepositoryCustom {
    @Autowired
    private ReactiveMongoTemplate mongoTemplate;

    @Override
    public Mono<Void> addFixedDeposit(String bankAccountId, int amount) {
        return mongoTemplate
                .findById(bankAccountId, BankAccountDetails.class)
                .map(account -> addFD(account, amount).subscribe()).then();
    }

    private Mono<BankAccountDetails> addFD(BankAccountDetails bankAccountDetails,
            int amount) {
        if (bankAccountDetails.getBalance() < amount) {
            throw new RuntimeException("Insufficient balance amount in bank account");
        }

        FixedDepositDetails fd2 = new FixedDepositDetails();
        fd2.setFdAmount(amount);
        .....
        bankAccountDetails.addFixedDeposit(fd2);
        bankAccountDetails.setBalance(bankAccountDetails.getBalance() - amount);
        return mongoTemplate.save(bankAccountDetails);
    }
}
```

In the above listing, we've autowired an instance of ReactiveMongoTemplate (defined by Spring Data MongoDB) to perform reactive operations on MongoDB. The addFixedDeposit method performs following actions:

- calls ReactiveMongoTemplate's findById method to obtain the BankAccountDetails entity whose id is bankAccountId. The findById method returns a Mono<BankAccountDetails> type (that is, a publisher that emits a single item of type BankAccountDetails).

- Mono's map method calls addFD method that:

    - throws RuntimeException if the balance in the bank account is less than the fixed deposit amount

    - creates a new FixedDepositDetails object and adds it to the BankAccountDetails entity returned by findById method, and

    - persists the modified BankAccountDetails entity into MongoDB by calling ReactiveMongoTemplate's save method. The save method returns a Mono<BankAccountDetails> type (that is, a publisher that emits a single item of type BankAccountDetails).

- calls Mono's then method that returns a Mono<Void> which represents a publisher that only emits a success or an error signal.

The implementation of addFixedDeposit method shows that Mono reactive type not only acts as a publisher of items but also defines methods that help process each item. For instance, you can use map method to transform the item, filter method to filter items, and so on. This is similar to how we process items using Java 8 Stream API (refer section 17-5 of chapter 17).

We saw in chapter 9 that a repository can extend QuerydslPredicateExecutor to create queries using Querydsl. Spring Data currently *doesn't* provide reactive support for queries created using Querydsl; therefore, your reactive repositories can't extend QuerydslPredicateExecutor interface.

Let's now look at how to configure Spring Data MongoDB to perform reactive operations on MongoDB.

Configuring Spring Data MongoDB

The following listing shows the DatabaseConfig class (an @Configuration annotated class) that enables use of reactive repositories for MongoDB:

Example listing 19-6 DatabaseConfig – configuring Spring Data MongoDB to use reactive repositories
Project – ch19-reactor3-webservice
Source location - src/main/java/sample/spring/chapter19/bankapp

```
package sample.spring.chapter19.bankapp;

import org.springframework.data.mongodb.ReactiveMongoDatabaseFactory;
import org.springframework.data.mongodb.core.*;
import org.springframework.data.mongodb.repository.config.EnableReactiveMongoRepositories;
.....
@Configuration
@EnableReactiveMongoRepositories(
     basePackages = "sample.spring.chapter19.bankapp.repository ")
public class DatabaseConfig {
    @Bean
    public MongoClient mongoClient() throws UnknownHostException {
        return MongoClients.create("mongodb://localhost");
    }
```

```
    public ReactiveMongoDatabaseFactory mongoDbFactory() throws UnknownHostException {
        return new SimpleReactiveMongoDatabaseFactory(mongoClient(), "test");
    }

    @Bean
    public ReactiveMongoTemplate reactiveMongoTemplate() throws UnknownHostException {
        return new ReactiveMongoTemplate(mongoDbFactory());
    }
}
```

@EnableReactiveMongoRepositories annotation enables use of reactive MongoDB repositories. The basePackages attribute specifies the packages to scan for reactive MongoDB repositories. @Bean-annotated mongoDbFactory method creates and returns an instance of SimpleReactiveMongoDatabaseFactory. SimpleReactiveMongoDatabaseFactory's constructor accepts an instance of MongoClient and the name of the database (which is test in our case). @Bean-annotated reactiveMongoTemplate method configures an instance of Spring Data MongoDB's ReactiveMongoTemplate that is used by repositories for performing reactive operations on MongoDB.

Testing the data access layer

In ch19-reactor3-webservice and ch19-rxjava2-webservice projects, repository methods are accessed through BankAccountService interface. The following listing shows the BankAccountService interface of ch19-reactor3-webservice project:

Example listing 19-7 BankAccountService – service interface
Project – ch19-reactor3-webservice
Source location - src/main/java/sample/spring/chapter19/bankapp/service

```
package sample.spring.chapter19.bankapp.service;
.....
public interface BankAccountService {
    Mono<String> createBankAccount(BankAccountDetails bankAccountDetails);
    Mono<BankAccountDetails> saveBankAccount(BankAccountDetails bankAccountDetails);
    .....
    Flux<BankAccountDetails> findByCustomQuery(int balance);
    .....
    Mono<Void> addFixedDeposit(String bankAccountId, int amount);
}
```

As we don't want calls to BankAccountService methods are blocked, the methods defined in the BankAccountService interface return reactive types.

The following listing shows the DataAccessTest class of ch19-reactor3-webservice project whose main method calls BankAccountService methods to reactively interact with the MongoDB database:

Example listing 19-8 DataAccessTest – test for reactive repositories
Project – ch19-reactor3-webservice
Source location - src/test/java/sample/spring/chapter19/bankapp

```
package sample.spring.chapter19.bankapp;
.....
public class DataAccessTest {
  private static Logger logger = LogManager.getLogger(DataAccessTest.class);
  private static BankAccountService bankAccountService;

  public static void main(String args[]) throws Exception {
    .....
```

```
    bankAccountService = context.getBean(BankAccountService.class);
    BankAccountDetails bankAccountDetails_1 = getNewBankAccountDetails();
    bankAccountService
        .createBankAccount(bankAccountDetails_1)
        .subscribe(
            id -> {
              logger.info("createBankAccount: created bank account with id - " + id
                  + " and balance " + bankAccountDetails_1.getBalance());
            });
    .....
    BankAccountDetails bankAccountDetails_2 = getNewBankAccountDetails();
    bankAccountService
        .saveBankAccount(bankAccountDetails_2)
        .subscribe(bankAccountDetails -> bankAccountService.addFixedDeposit(
             bankAccountDetails.getAccountId(), 2000)
                     .subscribe(
                          item -> logger.info("Received item : " + item),
                          error -> logger.info
                             ("addFixedDeposit -> Exception occurred while adding fixed
                                deposit : '" + error.getMessage() + "'"),
                          () -> logger.info("Fixed deposit successfully added to "
                                 + bankAccountDetails.getAccountId())
                     )
        );

    bankAccountService.findByCustomQuery(1000)
        .map(account -> account.getBalance())
        .reduce(0, Integer::sum)
        .subscribe(totalBalance ->
            logger.info("findByCustomQuery(1000) -> Sum of all balances " + totalBalance));
    .....
  }

  private static BankAccountDetails getNewBankAccountDetails() {
    BankAccountDetails bankAccountDetails = new BankAccountDetails();
    bankAccountDetails.setBalance(1000);
    .....
    return bankAccountDetails;
  }
}
```

The following are the important points to note in the above listing:

- BankAccountService's createBankAccount method invokes BankAccountReactorRepository's save method that persists BankAccountDetails entity into MongoDB. The createBankAccount method returns a Mono that publishes the id of the persisted BankAccountDetails entity.

- BankAccountService's saveBankAccount method also invokes BankAccountReactorRepository's save method but returns a Mono that publishes the persisted BankAccountDetails entity. We add a new fixed deposit to the BankAccountDetails entity returned by the saveBankAccount method.

- BankAccountService's addFixedDeposit method invokes BankAccountReactorRepositoryCustom's addFixedDeposit method (refer listing 19-4 and 19-5). The addFixedDeposit method returns a Mono<Void> type. As addFixedDeposit method returns Mono<Void>, we use a variant of subscribe method to handle error and completion signals.

- BankAccountService's findByCustomQuery method invokes BankAccountReactorRepository's findByCustomQuery method that returns Flux<BankAccountDetails> type. Flux's map method is used to get account balance for each of the BankAccountDetails entities returned by findByCustomQuery method. As the map method returns a Flux<Integer> type, the Flux's reduce method is used to calculate the sum of account balances. As the reduce method returns a Mono<Integer> type that publishes the sum of account balances, Mono's subscribe method is called to write the sum of account balances on the console.

If you run DataAccessTest's main method, you'll see the following output:

```
createBankAccount: created bank account with id - 59ecddddf0d02d23c0985693 and balance 1000
removeByBalance(500) -> Nothing found to delete
.....
addFixedDeposit -> Exception occurred while adding fixed deposit : 'Insufficient balance amount in bank account'
findByCustomQuery(1000) -> Sum of all balances 2000
```

The call to BankAccountService's addFixedDeposit method results in RuntimeException (refer listing 19-5) because the bank account balance is 1000 and we attempt to create a fixed deposit of amount 2000 (refer listing 19-8). If you refer to listing 19-8, you'll notice that we didn't catch any exception thrown by calling BankAccountService's addFixedDeposit method. Instead, Mono's subscribe method specified how an error or completion signal is handled. For this reason, call to addFixedDeposit method results in the following message on the console:

```
addFixedDeposit -> Exception occurred while adding fixed deposit : 'Insufficient balance amount in bank account'
```

In this section, we saw how to develop and test the reactive data access layer using Reactor's reactive types and Spring Data MongoDB repositories. Let's now look at how develop and test the data access layer using RxJava 2's reactive types with Spring Data MongoDB repositories.

RxJava 2

To use RxJava 2's reactive types with Spring Data MongoDB repositories, ch19-rxjava2-webservice project's pom.xml file defines dependencies on rxjava, reactor-core, reactor-adapter, spring-data-commons and spring-data-mongodb JAR files.

Defining the reactive repository

If you want to use RxJava 2 reactive types for developing the data access layer, your repository interface must extend ReactiveMongoRepository (refer listing 19-2), and the methods must return reactive types defined by RxJava 2.

You can also create a custom reactive repository that contains methods that return reactive types defined by RxJava 2. For instance, the following listing shows the BankAccountRxJava2RepositoryCustom repository (equivalent to BankAccountReactorRepositoryCustom repository shown in listing 19-4) that defines an addFixedDeposit method:

Example listing 19-9 BankAccountRxJava2RepositoryCustom – a custom reactive repository
Project – ch19-rxjava2-webservice
Source location - src/main/java/sample/spring/chapter19/bankapp/repository

```
package sample.spring.chapter19.bankapp.repository;
```

```
import io.reactivex.Completable;

interface BankAccountRxJava2RepositoryCustom {
    Completable addFixedDeposit(String bankAccountId, int amount);
}
```

BankAccountRxJava2RepositoryCustom defines an addFixedDeposit method that returns RxJava 2's Completable reactive type (equivalent to Mono<Void> type of Reactor).

The following listing shows the BankAccountRxJava2RepositoryCustomImpl class (equivalent to BankAccountReactorRepositoryCustomImpl class shown in listing 19-5) that implements the BankAccountRxJava2RepositoryCustom interface:

Example listing 19-10 BankAccountRxJava2RepositoryCustomImpl – custom repository implementation
Project – ch19-rxjava2-webservice
Source location - src/main/java/sample/spring/chapter19/bankapp/repository

```
package sample.spring.chapter19.bankapp.repository;

import io.reactivex.Completable;
import io.reactivex.Maybe;
import reactor.adapter.rxjava.RxJava2Adapter;
.....
public class BankAccountRxJava2RepositoryCustomImpl implements
        BankAccountRxJava2RepositoryCustom {
    @Autowired
    private ReactiveMongoTemplate mongoTemplate;

    @Override
    public Completable addFixedDeposit(String bankAccountId, int amount) {
        return RxJava2Adapter.monoToCompletable(mongoTemplate
                .findById(bankAccountId, BankAccountDetails.class)
                .map(account -> addFD(account, amount).subscribe()).then());
    }

    private Maybe<BankAccountDetails> addFD(
            BankAccountDetails bankAccountDetails, int amount) {
        if (bankAccountDetails.getBalance() < amount) {
            throw new RuntimeException("Insufficient balance amount in bank account");
        }
        .....
        return RxJava2Adapter.monoToMaybe(mongoTemplate.save(bankAccountDetails));
    }
}
```

BankAccountRxJava2RepositoryCustomImpl is different from BankAccountReactorRepositoryCustomImpl class (refer listing 19-5) in the following ways:

- The addFixedDeposit method returns Completable type (instead of Mono<Void>), and addFD method returns Maybe<BankAccountDetails> type (instead of Mono<BankAccountDetails>)
- RxJava2Adapter utility class (defined in reactor-adapter JAR) is used for converting reactive types defined by Reactor to RxJava 2 types. For instance, in the addFD method, calling ReactiveMongoTemplate's save method returns a Mono<BankAccountDetails> type that is converted to RxJava 2's Maybe<BankAccountDetails> type by RxJava2Adapter's monoToMaybe method. Similarly, in the addFixedDeposit method, Mono<Void> type is converted to RxJava 2's Completable type by RxJava2Adapter's monoToCompletable method.

Testing the data access layer

In `ch19-reactor3-webservice` and `ch19-rxjava2-webservice` projects, repository methods are accessed through `BankAccountService` interface. The following listing shows the `BankAccountService` interface of `ch19-rxjava2-webservice` project:

Example listing 19-11 `BankAccountService` – service interface
Project – `ch19-rxjava2-webservice`
Source location - `src/main/java/sample/spring/chapter19/bankapp/service`

```
package sample.spring.chapter19.bankapp.service;

import io.reactivex.*;

public interface BankAccountService {
    Single<String> createBankAccount(BankAccountDetails bankAccountDetails);
    Single<BankAccountDetails> saveBankAccount(
            BankAccountDetails bankAccountDetails);
    .....
    Flowable<BankAccountDetails> findByCustomQuery(int balance);
    Completable addFixedDeposit(String bankAccountId, int amount);
}
```

As we don't want calls to `BankAccountService` methods are blocked, the methods defined in the `BankAccountService` interface return reactive types.

The following listing shows the `BankAccountServiceImpl` class that implements the `BankAccountService` interface shown in the above listing:

Example listing 19-12 `BankAccountServiceImpl` – service implementation
Project – `ch19-rxjava2-webservice`
Source location - `src/main/java/sample/spring/chapter19/bankapp/service`

```
package sample.spring.chapter19.bankapp.service;

import io.reactivex.*;
import reactor.adapter.rxjava.RxJava2Adapter;
.....
@Service
public class BankAccountServiceImpl implements BankAccountService {

    @Autowired
    private BankAccountRxJava2Repository bankAccountRepository;

    @Override
    public Single<String> createBankAccount(
            BankAccountDetails bankAccountDetails) {
        return RxJava2Adapter.monoToSingle(bankAccountRepository.save(
                bankAccountDetails).map(e -> e.getAccountId()));
    }
    .....
    @Override
    public Maybe<BankAccountDetails> findOne(String id) {
        return RxJava2Adapter.monoToMaybe(bankAccountRepository.findById(id));
    }
    .....
}
```

We saw in listing 9-3 that methods defined in BankAccountRxJava2Repository interface return reactive types defined by RxJava 2. But, the methods (like, save, findById, and so on) defined by Spring Data MongoDB's ReactiveMongoRepository return reactive types defined by Reactor. For this reason, the service methods (like, createBankAccount, saveBankAccount and findOne) that access ReactiveMongoRepository methods must perform the conversion from Reactor's reactive types to RxJava 2's reactive types using RxJava2Adapter.

The following listing shows the DataAccessTest class of ch19-rxjava2-webservice project whose main method calls BankAccountService methods to reactively interact with the MongoDB database:

Example listing 19-13 DataAccessTest – test for reactive repositories
Project – ch19-rxjava2-webservice
Source location - src/test/java/sample/spring/chapter19/bankapp

```
package sample.spring.chapter19.bankapp;
.....
public class DataAccessTest {
  private static Logger logger = LogManager.getLogger(DataAccessTest.class);
  private static BankAccountService bankAccountService;

  public static void main(String args[]) throws Exception {
    .....
    BankAccountDetails bankAccountDetails_2 = getNewBankAccountDetails();
    bankAccountService.saveBankAccount(bankAccountDetails_2).subscribe(
            bankAccountDetails -> bankAccountService.addFixedDeposit(
                    bankAccountDetails.getAccountId(), 2000)
                 .subscribe(() -> logger.info("Fixed deposit successfully added to "
                                  + bankAccountDetails.getAccountId()),
                      error -> logger.info("addFixedDeposit -> "
                                  + Exception occurred while adding fixed deposit : '"
                                  + error.getMessage()
                                  + "'")
                 )
        );
    .....
  }
  .....
}
```

DataAccessTest class of ch19-rxjava2-webservice is almost identical to DataAccessTest class of ch19-reactor3-webservice project (refer listing 19-8). The only difference is that the subscribe method of Completable (returned by BankAccountService's addFixedDeposit method) accepts 2 handlers (instead of 3) – one for processing completion signal and one for processing error signal.

Developing a reactive application requires that all the application layers are non-blocking in nature. In this section, we saw how to develop the data access and service layers of a RESTful web service. Let's now look at how you can develop the web layer of a RESTful web service using Spring WebFlux.

19-4 Developing the web layer using Spring WebFlux

Spring WebFlux module (introduced in Spring 5) supports developing reactive web applications and RESTful web services. As in the case of Spring Web MVC, you can use @Controller, @GetMapping, and so on, annotations to write reactive web controllers.

As `HttpServletRequest` and `HttpSerlvetResponse` objects of Servlet API are *non-reactive* in nature, WebFlux uses `ServerHttpRequest` and `ServerHttpResponse` (refer `org.springframework.http.server.reactive` package of Spring 5 API) to represent reactive HTTP request and reactive HTTP response objects, respectively. As reading from `InputStream` and writing to `OutputStream` are blocking in nature, `ServerHttpRequest` and `ServerHttpResponse` objects expose request body and response body as a `Flux<DataBuffer>` type. `Flux` is Spring Reactor's reactive type and Spring's `DataBuffer` type is an abstraction over *byte buffers*.

Let's look at how to write a reactive web controller.

Writing a reactive web controller

The following listing shows the `BankAccountController` class (a reactive web controller) of `ch19-reactor3-webservice` project that calls `BankAccountService`'s methods:

Example listing 19-14 `BankAccountController` – a reactive web controller
Project – `ch19-reactor3-webservice`
Source location - `src/main/java/sample/spring/chapter19/bankapp/controller`

```
package sample.spring.chapter19.bankapp.controller;

import org.springframework.web.bind.annotation.*;
import reactor.core.publisher.*;
.....
@RestController
@RequestMapping("/bankaccount")
public class BankAccountController {
    @Autowired
    private BankAccountService bankAccountService;

    @PostMapping("/createBankAccount")
    public Mono<String> createBankAccount(
            @RequestBody BankAccountDetails bankAccountDetails) {
        return bankAccountService.createBankAccount(bankAccountDetails);
    }
    .....
    @GetMapping("/findOne/{id}")
    public Mono<BankAccountDetails> findOne(@PathVariable("id") String bankAccountId) {
        return bankAccountService.findOne(bankAccountId);
    }
    .....
    @PutMapping("/addFixedDeposit/{bankAccountId}/{amount}")
    public Mono<Void> addFixedDeposit(@PathVariable("bankAccountId") String bankAccountId,
            @PathVariable("amount") int amount) {
        return bankAccountService.addFixedDeposit(bankAccountId, amount);
    }
}
```

The above listing shows that the only difference between reactive and non-reactive web controllers is that the methods of a reactive web controller return reactive types.

> The only difference between `ch19-rxjava2-webservice`'s `BankAccountController` and `ch19-reactor3-webservice`'s `BankAccountController` is that the methods of `ch19-rxjava2-webservice`'s `BankAccountController` return reactive types defined by RxJava 2.

Configuring Spring WebFlux

The following listing shows the WebConfig class of ch19-reactor3-webservice project that configures WebFlux:

Example listing 19-15 WebConfig – configuring WebFlux
Project – ch19-reactor3-webservice
Source location - src/main/java/sample/spring/chapter19/bankapp

```
package sample.spring.chapter19.bankapp;

import org.springframework.web.reactive.config.EnableWebFlux;
.....
@EnableWebFlux
@Configuration
@ComponentScan(basePackages = "sample.spring.chapter19.bankapp.controller")
public class WebConfig { }
```

In the above listing, @EnableWebFlux annotation configures WebFlux for the project. @ComponentScan specifies the packages that contain the classes specific to the web layer. As controllers are defined in the sample.spring.chapter19.bankapp.controller package, it is specified as the value of basePackages attribute of @ComponentScan annotation.

Configuring the ServletContext

You can programmatically configure the ServletContext of a WebFlux-based web application (or RESTful web service) by using Spring's AbstractAnnotationConfigDispatcherHandlerInitializer class, as shown in the following example listing:

Example listing 19-16 BankAppInitializer – configuring ServletContext
Project – ch19-reactor3-webservice
Source location - src/main/java/sample/spring/chapter19/bankapp

```
package sample.spring.chapter19.bankapp;

import .....web.reactive.support.AbstractAnnotationConfigDispatcherHandlerInitializer;
.....
public class BankAppInitializer extends
        AbstractAnnotationConfigDispatcherHandlerInitializer {

    @Override
    protected Class<?>[] getConfigClasses() {
        return new Class[] { WebConfig.class,
             DatabaseConfig.class, BankAccountServiceImpl.class };
    }
}
```

getConfigClasses method returns @Configuration (or @Component) classes that we want to register with the application context. WebConfig.class registers beans in the web layer and DatabaseConfig.class registers beans in the data access layer. As BankAccountServiceImpl is the only service implementation in the project, it is also returned by the getConfigClasses method.

If you deploy ch19-reactor3-webservice (or ch19-rxjava2-webservice) project on Tomcat, you can use the Spring's WebClient class (introduced in Spring 5) to reactively call the BankAccountController methods.

Interacting with a reactive RESTful web service using WebClient

Spring's WebClient class (unlike RestTemplate) allows you to reactively interact with a reactive RESTful web service. In Spring 5, WebClient is also the preferred way to asynchronously interact with non-reactive RESTful web services.

> Both ch19-reactor3-webservice and ch19-rxjava2-webservice projects contain a ReactiveWebClient class (in src/main/test source folder) that uses WebClient to reactively interact with the webservice

The following listing shows the ReactiveWebClient class of ch19-reactor3-webservice project that uses WebClient to interact with the RESTful web service represented by ch19-reactor3-webservice project:

Example listing 19-17 ReactiveWebClient – a reactive web service client
Project – ch19-reactor3-webservice
Source location - src/test/java/sample/spring/chapter19/bankapp

```
package sample.spring.chapter19.bankapp;

import org.springframework.http.MediaType;
import org.springframework.web.reactive.function.BodyInserters;
import org.springframework.web.reactive.function.client.WebClient;
.....
public class ReactiveWebClient {
  .....
  private static WebClient webClient =
       WebClient.create("http://localhost:8080/ch19-reactor3-webservice/bankaccount");

  public static void main(String args[]) throws InterruptedException {

    // --create a new BankAccountDetails entity
    webClient.post().uri("/createBankAccount")
        .accept(MediaType.APPLICATION_JSON)
        .body(BodyInserters.fromObject(getNewBankAccountDetails()))
        .retrieve()
        .bodyToMono(String.class)
        .subscribe(id -> logger.info("createBankAccount method. returned id is -> " + id));

    // --find BankAccountDetails entities with balance 1000
    webClient.get().uri("/findByBalance/{balance}",1000)
        .accept(MediaType.APPLICATION_JSON)
        .retrieve()
        .bodyToFlux(BankAccountDetails.class)
        .subscribe(account -> logger.info("account with balance 1000 -> "
          + account.getAccountId()));
    .....
  }
  .....
  private static BankAccountDetails getNewBankAccountDetails() {
    BankAccountDetails bankAccountDetails = new BankAccountDetails();
    bankAccountDetails.setBalance(1000);
    .....
  }
}
```

WebClient's create method creates an instance of WebClient with base URL, host and port information. As ch19-reactor3-webservice is deployed locally on port 8080 and the BankAccountController is mapped to

/bankaccount request path, the following URL is passed to the create method: http://localhost:8080/ch19-reactor3-webservice/bankaccount.

The above listing shows how ReactiveWebClient invokes BankAccountController's createBankAccount and findByBalance methods. The following are the important points to note in the above listing:

- WebClient's post method creates an HTTP POST request, and WebClient's get method creates an HTTP GET request.
- After the HTTP request is created, the uri method specifies the request URI template. If the URI template contains variables, the first method argument is the URI template, followed by values of the URI variables. For instance, in the uri("findByBalance/{balance}", 1000) method call, "findByBalance/{balance}" is the URI template and 1000 is the value of {balance} URI variable.
- The accept method specifies values for the Accept request HTTP header. The value of MediaType.APPLICATION_JSON constant is "application/json", which means that the response data from the web service must be in JSON format.
- The body method (specific to POST, PUT and PATCH HTTP requests) sets the request body. The call to BodyInserters.fromObject method writes the given object to the request body. In the above listing, BodyInserters.fromObject(getNewBankAccountDetails()) writes the BankAccountDetails object returned by getNewBankAccountDetails method to the HTTP request body.
- The retrieve method sends the HTTP request and retrieves the response body.
- The bodyToMono method extracts the response body to a Mono. The type of the response body is specified as an argument to bodyToMono method. As BankAccountController's createBankAccount method returns Mono<String> type, the bodyToMono(String.class) method is called to convert response body to Mono<String>.
- The bodyToFlux method extracts the response body to a Flux. As BankAccountController's findByBalance method returns Flux<BankAccountDetails> type, bodyToFlux(BankAccountDetails.class) method is called to convert response body to Flux<BankAccountDetails>.

We saw earlier that BankAccountReactorRepositoryCustom's addFixedDeposit method throws a RuntimeException (refer listing 19-5) if the account balance is less than the fixed deposit amount. The following listing shows that the ReactiveWebClient's main method first creates a BankAccountDetails with 1000 balance and then attempts to create a fixed deposit of amount 2000 (which results in exception thrown by the web service):

Example listing 19-18 ReactiveWebClient – calling BankAccountController's addFixedDeposit method
Project – ch19-reactor3-webservice
Source location - src/test/java/sample/spring/chapter19/bankapp

```
package sample.spring.chapter19.bankapp;

import org.springframework.http.HttpStatus;
import sample.spring.chapter19.bankapp.exception.NotEnoughBalanceException;
.....
public class ReactiveWebClient {
  private static WebClient webClient =
         WebClient.create("http://localhost:8080/ch19-reactor3-webservice/bankaccount");

  public static void main(String args[]) throws InterruptedException {
```

```
    .....
    webClient.post().uri("/saveBankAccount").
        .....
        .subscribe(accountId -> addFixedDeposit(accountId, 2000)
            .subscribe(
                item -> logger.info("Received item : " + item),
                error -> logger.info("addFixedDeposit -->
                  Exception occurred while adding fixed deposit : '"
                  + error.getMessage() + "'"),
                () -> logger.info("Fixed deposit successfully added to " + accountId)));
    .....
  }

  private static Mono<Void> addFixedDeposit(String accountId, int amount) {
    return webClient
        .put()
        .uri("/addFixedDeposit/{bankAccountId}/{amount}", accountId, amount)
        .accept(MediaType.APPLICATION_JSON)
        .retrieve()
        .onStatus(statusCode -> HttpStatus.INTERNAL_SERVER_ERROR.equals(statusCode),
            clientResponse ->
              Mono.error(new NotEnoughBalanceException("Not enough
                  balance in the bank account")))
        .bodyToMono(Void.class);
  }
  .....
}
```

In the above listing, POST HTTP request to /saveBankAccount URI invokes BankAccountController's saveBankAccount method that creates a BankAccountDetails entity with balance amount as 1000. A PUT HTTP request is then sent to /addFixedDeposit/{bankAccountId}/{amount} URI (where {bankAccountId} is the bank account Id of the newly created BankAccountDetails entity and {amount} is 2000) that invokes BankAccountController's addFixedDeposit method. As account balance is 1000 and we are attempting to create a fixed deposit of 2000, RuntimeException is thrown by the BankAccountReactorRepositoryCustomImpl's addFixedDeposit method (refer listing 19-5).

A couple of important things to notice in the addFixedDeposit method shown in the above listing:

- WebClient's put method is used to create an HTTP PUT request
- The uri method specifies /addFixedDeposit/{bankAccountId}/{amount} as the URI template. The values for {bankAccountId} and {amount} URI variables are supplied as method arguments.
- If the HTTP response status code is 4xx or 5xx, the bodyToMono (or bodyToFlux) method creates a Mono (or Flux) with WebClientResponseException (an exception specific to Spring WebFlux) that contains the *actual* HTTP response data. You can customize this behavior by using the onStatus method. The first argument to onStatus method specifies the exception condition in which the exception function (specified by the second argument) is executed. The exception condition receives the HTTP response status code as an input. In the above listing, statusCode -> HttpStatus.INTERNAL_SERVER_ERROR.equals(statusCode) expression specifies that the exception function is executed only when the HTTP response status code received from the web service is 500 (that is, 'Internal Server Error'). The exception function receives a ClientResponse object (that represents the HTTP response) as an input which the exception function can use to retrieve HTTP status code, headers and response body. The exception function must return a Mono containing a Throwable. In the above listing, the exception function creates an instance of

NotEnoughBalanceException (a custom exception) and wraps it inside a Mono by calling Mono's error method.

- We create a Mono<Void> by simple calling bodyToMono method with Void.class as argument

If you run ReactiveWebClient's main method, you'll notice that the following message is written to the console when the request is sent to /addFixedDeposit/{bankAccountId}/{amount} URI:

```
INFO  sample.spring.chapter19.bankapp.ReactiveWebClient - addFixedDeposit --> Exception
occurred while adding fixed deposit : 'Not enough balance in the bank account'
```

Notice that the custom exception message 'Not enough balance in the bank account' is written to the output.

If you remove the onStatus method and re-run ReactiveWebClient's main method, you'll see the following output on the console:

```
INFO  sample.spring.chapter19.bankapp.ReactiveWebClient - addFixedDeposit --> Exception
occurred while adding fixed deposit : 'ClientResponse has erroneous status code: 500
Internal Server Error'
```

Notice that now the exception message is quite generic in nature that simply describes the HTTP response status code received from the web service.

Let's look at how web browsers receive data published by a reactive web service using *Server-Sent Events*.

Receiving data using Server-Sent Events (SSE)

Server-sent events allow a web browser to automatically receive updates from a server. You can send server-sent events from a Spring Web MVC application by using the SseEmitter class (defined in org.springframework.web.servlet.mvc.method.annotation package). If you are using Spring WebFlux, any controller method that returns a Flux (or Flowable) type can be used to send server-sent events.

The following listing shows the BankAccountController's findByCustomQuerySse method that sends server-sent events:

Example listing 19-19 BankAccountController – sending server-server sent events
Project – ch19-reactor3-webservice
Source location - src/main/java/sample/spring/chapter19/bankapp/controller

```
@GetMapping(path = "/findByCustomQuerySse/{balance}",
      produces = MediaType.TEXT_EVENT_STREAM_VALUE)
public Flux<BankAccountDetails>
         findByCustomQuerySse(@PathVariable("balance") int balance) {

  return bankAccountService.findByCustomQuery(balance).doOnNext(account -> {
    try {
      Thread.sleep(1000);
    } catch (InterruptedException e) {
      e.printStackTrace();
    }
  });
}
```

In the above listing, @GetMapping's produces attribute specifies that the findByCustomQuerySse method returns an *event stream*. The value of MediaType.TEXT_EVENT_STREAM_VALUE is 'text/event-stream', which means that the findByCustomQuerySse method is invoked only if the value of Accept request header is of 'text/event-stream'. To simulate an event stream, we've added a delay of 1 second between emissions using Flux's doOnNext method.

If you now open a web browser that supports server-sent events (like Chrome, Firefox and Safari) and hit the URL http://localhost:8080/ch19-reactor3-webservice/bankaccount/findByCustomQuerySse/1000, you'll notice that the bank account data is *streamed* from the server.

You can also use Javascript's EventSource object (in supported browsers) to receive server-sent events. For instance, the following listing shows how to receive server-sent events from BankAccountController's findByCustomQuerySse method:

Example listing 19-20 Receiving server-sent events using EventSource object

```
var eventSource = new EventSource(
        "/ch19-reactor3-webservice/bankaccount/findByCustomQuerySse/1000");
eventSource.onmessage = function(sse) {
    var newElement = document.getElementById("sseData");
    newElement.innerHTML += sse.data + "<br><br>";
}
```

The above listing shows that you create an EventSource object by passing the URI to BankAccountController's findByCustomQuerySse method. Each time an event is received from the server, EventSource's onmessage handler is called. As shown above, you can obtain the event data using the event's data attribute and use it update the user interface.

Let's now look at how you can secure a WebFlux application using Spring Security.

IMPORT **chapter 19/ch19-reactor3-secured-webservice** (This project is a variant of ch19-reactor3-webservice project that uses Spring Security 5 for securing web requests and methods.)

19-5 Securing a WebFlux application

Spring Security 5 provides support for *reactively* securing WebFlux applications. As with Spring Web MVC, you can use Spring Security to add web request security and method-level security to WebFlux applications.

The following listing shows the SecurityConfig class of ch19-reactor3-secured-webservice project that configures web request security and method-level security for the web service:

Example listing 19-21 SecurityConfig – web request security and method-level security configuration
Project – ch19-reactor3-secured-webservice
Source location - src/main/java/sample/spring/chapter19/bankapp

```
package sample.spring.chapter19.bankapp;

import org.springframework.security.config.annotation.method.configuration
.EnableReactiveMethodSecurity;
import org.springframework.security.config.annotation.web.reactive.EnableWebFluxSecurity;
import org.springframework.security.core.userdetails.ReactiveUserDetailsService;
import org.springframework.security.config.web.server.ServerHttpSecurity;
.....
@EnableWebFluxSecurity
@EnableReactiveMethodSecurity
@Configuration
public class SecurityConfig {
    @Bean
```

```
    public ReactiveUserDetailsService userDetailsService() {
        UserDetails user =  User.withDefaultPasswordEncoder()
                                  .username("user").password("user").roles("USER")
                                  .build();
        UserDetails admin = User.withDefaultPasswordEncoder()
                                  .username("admin").password("admin").roles("ADMIN")
                                  .build();
        return new MapReactiveUserDetailsService(user, admin);
    }

    @Bean
    public SecurityWebFilterChain springSecurityFilterChain(ServerHttpSecurity http) {
        return http.authorizeExchange().anyExchange().authenticated()
                .and().httpBasic()
                .and().csrf().disable()
                .build();
    }
}
```

In the above listing, `@EnableWebFluxSecurity` (similar to `@EnableWebSecurity` annotation) enables security for WebFlux applications, and `@EnableReactiveMethodSecurity` (similar to `@EnableGlobalMethodSecurity` annotation) enables method-level security.

The `userDetailsService` method returns a `ReactiveUserDetailsService` (a reactive version of `UserDetailsService`) bean that is used for authentication by Spring Security. The above listing shows that we create two `UserDetails` objects (one for a user with `"USER"` role and one for a user with `"ADMIN"` role) and add them to `MapReactiveUserDetailsService` (an implementation of `ReactiveUserDetailsService`).

The `springSecurityFilterChain` method returns a `SecurityWebFliterChain` bean that reactively applies web request security. Unlike servlet filters (which are *blocking* in nature), `SecurityWebFilterChain` consists of `WebFilters` (refer to `org.springframework.web.server.WebFilter` interface in Spring Framework API) that reactively process requests. The `springSecurityFilterChain` method is supplied with the `ServerHttpSecurity` object (introduced in Spring Security 5) that is used for reactively configuring the web request security. In the above listing, `authorizeExchange().anyExchange().authenticated()` specifies that only authenticated web requests are allowed, `httpBasic()` configures HTTP basic authentication, and `csrf().disable()` disables CSRF protection.

The following listing shows the `BankAccountService` class whose `findByCustomQuery` method is annotated with Spring Security's `@PreAuthorize` annotation:

Example listing 19-22 `BankAccountService` – securing methods with `@PreAuthorize` annotation
Project – `ch19-reactor3-secured-webservice`
Source location - `src/main/java/sample/spring/chapter19/bankapp/service`

```
package sample.spring.chapter19.bankapp.service;

import org.springframework.security.access.prepost.PreAuthorize;
.....
public interface BankAccountService {
    Flux<BankAccountDetails> findByBalance(int balance);
    .....
    @PreAuthorize("hasRole('ADMIN')")
    Flux<BankAccountDetails> findByCustomQuery(int balance);
    .....
}
```

@PreAuthorize("hasRole('ADMIN')") annotation on findByCustomQuery method specifies that the method can only be invoked by an authenticated user with role "ADMIN". On the other hand, a method like findByBalance (which is not annotated with @PreAuthorize annotation) can be invoked by any user.

The following listing shows the ReactiveWebClient class of ch19-reactor3-secured-webservice project that uses WebClient to call BankAccountController's methods:

Example listing 19-23 ReactiveWebClient – accessing the secured web service
Project – ch19-reactor3-secured-webservice
Source location - src/test/java/sample/spring/chapter19/bankapp

```
package sample.spring.chapter19.bankapp;

import static org.springframework.web.reactive.function.client.ExchangeFilterFunctions
.basicAuthentication;
.....
public class ReactiveWebClient {
  private static WebClient unauthenticatedWebClient = WebClient.
       create("http://localhost:8080/ch19-reactor3-secured-webservice/bankaccount");

  private static WebClient userWebClient =
    WebClient.builder().filter(basicAuthentication("user", "user"))
    .baseUrl("http://localhost:8080/ch19-reactor3-secured-webservice/bankaccount").build();

  private static WebClient adminWebClient =
    WebClient.builder().filter(basicAuthentication("admin", "admin"))
    .baseUrl("http://localhost:8080/ch19-reactor3-secured-webservice/bankaccount").build();

  public static void main(String args[]) throws InterruptedException {
    unauthenticatedWebClient.get().uri("/findByBalance/{balance}", 1000)
       .....
       .subscribe(
            account -> logger.info("Unauthenticated  /findByBalance/{balance} ->
                        account with balance 1000 -> " + account.getAccountId()),
            error -> logger.info("Unauthenticated  /findByBalance/{balance} -> error -> "
                        + error));

    userWebClient.get().uri("/findByBalance/{balance}", 1000)
       .....
       . subscribe(
            account -> logger.info("USER  /findByBalance/{balance} ->
                        account with balance 1000 -> " + account.getAccountId()),
            error -> logger.info("USER /findByBalance/{balance} -> error -> " + error));

    userWebClient.get().uri("/findByCustomQuery/{balance}", 1000)
       .....
       .subscribe(
            account -> logger.info("USER /findByCustomQuery/{balance} ->
                        account with balance 1000 -> " + account.getAccountId()),
            error -> logger.info("USER /findByCustomQuery/{balance} -> error -> "
              + error));

    adminWebClient.get().uri("/findByCustomQuery/{balance}", 1000)
       .....
       .subscribe(
          account -> logger.info("ADMIN /findByCustomQuery/{balance} ->
                        account with balance 1000 -> " + account.getAccountId()),
```

```
            error -> logger.info("ADMIN /findByCustomQuery/{balance} -> error -> "
                  + error));
  }
}
```

In the above listing, we create the following WebClient instances:

- unauthenticatedWebClient - a WebClient that doesn't add any Authorization header to the request
- userWebClient - a WebClient that adds Authorization header for a user with role "USER"
- adminWebClient - a WebClient that adds Authorization header for a user with role "ADMIN"

Notice that the unauthenticatedWebClient instance is created differently than userWebClient and adminWebClient instances. When creating userWebClient and adminWebClient instances, a WebClient builder (returned by builder() method) is used to create the WebClient instances, and ExchangeFilterFunctions's baseAuthentication static method is used to add the Authorization header.

Let's look at what happens when requests are sent to the secured web service using unauthenticatedWebClient, userWebClient and adminWebClient instances:

- when the unauthenticatedWebClient is used to send a request to /findByBalance/{balance}, it is restricted by Spring Security because we've specified in the security configuration (refer listing 19-21) that only authenticated requests are allowed
- when the userWebClient is used to send a request to /findByBalance/{balance}, the request contains the Authorization header for a user with "USER" role. When the request is successfully authenticated against the configured ReactiveUserDetailsService (refer listing 19-21), Spring Security allows access to /findByBalance/{balance}.
- when the userWebClient is used to send a request to /findByCustomQuery/{balance}, the request contains the Authorization header for a user with "USER" role. When the request is successfully authenticated, Spring Security allows access to /findByCustomQuery/{balance} request URI. Now, when it comes to executing BankAccountService's findByCustomQuery method, Spring Security finds that the authenticated user has "USER" role (and not "ADMIN"). As findByCustomQuery method is annotated with @PreAuthorize("hasRole('ADMIN')"), Spring Security denies access to the findByCustomQuery method.
- when the adminWebClient is used to send a request to /findByCustomQuery/{balance}, the request contains the Authorization header for the user in "ADMIN" role. When the request is successfully authenticated, Spring Security allows access to /findByCustomQuery/{balance} request URI. As the authenticated user has "ADMIN" role and the findByCustomQuery method is annotated with @PreAuthorize("hasRole('ADMIN')"), Spring Security allows access to the findByCustomQuery method.

If you run ReactiveWebClient's main method, you'll see the following output:

```
Unauthenticated /findByBalance/{balance} -> error ->
org.springframework.web.reactive.function.client.WebClientResponseException: ClientResponse
has erroneous status code: 401 Unauthorized

USER /findByCustomQuery/{balance} -> error ->
org.springframework.web.reactive.function.client.WebClientResponseException: ClientResponse
has erroneous status code: 403 Forbidden
```

```
ADMIN /findByCustomQuery/{balance} -> account with balance 1000 -> 59fc023fb533e71150514aa8
USER  /findByBalance/{balance} -> account with balance 1000 -> 59fc023fb533e71150514aa8
```

> Notice that the web service responses are not in the same order in which we called the web service. As reactive RESTful web services are non-blocking and asynchronous in nature, the responses are typically interleaved.

The output shows:

- when an unauthenticated user accesses `/findByBalance/{balance}` URI, the web service returns 401 (Unauthorized) HTTP response code
- when an authenticated user in `"USER"` role accesses `/findByCustomQuery/{balance}` URI, the web service returns 403 (Forbidden) HTTP response code
- the web service responds with data when an authenticated user with `"USER"` role accesses `/findByBalance/{balance}` URI
- the web service responds with data when an authenticated user with `"ADMIN"` role accesses `/findByCustomQuery/{balance}` URI

19-6 Summary

In this chapter, we looked at how to create a reactive RESTful web service in which all the application layers and the database driver are reactive in nature. We specifically looked at how to use Spring Data MongoDB's reactive support to build the data access layer of the web service, and Spring WebFlux module to build the web layer of the web service. We also looked at how Spring Security's reactive support can be used to implement web request and method-level security in WebFlux-based applications.

Appendix A – *Downloading and installing MongoDB database*

In this appendix, we'll look at how to download and install MongoDB database and access it on Windows.

A-1 Downloading and installing MongoDB database

Go to `https://www.mongodb.com/download-center` and download the MongoDB database that is applicable to your operating system. For instance, if you are using Windows, download the msi file for installing MongoDB. To install MongoDB on Windows, simply double-click the downloaded msi file and follow the setup wizard.

Starting MongoDB database server

On Windows, the MongoDB installation directory contains a `bin` folder that contains executable files. Go to the `bin` folder and execute the `mongod` command, as shown here:

```
C:\>cd C:\Program Files\MongoDB\Server\3.4\bin
C:\Program Files\MongoDB\Server\3.4\bin>mongod --dbpath C:\data
```

The `mongodb` command starts the server, and `--dbpath` argument specifies the folder in which MongoDB data is stored. If MongoDB is successfully started, you'll see the following message on the console:

```
waiting for connections on port 27017
```

A-2 Connecting to the MongoDB database

In this section, we'll look at the Nosqlclient (`https://github.com/nosqlclient/nosqlclient`) tool for accessing the MongoDB database. You can download Nosqlclient ZIP file for Windows from here: `https://github.com/nosqlclient/nosqlclient`.

Unzip the downloaded Nosqlclient ZIP file and start Nosqlclient by clicking the `Nosqlclient.exe` file. When the user interface shows up, select the 'Connect' option to open the list of MongoDB connections. As we have not configured any connection so far, no connections are shown in the list:

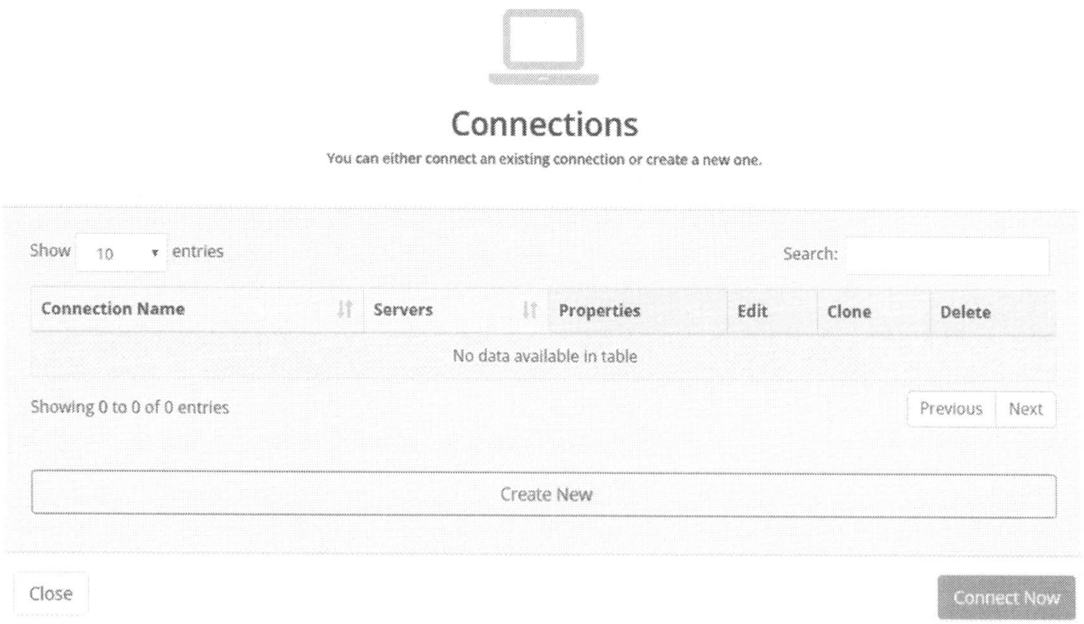

Figure A-1 Select 'Create New' option to configure a new MongoDB connection

Selecting the 'Create New' option opens the 'Add Connection' dialog for configuring a new MongoDB connection. Enter connection details as shown in the following figure and click 'Save changes' button:

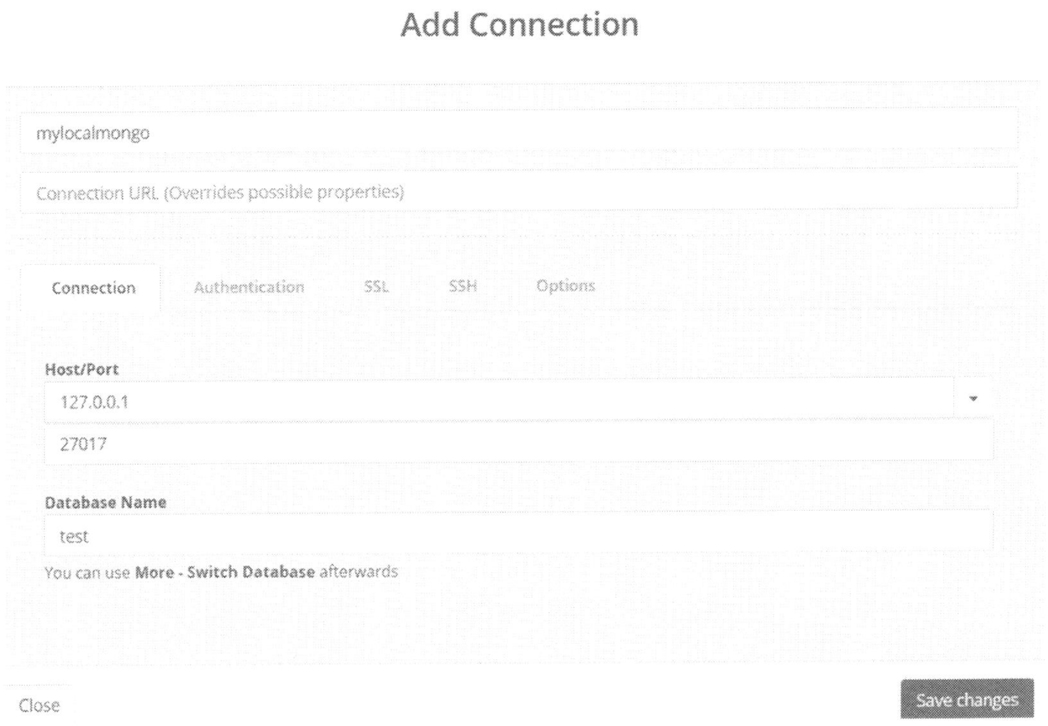

Figure A-2 Enter connection details and click 'Save changes' button

The above figure shows that we've entered Connection Name as mylocalmongo, Hostname as 127.0.0.1 (which means localhost), 27017 as the port number on which MongoDB instance is running, and the DB Name as test. The test database is created by default when you install MongoDB. Once you click 'Save changes', the connection details are saved and displayed in the list of configured MongoDB connections:

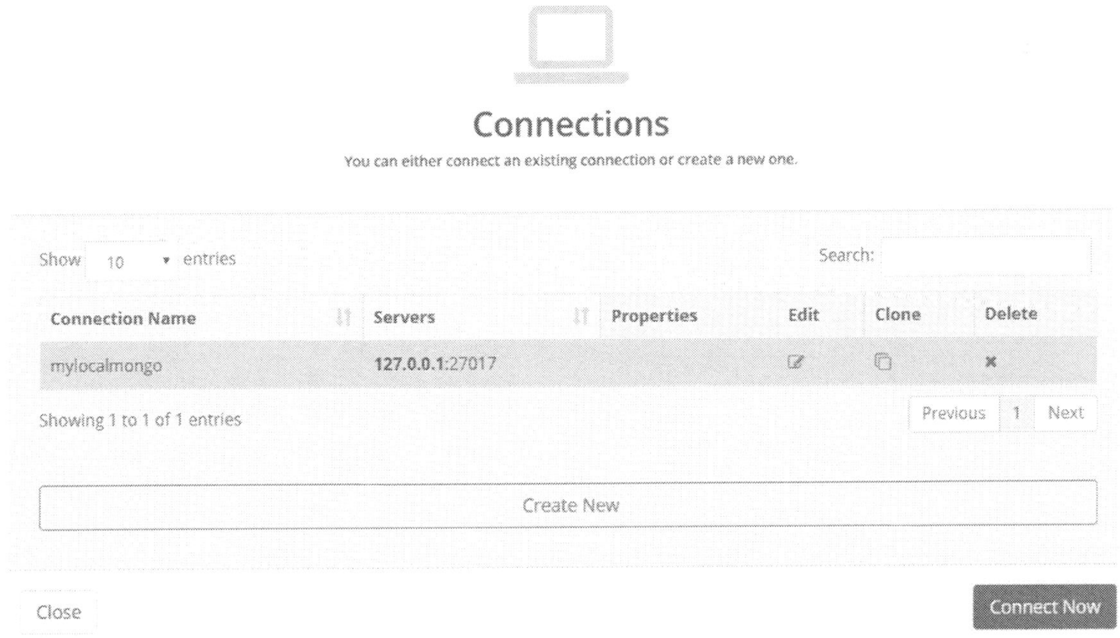

Figure A-3 The newly configured connection is displayed in the list of connections

Now, to connect to the MongoDB instance, select the mylocalmongo connection from the list of connections and click 'Connect Now' button.

Appendix B – *Importing and running sample projects in Eclipse IDE*

In this appendix, we'll look at how to setup the development environment, import a sample project into Eclipse IDE, and run it as a standalone application (if the sample project represents a standalone Java application) or deploy it on Tomcat 9 server (if the sample project represents a web application or a web service).

B-1 Downloading and installing Eclipse IDE and Tomcat 9

Before setting up the development environment, you need to do the following:

- **Download and install Eclipse IDE** – You can download the Eclipse IDE for Java EE Developers (4.7.1a release) from http://www.eclipse.org/downloads/packages/eclipse-ide-java-ee-developers/oxygen1a. To install Eclipse IDE, all you need to do is to unzip the downloaded ZIP file into a directory.
- **Download and install Tomcat 9 server** – You can download the Tomcat 9 server from https://tomcat.apache.org/download-90.cgi. It is recommended that you download the Tomcat 9 bundled as ZIP file, and unzip the bundle into your local file system.

Let's look at how to import a sample project into Eclipse IDE.

B-2 Importing a sample project into Eclipse IDE

It is recommended that you download the sample projects that accompany this book from the following Google code project:

https://github.com/getting-started-with-spring/4thEdition

To successfully import a sample project, you need to do the following:

- import the project to Eclipse IDE
- configure an M2_REPO classpath variable in the Eclipse IDE. M2_REPO variable points to the local *maven repository* that contains the JAR files on which the project depends.

Importing a sample project into Eclipse IDE

Follow these steps to import a sample project into Eclipse IDE:

- Go to File → Import option.
- Select Maven → Existing Maven Projects option from the dialog box, and click Next.
- Select the sample project *directory* (ex. ch01-bankapp-xml) from the file system, and click Finish. You *must* be connected to the internet at this time to allow Eclipse IDE to download project dependencies (as specified in the pom.xml file).

Configuring the M2_REPO classpath variable in the Eclipse IDE

When you import a project into Eclipse IDE, dependencies of the project are downloaded into the <home-directory>/.m2/repository directory. Here, <home-directory> is the home directory of the user. On Windows, this refers to C:\Documents and Settings\<*myusername*>\ directory. By default, the .classpath file of an imported project refers to the JAR dependencies of the project using M2_REPO classpath variable. For this reason, you need to configure a new M2_REPO classpath variable in Eclipse IDE that refers to <home-directory>/.m2/repository directory.

To configure a new M2_REPO variable, follow these steps:

- Go to Windows → Preferences option. This will show the Preferences dialog box.
- Select the Java → Build Path → Classpath Variables option in the dialog box to view the configured classpath variables.
- Now, click New button to configure a new M2_REPO classpath variable. It is important to note that you set the M2_REPO classpath variable to <home-directory>/.m2/repository directory.

We have now successfully imported the sample project into the Eclipse IDE and set the M2_REPO classpath variable. If the project represents a standalone application, you can run the application by following these steps:

- In Eclipse IDE's Project Explorer tab, right-click on the Java class that contains the main method of the application. You'll now see the list of actions that can be performed on the selected Java class.
- Select Run As → Java Application option. This will execute the main method of the Java class.

Let's now look at how Eclipse IDE is configured to work with Tomcat 9 server.

B-3 Configuring Eclipse IDE with Tomcat 9 server

You need to open Eclipse IDE's Servers view to configure Eclipse IDE with Tomcat 9 server. To open the Servers view, select Window → Show View → Servers option from the Eclipse IDE's menu bar. To configure a server with Eclipse IDE, first go to the Servers view, right-click in the Servers views, and select New → Server option. You'll now see a New Server wizard which allows you to configure a server with Eclipse IDE in a step-by-step fashion. The first step is 'Define a New Server', wherein you need to choose the *type* and *version* of the server with which you want to configure your Eclipse IDE. The following figure shows the 'Define a New Server' step:

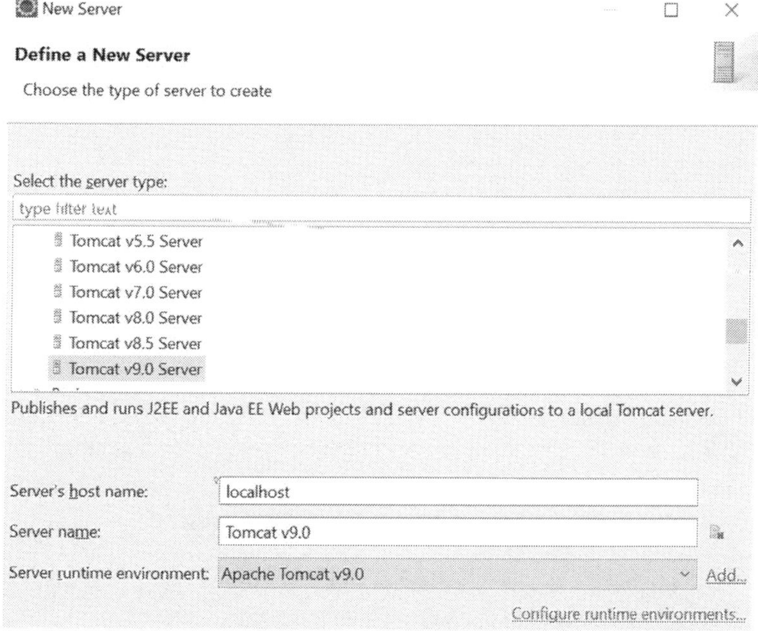

Figure B-1 Select the Tomcat server version that you want to use with Eclipse IDE

Select Apache → Tomcat v9.0 Server as the server, and set 'Apache Tomcat v9.0' as the server name. Click the Next button to go to the next step of configuring Tomcat 9 server with Eclipse IDE. The next step is to specify installation directory of Tomcat 9 server, as shown in the following figure:

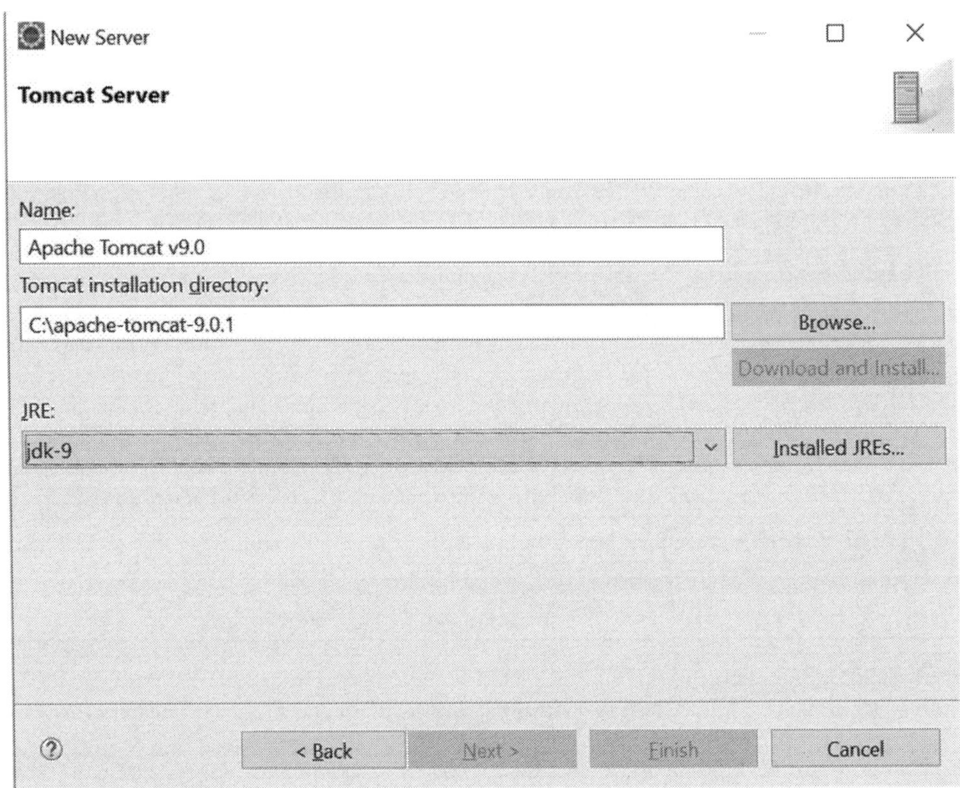

Figure B-2 Specify Tomcat server installation directory and set the Java SDK to be used by the server.

To set the Tomcat installation directory, click the Browse button and select the directory in which you unzipped the Tomcat ZIP file. Also, click the Installed JREs button and configure the Java SDK to be used by Eclipse IDE for running the Tomcat server. Click the Finish button to complete configuration of Tomcat 9 server with Eclipse IDE. You'll now be able to see the newly configured Tomcat 9 server in the Servers view, as shown in the following figure:

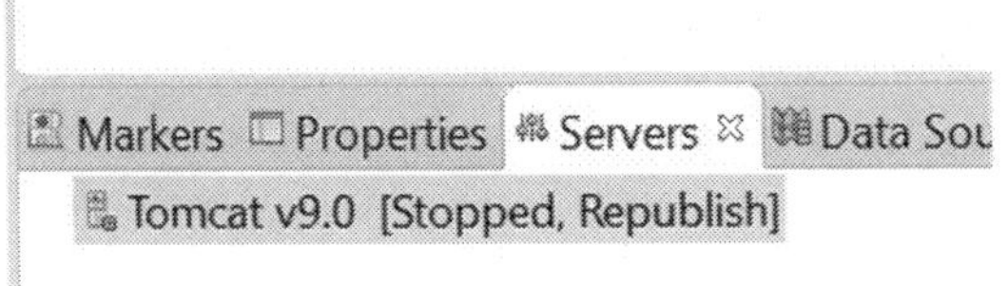

Figure B-3 The Servers view shows the newly configured Tomcat 9 server

Now that we have configured Tomcat 9 server, let's look at how to deploy a sample web project to the configured Tomcat 9 server.

B-4 Deploying a web project on Tomcat 9 server

To deploy a web project (ex. ch12-helloworld) on Tomcat 9 server, follow these steps:

- Right-click on the sample web project in Eclipse IDE's Project Explorer tab. You'll now see the list of actions that can be performed on the selected web project.

- If you want to simply deploy the web project, select `Run As` → `Run on Server` option. This will deploy the web project on the Tomcat 9 server that we configured in section B-3.

  OR

- If you want to deploy and *debug* the web project, then select `Debug As` → `Debug on Server` option. This will deploy the web project on the Tomcat 9 that we configured in section B-3, and allow you to debug the web project by setting breakpoints in the Eclipse IDE.

If Tomcat 9 server is configured correctly with Eclipse IDE, you'll notice that Tomcat 9 server is started and the web project is deployed on it. If you now open a web browser and go to `http://localhost:8080/<sample-project-folder-name>`, you'll see the home page of the web project. Here, `<sample-project-folder-name>` refers to the name of the folder of the sample project.

INDEX

@

<

A

B

C

D

E

F

G

H

I

J

S

T

U

V

W

X

Made in the USA
Lexington, KY
27 April 2019